Asia-Pacific Legal Development

In this age of globalization many legal experts see evidence of swift global movement towards an eventual single "world legal system." Yet the trend to political and economic integration in some parts of the world is matched by a trend to disintegration in others, where strong cultural and political resistance to external influences exists. *Asia-Pacific Legal Development* traces current and prospective developments in several legal systems of the Asia-Pacific region to make sense of these trends and counter-trends.

The contributing authors represent a wide variety of specialist expertise, both "public" and "private," and together encompass the three sectors that constitute a modern system of formal law: the economic, the civic, and the behavioural. Taking into account the opinions and perspectives of both indigenous and non-indigenous experts on topics ranging from prostitution to constitutional law, the book surveys how several ASEAN nations, as well as Canada, Australia, and New Zealand, are confronting social, economic, and legal change. In the first three parts, chapters are grouped along general sectoral lines to cover economic, civic, and behavioural themes, while the fourth addresses cross-sectoral contexts. With the introduction and concluding chapter, the editors provide an integrating framework as well as provocative insights into trends in legal development in the Asia-Pacific region, and on comparative legal research and writing in general.

Asia-Pacific Legal Development is not only an exemplary model for co-operative and comparative legal research and scholarly pluralism, but also a rich study of the increasingly relevant issue of convergence and divergence of legal systems, with a unique Asian focus.

Douglas M. Johnston was the Chair in Asia-Pacific Legal Relations at the University of Victoria until his retirement in 1995. Currently he is Director of the Policy Research Programme at the National University of Singapore, and Co-Director of the Southeast Asian Programme in Ocean Law, Policy, and Management, based in Bangkok. He is a specialist in international and comparative law and has published extensively on the law of sea and international environmental law.

Gerry Ferguson is a Professor of Law at the University of Victoria Faculty of Law, has been a visiting professor at a number of law faculties in the Asia-Pacific region, and is a member of the Board of Directors of the International Centre for Criminal Law Reform and Criminal Justice Policy and of the Advisory Council of the Law Commission of Canada. He is a specialist in criminal law and mental health law.

Edited by Douglas M. Johnston
and Gerry Ferguson

Asia-Pacific Legal Development

UBCPress / Vancouver

Printed in Canada on acid-free paper ∞

ISBN 0-7748-0673-7

Canadian Cataloguing in Publication Data

Main entry under title:
Asia-Pacific legal development

Includes bibliographical references and index.
ISBN 0-7748-0673-7

1. Law – Pacific Area. 2. Comparative law. I. Johnston, Douglas M., 1931-
II. Ferguson, Gerry.
K561.A84 1998 340.2 C98-910801-5

The editors of this book thank the Law Foundation of British Columbia for its generous publication grant and the Canada-ASEAN Centre in Singapore for financial assistance for the research of parts of this book.

UBC Press gratefully acknowledges the ongoing support to its publishing program from the Canada Council for the Arts, the British Columbia Arts Council, and the Multiculturalism Program of the Department of Canadian Heritage.

UBC Press
University of British Columbia
6344 Memorial Road
Vancouver, BC V6T 1Z2
(604) 822-5959
Fax: 1-800-668-0821
E-mail: orders@ubcpress.ubc.ca
www.ubcpress.ubc.ca

Contents

Acknowledgments

Ten years ago, publication of this book was little more than a twinkle in the eye of the first-named co-editor. The challenging road which led to its completion is described more fully in the Introduction. Along that road we have incurred a number of debts, which we now gratefully acknowledge.

To our co-authors, we are truly thankful for their sense of collegiality and their faith in the project, their dedication in researching and writing their chapters, and their patience and good humour in enduring the twists and bumps that such projects inevitably encounter.

To Rosemary Garton, our ever faithful and efficient secretary, we send a bouquet of thanks for her tireless typing, retyping, formatting, and reformatting of nearly every part of the book.

We are also grateful to Caron Rollins, our Associate Law Librarian at the University of Victoria, for her assistance in tracking down some of the more obscure citations in the book, and to Michael Penner, a University of Victoria law student, for his hard work on the index.

We would like to thank all the staff at UBC Press who so diligently worked on the production of this book. In particular, we would like to express our gratitude to Laura Macleod for her encouragement and support in ensuring that our book proposal was accepted by UBC Press and to Holly Keller-Brohman for the countless tasks that a managing editor performs.

We are also greatly indebted to the Law Foundation of British Columbia for its generous publication grant and to the Canada-ASEAN Centre in Singapore for financial assistance for research for Chapters 2 and 7 of this book.

Finally, and most importantly, we thank our spouses, Judith and Sharon, for their assistance, encouragement, and forbearance.

Douglas M. Johnston
Gerry Ferguson

Asia-Pacific Legal Development

Introduction: The Evolution of the Project

Douglas M. Johnston

ACCEPTING THE CHALLENGE OF ASIANIZATION

In the mid to late 1980s Canada "discovered" Asia. Economic recalculation of the national interest resulted in our official adoption of the Asia-Pacific region as the focus of our newest aspirations on the world stage. The westward-looking province of British Columbia became the primary beneficiary of federal funds made available to support a variety of Canadian Asia-Pacific initiatives, supplemented by substantial contributions from the provincial government.

This government-programmed emphasis on the Asia-Pacific region was quickly reflected in a re-ordering of priorities on the campuses of British Columbia. Included among these developments was the establishment of the Centre for Asia-Pacific Initiatives (CAPI) at the University of Victoria (UVic), a relatively youthful institution located conveniently close to the heart of the provincial government. Another of the UVic innovations was the creation of the Chair in Asia-Pacific Legal Relations.

On assuming that Chair in the summer of 1987, this author accepted the challenge of "Asianizing" the Law Faculty. It was agreed that the first stage of that Asianization process should involve the cultivation of a special interest in Southeast Asia and the legal systems of the ASEAN region. Apart from new courses and exchange agreements, a central component of the Asianization challenge involved an attempt to persuade a significant number of UVic law school colleagues to embark on a collective research project in the unfamiliar field of Asia-Pacific legal studies. At that time only two colleagues, William Neilson and Ted McDorman, had any sustained professional association with Asia. The road upward to this new plateau of collegial collaboration looked pretty steep. The challenge was to find a way of inducing our colleagues to share the excitement of our involvement in these remarkable cultures. But could we reasonably expect to attract our colleagues to this goal of collaboration in Asian legal studies?

CONFRONTING THE DIVERSITY OF COMPARATIVE LAW

Seduction of our colleagues on this scale was, after all, a fairly cheeky presumption. Even in the most favoured of circumstances, the organization of one's fellow academics has been likened to the "herding of cats." Ask any dean. Usually it is wise to treat one's colleagues as beyond the reach of any ambitious effort at institutionalization. Ask any university president. In this particular project, the usual problem of organizing a large-scale collaboration was compounded by its orientation. To some UVic colleagues "down the hall," serious commitment to legal scholarship in unfamiliar countries, and especially in "radically different" legal cultures, might have appeared to require immersion in exotica. An effort was made to meet this objection by suggesting that the quest was for conceptual insights ("sophistication") rather than in-depth erudition ("rigour"); and that the chief benefit of comparative inquiry would be the provision of fresh insights into the Canadian, or North American, legal culture.

Those left unmoved by the elegance of this sophistry, and reluctant to be converted into comparative lawyers, were asked to reflect on the many changes that have taken place in the history of comparative law, and to reconsider the academic challenge to Northwest Pacific law teachers in the 1990s. To encourage reflection on the proposition that the field of comparative legal studies is a diverse, eclectic, and vibrant one, the author prepared and circulated to his colleagues an introductory paper setting out a conceptual overview of the field. In particular, it was suggested that comparative law has evolved through nine generations; that none of the earlier stages of comparative legal studies has been entirely replaced; that each new generation has been added to its predecessors in the manner of a multilayered sponge cake; and that each generation has some continuing value as a mode of comparative inquiry.

The current diversity, some might say "disorderliness," in comparative legal studies has not repelled, but seems rather to have acted as a magnet in attracting legal scholars to the field. In addition, pressures of globalization have forced more lawyers and law and policy makers to acquire a degree of sophistication in the transnationalization of law. The existence of diversity within the field, and our acceptance of the legitimacy of that diversity, allowed our colleagues to come to the project from whatever schools, ideologies, or modes of scholarship they represent. Although eclecticism may not always be in fashion within the academic community, the advantages of eclecticism for the purposes of our project outweighed the disadvantages.

As we explain in Chapter 12, the eleven separate studies in this book exemplify six of the nine models of comparative law scholarship. The first generation, *descriptive comparative law,* can be seen to come down from antiquity, or at least from the time of Solon, the first law reformer, who is said to have surveyed the laws of various city-states in the sixth century BC, as did Aristotle two centuries later. These and subsequent evidences of comparative erudition were merely descriptive, lacking any pretence at systematic, analytical, or explanatory scholarship. Yet descriptive comparative law is still a conspicuous branch of modern legal research, not least in the form of transnational compilations of national legislation composed or commissioned by the United Nations.

The line between description and analysis is not always easy to discern, but the potentiality for "true" comparative law in the form of *comparative textual analysis* might be traced, in the second generation, to the promulgation of the French Napoleonic Code in 1806, which provided the first focus for comprehensive juridical modelling. The French contribution to the era of codification provided a model framework for the selective but systematic imitation of legal rules and institutions derived from the civil law of ancient Rome. However, by the 1840s this first, strictly European, cross-jurisdictional experiment in comparative textual analysis was flickering like a spent candle, and by the end of the decade the field of comparative legal inquiry was thrust back into the dark.

The restoration of comparative method in legal scholarship, in the third generation, may be attributed to the growth of a critical mass of like-minded scholarly enthusiasts who started to meet regularly in academic symposia. The most catalytic of these professional meetings was the First International Congress of Comparative Law, held in Paris in 1900 in association with the World Exposition), which had been designed to welcome the new dawn. This famous conjunction of scholars was inspired by the organizers' imperturbable faith in progress and a vision of a common law of mankind (droit commun de l'humanité, which would be realized through *comparative legislative studies* placed on a scientific foundation. This tradition of a scientific quest for a common core is alive and well today in the unification movement and in the concept of universally shared legal principles, which took root in Article 39(1) of the Statute of the World Court adopted in 1919, as an accredited source of public international law.

Fourth-generation reactions against excessive formalism and positivism in the early schools of comparative law began with the pioneering work of *legal ethnology* developed by scholars such as Sir Henry Maine (1822-88), whose *Ancient Law* became the first best-seller in the field of comparative legal studies. Despite snipings by critics with a fetish for historical accuracy, Maine's conceptual framework and probing insights and hypotheses were to inject a measure of creative imagination into the textualist and rather sterile literature of comparative law, inviting controversy but generating an interest that continues to transcend the level of technicality.

Karl Marx (1818-83) was only four years older than Maine, and most of his adult life was spent in London, just down the line from Oxford. Yet it would be difficult for two close-living contemporaries to differ more markedly in their manner of conducting class warfare against legal formalism. Although not perhaps the founder of the *sociology of law,* nor of the governing concepts of social class and class struggle, Marx popularized the idea of these historic forces as the central fact in the theory of social change and as the premise of the fifth generation of comparative legal studies. For Marxists, formal state law at any one point in social history is the coercive instrument of the ruling class or dominant elite, and formal law is part of the superstructure imposed on society by power-holders who control the economic base or infrastructure. Power-holding theory continues today to reverberate throughout academe, offering analogies to legal comparatists who frame their investigations with concepts of dominant and dependent legal cultures.

Thirty years after the Bolshevik Revolution of 1917, a family of socialist legal systems began to grow up, each member owing fidelity to its Marxist ancestry, thus giving promise to a new field of *comparative socialist studies* and a sixth-generation dimension to the comparison of legal systems. The lack of a clearly defined and wholly acceptable Soviet model of socialist legality and justice meant that the newer members of the family were left to develop their own variations. However, the Stalinist tradition of intolerance in the face of deviation was hard to shake off, and open inquiry was discouraged in most of the Soviet bloc countries lest it lead to a weakening of the ideological union. Both inside and outside the socialist academic community, controversies arose over the comparability of legal systems serving different (socialist and capitalist) interests, classes, and elites, adding a stimulating but often polemical vigour into the discourse on the theory of legal development.

In the late 1960s, when intergenerational divisions reached a new level of social significance, the evidence of dominance and dependency in international relations attracted the attention of radicalized legal scholars. Somewhat in the Marxist tradition, these younger and more critical scholars looked at formal law as essentially a coercive instrument that was likely to turn a generalized policy of Third World nation-building to the special advantage of the dominant class or the urban elite, and to the general benefit of foreign capitalists. There is evidence that this process is still continuing, for example, in the area of trade law with recent GATT negotiations. Most comparative lawyers, or at least those with a formalist or positivist orientation, were perceived to be serving these non-proletarian and chiefly American interests behind the façade of objective scholarship. This seventh mode of comparative law, the *law and development movement,* challenged all existing development assistance programs that focused on the goal of modernization and depended on the use of imported Western models of formal law as the vehicle of implementation. This ideological approach to comparative law coincided with post-independence resentments in many former colonies against the evidences of exploitative policies, which were seen to motivate the use of Western legal models. But wounds inflicted within the school of law and development theory could not be healed, and the movement failed to survive the early 1980s.

Some of the same suspicions of formal state law as a special interest, if not oppressive, mechanism continue to maintain an undercurrent in the mainstream of contemporary comparative law. But the eighth-generation model, focusing on such constructs as informal justice, legal pluralism, aboriginal rights, and governance is reflected more clearly in the domestic sphere of *law and society and legal history studies*. Today, problems in gaining research access to radically different legal cultures are often seen to prevent comparative lawyers from testing internationally the hypotheses at the bottom of critical legal theory, and from engaging in empirically rigorous studies of the state-society relationship in unfamiliar cultural settings.

The ninth generation – the most recent layer on the cake – is perhaps the most creatively interventionist of the newer approaches to comparative legal studies. The European Community has demonstrated how far the adhesive policy of *legal harmonization* can be applied in designated areas of common purpose. To a lesser extent, a much larger and growing membership of European countries has embarked on the same road within the framework of Council of Europe treaties, not least under the European Convention on Human Rights. Outside Europe the trend to legal harmonization is a more modest undertaking, but there is no lack of recent evidence that the United States, as the unipolar power, is now strongly motivated to induce other countries to bring more and more of their legislation into conformity with the U.S. model. The turn-of-the-century prospect of regional trade blocs, such as APEC, NAFTA, the Andean Economic Community, and AFTA, and of course the emergence of a reinforced global system of GATT trade rules under the supervision of the WTO, seem to guarantee that comparative lawyers of the next generation will devote more and more of their attention to the tasks of designing and implementing harmonization strategies across the lines of national jurisdiction.

ACCOMMODATING THE DIVERSITY WITHIN THE LAW SCHOOL COMMUNITY

The diversity of these models of comparative law is matched by the diversity of the North American law school community. Consensus on how to proceed with an ambitious collaborative project is difficult to develop among colleagues who, like all law school colleagues, reflect a wide variety of specialized areas of knowledge, styles of scholarship, and professional mindsets, influenced as these all are in some degree by temperament, training, and ideological or jurisprudential bias. All of these differences can be seen, in retrospect, to have had some effect on the final shaping of this project.

The literature produced by colleagues at UVic Law School, and perhaps at most North American law schools, might be divided into six principal groups. Admittedly there is a good deal of crossing of these lines, and some scholars may be seen to operate in two or more of these modes. Nevertheless it may not be too distortive to suggest the distinctiveness, if not mutual exclusiveness, of these six approaches. Reflections of all of these approaches, except perhaps the first, can be seen in one or more of the chapters in this book. The most practical of law school writing strives primarily to provide *legal advice* to those with responsibilities to clients in law firms, government departments, corporate enterprises, and other sectors of the legal profession. Often these writings are confidential and remain unpublished, but when legal advisers in the academic community do publish, their preference is generally to focus as sharply as possible on real, but usually technical, problems that have to be addressed. Contributions of this kind to comparative law, addressed to the profession, tend to deal with the latest legislation in a country that is foreign in the eyes of the reader for whom it is written, and it is likely that explanation of the legislation will be provided at the institutional rather than the doctrinal level.

As an extension of the professional service offered by legal scholars, much Western law school research, especially in the domain of private law, consists of *doctrinal analysis* focused on recent judicial decisions. This kind of highly technical micro-analysis is less concerned with advice to any particular addressee than with scrutiny of the most recent and significant case-to-case adjustments of doctrine within the judicial process. Contributions of this kind to comparative law tend to be confined to cognate jurisdictions of the common law or civil law family, and thus to countries with comparable traditions in the use of judicial institutions and procedures. Writings of this textualist orientation may be the most likely to be regarded by the author, and perhaps by the reader, as objective and value-neutral, but possibly also the least likely to reflect cross-cultural awareness of the interplay between text and context.

A rather sharp contrast can be drawn between the first two approaches and the remaining four. The most generic of these four might be described as *contextual analysis:* a kind of scholarship that attempts to extract themes, features, and factors of legal development from the milieu of economic, social, political, historical, and other variables. The focus is on what might be conceptualized as the legal system, culture, or tradition of the country subjected to study for purposes of comparative evaluation. Such macro-analytical scholarship seeks justification through the provision of conceptual insights (sophistication) rather than through that of in-depth erudition (rigour). It is vulnerable to the charge of subjectivism, but has the merit of offering the criteria by which it might be criticized by equally subjective commentators operating at the same level of analysis.

Of the remaining three approaches, *policy-oriented scholarship* provides the sharpest focus by concentrating on specific public policy issues of the day. Typically, these issues have not been created in the mind of the author, but have already been projected by the publicized interaction of interests and values. More often than not, they are included on the agenda of the relevant decision-making institution. Legal scholarship of this fourth kind tends therefore to be addressed to the decision-making arena as much as to the author's academic colleagues, and technical considerations may have to compete with political ones. Today this kind of writing is an increasingly familiar entree into the field of comparative, as well as international, law; indeed, the complexity of current problems associated with the implementation of globally or regionally negotiated instruments serves to restore the old linkages between these two fields of legal scholarship.

Macro-analysis of the sort that proceeds from the author's prior commitment to a set of strongly held political and social values might be described, somewhat clumsily, as *ideology-based legal analysis*. Usually this fifth approach to legal scholarship makes the author's value predispositions more or less explicit, to a much greater degree than in the other five approaches. Like policy-oriented scholarship, it has a persuasive purpose. As an approach to comparative legal studies, it often takes an *a priori* position between the interests of developed or Western countries, on the one hand, and of developing non-Western countries, on the other. Not infrequently, however, the author's personal value orientation appears to be culturally derived, and ideological commitment does not necessarily save this kind of scholarship from ethnocentric bias.

Finally, it is possible to distinguish what might be characterized as *theory-based legal analysis*. Like ideology-based legal analysis, this approach begins with concepts, but these concepts are intellectual constructs and categories rather than political or social values. Given the difficulty of separating ideology from theory, many writers in the field today might be regarded as exemplifying both approaches or as working on the interface between the two. Like all conceptualists, legal theorists might be accused of imposing their mind-set on social reality, and, when applied to a foreign legal system, this may be only one step away from imposing one of the intellectual styles associated with one's own culture. To this it may have to be argued that any approach to comparative law involves, to some degree, the push or pull of the author's cultural origin.

On the assumption that it is valuable to embrace, rather than shun, diversity, it was agreed at an early stage of this project that the contributors were free to rely upon whatever schools or modes of scholarship seemed most appropriate to them. The commonality of purpose was limited to two propositions that seemed to receive general acquiescence from the project participants. The first, as argued in the author's initial overview, was that the collective initiative should be "scoped" around the concept of *legal development.* This concept envisages law as a process by which legal norms, standards, institutions, and procedures are, more or less consciously, created, adapted, rationalized, improved, and terminated by human agency. Applied to comparative studies, the "legal development" orientation requires the investigator to deal with legal change as concomitant with social, economic, political, technological, and other kinds of change in human affairs. This, it was agreed, would be a sufficient objective for a collective initiative drawing upon the normal diversity that resides within any North American law school. A final chapter, to be written after receipt of the other chapters, would evaluate in a more generic way the numerous factors that seem to facilitate or obstruct legal change.

The second kind of bonding was agreement to use, as a principle of organization, the concept that legal systems consist, in large part, of *sectors.* If overgeneralization is one of the causes of superficiality in comparative legal studies, more might be gained than lost by lowering the level of comparison from the systemic to the sectoral. The sectoral level is intermediate between that of micro-comparison, which arguably offers too little insight into the functioning of law in its larger purposes, and that of cross-systemic comparison, which in a sense offers too much to be convincing. For the purpose of this collaboration, it was accepted that the substantive content of formal legal systems would be treated in three distinguishable, if overlapping, sectors: the economic, the civic, and the behavioural.

First, the largest part of a modern legal system consists of an *economic sector,* which encompasses all subject areas of property and transactional law that can be said to contribute to the development and maintenance of the economic system. In the eye of the ideologist, this sector of a formal legal system is derived from the need to use state institutions to buttress the capitalist, socialist, or hybrid ethos of the political economy. Joining commercial and corporate law at the core of the economic sector are contract law and other transactional subjects, such as agency, insurance, banking law, competition law, debtor-creditor, employment law, and of course the cluster of property law areas, both real and personal, that are even more basic to the protection and regulation of the economic system. At the present stage of economic history, when so much emphasis is now placed on the generative potentiality of globalization, it seems particularly valuable to trace the transnational effects of current trends in topics drawn from areas such as intellectual property and securities regulation. The scope of the economic sector might be viewed even more broadly as including ancillary areas of formal law, such as taxation, trusts, and estate succession, and more peripheral fields that contribute partially to the development of economic (i.e., property and transactional) law: for example, trade union law, environmental law, conflict of laws, and several subdivisions of public international law. Perhaps over half of the faculty members in a typical North American law school are primarily specialists in one or more of these economically significant areas of law; and at least one-third of the contributors to this book might be willing to be so designated.

The second largest part of formal state law can be characterized as the *civic sector,* consisting of those subject areas concerned with the structure and process of government and the relationship between the individual citizen and the state. Constitutional law sits at the centre of the civic sector, but it is buttressed by administrative law and other components of public law. However, since civic law serves symbolic as well as operational purposes in modern society, one of the tasks of comparative legal inquiry is to keep both of these two functions in mind when attempts are made to evaluate the significance of civic law in the different systems compared, and the differing relationships between the legislative, executive, and judicial branches of government. In early discussions with our public law colleagues, it was suggested that one of the benefits of cross-cultural analysis of developments in the civic sector was the generation of insights into the long-term effect of the current effort to impose Western models of democracy, governance, and constitutionalism on non-Western legal cultures and traditions; and that the quest for sophistication in this context would require a conscious departure from the older formalistic approaches to comparative law. Civic values and public institutions seem more likely to reflect reality than the texts of formal law, especially in non-litigious cultures with a tradition of limited resort to judicial process for civic purposes. Legal inquiry of this kind would, therefore, seem to require a healthy dose of "techno-scepticism," not least in interpreting recent changes in formal civic law in transitional political cultures such as those of Thailand and Vietnam.

Finally, the tripartite framework designed for this collaboration included those areas and issues that can be said to make up the *behavioural* sector, which is concerned with more intimately personal and interpersonal aspects of human experience than the transactional and civic sectors. In both of the latter, it is generally accepted that the state has a central role as the preserver of public order, the maintainer of services and standards, and if necessary the settler of disputes. But the behavioural sector is the farthest removed from the public domain, and is the sector that touches upon the most sensitive of cultural issues and the most highly esteemed of cultural values. The behavioural sector is the smallest of the three sectors in all systems of formal law, and indeed in many societies large segments of behavioural law are kept outside the ambit of formal law altogether. Certain social-behavioural issues, such as those associated with prostitution and mental disorder, sit uncomfortably on the fence between formal and informal modes of social control. Here especially the comparative lawyer should be on guard against the danger of ethnocentricity; but here too the foreign investigator might expect to learn the most about the role of law in markedly distinct societies.

Sophistry of this sort deserves to be punished rather than rewarded, but benevolence prevailed. More out of collegial generosity than from the power of logic or the elegance of theory, it was agreed to proceed within the suggested tri-sectoral framework. It was recognized, I think, that the approach advocated by the author had at least the virtue of being all-inclusive. However, the arbitrariness of the threefold classification suggested the need for a fourth, cross-sectoral part of the book. Three areas under study in this book seem to suit a cross-sectoral classification. The area of alternative dispute resolution lends itself to cross-cultural study, and yet applies equally to all three sectors. The law's treatment of indigenous peoples, when viewed as a discrete area of inquiry, as it is in this book, clearly straddles all three sectors of the modern system of formal law. The increasingly expansive area of environmental law seems also to be best approached as cross-sectoral in its scope and significance.

To the extent that anything as brittle as theory was passed around, other than the tri-sectoral concept that had been accepted as the principle of organization, it was the general hypothesis that the present tendency to promote a convergence of legal systems is likely to be most evident and most successful in the economic sector, and least likely in the behavioural sector, in which cultural resistance to external influences is expected to remain intense. The pact was, however, that each author or set of co-authors was free to deal with this hypothesis as seemed appropriate within their chosen context.

ACHIEVING THE GOAL

After circulating the overview paper, organizing a few general brainstorming sessions, and strong-arming colleagues in their offices one by one, it became apparent that half the faculty were committed, with varying degrees of scepticism, to this experiment in institutional writing. The fact that each contributor was free to "Asianize" his or her own area of domestic interest and expertise, with little or no constraint on the theory or style of scholarship to be applied, was clearly important in convincing many colleagues to join the project. In this way it was possible to avoid the clash of ideologies and philosophies that would surely have resulted from even a light-handed effort to secure consensus on a particular theory or approach to the book. Instead it was agreed that any fanciful hypothesizing could await the final chapter, where the tasks of integration and linkage-making would also be undertaken.

Although initial commitments to join the project were now in hand, "herding the cats" was not without its difficulties. The first challenge was to find ways for a number of contributors to extend their expertise to one or more Asian countries. A number of techniques were employed. Several contributors used all or part of their sabbatical leaves to acquire Asian expertise on the subjects under discussion. For others, shorter site visits and consultations with Asian experts, often "piggy-backed" to some other funded project in Asia, provided necessary expertise and insights. And, for two of the chapters, the authors sought out Asian country experts to act as direct collaborators in their writing. Using this variety of techniques, we were able to undertake this institutional research project without first having to secure substantial funding for either research or travel. This fact may serve as an encouragement to other law faculties contemplating such a project. Although funding was not initially seen as a prerequisite to undertaking this project, we are nonetheless greatly indebted to the Canada-ASEAN Centre in Singapore for financing two author-collaborator workshops, which greatly facilitated the completion of Chapters 2 and 7 of this book.

Setting a timetable for focusing our colleagues' scholarly interests on Asia was also problematic. Efficiency had to give way to patience; taking the long view for completion of the project was essential. Each contributor had different sorts of personal and professional obstacles to Asianizing their own scholarly research. These differences had to be respected. Deadlines were set in good faith, but were missed by most contributors, only to have new deadlines set that could once again be missed. Indeed, a few of the original participants dropped out entirely, but a few new ones also came aboard. At a few points it seemed the project was bound to miscarry. Fortunately, the author acquired a co-editor, Gerry Ferguson, soon after the project was under way, to share in the tasks of design, advocacy, consultation, diplomacy, business management, and editing that arise from this kind of venture. Complementarity and role-sharing, it was discovered, were effective survival techniques to endure the disappointment of broken promises and to drive the project forward. With the Faculty's two most stubborn members acting as co-editors, the end of the tunnel was bound to appear, and finally it did.

Fortune favoured the project in other ways. Pitman Potter, a friend and respected colleague from outside UVic, agreed to join as guest contributor, enhancing the collaboration with his expertise in Chinese law and other legal systems of Northeast Asia. Moreover, a superior UVic student paper on the Vietnamese constitution, written by Joanna Harrington – later a doctoral student at Cambridge University – provided the foundation for one of our four co-authored chapters.

What has emerged, then, is a set of diverse but back-linked studies that reflect the westward-looking scholarship of a North American west coast law school committed to collaboration in the Asia-Pacific. Individually, each of these expert studies stands on its own as an unique piece of transnational legal or cross-disciplinary scholarship. Collectively, they stand or fall as a carefully negotiated and coordinated collection of studies by half the full-time faculty of a North American law school, supplemented by a final chapter that draws out longer term implications within a conceptual framework of legal development. This collection is offered as an institutional work and as a possible foundation for other North American collaborations as we move into the "Asian century."

Part I: The Economic Sector

1
The Convergence of Securities Laws in Asia: Case Studies of Malaysia, Singapore, Japan, and China

Mark Gillen and Pitman Potter

INTRODUCTION

Securities laws can be characterized as laws belonging to what has been described as the "economic sector." The economic sector "encompasses all subject areas of law which can be said to contribute to the development and maintenance of the economic system."[1] This chapter considers securities laws to assess the hypothesis suggested in the Introduction to this book "that the present tendency to promote a *convergence of legal systems* is likely to be most evident and most successful in the economic sector."[2]

The chapter describes various factors that may contribute to the convergence of securities laws and various factors that may contribute to differences in these laws. Subsequently, it considers the influence of these factors on certain key aspects of securities laws in Malaysia, Singapore, Japan, and China. These countries provide useful contrasts in terms of legal systems, prevailing ideologies, cultures, and stages of economic development.

The aspects of securities laws that are considered in the country case studies below are the disclosure requirements on the distribution of securities, subsequent ongoing disclosure requirements, the regulation of subsequent trading (including insider trading, market manipulation, and takeover bids), and the regulation of securities market services such as underwriting, brokerage, portfolio management, and investment advice.

The analysis focuses primarily on the written laws of the countries considered. Where possible, attention is given to how the law works in practice and the extent to which the practice is consistent with the written law. However, in the area of securities laws, even where the law and practice differ, the law will set boundaries on the extent to which the practice can deviate and, over time, will affect the pattern of administrative practice.[3]

---

1 See D. M. Johnston, "Introduction: The Evolution of the Project," at 10.

2 *Ibid.* at 12.

3 Political pressures that are likely to arise in the context of securities markets will tend to put pressure on administrators to apply securities laws in a consistent, and therefore

Thus an analysis of the degree of convergence in securities laws will be relevant even where administrative practice currently deviates from the apparent letter of the law.

The next section sets out the various factors considered in the case studies. This is followed by the case studies themselves.

REASONS FOR SIMILARITIES AND DIFFERENCES IN SECURITIES LAWS

This section sets out various reasons for similarities in securities laws and factors that contribute to the differences in these laws.

Why Are There Similarities in Securities Laws?

A substantial degree of similarity is found in the securities laws of different jurisdictions. Securities laws typically have mandatory disclosure requirements on the distribution of securities to the public.[4] They also typically have ongoing mandatory disclosure requirements to provide information in support of the post-distribution trading of securities.[5] Insider trading and market manipulation techniques are usually prohibited in some manner.[6] Takeover bids are generally subject to rules governing the manner in which bids are made, the period over which bids must be kept open, and the information that must be provided to offeree shareholders.[7] Securities market services are usually subject to record keeping requirements, duties to clients, minimum competency standards, and minimum capital requirements

---

predictable, fashion. Investment is likely to be deterred by administrative practices that deviate significantly from promulgated securities laws that formed part of the basis for investment decisions.

4 See e.g. S. D. Cohen, "Survey of Registration and Disclosure Requirements in International Securities Markets" (1988) 9 *Michigan Yearbook of International Legal Studies* 243-61. See also the discussion of this aspect of the securities laws of the various countries discussed in the case studies below.

5 See, for instance, the discussion of this aspect of the securities laws of the various countries discussed in the case studies below. For a discussion of such requirements in Canadian securities legislation, see e.g. M. R. Gillen, *Securities Regulation in Canada* (Toronto: Carswell, 1992) c. 6. For a discussion of such requirements in U.S. securities laws, see e.g. T. L. Hazen, *Treatise on the Law of Securities Regulation*, vol. 1, 3d ed. (St. Paul, Minn.: West, 1995) at 514-27. See also the German *Securities Exchange Act*, ss. 44-44d.

6 See e.g. H. Lee, "An International Perspective on Market Manipulation," in C. Lye and R. Lazar, eds., *The Regulation of Financial and Capital Markets* (Singapore: Singapore Academy of Law, 1991) at 201-204. See also e.g. M. J. Houle, "Survey of National Legislation Regulating Insider Trading" (1988) 9 *Michigan Yearbook of International Legal Studies* 209-42.

7 See, for instance, the discussion of this aspect of the securities laws of the various countries discussed in the case studies below. On such provisions in Canada see Gillen, *supra* note 5, c. 11, and in the United States see Hazen, *supra* note 5, vol. 2, at 266-72, 290-309. See also D. A. DeMott, "Comparative Dimensions of Takeover Regulation" (1987) 65 Wash. Univ. L. Quarterly 69 comparing U.S. and U.K. approaches to takeover bid regulation.

that are enforced, in part, through a licensing requirement.[8] In many countries there has also been a gradual shift towards a greater degree of public regulation.[9] The securities laws of the countries discussed in the case studies below generally follow a very similar pattern that suggests a convergence of securities laws. These case studies also provide evidence of direct verbatim, or near verbatim borrowing of securities laws.

Similarities in securities laws evolve for a number of reasons. Perhaps the laws move towards similar solutions simply because these are the only practical solutions. Perhaps similar interest groups arise in securities markets wherever they develop, bringing about political pressures that lead to similar laws. The similarities may result from competitive pressures associated with attracting investment capital. Such competition may have become particularly more pronounced in the face of the increasing internationalization of securities markets.[10] Other factors that may have a bearing on the similarities are pressures from U.S. regulators to have U.S.-style securities laws adopted in other countries, the effects of proximity or of sharing the same language, or close business or educational contacts. The importance of the roles played by particular persons in the development of securities laws may also be a factor, as well as simple coincidences that lead to the following of one country's laws over those of another. These factors are briefly noted below. The factors are not necessarily consistent. They are raised here simply as possibilities to be considered in the case studies discussed below.

Convergence towards Optimal Solutions

Securities laws may have a tendency to converge because securities markets develop similar problems for which there are optimal solutions towards which markets gravitate. Each jurisdiction thus works its way to these optimal solutions as securities markets in the jurisdiction develop. While the details of the laws may differ from one jurisdiction to another, the broad

---

8 In the Canadian context, see e.g. Gillen, *supra* note 5, at 368-90. In the U.S., see e.g. Hazen, *supra* note 5, vol. 2, at 10-16, 33-46, and 91-102. In the context of Malaysia, Singapore, and Japan see case studies below.

9 See the discussion with respect to Malaysia and Singapore, *infra* notes 73 to 77 and the accompanying text.

10 For a summary of the effects of internationalization on the Canadian securities market, see e.g. H. Lazar, A. Mayrand, and K. Patterson, "Global Competition and Canadian Federalism: The Federal Sector" (1992) 20 C.B.L.J. 1. The extent of internationalization is also documented in e.g. J. A. Grundfest, "Internationalization of the World's Securities Markets: Economic Causes and Regulatory Consequences" (1990) J. of Financial Services Research 349; K. Y. Testy, "Comity and Cooperation: Securities Regulation in a Global Marketplace" (1994) 45 Alabama L. Rev. 927; J. Futterman, "Evasion and Flowback in the Regulation S Era: Strengthening U.S. Investor Protection While Promoting U.S. Corporate Offshore Offerings" (1995) 18 Fordham Int'l L.J. 806.

thrust of the laws will be similar. For instance, mandatory disclosure may be the best solution to the problem of asymmetrical information and potential frauds on the public distribution of securities,[11] or it may provide a more comparable standard of disclosure that might not be produced in the private market.[12]

Such inevitable solutions are, at best, only part of an explanation of similarities in securities laws. First, doubt has been expressed as to whether the solutions securities laws typically provide are in the public interest. For instance, it has been suggested that the costs of mandatory disclosure outweigh the benefits,[13] and the evidence on the effect of mandatory disclosure suggests that it has brought little, if any, benefit.[14] The benefit of regulating insider trading or takeover bids has also been questioned.[15] Some empirical evidence suggests that takeover bids result in net gains in wealth that are not wholly due to pure wealth transfers[16] and that takeover bid regulation deters these socially beneficial takeovers.[17]

---

11 See *infra* notes 32 to 36 and the accompanying text.

12 See *infra* note 37 and the accompanying text.

13 See e.g. F. H. Easterbrook and D. R. Fischel, "Mandatory Disclosure and the Protection of Investors" (1984) 70 Virginia L. Rev. 669.

14 See e.g. tests of the effects of the U.S. *Securities Act* of 1933 and the *Securities Exchange Act* of 1934 in G. J. Stigler, "Public Regulation of Securities Markets" (1964) 37 J. of Bus. 117; G. A. Jarrell, "The Economic Effects of Federal Regulation of the Market for New Security Issues" (1981) 24 J. of Law and Econ. 613; C. J. Simon, "The Effects of the 1933 Securities Act on Investor Information and the Performance of New Issues" (1989) 79 Amer. Econ. Rev. 295; and G. J. Benston, "Required Disclosure and the Stock Market: An Evaluation of the Securities Exchange Act of 1934" (1973) 63 Amer. Econ. Rev. 132. For critiques of Stigler see I. Friend and E. S. Herman, "The S.E.C. Through a Glass Darkly" (1964) 37 J. of Bus. 382; and S. Robbins and W. Werner, "Professor Stigler Revisited" (1964) 37 J. of Bus. 406. For a critique of Benston see I. Friend and R. Westerfield, "Required Disclosure and the Stock Market: Comment" (1975) 65 Amer. Econ. Rev. 467.

15 With respect to insider trading see e.g. H. G. Manne, *Insider Trading and the Stock Market* (New York: Free Press, 1966); H. G. Manne, "Insider Trading and the Law Professors" (1970) 23 Vanderbilt L. Rev. 547; D. W. Carlton and D. R. Fischel, "The Regulation of Insider Trading" (1983) 35 Stan. L. Rev. 857. With respect to takeover bid regulation see e.g. D. R. Fischel, " Efficient Capital Market Theory, the Market for Corporate Control, and the Regulation of Cash Tender Offers" (1978) 57 Tex. L. Rev. 1; F. H. Easterbrook and D. R. Fischel, "The Proper Role of a Target's Management in Responding to a Tender Offer" (1981) 94 Harv. L. Rev. 1161; and A. Schwartz, "Search Theory and the Tender Offer Auction" (1986) 2 J. L. Econ. and Org. 2.

16 This has generally been the conclusion of reviews of the considerable empirical literature on the effects of takeovers. See e.g. G. A. Jarrell, J. A. Brickley and J. M. Netter, "The Market for Corporate Control: The Empirical Evidence Since 1980" (1988) 2 J. of Econ. Perspectives 49; R. Romano, "A Guide to Takeovers: Theory, Evidence and Regulation" (1992) 9 Yale Yearbook on Regulation 119; M. C. Jensen and R. S. Ruback, "The Market for Corporate Control: the Scientific Evidence" (1983) 11 J. of Fin. Econ. 5.

17 Empirical evidence to this effect is reviewed in the articles cited *supra* note 16. For articles arguing that takeover bid regulation does deter beneficial takeovers, see e.g. D. R. Fischel, "Efficient Capital Market Theory, the Market for Corporate Control, and the Regulation of Cash Tender Offers" (1978) 57 Texas L. Rev. 1; F. H. Easterbrook and D. R.

Second, there are conceivable alternatives to the types of securities laws that are most prevalent. For instance, the concern for asymmetrical information and potential frauds has been addressed in a variety of ways at different times. Initially, at least, there was very little in the way of what one would recognize as modern day securities regulation. Markets and implicit market forces served to limit the extent of the problem.[18] The early response in England was to expand the scope of civil or criminal sanctions against misrepresentations by issuers.[19] Another approach has been to provide a mechanism to facilitate the investigation of frauds backed up by civil, administrative, or penal sanctions.[20] Yet another approach has been to require the disclosure of certain information to a private or public administrative body that would assess the merits of investment in the securities and allow the distribution only if investment in the securities met some minimum quality standard.[21]

It has also been argued that many aspects of securities regulation served the particular rent-seeking interest of various participants in securities markets[22] or responded to the bureaucratic pressures present in securities regulatory organizations.[23] In responding to such interests and pressures, various

---

Fischel, "The Proper Role of a Target's Management in Responding to a Tender Offer" (1981) 94 Harv. L. Rev. 1161; A. Schwartz, "Search Theory and the Tender Offer Auction" (1986) 2 J. L. Econ. and Org. 2; and H. Manne, "Mergers and the Market for Corporate Control" (1965) 73 J. Pol. Econ. 110.

18 Such an approach is not unreasonable given the evidence on the effectiveness of mandatory disclosure and arguments on the cost of mandatory disclosure relative to the benefits. See the articles cited *supra* notes 13 to 17.

19 See e.g. *Directors' Liability Act*, 1890 (U.K.), 53 and 54 Vict., c. 64.

20 See e.g. the Ontario *Securities Fraud Prevention Act*, S.O. 1928, c. 24.

21 This was the approach of early state "blue sky" legislation in the United States that was first enacted in the state of Kansas (Kans. Laws 1911, c. 133). This legislation was later adopted in several states (see J. R. Macey and G. P. Miller, "Origin of the Blue Sky Laws" (1991) 70 Texas L. Rev. 347 for a review of the development of state blue sky laws) and in other jurisdictions (see e.g. the Manitoba *Sale of Shares Act*, S.M. 1912, c. 75).

22 On public choice theories, see e.g. S. M. Phillips and J. R. Zecher, *The SEC and the Public Interest* (Cambridge, Mass.: MIT Press, 1981) (arguing that the securities laws in the U.S. amount to a substantial subsidy to securities analysts and institutional investors); H. G. Manne, "Economic Aspects of Required Disclosure Under Federal Securities Law," in H. G. Manne and E. Solomon, *Wall Street in Transition: The Emerging System and its Impact on the Economy* (New York, N.Y.: New York University Press, 1974) at 21 (arguing that securities regulation in the U.S. worked to the advantage of larger issuers of securities by imposing much more substantial burdens on smaller issuers than on larger issuers); J. R. Macey and G. P. Miller, "Origin of the Blue Sky Laws" (1991) 70 Texas Law Rev. 347 (arguing that smaller local banks, local industries, and farmers lobbied for state blue sky regulation at the expense of large Wall Street banks, investment banking firms, and major issuers of securities in manufacturing, railroad, and public utility companies); and D. D. Haddock and J. R. Macey, "Regulation on Demand: A Private Interest Model, with an Application to Insider Trading Regulation" (1987) 30 J. of L. and Econ. 311 (arguing that the interests of professional traders and insiders coalesced to bring about the particular pattern of insider trading regulation).

23 See e.g. D. C. Langevoort, "The SEC as a Bureaucracy: Public Choice, Institutional Rhetoric, and the Process of Policy Formulation" (1990) 47 Wash. and Lee Law Rev. 527; N.

aspects of securities regulation may not, in fact, be consistent with the broader public interest.

Thus, while similarities in securities laws may be partly explained as a gradual movement towards optimal solutions to common securities market problems, other factors may also play an important role in the convergence of securities laws. Given the plausible alternatives to the most prevalent types of securities laws, it is not clear that the most prevalent types are the best. Further, securities laws arguably serve interests other than a broad public interest.

Political Pressures Leading to Similar Securities Laws

An alternative explanation of similarities in securities laws is that similar political pressures may exist in different countries where securities markets develop.[24] First, similar political pressures may arise in different jurisdictions quite independently of competitive pressures that arise in the context of international competition in securities markets. Second, competition for capital in international securities markets may also affect the shape of domestic securities laws. Third, foreign securities market interests may attempt to influence domestic securities laws to protect economic rents in existing markets against competition and secure similar economic rents in the host jurisdiction.

Similarities in Developing Securities Markets Leading to Similar Political Pressures

Similar political pressures may arise due to common features in the development of securities markets that lead to similar interest groups applying political pressure in search of economic rents.

Similar Securities Market Participants Forms of organization involving multiple investors are likely to arise in response to economic pressures to capture economies of scale by producing on a large scale, or else engage in enterprises that require very large capital outlays. The benefits of liquidity tend to encourage forms of investment that can be freely traded.[25] An industry with expertise in the trading of these investments is likely to

---

Wolfson, "A Critique of the Securities and Exchange Commission," [1981] Emory L.J. 119.

24 See *supra* notes 22 and 23 with respect to public choice theories of securities regulation. These explanations of securities regulation might apply in other countries if similar political pressures exist in those countries.

25 The benefits of limited liability in the form of increased liquidity are discussed in P. Halpern, M. Trebilcock, and S. Turnbull, "An Economic Analysis of Limited Liability in Corporation Law" (1980) 30 U. of Toronto L.J. 117; and F. H. Easterbrook and D. R. Fischel, "Limited Liability in the Corporation" (1985) 52 U. Chi. Law Rev. 89.

develop.[26] Consequently, many different countries are likely to end up with securities markets that have broadly similar structural characteristics. There will be promoters, investors, brokers, dealers, underwriters, portfolio managers, and investment advisers. To manage risk and capture the benefits of diversification, various forms of financial intermediation will also be likely to develop. Exchanges are likely to be formed as brokers find that they can increase their business by facilitating trading through an exchange.[27] Accountants are likely to become involved as issuers of securities attempt to signal the quality of their investments to investors by calling upon accountants to put their reputational capital at stake in lending their seal of approval to the issuer's financial statements.[28] Other experts may be called upon to put their reputations at stake by lending their seal of approval to claims made by issuers of securities.[29] Lawyers will tend to become involved in developing the contractual framework within which securities trading takes place and in settling the legal disputes that frequent securities trades are bound to bring about.

Common Investor Protection Interests The above-listed market participants may have a common interest in protecting investors. Investor protection that increases the expected values of securities encourages capital formation through the issuance of securities and increases business for promoters, underwriters, accountants, and lawyers.[30] The increased capitalization of the market will tend to lead to more trading and thus more business for brokers and exchanges. Increased investment and trading is also likely to lead to more business for portfolio managers and investment advisers. Participants in securities markets at the time of an expansion in investment

26 Stories of the development of stock exchanges and other markets are often quite similar. See e.g. F. Braudel, *Civilization and Capitalism, 15th-18th Century*, Vol. II, *The Wheels of Commerce* (London: Collins, 1982) at 97-114.

27 Stories of the development of stock exchanges often involve brokers meeting in a given place where they would inquire whether their fellow brokers had clients interested in buying what their clients were interested in selling. See *ibid.* Braudel. On the development of the Singapore and Kuala Lumpur Stock Exchanges, see e.g. Tan Pheng Theng, *Securities Regulation in Singapore and Malaysia: A Primer on the Laws of the Stock Market with Cases and Materials* (Singapore: Stock Exchange of Singapore, 1978) at 1-4; and R. Gill, *The Making of Malaysia Inc.* (Singapore: Pelanduk Publications, 1985) at 30-35.

28 On the use of accountants as a signal of accuracy of financial statements, see e.g. R. L. Watts and J. L. Zimmerman, "Agency Problems, Auditing, and the Theory of the Firm: Some Evidence" (1983) 26 J.L. and Econ. 613. See also Easterbrook and Fischel, *supra* note 13 at 687-89.

29 These other experts might include rating organizations, engineers, geologists, or lawyers rendering legal opinions.

30 Suppose investors require a return of 10% per annum on an investment of a given risk. Suppose that there is a project of the given risk requiring $1,000,000 of capital and which will yield $110,000 of profit per annum (or 11%). At a 10% required rate of return, this project seems worthwhile. However, if investors are concerned that the facts on which the potential returns are based may be the result of a fraud or

through investor protection will gain temporary economic rents until a competitive response restores normal profits.[31]

The various market participants can use market mechanisms to address problems of asymmetric information that can cause investors to discount the value of securities.[32] Indeed, certain participants in securities markets may have come into existence largely to address these concerns. For instance, as noted above, issuers of securities may engage underwriters, accountants, and other experts in an attempt to assure investors of the quality of their securities.[33] Securities exchanges can also protect investors by subjecting issuers to certain criteria in exchange for listing privileges.[34] A listing

---

misrepresentation, they may adjust their estimate of the potential returns accordingly. If they adjust their expectations of the returns down to $90,000 per annum, the project will not be worthwhile to investors and project promoters will not proceed with the project. Investors are expecting only $90,000 on an investment of $1,000,000, or a 9% return, which is less than the required 10%. If one were to sell shares on such a project, and the market was reasonably efficient, the most one could expect to raise (no matter what the number of shares sold) would be $900,000.

If investors were more confident that the facts on which the $110,000 per annum return was based were accurate they would be willing to pay up to $1,100,000 on the financial instruments sold to raise the required capital investment funds. The project promoters would be able to proceed with the project. In other words, if investor confidence in the accuracy of information concerning investment projects could be increased through investor protection, then more investment projects would proceed with more securities being sold to raise the capital, thus creating more business for securities industry participants.

31 Economic rent has been described as follows: "The amount that a factor must earn in its present use to prevent it from moving (i.e. transferring) to another use is called its *transfer earnings*. Any excess it earns over this amount is called its *economic rent*": R. G. Lipsey, D. O. Purvis, and P. O. Steiner, *Economics* (New York: Harper and Row, 1988) at 180. Normal profits are "the imputed returns to capital and risk taking just necessary to prevent the owners from withdrawing from the industry": *ibid.* at 336. In other words, normal profits are the profits that are just sufficient to keep persons in an industry from pursuing other ventures that would yield approximately the same profits. Economic rents accrue when the resources used in the business earn more than the amount that is just sufficient to prevent the owners of those resources from transferring them to other uses.

32 Assymetry in information occurs when issuers of securities have more information about the value of their securities than investors have. Investors and issuers can attempt to reduce the assymetry. Issuers can try to provide investors with information and investors can try to gather and assess information. However, these activities involve costs. At some point the cost of further reductions in the assymetry in information will outweigh the benefits. Investors will be left with a residual inability to distinguish between better quality and poorer quality securities. They will adjust for the uncertain quality by an across-the-board discount in the prices of securities. This will tend to drive the higher quality securities out of the market. The seminal paper on this "adverse selection" process is Ackerloff, "The Market for 'Lemons': Qualitative Uncertainty and the Market Mechanism" (1970) 84 Quarterly J. Econ. 488. For an application to securities markets, see e.g. Easterbrook and Fischel, *supra* note 13 at 673-74.

33 See *supra* notes 28 and 29 and the accompanying text.

34 See e.g. Easterbrook and Fischel, *supra* note 13 at 689-90; and Easterbrook and Fischel, *The Economic Structure of Corporate Law* (Cambridge, Mass: Harvard Univ. Press, 1991) at 294-95.

on a securities exchange can thus serve as a signal of the investment quality of listed securities. However, there may be limitations to these market mechanisms.[35] The general reluctance of societies to allow private parties to impose punitive sanctions limits the capacity of markets to enforce mechanisms that would address problems resulting from asymmetric information.[36] Market participants may therefore need the assistance of public forms of enforcement.

Public enforcement may also serve a common investor protection interest by providing a more comparable standard of disclosure that might not be produced in the private market.[37] Investors, issuers, and persons in the securities business can benefit from a standard form of presentation of information. However, an individual issuer may not have an incentive to adopt a standard form of disclosure to the optimal extent because that issuer could not capture the benefits that other issuers would derive from that issuer's adoption of a standard form of disclosure. This might be addressed through a mechanism such as membership in a stock exchange that would require compliance with a standard disclosure format. However, limits on allowable methods of private enforcement may justify some public involvement in this area.

Anti-Investor Protection Rent Seeking Activities The various participants are also likely to promote regulation that will provide them with economic rents. This may not, however, be conducive to maximizing the value of securities. For instance, securities industry participants may seek regulation that controls entry into their particular business. Licensing regimes for various types of market participants, such as brokers, underwriters, portfolio managers, and investment advisers, might, in part, be interpreted as an attempt to control entry into these businesses. It has been suggested that mandatory disclosure gives larger issuers a competitive advantage over smaller issuers because the cost of compliance with disclosure requirements is, to a large extent, a fixed cost. Thus the costs of compliance for larger issuers is a smaller percentage of the value of its outstanding securities than is the case for a smaller issuer.[38] It has also been suggested that financial analysts benefit

35 See the discussion in Easterbrook and Fischel, *The Economic Structure of Corporate Law*, *supra* note 34 at 300-303.

36 Imprisonment of individuals under private agreements is generally not allowed, and courts are reluctant to enforce liquidated damages provisions in private agreements that are punitive in nature. See e.g. S. M. Waddams, *The Law of Contracts*, 3d ed. (Toronto: Canada Law Book, 1993) at 301-308; G. H. Trietel, *The Law of Contract*, 7th ed. (London: Stevens and Sons, 1987) at 768-72; and S. Williston, *A Treatise on the Law of Contracts*, 3d ed. (Mount Kisco, N.Y.: Baker, Voorhis and Co., 1961) at 667-79.

37 See Easterbrook and Fischel, *supra* note 13 at 686-87; and J. Azzi, "Disclosure in Prospectuses" (1991) 9 Co. and Sec. L.J. 205 at 215-16.

38 See Manne, *supra* note 22 at 28-36.

from having information gathered and formatted under mandatory disclosure laws[39] while underwriters, accountants, lawyers, and other experts also gain from their involvement in complying with mandatory disclosure laws without corresponding benefits to investors.

Other interests that are less directly involved in securities markets but instead offer competing modes of raising capital may also play an important role in the regulation of securities markets. For instance, it has been argued that state banks, which stood to lose loan business from an increased use of stocks and bonds in capital formation, were a significant source of pressure for the adoption in the United States of the so-called "blue sky laws," under which the investment merits of securities were subjected to a regulatory review before the securities could be sold.[40]

Summary With broadly similar groups of market participants becoming involved in securities markets in different countries, and with similar forms of competing interests, the kinds of political pressures that lead to the adoption of securities laws may be quite similar in different countries. Accordingly, securities laws taking broadly similar approaches to the regulation of securities markets may occur quite independently. The securities regulation that results from these political pressures may or may not be in the public interest.

Competition for Capital and the Internationalization of Securities Markets

While similar political pressures that develop independently within different countries may lead to the adoption of similar securities laws, international pressures have probably also contributed to this trend. For example, international competition for capital is a potential source of political pressure that has probably increased in recent years with the trend towards the globalization of securities markets.

Securities Laws and the Competition for Capital Capital directed to investment promotes economic growth and development.[41] The necessary capital for investment can come from encouraging a country's residents to channel their savings into investment, or it can come from foreign investors. Countries compete for the scarce funds of investors in the international market

39 See Phillips and Zecher, *supra* note 22.

40 See Macey and Miller, *supra* note 22.

41 Investment is necessary for economic growth. See e.g. Lipsey et al., *supra* note 31 at 828. The resulting capital formation can result in increases in labour productivity. See e.g. R. V. Cherneff, *Macroeconomics* (Scarborough, Ont.: Prentice-Hall, 1993) at 336-38.

place. Funds tend to move to the country that is perceived to provide the best return on investment for a given level of non-diversifiable risk.[42] Local entrepreneurs will therefore influence policy makers to provide conditions that encourage investment by both locals and foreigners by maximizing return on investment and minimizing non-diversifiable risk.

A country's legal infrastructure will be among the factors that will affect the country's investment climate.[43] A country's securities laws are part of that legal infrastructure. To attract investment, countries will be motivated to enact securities laws that are most likely to fulfil that purpose.[44]

Increasing International Competition A significant trend has emerged in recent years towards the "globalization" or "internationalization" of securities markets.[45] Large issues of securities are increasingly floated in more than one country,[46] issuers of securities frequently float issues in foreign countries,[47] and investors invest increasing amounts in foreign markets.[48] This

---

42 Risk and return are the two essential elements in assessing the value of an investment. An efficient portfolio of investments consists of investments that produce the greatest return for a given level of risk. See generally J. F. Weston and T. E. Copland, *Managerial Finance*, 9th ed. (Fort Worth: Dryden Press, 1992) at 357-92.

43 See e.g. M. J. Trebilcock, "What Makes Poor Countries Poor?: The Role of Institutional Capital in Economic Development," University of Toronto, Faculty of Law, Law and Economics Working Paper Series, WPS-38 (1995) at 45-52. On the importance of a legal infrastructure to economic prosperity, see also D. North, *Institutions, Institutional Change and Economic Performance* (Cambridge: Cambridge University Press, 1990) at 54-60.

44 This is similar to the argument that competition in corporate law would cause different jurisdictions to gravitate to similar corporate laws in what might be a "race to the bottom." The seminal article on this subject is W. L. Cary, "Federalism and Corporate Law: Reflections upon Delaware" (1974) 88 Yale L.J. 663. On a "race to the top," see R. K. Winter, "State Law, Shareholder Protection, and the Theory of the Corporation" (1977) 6 J. of Legal Studies 251. For a general discussion of corporate chartering competition see e.g. R. Romano, *The Genius of American Corporate Law* (Washington: American Enterprise Institute, 1993) at 14-51. Similar arguments have been made with respect to securities regulation. See e.g. Easterbrook and Fischel, *supra* note 34 at 295-96 and 300-302.

45 See *supra* note 10.

46 A number of large issues that were sold in several jurisdictions in the 1980s involved privatizations of British Crown companies: namely, British Petroleum in 1977 and 1987, British Telecom in 1984 and 1985, British Gas in 1986 and British Airways in 1987. Since then, international issues of securities have become more and more common.

47 North American issuers have sought increasing amounts of capital overseas. For instance, U.S. private issuers offered $U.S. 3.5 billion in debt securities in the Eurobond market during the first nine months of 1986: see M. Q. Connelly, "Multinational Securities Offerings: A Canadian Perspective" (1987) 50 Law and Contemporary Problems 251 at 252. In Canada the sales of new issues of securities to non-residents increased from $6.5 billion in 1978 to $22.3 billion in 1989: see H. Lazar et al., *supra* note 10.

48 For instance, in Canada sales of outstanding issues to non-residents grew from $2.6 billion in 1978 to $107.9 billion in 1989, and purchases of outstanding issues from non-residents grew from $3.0 billion in 1978 to $95.4 billion in 1989. See Lazar et al., *supra* note 10 at 5.

trend has been encouraged by numerous factors. For example, advances in communications technology and the development of computer technology in the processing of transactions have facilitated the trading of securities and settlement of securities transactions in remote markets. Also, developments in finance theory have favoured increased international portfolio diversification and new types of securities, such as derivative securities, that can be used to achieve the benefits of international diversification with smaller levels of investment while circumventing local restrictions on foreign ownership. Further, the growth of institutional investment has increased the number of investors that can spread the information and transaction costs of international diversification across a large dollar value portfolio. Deregulation in areas such as foreign exchange controls in many countries and a reduction in restrictions on investor participation in foreign securities markets have also facilitated the internationalization of securities markets.[49]

The internationalization of securities markets has increased the availability of funds from foreign investors and facilitated the flight of funds from local markets. Internationalization tends to increase competition between countries for investment funds, and induces countries to adopt securities laws that are perceived as being most likely to attract investors.

Foreign Interests Protecting Economic Rents from International Competition

The development of a country's securities laws may also be affected by political pressure from a foreign country that has well-developed securities markets and securities laws. The securities laws in the foreign country may provide market participants in that country with economic rents that could be lost in the face of foreign competition. It may then behoove the foreign country's market participants to exert political pressure for the adoption of similar securities laws in developing securities markets so that the economic rents they earn in the domestic market will not be subject to dilution through competition. In the context of the internationalization of securities markets, such political pressure may also be brought to bear to secure similar economic rents for securities market operations carried on in developing securities markets.

In recent years the United States has applied diplomatic pressure to get assistance in the enforcement of U.S. securities laws and to encourage other countries to adopt securities laws similar to those in the United States. This

49 See e.g. B. Asher, "The Development of a Global Securities Market," in F. Oditah, ed., *The Future of the Global Securities Market: Legal and Regulatory Aspects* (Oxford: Clarendon Press, 1996) 3 at 5-8; and J. G. MacIntosh, "International Securities Regulation: Competition, Cooperation, Convergence, and Cartelization" (paper presented at the Consumer and Commercial Law Workshop, Oct. 20-21, 1995) at 1-8.

is perhaps most notable with respect to insider trading.[50] These diplomatic endeavours may be the result of political pressure that has been brought to bear in the United States by those who earn economic rents brought about by U.S. securities laws.[51] The concern is that these rents will be dissipated with the flight of funds from the United States to countries with securities laws that impose fewer restraints on securities transactions.

The desire to protect economic rents obtained through U.S. securities regulation may also account for the pressure to give U.S. securities laws an increasingly extraterritorial effect.[52] Following U.S.-style securities laws may be a straightforward step for a country in which U.S. securities laws are already effectively being applied. Enacting U.S. securities laws may, in part, be a means of protecting some degree of sovereignty in enforcement. The desire to protect economic rents from foreign competition may also be a factor in U.S. attempts to obtain a greater degree of harmonization of securities laws through the International Organization of Securities Commissions (IOSCO).[53]

Transactions Costs, Information Costs, Uncertainty, and the Source of Borrowing

As the case studies below suggest, there is not only evidence of a trend to convergence in securities laws but also evidence of a tendency to borrow substantial elements of securities laws from other jurisdictions. While political pressures in both the domestic and international context may lead to a convergence of securities laws, they do not explain this tendency to borrow securities laws. Nor do they explain a pattern of borrowing that appears to be dominated by borrowing from a very limited set of existing securities laws.

---

50 See e.g. G. R. Raifman, "The Effect of the U.S.-Swiss Agreement on Swiss Banking Secrey and Insider Trading" (1985) 16 Securities L. Rev. 423-69; M. S. Klock, "A Comparative Analysis of Recent Accords which Facilitate Transnational SEC Investigations of Insider Trading" (1987) 11 Maryland Journal of Int'l L. 243-81; J. J. Ryan IV, "International Enforcement of Insider Trading: The Grand Jury Process, Court Compulsion and the U.S.-Switzerland Treaty on Mutual Assistance in Criminal Matters" (1988) 26 Amer. Crim. L.J. 247-93; G. A. Polcari, "A Comparative Analysis of Insider Trading Laws: The U.S., the U.K. and Japan – the Current International Agreements on Securities Regulation" (1989) 13 Suffolk Transnational L. J. 167-200.

51 For instance, one explanation for U.S. efforts to obtain treaties dealing with insider trading is that this was a response to political pressure from members of the securities industry in the United States to protect economic rents they obtain through insider trading laws from being dissipated by competition from foreign securities markets. On the potential economic rents to securities industry participants from the regulation of insider trading, see Haddock and Macey, *supra* note 22.

52 See e.g. Hazen, *supra* note 5, vol. 3 at 59-75 on the extraterritorial application of U.S. securities laws.

53 On the increasing U.S. influence in IOSCO see e.g. MacIntosh, *supra* note 49 at 25-26. See also "U.S. SEC Forges New Global Role Within IOSCO: Breeden Chairs Strengthened Technical Committee" (1990) 3(24) Int'l Sec. Reg. Rep. 1; and "U.S. SEC Would Cut Futures Group From IOSCO Working Party Structure" (1990) 3(16) Int'l Sec. Reg. Rep. 1.

Why Borrow?

Avoids Cost of Political Compromise A country could start from scratch creating securities laws to respond to political pressures from local interest groups. However, this would involve a potentially prolonged process of political compromise while various interest groups lobbied for their particular interests. Instead, foreign laws can be invoked in the political dialogue, in part as a form of rhetoric and in part as a starting point representing a compromise between similar interest groups in the foreign country. With the foreign compromise as a starting point, much of the prolonged process of political compromise might be avoided. The borrowed foreign laws can then be modified to accommodate differences in the structure of local interest groups.

Uncertainty Discourages Experimentation The uncertain results of creating unique securities laws may cause states to borrow from other jurisdictions. A country can get some sense of the effects the laws will have by looking to their effects in other countries. It may be nearly impossible to predict the effect of a unique set of laws, and the consequent uncertainty will tend to discourage the adoption of approaches that radically differ from those in other countries. This uncertainty is likely to be an important factor in the context of securities laws in the face of international competition for investment.

Even if a country were to accept the uncertainty associated with the effects of a radically different approach to securities laws, it would face the added costs of communicating the unique approach to investors and overcoming the uncertainty of investors as to the effect of the new laws. Borrowed securities laws can reduce the costs of overcoming investor uncertainty where the borrowed laws are ones with which investors are already familiar and have developed a level of comfort.

Information Costs and the Number of Sources of Borrowing

One approach to borrowing securities laws would be to consider all existing securities laws in other jurisdictions. However, this process would likely be inordinately costly. While the costs of gathering securities laws, translating them into the local language, and even comparing them at some general level might be manageable, it would be virtually impossible to assess the likely effect of these laws if they were adopted. Thus such a comprehensive approach cannot realistically be undertaken. A choice will have to be made as to which laws will be considered.

Factors Affecting the Source of Borrowing

Several factors may affect a country's choice of the source from which to borrow securities laws. These factors might, in general terms, be said to relate to information costs involved in the choice of the source of borrowing. These factors tend to encourage a relatively narrow focus in seeking potential sources for the borrowing of securities laws. Factors governing the choice may include how well known and apparently successful a particular set of foreign securities laws is, educational links, language, the extent of intercountry commercial links, and possibly the extent of parallel legal structures in the borrowing and source countries.

Uncertainty and the First-Mover Advantage As noted above, uncertainty over the effect of different securities laws and the difficulty of overcoming investor uncertainty towards radically different securities laws tends to discourage fundamental deviations from an existing set of securities laws. This uncertainty also favours a focus on the set of securities laws that is perceived, correctly or incorrectly, to be most closely linked to success in attracting investment or earning economic rents for influential market participants. Adopting these laws reduces the uncertainty associated with developing unique securities laws and avoids the costly and virtually impossible task of assessing the effects of a variety of other possible approaches while adopting what *ex ante* appear to be the laws most likely to achieve the desired effect. It is also likely to reduce the cost of communicating the nature and likely effect of the laws to investors by allowing the borrowing country to point to the existing securities laws of another country with which investors are likely to have some familiarity or level of comfort. The success of the country that is the source of the securities laws may also provide an effective form of rhetoric for market participants who seek economic rents similar to those enjoyed by their counterparts in the source country. A country that is first in developing an apparently successful set of securities laws thus has a considerable edge in being the source country of choice, given the likely reluctance of countries to experiment with different approaches to securities laws.

The U.S. securities laws of the 1930s appear to fit the role of such a first-mover. Other countries adopting securities laws, daunted by the empirical task of assessing the effects of a wide variety of possible securities laws, and noting the success of the U.S. economy, may have tended to look to U.S. securities laws. Also, the U.S. is an important source of investors. U.S. investors may be generally familiar with U.S. securities laws and have some confidence in the protection they provide. They may be more inclined to invest in countries having similar securities laws. This may be another important factor in the tendency to follow the approach of U.S. securities laws.

Educational Links The source of borrowing of securities laws may also be affected by the educational background of lawyers and policy makers. If a substantial number of lawyers either received their basic legal training or pursued graduate studies in law in a particular jurisdiction, they would be inclined to turn to what they were familiar with from their earlier education when searching for a starting point to draft laws in their own jurisdiction. There can be other advantages from having securities laws that lawyers may be familiar with from their earlier education. Lawyers should more readily be able to assimilate such securities laws, thereby lowering the cost of legal services associated with compliance.

Certain countries may occupy a leading position in education resulting, to some extent, in a convergence of ideas. The United States and the United Kingdom arguably occupy such leading positions, and this may account, in part, for the relative dominance of U.S. or U.K. securities laws in several countries.

Language Closely related to the effects of educational links is the effect of sharing a common language. There may be a tendency to copy the laws of a country in which securities laws can be more readily understood because they are set out in a language that is understood in the country borrowing the securities laws. Sharing a common language may also affect the way people think about securities law issues.

As with education, one or more languages tend to dominate in the international setting. For instance, English has arguably taken such a dominant position in the world.[54] This may contribute to a convergence of ideas that are linked to the way problems are conceived of in English. The dominance of English may also facilitate the adoption of securities laws from other English-speaking countries such as the United States and the United Kingdom. Many countries will have a group of persons who are sufficiently conversant in English to read the securities laws of English-speaking jurisdictions. This makes the laws of English-speaking jurisdictions more accessible than those of other jurisdictions.[55]

54 In terms of the language persons speak as their native tongue, English ranks fourth (with Mandarin, Hindi, and Spanish ranking first, second, and third). See *World Almanac and Book of Facts* (1997) at 642-43. However, English is spoken by between 700 million and 1 billion persons as a native, second, or foreign language. English is used in over 60 countries as an official or semi-official language. It is prominent in a further 20 countries and is either dominant or well established on six continents. See A. Pennycock, *The Cultural Politics of English as an International Language* (New York: Longman, 1994) at 7-8. By 1980, two-thirds or more of the world's scientists were writing in English and 80% of the world's electronically stored information was in English. See *Encyclopedia of Language and Linguistics*, vol. 3, at 1120-24. On the current importance of English in Asia see W. McGurn, "English in Asia: Money Talks," *Far Eastern Economic Review* (21 Mar. 1996) at 40-42.

55 The securities laws of other jurisdictions are also becoming more readily available in English. This may facilitate borrowing from other jurisdictions. However, U.S. and U.K. securities laws are likely to continue to dominate, due to the effect of the various other factors mentioned in the text.

Extent of Commercial Links Close commercial links, whether due to the proximity of countries or otherwise, may encourage similarities in laws in commercial areas such as the regulation of securities markets. Close commercial links, particularly where they involve capital flows between the countries, may bring political pressure from securities industry participants and investors to make the securities laws of the two countries at least compatible. Compatibility can reduce the transactions costs associated with raising capital and therefore increase the amount of capital that is likely to be raised. The compatibility of Canadian and U.S. securities laws, joint U.S.-Canadian interjurisdictional policy releases, and memoranda of understanding on securities law matters are good examples of attempts to achieve compatibility where there are significant commercial links between the countries.[56]

Common Legal Tradition The similarity between the securities laws of Singapore and Malaysia and their borrowing from Australian, British, and U.S. securities laws, discussed below,[57] suggests that policy makers may have a tendency to look to jurisdictions that have similar legal systems and traditions. It may be easier for policy makers to understand and assess the likely effects of the laws of jurisdictions with similar legal traditions thus lowering the information costs associated with such assessments. It may also be easier to incorporate the laws of such jurisdictions into the domestic legal system thereby lowering the costs of implementing borrowed laws. Thus, for instance, common law jurisdictions may tend to follow other common law jurisdictions and civil law jurisdictions may tend to follow other civil law jurisdictions.

The Roles of Particular Individuals and the Element of Chance In the process of developing a set of laws responding to political pressures, it may make sense to assign tasks to a particular individual or small group of individuals. This can avoid the transactions costs likely to be encountered in coordinating an unwieldy network of interest group representatives and reaching a joint position over a wide array of possible issues. Instead, the individual or small group can work to a solution that, while not representing the optimal solution for each participant, is one for which no interest

---

56 See e.g. the Canadian Securities Administrators National Policy #45. See also Sec. Exch. Act Rel. No. 33-6902, [1991 Transfer Binder] Fed. Sec. L. Rep. (CCH) ¶ 84,812 (SEC 21 June 1991). This allows, in certain circumstances, distributions of securities in Canada on the basis of compliance with U.S. disclosure laws and allows distributions of securities in the U.S. on the basis of compliance with Canadian disclosure laws. It also allows for takeover bids involving shareholders in the U.S. and Canada to proceed, in certain circumstances, on the basis of compliance with Canadian takeover bid requirements or, in certain circumstances, on the basis of compliance with U.S. takeover bid requirements.

57 See notes 78 to 93 and the accompanying text.

group is willing to incur the costs involved in defeating it. There may be several solutions that meet such a criterion. Consequently the individual, or small group of individuals, may have a significant influence on the choice of a solution. The background of the persons involved may then be of some significance in the source of and extent of borrowing. For instance, where the person worked or did graduate studies may be significant in his or her choice of a source jurisdiction, since the person may feel he or she is in a better position to understand and communicate the impact of the source country's laws.

An element of chance may be involved in the choice of individuals heading up the development of a particular set of laws. There may be a limited set of persons having credible expertise for such positions. The choice among this limited set may be based in part on chance connections between the person making the appointment and the appointee. The person or group of persons may have become influential in the development of securities laws through a series of coincidences that may involve contacts or friendships fostered professionally, during school years or through chance meetings. Personal characteristics of the appointee may also influence the choice of the person making the appointment.

Factors Contributing to Differences

In spite of evidence of similarities between the securities laws of different countries, there remain differences of varying degrees of significance. It is implicit in the analysis above concerning information and transactions costs that there may still be scope for some degree of experimentation by individual countries, which may include the creation of uniquely local laws, variations on borrowed laws, and laws that consist of unique forms of multi-source borrowing. In addition, several factors may affect the kinds of political pressures that may be brought to bear in the country and lead to different political pressures and thus different features in the laws that are the outcome of the political process. In the context of securities laws, these factors include the stage of a country's development, differences in legal systems, ideology, culture, local market conditions, and path dependence. These are canvassed below as possible explanations for observed differences in securities laws.

Experimentation

Some differences in securities laws may be due to experimentation, where policy makers take note of perceived deficiencies in the securities laws of other countries and seek to correct them with their own home-grown approach. There will still be variation, given uncertainty over the set of laws that will best attract investment. Thus there may be continuous experimentation in an attempt to identify the set of laws that best attracts investment.

The securities laws may also be complicated by attempts to achieve other policy goals through the regulation of securities markets.

Stage of Development

The stage of development may contribute to differences in the securities laws. Countries in which the development of securities markets is relatively recent will not have the experience of a long history of securities market developments to draw on in developing their securities laws. Consequently, their laws may be less finely nuanced with, perhaps, less regulatory detail.[58]

The borrowing of securities laws can, to some extent, overcome the lack of experience with securities markets by drawing on the securities market experiences of other countries. However, a lack of securities market expertise for the effective enforcement of securities laws may also be a factor that limits the regulatory complexity of securities laws. Countries in the early stages of development, facing strong pressures to provide higher standards of living and pressures from entrepreneurs and foreign investors, may also be inclined to avoid putting undue regulatory hurdles on the sale of securities that provide the necessary funds for investment to promote development.

Further, less developed securities markets may have yet to develop the same institutional structures as more developed securities markets. Thus the kinds of political pressures that are brought to bear on the creation of securities laws may not be the same as those in more developed securities markets. The different political pressures can lead to variations in the nature of the securities laws that the country develops.

Legal System Differences

Differences in the legal system may be another source of differences in securities laws. As noted above, it may be easier to assess the effect of and implement securities laws that are drawn from a country having a similar legal system.

If common law countries borrow primarily from other common law countries while civil law countries borrow from other civil law countries, then one might expect to find at least two securities law models with differences in approach attributable to the different characteristics of the legal system. However, the fact that securities regulation in common law countries has become predominantly a matter of statute law administered largely

58 It has been suggested that securities commissions, once in place, have a tendency to steadily increase in the amount of regulatory detail. See N. Wolfson, "A Critique of the Securities and Exchange Commission" [1981] Emory L.J. 119 at 124-27 and D. C. Langevoort, "The SEC as a Bureaucracy: Public Choice, Institutional Rhetoric, and the Process of Policy Formulation" (1990) 47 Wash. and Lee L. Rev. 527 at 531-32. The more recently developed regulatory frameworks are less likely to have developed the same degree of regulatory detail.

by regulatory bodies tends to reduce the significance of the distinction between the civil law and common law approaches.

Ideology

Ideology may also play a role in some differences in securities laws. For instance, the development of securities laws in transitional economies, such as China and Vietnam, may be affected by a continuing controlled economy mentality in the minds of some influential bureaucrats. Securities laws might thus be more inclined to constrain securities market trading or to direct securities markets towards achieving a particular economic outcome. For instance, trading in the securities of companies in specific industries that the government wants to promote might be encouraged over the trading in securities of companies in other industries. A controlled economy mentality might also emphasize government access to information at least as much or more than investor access to information, since information is a key component in effective control over the economy. Generally, where a Marxist ideology has prevailed there may be scepticism towards the adoption of capitalist concepts, particularly those associated with an aspect as seemingly central to capitalism as the trading of securities.

Countries that are in a process of transition from command economies are also likely to have a pre-existing set of political pressures that differ from those in a country in which securities markets are developing in a primarily market-based economy. The groups in the command economy that stand to gain or lose economic rents from the development of securities markets and related securities laws are likely to be different from the groups that might gain or lose economic rents in the development of securities markets and securities laws in primarily market-based economies.

Culture

Differences in culture or religion could also affect securities laws. Such differences may be reflected in different ethics towards business relations and impinge upon such matters as good faith in securities trading or in the provision of securities market services. These differences in culture or religion may result in differences in the political pressures that are brought to bear in the context of the development of securities laws.

Local Market Features

While securities markets may tend to develop similar structures with similar market participants, there may also be unique features to local securities markets. These unique features may create different problems that call for unique regulatory responses. Unique regulatory responses may also be due to somewhat different interest group pressures created by the unique features of local securities markets.

Path Dependency

The development of securities markets, while taking on similar overall characteristics, may, in some respects, have proceeded down different paths. As noted above, subtle variations in the development of securities markets resulting in different interest group pressures might lead to variations in securities laws. Once particular interest groups have something to lose through changes in securities laws, it may be difficult to closely follow the laws of another country. Also, once the securities laws have proceeded down one path, it may be difficult to follow the path taken by another country, because change will be resisted by those who believe they would suffer substantial losses as a result of any change.[59]

CASE STUDIES

This section considers several of the factors noted above in the context of the securities laws of Malaysia, Singapore, Japan, and China.

Malaysia and Singapore

The securities laws of Malaysia and Singapore are considered together in this section because they are quite similar and because the two countries share similar historical roots. Both countries are considered because the links between the two countries provide an interesting perspective on the sources of similarities and differences in their securities laws.

General Features of Malaysian and Singaporean Securities Laws

Mandatory Disclosure, Market Manipulation, Insider Trading, Takeover Bid Regulation, and Securities Industry Regulation

Securities laws in Malaysia and Singapore follow what is a fairly common pattern for securities laws in many other jurisdictions. In both countries

59 The concept of path dependence has been described in the following way in D. Stark, "Path Dependence and Privatization Strategies in East Central Europe," in D. Kincaid and A. Parks, eds., *Comparative National Development: Society and Economy in the New Global Order* (Chapel Hill, N.C.: Univ. of North Carolina Press, 1994) at 169-70:

> The strength of the concept of path dependence ... is its analytic power in explaining outcomes where strategic actors are deliberately searching for departures from long-established routines and attempting to restructure the rules of the game. Actors who seek to move in new directions find that their choices are constrained by the existing set of institutional resources. Institutions limit the field of action; they preclude some directions; they constrain certain courses. But institutions favor the perception and selection of some strategies over others ... Actors who seek to introduce change require resources to overcome obstacles to change. This exploitation of existing institutional resources is a principal component of the apparent paradox that even (and especially) instances of transformation are marked by path dependence.

See also the discussion of path dependence in North, *supra* note 43 at 92-100.

distributions of securities are subject to mandatory disclosure requirements[60] vetted by administrators[61] and backed up with penal sanctions for non-compliance[62] and statutory civil liability for misrepresentations.[63] Subsequent

60 The securities laws of Malaysia and Singapore require that a prospectus be registered by the Registrar of companies before a person can "issue, circulate or distribute any form of application for shares in or debentures of a corporation" (Malaysian *Companies Act 1965*, Laws of Malaysia 1965, Act 125, as amended (hereinafter MCA), s. 37(1); and the Singapore *Companies Act* (Act 42 of 1967), Statutes of Singapore, c. 50, 1990 ed. (hereinafter SCA), s. 43(1)). A prospectus must also be registered where there is "an invitation to the public" to deposit money with, or loan money to, a corporation or proposed corporation (MCA s. 38(1); SCA s. 44(1)). The legislation does not use the broad term "security" as the U.S. legislation does. However, the legislation has a potentially broad scope in that, in addition to requiring the registration of a prospectus with respect to "shares or debentures of a corporation," it requires the registration of a prospectus in connection with an offer or invitation to "the public" to subscribe for or purchase any "interest" (MCA s. 90(1); SCA s. 113(1)). The term "interest" is statutorily defined in a way that gives a broad scope to the term with elements of the definition being similar to the definition of "security" in the U.S. (see MCA s. 84; SCA s. 107).

The prospectus must include certain specific types of information (MCA 5th Sch.; SCA 5th Sch.). For instance, the prospectus must disclose such information as the nature of the business of the issuer, the rights attached to the securities being issued, the use of the proceeds of the issue, the dividend record for each class of shares, and information on the management of the issuer (MCA 5th Sch.; SCA 5th Sch.). Financial information in the form of audited statements of assets and liabilities and profit and loss must also be provided (MCA 5th Sch., para. 20; SCA 5th Sch., para. 20). In addition to information specifically required, the prospectus must disclose all other material facts, because the statutory civil liability provision makes certain persons liable for the "wilful non-disclosure therein of any matter of which he had knowledge and which he knew to be material" (MCA s. 46(1); SCA s. 55(1)). Representations with respect to securities offered to the public are to be limited to those contained in the prospectus. This is effected by deeming that any advertisement offering or calling attention to an intended offer of securities to the public to be a prospectus (MCA ss. 4(5), 40(1), and 90; SCA ss. 4(5), 48(1), and 113(1)). To facilitate the distribution of the securities, advertisements that simply provide basic information drawing attention to the issue are allowed (MCA s. 40(1); SCA s. 48(1)).

61 In both Malaysia and Singapore the prospectus must be filed with the Registrar of Companies. The Registrar can refuse to register the prospectus if it contains any statement or matter that is, in his opinion, misleading in the form and context in which it is included (MCA s. 42(2); SCA s. 50(2)(a)). The Registrar can also refuse to register a copy of the prospectus if it does not appear to comply with the requirements of the Act (MCA s. 42(2); SCA s. 50(2)). Where the prospectus relates to the listing of securities on either the Kuala Lumpur Stock Exchange in Malaysia or the Stock Exchange of Singapore in Singapore, the proposed listing and the prospectus must be approved by the stock exchange. In Malaysia there is a Securities Commission, which also has responsibility for examining and approving public issues of securities. See the *Securities Commission Act 1993*, Laws of Malaysia, Act 498, s. 32, as amended by the *Securities Commission (Amendment) Act 1995*, Laws of Malaysia, Act A926, s.11.

62 There are penal sanctions for failing to provide a prospectus where one is required, issuing a prospectus which has not been registered, issuing a prospectus without obtaining the required consents, and for advertisements disclosing other than permitted matters (For each of these offences the penalty is up to five years imprisonment or $M 100,000 (about $US 40,000) or both. There is also a penal sanction for the failure to comply with requirements as to the contents of the prospectus, for which the penalty is imprisonment for up to five years or a fine of up to $M 30,000).

periodic and continuous disclosure requirements apply once securities have been publicly distributed.[64] Trading on the basis of inside information is prohibited[65] and subject to penal and civil liability sanctions.[66] Various

63 MCA s. 46; SCA s. 55. These provisions are remarkably similar to the civil liability provisions in the U.K. *Companies Act, 1948*, 11 and 12 Geo. 6, cc. 38, 43 and in the early Australian uniform companies acts (e.g. New South Wales *Companies Act, 1961*, Act No. 71, 1961, s. 46; Victoria *Companies Act 1961*, 10 Eliz. 2, No. 6839, s. 46; South Australia *Companies Act, 1962*, Act No. 56 of 1962, s. 46; Queensland, *The Companies Act of 1961*, 10 Eliz. 2, No. 55, s. 46; Western Australia, *Companies Act, 1961*, Act No. 82 of 1961, s. 46; Tasmania *Companies Act 1962*, Act No. 66 of 1962, s. 46). The Malaysian and Singaporean provisions are also remarkably similar to the Canadian provisions on civil liability for misrepresentations in a prospectus (see e.g. the B.C. *Securities Act*, R.S.B.C. 1996, c. 418, s. 131) and the U.S. *Securities Act of 1933*, 15 U.S.C. § 77k, s. 11. These provisions are all descendants of the U.K. *Directors Liability Act*, 53 and 54 Vict., c. 64.

64 See MCA s. 165 and Schedule 8; SCA s. 197. There are also stock exchange requirements. Ongoing disclosure of material changes and periodic and annual reports are dealt with in the *Kuala Lumpur Stock Exchange Listing Requirements*, ss. 22-65 and in the *Stock Exchange of Singapore Limited Listing Manual*, ch. 9, clauses 901-25.

65 Although there is some variation in the specific provisions, both Malaysia and Singapore prohibit trades by insiders on the basis of inside information. In Malaysia an insider trade occurs where an insider makes improper use of specific confidential information acquired by virtue of his or her position, for the purpose of gaining an advantage for him or her self or other persons, where the specific confidential information might reasonably be expected to materially affect the price of the securities traded if it were generally known (Malaysian *Securities Industry Act 1983*, Laws of Malaysia, Act 280, as amended (hereinafter MSIA), s. 89(1), MCA s. 132A(1)). Trades by insiders of an issue in the securities of another issuer that may be subject to a takeover bid or substantial commercial transaction with the issuer to which the insiders are connected are also considered insider trades (MSIA s. 89(5), MCA s. 132A(5)). Singapore prohibits insiders, including tippees, from informing others of inside information where they reasonably ought to know that the person to whom the information is communicated will make use of the information for trading in the securities (Singapore *Securities Industry Act*, Statutes of Singapore, c. 289 (Act 15 of 1986), as amended (hereinafter SSIA), s. 103(5)). In Malaysia, persons who hold price-sensitive information by virtue of an official capacity, or former official capacity, are prohibited from making improper use of the information in dealing in securities of the issuer to gain an advantage for themselves or others when they know the information is unpublished and they would reasonably be expected not to disclose except in the performance of their official duties. (The information does not have to be "specific confidential information" but the person must know that the information is unpublished price-sensitive information. Enforcement for this provision is limited to a penal sanction (MSIA s. 90; MCA s. 132B).

The definition of "insider" in Malaysia includes directors, officers, and employees of the company (MSIA ss. 2(1) "director," 2(1) "officer," 89(1), (4); MCA ss. 4(1) "director," 4(1) "officer," 132(6), 132A(1), (4). Persons who have been directors or officers of the corporation within the preceding 12 months are also considered insiders (MSIA s. 89(4) "officer," MCA s. 132A(4) "officer"). Bankers, lawyers, auditors, accountants, or stockbrokers of the issuer are considered insiders (MSIA s. 89(4), MCA s. 132A(4)). Also included as insiders are other persons "knowingly connected" with the issuer (currently or within the previous six months), who hold information by virtue of their connection, which they know to be price-sensitive information, and which they would reasonably be expected not to disclose except in the performance of the functions of their position with the issuer (MSIA s. 89(4), MCA s. 132A(4)).

The definition of "insider" in Singapore includes directors, officers, and employees of a company (SSIA s. 103(9)(a) and (12)(a)), a receiver, receiver manager, judicial

specific market manipulation techniques are prohibited and a general anti-fraud provision covers other potential market manipulation techniques.[67] As in many other jurisdictions, takeover bids to all shareholders are mandatory under certain circumstances, and bids are subject to disclosure requirements,

---

manager, liquidator, or a corporation or trustee administering a compromise or arrangement between a corporation and other persons (SSIA s. 103(9)(a) and (12)(b)-(e)). It includes persons engaged in a professional or business relationship with a corporation (SSIA s. 103(9)(c)(i)). It also includes shareholders in a corporation holding 5% or more of the nominal amount of voting shares of a class of shares (SSIA s. 103(9)(b) and SCA s. 81) and shareholders of a related corporation holding 5% or more of the nominal amount of voting shares of a class of shares (SSIA s. 103(9)(b)). Directors, officers and employees of such a shareholder of the corporation, or of a related corporation, are also insiders (SSIA ss. 103(9)(c)(ii) and (12)). Tippees are also prohibited from trading on inside information in certain circumstances.

66 The persons defined to be insiders who engage in insider trades are subject to a penal sanction. In Malaysia the penalty is a fine of up to 50,000 Malaysian Ringit and seven years' imprisonment under the MSIA (s. 91) or 50,000 Malaysian Ringit and five years' imprisonment under the MCA (s. 132A(6)). In Singapore the penalty is a fine of up to 50,000 Singapore dollars or imprisonment for a term of up to seven years. For a body corporate, the penalty is a fine of up to 100,000 Singapore dollars (SSIA s. 104). In Singapore the penalty also applies to the communication of inside information and liability to persons with whom they traded.

In Malaysia the liability to persons with whom the insider trades is the difference between the consideration paid for the securities and the consideration that would have been paid if the information had been generally known at the time the trade was made (MSIA s. 89(1); MCA s. 132A(1)). There is no liability to a person who knew or reasonably ought to have known of the information. In Singapore a person who engages in a prohibited insider trade or communication of inside information is liable to compensate those who entered into a securities transaction with the person, or someone acting on the person's behalf, and who suffered a loss as a result (SSIA s. 105(1)). The loss is measured by the difference between the price at which the transaction occurred and the price at which the transaction would have occurred if there had been no contravention of the insider trading prohibition (SSIA s. 105(1)).

In both Malaysia and Singapore, directors, officers, and employees of a company and bankers, lawyers, and auditors of the company who make improper use of their position to gain an advantage for themselves or any other person, or to cause detriment to the company, are subject to a penal sanction and are liable to the company for any profit made or for any damage suffered by the company (MCA s. 132(2) and (3); SCA s. 4(1) "director" and "officer" and s. 157).

For discussions of the regulation of insider trading in Malaysia and Singapore, see e.g. Shahril Ridza Ridzuan, "Statutory Regulation of Insider Dealing in Malaysia, Singapore and Hong Kong – A Comparative Analysis" [1993] 2 Malayan L.J. xxv; Philip Koh Tong Ngee, "Insider Trading: Some Aspects of the Statutory Regulation in Malaysia" [1991] 2 Malayan L. J. lvii; Ter Kah Leng and Catherine Tay Swee Kian, "A Comparative Study of the Regulation of Insider Trading in Singapore, Malaysia, Australia, England and the United States" [1987] Malayan L. J. ciii; W. Woon, "The Statutory Control of Insider Trading – Section 103, Securities Industry Act 1986" (1986) 28 Malaya L. Rev. 275; P. N. Pillai, "Insider Trading in Singapore and Malaysia" (1974) 16 Malaya L. Rev. 333; and Puan Rafiah Salim, "Liabilities of Company Officials in Insider Trading," *Company Law and Securities Regulation in Malaysia – Current Developments* (Kuala Lumpur: International Law Book, 1989) 1.

67 In addition to the legislative provisions noted above, Malaysia and Singapore have added a broad securities fraud provision to their securities industry acts (MSIA s. 87A; SSIA s. 102) which is virtually identical to Rule 10b-5 promulgated under s. 10 of the

a minimum bid period, offeree withdrawal rights, a pro rata share take-up requirement, and a principle of equal consideration to all offeree shareholders.[68] Further, as in many other jurisdictions, the provision of securities market services is regulated through a licensing scheme,[69] accounting and record keeping requirements,[70] disclosure of potential conflicts of interest,[71] and contingency fund arrangements.[72]

Public and Private Regulation

The regulation of securities markets is usually divided between public and private (or quasi-private) regulation. Public regulation typically occurs in the form of statutes and subordinate legislation often administered by government regulatory agencies such as a securities commission. Private or quasi-private modes of regulation are effected through organizations such as securities exchanges or other securities quotation organizations, associations of brokers, financial analysts, and so on.[73]

Securities Exchange Act of 1934 (compare the provisions set out *infra* note 87). Rule 10b-5 has been the basis of the development of the law with respect to insider trading in the United States (see Hazen, *supra* note 5, vol. 2, at 598-619). This provision could be relied on by courts in Malaysia and Singapore to expand on the scope of the other insider trading provisions. This would depend on the willingness of the normally conservative courts in Malaysia to give a broad interpretation to the provision, particularly in light of other more specific provisions on insider trading.

68 In Singapore, takeover bids became subject to regulation under a provision of the *Companies Act 1967* (formerly s. 179 of the *Companies Act 1967*, Act 42 of 1967). This provision is discussed in P. Pillai, "Corporate Takeovers in Singapore" (1973) 15 Malaya L. Rev. 170. This legislative regulatory scheme was supplemented in 1973 by a non-statutory code on takeovers and mergers issued by the Minister of Finance (the *Singapore Code on Take-Overs and Mergers*). It is administered by the Securities Industry Council (See the *Companies Act 1967*, s. 213(18)). Thus takeover bids in Singapore are regulated partly by statute and partly by administrative guidelines.

In Malaysia, guidelines on takeovers were introduced in 1974. In 1987 an amendment to the *Companies Act 1965* empowered a panel to prepare a code governing takeovers and mergers (s. 179 added by the *Companies (Amendment) Act 1985*, Act A616). The creation of a panel on takeovers and mergers in Malaysia is discussed in D. A. Wishart, "Malaysian Code on Take-Overs and Mergers," *Company Law and Securities Regulation in Malaysia – Current Developments, supra* note 66 at 39. Thus takeover bids in Malaysia are now regulated under the *Malaysian Code on Take-Overs and Mergers 1987*. Both the Malaysian and Singaporean codes draw heavily on the London City Code on Take-Overs and Mergers: see Wishart, *ibid.* at 39. With respect to the Singapore code see Tan, *supra* note 27 at 596.

69 MSIA ss. 12-28; SSIA ss. 23-40.

70 MSIA ss. 29-35; SSIA ss. 41-47 and 56-73.

71 MSIA ss. 39-40; SSIA ss. 50-54.

72 MSIA ss. 60-83; SSIA ss. 74-96.

73 Securities exchanges in North America are often referred to as "quasi-private" organizations since they are typically incorporated under separate legislation (rather than a general statute of incorporation) and are said to serve public as well as private interests. They are subject to supervision by securities commissions. Other organizations, such as associations of brokers and investment dealers, are subject to securities commission supervision. See e.g. the discussion in Gillen, *supra* note 5 at 72-74 and the discussion in Hazen, *supra* note 5, vol. 2, at 10-27.

A common pattern in many jurisdictions as securities markets develop is a gradual shift from primarily private forms of securities market regulation to more public forms of regulation. In the United Kingdom, the United States, and Canada securities trading was largely regulated by stock exchanges against the backdrop of the common law of contract.[74] Although early forms of regulation made use of administrators, they did not call upon an administrative apparatus nearly as extensively as modern securities legislation does. Later securities laws created the Securities Exchange Commission in the United States and securities commissions in most provinces in Canada. These developments occurred in the 1930s in the United States and began in the late 1940s in Canada.[75]

Malaysia has only very recently created a securities commission,[76] and Singapore has yet to do so. Until the creation of a securities commission in Malaysia, such matters as the vetting of prospectuses and administrative decisions with respect to takeovers were handled by a Capital Issues Committee and a Takeover Panel that formed part of the Kuala Lumpur Stock Exchange.[77]

Foreign Sources of Malaysian and Singaporean Securities Laws

Although the general thrust of the securities laws of Malaysia and Singapore is similar to that of U.S. securities laws, the greater part of the securities laws of Malaysia and Singapore is modelled on British and Australian laws. The Malaysian *Company Act 1965*[78] and the Singapore *Companies Act*,[79] which

---

74 Stock exchanges and trading in company shares existed in Canada and the U.S. well before the adoption of the first securities laws. The first statute directly regulating securities sales in the U.S. was a 1911 Kansas statute (Kans. Laws 1911, c. 133). The first Canadian statute directly regulating the sale of securities was the Manitoba *Sale of Shares Act*, S.M. 1912, c. 75 which was modelled on the Kansas statute. Stock exchanges regulated securities issuers through listing agreements and regulated brokers through membership rules. Issuers agreed to listing rules and paid fees for the right to list shares on the exchange. Brokers complied with membership rules for the right to execute trades through the exchange. See the discussions of the law relating to stock exchanges in e.g. A. P. Poley and F. H. Carruthers Gould, *The History, Law, and Practice of the Stock Exchange* (London: Pitman and Sons, 1907); and R. E. Melsheimer and W. Laurence, *The Law and Customs of the London Stock Exchange* (London: Henry Sweet, 1879).

75 The U.S. Securities Exchange Commission was created by the *Securities Exchange Act of 1934*, 73rd Congress, 2nd Sess., 1933, c. 404, s. 4. The first Canadian securities commission was created in Ontario under the Ontario *Securities Act*, S.O. 1947, c. 98.

76 See the *Securities Commission Act 1993*, Laws of Malaysia 1993, Act 498.

77 *Ibid.* at s. 15 under which the newly formed Securities Commission was given a wide range of functions with respect to securities matters including regulating the issuance of securities and takeover bids. These were formerly the work of a Capital Issues Committee that had been set up by the Ministry of Finance in 1968 and formally established under the *Securities Industry Act 1983*.

78 *Supra* note 60.

79 *Supra* note 60.

80 See H. A. J. Ford, *Principles of Company Law*, 4th ed. (Sydney: Butterworths, 1986) at 15. The Australian uniform companies acts, containing virtually identical provisions, were enacted in 1961 and 1962: see the New South Wales *Companies Act, 1961*, Act No. 71,

contain provisions on the prospectus requirement, prospectus disclosure, and continuous disclosure, are modelled on the Australian uniform companies acts,[80] which were similar in many respects to the U.K. *Companies Act 1948*.[81] The Malaysia *Securities Industry Act 1983*[82] and the Singapore *Securities Industry Act*[83] are also very similar to corresponding Australian laws.[84] Although the regulation of takeover bids shares many features with the U.S. Williams Act,[85] it is based primarily on the London City Code.[86] Perhaps the clearest example of directly copying a U.S. provision in both Malaysia and Singapore is the almost word-for-word adoption of the general anti-fraud rule in U.S. Rule 10b-5.[87]

1961, ss. 37-47, 76-89; Victoria *Companies Act 1961*, 10 Eliz. 2, No. 6839, ss. 37-47, 76-89; South Australia *Companies Act, 1962*, Act No. 56 of 1962, ss. 37-47, 76-89; Queensland, *The Companies Act of 1961*, 10 Eliz. 2, No. 55, ss. 37-47, 76-89; Western Australia, *Companies Act, 1961*, Act No. 82 of 1961, ss. 37-47, 76-89; Tazmania *Companies Act 1962*, Act No. 66 of 1962, ss. 37-47, 76-89.

81 11 and 12 Geo. 6, c. 38. On the history of Australian company laws, see e.g. H. A. J. Ford, *Principles of Company Law*, 4th ed. (Sydney: Butterworths, 1986) at 13-15.

82 Laws of Malaysia 1983, Act 280 (hereinafter the "MSIA").

83 Act 15 of 1986.

84 Compare these statutes with, for example, the New South Wales *Securities Industry Act*, 1975, Act No. 3 of 1975 or the Commonwealth *Corporations Act*, Act 109 of 1989, c. 7. Certain amendments to Australian securities industry acts have been directly picked up in subsequent amendments to Singaporean and Malaysian securities industry legislation: see e.g. Khaw Lake Tee, "The Securities Industry Act 1983" [1984] J. of Malaysian and Comparative L. 93. See also *infra* notes 88 to 91 and the accompanying text.

85 See D. A. DeMott, "Comparative Dimensions of Takeover Regulation" (1987) 65 Wash. Univ. L. Q. 69 at 84-99.

86 Compare the London City Code (*Panel on Take-Overs and Mergers, The City Code on Take-Overs and Mergers* (1985)) to the Malaysian *Code on Take-Overs and Mergers 1987* (created under the authority given in s. 33A of the *Securities Commission Act, 1993*, Laws of Malaysia, Act 498) and the Singapore *Code on Take-overs and Mergers* (created under the authority given in s. 213(18) of the Singapore *Companies Act*).

87 U.S. Rule 10b-5 (17 C.F.R. § 240) provides that:

> It shall be unlawful for any person, directly or indirectly, by the use of any means or instrumentality of interstate commerce, or of any mails or of any facility of any national securities exchange,
> (a) To employ any device, scheme, or artifice to defraud,
> (b) To make any untrue statement of a material fact or to omit to state a material fact necessary in order to make the statements made, in light of the circumstances under which they were made, not misleading, or
> (c) To engage in any act, practice, or course of business which operates or would operate as a fraud or deceit upon any person, in connection with the purchase or sale of any security.

The corresponding provisions in Malaysia (MSIA s. 87A) and Singapore (SSIA s. 102) provide that,

> It shall be unlawful for any person directly or indirectly in connection with the puchase or sale of any securities
> (a) to emply any device, scheme or artifice to defraud;
> (b) to engage in any act, practice or course of business which operates or would operate as a fraud or deceit upon any person; or

Singaporean legislation on the regulation of the securities industry and market manipulation was developed at the same time similar legislation was being developed in Australia.[88] Discussions were held between Singapore and Australian State authorities who were facing similar concerns about their respective securities markets at the time.[89] Singapore delayed the introduction of its legislation to coordinate its introduction with virtually identically worded Malaysian legislation.[90] Although the general thrust was similar to that of the U.S. *Securities Exchange Act* of 1934, the approach in Singapore and Malaysia at the time was to avoid the creation of a commission similar to the U.S. Securities Exchange Commission and to rely more heavily on a self-regulatory approach to the securities industry.[91]

A noteworthy feature of Malaysian securities laws with respect to the source of borrowing is a prohibition of short sales of securities.[92] This provision has its origin in the short sale restrictions in Australian securities laws.[93]

Factors Contributing to Similarities

Convergence towards Optimal Solutions

The general similarity of the securities laws of Malaysia and Singapore to the securities laws of many other jurisdictions is consistent with the suggestion that securities laws converge towards optimal solutions to common securities market problems. The somewhat later development of Malaysian

---

(c) to make any untrue statement of a material fact or omit to state a material fact necessary in order to make the statements made in the light of the circumstances under which they were made not misleading.

88 See Singapore *Securities Industry Act*, 1970 (although it never came into force and was replaced by the *Securities Industry Act*, 1973: see Tan, *supra* note 27 at 8-10); Victoria *Securities Industry Act*, Act No. 7962, 1970; the Queensland *Securities Industry Act*, Act No. 2, 1971; New South Wales *Securities Industry Act*, Act No. 53, 1970; and the Western Australia *Securities Industry Act*, Act No. 118, 1970.

89 See Tan, *supra* note 27 at 32.

90 *Ibid.* at 32-33.

91 See G. M. Ferris, Jr., *A Study of the Securities Market in Singapore and Malaysia* (IESC Project #2067, 1969, known as the "Ferris Report") at 3-4; and Tan Boon Teik, "Forms of Control Exercised over the Securities Industry: A Comparative View" (1974) SES J. 4 at 5.

92 See MSIA s. 41.

93 The Malaysian provision was not included in the original *Securities Industry Act, 1973* but was introduced in the *Securities Industry Act, 1983.* It appears to have its origins in very similarly worded provisions of the Australian uniform securities acts (New South Wales *Securities Industry Act, 1975*, Act No. 3, 1975, s. 54; Victoria *Securities Industry Act*, Act No. 8788, s. 54; Queensland *Securities Industry Act*, Act No. 78, 1975, s. 54; Western Australia *Securities Industry Act*, Act No. 99, 1975, s. 54), which were carried forward into the uniform federal *Corporations Act 1989*, Act 109, 1989, s. 846. An early version of a short-selling provision appeared in the Queensland *Securities Industry Act*, Act No. 2, 1971, s. 41 although that section required only that the seller disclose to the dealer that he or she had no currently exercisable interest in a security that he or she proposed to sell.

and Singaporean securities laws in the form of U.S. and British securities laws may have been due to the later development of securities markets in Malaysia and Singapore.

Political Pressures Leading to Similar Securities Laws

On the other hand, the degree of general similarity of securities laws in Malaysia and Singapore to those of the United States and the United Kingdom is also consistent with similar political pressures that arose as securities markets developed. The development of securities markets in Malaysia and Singapore followed a similar pattern to the development of securities markets in the United States and United Kingdom. Similar market participants would have come into existence. Indeed, since the early days of securities market development in Malaysia and Singapore involved local trading in shares of British companies,[94] the early development of securities markets in Malaysia and Singapore probably involved the transplanting of security industry participants from the United Kingdom.

Competition for capital in the face of the increasing globalization of securities markets in recent years would have created incentives to tap foreign sources of investment capital, particularly with the demand for an "Asian play" as part of international investment portfolios. Issuers of securities and securities industry participants in Malaysia and Singapore would have supported a securities law regime that took a form foreign investors were familiar with in order to ease some of the uncertainty foreign investors might have associated with such investments, and thereby encourage foreign participation in the Malaysian and Singaporean securities markets.

Transaction Costs, Information Costs, Uncertainty, and the Source of Borrowing

With a similar securities market development to that of Britain, and possibly also the transplanting of British securities industry participants, it may have been simplest in Malaysia and Singapore to borrow a base set of securities laws that represented an existing political compromise between the very similar industry participants in the United Kingdom. This would have avoided the costs of prolonged negotiations and lobbying that might otherwise have been required to achieve a political compromise. Borrowing from relatively well known securities laws may have also reduced investor uncertainty as to the potential effect of such laws, and would have made the laws relatively easy for investors to assimilate.

The educational link between Malaysia and Singapore on the one hand and the United Kingdom and Australia on the other was also likely a significant

94 See Gill, *supra* note 27 at 30-35; Tan, *supra* note 27 at 1-4.

factor. This would have been particularly evident in legal education. Until relatively recently, most lawyers in Malaysia and Singapore received their basic legal education in either England or Australia.[95] This educational link has its roots in the history of the British colonization of the Malay peninsula.

The continued use of English in both Malaysia and Singapore is also an important factor. In Singapore, English is one of the four recognized national languages. In Malaysia it is an important second language widely taught in schools beginning at the primary level.

Borrowing from both the U.S. and British/Australian laws may be due in part to a preference for the laws of other common law jurisdictions. However, the general preference for borrowing from British and Australian laws suggests that factors such as educational links and language play a significant role.

The very close fit between the securities laws of Malaysia and Singapore may be due to more than just their common historical and educational links to the United Kingdom and Australia. The securities markets in Malaysia and Singapore have a common origin. The Kuala Lumpur and Singapore stock exchanges were once two trading floors of a single exchange that only formally separated as recently as 1973.[96] The proximity of the two countries and close business contacts contributed to the flow of funds between the two countries. The adoption of securities laws that would interfere with the ready flow of funds would probably be resisted by many investors. Laws interfering with investment in one of the two countries would be likely to cause a ready flight of capital to the other country. Laws favouring investment in one of the two countries, and thereby attracting capital from the other, would probably be quickly imitated in the other country. Indeed, this is consistent with the closeness in time of the adoption and major amendments of securities laws in both countries.[97]

Factors Contributing to Differences

Stage of Development

The timing of the adoption of securities laws in Malaysia and Singapore suggests that the stage of development of a country's securities markets is

95 See "Divided at the Bar, United on the Bench," *Far Eastern Economic Review* (21 July 1988) 15.

96 See Gill, *supra* note 27 at 30-35, 72-76; Tan, *supra* note 27 at 4-10.

97 The 1965 Malaysian *Companies Act 1965* and the 1967 Singapore *Companies Act* were enacted shortly after major amendments to company laws in Australia (see *supra* note 80). The first securities industry acts in Malaysia and Singapore were enacted in the early 1970s around the same time as similar Australian securities industry statutes were enacted (see *supra* notes 88 and 93). Amendments to Malaysian and Singaporean securities industry statutes in the 1980s also closely followed the amendments to Australian securities industry legislation at around the same time: see *supra* note 84.

also significant in the degree to which the securities laws of a country will be similar to those of other countries. For instance, the securities laws of Malaysia and Singapore are of relatively recent origin compared to those of, for example, the United Kingdom, the United States, and Canada. Statutory civil liability for misrepresentations in a prospectus appeared in the United Kingdom as early as 1890.[98] In the United States, legislation regulating the sale of securities appeared in Kansas as early as 1911[99] and federal regulation of securities markets developed in the 1930s.[100] In Canada, legislation on the sale of securities appeared in Manitoba as early as 1912[101] and similar legislation was enacted in several other provinces in the ensuing years.[102] In Malaysia and Singapore, securities laws similar in character and scope to securities laws in the United Kingdom, United States, and Canada were not adopted until the enactment of modified company laws in the 1960s and securities industry acts in the 1970s.[103] This pattern is consistent with the later development of securities markets in Malaysia and Singapore. Although trading in the shares of British companies in Malaysia and Singapore dates back to the turn of the century, active securities markets do not appear to have developed until the late 1940s.[104] Trading was still sporadic and more consistent trading did not appear until the 1960s.[105]

The development of insider trading laws is of relatively recent origin in North America.[106] It is of even more recent origin in Malaysia and Singapore. In part, this may reflect the stage of development of securities markets. Economies of scale may not make it worthwhile to regulate insider trading until the volume of trading is sufficient to justify the costs of monitoring for insider trading.[107] There may also be economic rents to be derived by particular

98 See the *Director's Liability Act*, 1890, 53 and 54 Vict. c. 64.

99 Kans. Laws 1911, c. 133.

100 See the *Securities Act of 1933*, 73rd Congress, 1st Sess., 1933, c. 38 and the *Securities Exchange Act of 1934*, 73rd Congress, 2d Sess., 1934, c. 404.

101 The Manitoba *Sale of Shares Act*, S.M. 1912, c. 75.

102 See Saskatchewan, *The Sale of Shares Act*, S.S. 1914, c. 18; Alberta, *The Sale of Shares Act*, S.A. 1916, c. 8; New Brunswick, *The Sale of Securities Act*, S.N.B. 1923, c. 19; Quebec, *An Act Respecting the Issue and Sale of Shares, Bonds and Other Securities*, S.Q. 1924, c. 64.

103 See *supra* note 97.

104 See Gill, *supra* note 27 at 30-35, 72-76; and Tan, *supra* note 27 at 1-4; and Tan Chwee Huat, *Financial Markets and Institutions in Singapore*, 7th ed. (Singapore: Singapore University Press, 1992) at 243.

105 Gill, *ibid.*

106 U.S. regulation of insider trading has arisen largely out of court decisions over the past 26 years on SEC Rule 10b-5. This case law development in the U.S. is discussed in Hazen, *supra* note 5, vol. 2, at 598 to 619. The statutory prohibition of insider trading was introduced in Canada for the first time in Ontario in 1966 in the *Securities Act*, S.O. 1966, c. 142.

107 See F. H. Easterbrook, "Insider Trading as an Agency Problem," in J. W. Pratt and R. J. Zechauser, eds., *Principals and Agents: The Structure of Business* (Boston: Harvard Business School Press, 1985) 82 at 93.

market participants from the regulation of insider trading. However, lobbying for this type of regulation may not come about until there is a sufficient volume of trading to provide economic rents from the regulation of insider trading that are sufficient to cover the costs of lobbying.

The more recent shift in Malaysia to the use of a securities commission, and generally to more public forms of regulation, may also be in part due to the more recent development of its securities markets in Malaysia.

The Effect of Cultural Differences

Cultural differences in Malaysia might well be expected to have some influence on securities laws. The Malay population is predominantly Islamic, and Islam has strict concepts of usury that could affect the nature of debt instruments used. However, these usury concepts have yet to find their way into the written law. This is probably due to the pluralistic nature of Malaysian society, given that its population is roughly 55% Malay, 35% Chinese, and 10% Indian.

Steps have also been taken to increase Malay control over the economy in response to the relative economic dominance of the Chinese. However, while these steps have had an impact on Malay control of companies, no specific provisions have been enacted in securities laws to favour Malays. One feature of the securities market that results from action to increase Malay control in the economy is the existence of a Bumiputera Stock Exchange. However, very few stocks have been listed on the Bumiputera Stock Exchange, and it has not had a significant impact on the market.

In Singapore roughly 85% of the population is Chinese with the remaining population being predominantly Malay and Indian. In spite of this quite different racial structure from that of Malaysia, the securities laws of the two countries remain quite similar and track the general character of securities laws in many other jurisdictions. This suggests that the culture has relatively little influence on securities laws.

Japan

General Features of Japanese Securities Laws

The securities laws of Japan have taken on characteristics similar to the securities laws of many other jurisdictions. Mandatory disclosure requirements must be met on a public offering of securities.[108] There are mandatory continuous

108 See Misao Tatsuta, "Japan," in H. S. Bloomenthal and S. Wolff, eds., *International Capital Markets and Securities Regulation* (New York, N.Y.: Clark Boardman, 1982 looseleaf) at para. 11.06; and K. Tsunematsu and Shuji Yanase, "Japan," in Robert C. Rosen, ed., *International Securities Regulation* (Dobbs Ferry, N.Y.: Oceana Publications, 1992) at 31-50. See the *Japanese Securities and Exchange Law*, Law No. 25, 13 Apr. 1948, as amended (hereinafter SEL), Chapter II, arts. 3-15.

disclosure requirements in the form of timely disclosure, periodic financial reports, and periodic updates of other information disclosed when a public offering is made.[109] Trading on the basis of inside information is prohibited and subject to penal and civil liability sanctions.[110] Takeover bids are also regulated with features such as disclosure requirements,[111] a minimum bid period,[112] withdrawal rights[113] and other aspects[114] that are quite similar to

---

109 Tatsuta, *ibid.* para. 11.09; Tsunematsu and Yanase, *supra* note 108 at 50-56. See SEL Chapter II, arts. 24, 24-2 to 24-5, 25 and 26.

110 See *infra* notes 119 to 130 and the accompanying text.

111 To make a takeover bid (or 'tender offer') the bidder must publish a notice of the bid in at least two Japanese daily newspapers that are either business newspapers or newspapers reporting general affairs (SEL art. 27-3, paras. 1 and 2; Tender Offer Ordinance (TO Ordinance) art. 10). The notice must set out the purchase price, the bid period, the number of securities the bidder intends to purchase, the percentage of securities of the target owned by the bidder before the bid, and the percentage that will be owned if the bid is successful (SEL art. 27-3, paras. 1 and 2; TO Ordinance art. 10). On the day notice of the bid is published, the bidder must also file a tender offer registration statement with the Minister of Finance and send a copy of the registration statement to the target company and the securities exchange on which the target company's securities are listed (or the securities dealers' association where the securities are not listed on a stock exchange but are traded in the over-the-counter market) (SEL art. 27-3, paras 3 and 4; SEL Order art. 11 and TO Ordinance arts. 12 and 13). Where the bid involves an exchange of bidder securities for securities of the target, a securities registration statement for the securities of the bidder to be exchanged must be filed with the tender offer registration statement (SEL arts. 4 and 27-4; TO Ordinance arts. 15 and 17).

If the bid is amended, notice of the amendment must be made and the tender offer registration statement must also be amended (SEL arts. 27-6 to 27-8; SEL Order art. 13; and TO Ordinance arts. 19, 21-23). The bid may not be amended in a way that is detrimental to target shareholders (SEL art. 27-5; SEL Order art. 12; and TO Ordinance art. 18).

In addition the bidder must prepare a tender offer explanatory statement which contains substantially all the information in the registration statement (SEL art. 27-9; TO Ordinance art. 24). The tender offer explanatory statement must be sent to each person who tenders securities of the target in response to the bid (SEL art. 27-9; TO Ordinance art. 24). If the tender offer registration statement is amended then the tender offer explanatory statement must also be amended.

When the bid period has expired, the bidder must send a notice to target security holders who tendered under the bid noting the amount of securities tendered (SEL Order art. 8, para. 5). The bidder must also publish a notice of the result of the bid and file a tender offer report with the Ministry of Finance (SEL art. 27-13; TO Ordinance arts. 30 and 31).

If the target company publicly expresses an opinion on the bid, it must file an opinion report with the Minister of Finance and send the report to the bidder and the stock exchange on which the target's securities are listed (or to the securities dealers' association where the securities are not listed on a stock exchange but are traded on the over-the-counter market) (SEL art. 27-10; TO Ordinance art. 25).

112 The bid must be left open for a period of at least 20 days and can not be left open for more than 60 days from the date of the commencement of the tender offer (SEL art. 27-8 para. 1). If there is an amendment of the registration statement or a change in the terms of purchase then the bid period is extended by ten days from the date of the filing of the amendment (SEL art. 27-8, para. 8; TO Ordinance art. 22, para. 2).

the Williams Act in the U.S. Market manipulation techniques such as wash sales or the creation of a false market are prohibited.[115] The securities industry is regulated through the licensing of securities companies with minimum capital requirements[116] and competency standards, and the potential revocation of the licence is a key method of enforcing a set of duties and restrictions on securities companies.[117]

Foreign Sources of Japanese Securities Laws

The U.S. Influence

The Japanese legislation on securities regulation draws extensively on U.S. securities legislation. The reopening of Japanese stock exchanges after the Second World War was permitted by the occupation forces after the enactment of U.S.-style securities laws modelled on the U.S. *Securities Act of 1933* and the *Securities Exchange Act of 1934*.[118] Consequently the structure of public offering requirements is similar to that in the United States with the filing of a registration statement and the distribution of a prospectus to prospective investors. Proxy solicitation requirements and other continuous disclosure requirements are also patterned on U.S. securities laws. The

---

113 Target shareholders who tender their shares under the bid may withdraw their shares at any time during the bid period without penalty (SEL art. 27-12; SEL Order art. 14-2).

114 The bidder is generally prevented from purchasing securities subject to the bid other than under the bid itself (SEL art. 27-5; SEL Order art. 12; and TO Ordinance art. 18).

Japanese regulation of takeover bids restricts the withdrawal of a takeover bid once it is made. A bid may only be withdrawn in the event of a material change in the business or assets of the target company or in the event of a change in a material fact relating to the target company, and then only if the bidder has made it clear in the published notice of the bid and in the registration statement that it reserves the right to withdraw the bid upon the occurrence of such an event (SEL art. 27-11; SEL Order art. 14; and TO Ordinance arts. 27 and 28).

The requirements noted above apply when there is a "tender offer." A tender offer is defined as an offer to buy (or the solicitation of an offer to sell) shares of stock and certain other types of publicly-traded securities (such as subscription warrants or convertible bonds), where the offer is not made on a securities market (such as a stock exchange or over-the-counter market), but is made through a public notice (SEL art. 27-2, para. 6). The regulations apply where the tender offer will result in the bidder, or persons related to the bidder, owning more than 5% of the aggregate outstanding shares of the issuer (SEL art. 27-2, para. 1, item 3; SEL Order art. 7, paras. 1, 3-5).

Violations of these requirements are criminal offences. See SEL arts. 197 items 1-3 and 1-4, art. 198 items 1-2 to 4, 6 and 7; art. 200 items 1, 2, 2-5 to 2-11 and art. 205 items 1, 2, 2-3, 3.

115 See e.g. SEL art. 125 modelled on s. 9(a) of the U.S. *Securities Exchange Act of 1934* and SEL art. 58 modelled on s. 10(b) of the U.S. *Securities Exchange Act of 1934*.

116 See SEL art. 28 on the requirement to have a licence and see SEL arts. 29 and 31 on the conditions for the granting of a licence.

117 On the potential removal of a licence, see SEL art. 32 and on duties and responsibilities of securities companies, brokers, and dealers see e.g. SEL arts. 41-66.

118 See Shen-Shin Lu, "Are the 1988 Amendments to Japanese Securities Regulation Law Effective Deterrents to Insider Trading?" [1991] Col. Bus. L. Rev. 179 at 181.

takeover bid requirements, as noted above, are similar in many respects to those of the Williams Act in the U.S., and the scheme for the regulation of the securities industry is also similar to that of the U.S. *Securities Exchange Act of 1934*.

Differences in the Development of Insider Trading Regulation

In spite of the early similarity between Japanese and U.S. securities laws, the insider trading laws in the two countries have developed along quite different paths. The post-war Japanese *Securities and Exchange Law* (SEL) contained an insider short-swing profit rule similar to s. 16 of the U.S. *Securities Exchange Act of 1934*.[119] It also contained a general anti-fraud rule based on s. 10(b) of the *Securities Exchange Act of 1934* and Rule 10b-5.[120] Rule 10b-5 has been the basis for the development of much of the U.S. law on insider trading.[121] Although Rule 10b-5 has been widely used in insider trading cases in the United States, it has never been used in an insider trading case in Japan.[122] Similarly, before 1988 there was only one case in Japan based on the Japanese equivalent of s. 16 of the U.S. *Securities Exchange Act of 1934*.[123]

Substantial amendments in Japanese securities laws with respect to insider trading were adopted in 1988. The 1988 amendments prohibited the purchase or sale of securities by insiders with knowledge of a material fact until the material fact has been made public.[124] A broad scope was given to

---

119 SEL art. 188. See Lu, *ibid.* at 185.

120 SEL art. 58. Lu, *supra* note 118 at 185-86. W. Swan, "The 1988 Japanese Insider Trading Amendments: Will Japan See Results from These Tougher Laws" (1991) 12 Univ. Penn. J. of Int'l Bus. Law 275 at 276-77.

121 See e.g. the discussion in Hazen, *supra* note 5 at vol. 2 at 598-619.

122 Lu, *supra* note 118 at 186. Indeed, to 1991 there had only been one case involving SEL s. 58. That case did not deal with insider trading: see Swan, *supra* note 120 at 277.

123 Lu, *supra* note 118 at 191. Two cases have been brought according to note, "Regulation of Insider Trading in Japan" (1986) 89 Col. L. Rev. 1296 at 1300.

124 Amendments to the Securities Exchange Law in 1988 prohibit the purchase or sale of securities by insiders who have knowledge of a material fact related to the business and related matters of a company unless the material fact has been made public (SEL art. 190-2(1) and (3)). Similarly, no insider who has obtained knowledge of a fact in relation to the execution of a tender offer shall purchase securities of the corporation subject to the tender offer unless the fact has been made public, and no insider who has obtained knowledge of a fact in relation to the termination of a tender offer shall sell securities of the corporation that is subject to the tender offer unless the fact has been made public (SEL art. 190-3(1)). The sanction for a violation of the prohibition is a period of up to six months' imprisonment or a fine of up to 500,000 Yen (SEL art. 200). Two cases involving insider trading since the 1988 amendments are discussed in Wataru Horiguchi, "Securities Malfeasance in Japan: The Need for an Independent Organization to Monitor Insider Trading, Price Manipulation, and Loss Compensation" (1993) 16 Hastings Int'l and Comp. L. Rev. 223 at 224-25.

The securities to which the insider trading prohibitions apply are shares or bonds listed on any Japanese stock exchange, any share subscription warrants issued by a listed issuer (whether or not the warrants are themselves listed), and any options to deal in the securities of a listed issuer (SEL art. 190-2(1)). The tender offer insider

persons considered to be insiders.[125] "Material facts" was given an extensive definition[126] as was the expression "made public."[127] The amendments also restored an insider trade reporting requirement.[128] Thus in addition to the

---

trading prohibition applies to shares or similar instruments (and options on shares or similar instruments) that are subject to a tender offer (SEL art. 190-3(1) and (3)). This requirement of officers and major shareholders to disgorge short-swing profits does not require proof that the officer or major shareholder was in possession of confidential information.

There are several exceptions to the insider trading prohibition. For instance, the acquisition of shares upon the exercise of a right to subscribe for shares or on the exercise of conversion rights is not a violation of the insider trading prohibition (SEL art. 190-2(5) items 1 and 2). Similarly, a trade in the securities of a company based on the exercise of an appraisal right by a dissenting shareholder does not constitute a prohibited insider trade (SEL art. 190-2(5) item 3). A trade pursuant to an agreement entered into before the person making the trade obtained knowledge of the material fact, a trade made pursuant to a plan fixed before the person obtained knowledge of the material fact, or a trade based on similar "special circumstances" does not constitute a prohibited insider trade (SEL art. 190-2(5) item 8). A trade between two "corporate insiders" that takes place outside a securities market is also exempt (SEL art. 190-2(5) item 7). A purchase at the request of a company of its own shares pursuant to a resolution of the board of directors taken in defence of a tender offer also does not constitute a prohibited insider trade (SEL art. 190-2(5) item 4). Similar exemptions are provided with respect to the prohibition of insider trading in the context of tender offers with an exemption being granted in respect of shares of the offeree purchased at the request of the offeror (SEL art. 190-3(6)).

125 The prohibition with respect to trading in securities on the basis of an undisclosed material fact applies to persons who are "corporate insiders." In general terms, "corporate insiders" are:

(1) officers, agents, employees, or other personnel of an issuer who obtain knowledge of a material fact about the issuer in connection with their office (SEL art. 190-2(1) item 1);
(2) shareholders holding more than 10% of the voting shares of an issuer where they obtain knowledge of a material fact about the issuer through the exercise of the right to inspect the issuer's accounting books and documents (SEL art. 190-2(1) item 2);
(3) persons (other than officers, agents, employees or other personnel of the company) who have entered into a contract with the issuer and have obtained knowledge of a material fact about the issuer in connection with the execution of the contract (SEL art. 190-2(1) item 4); and
(4) persons who obtain knowledge of a material fact about an issuer in connection with the exercise of a statutory authority over the issuer (SEL art. 190-2(1) item 3). The definition also covers persons who have access to an issuer's accounting books or documents or are officers, agents, employees, or other personnel of a person in a contractual relationship with the issuer (SEL art. 190-2(1)). Persons who have ceased to be "corporate insiders" but who had obtained knowledge of a material fact relating to the issuer are also prohibited from trading unless the material fact has been made public (SEL art. 190-2(1)). Tippees (persons to whom a material fact about an issuer has been communicated by a "corporate insider") are also prohibited from trading (SEL art. 190-2(3)).

Where a tender offer is involved, persons who are prohibited from trading are described as "tender offer insiders." The definition of "tender offer insiders" is very similar to the definition of "corporate insiders," replacing "issuer" with "offeror" and "knowledge of a material fact about the issuer" with "knowledge of a fact relating to the tender offer." In short, the term "tender offer insiders" includes officers, agents,

unused equivalent of Rule 10b-5 in the United States, Japanese securities laws include an insider trade reporting requirement, an insider short-swing profit provision,[129] an insider short sale prohibition,[130] and other prohibitions

---

employees, and other personnel of the offeror (SEL art. 190-3(1) item 1), major shareholders of the offeror (and their officers, agents, employees, and other personnel) who are exercising their right to inspect the accounting records of the offeror (SEL art. 190-3(1) items 2 and 5), persons in a contractual relationship with the offeror (and any officers, agents, employees or other personnel of that person) (SEL art. 190-3(1) Items 4 and 5), and persons who obtain knowledge of a fact relating to a tender offer in the exercise of a statutory authority over the offeror (SEL art. 190-3(1) item 3). Persons who were but have ceased to be in any of the situations described above continue, for a period of one year, to be prohibited from trading with knowledge of a fact relating to a tender offer that has not been made public (SEL art. 190-3(1)). Tippees (or persons to whom a fact relating to the tender offer has been communicated by one of the above-described tender offer insiders) are also prohibited from trading (SEL art. 190-3(4)).

126 An interesting aspect of the recent Japanese insider trading provisions is their attempt to define "material facts." Certain facts are presumed to be material subject to a Ministry of Finance Ordinance that specifies categories of facts that are deemed not to be material (SEL art. 190-2(2) item 1). Ministry of Finance Ordinance no. 10 of 1989 arts. 1 and 2 provides that a fact is not material if it affects less than 10% of the book value of the company's assets or less than 10% of the company's sales. See Swan, *supra* note 120 at 292-93 and K. Okamura and C. Takeshita, *Laws and Regulations Relating to Insider Trading in Japan* (Tokyo: Commercial Law Center, 1989). Facts that are presumed to be material are issuances of shares of stock, convertible bonds and bonds with warrants to subscribe for new shares, reductions of stated capital, stock splits, changes in the amount or method of distribution of dividends or cash distributions, mergers, transfers of the company's business to a third party either partially or in its entirety, acquisitions of a business from a third party, dissolution, commercialization of a new product or technology, damage arising out of a natural disaster or business operations, changes in the composition of those who are principal shareholders, any event that might cause the delisting of shares, and other similar matters prescribed by cabinet order (SEL art. 190-2(2) items 1 and 2).

Changes in sales, operating profit, or net income projections, or differences in recorded sales, operating profit, or net income from past projections or previous year results are also considered material facts subject to a test of materiality determined by a Ministry of Finance Ordinance (SEL art. 190-2(2) item 3). A catch-all provision includes any other facts "relating to the management, business, or property of the company, which may have a significant influence on the investment decisions of investors" (SEL art. 190-2(2) item 4). This catch-all definition looks very similar to the definition of "material change" that is commonly used in Canadian provincial securities legislation: see e.g. British Columbia *Securities Act*, s. 1(1); Ontario *Securities Act*, s. 1(1).

A fact relating to a tender offer is defined as a decision made by the tender offeror to execute the tender offer or a decision made by the tender offeror not to execute the tender offer (SEL art. 190-3(2)). The Ministry of Finance can determine by ordinance categories of facts that will not be considered facts relating to a tender offer where they are determined to have only an immaterial influence on the investment decisions of investors (SEL art. 190-3(2)).

127 Trading with knowledge of a material fact is prohibited unless the material fact has been "made public" (SEL art. 190-2(1) and (3)). A material fact is considered to have been made public where it is contained in a registration statement, or annual, semi-annual, or extraordinary securities report filed with the Minister of Finance and made available for public inspection as required by the *Securities and Exchange Law* (SEL arts. 190-2(4) and 25). Otherwise, a material fact is considered to be made public where it

against insider trading. The effect of the amendments was that in many respects Japanese securities legislation came to reflect the essential elements of much of the U.S. law on insider trading that had been developed by courts in the United States on the basis of Rule 10b-5.

Factors Contributing to Similarities

Convergence towards Optimal Solutions

It might be argued that the changes in insider trading reflect a convergence towards an optimal solution. Although this solution was adopted much later in Japan than it was in the United States, there may be good reasons for the delay. It has been suggested that there may be economies of scale in the regulation of insider trading.[131] It has also been suggested that the development of computer technology may encourage the regulation of

---

is disclosed by the company's management in at least two forms of mass media and at least 12 hours have elapsed since the disclosure (SEL art. 190-2(4) and SEL Operation Order art. 30). The forms of mass media are national daily newspapers, a national industry or economic newspaper, or a national radio or television broadcast (SEL art. 190-2(4) and SEL Operation Order art. 30): see Tsunematsu and Yanase, *supra* note 108 at 65; Lu, *supra* note 118 at 216. The definition of "made public for the purposes of a tender offer" is essentially the same as the definition of public filing of a tender offer registration statement or other public notice (SEL art. 190-3(5)).

128 Directors, auditors, and shareholders holding 10% or more of the issued shares of a company listed on a stock exchange are required to file reports of trades before the 15th of the month following the transaction. The reports apply to trades in shares, convertible bonds, bonds with share warrants, subscription rights, and options relating to such securities (SEL art. 188). The filing of an untrue report or the failure to file a report can result in a fine of up to 300,000 Yen (SEL art. 205). Exceptions to the reporting requirement are provided for fractional shares and unround blocks, employee securities purchase plans, employee trust funds, stock-index future transactions, and new issue stabilizations (SEL art. 188 and SEL Ordinance art. 4. These are briefly dicussed in Lu, *supra* note 118 at 201-203).

129 An officer of a listed company or a shareholder holding 10% or more of the issued shares of a listed company who buys and sells, or sells and buys, shares, convertible bonds, bonds with share warrants, subscription rights, or options relating to such securities is obliged to disgorge to the company any profits received thereby (SEL art. 189(1)). If the company fails to make a demand for recovery of the profits within 60 days, the shareholder is entitled to demand the disgorgement of the profits on behalf of the company (SEL art. 189(2)). A limitation period of two years commences on the date the profits were realized (SEL art. 189(3)). On finding that an officer or major shareholder has made a short-swing profit, the Minister of Finance is required to make a report to the company, subject to giving the officer or major shareholder an opportunity to file an objection (SEL art. 189(4)-(6)). If the profits have not been disgorged within 30 days of the date that the Minister's report is given to the company, the report is to be made available for public inspection (SEL art. 189(7)). The report is made public until the end of the two-year limitation period.

130 Officers and shareholders holding 10% or more of a listed company's shares cannot short sell the company's securities (SEL art. 190). There is a penal sanction for short sales by such insiders of up to 300,000 Yen (SEL art. 205).

131 See Easterbrook, *supra* note 107 at 93.

insider trading by reducing the cost of enforcement.[132] If so, it may be that the adoption of laws prohibiting insider trading occurred sooner in the United States because its securities markets developed a sufficient volume of trading to justify the costs of insider trading regulation, even on a much less sophisticated computer technology than was available in Japan in 1988, when it adopted a more extensive regulation of insider trading. The combination of more developed markets with more trading and improved computer technology may have sufficiently reduced the cost of insider trading regulation in Japan to make it worthwhile.

Political Pressures Leading to Similar Securities Laws

While one might explain the convergence of Japanese and U.S. securities laws as a convergence towards optimal solutions, other explanations are at least as plausible. The apparent imposition of U.S.-style securities laws, along with other U.S. legislation such as banking legislation designed to break up the powerful Japanese Zaibatsu,[133] appears to fit more with U.S. interests protecting domestic economic rents from being dissipated by powerful Japanese organizations such as the Zaibatsu.

The notion that similar securities laws might have resulted from similar political pressures caused by the development of similar market participants with common investor protection interests or from a compromise between various rent-seeking interests does not appear to fit in the case of Japan. The financial market structure of Japan before the U.S. occupation was significantly different from that of the U.S.[134] As noted below, this difference in market structure was probably a significant factor in the different development paths of laws with respect to insider trading in the United States and Japan following the U.S. post-war occupation.

The eventual adoption of an expanded regulation of insider trading in Japan may have been, in part, a result of the competition for capital in the context of increasingly internationalized securities markets. Explanations advanced for the 1988 amendments with respect to insider trading include the exposure of the Japanese securities market (with its growth and increasing importance as a major world securities market), Japan's negative image as a haven for insider trading, the world trend towards increasingly stringent insider trading regulations, and a major insider trading case that reinforced

132 *Ibid.*

133 See R. Clark, *The Japanese Company* (New Haven: Yale Univ. Press, 1979) at 42-44, 73-87; M. J. Roe, *Strong Managers Weak Owners: The Political Roots of American Corporate Finance* (Princeton, N.J.: Princeton University Press, 1994) at 216-18; and M. J. Roe, "Some Differences in Corporate Structure in Germany, Japan, and the United States" (1993) 102 Yale L. J. 1927 at 1972-73.

134 *Ibid.*

Japan's image as a haven for insider trading.[135] All of these explanations are consistent with a perceived need to improve the image of Japanese insider trading laws to maintain Japan's competitiveness in international securities markets.

Transaction Costs, Information Costs, Uncertainty and the Source of Borrowing

With the quite different institutional structure in Japan at the end of the Second World War, the imposition of U.S. securities laws would not have been likely to represent an approximation to political compromise among securities industry participants. Thus the adoption of U.S. securities laws would probably not have avoided a significant portion of the costs of reaching a political compromise between securities industry participants. Indeed, industry participants had probably already reached their own form of political compromise to which the imposed legal structure was antithetical.

What is curious then is why the imposition of a legal and institutional structure was not done away with once the U.S. occupation was over. One reason could be that a new institutional structure was, in fact, effectively imposed, and the law then reflected an approximate political compromise in the newly imposed institutional structure. However, it is clear that this did not happen. Instead, the institutional structure that arose was, in many respects, a reconstitution of the pre-war institutional structure created within and around the new legal framework. Once the institutional framework had been so reconstructed there was no need to change the legal framework. The political compromise reflected in the new institutional framework worked with the imposed legislation and there was no need to change the legislation.

Another reason why there may not have been much impetus in Japan to change its securities legislation once it was in place is that foreign investors, particular U.S. investors, had some familiarity with the Japanese legislation, which was essentially borrowed from the United States. The familiar investment environment may have facilitated foreign indirect investment in Japan, providing an additional source of capital funds for Japanese industry. Changing the legislation might have created unnecessary uncertainty for foreign investors (and possibly for local investors as well).

The first-mover advantage of U.S. securities legislation probably gave it a significant edge over alternative sources of securities legislation or over any significant degree of experimentation. The information costs associated with canvassing other potential sources of borrowing or experimentation, together

135 Lu, *supra* note 118 at 193-97. Swan, *supra* note 120 at 281-84. See also H. L. Pitt and D. B. Hardison, "Games Without Partners: Trends in the International Response to Insider Trading" (1992) 55 Law and Contemporary Problems 199 at 217-18.

with costs to investors of becoming informed of changes and the cost of getting securities industry support for any significant changes to the legislation, were probably not perceived by participants in the Japanese securities industry to be worthwhile. The growing commercial links between Japan and the United States over the years may have served to reinforce the use of U.S.-style securities legislation.

Factors Contributing to Differences

Legal System Differences

The difference in the legal system between the United States and Japan may, in part, account for the fact that Japan did not develop laws on insider trading on the basis of Rule 10b-5 as the United States did. Various reasons have been advanced for the lack of use of the Japanese Rule 10b-5 equivalent to curb insider trading.[136] Among the reasons advanced is the difficulty of applying the vague wording of the provision in the Japanese legal system compared to the U.S.-style common law system.[137]

While legal system differences may have had an effect on the use of the Japanese equivalent of the U.S. Rule 10b-5, they were apparently not considered sufficient to prevent the initial adoption of U.S.-style securities legislation. Legal system differences were also apparently not sufficient to lead to the repeal of U.S.-style securities legislation after the post-war occupation period had ended. Overall the legal system differences do not appear to have been a significant factor in the source of borrowing of Japanese securities laws.

Culture

Another reason suggested for the Japanese reluctance to develop insider trading regulation on the basis of its Rule 10b-5 equivalent is that Japanese attitudes towards insider trading are different from those in North America.[138] The argument is that Japanese people view the stock market as a kind of lottery – you pay your money and you take your chances, including the risk that there is some insider trading. Insider trading is viewed as a natural characteristic of securities markets and is not inherently immoral or unjust.

Local Market Features and Path Dependence

The much later adoption of extensive insider trading regulation in Japan as

---

136 See e.g. Lu, *supra* note 118 at 186-88. Swan, *supra* note 120 at 279-81. Pitt and Hardison, *supra* note 135 at 217. L. Zoglin, "Insider Trading in Japan: A Challenge to the Integration of the Japanese Equity Market Into the Global Securities Market" [1987] Col. Bus. L. Rev. 419 at 421.

137 Lu, *supra* note 118 at 186-88. For similar arguments with respect to political donations see Swan, *supra* note 120 at 280-81. See also Horiguchi, *supra* note 124 at 224.

138 *Ibid.*

compared to the United States may also be attributed to the unique features of the Japanese market and the consequent political forces. Another of the reasons advanced for the Japanese reluctance to develop insider trading regulation on the basis of its Rule 10b-5 equivalent is the importance that insider trading had in fund-raising by politicians.[139] Securities firms and corporate insiders lobbied against increased insider trading regulations and the Securities Bureau of the Ministry of Finance was said to be reluctant to change the law, preferring the status quo.[140] The amendments were ultimately facilitated by bundling them with other securities law amendments.[141] Thus local market features and political forces may have been significant in delaying the adoption of insider trading laws in Japan and may have been overcome only by increased pressure from international securities market competition.

Local market features and political forces may have also accounted for the return to the pre-war status quo on insider trading after the post-war U.S. occupation period. This is apparent in the constraints imposed on the use of the short-swing profit rule by the 1953 repeal of the equivalent of U.S. *Securities Exchange Act* s. 16(a), which required the filing of trading reports by directors, officers, and major shareholders.[142] Large corporate shareholders allegedly lobbied for the repeal of the disclosure requirement because it interfered with their pre-war insider trading practices and payoffs to politicians.[143]

China

An Overview of Chinese Securities Laws

The securities laws of China consist of laws at both the national level and the local level relating to the Shanghai and Shenzhen stock exchanges. These securities laws are a relatively recent phenomenon in China.[144]

139 *Ibid.*

140 Lu, *supra* note 118 at 194.

141 *Ibid.* at 194-95.

142 *Ibid.* at 190. Swan, *supra* note 120 at 278.

143 *Ibid.* at 191.

144 After an extended period of debate, the People's Republic of China (PRC) began in 1990 to erect a system of securities laws and regulations that brought to the finance sector reform policies enacted in other sectors of the economy. While the effort remains incomplete (as indicated by the failure as of early 1995 to enact a securities law) much has been accomplished – most notably the enactment of the *Company Law* of the PRC in 1993. Beginning in the late 1980s and gathering momentum with the establishment of securities exchanges at Shanghai and Shenzhen, this effort was fraught with policy conflicts over the goals of regulation. At the national level, the *Company Law* grew out of national-level regulations enacted as compromise measures in 1992-1993. These also reflected the context of the tentative draft of the securities law, and the debates surrounding it. See generally P. B. Potter, "The Legal Framework for Securities Markets in China: The Challenge of Maintaining State Control, and Inducing

Local Regulatory Regimes

With the opening of the Shanghai Securities Market in December 1990, China began a well-publicized effort to build a legal regime for regulating securities markets. The Shenzhen market was officially opened shortly thereafter, and for a time the regulatory frameworks in these two cities were the major if not the only basis for securities regulation in China. Subject to the limits of national regulations, the local measures applicable in Shanghai and Shenzhen remain effective in these locales.

The Shanghai Exchange The Shanghai Exchange Regulations,[145] enacted 26 November 1990, contain detailed provisions governing Shanghai Securities Exchange (SSE) operations and organization, all of which are subject to the authority of the People's Bank of China, Shanghai (PBOC, Shanghai).[146] The regulations cover such issues as the organization of the exchange, issuance of securities, delegated purchase and sale of securities, transactions at the exchange, auctions, liquidation and closing, detailed rules on related party transactions,[147] the regulatory and fee structures, trading procedures, accounting, and dispute resolution.

The 1990 regulations underscore the provisions of earlier measures concerning the authority of PBOC, Shanghai to approve all securities issuances and to control, suspend, and even terminate securities trading.[148] In addition the 1990 measures include many of the same policies expressed in prior enactments, retaining the disparate treatment given stock and bond issues, and the insistence that transactions in securities be limited to exchanges

---

Investor Confidence" (1992) 7 China L. Rep. 61; and P. B. Potter, "China Securities Regulation: A National System Begins to Emerge," *East Asian Executive Reports* (15 May 1993) 9.

145 The Shanghai regulations included primarily the Trial Regulations of the Shanghai Securities Exchange on the Activities of the Exchange Market (the Shanghai Exchange Regulations). See "Trial Regulations of the Shanghai Securities Exchange on the Activities of the Exchange Market," 26 Nov. 1990 (Shanghai: Shanghai Securities Exchange Board of Directors, 1990), issued by the Shanghai Securities Exchange (SSE) board of directors, and the Methods of Shanghai Municipality for Administration of Securities Transactions (the Shanghai Transaction Regulations). See "Methods of Shanghai Municipality for Administration of Securities Transactions," *Liberation Daily* (12 Dec. 1990) 3. An English translation appears as "Shanghai Securities Transaction Regulations" in *FBIS Daily Report – China* (20 Dec. 1990) 46, issued by the municipal government.

146 Article 5 of the Shanghai Exchange Regulations provides that the department in charge is PBOC (Shanghai), whose approval and supervisory authority are reiterated throughout.

147 Many of these details are needed because of the continuing absence of a comprehensive company law.

148 See "Provisional Methods for Issuing Stock," 10 Aug. 1984 (Shanghai: General Office of the Shanghai Municipal Government, 1984) and "Economic Laws and Regulations Research Centre of the Shanghai Municipal Government," *Compilation of Statutes and Regulations and Rules of Shanghai Municipality* (Shanghai: Shanghai People's Press, 1986).

controlled by PBOC, Shanghai.[149] Complementing the Exchange Regulations, the Shanghai Transaction Regulations govern the issuance and transfer of securities, and related matters such as the issuance and trading of securities, securities dealers, the role of the SSE in securities transactions, the brokerage guild, the administrative institute for securities, penalties, and supplemental provisions, thus focusing more specifically on the processes for issuance and transfers of securities and the parties involved.[150]

In November 1991, PBOC, Shanghai and the Shanghai municipal government issued administrative measures and implementing rules for "B shares" – that is, shares denominated in renminbi but able to pay dividends in foreign currency.[151] The Shanghai B Share Administrative Measures[152] address such issues as the administration of security issuance, administra-

---

149 Compare Shanghai Exchange Regulations, *supra* note 145 with "Shanghai shi gupiao guanli zanxing banfa" and "Shanghai shi zhaiquan guanli banfa," discussed in "Shanghai fabu shi zhaiquan he gupiao guanli zanxing banfa" ("Shanghai Issued Municipal Regulations on Administration of Bonds and Stocks"), in *Economic Reference* (1 July 1987) 2. Also see "Regulations Issued on Bonds," *China Daily Business Weekly* (12 July 1987) 2.

The 1990 regulations also reiterate provisions of other 1987 Shanghai municipal enactments, such as the "Experimental Methods for Stock Companies" and the "Administrative Methods of Shanghai Municipality for Securities and Their Exchanges," authorizing regulatory organs to collect detailed materials and information about the enterprises whose securities were being traded. See generally, Shi Qingkai, "A Study of the Development and Legislation of Our Stock System" (Graduation Thesis, Shanghai Academy of Social Sciences Institute of Law, 1989).

150 See "Methods of Shanghai Municipality for Administration of Securities Transactions," *Liberation Daily* (12 Dec. 1990) 3. An English translation appears as "Shanghai Securities Transaction Regulations," *FBIS Daily Report – China* (20 Dec. 1990) 46. While reiterating the theme of the Shanghai Exchange Regulations in maintaining PBOC control over securities transactions, the Shanghai Transaction Regulations also depart from the Shanghai Exchange Regulations by opening the possibility of a greater variety of securities being traded (see Shanghai Transaction Regulations, art. 3), and by minimizing the differential treatment of the issuance and trading of stock and bonds. For example, the standard information required to be disclosed for the issuance of stocks and bonds is more nearly equal under the Shanghai Transaction Regulations (arts. 9-11) than under the Shanghai Exchange Regulations.

151 The emergence of B Shares was predicated on the non-convertibility of the renminbi. Despite the restrictions on their offerings and trading, B Shares were for a time the only way to introduce foreign currency investment into Chinese domestic companies on a portfolio basis. However, with the introduction of H shares in 1993 and the American Depository Receipts (ADRs) listed by Chinese companies on the New York Stock Exchange (NYSE), alternative avenues have made the B Share market less attractive. See e.g. L. Weiling, "Experts Call for Moves to Revive B-Share Markets," *The China Daily* (15 Apr. 1994) 3; also D. Whittall, "Heavy Hitting H Shares," *The China Business Review* (May-June 1994) 44. With the reform of the Chinese foreign exchange system in December 1993, non-convertibility is on the way out, and with it the premise for limits on B Share markets. See "Announcement of the People's Bank of China on Further Reforming the Foreign Exchange Management System" (28 Dec. 1993) in *China Economic News* (10 Jan. 1994) 9.

152 "Measures of Shanghai Municipality for Administration of Special Renminbi-Denominated Shares" ("Shanghai B Share Administrative Measures") (22 Nov. 1991), enacted

tion of trading, administration of securities houses, and supplementary provisions. The Shanghai B Share Implementing Rules[153] address a wider range of issues including conversion rates, exchange accounts, securities dealers inside and outside China, issues and trading, clearance procedures, and taxation, fees, and penalties. In addition, the SSE issued a set of Supplementary Operating Rules in February 1992 governing transactions in "B shares," which address issues related to "B share" accounts, delegated purchase and sale, the mechanics of trade transactions, fees, dispute resolution, and other issues.[154] Taken together this group of regulations sets the basic framework for the B Share market in Shanghai.

The Shenzhen Exchange Another major exchange in China is the Shenzhen Exchange. The Shenzhen Exchange Rules set out the basic provisions for operation of the exchange.[155] These rules were adopted after lengthy negotiations between representatives of the Shenzhen Exchange, the Shenzhen Municipal Government, and the Shenzhen Branch of the PBOC.[156] The Shenzhen Exchange Rules are shorter and more general than the Shanghai Exchange Regulations.[157] They address: (1) general principles, such as the authority of the Shenzhen branch of the PBOC to supervise the exchange;

---

by the People's Bank of China and the Shanghai Municipal Government, translation by Baker & McKenzie.

153 "Detailed Implementing Rules for the Measures of Shanghai Municipality for the Administration of Special Renminbi-Denominated Shares" ("Shanghai B Share Implementing Rules") (25 Nov. 1991), enacted by the Shanghai Branch of the People's Bank of China, translation by Baker & McKenzie.

154 "Supplementary Operating Rules for the Trading Market (Special Renminbi-Denominated Shares) of the Shanghai Securities Exchange" ("Shanghai B Share Operating Rules") (18 Feb. 1992), enacted by the Shanghai Securities Exchange, translation by Baker & McKenzie.

155 In July 1990 the Shenzhen municipal government established a Leading Small Group, which began drafting regulations for the Shenzhen Exchange. See "Notice of the Shenzhen Municipal People's Government Concerning the Establishment of the Leading Small Group for the Shenzhen Securities Market," in *Annual Report on Shenzhen Securities Market 1990* at 229. Based on drafting work by the Leading Small Group, regulations governing the Shenzhen exchange were formally enacted in May 1991 with subsequent measures issued to address stock trading and other matters. For discussion of provisions for issuance and marketing of securities by the leading small group, see "Summary of Minutes of the Leading Small Group of the Shenzhen Securities Market: Selection Three," *Annual Report on the Shenzhen Securities Market 1990* at 113. Much of the text was incorporated in the Shenzhen Stock Transaction Regulations. Compare Section 4 of "Summary of Minutes of the Leading Small Group of the Shenzhen Securities Market: Selection Three," *Annual Report on the Shenzhen Securities Market 1990* at 113 with arts. 15 and 36 of the Shenzhen Transaction Regulations.

156 See "Articles of Association for the Shenzhen Securities Exchange" and "Provisional Methods of Shenzhen Municipality for the Issue and Transferring of Shares" (15 May 1991).

157 The Shanghai Exchange Regulations consist of 259 detailed articles while the Shenzhen Exchange Rules comprise 38 articles.

(2) registered capital of the exchange (RMB 10 million); (3) operations (e.g. establishment and operation of the exchange as well as sales, purchases, clearing accounts, payment of interest, and other matters); (4) membership (subject to PBOC approval, rights and obligations, penalties for violations); (5) congress of members (including functions as a representative organization for members); (6) board of directors (day-to-day managerial functions); (7) general manager (duties and functions); (8) supervisory committee (authority and functions); (9) finance and accounting rules (subject to state regulations); (10) liquidation of the exchange (withdrawal of state authorization, force majeure); and (11) supplementary provisions. The regulatory focus of these regulations is on the organization and administration of the exchange as an institution, separate and distinct from the transactions associated with it.

The Shenzhen Stock Transaction Regulations comprise 97 articles organized into eight chapters. The Regulations address matters such as (1) general principles; (2) stock; (3) stock issues; (4) stock transactions; (5) brokers, the Exchange and registered companies; (6) the organ in charge; (7) sanctions; and (8) supplementary principles. These rules are comparable to the provisions of the Shanghai Transaction Regulations and the provisions of the Shanghai Exchange Regulations that address matters of stock issues and trading. Unlike the Shanghai enactment, the Shenzhen measures delineate clearly the functional difference between the regulation of the exchange itself (through the Shenzhen Exchange Rules) and the regulation of stock transactions (through the Shenzhen Stock Transaction Regulations).

The Shezhen Exchange also adopted rules on B shares.[158] These rules differ in a number of respects from the Shanghai Exchange B share rules.[159]

National Regulatory Regimes

Despite the absence of a national Securities Law, China's securities regulations still operate at the national level, through the *Company Law*[160] and

---

158 In December 1991 the PBOC, PBOC (Shenzhen), and the Shenzhen municipal government issued Interim Procedures. See "Interim Procedures on Control of Shenzhen Special (B-Type) RMB Stocks" ("Shenzhen B Share Interim Procedures") in *China Economic News* (27 Jan. 1992) 7 and Implementing Rules "Rules for the Implementation of the Interim Procedures on Control of Shenzhen Special (B-Type) RMB Stocks" ("Shenzhen B Share Implementing Rules") in *China Economic News* (3 Feb. 1992) 7 for the Shenzhen Securities Market that are broadly similar to those issued for Shanghai.

159 The Shenzhen measures on B Shares differ from the Shanghai regulations on matters such as conversion rates, direct subscription by overseas investors, remittance of foreign exchange proceeds, clearing banks, and the appointment of foreign securities firms as members of the Shenzhen Exchange. See L. S. Liu and P. B. Potter, "Foreign Access to Securities Markets in Taiwan and the People's Republic of China" (1994) 19 Univ. of Melbourne L. Rev. 330.

160 In December 1993 the NPC (National People's Congress) promulgated the PRC *Company Law,* which not only formalizes the rules and procedures for company operations

through a series of national regulations on securities issuances.[161] These enactments provide the regulatory foundation upon which local regulations in Shanghai and Shenzhen operate.

---

but also redefines the regulatory system for company shares. See "Company Law of the People's Republic of China" (hereater "PRC *Company Law*") in *China Economic News*, Supplement No. 2 (7 Mar. 1994). A number of preliminary analyses have emerged addressing this legislation, including P. Torbert, "Broadening the Scope of Investment," *The China Business Review* (May-June 1994) 48 and D. Ho, "China's New Company Law: Something Concrete to Go By," *East Asian Executive Reports* (Feb. 1994) 9. The PRC *Company Law* was based on a draft that had been submitted in March after undergoing years of refinement and debate. See "Draft Corporate Law Submitted," *FBIS Daily Report – China* (16 Feb. 1993) 29; and "Speech by Qiao Shi at Closing of NPC," *FBIS Daily Report – China* (1 Apr. 1993) 22. One source from which many of the *Company Law*'s provisions were drawn is the Provisional Regulations of Shenzhen Municipality on Companies Limited by Shares (17 Mar. 1992), reprinted in *China Law and Practice* (7 May 1992) 12, and on various "opinions on stock companies and limited liability companies. See e.g. "Opinion on Standards for Limited Liability Stock Companies," *People's Daily* (19 June 1992), regarding e.g. bond issues, accounting issues, mergers, bankruptcy and liquidation, and responsibilities of branches of foreign companies.

Of particular importance for foreign investment in Chinese securities are the provisions concerning companies limited by shares (*gufen youxian gongsi*, also referred to as joint stock companies), which were previously authorized to issue B shares, and which under the PRC *Company Law* (art. 155) may now receive approval for listing their shares in foreign securities exchanges. The PRC *Company Law* also imposes restrictions on share issuances (arts. 130, 131), share transfers (art. 147), the listing of shares (arts. 152, 153), and the issuance of corporate bonds (arts. 159-63).

161 Following the opening of securities exchanges in Shanghai and Shenzhen, securities regulation in the PRC gradually extended to the national level through a series of eight separate regulations issued between June and August 1992. These included (1) Regulations on Enterprises' Shareholding System Experiment (15 May 1992); (2) Temporary Provisions on Several Issues Concerning Financial Management in Experimental Shareholding Enterprises (27 June 1992); (3) Temporary Provisions on Issues Concerning Tax Revenue of Experimental Shareholding Enterprises (12 June 1992); (4) Interim Procedures Governing the Supply and Marketing of Goods and Materials by Experimental Shareholding Enterprises (30 June 1992); (5) Provisional Regulations on the Macroeconomic Control of Experimental Joint-Stock Enterprises (6 July 1992); (6) Interim Regulations Governing Labor and Wages in Enterprises Experimenting With Share-Holding Systems (1 June 1992); (7) Provisional Regulations on Auditing at Experimental Shareholding Enterprises (19 July 1992); and (8) Interim Provisions on Administering Land Assets of Experimental Shareholding Enterprises (9 July 1992).

The most important of these measures, and one from which the others derived, was the Regulations on Enterprises' Shareholding System Experiment (hereinafter the Shareholder System Regulations), issued jointly by the State Commission on Restructuring the Economy, the State Planning Commission, the Ministry of Finance, the People's Bank of China, and the State Council Production Office. See "State Regulations on Shareholding Experiment," *FBIS Daily Report – China* (22 June 1992) 31. The Shareholder System Regulations set the broad parameters for expanding the use of shares as the basis for enterprise ownership. A key element of these regulations was protection of shareholder interests. Additional issues included (1) financial management (see "Temporary Provisions on Several Issues Concerning Financial Management in Experimental Shareholding Enterprises," in "Provisions on Financial Management of Stock Firms," *FBIS Daily Report – China* (6 July 1992) 52 and "Provisional Regulations on Auditing at Experimental Shareholding Enterprises,"

The Securities Committee of the State Council (SCOSC) and its subordinate organ, the China Securities Supervision and Control Committee (CSSACC) oversee securities regulation at the national level.[162] The SCOSC is the source of regulatory and policy guidance, drafting laws and regulations, formulating principles, policies, and rules, and devising plans and proposals while also offering general guidance and supervisory assistance. The State Planning Commission has responsibility for general planning for

---

in "Regulations on Shareholding Enterprise Auditing," *FBIC Daily Report – China* (22 July 1992) 37); (2) taxation (see "Temporary Provisions on Issues Concerning Tax Revenue of Experimental Shareholding Enterprises," in "Rules on Taxing Experimental Shareholding Firms," *FBIS Daily Report – China* (6 July 1992) 57); (3) commercial transactions (see "Interim Procedures Governing the Supply and Marketing of Goods and Materials by Experimental Shareholding Enterprises," in "Rules on Marketing by Pilot Shareholding Firms," *FBIS Daily Report – China* (6 July 1992) 58); and (4) the formation and supervision of joint stock companies (see "Provisional Regulations on the Macroeconomic Control of Experimental Joint-Stock Enterprises," in "Regulations on Forming Joint-Stock Enterprises," *FBIS Daily Report – China* (14 July 1992) 37).

In April 1993, the State Council issued a provisional regulation that provided formal nationwide standards for the issue and trading of stock. See "Interim Provisions on the Management of the Issuing and Trading of Stocks," *China Economic News* (7 June 1993) 7 and (14 June 1993) 7. See also *South China Morning Post* (8 June 1993) B4. Emerging from the State Council's January 1993 Circular on Further Strengthening Macro-Control of Securities Markets (see "State Council Circular on Securities Markets," *FBIS Daily Report – China* (25 Jan. 1993) 240), the State Council rules supplemented regulations already in place at the Shanghai and Shenzhen Securities Exchanges. The 1993 regulations addressed such matters as stock issues and trading; takeovers; custody, clearance and registration of shares; information disclosure; inspection and penalties; and dispute resolution. While they did not extend directly to foreign-invested B Shares, the regulations did establish a national set of rules that paved the way for listing Chinese domestic stocks on foreign markets such as Hong Kong. Additional regulations were planned for B Shares and for the overseas issue and trading of domestic Chinese shares.

Expanding upon the State Council Circular of January 1993, the mid-year regulations specified that the State Council Securities Policy Committee (SCSPC) was to have overall charge of administration of the national stock market, while the China Securities Regulatory Commission (CSRC) was to be SCSPC's executive agency responsible for supervision and regulation. The regulations granted CSRC broad authority to investigate individuals or companies suspected of violating the regulations, and to examine the business activities of any securities institution without cause. The CSRC has subsequently established a special Commission for examining and approving share issues. See "Overseer for share issues established," *South China Morning Post* (25 June 1993) B1.

See generally, P. Potter, "Securities Regulation: A National System Begins to Emerge" and "P.R.C. State Council Issues National Stock Regulations," *East Asian Executive Reports* (15 May 1993) 9 and (15 July 1993) 9, respectively.

162 See "State Council Circular on Securities Markets," *FBIS Daily Report – China* (25 Jan. 1993) 24. These organs effectively replaced the China Commission on Securities Supervision and Management, which had been touted as an independent semi-official regulatory body, and the State Council's Securities Administrative Conference, which had comprised a loose group of officials and experts appointed from the PBOC, Ministry of Finance, the State Commission on Economic Restructuring, and other organs. See "Stock Market Supervision Said to Be Accelerated" and "State Council Sets Up Securities Management Body," *FBIS Daily Report – China* (6 July 1992) 51 and 52.

the securities industry, while the PBOC exercises specific regulatory authority over securities organizations – that is, exchanges, brokers, etc. The Ministry of Finance, in coordination with the CSSACC, has responsibility for registered accountants, while the Economic Restructuring Commission is responsible for formulating laws and regulations on specific securities experiments.

Specific Regulatory Regimes

China's securities law regime may be compared with others in the East Asian region by reference to issues related to information disclosure, insider dealing, market manipulation, takeover bid regulation, and securities industry regulation. China's securities laws share many features with the securities laws of other jurisdictions such as Malaysia, Singapore, Japan, and the United States. For instance, mandatory disclosure is a significant feature of Chinese securities laws. However, China's securities law regime also has several unique features that, in comparison with the securities laws of Malaysia, Singapore, and Japan, shed some light on the relative importance of the various factors affecting similarities and differences in securities laws. These features are addressed below in the context of information disclosure, insider trading, market manipulation, takeover bid regulation, and securities industry regulation.

Information Disclosure

Similarity to Other Jurisdictions As noted above, the disclosure requirements under national laws share some broad similarities to those of Malaysia, Singapore, Japan, and other countries. The distribution of shares is subject to disclosure in the form of a prospectus.[163] Subsequent forms of continuous

---

163 Under national securities regulatory regimes, the PRC *Company Law* contains provisions on information disclosure that augment previous law and regulation. The prospectus for companies limited by shares must include information on (1) the number of shares subscribed for by promoters; (2) the par value and issue price of each share; (3) the total number of non-registered shares issued; (4) the rights and obligations of subscribers; and (5) the time limit for the public offer and for notifying subscribers of the right to revoke their subscription if the offer is under-subscribed: *ibid.* at art. 87. A new prospectus must be provided for each new share issuance (art. 140). Applications submitted to the State Council's securities administration department for approval of share offers must include additional information on the company's operating budget and other financial information: *ibid.* at art. 84.

The 1993 Interim Provisions on the Management of the Issuing and Trading of Stocks issued by the State Council also contained provisions on information disclosure. See *China Economic News* (7 June 1993) 7; (14 June 1993) 7; and (21 June 1993) 8. See also *South China Morning Post* (8 June 1993) B4. In applying for the issue of stock, enterprises must, under these provisions, supply the local government department in charge with a prospectus, financial reports from the previous three years, asset appraisal reports, and other documents. See Interim Provisions on the Management of the Issuing and Trading of Stocks, art. 13, in *China Economic News* (7 June 1993) 8. The

disclosure are also required for publicly traded shares.[164] The specific information required differs in many respects but appears to be generally directed to information that would assist in the valuation of the securities being traded. The disclosure requirements are backed by penal sanctions and rights of private compensation.[165]

The information disclosure regimes of the Shanghai and Shenzhen exchanges appear even closer to North American regimes than the information

---

prospectus must include information on the financial status of the issuer and a prediction of gains, losses, and risks: see Interim Provisions on the Management of the Issuing and Trading of Stocks, art. 15, in *China Economic News* (7 June 1993) 8-9. Article 16 of the Interim Provisions requires the promoter to guarantee the accuracy of the prospectus. When listing stock, the listed company must provide a prospectus, as well as a listing announcement containing additional financial disclosure. See Interim Provisions on the Management of the Issuing and Trading of Stocks, art. 34, in *China Economic News* (14 June 1993) 7.

164 Listed companies are required to make public their financial and operational conditions and to publish financial statements every six months of the fiscal year. See PRC *Company Law*, art. 156. Yearly financial reporting must include balance sheets, profit and loss statements, reports on financial conditions, and profit distribution statements: *ibid.* at art. 175. These reports must also comply with the PRC *Accounting Law*, which was revised in late 1993 in part to encompass the new forms of business organization brought on by the *Company Law*: see PRC *Accounting Law* (1985), as amended (1993), in *China Economic News* (24 Jan. 1994) 6.

Under the 1993 Interim Provisions on the Management of the Issuing and Trading of Stocks, listed companies are also required to provide to the regulatory authorities an interim mid-year report and an extensive annual report on financial conditions, company operations, accounts of shareholders, directors, and other personnel, and other issues. See the Interim Provisions on the Management of the Issuing and Trading of Stocks, arts. 58-59, in *China Economic News* (21 June 1993) 8-9.

Local regimes also have continuous disclosure requirements. For instance, under the Shanghai Exchange Regulations, after receiving approval for issuance of securities, stock and bond issuers alike are subject to continuous disclosure requirements. They must report a wide variety of changes in financial and operating circumstances, such as changes in capital structure, debt, operating losses, and so on. See Shanghai Exchange Regulations, *supra* arts. 40 and 41. In addition, securities issuers must provide PBOC (Shanghai) with yearly financial reports, which must also be made semiannually by issuers of stock. See Shanghai Transaction Regulations, art. 36. The occurrence of major events, such as major contracts, changes in operations, significant investments, large debts or losses, changes in managerial personnel or directors, or major litigation, must also be reported. See Shanghai Transaction Regulations, art. 37.

In contrast to the detailed reporting requirements imposed under the Shanghai Exchange Regulations, members of the Shenzhen exchange are subjected to rather general duties to uphold exchange rules, preserve the interests of the exchange and promote the stability and prosperity of the exchange, pay fees and interest as per regulations, and accept the supervision and administration of the exchange in connection with the listing of securities. Shenzhen Exchange Aricle, art. 10.

165 The Interim Provisions on the Management of the Issuing and Trading of Stocks impose penalties for making false or misleading statements or otherwise failing to comply with the information disclosure requirements. See Interim Provisions on the Management of the Issuing and Trading of Stocks, art. 74, in *China Economic News* (21 June 1993) 11. Under the *Company Law*, violations of the information

disclosure regimes in Malaysia, Singapore, and Japan. This is particularly evident in the case of the Shanghai exchange with its quite detailed prospectus and continuous disclosure requirements (including the timely disclosure of significant events).[166]

Uniquely Open-Ended Approach in Shenzhen The Shenzhen approach is unique in that it is somewhat more open-ended than the Shanghai approach. While employing the disclosure approach common to many jurisdictions, the Shenzhen approach appears to be somewhat experimental in its acceptance of a wide range of disclosure in the form of feasibility studies, stock valuation reports, asset valuation reports, and profit projections that are certified by licensed accounting firms.[167] Issuers of stock may rely on secondary reports and affirmations to a much greater extent than do stock issuers on the Shanghai Exchange. For example, instead of submitting original accounting reports and profit and loss statements, stock issuers on the Shenzhen exchange may submit financial reports, feasibility studies, stock valuation reports, asset valuation reports, and profit projections that are certified by licensed accounting firms.[168] For subsequent issues, the issuer may again

---

disclosure provisions (including false or fraudulent reporting) are dealt with by fines and a right to private compensation. See PRC *Company Law*, c. 10.

166 The Shanghai Transaction Regulations require securities issuers to provide information to purchasers through the prospectus for soliciting shareholders, including predicted economic results, prospects for company development, assets, and liabilities for false statements in connection with the issuance of securities (see Shanghai Transaction Regulations, art. 20). These regulations are intended to permit recovery on the broadest possible level by investors. The Shanghai Exchange Regulations impose other extensive information disclosure requirements on the enterprises that issue and trade securities: see arts. 29 *et seq.*, 33 *et seq.*, and 59 *et seq.* Issuers of securities must provide PBOC (Shanghai) with extensive information during the process of seeking approval for the issuance. Stock issuers are required to provide balance sheets and other primary financial data. See Shanghai Exchange Regulations, *supra* art. 30, concerning information disclosure in applications for stock issuance and on matters that are likely to affect the price and marketability of the stock. While the rules limiting daily price fluctuations to .5% per day would appear to lessen the importance of the availability of information likely to affect bond prices, they also would seem to obviate the need for the requirement in connection with stock issuing.

167 The Shenzhen Stock Transaction Regulations contain several provisions related to information disclosure that are generally similar to the regulations issued for Shanghai. The Shenzhen Stock Transaction Regulations, for example, require that the prospectus issued to potential purchasers contain extensive information about the issuer, verified by certified accounts and confirmed by PBOC (Shenzhen). See Shenzhen Stock Transaction Regulations, art. 18. However, in contrast to the detailed reporting requirements imposed under the Shanghai Exchange Regulations, members of the Shenzhen exchange are subjected to rather general duties to uphold exchange rules, preserve the interests of the exchange, promote the stability and prosperity of the exchange, pay fees and interest as per regulations, and accept the supervision and administration of the exchange in connection with the listing of securities: Shenzhen Exchange Articles, art. 10.

168 Shenzhen Stock Transaction Rules, art. 17.

rely on affirmation and secondary accountant reports to establish such issues as the financial condition of the issuer and profit projections.[169] In addition, when seeking approval of a stock issue, companies are permitted to rely on certified statements rather than on primary documentation in matters such as the approval of company activities, proportion of ownership, valuation, number of shareholders, and compliance with legal and public interest requirements during the previous three years.[170]

Emphasis on Disclosure to Regulators over Investors Perhaps the most intriguing aspect of the disclosure regime is the extent to which the primary recipients appear to be regulators rather than investors. The origins of the primarily regulator focus of disclosure requirements lie in the regulations for the Shanghai and Shenzhen markets. In these markets the information disclosure provisions were aimed at ensuring PBOC control over stock issuers and over transactions in the shares themselves. For instance, the Shanghai Exchange Regulations also impose extensive information disclosure requirements on the enterprises that issue and trade securities.[171] Issuers of securities must provide PBOC (Shanghai) with extensive information during the process of seeking approval for the issuance. Stock issuers are required to provide balance sheets and other primary financial data,[172] as well as information on issues that are likely to affect the price and marketability of the stock.[173] These requirements enable PBOC (Shanghai) to maintain substantial surveillance over stock issuers.

Preference for State Enterprises and Financial Institutions over Private Enterprises The disclosure requirements for stocks are significantly stricter than the reporting requirements for bonds. Bond issuers are not required to provide balance sheets and other primary financial data, but may rely more heavily on audited reports as to bond values.[174] Bond issuers are also not required to report on matters likely to affect the future price and marketability of their securities.[175] This disparate treatment of stock and bond issuers permits state

---

169 Shenzhen Stock Transaction Regulations, arts. 19, 20.

170 *Ibid.* at art. 15.

171 Shanghai Exchange Regulations, *supra* note 145 arts. 29 *et seq.*, arts. 33 *et seq.*, and arts. 59 *et seq.*

172 *Ibid.* at art. 30 (concerning information disclosure in applications for stock issuance).

173 *Ibid.* While the rules limiting daily price fluctuations to 0.5% per day appear to lessen the importance of making information available where it is likely to affect bond prices, the same rules appear to lessen the information requirement in connection with the issuance of stock.

174 Shanghai Exchange Regulations, *supra* note 145 art. 31. As with other accounting requirements, the audit must be performed by a licensed Chinese accountancy firm. See e.g. Shanghai Transaction Regulations, art. 48 concerning the certification of securities firm records by certified accountants.

175 Shanghai Exchange Regulations, *supra* note 145 art. 32.

enterprises and financial institutions (the enterprises authorized to trade in bonds) to obtain approval for securities issues more easily without the extensive information disclosure requirements and likely delays that will ensue for private enterprises that are the main issuers of stock.[176]

The information disclosure provisions of the Shenzhen Stock Transaction Regulations, on the other hand, tend to limit the surveillance powers of PBOC (Shenzhen). While PBOC (Shenzhen) is permitted to obtain information on the business and financial conditions of stock companies and stock issuers, this must be "in accordance with the law" and only "in order to protect the lawful rights and interest of investors."[177]

Comparison to Other Jurisdictions As noted above, China's securities laws are similar to those of Malaysia, Singapore, Japan, and many other jurisdictions in mandating certain types of disclosure. Specific required information appears directed at facilitating the valuation of securities and is supported by penal and civil sanctions as in many other jurisdictions. What is particularly unique about China's securities law disclosure requirements is their greater emphasis on disclosure to the People's Bank of China than disclosure to investors and the degree to which financing of state enterprises and financial institutions face less extensive disclosure requirements than those faced by private enterprises. The other interesting feature of the disclosure regime is the apparently greater willingness of the Shenzhen exchange to experiment with its approach to disclosure and the apparently greater limitations on the surveillance powers of PBOC, Shenzhen.

Insider Trading

Insider trading is addressed in the *Company Law*, as well as in the local regulations governing the Shanghai and Shenzhen exchanges.

Company Law The *Company Law* sets forth a general principle that issues of shares must be public, fair, and impartial,[178] and imposes fines for improper share issues.[179] These are reminiscent of the antecedent national regulations.

National Securities Regulations The Interim Provisions on the Management and Trading of Stocks articulate in Article 3 a general principle that stock

176 "Strengthen and Perfect Administration of Stocks and Bonds, *Chinese Legal System Gazette* (8 Apr. 1987) 1; and "The State Council Notifies Localities to Strengthen Administration of Stocks and Bonds," *Economy Daily* (7 Apr. 1987) 1, which provide that state enterprises issue bonds and collective and private enterprises issue stock.

177 Shenzhen Stock Transaction Regulations, art. 32.

178 PRC *Company Law*, art. 129.

179 *Ibid.* at art. 207.

issues must be open, fair, honest, and trustworthy.[180] The Interim Provisions also restrict professional personnel with access to inside information from buying or holding stocks during particular periods during and after the preparation of appraisal and audit reports.[181] The Interim Provisions also contain a short-swing profit rule requiring disgorgement of profits from sale of stock within six months of its purchase by directors and officers or by shareholders with more than 5% ownership of voting stocks.[182] Violations of these insider dealing provisions can result in fines of up to RMB 500,000 and confiscation of the shares illegally obtained.[183]

Local Regulations The Shanghai Transaction Regulations contain provisions prohibiting insider trading.[184] The prohibition against trading by regulatory officials, exchange officials, personnel at securities dealers, and personnel with organizational ties to securities issuers is also intended to protect investors from abuses.[185]

The potential for insider trading and official abuse of information is addressed through the prohibition against purchasing or selling stock by party, government, or army officials, or by officials at the Exchange.[186] In the light of their potential access to non-public information, securities dealers are also subject to limitations on the proportion of any given issue they may hold on their own account, and are under direct PBOC (Shenzhen) scrutiny.[187] Similarly, the exchange itself is prohibited from trading stock for its own account.[188] Finally, the Shenzhen Stock Transaction Regulations prohibit a variety of abuses such as insider trading, market manipulation, and others that are addressed in the Shanghai regulations.[189]

---

180 Interim Provisions on the Management of the Issuing and Trading of Stocks, art. 3 in *China Economic News* (7 June 1993) 7.

181 Interim Provisions on the Management and Trading of Stocks, art. 40, in *China Economic News* (14 June 1993) 7-8.

182 *Ibid.* at art. 38, in *China Economic News* (14 June 1993) 7.

183 *Ibid.* at art. 38, in *China Economic News* (21 June 1993) 10. Insiders are defined as persons who have access to inside information by way of holding shares of an issuer or serving as director or other senior official of an enterprise, by reason of professional position or other method. Insider information is defined as including major information that is secret but in the possession of related issuers, securities organizations, control organs, or other bodies. Interim Provisions, art. 81(14) and 81(15), in *China Economic News* (21 June 1993) 12.

184 Shanghai Transaction Regulations, *supra* note 145 art. 39.

185 *Ibid.* at art. 40.

186 *Ibid.* at art. 29, which suggests that exceptions might be made under specific administrative methods to be enacted in the future with the approval of PBOC and the Shenzhen municipal government.

187 Shenzhen Stock Transaction Regulations, arts. 49 and 53.

188 *Ibid.* at art. 58.

189 *Ibid.* at arts. 43 and 62, and c. 7.

Comparison to Other Jurisdictions China's insider trading regulation is similar to that of Malaysia, Singapore, Japan, and North America in several respects. First, there has been a conscious decision to prohibit certain forms of so-called "insider trading." This is not insignificant, given that the regulation of insider trading in most countries is of relatively recent origin. Second, the Shanghai exchange approach of defining a group of persons who are prohibited from trading in certain circumstances is similar to the approach taken in Malaysia, Singapore, and Japan.[190] The short-swing profit rule under the national securities regulations, which was also adopted in Japan, was no doubt drawn from the similar the U.S. *Securities Exchange Act* provision.[191] One important difference is the apparent reliance on penal and administrative sanctions without the corresponding civil rights of action for alleged victims of insider trading that are available under the insider trading laws of Malaysia, Singapore, Japan, and North America.

Market Manipulation

Company Law In addition to the *Company Law's* general provisions for sanctions against improper issues of stock, the law also provides penalties for potentially manipulative activities such as false reporting, failing to complete delivery of a sold stock, and other activities.[192]

National Securities Regulations The Interim Provisions on the Management of the Issuing and Trading of Stocks impose penalties including fines and disgorgement of profits for various kinds of market abuses, including monopolizing stock prices through collaboration or concentration of funds, disrupting the market by offering or selling shares not actually held, manipulation of stock prices by collaborating with others to hold back actual transfer of ownership, fake buy/sell orders, and other methods.[193] Criminal penalties and civil remedies are also available.[194]

Local Regulations The Shanghai Transaction Regulations contain prohibitions against issuing false or misleading statements or information, creating false impressions concerning the supply or demand or price of securities,

---

190 It is also the approach taken in Canada (see e.g. *Securities Act*, S.B.C. 1996, c. 418, s. 3, which describes persons who are in a "special relationship" who are prohibited from trading in certain circumstances under s. 68), and under the Insider Trading Directive of the European Community.

191 Section s. 16(b).

192 PRC *Company Law*, arts. 207 *et seq.*

193 Interim Provisions on the Management of the Issuing and Trading of Stocks, art. 74, in *China Economic News* (21 June 1993) 11.

194 *Ibid.* at arts. 77, 78, in *China Economic News* (21 June 1993) 11.

and market manipulation.[195] The Regulations also prohibit market manipulation, issuing false information, and similar acts.[196]

The Shenzhen Stock Transaction Regulations expressly prohibit a number of market manipulation activities such as collusion in the coordinated selling and purchase of the same securities to affect market demand and price, failing to complete delivery of sold securities, false sales, successive high price purchases, and low price sales of the same security to affect market price.[197] Penalties including fines, forfeiture of the securities obtained, and other administrative sanctions are imposed for violations of the market manipulation provisions.[198]

Comparison with Other Jurisdictions The regulation of market manipulation in China is similar to that in other jurisdictions in the types of transactions that are regulated. The regulation of market manipulation in most jurisdictions covers issues such as the cornering or monopolizing of the market and the creation of false impressions of the price or value of a security (especially through "wash sales" or what might be described as "fake buy or sell orders"). An interesting feature of China's regulation of market manipulation is the prohibition of short selling. Short selling is also prohibited in Malaysia, apparently drawing on similar restrictions in Australian laws. Short sales are not prohibited in other jurisdictions such as Japan, the United States, and Canada.

Takeover Bid Regulation

National Securities Regulations The Interim Provisions on Stock Issues and Trading set forth general provisions governing takeovers.[199] Under these regulations, when a party other than promoters holds directly or indirectly more than 5% of the common shares issued by a listed company, written notice must be given to the regulatory authorities and to the company whose shares are held.[200] When 30% or more of the shares are held, the holder must submit a buyout offer in cash at a price which is the higher of (1) the highest price paid for the shares in any buyout within the previous twelve months or (2) the average market price within 30 days prior to the offer.[201] The offer must remain open for not less than 30 days, it must apply equally to all

195 Shanghai Transaction Regulations, arts. 39(1), (3), and (6).
196 *Ibid.* at art. 39.
197 Shenzhen Stock Transaction Regulations, art. 43.
198 *Ibid.* at art. 93.
199 Interim Provisions on the Management of the Issuing and Trading of Stocks, Ch. 4, in *China Economic News* (14 June 1993) 8.
200 *Ibid.* at art. 47, in *China Economic News* (14 June 1993) 8.
201 *Ibid.* at art. 48, in *China Economic News* (14 June 1993) 8.

holders of the same classes of stock, and a written report of the offer must be submitted to the regulatory authorities and to the target company.[202] The buyout is considered to have failed if the offeror holds less than 50% of the total amount of common shares issued by the target company at the expiry period of the offer.[203]

Comparison with Other Jurisdictions The national Interim Provisions share some similarities with takeover bid regulation in other jurisdictions. For instance, securities legislation in both Canada and the United States requires notification of significant direct or indirect ownership of shares (the so-called "early warning" provisions because they give an early warning of a potential takeover). Indeed, the 5% threshold is also the threshold for early warning under the U.S. *Securities Exchange Act*. The Interim Provisions are also similar to those of Malaysia, Singapore, Japan, and North American in requiring that the offer remain open for a minimum period, that the offer apply equally to all holders of the same class of stock, and that disclosure of the offer be made to both the regulatory authorities and the target company.

The Interim Provisions are unusual in providing for a minimum price for a bid. However, the concept appears to be one of assuring equal treatment of shareholders by making sure that the price paid for shares under the bid is at least as high as the price paid to shareholders who sold their shares to the bidder in the market before the bid. Somewhat different provisions that are intended to fulfil the same purpose are present in takeover bid regulations in other jurisdictions.

It is not uncommon for bidders to make the acquisition of at least 50% of the shares a condition that must be fulfilled for the bid to proceed. The Interim Provisions make this a mandatory condition. This is not a common feature of takeover bid regulations in other jurisdictions.

Securities Industry Regulation

China's securities regulatory apparatus continues to emphasize state control. This is particularly evident in the rules governing the Shanghai Securities Exchange and in the *Company Law*'s provisions on state supervision of the issue and trading of shares and bonds. The Shenzhen exchange for a time stood out as an exception, but has gradually conformed to a more state-centred approach.

Shanghai Exchange Regulations The Shanghai securities regulations establish a high degree of government control over the issuance and trading of

---

202 *Ibid.* at arts. 49, 50, in *China Economic News* (14 June 1993) 8.
203 *Ibid.* at art. 51, in *China Economic News* (14 June 1993) 8.

securities. While the regulations express concern with building investor confidence by proscribing a variety of market abuses, these efforts appear to be incidental to the larger objective of maintaining the regulatory authority of PBOC (Shanghai).

The Shanghai Exchange Regulations subject the SSE and its activities to the direct regulatory authority of the PBOC's Shanghai Branch,[204] while the Shanghai Transaction Regulations state that the routine operations of the SSE are subject to direct control by the Financial Administration and Management Department of PBOC (Shanghai).[205] Neither the Exchange Regulations nor the Transaction Regulations provide for intervening organizations through which PBOC direction might be filtered. Moreover, the SSE Board of Directors is largely, if not exclusively, staffed with PBOC (Shanghai) officials.[206] Thus, the control exercised by PBOC (Shanghai) over the SSE is direct and relatively unfettered by intervening institutions.

Under the Shanghai Transaction Regulations, PBOC (Shanghai) has authority to regulate the Exchange and its dealers, conduct examination and verification of financial reporting by issuers and brokerage houses, investigate illegal activities, and perform various other regulatory functions.[207] The issuance of securities is prohibited without approval from PBOC (Shanghai).[208] Such approval is also required for buying and selling securities, whether over the counter or on the market.[209] All transactions in securities must take place through an exchange approved by PBOC (Shanghai).[210] In addition, PBOC power to control price fluctuations is evident, reinforcing concerns raised by Gong Haocheng, Chief of the PBOC's Shanghai Branch, over potentially volatile stock prices as obstacles to further development of the Shanghai exchange.[211] PBOC (Shanghai) also is charged with administering penalties for violations of reporting and trading rules, ranging from warnings to fines of up to RMB 200,000 and the potential for further administrative or criminal sanctions.[212]

---

204 Shanghai Exchange Regulations, *supra* note 145 art. 5.

205 Shanghai Transaction Regulations, *supra* note 145 art. 4.

206 Interviews with officials from the Securities Exchange Executive Council, Beijing, 31 Aug. 1991, 24 Oct. 1991. Interview with officials from Shanghai Securities Exchange, 4 Sept. 1991.

207 Shanghai Transaction Regulations, *supra* note 145 arts. 72 *et seq.*

208 *Ibid.* at art. 7. Violations of this requirement are punishable by fines ranging between 50,000 and 100,000 yuan, although it does not appear that the transaction would be voided for such a violation. Shanghai Transaction Regulations, *supra* note 145 art. 75(1).

209 Shanghai Transaction Regulations, *supra* note 145 art. 29.

210 *Ibid.* at art. 27.

211 Gong Haocheng, "Speaking about the Securities Exchange," *Economy Daily* (12 Jan. 1991).

212 Shanghai Transaction Regulations, *supra* note 145 arts. 75 *et seq.*

Under the Shanghai Transaction Regulations, securities dealers are prohibited from such potentially abusive conduct as issuing opinions on securities, guaranteeing client positions, accepting deposits or making loans, engaging in unfair competition against other dealers, permitting their senior staff to divulge inside information, and so on.[213]

PBOC (Shanghai's) control over transactions at the SSE is also exercised through provisions on the delegated purchase and sale of securities. Registration is required for the person authorizing the delegated transaction, and from the securities dealer receiving the authorization.[214] This permits PBOC (Shanghai) to be informed as to the identity of all parties with interests in securities transactions. The delegated person handling the transaction must be a member of the exchange,[215] ensuring again that PBOC (Shanghai), which approves SSE memberships, retains supervisory authority over the conduct of transactions. The potential extent of control by PBOC (Shanghai) is also evident in provisions permitting suspensions and terminations of stock and bonds issuances for operational and financial reasons or for violations of exchange rules,[216] or for any additional "reasons that require [it]."[217]

PBOC (Shanghai) also has the authority to approve and supervise the formation and performance of securities dealers, which must provide ongoing reporting on business operations.[218] Since the bulk of transactions are handled through securities dealers, often through underwriting, the control of PBOC (Shanghai) over these entities gives it the power to supervise the vast majority of securities transactions. This mechanism for control is augmented by the provisions of the Shanghai Transactions Regulations concerning the "guild of brokerage houses," membership in which is mandatory, and which is under the guidance of PBOC (Shanghai).[219]

Shenzhen Exchange Rules The Shenzhen Exchange Rules provide that the organ in charge of the Shenzhen Exchange is the local branch of the PBOC (Shenzhen),[220] which has the authority to investigate and supervise virtually all aspects of the Exchange's activities.[221] While subject to the requirement that it be exercised in accordance with law and under the principles of openness, fairness, and impartiality, the regulatory authority of PBOC (Shenzhen) remains significant.[222]

---

213 *Ibid.* at arts. 44, 51, and 52.
214 Shanghai Exchange Regulations, *supra* note 145 arts. 53 *et seq.*
215 *Ibid.* at arts. 72 *et seq.*
216 *Ibid.* at arts. 43-52.
217 *Ibid.* at arts. 45(9) and 50(4).
218 Shanghai Transaction Regulations, *supra* note 145 arts. 41 and 48.
219 *Ibid.* at arts. 68 *et seq.*
220 Shenzhen Exchange Rules, art. 3.
221 Shenzhen Stock Transaction Regulations, arts. 79, 80.
222 *Ibid.* at art. 81.

The Shenzhen Stock Transaction Regulations also include measures aimed at preventing abuses in the securities industry. The conditions for issuance of stock include provisions for capitalization and minimum ownership requirements for the issuer, thereby attempting to ensure that the issuer has a vested interest in the long-term health of the stock.[223] The Transaction Regulations prohibit domestic purchasers from using their enterprise or unit budgets to purchase securities,[224] thus addressing an ongoing problem which undermines not only local budgetary management but also confidence in investor access to the market and in the validity of stock prices.

The Provisional Regulations of Shenzhen Municipality for the Administration of Securities Organs (the Shenzhen Securities Organ Regulations)[225] expand the authority of PBOC (Shenzhen) over the securities industry in Shenzhen. The Provisional Regulations contain provisions subjecting the establishment and operation of securities management organs to PBOC (Shenzhen) approval, supervision, and sanctioning authority.[226] By authorizing securities management organs to conduct, subject to the supervision of PBOC (Shenzhen), virtually all aspects of securities market activity, including underwriting, purchase and sales of shares, valuation and certification of stock and financial information, consulting on securities investments, and other activities, these regulations permit more direct PBOC (Shenzhen) control over securities activities at the Shenzhen Exchange than would have been possible under the Shenzhen Exchange Rules and the Shenzhen Stock Transaction Regulations alone.[227]

Comparison with Other Jurisdictions The general approach to regulation of the Chinese securities industry, particularly the local regime for Shanghai, is similar to that in other jurisdictions. Trading in securities is regulated by a registration requirement coupled with restrictions that purport to control various abuses. The restrictions are then enforced through suspension or

---

223 *Ibid.* at arts. 15.3 and 15.5.

224 *Ibid.* at art. 29.

225 See "Provisional Regulations of Shenzhen Municipality for the Administration of Securities Organs," *Shenzhen SEZ News* (15 June 1991) 2. By contrast, the Shenzhen Stock Transaction Regulations were issued by the Shenzhen Municipal Government, while the Shenzhen Exchange Rules were subject to approval by the Membership Council of the Exchange before they were issued. "Shenzhen zhengquan jiaoyi suo zhangcheng" (Articles of Association for the Shenzhen Securities Exchange), art. 38 and "Shenzhen shi gupiao faxing yu jiaoyi guanli zanxing banfa" (Provisional Methods of Shenzhen Municipality for the Issue and Transferring of Shares). These regulations were patterned after PBOC central branch's Provisional Regulations on Management of Securities Companies, issued in March 1991.

226 Shenzhen Securities Organs Regulations, c. 6.

227 *Ibid.* at arts. 23 *et seq.*

termination of registration and a series of penal and administrative sanctions. However, in other jurisdictions it is common to delegate aspects of the regulation and enforcement to self-regulatory organizations of securities industry members. What appears to be unique about the approach in China is the extent of government control, particularly through the PBOC.

Foreign Sources of Law

As has much of China's reform policies over the past decade, the Chinese securities law regime has been subject to conflicting influences. Anglo-North American influences have been merged with a Soviet-style system of banking and finance.

Soviet-style System of Banking and Finance

As its baseline, the People's Bank of China has continued to advocate a Soviet-style banking and finance system, aptly described by Paul Bowles and Gordon Bennett as the "Monobank" system. This approach continues to vest in PBOC the ultimate authority to direct finance and monetary policy towards planned development goals. Thus we can detect in the policies and proposals of PBOC regarding the Chinese securities markets goals of preserving the Bank's bureaucratic prerogatives, while also ensuring that China's securities markets serve national development goals.

PBOC's concern with maintaining its control over investment targeting and ensuring that investment in stocks did not jeopardize the planned targeting of bond investments is evident in statements by PBOC officers that "bank credit would remain the main form of financing in China," and that, while government bonds would take on greater significance, "stocks are unlikely to gain momentum in the near future." Concerns that securities issues satisfied the imperatives of state planning were also expressed through regulations issued in March 1990 that restricted enterprises from issuing their own bonds without the approval and coordination of PBOC and the state planning authorities. In May, regulations were issued concerning state treasury bonds and "special state bonds" (primarily for construction projects) that made clear that these securities should be the mainstay for government and enterprise investments. PBOC's basic position was expressed earlier in the Provisional Regulations on Administration of Enterprise Bonds (March 1987), which placed enterprise bond issues under the strict control of PBOC. The regulations provided that bonds could be sold only by the issuing enterprise or by designated financial institutions (which would be subject to PBOC control). As indicated by the subsequent Notice on Strengthening Administration of Stock and Bonds (April, 1987), which subjected securities issuances to still greater PBOC control, a key purpose of PBOC supervision was to ensure that investment was targeted at state construction projects.

U.S. and British Influences on Securities Markets and the Regulatory System

The proponents of expanding China's securities markets and regulatory system have been strongly influenced by a variety of foreign jurisdictions, most notably the United States. The Chinese experts most closely associated with the securities regulatory system received their legal education in the United States and have continued to look to the NYSE and the SEC system as models for markets and regulatory regimes. Thus it is not surprising to find, in both the Shenzhen and Shanghai exchange regulations, provisions on information disclosure and insider dealing that reflect ideals drawn from the U.S. regulatory regime. As well, the Hong Kong stock market with its British lineage has been a source of inspiration, although this source too has been strongly affected by the United States model of regulation, particularly where information disclosure and insider dealing issues are concerned.

European and Anglo-North American Influences on Company Law

The Chinese *Company Law* reflects a curious blend of European and Anglo-North American approaches to securities regulation. The Anglo-North American approach, which centres on concession theory and the status of the corporation as a creation of the sovereign, is evident in the close state regulation that has been the centrepiece of PBOC regulation of Chinese corporate finance. Similarly, the *Company Law*'s provisions on mergers and acquisitions, and on shareholder rights, appear to reflect Anglo-American influences. On the other hand, by focusing on specific forms through which a business organization can be formed, the *Company Law* tends to adopt the civilian approach that emphasizes classification as a basis for legal capacity. Also, the enforcement provisions of the *Company Law* appear to reflect European civilian influences, in that overwhelming attention is given to the imposition of administrative and penal sanctions rather than private rights of action. The *Company Law*'s provisions to the effect that more information is required to be disclosed to government regulators than to market participants appears to be uniquely Chinese, since both the European and Anglo-North American approaches tend to favour extensive provision of information to individual shareholders.

Factors Affecting the Foreign Sources of Securities Laws in China

The Competition for Capital and Convergence to Optimal Solutions

The conscious effort of China to develop securities markets, and in particular its creation of B shares for foreign investors, suggests that securities laws in China are directed towards competition for capital. In other jurisdictions, securities laws came into existence after the initial development of securities markets and then developed as securities markets developed. In

China, securities laws were created as part of the process of developing securities markets. Consequently, the adoption in principle of foreign securities laws was not a gradual convergence towards optimal solutions to problems encountered in the market.

Avoiding Uncertainty Associated with Experimentation

Instead, if there was a sense that the securities laws in China were optimal solutions to common securities market problems, it was not based on prolonged experience with securities markets but on an assessment that the securities laws borrowed from other jurisdictions were optimal solutions. However, China's securities laws may well not have been seen as a borrowing of perceived optimal solutions. Instead, the borrowing of securities laws may have made just as much sense as an attempt to encourage investment by presenting foreign investors with a securities law regime they would be familiar with. It may also be the case that, in the desire to encourage capital formation, China was unwilling to risk the consequences of any radical experiments in securities laws.

Shenzhen's approach to regulation may be exceptional in this regard. The more open-ended approach to regulation with apparently less specific disclosure provisions than Shanghai, and less specific than one normally finds in other jurisdictions, might be regarded as a somewhat experimental approach.

Similar Political Pressures

The borrowing of securities laws in China was probably not an attempt to borrow a set of laws that would be a good starting point for accommodating a pre-existing set of interest groups in China's securities market. In fact, China's securities laws, in their current form, did not come into existence in the face of a reasonably well-developed and pre-existing securities market. Instead, China's securities laws have been developed in a relatively short space of time more or less at the same time as fledgling securities markets were developing in China. This is not to say that political dynamics have not affected securities laws in China. However, the pre-existing political structure in China, as discussed below, appears to account for several unique features of Chinese securities law that have been grafted on to an otherwise borrowed model.

Foreign Interests Protecting Economic Rents

China's securities laws are also not likely to be the result of foreign interests protecting economic rents from international competition in the securities business. China appears to be particularly reluctant to allow its domestic policies to be guided by foreign political pressure. Thus the borrowing that has occurred is more likely to be the result of China's competing for investment capital by adopting a generally accepted form of securities laws while avoiding the uncertainty associated with substantial variations from such a generally accepted form of securities laws.

The Importance of Existing Commercial Links

Existing commercial links are not likely to have been important in the source of borrowing in China, since securities markets were being developed in China at a relatively early stage in the development of China's commercial links. Nonetheless, it may well have been expected that its most significant commercial links would be with countries such as the United States, Japan, and the United Kingdom, which were also the likely sources of most potential foreign investment. U.S. (and to some extent British) sources of borrowing therefore may have made sense, particularly given that Japan also has securities laws that largely reflect U.S. influences.

Language: The Roles of Particular Individuals and Education

Since China's securities laws have largely been borrowed from the United States and influenced by British securities laws via Hong Kong, it does not appear that borrowing from a source sharing a common language was an important factor in China's choice of a source of borrowing. However, the roles of particular individuals in the drafting of China's securities laws and the place where they received their education in securities matters does appear to have had a significant influence on the development of China's securities laws. As noted above, the Chinese experts most closely associated with the securities regulatory system received their legal education in the United States, and have continued to look to the NYSE and the SEC system as models for markets and regulatory regimes. It is therefore not surprising to find, in both the Shenzhen and Shanghai exchange regulations, provisions on information disclosure and insider dealing that reflect ideals drawn from the U.S. regulatory regime.

Legal System

The fact that China's legal system is, in principle, quite different from the common law system in the United States or United Kingdom did not seem to daunt China in its choice of jurisdictions from which to borrow securities laws. Apparently, any advantage that China might have gained by implementing a borrowed securities law from a country with a similar legal system was not a factor in its choice of a source of borrowing.

Political Structure and Ideology

The political structure and ideology of a command economy appear to be important factors with respect to certain characteristics of China's securities laws. This is apparent in the extent to which disclosure requirements call for a significant amount of disclosure that is directed primarily to government departments rather than to investors. This is not a common feature of securities regulation in many other jurisdictions, including Malaysia, Singapore, Japan, and North American jurisdictions. The influence of the preexisting political structure and the importance of government control is also apparent in the amount of control that the People's Bank of China appears to retain. While the PBOC appears to have accepted the need to develop bond markets and equity capital markets, its control over the securities industry and over dividends on shares suggests a concern that a very successful development of such markets without PBOC control could seriously diminish the influence of the PBOC.

SUMMARY

The case studies discussed above indicate that the securities laws of Malaysia, Singapore, Japan, and China share many features that are common to the securities laws of other countries such as the United States, Canada, the United Kingdom, and Australia. These common features are present despite differing ideologies, cultures, legal systems, and stages of development.

These common features might be the result of a gradual iteration of securities laws towards optimal solutions. However, as noted above, it is also possible that securities laws are the result of rent-seeking behaviour that produces less than optimal results. In the case of China, the relatively recent development of securities markets and the almost simultaneous introduction of securities laws suggest that these laws, with their similarities to securities laws in other countries, could not have been the result of a gradual iteration to optimal solutions.

Other explanations of similarities seem equally as plausible as the iteration towards optimal solutions. For instance, the similarity of the development of securities markets in Singapore and Malaysia to that in other countries such as the United Kingdom, Canada, and the United States may have led to similar market participants creating similar domestic political pressures for securities laws. International competitive pressures may have also been a significant factor in the developments of securities laws in the countries considered. The recent level of interest in Asian markets such as Malaysia and Singapore may have been facilitated by these countries having enacted securities laws that share many features with the securities laws of the United Kingdom and the United States. Japan's apparent willingness to retain securities laws imposed on them under U.S. occupation may have also been a result of the benefits such laws provided in attracting foreign investment. China's B share development was also directed at foreign investors. Its choice of securities laws that were, at least on their face, similar to the securities laws of other countries also lends support to the notion that international competitive forces lead to similar securities law features in different countries.

The apparent tendency of the countries considered to borrow securities laws from relatively well-known sources is consistent with the concept that borrowing securities laws can avoid the costs of assessing the potential effects of different or experimental securities laws and the costs of communicating different or experimental securities laws to investors. The decision to borrow from a limited number of well-known sources of securities laws, namely British and American, is also consistent with the notion that the early success of these securities laws may have given them a first-mover advantage.

Educational links and commercial ties seem to have been a significant factor in the development of securities laws in Malaysia, Singapore, and Japan. Early commercial links between the United Kingdom, Singapore, and Malaysia led to similar market participants. The British legal education of most lawyers in Singapore and Malaysia no doubt played a significant role in the adoption of the British approach to securities regulation with which the British-trained lawyers were familiar. The continued commercial links between Singapore and Malaysia probably account for the closeness in time of the adoption and amendment of securities laws in those countries. The educational and commercial links that developed between Japan and the United States in the years after the imposition of U.S. securities laws during the post-war occupation may have discouraged the replacement of these laws with other approaches to securities regulation in Japan.

On the other hand, educational, commercial, and linguistic links would not have been a significant factor in the development of securities laws in China. Educational and commercial links with countries such as the United States were just developing at the time securities markets and securities laws were being developed. In China, the educational links may have been more coincidental, in that the persons assigned to address securities law matters had been educated in the United States (although this may have been by design).

While the securities laws of the countries considered share many common features, there are also several unique features. A number of factors may explain the existence of these features. For instance, the later development of securities markets in Singapore and Malaysia may account for their later development of securities laws, their later adoption of insider trading restrictions, and their later expansion of reliance on public, as opposed to private, forms of regulation. Cultural differences may account for the apparent reluctance of Japanese courts to use Japan's U.S. rule 10b-5 provision to develop a body of law on insider trading. Political and ideological differences may also account for China's restrictions on takeovers to preserve Chinese government control, the tendency to require substantial disclosure directed to Chinese government departments rather than to investors, and the development of bond markets relied on by government-controlled enterprises over share markets relied on by private enterprises.

2
Parallel Importation of Wares and Reputation Spillover: Examples of Transnationalization of Law

*Robert G. Howell, in collaboration with Khaw Lake Tee**

THEMES AND PERSPECTIVES

Introduction

This chapter deals with two examples of economic or marketplace matters involving the usage of trademarks that present a choice between strict territoriality and recognition and accommodation, to some extent, of a transnational perspective.

Trade is driven by supply, demand, and the potential for profit. It establishes its own pattern with minimal regard to political territory, subject to outright political exclusion or restriction.[1] The internationalism of today presents a macrocosm of the market changes of the nineteenth century industrial revolution in Europe and North America. At that time, improved transport and communications caused local town or village markets to expand to national markets. A particular consequence of this was the emerging practice and use of trademarks. The historical and primary function of trademarks – that is, to identify and distinguish the source of goods – fell into confusion when almost identical marks, from formerly isolated marketplaces, came to be used in larger merged marketplaces. In effect, improvements in technology and communications had created a need for the legal

* The author wishes to thank Dr. Khaw Lake Tee, Associate Professor, Faculty of Law, University of Malaya, Kuala Lumpur, Malaysia, who provided considerable assistance in researching the law of Malaysia and Singapore and providing the author with copies of relevant judgments and other materials from the region. The author also acknowledges the assistance of his research assistants, Mr. David Mitchell (UVic 1996) and Mr. Kerry Hillier (UVic 1998) and, for secretarial contributions, Mrs. Sheila Talbot. The topic of this chapter was discussed at a symposium, "Intellectual Property Law and Policy," Guild House, National University of Singapore, 19-21 April 1993, organized by the author and funded by the Canada-ASEAN Centre in Singapore. Mr. Alban Kang of the Singapore Bar presented helpful comments on the position at that time.

1 North Korea is the most obvious example of a jurisdiction falling within this category, although even in this instance a thaw is in process.

regulation of trademarks at a national level. The result was the establishment of national schemes of statutory trademark registration,[2] which have continued to the present time. An international connection was, of course, provided in the Paris Union of 1883.[3] However, that Convention did not internationalize trademark law. On the contrary, it embraced national territoriality, while facilitating, in a very limited way, certain accommodations, such as convention priorities, between registrants for trademarks from signatory jurisdictions.[4]

The greater improvements and diversity in the technologies of transport and communications that have occurred in the second half of this century, particularly within the past ten years, have globalized, or at least transnationalized, the marketplace for products and services. National jurisdictions must now accommodate their domestic law, or create some transnational law, to regulate competitive practices at an international or transnational level.

The two aspects of transnationalism with respect to trademarks to be discussed are (1) the "parallel importation" or "grey marketing" of goods; and (2) extraterritorial recognition of business goodwill, or so-called "reputation spillover." The nature of these topics is described below. They demonstrate within common law jurisdictions a transnational accommodation by judicial incremental decision-making. This affords a slow-motion glimpse at an evolution in progress. Ultimately, of course, treaty or legislative measures may be needed to regularize the position in a comprehensive manner.[5]

The jurisdictions chosen for comparison are primarily Canada, Malaysia, and Singapore, all Commonwealth members and all sharing a heritage of English common law. Necessarily some drawing upon authorities from other Commonwealth jurisdictions and, where appropriate, the United States is involved.

Context of Competition

Both parallel importation and reputation spillover concern competition, the issue of fair and unfair competition. In the Commonwealth, unfair competition is not a legal term of art. It rather describes a state of affairs where

---

2 See *General Electric Co. (of U.S.A.) v. General Electric Co. Ltd.*, [1972] 1 W.L.R. 729 at 741-52 (H.L.), Lord Diplock.

3 International Union for the Protection of Industrial Property 1883 (the Paris Convention). See Marshall A. Leaffer, ed. *International Treaties on Intellectual Property* (Washington, D.C.: Bureau of National Affairs, 1990) at 17.

4 Trade secret and patent protection is similarly territorial. Copyright, however, under the International Union for the Protection of Literary and Artistic Works 1886 (the Berne Convention) (Leaffer, *ibid.* at 339), provided some measure of transnationalism with respect to copyright by providing protection under qualifying circumstances throughout the Union.

5 Cf. parallel importation of works protected by copyright. See *infra* note 169.

existing and accepted market practices, as reflected in existing categories of law, are violated. These categories of law are predicated upon the preservation of fair competition. Activity violating the legal parameters is termed unfair or destructive of fair competition. The difficulty lies in the formulation or development of an applicable law to establish the demarcation between fair and unfair, particularly in the context of trademarks or usage of other indicia to identify the origin or source of a product. Within the framework of competition, the proprietary focus is upon the plaintiff's business reputation or goodwill identified by the indicia.

Parallel Importation

Parallel importation broadly describes a situation in which an international manufacturer or supplier distributes products through an authorized distributorship network with geographic regions being allocated to each distributor. An alleged parallel importer will acquire quantities of a product from an international supplier in one jurisdiction and export it to a second jurisdiction for the purpose of resale. Should the authorized distributor in the second jurisdiction be given trademark and unfair competition protection against such importation on the basis that the product is the same as that supplied by the authorized distributor (therefore, being said to be a "genuine" item), and is bearing the trademark or other indicia of the manufacturer or supplier? An unqualified affirmative would grant to an authorized distributor, within its territory, a monopoly in the nature of a patent,[6] and would cause an inevitable collision with restraint on trade and free competition.[7] Yet the authorized distributor will have invested substantially in the local territorial jurisdiction and will have created business goodwill in the area. The parallel importer has merely purchased the product elsewhere at a lower price. It has made no investment in establishing goodwill in the national or international marketplace and usually cannot service customers, for instance, in relation to the honouring of any international warranty.

The demarcation between fair and unfair competition in this situation is difficult to draw. The cost and pricing structure of each authorized distributor depends upon local conditions. These, of course, can be manipulated by supply side monopoly practices to sustain price at a level that will ensure the highest economic return to the distributor. Fair competition clearly includes another supplier creating a product, or supplying a service, of the same nature as that of the authorized distributor; but does fair competition encompass a third party parallel importer as described above? If the

---

6 See *Consumers Distributing Co. v. Seiko Time Canada Ltd.* (1984), 1 C.P.R. (3d) 1 at 14 (S.C.C.) [hereinafter *Seiko*].

7 *Ibid.* at 15.

authorized distributor has been manipulating supply and price for simply profit maximization, an initial response is to applaud the competitive importation. On the other hand, the authorized distributor may simply be using its monopoly to meet the high costs of market development and service and to allow a moderate and reasonable return on that investment. The response is then one of sympathy for the authorized distributor and concern that should the distributor be driven out of business by the importer's (unfair) competition, the entire market for the product will collapse, because the importer does not contribute to the structural costs of developing and maintaining the market.

A conceptual perspective relevant to this scenario is the theory of exhaustion of proprietary protection, or the first sale principle, drawn by analogy from patent law. It seeks to rationalize the relationship between intellectual property rights and the rights of a product purchaser to resell that product in the marketplace. It has not been adopted expressly in a context of trademarks by any Commonwealth court. However, it has been expressly considered in this context in the United States.[8] The exhaustion principle would establish that, once a product has been released into a marketplace, the purchaser cannot be prevented by the law of trademarks, or other proprietary sanction, from reselling that product. The Supreme Court of Canada has noted in this respect: "the distribution of a trade marked product lawfully acquired is not, by itself, prohibited under the *Trade-Marks Act* of Canada, or indeed at common law"[9] and that any purported right to "entail and control the sale of personal property ... is foreign to our law."[10] Implicitly, this is an adoption of the exhaustion principle. Indeed, its application is axiomatic with respect to products released in a domestic marketplace by a domestic manufacturer or supplier and resold in the same marketplace. It becomes problematic only when the product is released in an extraterritorial marketplace and later imported and resold in a domestic marketplace. The essential question is whether the principle of exhaustion should apply universally, so that a release into any marketplace in the world is sufficient to exhaust the proprietary rights of the manufacturer or supplier on a worldwide basis, or transnationally, so that marketplaces that in some way are related or connected provide an encompassment for an application of the principle.

In the latter situation, any relation or connection between these marketplaces could be determined upon factors such as free (or freer) trade areas,

---

8 For a comprehensive discussion of these principles, see *Bell & Howell: Mamiya Co. v. Masel Supply Co.* (1982), 548 F. Supp. 1063 at 1070-73 (E.D.N.Y.) (vacated on other grounds (1983), 719 F. 2d 42 (2d Cir.)).

9 *Seiko, supra* note 6 at 9.

10 *Ibid.* at 14.

trading patterns, goodwill zones, or, as expressly agreed, in multilateral or bilateral trade pacts.

In addition to the need to establish a relevant geographic area, the nature of the relationship between the manufacturer or supplier on the one hand and the authorized distributors on the other will be of major importance. For example, it may be significant as to which party actually released the product into a marketplace. Was it the foreign authorized distributor? Was it the principal manufacturer or supplier? If the principal manufacturer wholly or partially owns or controls the distributor, should both be treated as being one entity? Similarly, should the authorized distributor in the territory into which the parallel importation occurs be deemed to have participated in the initial release of the product by the principal manufacturer, if it is wholly or partially owned or controlled by the principal manufacturer?

These considerations reflect clearly the difficulties of transnationalization and the need for theories of unfair competition to be rationalized within transnational, rather than merely national, marketplace boundaries.

Reputation or Goodwill Spillover

Extraterritorial trading, or reputation spillover, presents similar issues. They involve a business reputation earned in one jurisdiction "spilling" across to another jurisdiction. Should this reputation be protected in the second or subsequent jurisdictions? Does it constitute protectable goodwill in another jurisdiction?

Traditionally, a territorial perspective has prevailed in the United Kingdom. Classic authorities require an actual carrying on of business in the domestic territory (the United Kingdom) as a prerequisite to establishing both goodwill and (upon being consequently deprived of this goodwill) the essential element of damage in the tort of passing off.[11] Less traditional approaches ameliorate or reduce the requirement of actual business in the territory in which protection is claimed to some token presence such as a booking agency or business agent or actual importation of wares by territorial residents.[12] A third approach, found predominantly outside the United Kingdom, dispenses even with this symbolism and, in certain circumstances, will protect a business reputation that has been established by cross-border advertising and extraterritorial travel by residents of the domestic territory.[13]

---

11 See *Erven Warnink Besloten Vennootschap v. J. Townend & Sons (Hull) Ltd.*, [1979] A.C. 731 at 742 (H.L.), Lord Diplock and at 755-56, Lord Fraser. Lord Fraser's formulation is more particularly focused upon the territorial situation. See also *Star Industrial Co. v. Yap Kwee Kor*, [1976] F.S.R. 256 (P.C.).

12 See generally *The Athletes Foot Marketing Associates Inc.* v. *Cobra Sports Ltd.*, [1980] R.P.C. 343 (Ch.) for a useful summary of the principal cases in the United Kingdom illustrating these situations.

13 See e.g. *Sund v. Beachcombers Restaurant Ltd.* (1960), 25 D.L.R. (2d) 54 (B.C.S.C.), rev'd on other grounds (1961), 27 D.L.R. (2d) 434 (B.C.C.A.). A number of cases may be

This approach presents a transnational response. It is now the prevailing perspective in Canada.[14]

PARALLEL IMPORTATION

The Position in Canada

The Common Law Response

An authorized distributor's primary common law response to parallel importation is the "passing off" tort. The essence of passing off is one trader misrepresenting his goods or services as those of another trader, or misrepresenting that his business is in some way associated or connected with the business or product of the other. The trader misrepresenting the position is taking or usurping the business reputation or goodwill of the other trader. It is not, however, a taking or misappropriation *simpliciter*. It must be through the means of a misrepresentation, meaning that the public must be confused or deceived as to the origin of the goods or services. An authorized distributor has very limited scope to establish this element against a parallel importer.

The leading Canadian authority is *Consumers Distributing Co. Ltd. v. Seiko Time Canada Ltd.*[15] The plaintiff was the authorized distributor for Canada of the Seiko quartz watches marketed by the Japanese company K. Hattori & Company through a system of authorized distributors. The defendant purchased Seiko watches from an offshore authorized distributor, but the latter was selling outside the authorized distributor network (this party is described as "a diverter"), and imported the watches into Canada where they were sold from discount stores at a price less than that charged by the plaintiff-authorized distributor in the more "up market" stores. Because the imported watches were genuine Seiko watches, there was no significant basis for a misrepresentation. The only possibility of establishing misrepresentation involved establishing differences between the products and the circumstances of sale. The noted differences were:

---

interpreted to provide various degrees of support. A strong indication of support for protecting extraterritorial reputation was given by the Supreme Court of Canada as early as 1931: *Brewster Transport Co. v. Rocky Mountain Tours & Transport*, [1931] 1 D.L.R. 713 (S.C.C.).

14 See *Orkin Exterminating Co. v. Pestco Co. of Canada* (1985), 5 C.P.R. (3d) 433 (Ont. C.A.) and *Walt Disney Productions v. Triple Five Corp.* (1994), 53 C.P.R. (3d) 129 (Alta. C.A.) (leave to appeal to S.C.C. denied (1994), S.C.C. Bulletin 1210). The proceedings in *Walt Disney Productions* concerned the use of the expression "Fantasyland" in a mall. Later proceedings concerned use of that expression in a hotel in the mall. See *infra* note 122.

15 *Seiko, supra* note 6. The issue of trademarks and parallel importation particularly in Canada is considered by H. P. Knopf, "Trade-marks Law and the Free Flow of Goods in Canada," in G. F. Henderson *et al.*, eds. *Trade-marks Law of Canada* (Scarborough, Ont.: Carswell, 1993) at 333.

(1) The sale was not by an Hattori-appointed authorized dealer.
(2) These Seiko watches were not therefore sold with the international guarantee or warranty (the warranty form had to be properly completed by an authorized distributor).
(3) There was no point of sale service or supply of Seiko warranty booklets, nor was there an adjustment service for customers, and the selection of models of Seiko watches was limited to eleven so-called "grey" models, instead of 250 authorized models.
(4) There was no after-sale service, such as a repair service.[16]

Item 3 (and probably item 4, apart from any issue as to repairs under the warranty) was disregarded as merely a merchandising style and not something that should be considered an element of the product.[17]

In the result there were two different products. First, a Seiko watch *simpliciter* and second, a composite product of a Seiko watch sold by an authorized Hattori distributor and with the Hattori international warranty. A misrepresentation would therefore have occurred if the parallel importer had represented that the Seiko watches it had imported and was selling were in fact the composite product. However, any potential misrepresentation to this effect was negated after the importer complied with an interlocutory injunction to provide a notice at each point of sale disclaiming any composite elements. This requirement was not contested during the remainder of the proceedings. The trial and appeal courts would still, however, have prevented parallel importation.[18] The Supreme Court of Canada reversed, finding the disclaimer to be sufficient to negate any misrepresentation, thereby denying passing off.[19] The court subsequently articulated an essential policy behind the decision – that consumers want choice. They are prepared to risk having to arrange at their own expense any after-sale service (such as repair) if they receive a price benefit at the time of purchase.[20]

Any potential relief at common law could have been given only by reformulating the passing off tort to eliminate from it the element of misrepresentation and to substitute misappropriation with respect to the goodwill built up by the authorized distributor in creating and continuing market support initiatives. Traditionally, such relief has not been available in the Commonwealth,[21] and, it is suggested, is denied by the Supreme Court of

16 *Ibid.* at 7-8.
17 *Ibid.* at 16.
18 *Ibid.* at 7.
19 *Ibid.* at 17-18. The terms of the interlocutory injunction are set out *ibid.* at 6.
20 *Ibid.* at 22.
21 This issue has not been considered directly in Canada, but the tort has been rejected elsewhere. See *Victoria Park Racing & Recreational Grounds Co. v. Taylor* (1938), 58 C.L.R. 479 (H.C. Aust.); *Lorimar Productions Inc. v. Sterling Clothing Manufacturers (Pty) Ltd.*, [1982] R.P.C. 395 at 418-22 (S.C. S. Africa); *Cadbury Schweppes Pty Ltd. v. Pub Squash Co. Pty.*, [1981] 1 All E.R. 213 (P.C.); and *Moorgate Tobacco Co. v. Philip Morris Ltd.* (1984), 56

Canada in *Seiko*. However, common law relief to this effect was contemplated by Joyal J. in the Federal Court of Canada (Trial Division) in *Mattel Canada Inc. v. GTS Acquisitions Ltd.*,[22] but this case subsequently has been overruled by the Federal Court of Appeal in *Smith & Nephew Inc. v. Glen Oak Inc.*[23] It is useful to contrast the conceptual and policy approach in *Mattel* with the current position. In *Mattel*, the plaintiff had been the exclusive authorized distributor of Nintendo video games and related products in Canada since 1986. The defendant imported into Canada identical Nintendo games acquired in the United States. There was no misrepresentation, since the products were identical. Joyal J. interpreted dicta in *Seiko* as nevertheless allowing relief if the public interest in free competition is affected or some other situation of unfair competition is involved.[24] He found this to have occurred because "the plaintiff [had] exerted strong efforts and expended large sums of money to create a market in Canada for Nintendo products [and] it was only when, through the plaintiff's efforts, Nintendo became the hottest game in town that it started to face the 'grey' market penetration."[25] In effect this would amount to relief for misappropriation without the requisite of a misrepresentation. This result was then linked with other areas of law not of direct significance in this comparative survey.[26]

Aust. L.R. 193 at 209-14 (H.C. Aust.). In Canada, a misappropriation theory of this nature was referred to by Laskin C.J.C. for the majority in *MacDonald v. Vapor Canada Ltd.*, [1977] 2 S.C.R. 134 at 149 in the context of speculation on the scope of s. 7(e), *Trade-marks Act*, R.S.C. 1985, c. T-13, a provision constitutionally suspect on other grounds. See also *Canada Safeway Ltd. v. Manitoba Food & Commercial Workers Local 832* (1983), 25 C.C.L.T. 1 (Man. C.A.), which created a new tort from the "action on the case" to deal with a misappropriation that did not fit into the existing categories of relief.

22 (1989), 25 C.I.P.R. 150 (F.C.T.D.).

23 (1996), 68 C.P.R. (3d) 153 at 156 (F.C.A.).

24 See *ibid.* at 158, where Joyal J. states that *Seiko* "not only leaves the door open to other considerations if a registered trademark owner or registered user is involved, but also opens wider the same door to other tests whenever some kind of unfair competition is raised."

25 *Ibid.* at 158. At 159 Joyal J. notes that the defendant parallel importer had "incurred no risk," nor "any investment of capital" nor assisted "to keep or finance inventory."

26 See *ibid.* at 155-56 where Joyal J. interpreted the decision of the Supreme Court of Canada in *Seiko* as allowing relief in instances of, broadly speaking, "unfair competition." This interpretation was, in turn, linked expressly with s. 7(e) of the *Trade-marks Act*, R.S.C. 1985, c. T.-13, which contained the following proscription: "[no person shall] do any other act or adopt any other business practice contrary to honest industrial or commercial usage in Canada." A purpose of s. 7 (as a whole) was seen by Joyal J. as to "regularize the whole field of trademark ownership" and to incorporate the notion of "unfair competition." Since *Mattel* was merely an interlocutory proceeding, no final conclusion was reached as to the application of "the strong moral arm" of s. 7(e). It was merely given "some weight" in the decision to grant the injunction. However, there was *obiter dicta* speculating that should legality be the appropriate test of s. 7(e), the U.S. exporters (selling, presumably, in breach of contract with the manufacturer) but not the Canadian importers would be caught by s. 7(e). See generally *Mattel*, *ibid.* at 158-59. While an evaluation of s. 7(e) is beyond the scope and purpose of this

The approach of Joyal J. is territorial. It would provide a common law monopoly to an authorized distributor within the jurisdiction. It is contrary to the policy analysis of the Supreme Court of Canada in *Seiko*, which emphasized a choice of products – a watch by itself or a watch within a composite of service factors – that parallel importation would give to the public. *Seiko* also finds fair competition to include the resale of the genuine products, and emphasizes that resale cannot be prevented through common law proprietary means (resale may, of course, be contractually prevented in particular cases). In this respect, the reference in *Seiko* that "the manufacturer had placed the watches in question [i.e. the grey market watches] in the market stream just as was done by the manufacturer with [respect to] the watches sold to the public by the [authorized distributor]"[27] strongly suggests an application of the exhaustion principle upon a universal basis.[28] This essentially reflects the policy position of the Federal Court of Appeal in *Smith & Nephew*, considering the position in a statutory trademark context.

Infringement Proceedings: The Canadian Trade-Marks Act

Unlike the tort of passing off, statutory trademark protection is not predicated upon a misrepresentation. Instead, sections 19 and 20 of the *Trade-Marks Act*[29] establish, in favour of a registered owner, rights in the registered mark itself. A mere use (i.e. taking or misappropriation) of a registered mark, or use of a mark that can be confused with a registered mark, in conjunction with the wares or services with which it is registered, provides the registered owner with a statutory infringement action. If an authorized distributor is the owner or licensee of a registered trademark, can it prevent parallel imports by infringement proceedings? Section 19 stipulates the rights conferred by registration as follows:

> the registration of a trademark in respect of any wares or services, unless shown to be invalid, gives to the owner of the trademark the exclusive right to the use throughout Canada of the trademark in respect of those wares or services.

---

current chapter, it is important to note that Joyal J. did not consider the constitutional uncertainty as to whether and under what circumstances s. 7 (especially s. 7(e)) is a valid exercise of federal legislative jurisdiction, most particularly if invoked as a stand alone remedy without any linkage or rounding out of any valid federal legislative jurisdiction. The seminal authority is *MacDonald v. Vapor Canada,* [1977] 2 S.C.R. 134. Subsequent cases present different interpretations, including that s. 7(e) is unconstitutional in any circumstance.

27 *Seiko, supra* note 6 at 18.

28 See also *Nestle Enterprises Ltd. v. Edan Food Sales Inc.* (1991), 37 C.P.R. (3d) 480 (F.C.T.D.).

29 *Trade-marks Act,* R.S.C. 1985, c. T-13, ss. 19, 20.

30 A use can additionally occur upon the exportation of wares marked in Canada (s. 4(3)). Note also that the expression "confusing" is a term defined in ss. 2 and 6.

In turn, "use" is defined by sections 2 and 4 as a use "in association with wares [or services]," with the added condition:

> if, at the time of the transfer of the property in or possession of the wares, in the normal course of trade, it is marked on the wares themselves or on the packages in which they are distributed or it is in any other manner so associated with the wares that notice of the association is then given to the person to whom the property or possession is transferred; or [with respect to services] if it is used or displayed in the performance or advertising of those services.[30]

Any resale of a product in the normal course of trade would, literally speaking, constitute an infringement. The person re-selling would be making a use of the owner's trademark. This rule enables an authorized distributor who is owner or licensee of a registered mark to claim the resale of parallel imported goods as an infringement by the importer.

As noted earlier, such a position has not, however, been taken in respect of wares released into a domestic market and resold within that market. Rights under trademark law are generally considered to be exhausted upon first sale.[31] The possible application of this principle in a transnational parallel importation context was left undecided by Jackett P. in the Exchequer Court in *Wilkinson Sword (Canada) Ltd. v. Juda*,[32] a case involving the parallel importation to Canada of genuine Wilkinson Sword razor blades acquired in the United Kingdom. The plaintiff, Wilkinson Sword (Canada) Limited, failed on technical grounds,[33] but Jackett P. suggested that a valid ownership of the trademark by Wilkinson Sword Canada would not have operated "to prevent persons who had acquired such goods in the ordinary course of trade from selling them."[34]

Since the initial release of these goods was made extraterritorially (in the United Kingdom) by the parent company, this *obiter dictum* of Jackett P. suggested a preference for exhaustion upon a universal basis, at least in the circumstances where the release has occurred before the assignment of the mark.[35]

---

31 See *supra* text accompanying note 8 *et seq.*

32 (1966), 34 Fox's Pat. Cas. 77 at 93 (Ex. Ct.).

33 Wilkinson Sword (Canada) Ltd. was the owner (by assignment from Wilkinson Sword U.K.) of the trademark, yet that mark was found to be still distinctive in the public mind of the parent Wilkinson Sword U.K. rather than Wilkinson Sword (Canada) Ltd. and therefore invalid (and struck out) with respect to the latter.

34 *Supra* note 32 at 92 n. 8.

35 This perspective was not pursued in the later case of *Breck's Sporting Goods Co. v. Magder* (1975), 17 C.P.R. (2d) 201 (S.C.C.). In an identical situation to that in *Wilkinson Sword*, the mark was simply found to be not distinctive of the distributor/owner without any analysis of broader conceptual or policy issues as to *exhaustion* of proprietary rights.

Other cases have allowed an owner of a valid Canadian trademark to use its registered ownership of a mark to prevent parallel importation. The principle of exhaustion has not been considered in these instances. They present clear examples of territoriality. The first is *Remington Rand Ltd. v. Transworld Metal Co.*[36] The plaintiff was the authorized distributor for Canada of shavers manufactured in the United States by the Sperry Rand Corporation, and was a wholly owned subsidiary of Sperry Rand. The defendant purchased essentially identical Sperry Rand shavers in the United States and West Germany and imported them to Canada for sale. The parallel importation was enjoined upon a pre-trial motion. The validity of the registered marks was not challenged. The second case is *H. J. Heinz Co. of Canada Ltd. v. Edan Food Sales Inc.*[37] Heinz U.S. assigned the trademark HEINZ to Heinz Canada, a subsidiary company, with respect to the geographic area of Canada. Subsequently, various combinations of marks involving the word HEINZ were registered and used by Heinz Canada and substantial expenditure kept the product and packaging abreast of changes in tastes in the Canadian market (i.e. the product was Canadianized).[38] The parallel importation carried the trademark HEINZ. Cullen J. expressly adopted a passage from *Remington Rand* that, in turn, had emphasized the territoriality of registered trade marks in reliance upon the following dictum of the English Chancery Division in 1926 concerning the multinational operations of the Dunlop tire enterprise:

> The "Dunlop" tyre business is conducted under a system whereby in different countries there are different Companies, so that the English Company owns in this country a number of Trade Marks and the French "Dunlop" company in France holds Trade Marks in France which are identical with the English Trade Marks, and I gather that a similar condition of affairs obtains in Italy and possibly in other countries. It follows from that that a French "Dunlop" tyre having upon it the Trade Marks which are identical with the English Trade Marks cannot be imported for sale into this country without infringing the English Trade marks.[39]

This position was strengthened by the plaintiff's ketchup being accepted as a "distinctly 'Canadian' product."[40]

A very significant move towards universality was, however, taken in 1996 in *Smith & Nephew*[41] The plaintiff and authorized distributor was the licensee

36 *Remington Rand Ltd. v. Transworld Metal Co.*, [1960] Ex. C.R. 463 (T.D.).
37 *H. J. Heinz Co. of Canada v. Edan Food Sales Inc.* (1991), 35 C.P.R. (3d) 213 (F.C.T.D.).
38 *Ibid.* at 215-16.
39 *Ibid.* at 220. See also *Remington Rand, supra* note 36 at 464 citing this passage from *Dunlop Rubber Co. v. A. A. Booth & Co.* (1926), 43 R.P.C. 139 (Ch. D).
40 *Ibid.* at 216.

of the Canadian trademark NIVEA for facial cream and soap. The trademark owner in Canada was the German corporation Beiersdorf AG. The parallel importer had acquired products bearing the trademark NIVEA and placed in the international market by "a Mexican affiliate or subsidiary of [Beiersdorf]."[42] Hugessen J.A. (for the Federal Court of Appeal) in effect found trademark rights to be exhausted. "[A] Canadian licensee and importer of goods bearing [Beiersdorf AG's] trademarks cannot complain of the sale in Canada of other goods which are also manufactured by or under license from [Beiersdorf] and bear the same trademarks."[43] The court emphasized first the lack of deception as to the origin of the goods, and second the fact that the plaintiff-authorized distributor was only a *licensee*. No determination was made as to the position of local distributors as territorial *owners* of trademarks of a multinational group. These were considered to give rise "to different considerations and different problems."[44] A third consideration involved a favourable analogy with the analysis in *Revlon Inc. v. Cripps & Lee Ltd.*[45] in the United Kingdom, to be discussed later in this chapter.

The Overall Position

Statutory infringement proceedings by territorially based authorized distributors who own (by assignment or otherwise) a registered trademark for a particular product have been successful in preventing parallel importation, so long as the trademark is upheld as valid. This presents a territorial application of statutory trademark law. A parallel importer's most successful strategy is to challenge the validity of the trademark. This is usually done by demonstrating that the trademark of the registered owner/authorized distributor is not "distinctive," because the public, upon viewing the mark, links the origin of the product not to the authorized distributor but to the foreign manufacturer or supplier. It is trite that a trademark must be distinctive of the actual owner of the mark.

The predominant emphasis on territoriality in a statutory infringement context is consistent with the historical and traditional focus of the legislation. A sharp contrast is, however, to be drawn with developments at common law where greater doctrinal and judicial flexibility has enabled the Supreme Court of Canada to respond to the modern reality of transnationalization and to present a predominantly universal or, at least, transnational perspective to the application of the principle of exhaustion.

---

41 *Smith & Nephew Inc. v. Glen Oak Inc.*, *supra* note 23.

42 *Ibid.* at 155.

43 *Ibid.* at 160.

44 *Ibid.*

45 See *Revlon Inc. v. Cripps & Lee Ltd.*, [1980] F.S.R. 85 (C.A. 1979) discussed *infra* note 56 and accompanying text. The court in *Smith & Nephew* did not, however, refer to the later English authority, *Colgate-Palmolive Ltd. v. Markwell Finance Ltd.*, [1989] R.P.C. 497

The predominantly territorial perspective of statutory infringement proceedings may yet be challenged in the context of parallel importation if the overall policy question posed by Jackett P. in *Wilkinson Sword* in 1966[46] were to be considered expressly by the Supreme Court of Canada. The *obiter dictum* reflects an exhaustion of rights either universally or transnationally. In policy, this is consistent with that in the 1984 pronouncements of the Supreme Court of Canada in *Seiko,*[47] and was adopted in *Smith & Nephew* with respect to territorial licensees.

Smith & Nephew will likely preclude an action by an authorized distributor who is a licencee. It is not necessary for a trademark to be distinctive of a licensee, since section 50(1) of the Act prescribes that a licence "to use [a] trade-mark *in a country* [and a consequential] use advertisement or display of the trade-mark *in that country* ... by that [licensee] has, and is deemed always to have had, the same effect as a use, advertisement or display of the trade-mark *in that country* by the owner."[48] (Emphasis added.) The above-emphasized phrases were not in the earlier provision concerning the registered user scheme of trademark licensing in Canada,[49] and, arguably, may reinforce a territorial interpretation to afford a licensee/authorized distributor in Canada with *territorial* rights of a trademark owner in Canada. A licensee, however, is unlikely to be afforded any greater protection or be placed in a better position than the registered owner,[50] and ought, therefore, to be bound by any disability of, or defence available against, the registered owner. This would ordinarily mean that, should a registered owner be unable to enforce its trademark rights because of it having released the particular product in the marketplace (that is, if the exhaustion principle were to apply extraterritorially), the licensee would likewise be unable to enforce the mark.[51] This reflects the position in *Smith & Nephew*.

(C.A.) that took a more territorial approach, retracting somewhat from the earlier position in *Revlon*. See *infra* text accompanying note 63 *et seq*. Both *Revlon* and *Colgate-Palmolive* involved licensees.

46 See *supra* text accompanying note 34.

47 See *supra* text accompanying note 27.

48 *Trade-marks Act*, s. 50(1) [am. *Intellectual Property Law Improvement Act*, S.C. 1993, c. 15, s. 69] (with effect from 9 June 1993). Section 50(1) stipulates as a pre-condition that the trademark owner "has, under the licence, direct or indirect control of the character or quality of the wares or services."

49 Before 9 June 1993, then s. 50(3) provided, with respect to "registered users," that "[a] permitted use of a trade-mark has the same effect for all purpose of [the] Act as a use thereof by the registered owner." Generally, with respect to this provision, see *S. C. Johnson & Son Ltd. v. Marketing Internat. Ltd.*, [1980] 1 S.C.R. 99.

50 See W. L. Hayhurst, "Intellectual Property as a Non-Tariff Barrier in Canada, with Particular Reference to Grey Goods and Parallel Imports" (1990) 31 C.P.R. (3d) 289 at 308.

51 See *infra* note 99 that refers to the possibility of territorial legislation granting a territorial licensee greater rights than the owner. This would not seem to be an available option in Canada after the decision in *Smith & Nephew, supra* note 23.

Parallel Importation in Malaysia and Singapore

English-Law Basis

Because Malaysia and Singapore appear to have closely followed English authorities, some attention must be given to this source. There are two classic cases. The 1926 case of *Dunlop Rubber Co. Ltd. v. A. A. Booth & Co.*[52] enabled the English Dunlop Company, the holder of a United Kingdom trademark, to prevent the importation of tires bearing the Dunlop trademark affixed by its associated French Dunlop Company. Emphasis in this case was given to the local nature of goodwill. It is a primary authority favouring territoriality. The second case is *Champagne Heidsieck et cie Monopole Societé Anonyme v. Buxton*[53] in 1930. It supports universality. The plaintiffs were producing champagne for sale in England and France. The defendants imported and sold it in England. Since the champagne was a genuine product, there was no misrepresentation or confusion that might constitute passing off. Both passing off and infringement were denied. There was no deception. The goods were genuine and therefore the trademark correctly indicated the origin of the product.[54]

The 1938 legislation in the United Kingdom partially established some universality to the principle of exhaustion. Section 4(3) of the *Trade Marks Act*, 1938 (U.K.) provided that infringement could not occur by the use of any mark:

> (i) in relation to goods connected in the course of trade with the proprietor or registered user of the mark; [and where]
> (ii) the proprietor or a registered user [has] applied the trademark and has not subsequently removed or obliterated it; or
> (iii) [the proprietor or a registered user] has at any time expressly or impliedly consented to the use of the trade mark.

Paragraphs (ii) and (iii) provided a basis for a parallel importer to avoid infringement. The particular trademark "used" by the parallel importer might have been "applied" by the registered proprietor or user, or be so deemed by the court. Similarly, a consent might be implied by the court. These approaches would involve an assessment of the same policy factors as applicable to imposing exhaustion through operation of law, except that upon an implied consent theory it can be negated by an express denial of consent. They were demonstrated in the seminal case of *Revlon Inc. v. Cripps & Lee Ltd.*[55]

---

52 *Supra* note 39.
53 [1930] 1 Ch. 330 (Ch.).
54 *Ibid.* at 339.
55 *Revlon Inc. v. Cripps & Lee Ltd.*, *supra* note 45.

Revlon U.S. was the parent company manufacturing many Revlon products. It distributed them through authorized distributors, including subsidiaries registered as owners of various Revlon trademarks in the United Kingdom. A Revlon brand shampoo manufactured by Revlon U.S. was not available in the United Kingdom, but was imported to that country by a third party. The importation was allowed to continue. Passing off was denied.[56]

More significantly, an infringement proceeding was denied because, in terms of section 4(3) of the U.K. Act: (1) the imported goods were "connected in the course of trade" with the U.K. owners or registered users by virtue of the control exercised over them by the parent, Revlon U.S., which had affixed the mark to the goods;[57] and (2) in the circumstances, the court implied a consent given by the U.K. subsidiary owners or registered users of the mark to the use of the mark in the U.K. by the parent, Revlon U.S., thereby meeting the terms of Section 4(3).[58] Buckley and Bridge L.J. were not prepared to go further and invoke the other statutory option of deeming the use by the U.S. parent to be a use by the U.K. subsidiaries.[59] Templeman L.J., however, was prepared to invoke this additional basis.[60] He saw it to be a logical (albeit converse) extension of the earlier decision of the Court of Appeal in *G.E. Trade Mark* where a use by a wholly owned subsidiary was deemed to be a use by the parent. Disagreeing with this converse extension, Buckley L.J. (with Bridge L.J. concurring) stated that "it [is] more difficult to say that an act of the parent company can legitimately be regarded as the act of a wholly-owned subsidiary who cannot in any way control the parent."[61] *Revlon*, therefore, presents a policy perspective of universality, through essentially a theory of imputed consent and (per Templeman L.J.) deemed user.[62]

---

56 The essential features denying relief by passing off were: (1) the imported products were of the same broad nature as those dealt with by the Revlon group internationally; (2) the public did not distinguish between the various entities in the multinational group, but relied upon the reputation of the composite entity; (3) there was no quality differential between the products; and (d) there was no public confusion because, while the products were seen as different types, their source was seen as that of the composite multinational group. See *ibid.* at 102-104, Buckley L.J., Bridge L.J. concurring, and at 112-13, Templeman L.J.

57 *Revlon Inc. v. Cripps & Lee Ltd., supra* note 45 at 106-107, Buckley L.J., Bridge L.J. concurring, and at 114-15, Templeman L.J.

58 *Ibid.* at 106, Buckley L.J., Bridge L.J. concurring, and at 117, Templeman L.J.

59 *Ibid.* at 107.

60 *Ibid.* at 115-16. Templeman L.J. found this to be a logical (albeit converse) extension of the earlier decision of the Court of Appeal in *G.E. Trade Mark,* where a use by a wholly owned subsidiary was deemed to be a use by the parent. Disagreeing with this converse extension, Buckley L.J., with Bridge L.J. concurring, found: "it is more difficult to say that an act of the parent company can legitimately be regarded as the act of a wholly-owned subsidiary who cannot in any way control the parent": *ibid.* at 107).

61 *Ibid.* at 107.

62 Most of the subsequent cases in the United Kingdom can be distinguished on their facts. In *Wilkinson Sword Ltd. v. Cripps & Lee Ltd.,* [1982] F.S.R. 16 at 28 (Ch.), the imported product was of a significantly inferior quality and constituted passing off within

Some ten years later, a more territorial focus was taken in *Colgate-Palmolive Ltd. v. Markwell Finance Ltd.*[63] The parent and manufacturer was Colgate U.S. It beneficially owned, through an intermediate company, Colgate U.K. It also operated worldwide subsidiaries including Colgate Limitada in Brazil (Colgate Brazil). The defendant obtained and imported into the United Kingdom products from Colgate Brazil that were not otherwise supplied in the United Kingdom and that were inferior to the Colgate products in the United Kingdom. Both Colgate U.K. and Colgate U.S. sued under passing off. Colgate U.S. sued additionally for infringement of its U.K.-registered trademarks. The defendant had acquired its Colgate products from the open market in Brazil and from Nigeria, a location to which Colgate Brazil was entitled to export. The plaintiffs succeeded in passing off.[64] The infringement claim of Colgate U.S. also prevailed. In this respect, the following findings emphasize the territorial perspective:

(1) a reiteration of the traditional authorities in the related context of reputation spillover and extraterritorial reputation, to emphasize that goodwill is territorial – that is, being "local in character and divisible";[65]

(2) an acknowledgment that simply a use of a registered trademark is sufficient to constitute infringement;[66]

(3) a more restricted interpretation of the defence in section 4(3) of the U.K. statute finding that

 (a) it must be the actual U.K. registered marks that are physically applied by the proprietor (or registered user) to the goods elsewhere and subsequently imported to the United Kingdom. Here Colgate U.S. applied the Brazilian trade marks "even though these happened to be the same as the relevant United Kingdom marks."[67] The defence in section 4(3) was held to be territorial in scope.[68]

---

the principle of *Erven Warnink, supra* note 11. In *Castrol Ltd.* v. *Automotive Oil Supplies Ltd.*, [1983] R.P.C. 315 at 324 (Ch.) the terms of the licence from the U.K. company to a related company in Canada expressly negated any consent for the Canadian company to affix the mark outside Canada. There was also a quality differential between the products.

63 *Colgate-Palmolive Ltd. v. Markwell Finance Ltd., supra* note 45. See also A. Firth, "Colgate-Palmolive Finance" [1988] 9 EIPR 278 for a helpful case note and historical survey.

64 *Ibid.* at 517, Slade L.J. and at 530-31, Lloyd L.J. The action focused upon the lower quality of the Brazilian product and the fact that it was manufactured from different raw materials, designed for tropical countries. Slade L.J. noted in *obiter* that the claim would have failed if it had been brought simply on the basis of a misrepresentation as to the commercial origin of the products, because the "get up" was of the Colgate group as a composite whole (*ibid.* at 515-16).

65 *Ibid.* at 535. Lloyd L.J. noted that this view of goodwill ought to prevail with respect to trademark infringement. See also *ibid.* at 508, Slade L.J. (citing *Star Industrial Co. Ltd. v. Yap Kwee Kor, supra* note 11) and at 531, Lloyd L.J.

66 *Ibid.* at 518-19, Slade L.J.

67 *Ibid.* at 522, Slade L.J. and at 533, Lloyd L.J.

68 *Ibid.* If an overseas mark is identical with the U.K. mark, what must be established to show that the affixing ought to be deemed to be an application of the U.K. mark

(b) an application of the trademark by the Brazilian wholly owned subsidiary would not *ipso facto* be deemed to constitute an application of the mark by the parent owner Colgate U.S., despite the implication to this effect in *Revlon*.[69] The only possibilities of this being so would be if the subsidiary, Colgate Brazil, could be found to be an agent of the parent, Colgate U.S., for the purpose of applying the mark, or if the separate corporate entities could be said to be a "mere facade."[70]

(c) the application by the subsidiary, Colgate Brazil, could not be said to have been with the consent of the parent, Colgate U.S. because there was no evidence to this effect. The absence of any prohibition, restriction, or disclaimer could not be interpreted as positively implying a consent to apply the mark. In effect, actual consent might be necessary. The assumption in *Revlon* that this implication could be made upon a point of policy to avoid suing upon a trademark (territorially) against a parallel importer was rejected, at least in instances where the products were different.[71]

Overall, therefore, the position in the United Kingdom is moving away from the relatively universal approach revealed by *Revlon* in 1979 to a more territorial emphasis presented in *Colgate-Palmolive* in 1989. Most interestingly, the Court of Appeal in *Colgate-Palmolive* saw fit to expressly link the policy choices behind parallel importation with those behind the potentially related area of reputation, that is, spillover or extraterritorial reputation. In this regard, note has been made earlier that the United Kingdom has traditionally taken a territorial approach to this issue, requiring an actual business presence in the United Kingdom in order to have protectable goodwill and consequent damages from loss of that goodwill.[72] The most insistent authorities to this effect were cited by the Court of Appeal in support of territorial goodwill for the purposes of parallel importation.[73]

---

within s. 4(3) of the legislation? Lloyd L.J. suggests that this must depend on the subjective intention of the entity that is applying the mark (*ibid.* at 534).

69 See *supra* text accompanying notes 58-61, where doubt was expressed that an application by a parent company could be deemed to be an application by a subsidiary, but the *vice versa* position (an application by the subsidiary being deemed to be an application by the parent) was impliedly accepted.

70 *Colgate-Palmolive Ltd. v. Markwell Finance Ltd., supra* note 45 at 523, Slade L.J. and at 533, Lloyd L.J.

71 *Ibid.* at 526-27, Slade L.J. and at 534-35, Lloyd L.J.

72 See *supra* text accompanying note 11.

73 A similar trend in infringement proceedings in a parallel importation context can be found in Australian case law. An earlier emphasis upon a relatively universal application of what can be seen as an exhaustion principle has moved toward a more territorial focus. Interestingly, while there is some direct reference to a principle in the nature of exhaustion, the prevailing mechanism of application also encompasses an implied consent theory, notwithstanding the absence of a direct legislative provision similar to that in the United Kingdom. The proximity of and political and economic links

Malaysia and Singapore have been said not to prohibit parallel importation of trademarked goods.[74] This conclusion requires more analysis. The jurisprudence of both countries has been noted as following English law.[75] The fact that English law has shifted to a more territorial focus in *Colgate-Palmolive* may, therefore, cause some readjustment in these jurisdictions. At least some conditional or qualifying criteria may now need to be contemplated.

Developments in Malaysia

In 1988, prior to the *Colgate-Palmolive* decision in the United Kingdom, the Malaysian High Court in *Winthrop Products*[76] found for a parallel importer upon favourable facts, but included dicta unequivocally preferring proprietary exhaustion on a universal basis. The product was the analgesic "Panadol." The first plaintiff was the owner of the trademark in Malaysia. It was part of the multinational Sterling Drug group and wholly owned by the U.S. parent, which also wholly owned the British distributor from whom the defendant parallel importer acquired the product and imported it to Malaysia. There was no differentiation in the mark between various distribution territories. There was a divergence in the colour of the packaging. The second plaintiff, the registered user in Malaysia, distributed the product in white packs, labelled as manufactured in Malaysia by the second plaintiff. The parallel imports were blue packs, intended for the United Kingdom domestic market but exported to some overseas distribution areas.[77]

The court focused primarily upon the alleged infringement of registered trademark rights. This was seen as presenting a stronger claim for the plaintiffs than a weaker claim for passing off.[78] This assessment is consistent with the position in Canada where, it will be recalled, the passing off tort has been interpreted as providing no relief for authorized distributors, as long as there is no misrepresentation.[79] By contrast, statutory infringement proceedings by authorized distributors have succeeded against parallel importers, with the overall policy and enforcement question having been posed in the *Wilkinson Sword* case but left unanswered.[80] The High Court in Malaysia

---

between Southeast Asia and Australia should encourage legal and policy comparisons between these jurisdictions.

74 See A. Wineburg, ed., *Intellectual Property Protection in Asia* (Salem, N.H.: Butterworths, 1991) at s. 7.22 (Malaysia) and s. 8.29 (Singapore).

75 See G. Wei Sze Shun, "Parallel Imports and the Tort of Passing-Off and Trade Mark Infringement" (1989) 31 Mal. L. Rev. 284.

76 *Winthrop Products Inc. v. Sun Ocean (M) Sdn. Bhd.*, [1988] 2 M.L.J. 317 (V.C. George J.).

77 *Ibid.* at 319. The so-called "blue packs" were not labelled to suggest any territorial restriction in respect of sale. They could be readily purchased from the British distributor, wholesalers, and retailers in the United Kingdom. They had also been exported to Ireland, eastern Europe and, in particular, Yugoslavia.

78 *Ibid.* at 322.

79 See *supra* text accompanying note 15 *et seq.*

80 See *supra* text accompanying notes 40-43.

not only posed but explicitly answered and applied this question in favour of exhaustion and universality as follows: "proprietorship or user right [of a registered trademark] per se does not give a right to control dealings with the goods ... some measure of contractual control may be provided for but trade mark laws certainly do not give rights of control."[81] In support of this position, the High Court relied upon the 1930 English decision of *Champagne Heidsieck*, already noted as the classical authority in support of universality.

More analytically, the High Court applied the English *Revlon* case, finding similarity between the terms of the English *Trade Marks Act* 1938[82] and the Malaysian *Trade Marks Ordinance* of 1950.[83] The key findings were that (1) the trademark had been "attached" to the product "by a Sterling company"; (2) the Malaysian owner and registered user was taken to have "impliedly consented" to the affixation; and (3) as a result, Malaysian trademark law could not prevent parallel importation into Malaysia.[84]

The claim in passing off was dismissed in the absence of misrepresentation,[85] essentially the same as in *Seiko* in Canada.

However, in 1992, after *Colgate-Palmolive*, parallel importation was again before the Malaysian High Court in *Hai-O Enterprise Bhd.*[86] A medicated wine, produced in the People's Republic of China, had been distributed in Malaysia by the plaintiff. The parallel importer acquired the same product through Hong Kong. The plaintiff had registered itself as the owner of the trademark in Malaysia. It sought to prevent the parallel importation, but failed upon its non-entitlement to registration of the trademark. Attempts to substitute the Chinese owner failed for uncertainty as to who was the owner. It was, therefore, a weak case. Nevertheless, the court, referring to Australian and English precedents including *Colgate-Palmolive*, noted the following factors (in addition to the absence of lawful registration):

(1) The parallel imports were of inferior quality to the product of the authorized distributor.
(2) There were contractual restrictions upon export and subsequent import of which the parties concerned [importantly, the parallel importer] had notice.
(3) The registered owner in the jurisdiction into which the product was imported was "different from the trademark owner in the country of export."[87]

---

81 *Winthrop, supra* note 76 at 321.
82 See *supra* text accompanying notes 32-34.
83 *Winthrop, supra* note 76 at 322.
84 *Ibid.*
85 *Ibid.* at 322-23.
86 *Hai-O Enterprise Bhd. v. Nguang Chan/Nguang Chan Liquor Trader*, [1992] 4 C.L.J. 1985 (Mal. H.C.).
87 *Ibid.* at 2006.

Despite the factual weakness of this case, the factors stipulated by the court provide important policy criteria that may limit the earlier trend towards a more universal application of the exhaustion principle.

The Position in Singapore

While a number of authorities in Singapore address the protection of extraterritorial goodwill, there appears to be no reported instance of proceedings for parallel importation of trademarked goods to Singapore. However, it does appear that any developments in Singapore will follow the position in the United Kingdom.[88] A similar position to that in Malaysia should, therefore, prevail.

Conclusions

A reflection upon parallel importation concerning trademarked goods in the jurisdictions under review – Canada, Malaysia, and Singapore, with incidental reference to the United Kingdom – presents some equivocation in the balance between territorial and transnational influences. This is not surprising, given the medium of common law judicial incrementalism as the vehicle of change in this area. Principal themes can, however, be identified.

There have been strong declarations of judicial policy that proprietary rights in trademarks ought not to be available to restrict resale of trademarked items. This proposition is, by tradition and custom, unimpeachable within a domestic or territorial marketplace. It can be described as the principle of exhaustion of proprietary rights upon the release of the trademarked product into the marketplace – that is, after "first sale." Policy recognition in *Seiko, Smith & Nephew, Winthrop Products*, and in *obiter* (being left unanswered) in *Wilkinson Sword* would apply the exhaustion principle universally, or at least transnationally.[89] In *Smith & Nephew* a distinction was made between territorial licensees and territorial owners.

The common law tort of passing off, being the remedial vehicle for unregistered trademarks and other indicia of business goodwill, readily accommodates exhaustion and transnationalism. The essential factor is the avoidance of a misrepresentation of the public in the territory of import as to the origin of the goods. This can be achieved by an effective notice or disclaimer. Indeed, to provide common law protection to a territorially focused authorized distributor, a court must be quite overt in its suspension of this key element of misrepresentation in favour of one of pure misappropriation. This was done in Canada in *Mattel*.[90] If it had not been overruled,[91] it would stand in some isolation from the otherwise accepted position that

88 See Wei Sze Shun, *supra* note 75.
89 See *supra* text accompanying notes 32-35 and 81.
90 See *supra* text accompanying notes 22-26.
91 See *supra* text accompanying note 23.

the Commonwealth, unlike the United States,[92] does not have a general misappropriation tort.[93] Future emphasis upon territorialism could, of course, result in a misappropriation tort being recognized. A common law trend in this direction may be perceived in the related area of extraterritorial goodwill or reputation "spillover," which is also discussed in this chapter.[94]

A more equivocal position is revealed for statutory infringement proceedings. This, no doubt, results from the territorial focus of trademark enactments. An infringement occurs merely upon an unauthorized use by a parallel importer. Such usage is obvious.[95]

The key issue is whether, despite this literal violation, the court will apply the statute to control or prohibit the resale of trademarked items. This is not done for goods acquired and resold within a territorial market. A policy of exhaustion of proprietary rights may be said to apply. The global or transnational context of commerce that prevails today presents this question in an extraterritorial context.

English courts have considered the issue. Aided by the structure of the 1938 trademark legislation in the United Kingdom, the English Court of Appeal in *Revlon* in 1980 adopted an implied consent theory to achieve an exhaustion of statutory trademark rights. The Federal Court of Appeal in Canada in 1996 endorsed *Revlon* and found statutory trademark rights to be exhausted in a territorial licensee. The court made no reference to the subsequent retraction from this position in the United Kingdom in *Colgate-Palmolive* in 1992. This retraction is a reminder of the common law style of judicial analysis, which avoids broad theories (territoriality or universality) in favour of incremental development with regard to the particular facts of each case. Accordingly, universality or transnationalism will occur only in certain circumstances. This trend to a more analytical, factually related, approach is also reflected in Malaysia and is very likely to be the position in Singapore.

Factors to consider will likely include the following:

(1) Whether the owner/manufacturer and the authorized distributor are part of a corporate group, or possessed of some other relationship of control. This may be relevant in determining whether the authorized distributor might be deemed bound by some activity of the parent or corporate group. For example, an authorized distributor may be found

92 A tort in the nature of "misappropriation of business values" was recognized by the United States Supreme Court in *International News Services v. Associated Press* (1918), 248 U.S. 215. See J. T. McCarthy, *McCarthy on Trademarks and Unfair Competition,* 4th ed. (New York: Clark Boardman Callaghan, 1996 updated by looseleaf) at ss. 10.47 *et seq.* and D. G. Baird, "Common Law Intellectual Property and the Legacy of International News Service v. Associated Press" (1983) 50 U. Chi. L. Rev. 411.

93 See *supra* note 21 and accompanying text.

94 See *infra* text accompanying notes 120-22.

95 See *supra* text accompanying note 29 *et seq.*

to have consented to the mark being affixed by the extraterritorial distributor (from which the parallel importer acquired the product), or to have been party to the release of the product in the marketplace by the extraterritorial distributor.[96]

(2) Linked with the above factor is the relevance of any contractual restrictions upon the extraterritorial distributor that prohibit export to the particular domestic territory. In themselves, these would not bind a parallel importer, who would not be party to the contract, but the possibility of invoking the equitable principle of notice to effect a binding obligation against a parallel importer has been suggested.[97]

(3) Are the products identical? Even small differences may be sufficient to bring about a different result.[98]

(4) Can a non-related territorial licensee (or registered user) of a trademark be deemed to have in the territory, enforcement rights unencumbered by any legal disability (such as the consequence of first sale or other release to the market) that might appertain to the extraterritorial owner of the trademark? Or, is a territorial licensee strictly in no better position than the extraterritorial owner of the mark?[99]

---

96 See *supra* text accompanying notes 83 and 84 concerning implied consent and the cases of *Revlon* (U.K.) and *Winthrop Products* (Malaysia).

97 See *Hai-O Enterprise Bhd. v. Nguang Chan/Nguang Chan Liquor Trader, supra* note 86 at 2006 (Mal. H.C.). In effect, this would amount to notice constituting a *proprietary* obligation on a third party comparable to, say, a restrictive covenant on land as established in the classic authority of *Tulk v. Moxhay* (1848), 41 E.R. 1143 (Ch.). Later cases, of course, refined the restrictive covenant with respect to land in a more restrictive, but focused, manner consistent with related areas of land law (i.e. the common law covenant and the negative easement). *Tulk v. Moxhay*, however, provided the breakthrough establishing a binding proprietary obligation on a third party by a "mere equity" from notice of a contract binding a vendor and restricting use of the land being acquired. It is unclear how far the *Tulk v. Moxhay* principle might be utilized with respect to personal property. Notice to a third party has bound that party with respect to its dealings with a person in breach of an obligation of confidence.

98 The essence of parallel importation is that the product is a genuine product, or the same product as that of the authorized distributor. Importing and selling an exactly identical product will prevent any claim of misrepresentation in passing off: see *supra* text accompanying note 16 concerning *Seiko*. On the other hand, an identical product displaying a registered trademark will ordinarily be fatal to a parallel importer, since mere use of a registered trademark on products of the categories covered by the mark will amount to an infringement, subject to the validity of the trademark and any application of the exhaustion principle. See *supra* text accompanying notes 29-31. Yet again, a significant difference will mean the imported product is an entirely distinct product from the product of the authorized distributor, therefore not amounting to parallel importation. If, however, the product is still of the same type for which a registered trademark pertains, then statutory registration rights will still be available to a defendant authorized distributor. It presents a fine line. An authorized distributor might differentiate the product to ensure that a trademark is distinctive of the distributor in the territory concerned. Yet, if too different, it may constitute an entirely separate product, different from that being imported.

99 As a matter of principle, a territorial licensee can be "in no better position" than the licensor. The licensee is subject to any disability of, or proprietary defence available

(5) Should there be a distinction between a territorial *licensee* (in circumstances described in paragraph 4 above) and a territorial *owner* by assignment?[100]

These factors will be evaluated below in the formulation of propositions for transnational marketplaces in the contexts set out in this chapter.

EXTRATERRITORIAL GOODWILL OR REPUTATION "SPILLOVER"

This chapter has already referred to the linkage expressly made by the English Court of Appeal in *Colgate-Palmolive* between the policy perspectives inherent in parallel importation and those relevant in the context of extraterritorial reputation or reputation "spillover" between territorial jurisdictions.[101] Note has also been made of the various levels of response to the protection of extraterritorial business reputation or goodwill, each demarcated by the degree of presence (or absence) of business activity in the territorial jurisdiction.[102] The principal context for transnationalism issues of this kind is the common law proceeding in passing off.

The Position in Canada

The Common Law

Recent appellate decisions of *Orkin* in Ontario and *Disney* (mall proceedings) in Alberta[103] have confirmed an already discernible trend[104] to interpret the tort of passing off broadly enough to afford transnational, if not universal, protection to extraterritorial business goodwill or reputation. Both cases involved plaintiffs based in the United States and possessing considerable transborder reputation in Canada. Neither carried on business in Canada, but each enjoyed business custom, to a greater or lesser extent,

---

against, the licensor. See *supra* text accompanying notes 50 and 51. However, territorial legislation may provide a licensee in that territory with greater protection. For example, in Canada, s. 50(3) of the *Trade-marks Act* enables (subject to any contract between the licensee and the owner of the mark), a licensee to request the owner of the trademark to take proceedings for any infringement. A failure of the owner to do so within two months enables the licensee to "institute proceedings for infringement in the licensee's own name as if the licensee were the owner, making the owner a defendant." This provision could bear an interpretation as granting *sui generis* rights to the licensee in Canada *as a territorial user*, independent of the rights of the trademark owner. However, an opposite interpretation was reached by the Canadian Federal Court of Appeal in *Smith & Nephew* to the effect that the licensee is bound by any defences which would be available to the owner for trademark infringement. See *supra* text accompanying notes 41-45.

100 See *supra* text accompanying note 44.

101 See *supra* text accompanying notes 72-73.

102 See *supra* text accompanying notes 11-14.

103 *Orkin Exterminating Co. Inc. v. Pestco of Canada* and *Walt Disney Productions v. Triple Five Corp., supra* note 14.

104 This trend was apparent in earlier cases in Canada, perhaps as early as 1931 in *Brewster Transport Co. v. Rocky Mountain Tours & Transport, supra* note 13.

from Canadians while travelling in the United States. The circumstances, therefore, did not involve even the symbolism of an agency or booking office in the territorial area. There were local clients, reflecting extraterritorial business. The cases present the third level of response in the spectrum (1) from actual business in the territory; (2) through some token or symbolic presence in the territory; and (3) to no presence in the territory – that is, entirely extraterritorial goodwill, with reputation alone extending into the territory.[105]

The writer suggests that the *Disney* decision (mall proceedings) in the Alberta Court of Appeal diminishes the substance or content of the element of misrepresentation in passing off to almost non-existence, constituting the real basis of relief to be a mere taking or misappropriation of reputation without any significant public confusion. The position may be simply a matter of preventing the unjust enrichment of the defendant.[106] Earlier, however, the Ontario Court of Appeal in *Orkin* restructured the common law to encompass relief against the taking of extraterritorial goodwill or reputation, but still, in substance, within the admittedly stretched confines of passing off.

The analysis involved confronting the two principal conceptual elements that have been used, especially in the United Kingdom, to justify a territorial limitation for passing off. These elements are (1) the need for the extraterritorial trader to demonstrate goodwill in the domestic territory, and (2) the need for the extraterritorial trader to have suffered damage in the domestic territory, the element of damage being accepted as a formal requisite in a passing off proceeding.[107]

The first requirement in redefining business goodwill as a transnational, rather than territorial, concept was established by:

(1) rejecting earlier definitions of goodwill (requiring an actual business presence) as inappropriate to passing off, predicated as they were upon a 1901 decision of the House of Lords upon matters of taxation.[108]

---

105 See *supra* text accompanying notes 13 and 14.

106 See *infra* note 122.

107 The accepted test in the Commonwealth is that of Lord Diplock in *Erven Warnink, supra* note 11 at 742 to the effect that there must be a misrepresentation that as "a reasonably foreseeable consequence" will cause "actual damage to a business or goodwill of the trader by whom the action is brought or (in a *quia timet* action) will probably do so." However, the practical focus is really upon what will constitute damage and when this might be implied or when only nominal damages might be awarded. See *Draper v. Trist*, [1939] 3 All E.R. 513 at 518-19 (C.A.) and *Habib Bank Ltd. v. Habib Bank AG Zurich*, [1981] 2 All E.R. 650 at 663-64 (C.A.). See also C. P. Best, "Damages Against the Innocent Infringer in Passing Off and Trade Mark Infringement" (1985) [Can.] I.P.J. 201.

108 See *Orkin Exterminating Co. Inc. v. Pestco of Canada, supra* note 14 at 450. The classic authority defining goodwill was *Commissioners of Inland Revenue v. Muller & Co.'s Margarine Ltd.*, [1901] A.C. 217 at 223-24 and 225 (H.L.). Earlier, Lord Diplock in *Erven Warnink, supra* note 11 at 741 had expressly adopted the test for goodwill from *Muller*

(2) finding the interrelatedness of the societies of Canada and the United States, through travel and mass advertising in electronic and print media, to create an "almost inevitable" flow of goodwill throughout North America. The more conservative and territorial position in the United Kingdom was, therefore, distinguished upon geographic criteria.[109]

(3) rejecting any distinction between goods and services. Ordinarily consumers can readily import to a domestic territory goods produced extraterritorially, but this potential is not available for extraterritorial services except by means of a symbolic presence such as a booking agency. A resort to such symbolism was not favoured.[110] Goods and services are therefore to be treated similarly.

(4) declaring the likelihood of public confusion as to some association or linkage between the parties to be the main consideration to establishing goodwill. The court noted simply: "where there is such confusion there is goodwill deserving of protection."[111] Since confusion itself is predicated upon reputation, mere extraterritorial reputation will constitute goodwill and the subject of protection.

The breadth of such protection of extraterritorial "mere reputation" is, however, likely limited by other dicta as follows:

(1) Any broadening (in effect, transnationalizing) of this area should proceed by resolving "competing contentions on relatively narrow grounds which are responsive to particular facts,"[112] while at the same time affording adequate protection to international trade and transnational commerce from local usurpers.[113] The particular circumstances in *Orkin* involved not only customers (for extraterritorial services) from Ontario,[114] but also a documented intention on the part of the U.S.-based Orkin Exterminating Company to enter business (presumably relatively soon) in Ontario. This

---

& Co.'s Margarine case, describing it as "best expressed" in that case. It is suggested that the divergence from this in *Orkin* demonstrates how extensive global or transnational business arrangements have become since as recently as 1979. A test found acceptable in 1979 by one of the highest courts in the Commonwealth was found inadequate and unacceptable in a transnational context in 1985.

109 See *Orkin, ibid.* at 450.

110 *Ibid.* at 446-47.

111 *Ibid.* at 450.

112 *Ibid.* at 444.

113 *Ibid.* The court noted: "If the plaintiff's trade name has a reputation in the defendant's jurisdiction, such that the public associates it with services provided by the plaintiff, then the defendant's use of it means that the plaintiff has *lost control* over the impact of its trade name in the defendant's jurisdiction" (emphasis added).

114 Orkin Exterminating (or its predecessors) had been in business in the United States since 1901. Canadians came into contact with the company when travelling in the United States and being "exposed to Orkin's extensive advertising and use of its trade marks in that country." It was estimated that millions of Canadians travel every year in the United States and especially in the warmer areas (the southern states) where Orkin's activities were extensive. Also, there were advertisements by Orkin in Ameri-

factor was emphasized by the Court, but expressly without stipulation as a prerequisite.[115]

(2) A boundary should be recognized, more limited than the earlier sweeping reference to North America,[116] to demonstrate goodwill zones (with subzones of selling, advertising, and reputation), reflecting a territory set by commercial or trade activity rather than political control.[117] This may necessitate some inquiry as to a trading pattern or area within which goodwill is established and protection is afforded.

The requirement in *Orkin* that the extraterritorial trader must have suffered damage in the domestic territory was dealt with very briefly, by finding the extraterritorial plaintiff to have sustained a "loss of control over the impact of its trade name" causing a "potential impediment" to its use in Ontario.[118]

The facts in *Orkin* made it easy for the Court to recognize extraterritorial goodwill, but within the framework of passing off, as expanded.[119] Perhaps unfortunately, the judgment also contained reference to misappropriation by the defendant,[120] and to the defendant's blatant intent to use the plaintiff's goodwill.[121] These dicta suggest a refocusing of common law relief beyond passing off to more of a remedy for misappropriation in an extraterritorial context. In *Orkin*, this was simply speculation. However, as earlier described, more recently the Alberta Court of Appeal in litigation by Walt Disney Productions concerning Disney's claimed exclusivity in the expression "Fantasyland" seemed to extend remedial action beyond the traditional ambit of passing off to substantially a proceeding for misappropriation *simpliciter*.[122]

---

can publications circulating in Canada. Finally, Canadians had used Orkin's services with respect to property owned by Canadians in the United States. This gave exposure to both bills for work rendered and advertising material. See *Orkin, ibid.* at 435-37.

115 *Orkin, supra* note 14 at 444. The court noted the existence of customers (in Canada for their properties in the United States) and the intent of the company to enter into business in Ontario, as important factors, but added that it "did not intend to indicate that a case ... could not be decided on more general grounds" than those concerning customers and intent to enter Ontario.

116 See *supra* note 109.

117 Orkin, *supra* note 14 at 450. In addition to goodwill zones, there may be potential goodwill, or expansion, zones.

118 *Ibid.* at 454. Cf. *supra* note 113.

119 The principal expansions of the tort of passing off in *Orkin* were the redefining of goodwill to mean simply evidence of confusion (see *supra* note 111 and accompanying text) and the constituting of damage by lost control (see *ibid.* note 120). The primary elements of passing off – a misrepresentation and public or consumer confusion – were clearly established.

120 *Ibid.* at 448.

121 *Ibid.* at 448 and 449. At 449, Morden J.A. for the court commented: "I need not, and do not, say that the defendant's bad faith alone will confer a cause of action on a foreign plaintiff ... but it surely must be a relevant factor to take into account in adjusting competing interests."

122 See *Walt Disney Productions v. Triple Five Corp., supra* note 14. Walt Disney Productions succeeded in preventing the owners of the West Edmonton Mall in Alberta, reputed

Statutory Infringement

The inherently territorial nature of statutory trademark legislation limits any similar broad transnational or universal thrust with respect to statutory infringement involving extraterritorial traders. The two principal statutory contexts raising extraterritorial issues similar to those discussed at common law are:

(1) A proceeding by an extraterritorial trader to challenge the validity of a registered trade mark of a domestic trader on the basis that the mark lacks the requisite distinctiveness in the domestic trader because the local public associate it with the extraterritorial trader. Mere extraterritorial reputation (without any actual business within the territory) has been sufficient to validate this challenge,[123] and produces a result very similar to that at common law for passing off. However, the scope of such a proceeding is limited to expunging or denying a domestic producer the right to register a trademark. It does not ensure any rights in the extraterritorial trader to itself use the mark within the territory, nor does it prevent the domestic user from carrying on business in the territory using that mark or name as an unregistered trademark or trade name.[124]

(2) Apart from Convention priority registration,[125] an extraterritorial trader seeking to have its extraterritorial reputation in a trademark obtain a priority for previous usage must establish that its mark was used or made known in Canada under provisions of the Act[126] that have been

---

to be the largest shopping mall in North America, from using the expression "Fantasyland" in the amusement area of the mall. While there was certainly evidence that the mall owner had copied and sought an association or linkage with the plaintiff's theme parks, known as Disneyland, the elements of passing off were not, arguably, established. Yet the cause was found to be established. An apparent primary emphasis in the judgment was the prevention of unjust enrichment. This accommodated particularly the absence of damage in the territory, given that Disney had no apparent plan or intention to enter into future business in Alberta or elsewhere in Canada. The test as to an association between the parties was minimized to simply whether Disney would be seen to have consented to or authorized use of the name Fantasyland. Furthermore, the percentage of population that was confused, even to this minimal extent, was certainly less than 10%. A subsequent decision at trial level allowing a related hotel within the West Edmonton Mall to continue to be known as the Fantasyland Hotel provides some balance. See *Walt Disney Productions v. Fantasyland Hotel Inc.* (1994), 56 C.P.R. (3d) 129 (Ala. Q.B.), aff'd (1996), 67 C.P.R. (3d) 444 (Alta. C.A.). However, the essential *misappropriation* and *unjust enrichment* thrust of the earlier proceeding at appellate level reflects the substantial judicial preference for transnational, if not universal, protection for extraterritorial business goodwill.

123 See e.g. *E & J Gallo Winery v. Andres Wines Ltd.*, [1976] 2 F.C. 3 (C.A.).

124 To prevent a domestic entity from carrying on business, a foreign plaintiff must either obtain a registered trademark and bring an infringement proceeding or invoke the tort of passing off.

125 See ss. 31 and 16(2), *Trade-marks Act*, R.S.C. 1985, c. T-13, as am.

126 *Ibid.* s. 5.

interpreted far more strictly than in the corresponding proceeding at common law as earlier described.[127]

The Position in Malaysia

Two recent cases in Malaysia have tended towards transnationalism by protecting extraterritorial business goodwill or reputation.[128]

In 1992, the French multinational company of some 130 years standing, Compagnie General Des Eaux, succeeded in the Malaysian High Court in a passing off proceeding against a domestic enterprise that was using its name.[129] The defendant local enterprise denied that the plaintiff multinational had goodwill in Malaysia or had suffered damage in Malaysia. The respective business activities were reported as "different and diverse."[130] However, strong factors supported the multinational plaintiff, including the following:

(1) It had, since 1986, engaged in joint venture projects in Malaysia, holding a 20% share in a Malaysian-based company since that time, and having established a representative office (but apparently not an actual business)[131] in Malaysia in July 1988.

(2) It had decided in 1991 to expand its business to Malaysia and had sought registration of its name with the Malaysian Registry of Companies in October 1991, only to have found that the defendant had obtained a registration with the Registry for that name as recently as September 1991.[132]

(3) Both parties had an identical name in the French language. Since Malaysia was not a French language jurisdiction, this in itself would have caused public confusion between the parties, notwithstanding the general or generic nature of the name.[133]

An identical instance to Item 3 above occurred in 1993 before the same judge.[134] The plaintiffs in that case were the United Kingdom parent and its

127 See e.g. the classic Canadian authority, *Robert C. Wian Enterprises Inc. v. Mady* (1965), 49 D.L.R. (2d) 65 (Ex. Ct.).

128 An early instance of interlocutory proceedings before the Malaysian High Court in *Roadstar-Anseach Investments Pte Ltd. v. Thian Hock Electric Sdn. Bhd.*, [1990] 1 C.L.J. 1219, 1221 (H.C., Kuala Lumpur, 1989) suggested a strict territorial approach in requiring a plaintiff in passing off proceedings to plead "that it was carrying on business in respect of the product in Malaysia and that its product had acquired substantial reputation and goodwill in [Malaysia]."

129 *Compagnie Generale Des Eaux v. Compagnie Generale Des Eaux Sdn. Bhd.*, [1992] 4 C.L.J. 1979 (H.C. Kuala Lumpur).

130 *Ibid.* at 1980.

131 In a subsequent case before the same judge, this case was described as not involving the plaintiff "actually hav[ing] an office in Malaysia." See *infra* note 134 at 39.

132 *Compagnie Generale des Eaux, supra* note 29.

133 *Ibid.* at 1981.

134 *Dun & Bradstreet (Singapore) Pte Ltd. v. Dun & Bradstreet (Malaysia) Sdn. Bhd*, [1994] 1 M.L.J. 32 (H.C. Kuala Lumpur) (appealed to Sup. Ct. Malaysia, number 02-448-93).

Singapore subsidiary in the multinational Dun & Bradstreet group, which was involved in financial services, particularly credit information services. A subsidiary was proposed to be incorporated in Malaysia, where the defendant was discovered to be carrying on a general trading business under the plaintiff's name. The plaintiffs succeeded. Important factors included:

(1) the noted intention to enter into business in Malaysia
(2) the distinctiveness of the names "Dun" and "Bradstreet," both individually and even more so when combined[135]
(3) the fact that the plaintiffs had an international reputation established from 1857 with two million customers worldwide and a turnover in excess of $U.S.5 million[136]
(4) the fact that the plaintiff Singapore subsidiary had extended its services (although not its physical presence) to Malaysia by contracting with local Malaysian entities, "which had resulted in [the Singapore entity] acquiring a substantial reputation and goodwill in [Malaysia]"[137] over the previous three years[138]
(5) the geographic proximity between Malaysia and Singapore[139]
(6) the likelihood that the defendant's business of general trading would be confused with the plaintiff's business of financial services. Despite the high literacy level of the public, each of these companies would be seen as a branch or extension of the other.[140]

The strict English position (requiring actual business in the domestic jurisdiction) was distinguished on the basis of the contractual connections with the Malaysian companies with a broad test of reputation plus some market activity in the jurisdiction being sufficient to establish sufficient presence and goodwill in Malaysia.[141] The Court also drew comparisons with other jurisdictions that have adopted tests more liberal than the English position.[142]

The position prevailing in Malaysia is, therefore, more transnational than the strict territorial position historically favoured in the United Kingdom, but not as broad as that espoused in *Orkin* in Canada, since it requires an

135 *Ibid.* at 35. Abdul Malek J. considered that "Dunn" or "Dunne" might be more common than "Dun" and that the combination of "Dun & Bradstreet" was a rarity.
136 *Ibid.* at 38.
137 Ibid. at 36. These contacts were described as "subscription agreements" and had been entered into with at least 31 Malaysian companies from 1989 until the time of the hearing (*ibid.* at 39).
138 *Ibid.* at 41.
139 *Ibid.*
140 *Ibid.* at 39.
141 *Ibid.* The fact that the plaintiffs did not pay taxes locally, nor have Malaysian government approval to underwrite businesses in Malaysia, was found to be irrelevant to the establishment of goodwill in Malaysia. Earlier (at 38), the defendant had argued that the absence of these factors was an important consideration in denying sufficient presence in Malaysia.
142 *Ibid.* at 38.

extraterritorial entity to have some market activity with Malaysia. However, there would seem to be a very close affinity between the position in Malaysia and that in Canada.

The Position in Singapore

Passing Off

The position in Singapore, reflects a stringent territorial perspective, similar to the predominant position in England, which requires actual business in the territory. A recent commentator, Ng Siew Kuan, has persuasively urged that the perspective should change from actual business to actual customers, so as to achieve closer alignment with the broader jurisprudence in other parts of the Commonwealth.[143] The policy arguments in support of this position reiterate the universality of the globalization of trade, mass communication, and worldwide travel, as well as Singapore's international and regional importance in trade and commerce,[144] and the need for greater commercial morality.[145]

This apparently strict territorial position in Singapore, in contrast with a broader, more transnational position in Malaysia, may not be so surprising. It will be recalled that the decision in 1976 of the Privy Council in *Star Industrial*, one of the classic territorial decisions, was an appeal from Singapore.[146] It did not present the usual reputation or goodwill spillover scenario. The plaintiff was a Hong Kong manufacturer of toothbrushes that were marketed in a distinctive guise. It had exported its products to Singapore from 1953 to 1965 when it ceased business in Singapore. In 1968 the defendant, using a tradename and guise similar to those that had been

---

143 See Ng Siew Kuan," Foreign Traders and the Law of Passing Off: The Requirements of Goodwill Within the Jurisdiction," [1991] S.J.L.S. 372 at 405. The protection of actual customers is presented by Ng Siew Kuan as a compromise between actual business and mere reputation, the latter being seen as insufficient to warrant protection, although the need for flexibility in determining if goodwill exists is also urged (*ibid.* at 405 and 408).

144 *Ibid.* at 407-408. In addition to the international importance of Singapore, Ng Siew Kuan notes the regional proximity of Singapore to Malaysia, Indonesia, Thailand, Hong Kong, and Japan and, more locally, refers to the "Growth Triangle Co-Operation of Singapore – Johor – Riau Islands" (*ibid.* at 408).

145 *Ibid.* at 408-409 relying upon dicta of Lord Diplock upon this theme in a different context. Lord Diplock's comments are from *Erven Warnink, supra* note 11 at 743, where the House of Lords recognized the extension of the passing off tort to include misrepresentations as to the ingredients of a product. Lord Diplock considered development of the tort should parallel rather than diverge from new legislative initiatives, which were essentially consumer protection provisions (re the content or nature of actional misrepresentations to the public). Ng Siew Kuan would apply a similar parallel with the commercial reality of global, transnational, or regional commerce of today and expand the passing off tort accordingly.

146 *Star Industrial Co. v. Yap Kwee Kor, supra* note 11.

previously used by the plaintiff, began selling toothbrushes in Singapore. The plaintiff's proceedings in passing off failed for the lack of current goodwill in Singapore. There was little focus upon any reputation spillover in Singapore from 1953 to 1965. The imposition of an excise duty in 1965 caused a cessation of the imports. The plaintiffs were held to have no goodwill in Singapore.

The judgments do not provide any analysis of any reputation spillover to Singapore from Hong Kong. The focus was upon whether goodwill had been acquired by the importations from 1953 to 1965 and whether it continued after the cessation in 1965.[147] This might afford a basis to distinguish *Star Industrial* from the regular reputation spillover authorities.[148] However, the Privy Council was prepared to assume that the plaintiff had acquired goodwill in Singapore by 1965,[149] but lost it immediately upon its abandonment of its export and sale to Singapore.[150] This clear territorial assertion was reiterated based on the principle that goodwill can exist only when attached to a business and "is local in character and divisible; if the business is carried on in several countries a separate goodwill attaches to each" and "perishes" in a country where business is abandoned, even though the business may continue to be carried on in other countries.[151]

Star Industrial was affirmed as recently as 1991 as to the requirement of a territorial definition of goodwill,[152] but later in 1991 doubt was expressed as to whether *Star Industrial* really prevented the establishment of goodwill in Singapore without an actual business presence in the jurisdiction.[153]

Trade-Marks Act

Extraterritorial goodwill is more likely to be recognized in proceedings to

---

147 Choor Singh J. at trial (Singapore H.C.) found insufficient sales in Singapore. Apparently, Singapore was used only as a centre of collection and redistribution by re-export to other countries in the region. See *Star Industrial Co. v. Yap Kwee Kor*, [1976] 1 M.L.J. 149 at 151. The Singapore Court of Appeal agreed, finding that the plaintiff "could not, on any view, have acquired a right of property in Singapore by 1965 in respect of [the imports from Hong Kong]": *ibid.* at 154.

148 See Megarry V.C. in *Metric Resources Corp. v. Leasemetrix Ltd.* (1979), F.S.R. 571, noting this distinction. See also *Baskin-Robbins Ice Cream Co. v. Gutman* (1976), F.S.R. 545 at 547, in which Graham J. doubted that Lord Diplock in *Star Industrial* meant his words to be interpreted in a narrow territorial sense.

149 *Star Industrial*, *supra* note 11 at 268 and [1976] 1 M.L.J., *supra* note 147 at 154.

150 *Ibid.* at 270 and M.L.J. 155.

151 *Ibid.* at 269 and M.L.J. 155. See also the Singapore Court of Appeal (*ibid.* at M.L.J. 154) and Choor Singh J. at trial (*ibid.* at M.L.J. 152) to the same effect, noting the absence of business to be conclusive.

152 See *Tan Gek Neo Jessie v. Minister for Finance*, [1991] 2 M.L.J. 301 at 306 (H.C. Singapore), Thean J. This case involved the American multinational corporation "J.C. Penn[e]y Company Inc.," but proceeded upon issues of validity of registration under the Singapore *Trade Marks Act* rather than passing off. See *infra* text accompanying notes 158 and 159. Contrast the proceedings in Hong Kong in *J.C. Penn[e]y Co. Inc. v. Punjabi Nick*, [1979] F.S.R. 26 (S.C. H.K.).

expunge or deny registration for statutory trademark protection. These proceedings are similar to those in Canada, where a local registrant cannot claim a mark to be distinctive of its wares if it is associated by the public with a foreign owner or user.[154]

The Singapore *Trade Marks Act* requires that only a proprietor of a trademark can obtain registration, and the mark must not be likely to deceive or confuse the public.[155] Under these provisions, authorities in the 1980s denied registration by local traders of marks possessing a substantial extraterritorial reputation, so long as there was some use (by way of sales, but without an established business) in Singapore.[156] Similarly, an infringement proceeding by a United States corporation with respect to its mark of international reputation (Jordache jeans) succeeded in *Jordache Enterprises Inc. v. Millennium Pte Ltd.*, notwithstanding a rejection of a claim in passing off for failure of the plaintiff to establish goodwill in Singapore.[157]

More recent cases have, however, been more equivocal. In *Tan Gek Neo Jessie v. Minister of Finance*, the High Court quashed a direction by the Registrar of Business that a local trader cease to use the expressions "J. C. Penn[e]y" or "Penn[e]y" in its business known as "J. C. Penn[e]y Collections." The United States' multinational, J. C. Penney Company Incorporated, failed for reasons that included the expiry some years earlier of its registered trademark in Singapore, and its failure to have used, or currently to be using the mark in Singapore.[158] Therefore, it had "no reputation [in Singapore] in relation to its business."[159]

Yet in 1992 the United States' multinational, R. H. Macy & Company, succeeded in a similar context. The trademark MACY's registered by a local

153 See *Haw Par Brothers Internat. Ltd. v. Jack Chiarapurk*, [1991] 2 M.L.J. 428 at 437-38 (H.C. Singapore), which relied on indications of a less stringent approach possibly developing in the United Kingdom. See *supra* note 148, citing the English cases that suggest this amelioration of the strict territorial approach.

154 See *supra* text accompanying notes 123 and 124.

155 See *Trade Marks Act* (Singapore), s. 11(1) (before 1 Mar. 1991); s. 12(1) (from 1 Mar. 1991) and s. 15(1), noted in Ng-Loy Wee Loon, "Protection of Foreign Traders' Rights in Their Trade Marks Registered Outside Singapore" [1992] S.J.L.S. 221 at 222.

156 See *Davidoff Extension S.A. v. Davidoff Commercio E. Industria Ltda*, [1988] 1 M.L.J. 234 (H.C. Singapore) and *Karrimor International Ltd. v. Ho Choong Fun*, [1989] 3 M.L.J. 467 (H.C. Singapore), both of these cases being brought to attention by Ng-Loy Wee Loon, *supra* note 155 at 223-24.

157 See *Jordache Enterprises Inc. v. Millennium Pte. Ltd.*, [1985] 1 M.L.J. 281 at 284-85 (H.C. Singapore), Thean J. The plaintiff had registered its mark "Jordache" in Singapore on 3 Oct. 1979. The defendant's unregistered mark "Jordane" too closely resembled the plaintiff's mark and would cause confusion and thereby statutory infringement.

158 See *Tan Gek Neo Jessie v. Minister of Finance, supra* note 152 at 305. The failure of the extraterritorial plaintiff to use the mark in Singapore was held to deny any possibility of a use by the defendant causing any deception or confusion of the public. Additionally, Thean J. (at 306) found the marks to be not sufficiently similar to cause confusion.

159 *Ibid.* at 306. See also Ng-Loy Wee Loon, *supra* note 155 at 228-29.

Singapore trader was expunged.[160] The American multinational did not itself carry on business in Singapore, nor did it advertise or promote its trademark in Singapore. Instead, it appeared to have had since 1982 a licensing arrangement with a representative office in Singapore to which customers placed orders for clothing. This clothing was made locally, but, with the apparent permission of the representative office, displayed the mark "MACY's."[161] The case has been interpreted in Singapore as a trend towards protecting foreign trademark holders by clarifying that actual business is not necessary when using the particular statutory provisions to prevent a local trader from obtaining registered mark privileges in usurpation of foreign reputation or goodwill. Some use in Singapore by the foreign entity is still necessary, but of a more limited and incidental extent.[162]

The extent to which this trend will influence the strictly territorial position taken in *Star Industrial* in common law passing off in Singapore is unclear. It is, however, to be noted that an inference has been drawn from the *Macy* case that, if a local trader is permitted to obtain a registration of a foreign trademark, the foreign holder would not in the future be able to enter into business using that mark in Singapore – a result seen as undesirable and disadvantageous for Singapore.[163] This, it is suggested, presents a similar policy analysis to that adopted in Canada in *Orkin* in a passing off context, establishing the requisite element of damage as the loss of control by the foreign entity of prospective use of its mark in the domestic territory.[164]

Reputation Spillover: Conclusions

Singapore and the United Kingdom have largely retained a territorial, legal, and policy focus within the passing off proceeding, preventing any significant transnational recognition and protection of business goodwill or reputation. The pivotal analytical focus has been the nature and degree of any connection the extraterritorial trader has with the national or domestic jurisdiction in which the proceeding is brought. This reflects two key elements of the passing off proceeding in this extraterritorial context: the establishment of goodwill and the sustaining of damage within that territory. The finding of a sufficient connection or involvement within the domestic jurisdiction serves to meet these criteria. Singapore, following the United Kingdom, has required the extraterritorial trader to establish actual business, or some equivalent close connection, in the domestic jurisdiction.

160 See *R. H. Macy & Co. Inc. v. Trade Accents*, [1992] 1 S.L.R. 581 (H.C. Singapore), noted by Ng-Loy Wee Loon, *supra* note 155.

161 See Ng-Loy Wee Loon, *supra* note 155 at 221.

162 See Ng-Loy Wee Loon, *ibid.* at 221, 226, and 228-30 who, while acknowledging that the position of foreign holders of marks has been enhanced, suggests that even the minimal requirement of some use or commercial activity may still be too strict.

163 See Ng-Loy Wee Loon, *ibid.* at 221 n. 3.

164 See *supra* text accompanying notes 113 and 118.

The amelioration of this standard by recognition of connections less than an actual business presence begin to accord transnational recognition and protection. This has occurred in some U.K. decisions, and is illustrated in the Malaysian authorities that involve joint ventures between foreign and Malaysian companies, the holding of interests in Malaysian companies, or having a representative office in Malaysia.

The recent trend in *Orkin* in Ontario, Canada, from stretching or fictionalizing a territorial connection to include symbolic or token linkages, to redefining business goodwill so as to include extraterritorial business reputation that causes public confusion in the domestic territory, presents a major conceptual liberalization. This change, together with an acceptance of the further requirement of loss or damage being met upon merely a loss of control by the foreign trader over its mark in the domestic territory should substantially increase the transnational application of the proceeding in passing off. The Court made this change quite purposefully, expressly acknowledging the transnationalizing of business within commercial and trading zones and geographical regions that were quite distinct from political and jurisdictional territories.

The restraint noted in *Orkin* in recognizing this transnationalization as an evolving field of law, and warning that any development ought to proceed cautiously within the context of the particular facts of each case, was perhaps muted by other references that discouraged a local trader from intentionally taking by misappropriation the goodwill of an extraterritorial trader. The latter hint of judicial relief upon merely an unconsented and intentional taking or misappropriation might have influenced the later Canadian hearing in *Disney* (mall proceedings) before the Alberta Court of Appeal, which extended relief to a situation in which, arguably, there was no significant misrepresentation or public confusion. If this is so, then the mall proceedings[165] in *Disney* presents an instance of extraterritorial relief upon merely a misappropriation and related unjust enrichment upon a local trader's usurpation of an extraterritorial trader's greater reputation. It would accordingly be beyond the accepted confines of passing off, though reflecting the policy strength in this context of Canadian judicial acceptance of the need for transnational protection of business goodwill.

The treatment of this topic has included a brief reference to the Canadian *Trade-Marks Act* to demonstrate how comparable extraterritorial scenarios might arise and proceed under typical trademark legislation. It is seen to be possible, but more strict and confined than that of the broad evaluation of the common law proceeding in passing off. This reflects the focus upon the

---

165 See *supra* note 122 and accompanying text. The subsequent hotel proceedings in *Disney*, also referenced in note 122, are in the nature of a regular passing off proceeding.

interpretation of statutory provisions, drawn essentially from a territorial perspective of history.

CONCLUSIONS AND PROJECTIONS

The jurisdictions considered in this chapter – Canada, Malaysia, and Singapore – all have an inheritance of English common law involving judicial incremental development in response to changing economic, business, political, and social circumstances. All three judiciaries are responding to the transnational pressures presented with parallel importation and extraterritorial trading in the context of proprietary protection for trade marks and other indicia of business goodwill.

This incremental process causes some uncertainty, but it does foster a gradual development that enables competing interests to be balanced and legal regulation to be more clearly reflective of ongoing business and of economic changes. This glimpse at an evolution in progress produces an essentially micro analysis. Jurisdictions may, of course, opt for change by legislation or bilateral or multilateral treaty, but there has been little movement in this regard.[166]

Both situations are governed by market boundaries. The market in business or factual terms is broader than the political or juridical territory. Should business interests within the narrower political or juridical territory be protected from influences in the wider business or factual marketplace? Before examining some policy considerations and projections it is necessary to reflect upon the relationship between parallel importation and extraterritorial business reputation. As noted, the English Court of Appeal expressly finds the linkage to be appropriate,[167] but to what extent is this supportable? Is it useful? Any projection of how these situations may develop, particularly concerning Canada, Malaysia, and Singapore, must recognize both the similarities and the differences between parallel importation and extraterritorial reputation.

Conceptually, there is some commonality, and the linkage of the two situations does create a useful analogy, but with inherent limitations. Both situations involve

166 See e.g. E. Miller, "NAFTA: Protector of National Intellectual Property Rights or Blueprint for Globalization? The Effect of NAFTA on the First Sale Doctrine in Copyright" (1995) 16 Loy. L.A. Ent. L.J. 475 finding NAFTA to have "left a palpable regulatory gap in the area of parallel imports" (at note 228). See also H. A. Kremen, "Caveat Venditor: International Application of the First Sale Doctrine" (1997) 23 Syracuse J. Int'l L. and Com. 161, lamenting that the GATT/WTO Uruguay Round left the issue of parallel importation to be resolved bilaterally because of the significant divergence of opinion (at note 75). In this regard, see Article 6, Agreement on Trade-related Aspects of Intellectual Property Rights (TRIPs) (W.T.O.), providing "nothing in this Agreement shall be used to address the issue of the exhaustion of intellectual property rights."

167 See *supra* text accompanying notes 72, 73, and 101.

(1) A local trader in competition with a trader who enjoys an extraterritorial benefit – either a source of a product at a price less than that charged by the local distributor (parallel importation) or a reputation gained extraterritorially.

(2) A need to demarcate a boundary for the marketplace – either for determining the existence of goodwill or damage or to determine if a product was released in a relevant market so to invoke a principle of exhaustion of proprietary relief. In *Orkin*, the recognition by the Ontario Court of Appeal of goodwill zones (with sub-zones of selling, advertising, and reputation) that reflected a territory set by a business or commercial activity instead of political or governmental jurisdiction may be useful in establishing a more extensive marketplace in which the principle of exhaustion might apply to the initial release of a product.

(3) A conceptual similarity focused upon:

  (a) In statutory trade mark, infringement proceedings in which the mere usage (i.e. taking or misappropriating) of the registered mark (or a mark that is confusing with the registered mark) in the domestic jurisdiction by another is sufficient to establish relief.

  (b) In common law passing off, the interrelationship between a taking through misrepresentation and a taking by misappropriation *simpliciter*. The Supreme Court of Canada in *Seiko* demonstrated that a misrepresentation could not exist if it had been expressly negated by a statement or disclaimer. As a result, the passing off tort was ineffective to prevent parallel importation of genuine products disclaimed to possess any of the ancillary benefits provided by an authorized distributor. To avoid this consequence, so as to protect an authorized distributor, Joyal J. in *Mattel* (subsequently overruled) had to modify the tort of passing off to provide relief to an authorized distributor simply upon its reputation being misappropriated. There was no misrepresentation of the Nintendo games, which were genuine and identical to those of the authorized distributor. Similarly, with extraterritorial business reputation, the Alberta Court of Appeal in *Disney* in effect gave relief for misappropriation when, arguably, there was little or no misrepresentation or confusion of the public in Alberta or elsewhere in Canada and any possible damage would have occurred outside Canada. Otherwise, as in *Orkin*, the element of misrepresentation has been respected, but other elements of the tort, such as the need for, and meaning of, goodwill, and the need for damage, have been ameliorated, and factors such as the defendant's intent or enrichment have been emphasized. This emphasis is more suggestive of misappropriation than of misrepresentation. The tort is therefore being modified to accommodate the extraterritorial factor.

While the above factors would support a linkage of parallel importation and extraterritorial business reputation to establish a paradigmatic framework, the following factors limit its usefulness:

(1) Relief for (in effect) misappropriation protects the territorial or local authorized distributor in a parallel importation context, but protects the extraterritorial or foreign trader in an extraterritorial reputation context. The latter is consistent with transnationalization, but the former is not.

(2) Parallel importation is a far more diverse and complex phenomenon than extraterritorial reputation. In addition to whatever the position may be concerning trademark and unfair competition, prohibitions or restrictions on parallel importation also exist in patent[168] and copyright law.[169] Furthermore, it is a highly divisive issue, legally and economically, and with no obvious consensus as to a choice one way or the other.[170] The core issue concerns whether domestic proprietary protection (including statutory trademark laws) should be interpreted as "exhausted" as against "unauthorized" imports. A decision, whether affirmative or negative, will have a significant impact on many economic interests in many jurisdictions. By contrast, extraterritorial reputation is relatively self-contained, and ordinarily the morality of the situation favours a foreign trader whose indicia and reputation have been usurped by a local trader.[171]

---

168 See generally, H. G. Fox, *The Canadian Law and Practice Relating to Letters Patent for Inventions*, 4th ed. (Toronto: Carswell, 1969) at 391-93.

169 For example, in Canada see *Copyright Act*, R.S.C. 1985, c. C-42, ss. 44, 44.1, 44.2, 44.3, and 45 as am. Significant amendments were made by the *Copyright Amendment Act 1997*, S.C. 1997, c. 24, s. 26. These provisions concern works copied in a country *without* the consent of the copyright owner in the country where the copies were made, or where the copies were made outside a treaty country. The position is, therefore, not one of true parallel importation. However, true parallel importation is prevented by s. 27.1 (en. 1997, c. 24, s. 15) in respect of the importation of a book "made with the consent of the owner of the copyright in the book in the country where the copies were made, but imported without the consent of the owner of the copyright in the book in Canada" (s. 27.1(a)). Exceptions are provided in s. 45.

170 See *infra* note 189 and accompanying text, which set out a recent decision in Japan allowing parallel importation in a patent context and referring to a thorough analysis of policy arguments for and against this position in a publication by the Institute of Intellectual Property in Tokyo.

171 In addition to the local trader being seen as "taking," "usurping," or "copying" in order to gain an advantage for itself, there is no corresponding advantage to the public or to consumers in the domestic jurisdiction. Indeed, the ordinarily required element of misrepresentation in a passing off proceeding means that there is some public deception or confusion, which raises a consumer protection issue. Although the principal role of the tort of passing off is the protection of a competitor's business goodwill, recently it has been seen as parallel to the protection of consumers. See e.g. *Erven Warnink, supra* note 11 at 742-43, and Lord Diplock in *Ciba-Geigy Canada Ltd. v. Apotex Inc.* (1992), 44 C.P.R. (3d) 289 at 300 (S.C.C.). Parallel importation, on the other hand, although injuring the authorized distributor in the domestic jurisdiction,

Reputation Spillover: A Projection

The trend towards wider protection of extraterritorial business reputation seems likely to continue. It has a broadly based consensus in common law jurisdictions.[172] There may also be a possibility of some movement in the United Kingdom away from a strict territorial definition of business goodwill.[173] In Singapore, this strict perspective in interpreting the tort of passing off is likely to be seen as precedent-driven,[174] and the future position is likely to be influenced more by the greater transnational focus reflected in Singapore when applying the jurisdiction's trademark legislation.[175] Additionally, Singapore's strong international trading and commercial reputation, along with its close geographic proximity to other regional jurisdictions, provides strong policy support for a move to a more transnational perspective, similar to that of Malaysia.[176] At the other end of the spectrum, the analysis in the *Disney* mall proceedings before the Alberta Court of Appeal is too far removed from the established elements of passing off.[177]

Negating the extremities of *Disney* (mall proceedings) on the one hand and the strictly territorial position of Singaporean common law on the other, the issue for Malaysian and Singaporean courts will be whether to

(1) require, but minimize or even fictionalize, some territorial connection between the jurisdiction and the plaintiff's business or product, as appears to be the current Malaysian position[178]

(2) or avoid any need for finding such territorial linkage by redefining goodwill and the requirement of damage, but retaining a strong requirement

---

does provide a choice for consumers of receiving a genuine item, albeit often without the same sales service at a lower price. See *Seiko, supra* note 6 at 15.

172 See *ConAgra Inc. v. McCain Foods (Aust.) Pty Ltd.* (1992), 33 F.C.R. 302, 106 A.L.R. 465 (Aust. Full Ct.) for a survey of precedents from Australia, Hong Kong, Ireland, and the United Kingdom, as well as some reference to Canada and the United States.

173 See *ConAgra Inc. v. McCain Foods (Aust.) Pty Ltd., ibid.* at A.L.R. 489-90, in which Lockhart J. referred to the recent decision of the House of Lords in *Reckitt and Coleman Properties Ltd. v. Borden Inc.* (1990), 1 W.L.R. 491 at 499, Lord Oliver, and 511, Lord Jauncey, discussing goodwill in another context and not including any local requirement in the definition. Lockhart J. saw this as reflecting some amelioration of a strict territorial position. Any such redefinition would be consistent with an early comment of Megarry V.C. in *Metric Resources Corp. v. Leasemetrix Ltd., supra* note 148 at 577 from a policy perspective: "I do not see why the filching of a reputation acquired in England should not be regarded as an injury to a business carried on in France, and in France alone."

174 The decision of the Privy Council in *Star Industrial Co. v. Yap Kwee Kor, supra* note 11, in which the Board stipulated a strict territorial approach, requiring the plaintiff to have actual business in the domestic jurisdiction, was on appeal from the courts of Singapore. See *supra* text accompanying notes 146 to 151.

175 See *supra* text accompanying notes 160 to 163.

176 See *supra* text accompanying note 138.

177 See *supra* text accompanying note 122.

178 See *supra* text accompanying notes 141 and 142.

of misrepresentation. This presents the Canadian option of *Orkin* in Ontario.[179] In effect, mere reputation (and perhaps an intention to enter into the local market)[180] will establish goodwill in the territory, and the plaintiff's loss of control over the mark or indicia will establish damage.

It is suggested that the *Orkin* option be adopted. *Orkin* provides, in addition to the conceptual fluidity just described, a formula (from U.S. sources) to recognize goodwill zones.[181] This option will allow the business and economic market to correspond with that applicable to the juridical evaluation. It is of particular importance to Malaysia and Singapore, given the close geographic and regional trading in Southeast Asia, and to Canada and the United States.[182] Both regions present trading or business zones although there ought to be actual evidence pointing to the existence of a goodwill zone with respect to the particular products and business activities that are involved in a proceeding. This reflects the warning given in *Orkin* that each instance ought to be determined on a case by case basis.[183]

This trend is also reflected, and is projected to continue, in proceedings under statutory trademark legislation brought by an extraterritorial trader to challenge the validity of a registered trademark (or an application for a registered trademark) held by a domestic trader, on the basis that the mark lacks distinctiveness in the domestic territory because it is recognized by the public as attributable to the extraterritorial trader. Canadian recognition of the sufficiency of mere reputation in the domestic territory[184] is broader than the position in Singapore, where some minimal or incidental use in the territory is required, but the trend is similar.[185] It is also consistent with common law, although conceptually less difficult, because the extraterritorial trader need not establish goodwill in the domestic territory, but merely that it has sufficient reputation in the territory to prevent the domestic registrant or applicant from claiming it has that goodwill or distinctiveness.

A distinction is, however, likely to continue between an extraterritorial challenge to the validity of a domestic registered mark (or application to register) as just described, and the application of an extraterritorial trader to acquire a domestic priority to obtain a registered mark. The latter is a sovereign grant by the territory of a statutory proprietary right. In this circumstance, the statutory criteria have been, and will likely continue to be strictly

179 See *supra* text accompanying note 111.
180 See *supra* text accompanying note 115.
181 See *supra* text accompanying note 117.
182 The establishment of goodwill zones may be assisted by regional trading treaties or other formal trading arrangements.
183 See *supra* text accompanying note 112.
184 See *supra* text accompanying note 111.
185 See *supra* text accompanying note 162.

applied by the courts.[186] Making this grant represents a territorial regulation of the extent to which an extraterritorial entity will gain a territorial statutory right. It is beyond the common law tradition for courts to directly modify detailed statutory criteria, subject to differing emphases in interpretation.

A projection within this area might include the possibility of regional trademarks being created within formal trading blocks. This could be achieved only by bilateral or multilateral negotiation. It would involve both a substantial harmonization of registered trademark law and a compromise of the sovereignty of the participant jurisdictions.

Parallel Importation: A Projection

Although this analysis is focused on trademarks and unfair competition, parallel importation in the related areas of copyright and patent law cannot be isolated entirely from policy considerations, despite the different nature of protection afforded by these other categories of intellectual property. For example, the traditional position in patent law is trite. It is strictly territorial, with parallel importation of patented items being prohibited.[187] However, in March 1995 the Tokyo High Court (subsequently affirmed by the Supreme Court of Japan) rejected this principle and allowed in that case parallel importation to Japan of products subject to domestic patents.[188] This position could bring both advantages and disadvantages, depending on whether freer trade or territorial protectionism is desired. It certainly exposes a territorial patent owner or licensee to universal or transnational competition. The decision has been the subject of considerable debate with no consensus being reached, even in Japan, as to the acceptability or otherwise of this development.[189] From the opposite perspective, the Parliament of Canada in the *Copyright Amendment Act*, 1997, significantly restricted parallel importation to Canada of books, in order to protect Canadian publishers and thereby, it is said, Canadian culture.[190] These examples, although not directly relevant in the context of this chapter, reflect the policy

186 See *supra* text accompanying note 127.

187 See *supra* note 168 and accompanying text.

188 See *Aluminum Automobile's Wheel Case* (Tokyo Dist. Ct., 22 July 1994 [1992 (wa) No. 16565]; Tokyo High Ct., 23 Mar. 1965 [1994 (ne) No. 3272]; Supreme Court of Japan, 1 July 1997 [1995 (o) No. 1998].

189 See Y. Tsuda & S. Sakuma, "Research on Parallel Trade of Patented Products" (1996) 5 I.I.P. Bulletin 10-16, which summarized the arguments presented, from different perspectives, for and against such parallel importation. The writer would like to thank the Institute of Intellectual Property (Tokyo, Japan) for providing him with this material and other information on the topic. See also Kremen, *supra* note 166 for further reference to this case and an analysis of the conflicting perspectives that it presents.

190 See s. 15, *Copyright Amendment Act 1997*, S.C. 1997, c. 24 inserting s. 27.1 in the *Copyright Act*, R.S.C. 1985, c. C-42, discussed *supra* note 169.

ambivalence of jurisdictions towards parallel importation and render any accurate projection to be quite uncertain.

Trademarks and unfair competition might, however, be distinguished from patent and copyright protection. They do not provide a monopoly in an item (patent) or in a specific form of expression (copyright), but rather simply prevent a confusing usage of marks or other indicia of source or origin. This distinction is more apparent with the tort of passing off (unfair competition) where the key element of misrepresentation can be negated by a statement or disclaimer as in *Seiko*. Given this ability and the explicit policy emphasis of the Supreme Court of Canada and the High Court of Malaysia rejecting proprietary restraint upon resale of personalty, the prospect of passing off being an effective remedy against parallel importation is slim. Furthermore, in *Seiko*, the principle of exhaustion was impliedly applied on a transnational (or even universal) basis, but without explicit analysis to this effect. It is, however, suggested that any detailed analysis of the exhaustion principle will be unnecessary in a passing off context. The primary issue will likely always be the presence or absence of a misrepresentation. A misrepresentation will usually exist in circumstances where (1) the parallel importer has not sufficiently differentiated itself from the authorized distributor and the before and after sales services of that distributor, or (2) the parallel imported product is dissimilar to the genuine product, but is expressly or implicitly represented as the genuine product.

Any common law relief for unfair competition could exist outside these situations only if the test of misappropriation were to be substituted. This test was attempted in *Mattel* in Canada.[191] It protects the domestic or territorial authorized distributor, but is unfavourable to freer global trade.

Statutory infringement proceedings, predicated upon merely an unauthorized use of the mark (or of a confusing mark), is in essence a misappropriation proceeding. There is no element of misrepresentation in which to escape the fundamental issue of exhaustion. It is projected that, despite a literal violation of trademark legislation, courts in common law jurisdictions will ultimately interpret the legislation as not preventing resale of a trademarked item. A principle of exhaustion will be applied to prevent an authorized distributor from using literal infringement to prevent parallel importation, but only in circumstances in which the local or domestic authorized distributor can be linked with the initial (or at least some antecedent) release of the trademarked product in a relevant marketplace. This linkage will likely be established upon any or all of the factors set out earlier in this chapter, emphasizing the presence (or absence) and extent of control that exists between the manufacturer or extraterritorial distributor

191 See *supra* text accompanying note 22 *et seq*. As noted, *Mattel* was subsequently overruled in *Smith & Nephew*. See *supra* text accompanying note 23.

and the particular territorial distributor, in addition to any contractual restrictions that the extraterritorial distributor may have imposed on territorial distributors concerning re-exporting to other territories.[192] The factors are drawn from the authorities noted to comprise two broad perspectives, each of which goes back in English precedent to 1926-30, and presents competing views between universality and territoriality of goodwill.[193] These competing views were replicated in Malaysia in, respectively, *Winthrop Products* (1988) and *Hai-O Enterprise Bhd.* (1992).[194] The more recent trend has been to limit a broad theory of universality in favour of an analytical, factually related, case by case approach,[195] and with the position under the *Trade-Marks Act* in Canada being equivocal, despite policy factors favouring universality.[196]

Applying the factors, it may be projected:

(1) If a distributor is the territorial registered owner of a relevant trademark, but has itself released the trademarked product into an extraterritorial marketplace, it will likely not be able to enforce territorially its trademark rights against a parallel importer of that product.

(2) If an authorized distributor is a territorial licensee, although wholly independent of control by the manufacturer or extraterritorial supplier, it is likely to be similarly prevented from enforcing its territorial licence against a parallel importer by virtue of the principle of a licensee being in no better position than the extraterritorial supplier who released the product in the marketplace and thereby may have exhausted its proprietary remedies.

(3) If an authorized distributor in a particular territory does not release the trademarked product extraterritorially and is the territorial registered owner of the relevant trademark, but is also a wholly owned subsidiary of the manufacturer or extraterritorial supplier, or part of a corporate group, it may not be protected against parallel importation, because it may through its wholly owned status be linked with the initial distribution of the product, and exhaustion may apply directly or through a theory of implied consent. This factor may also apply to *control* of the authorized distributor by the manufacturer or extraterritorial supplier through majority ownership, or even some effective controlling influence, say through ownership of a block of shares (with other shareholding being dispersed) or through common directorships.

---

192 See *supra* text accompanying notes 96 and 97.

193 See *supra* text accompanying notes 52-53.

194 See *supra* text accompanying notes 81 (*Winthrop Products*) and 86 (*Hai-O Enterprise Bhd.)*.

195 This trend was established in *Colgate-Palmolive* in the United Kingdom. See *supra* text accompanying notes 63 *et seq.*

196 For a summary, see *supra* text accompanying notes 46-51.

(4) If an authorized distributor in a particular territory does not release the trademarked product extraterritorially, and is the local or territorially registered owner of the relevant trademark, but is wholly independent of the manufacturer or extraterritorial supplier or seller, then it is likely that it will be able to enforce its trademark rights against a parallel importer of a product bearing that trademark.

(5) In many instances it may be necessary to demarcate a marketplace. Here a direct analogy may be drawn with extraterritorial reputation. The recognition in *Orkin* of goodwill zones (with sub-zones of selling, advertising, and reputation) that reflect a relevant business or commercial territory might be extended to the context of parallel importation, to establish a marketplace for the purpose of applying an exhaustion principle.

The above projections, which are focused on regulation of parallel importation as a distinct legal topic, reflect some considerable uniformity or convergence of analysis by courts in each sovereign jurisdiction – that is, the development of a consensus between independent judicial hierarchies. As likely as this projection is, the containment of parallel importation as a discrete topic is not so likely. More probably, it will be significantly influenced by two greater forces of extraterritorial legal development in response to the globalization of markets, the spreading influence of digitized technologies, and the diminishing significance of political territorial boundaries. These two forces are

(1) movements within the body of law that describe private international law or conflict of laws whereby a territory might assume a judicial jurisdiction to determine alleged infringement of intellectual property rights occurring extraterritorially with attendant "choice of law" issues[197]

(2) a developing recognition of an interface between the protection of exclusivity (or monopoly) through intellectual property law and the dispersion of monopolies through antitrust or competition law. To date, this interface has occurred principally in the European Union and, to a lesser extent, the United States,[198] but also has been the subject of

---

197 See R. G. Howell, "Intellectual Property, Private International Law, and Issues of Territoriality" (1997), 13 C.I.P.R. 209.

198 In the European Union, the focus of the growing interface between intellectual property and competition law is focused on the distinction between the *existence* of intellectual property rights (being a jurisdiction of the member states) and the *exercise* of those rights with a consequent impact on competition (being a jurisdiction of the Community). With respect to parallel importation and trademark infringement or unfair competition, the principle of exhaustion upon first sale in the European Union applies under art. 85, para. 1(c), Treaty of Rome. See McKeough, "Intellectual Property Protection and Freedom of Competition: Competing Policies Under the Treaty of Rome: Copyright" (1985) 1 [Can.] I.P.J. 237 at 262-63; and J. Phillips, *Introduction to Intellectual Property* (London: Butterworths, 1986) at s. 27.5(vi). More generally, see J. Flynn, "Intellectual Property and Anti-Trust: E. C. Attitudes," [1992] 2 E.I.P.R. 49 and T. C.

commentary in Canada.[199] It has considerable potential in the context of parallel importation, given that the availability of parallel imported goods increases consumer choice. It may possibly also be said to increase competition, although this will present the difficulty of what is competition, or what is *fair* competition, or whether parallel importation is anticompetitive by destroying the territorial market infrastructure that is created only by an incentive to an authorized territorial distributor to invest in that territory.

Within all of these converging areas of substantive law, the formality of a bilateral or regional trade agreement or political consortium may also be relevant in projecting future trends. A universal agreement on parallel importation is unlikely, given the breadth and diversity of interests involved, but a regional or bilateral arrangement, even if merely to stipulate factors of the type just noted, would be a significant step, especially between close trading partners. Indeed, the relationship of parallel importation to regional trade has been suggested as a matter for determination through a regional dispute resolution mechanism of a trading arrangement.[200] The influence of such international judicial incrementalism should not be overlooked.

Conclusion

Parallel importation (grey marketing) of goods and extraterritorial business goodwill (reputation spillover) are two areas of dynamic economic or marketplace activity in a global or transnational environment. The jurisdictions of Canada, Malaysia, and Singapore, being Commonwealth common law jurisdictions, possess similar legal institutions and legal methodology. All three jurisdictions are also established trading nations

---

Vinje, "The Final Word on Magill: The Judgment of the ECJ," [1995] 6 E.I.P.R. 297. In the United States, see U.S. Department of Justice/Federal Trade Commission "Antitrust Guidelines for the Licensing of Intellectual Property" available in [1995] 7 E.I.P.R. Supplement and *United States v. Microsoft Corp.* (1995), 56 F. 3d 1448 (D.C. Cir.). With respect to this topic of intellectual property and competition law, I would like to acknowledge the research assistance of Mr. S. J. Ferance (U.Vic. 1998).

199 See generally, *Massie & Renwick Ltd.* v. *Underwriters' Survey Bureau Ltd.*, [1937] S.C.R. 265 at 268, [1937] 2 D.L.R. 213, which discusses copyright and competition law; *Visx Inc. v. Nidek Co.* (1994), 58 C.P.R. (3d) 51 (F.C.T.D.), which discusses patent and competition law; and *Director of Investigation and Research v. Tele-Direct (Publications) Inc.* (1997), 73 C.P.R. (3d) 1 at 30-33, which discusses trademark protection and competition law. See also R. J. Roberts, "Technology Transfer Agreements and North American Competition Law" (1995), 9 I.P.J. 247. In neither Canada nor the United States has parallel importation for reputation spillover been considered specifically in a competition law context.

200 See *Nestle Enterprises Ltd. v. Edan Food Sales Inc., supra* note 28 at 482 and 487-88, in which a defendant parallel importer sought an order of the court to the effect that the dispute mechanism under the *Canada-United States Free Trade Agreement* (1988) art. 1808 should be invoked. There was, however, no need for the Court to deal with the defendant's motion. See also Hayhurst, *supra* note 50.

and are closely juxtaposed to other developed and active trading nations. The response of each jurisdiction, all through the common law technique of judicial incrementalism, is remarkably similar. Of the three, Canada appears overall to be the most universal in the application and development of these topics in law and policy, although it shows some equivocation with parallel importation. Malaysia, although not citing or relying on Canadian authorities, is more universal than Singapore, which has to date relied more on the traditional territorial position most often depicted in the United Kingdom. However, recent developments in Singapore suggest some fluidity and prospect of being less territorial and closer to the position presented in Malaysia.

The topics of parallel importation and extraterritorial business goodwill are almost exclusively economic or commercial in their impact and influence on each society. Any moral or social issues that might be included are essentially peripheral or of marginal significance. The position therefore is one of economic transnationalism in a pursuit of trade and business profits. Substantial convergence is evidenced in the approaches or trends presented in each jurisdiction. This convergence is projected to continue and to be influenced by future potential convergence of other broad areas of law that are predicated upon the interface of territoriality and universality – that is, on transnationalism.

3
Vietnam's Economic Law Transformation within the ASEAN Community

William A. W. Neilson

> As Lenin taught, we are not afraid of capitalist enterprises, but of not being able to supervise and control them.[1]

> By joining ASEAN, Vietnam is conforming with the policy on multilateralism and diversification, and it has helped accelerate the process of Vietnam integrating into the regional and world economy.[2]

INTRODUCTION

Barely ten years ago, Vietnam was an isolated state, paralyzed by the perils of a rigid command economy and largely dependent on military and economic aid from the former Soviet Union. In desperation and after much internal conflict, the Vietnamese Communist Party in 1986 embraced a program of economic liberalization called *doi moi* or "renovation," first reflected in the 1987 Law on Foreign Investment. With this measure, the first steps were taken to attract foreign capital and technology which, it was hoped, would be joined with state enterprises to jump-start Vietnam's economic recovery.

In this chapter, the origins and evolution of the *doi moi* strategy are assessed, with an emphasis on the influences of gradualism and localism that dominated its implementation until 1992. In that same year, the new Constitution codified the legal principles of Vietnam's new multi-sectoral commodity economy. As well, also in 1992, by the Singapore Declaration, the Association of Southeast Asian Nations (ASEAN) established the ASEAN Free Trade Area (AFTA). Barely three years later, Vietnam became the seventh member state of ASEAN. In this chapter, I will also assess the likelihood and significance of ASEAN-prompted economic law changes for Vietnam. The advent of ASEAN Framework Agreements, combined with accelerated AFTA

1 *Far Eastern Economic Review* (6 Jan. 1996) 4, quoting a senior Party official.
2 Vice-Minister of Commerce Mai Van Dau, *Vietnam Investment Review* (29 July 1996).

tariff reductions, will prompt further economic law reforms in Vietnam, most likely in state enterprise, import-export, investment, and competition law areas. Even allowing for the more informal, consensus-based ASEAN decisional culture, the regionalization of economic policy directions poses significant challenges for Vietnam's party-state duopoly. The "ASEAN factor" will be a significant force in *doi moi's* second decade.

THE ORIGINS OF *DOI MOI*

Ten years ago, the Sixth Congress of the Vietnamese Communist Party (VCP) committed Vietnam to a program of economic liberalization, otherwise known as *doi moi* (translated loosely as "renovation"). Under the "leadership of the Party, mastery of the People and management by the State,"[3] economic but not political pluralism was now to be encouraged.

The principles of *doi moi* are codified in the second chapter of the 1992 Constitution, entitled "The Economic System."[4] In a series of amendments that revised significantly the terms of the 1980 Constitution,[5] private firms and family businesses are authorized to "choose their own forms of production" and to set up "trade businesses without any limit on scope and areas of operation provided they engage in branches and trade beneficial to the nation and people." Five different economic interests are recognized: "state, collective, individual, private capitalists and state capitalists."[6] The "potentialities" of these five economic sectors, including the private sector, are to be brought "into full play" by the directing hand of state economic policy (article 16). The complex essence of *doi moi* is found in article 15:

> The State develops the multisectoral commodity economy in accordance with the market mechanism based on state management and socialist orientations. The multisectoral economic structure with its various diverse forms of production organization depends on the system of ownership of the entire people, of collectives, and of private parties with the system of ownership of the entire people and collectives being at the core.

The adoption of *doi moi* by the Sixth Party Congress was a political response to a collapsing command economy.[7] During the 1980s, Vietnam

---

3 See W. S. Turley, "Party, State and People: Political Structure and Economic Prospects," in W. S. Turley, ed., *Reinventing Vietnamese Socialism* (Ithaca, N.Y.: Cornell University Press, 1993) 257 at 259.

4 *1992 Constitution of the Socialist Republic of Vietnam*, trans. Phuong-Khanh Nguyen, in A. P. Blaustein & G. H. Flanz, eds., *Constitutions of the Countries of the World* (Dobbs Ferry, N.Y.: Oceana, 1992) [hereinafter 1992 Constitution].

5 Levien Do, "Vietnam's Revised Constitution: Impact on Foreign Investment," in C. A. Thayer & D. G. Marr, eds., *Vietnam and the Rule of Law* (Canberra: Australian National University Monograph 19, 1993) at 123.

6 1992 Constitution, art. 16.

suffered from hyperinflation, widespread hunger, and serious emigration. Between 1985 and 1988, the annual inflation rate increased to 700% with unemployment running close to 50% of the industrial work force. Foreign observers estimated that over three million Vietnamese were near starvation in 1988, an additional five million were malnourished, while close to two million others had fled the country. With the breakup of the Soviet Union in 1989, Vietnam lost the equivalent of nearly one-third of its annual state budget plus its largest trading partner. Its powerful neighbour, China, had started its economic reforms some eight years prior to the Sixth Party Congress and even the conservatives in the VCP could see that their Chinese Party counterparts still held the reigns of political power in Deng's China. Just as significantly, the gap between Vietnam's economic stagnation and the bustling economies of its ASEAN neighbours was becoming painfully obvious.

The abysmal isolationism of the Socialist Republic of Vietnam (SRV) in the mid 1980s needs to be noted, if only to appreciate the political and social context within which *doi moi* was born, and to better understand the present-day constraints on the emergence of a civil society in Vietnam.

By 1986, 11 years after reunification, the SRV had 24 ministries, 9 state commissions, and another 27 general offices and agencies directly attached to the central state Council of Ministers.[8] The government also included the lesser jurisdictions of 40 provinces and municipalities (now 61), each having 34 to 46 government departments, 500 counties (each one with 22 to 25 bureaus and committees) and nearly 10,000 villages (each with 5 to 10 committees). As well, these did not include the additional management structures of more than 300 institutes and about 130 mass organizations governing specific groups such as workers, women, journalists, teachers, and youth. In the words of one observer, the state had become "absolutized" and, in addition, had become almost totally unconnected to the non-communist world around it, to the extent that government policy makers relied on Soviet interpretations of Chinese and ASEAN economic policies and developments.[9]

As we shall see, there is little doubt that "Vietnam's renovation reform since 1986 has ended the introversion of an autarkic state which was folding in upon itself."[10] Vietnam's ASEAN membership, burgeoning investment

7 Discussed in Huynh Kim Khanh, "Revolution at an Impasse: Impressions of Vietnamese Communism circa 1990," in R. Stubbs, ed., *Vietnam: Facing the 1990s* (Toronto: Joint Centre for Asia Pacific Studies, 1989) and K. M. Schellhorn, "Political and Economic Reforms in Vietnam" (1992) 14:3 *Contemporary Southeast Asia* 231.

8 A. Woodside, "The Struggle to Rethink the Vietnamese State in the Era of Market Economics" (Paper for the conference on Economy and Culture in Eastern Asia, 15-17 Apr. 1994) (Toronto: Joint Centre for Asia Pacific Studies), mimeo at 4-5.

9 *Ibid.*

by Singapore and Malaysia, and bilateral investment treaties with countries as diverse as Indonesia, China, and Australia need only be cited. As a Canadian colleague observed, "imported Soviet prejudices about overseas Chinese capital have evaporated and Vietnamese economists no longer have to go to Moscow to study Singapore."[11]

ASEAN, ECONOMIC REGIONALISM, AND VIETNAM'S MEMBERSHIP[12]

The Association of Southeast Asian Nations (ASEAN) came into being in August 1967, primarily as an anti-communist containment pact, with the signing of the Bangkok Declaration by its five original member states – Indonesia, Malaysia, the Philippines, Singapore, and Thailand. Brunei joined ASEAN in 1984. Vietnam became the seventh member on 28 July 1995, followed by Laos and Myanmar (Burma) in 1997.[13]

Three months before the National Assembly adopted the 1992 Constitution, ASEAN leaders, at their Singapore Summit of 27-28 January 1992, adopted a legal framework to promote economic cooperation in their region. The system is reflected in three documents, beginning with the Singapore Declaration,[14] which summarizes agreements in a variety of fields, including communications and education. The Declaration also outlined a broad-based program for economic integration adaptable enough to encompass the needs of the various ASEAN nations.[15] The second document, The Framework Agreement on Enhancing ASEAN Economic Cooperation, established the ASEAN Free Trade Area (AFTA) which is implemented primarily through the provisions of the third document, entitled The Agreement on the Common Effective Preferential Tariff Scheme (CEPT).[16]

Taken together, the three ASEAN documents provide a remarkably flexible legal framework for regional economic cooperation and integration. The Framework Agreement anticipated future cooperation in a variety of fields, such as finance, forestry, communications, technology transfer, human resources, and tourism. For its part, the CEPT-AFTA Agreement, through its flexible but binding provisions, was designed to ensure the participation

10 *Ibid.*

11 *Ibid.* at 6a.

12 For an earlier treatment of this topic, see W. A. W. Neilson, "Some Economic Law Implications of Vietnam's ASEAN Membership," in J. Gillespie, ed., *Commercial Law Development in Vietnam: Vietnamese and Foreign Commentaries* (Singapore; Butterworths Asia, 1997) at 413-30.

13 Cambodia had been expected to join with Myanmar and Laos but its membership was put in abeyance pending negotiations with ASEAN over the coup by the Hun Sen forces: "ASEAN Admits Burma, Laos; Cambodia waits," *The [Toronto] Globe & Mail* (24 July 1997) A7.

14 "The ASEAN Singapore Declaration" (1992) 31 I.L.M. 498.

15 Note, "Flexible Free Trade: The ASEAN Free Trade Area" (1993) 34 Harvard Int'l L.J. 224.

16 (1992) 31 I.L.M. 506 and "CEPT-AFTA Agreement" 31 I.L.M. 513 (1992), respectively.

of all the ASEAN states, regardless of their various levels of economic development, in the tariff reduction plan. The plan covers intra-ASEAN tariffs on both capital goods and processed agricultural products and, in its 1992 version, anticipated significant tariff reductions to the 0%-5% level by January 2003.

ASEAN's population, with Vietnam's accession to membership, now exceeds 420 million, and it is obvious by any statistical measure that, after its inception in January 1993, AFTA made notable economic progress.[17] For instance, total ASEAN trade with the rest of the world grew as much as 21% (to US$543 billion) in 1994, while intra-ASEAN trade expanded by 24% to US$110 billion in the same year. According to WTO trade data, ASEAN had become the world's fourth largest trading group, ranking behind the United States, the European Union, and Japan. By early 1997, ASEAN's trade was expanding at a faster rate than that of the top three trading areas.

The readiness of its member states to entrust greater linkage, coordinating, and decisional responsibilities to the ASEAN organization has led to the development of a regional administrative infrastructure to which member states must report on a regular and continuing basis. It is estimated, for example, that there are over 225 ASEAN officials' and ministerial meetings annually. These interactions amount to an extraordinary reversal of Vietnam's regional isolationism, which prevailed well into the 1980s. ASEAN's working language is English. With the assistance of ASEAN member and observer states, hundreds of Vietnamese public servants are taking advanced training programs in trade law, English language, ASEAN diplomatic relations, and economic terminology.[18]

All ASEAN members, under the terms of article 2 of the 1992 Economic Cooperation Framework Agreement,"agree to establish and participate in the ASEAN Free Trade Area (AFTA)." AFTA's implementation is to be supervised, coordinated, and reviewed by a Ministerial-level Council and the Common Effective Preferential Tariff (CEPT) Scheme "shall be the main mechanism for the AFTA." The CEPT covers all manufactured products, including capital goods and processed agricultural products. In order to be considered an ASEAN/AFTA product, the good must have at least 40% of its content originating from an ASEAN member. At least 25% of the content must be manufactured by the last exporting country, with the remaining 15% manufactured by any other ASEAN country. The rule of origin is expected to encourage further foreign investment in ASEAN states by allowing producers locating a significant portion of their manufacturing process outside of ASEAN to gain access to the preferential tariff scheme. The Ministry

17 J. L. H. Tan, "Introductory Overview: AFTA in the Changing International Economy," in M. Ariff, ed., *AFTA in the Changing International Economy* (Singapore: Institute of Southeast Asian Studies 1996) at 6-7.

18 "Implementation of CEPT by Vietnam" (1996) 5:1 Indochina L. Q. 44.

of Trade recently announced its intention to issue a Certificate of Origin Form D for exported products on the list that Vietnam has registered with the CEPT scheme.[19]

Under the CEPT, the AFTA member states agreed to reduce tariffs on manufactured goods traded between themselves to between 0%-5% over a ten-year period, beginning January 1993. Given its less developed economy, Vietnam was given more time to reduce its tariffs when it joined AFTA in 1995. Under these terms,[20] within three years of the ten-year deadline for other ASEAN members, Vietnam must extend its tariff reduction list to cover 85% of all goods, and almost all goods in a further five years. Vietnam started its tariff reductions on 1 January 1996 and must have an AFTA tariff rate of 0%-5% by 1 January 2006.[21] Vietnam cut import tariffs to below 60% on a list of 857 goods or commodities under the CEPT scheme. For those products that Vietnam has temporarily excluded from tariff reductions, beginning on 1 January 1999 and ending 1 January 2003, Vietnam must phase in tariff reductions on these products in five equal instalments. Agricultural products, on the other hand, are temporarily excluded from the mandatory tariff reductions through 1999 at which time a five-year instalment plan of tariff reductions must commence. Already, however, the other ASEAN/AFTA members have agreed to accelerate the implementation of the CEPT, calling for the 0%-5% target to be reached by the year 2000, rather than 2003.[22] It appears, however, that Vietnam's deadline of 2006 remains unchanged.[23] There is every indication that Vietnam will abide by its original three-year extension (to 2006), thereby affording its domestic enterprises, including state-owned enterprises (SOEs) more time, sometimes through joint ventures with foreign equity partners, to become more regionally competitive as tariff protection is reduced in stages over the next ten years.

DOI MOI AND THE CONTINUING FORCE OF STATE ECONOMIC MANAGEMENT

The absolutism of the state, previously synonymous with the pre-*doi moi* Vietnam, undoubtedly will be affected by the forces of economic regionalism inherent in ASEAN membership. However, in terms of state economic management in the provincial and national sense, the determinative role of

19 *Vietnam Investment Review* (3 June 1996) 5.

20 "Vietnam Nears Asean's Tariff Implementation," *Vietnam Investment Review* (1 Apr. 1996) 1.

21 Protocol for the Accession of the Socialist Republic of Vietnam to the Agreement on the Common Effective Preferential Tariff Scheme (CEPT) for the ASEAN Free Trade Area (AFTA), ASEANWEB's – The Official ASEAN Secretariat Homepage, 15 Dec. 1995.

22 "ASEAN-Bangkok Summit Declaration" (1992) 5:1 Indochina L. Q. 52.

23 "ASEAN Mulls Proposal by Philippines to Open AFTA to All Trading Partners" *Asian Wall Street Journal Weekly* (13 May 1996) 2.

state authority has been only partly diminished by *doi moi*. Its formidable presence at both the central and local levels, practised under the principle of unified state management,[24] pervades the economic and political life of Vietnam. At the local level, the People's Committees effectively control foreign direct investment (FDI) entry into the new market economy through their control over business entry, land use rights, and labour supply contracts. The same government ministries and local People's Committees that are engaged in the administrative approval and supervision of all business activity also own and operate companies that engage in commerce. These companies are the predominant local partners in foreign-invested joint ventures. This means that the market gatekeepers and regulators in many cases are also partners or major shareholders in companies within their regulatory responsibilities. Sporadic efforts by the central government to separate business and regulatory responsibilities have been successfully resisted, in large part, by local departments and their host People's Committees.[25]

The tensions between business and regulatory interests are exacerbated by the legacy of pre-*doi moi* bureaucratic obstructionism to both foreign and domestic private enterprise and commercial activity. This obstructionism has been described by Prime Minister Vo Van Kiet as "intolerable," and the government has attempted to break the bottlenecks and curtail the abuses of discretionary power in the national and local bureaucracies).[26]

COMMERCIAL RIGHTS AND THE REGULATORY STATE

Before 1986, the Soviet-modelled legal system refused to recognize non-state economic interests. The VCP legal policy was preoccupied with class and nationalism. Few laws in the 1970s were enacted, many were not made public, and few were strictly followed. What passed for commercial law usually took the form of administrative regulations and decrees fixing production targets and product prices. As a result, when *doi moi* was adopted as state policy in 1986, there was almost a complete absence of a commercial rights-based legal system in Vietnam.[27]

---

24 By art. 6, the principle of "democratic centralism" governs the organization and operation of all state agencies, the People's Councils, and the National Assembly. Provinces and municipalities are "administrative units" that are "subordinate to the central government" (art. 118). The VCP is "the leading force of the state and society" (art. 4) and by art. 26, "the State shall exercise its *unified management* over the national economy."

25 Ha Anh, "Provincial Offices to be Reorganized Nation-wide," *Vietnam Investment Review* (8 Jan. 1996) 2.

26 *Vietnam Investment Review* (25 July 1994) 5; Quoc Vinh, "New Ministry Makes One Stop Investment Promise," *Vietnam Investment Review* (20 Nov. 1995) 1; R. Chua, "Vietnam Initiates Ministry Shuffle to Ease Investment," *Asian Wall Street Journal Weekly* (30 Oct. 1995) 20.

27 See J. Gillespie, "Private Commercial Rights in Vietnam: A Comparative Analysis" (1994) 30 Stanford J. of Int'l Law 325.

To this day, most government and legal experts espouse the view that, if there is no law that expressly permits a business activity, then that enterprise cannot be lawfully carried out. Conversely, if private persons cannot legally engage in commercial activities unless they are expressly authorized to do so (in detail), then only the state may act in their place. This conception of legal capacity undermines any chance of flexibly interpreting commercial legislation to fit changing circumstances to deal with new business opportunities or to negotiate constructive solutions with state bureaucracies charged with the regulatory oversight of all economic sectors. Another result is the realization that comprehensive law reform will be necessary if commercial rights are to be recognized by the state bureaucracies, credit providers, and courts.[28]

Under the Vietnamese legal system, the declaration or recognition of a commercial right or legal capacity in the constitution or even in a law[29] or Ordinance will *not*, of itself, confer an enforceable right on the beneficiary class (e.g., the right of private business enterprises to co-exist with state companies or to enter into contracts that are binding on such enterprises). The legal recognition must be brought into existence by a separate legislative instrument, most often a decree, directive, or circular, issued by the agency or ministry responsible for administering the legislation in question. Assuming that implementing instructions are then put in the hands of the line officials, the legislation will then come into effect. Since Vietnamese courts[30] are not empowered to adjudicate the constitutionality or legality of legislation, investors and other claimants are often left to negotiate any questions of coverage or compliance interpretation with the officials whose departments or ministries issued the regulations in the first place.

The end result vests substantial subjective authority in the bureaucracy for the interpretation and implementation of normative commercial legislation, with consequent results for foreign investors.[31] In the words of an experienced Australian observer,

---

28 W. A. W. Neilson, "Vietnam's *Doi Moi* Legal System: Pushing the Limits of Rapid Legal Change," in B. Duffield, ed., *Vietnam and Japan – Japanese Investment and Aid Strategies in Vietnam* (Victoria: UVic Centre for Asia Pacific Initiatives, 1995) 41 at 50.

29 For example, the new Commercial Law passed by the National Assembly on 10 May 1997 purports in art. 12 to extend equality of legal status to traders in the "individual and private capitalist economic sectors." However, recognition of this status awaits separate implementation enactments.

30 Discussed in W. A. W. Neilson, *The Vietnam Investment Manual* (Hong Kong: Asia Law & Practice 1995) at 126-27, the Standing Committee of the National Assembly rules on issues of constitutionality but the cases are not formally argued in the court sense. See *Law on the Promulgation of Statutory Instruments* (Vietnam), 1996, s. 10.

31 Subject to the limited possibility for review by the new Administrative Court, which commenced operations in July 1996, initially in Hanoi and Ho Chi Minh City: see *Vietnam Investment Review* (22 July 1996) 12.

32 Gillespie, *supra* note 27 at 328.

Rather than mapping a public commercial space, legislation in Vietnam has in general reinforced an interlocking system of administrative licences; a legacy of Vietnam's socialist legal system. Considerable effort is now devoted to enacting legislation (e.g., Civil Code and Commercial Code) that defines public-private property and contractual rights with the precision required by a law-governed society. No matter how clearly they are delineated, however, normative laws are administered by regulators accustomed to a socialist legal system.[32]

VIETNAM'S FOREIGN DIRECT INVESTMENT STRATEGY: "THE MARKET MECHANISM BASED ON STATE MANAGEMENT AND SOCIALIST ORIENTATIONS"

Until fairly recently, Vietnam's *doi moi* policy was to move slowly in filling in the legal details of a rights-based market system (such as private property rights, bankruptcy rules, legal services, workers' rights, and economic courts to adjudicate commercial contracts). Early reform initiatives on any of these "very complex issues of domestic institutional change"[33] were judged unwise, because they were too difficult or controversial (between 1987 and 1993) to win over substantial opposition within the VCP, the government, and the senior bureaucracy. During the same period, it was politically prudent for the Vietnamese leadership to push FDI as the major *doi moi* policy initiative because, as in China,[34] "it was relatively easy in the context of Vietnam's political economy."[35]

Under that approach, it was first necessary to promulgate a favourable legal framework for the attraction and protection of foreign direct investment, linking capital and technology inflows to favoured state companies. The state enterprises were devoid of either input, but were relatively blessed with land use rights, trade permits, local monopolies, and licensing connections.

It is no accident that the first major piece of *doi moi* legislation was the Foreign Investment Law (FIL), which was passed by the National Assembly in 1986 and came into effect the following December.[36] Amended several times and under constant review for improvement and revision,[37] the FIL

33 C. Gates, "Foreign Direct Investment, Institutional Change and Vietnam's Gradualist Approach to Reform," *Southeast Asian Affairs 1995* (Singapore: Institute for Southeast Asian Studies) 382 at 396.

34 S. Shirk, *The Political Logic of Economic Reform in China* (Berkeley: University of California Press, 1993) at 333-50; and Gates, *ibid.* at 385-86.

35 Gates, *supra* note 33.

36 *The Law on Foreign Investment in Vietnam,* 29 Dec. 1987.

37 The 1987 Law was first amended in June 1990 to allow joint ventures to cooperate with their foreign partners in setting up these ventures. Another 1990 amendment allowed joint venture enterprises producing import substitutes to enjoy tax incentives equal to that of joint ventures producing exports. In December 1992, the FIL was amended again, allowing, *inter alia,* Vietnamese individuals to co-invest with Vietnamese SOEs

remains the pillar for foreign investors in Vietnam, now under the principal administration of the Ministry of Planning and Investment.[38]

Seen in this light, Vietnam's FDI reforms are located in the earlier phases of reform sequencing adopted by economies in transition to market (or partial market) systems. This sequencing[39] puts Vietnam in the Chinese camp of gradualist reformers, "liberalizing inward capital flows before establishing a domestic market-oriented institutional framework of property rights, contracting company law, and legislation regulating (or deregulating) factors markets."[40]

Vietnam's target for FDI is to attract up to US$25 billion by the year 2000 in its quest to double Gross Domestic Product by the same year. Domestic savings and foreign aid, in an equal total amount, round out the capital infusion targets, although the first element (domestic savings) is a much more dubious proposition than the second contributor (foreign aid).[41]

Asian neighbours dominate the list of licensed FDI projects. Out of a total of almost 1400 projects totalling US$20 billion, nearly 900 projects valued at US$14 billion or 70% of total licensed value (as of mid-March 1996) have involved investors from Taiwan, Hong Kong, Japan, Singapore, South Korea, and Malaysia in descending order.[42] Taiwan's policy of "going down south" has strengthened its ties with Vietnam since 1988 when the first Taiwanese investment was approved by the State Committee on Cooperation and Investment (SCCI). Over 15 flights weekly connect Hanoi and Ho Chi Minh City to Taipei and Kaoshiung, carrying nearly 10,000 investors and tourists from Taiwan every month.[43] There is some evidence that East Asian investors are prepared to take over higher risk Vietnamese investments from skittish Western investors[44] and except for the larger

---

to form the Vietnamese party in joint ventures with foreign parties. The latest FIL came into effect in late 1996: *The Law on Foreign Investment in Vietnam*, 12 Nov. 1996, implemented by Decree No. 12-CP, 18 Feb. 1997.

38 The Ministry of Planning and Investment (MPI) was formed from the merging of the State Planning Committee and the State Committee on Cooperation and Investment. According to the Decree detailing the duties and structures of the MPI, it is "entrusted with socio-economic master planning, management of domestic and foreign investment and drafting laws, ordinances, and other legal documents relating to economic management." The MPI is now the licensing body for both foreign and domestic investment and will also manage and distribute Official Development Aid: "Decree Sets MPI Agenda," *Vietnam Investment Review* (6 Nov. 1995) 2.

39 Gates, *supra* note 33 at 383-85.

40 *Ibid.*, subject to the shock therapy measures taken to reduce inflation in 1989.

41 N. Freeman, "Saving for a Rainy Day, Vietnamese Style," *Singapore Business Times* (24-25 Feb. 1996) 3; Quoc Dinh, "Local Investment Far Below Target," *Vietnam Investment Review* (18 Dec. 1995) 15.

42 *Vietnam Economic Times* (Apr. 1996) 13. In 1997, Singapore-based investors pulled ahead of Taiwan in terms of total capital committed (US$5.3 billion), compared to Taiwan's US $4 billion; *Vietnam Economic Times* (Oct. 1997) 13.

43 "Taiwan Still Tops the Charts," *Vietnam Investment Review* (6 Mar. 1995) 12.

Japanese corporations,[45] are willing to cope with Vietnam's fledgling *doi moi* legal system.

The United States presently ranks as the sixth largest investor just ahead of Malaysia, with 53 projects for US$1.2 billion, two years after the lifting of its trade embargo on Vietnam. Talks between the two countries on economic normalization are continuing, but the United States does not yet offer most-favoured-nation treatment for Vietnamese exports. Since the United States also does not provide access to government programs such as the Overseas Private Investment Cooperation Insurance and Export-Import Bank financing, U.S. traders and investors remain seriously disadvantaged vis-à-vis their competitors from other FDI states.[46] Canada, for the past several years, has settled in as a relatively uninvolved investor in Vietnam, currently standing in twenty-second place among national investors in Vietnamese licensed ventures.[47]

THE VIET KIEU

Article 25 of the 1992 Constitution commits the State to create "favourable conditions for overseas Vietnamese to invest in Vietnam." The volume of overseas Vietnamese, or Viet Kieu, visitors is quite impressive, rising from 30,000 in 1990 to over 265,000 in 1995, but declining to 183,000 the following year.[48] About 2 million Vietnamese live in 80 countries around the world, with almost half residing in the United States, 150,000 each in Canada and Australia, 120,000 in France, and at least 80,000 in Germany, according to the Vietnamese government's Central Committee for Overseas Vietnamese.[49] Most of the Viet Kieu visitors are coming back to visit family. Nearly 50,000 Viet Kieu returned to Saigon (Ho Chi Minh City) for the Tet (New Year) celebrations in 1995. Remittances by overseas Vietnamese are estimated at US$700 million to $1 billion, with up to US$600 million being sent from U.S. Vietnamese to their extended families in Vietnam. It is believed that only a small fraction of the remitted funds are ever placed in

---

44 "Total Quits Refinery," *Vietnam Investment Review* (11 Sept. 1995) 1; "BHP Oil Rethink," *Vietnam Investment Review* (2 Oct. 1995) 1.

45 "Japanese Critical of Investment in Vietnam," *Vietnam Investment Review* (22 Apr. 1996) 17.

46 A. Schwarz, "Vietnam Syndrome," *Far Eastern Economic Review* (28 Mar. 1996) 50-52; S. Michel, "Halfway There," *Far Eastern Economic Review* (28 Mar. 1996) 52. In early November 1997, reports indicated that Vietnam would soon be removed from a list of countries barred from receiving the benefit of U.S. government credit and political risk insurance: "US Ready to Lift Finance Restrictions," *South China Morning Post* (1 Nov. 1997) B4. This obstacle was finally removed in February 1998.

47 Vietnam Law & Legal Forum (July 1995) 4.

48 S. Korsmoe, "Coming Home," *Vietnam Economic Times* (Feb. 1996) 16-21; *Vietnam Investment Review* (20 Oct. 1997) 25.

49 F. Murata, "Vietnam Returnees Get Mixed Welcome," *Nikkei Weekly* (12 Feb. 1996) 20.

Vietnam's fledging and largely distrusted domestic banks. Observers suggest that there could be upwards of US$2 billion being held by Vietnamese residents outside official banking channels. [50]

Most remittance funds, it is believed, are used for basic living expenses. Some funds undoubtedly are undisclosed offshore investments in small family enterprises in which the overseas Vietnamese relative is a silent partner. Despite efforts by the government to attract substantial Viet Kieu investments, current Viet Kieu investment is estimated at only US$150 million, less than 1% of total foreign invested capital, and comprised of approximately 50 Viet Kieu companies recognized under various licensing schemes.[51]

Several attempts have been made by the Vietnamese government to stimulate Viet Kieu investment in the private sector. In May 1993, Decree 29/CP promised tax incentives, multiple entry visas, and a provision qualifying Viet Kieu as local partners in foreign invested joint ventures. However, the implementing Circular issued ten months later omitted reference to the visa and local partner incentives. [52] The Law on Encouragement of Domestic Investment was then passed by the National Assembly in June 1994, becoming effective on 1 January 1995.[53] The Law reiterates preferential tax treatment, provisions for loan guarantees and export credits, allowance for the employment of overseas Vietnamese to assist in the implementation of FDI projects, and, in the case of Viet Kieu investors, special profit patriation advantages. However, the implementation of the Domestic Investment Law proceeds at a very slow pace and it is too early to gauge its effect on Viet Kieu investment decisions.

In addition to the serious uncertainties of both coverage and administration of the Viet Kieu investment regulations, a number of other factors limit the amount of Viet Kieu direct investment in Vietnam. Personal security concerns deter some potential Viet Kieu investors, who are mindful of their being considered Vietnamese citizens under local law even though they have acquired new citizenship in other countries like the United States or Canada. Unlike the expatriate Chinese, the Viet Kieu are often single generation entrepreneurs who have not accumulated sufficient funds for business investment. In those cases where family units have amassed equity capital, many Viet Kieu investors (and local Vietnamese partners) prefer to bypass the banking and project approval systems in setting up small and medium-sized enterprises. This suggests that the official Viet Kieu investment figures are substantially understated. It is suspected that a sizeable number of local businesses in the private sector have silent Viet Kieu

---

50 Cao Ly Dung, "Many Happy Returns," *Vietnam Economic Times* (Feb. 1996) 23.

51 Murata, *supra* note 49.

52 *Circular* 497/TTLB (Mar. 1994).

53 F. Burke, "New Domestic Investment Law," *Eastern Asian Investment Reports* (15 Dec. 1994).

partners. With their stronger capitalization, these small firms are better equipped to deal with government policies on business financing, trade monopolies, and land-use rights, and administrative regulations that generally favour state-owned companies over private firms.[54]

STATE-OWNED ENTERPRISES AND FOREIGN DIRECT INVESTMENT

There is little agreement on how many state-owned enterprises (SOEs) exist in Vietnam. The more popular estimate is in the 6,000 to 7,000 firm range, trimmed from some 12,000 a few years ago.[55] Even while the government has been closing down some failing SOEs since 1991, "hundreds of new ones have arisen, without regard to planning or quality control," in the words of the Chairman of the State Planning Committee.[56]

Some line ministries, like the Ministry of Defence, have been particularly energetic in establishing new businesses throughout the country. The Army Industrial Department has been a successful bidder through its construction and transport firms on nearly every important national infrastructure project (usually with ASEAN, Japanese, Taiwanese, or South Korean corporate partners) involving hydroelectricity, major roads, electric transmission lines and the Second Telecommunication Network (breaking the monopoly held by the Vietnam Post and Telecommunications Corporation, a decision ratified both by the Central Secretariat of the Communist Party and the government).[57] By the end of 1995, 32 army businesses had been awarded much-valued export and import licences. The commercialization of the army takes advantage of its extensive land-user assets, relatively skilled workforce, political connections, and the precedents offered by China and its ASEAN neighbour, Indonesia.[58] Similarly, army corporatization serves to replace declining state budget support and provides employment for the biggest land army in Southeast Asia (notwithstanding large scale demobilization).

Doi moi's gradualist approach to economic and institutional reform has produced some very interesting results for the state enterprise sector and its relationship to foreign direct investment. The core element of the Vietnamese FDI strategy is to join foreign capital and technology with state

54 See e.g. G. Torode, "Hanoi's Hard Road to the Private Sector," *South China Morning Post Weekly* (18 Nov. 1995).

55 J. Dodsworth, "State Owned Enterprise Performance," Occasional Paper 135 in International Monetary Fund, *Vietnam: Transition to a Market Economy* (Washington, D.C.: IMF, 1996) c. 3 at 11.

56 Do Quoc Sam, reported in *Vietnam Investment Review* (27 Mar. 1995) 7. Decree No. 38 – CP, 28 Apr. 1997 on The Establishment, Reorganization, Dissolution and Bankruptcy of State Enterprises attempts to control and restrict the establishment of new state enterprises without prior government approval.

57 Anh Vu, "Military Forces Play Big Role in Business," *Vietnam Investment Review* (26 Dec. 1994) 10.

58 *Ibid.*

companies. Government priority investment areas are directly tied to the development of state enterprises in key target sectors in heavy industry (steel, cement, chemicals, fertilizer, power generation, mining, oil and gas, and transport). It is no accident that the largest foreign-invested joint ventures are in these sectors. Two-thirds of the U.S.$25 billion investment planned to the year 2000 (incorporating both FDI and foreign aid) are to go to these heavy industry SOEs, nearly four times the investment level for light industry and six times that of agriculture. SOEs consume nearly 80% of the state investment budget and employ 90% of the skilled labour force.[59]

For several reasons, the statistics on SOEs bear close watching. Their number and alliances are in constant flux. SOE employment data are "subject to large margins of uncertainty,"[60] auditing standards are highly uneven, and their contribution to the economy is inflated by the SOEs' generous valuation of their land-user rights, which are their principal contributions to most foreign invested joint ventures.[61] Keeping these caveats in mind, the IMF nonetheless complimented the SOE sector on its "broadly favourable performance" in recent years, largely attributed to their transformation "into commercially operated companies with increasing foreign participation."[62] The same study concluded that locally managed SOEs had fared considerably worse, co-existent with the shedding of more than one million employees between 1988-92.

PEOPLE'S COMMITTEES AND SOEs

Nearly 80% of the 3100 industrial SOEs are owned and managed by local government bodies, the largest being the Ho Chi Minh City People's Committee which has over 100 companies and many more subsidiaries under its administration.[63] The Ho Chi Minh City SOEs have attracted nearly 40% of the joint venture equity capital supplied by foreigners.

The powerful role played by the local People's Committees in the three major cities (Hanoi, Ho Chi Minh City, and Haiphong) as FDI gatekeepers and chief regulators is a direct result of the decentralized and market-oriented economic order created by *doi moi*. Under central planning before it broke

---

59 A. Schwarz, "Withering State: The Way We Were," *Far Eastern Economic Review* (2 Mar. 1995) 56-58.

60 IMF Occasional Paper 135, *supra* note 55 at 12.

61 See S. Fahey, "Vietnam: Pivotal Year?" *Southeast Asian Affairs 1994* (Singapore: Institute for Southeast Asian Studies) 337 at 342-43 for an incisive discussion of the lack of "data transparency" in Vietnam.

62 IMF Occasional Paper 135, *supra* note 55 at 11.

63 See generally, "The Committee It Pays to Know," *Asiamoney* (Dec. 1994/Jan. 1995) 19-25 and "New Board to Advise Ho Chi Minh City Investors," *Vietnam Investment Review* (16 Oct. 1995); also G. Porter, "Bureaucratic Centralism and Economic Liberalization," in *Vietnam: The Politics of Bureaucratic Socialism* (Ithaca, N.Y.: Cornell University Press 1993) at c. 5.

down in the late 1980s, government departments at the national and provincial/city levels were entitled to create and own various kinds of production enterprises. These line departments directed SOEs economically and administratively and served as their protectors and advocates when they came into conflict with specialized national ministries such as Finance and Labour.[64] *Doi moi*, much like the Chinese experience under Deng Xiaoping, appealed to these bureaucratic-SOE alliances and secured their crucial political support because they became the main beneficiaries of the FDI-joint venture (JV) linkup. The decentralist tendencies of the early *doi moi* SOE/JV policy strengthened the power base of the People's Committees and have often thwarted the recurring attempts of the centre to focus FDI project approval authority in the Hanoi-based State Committee on Cooperation and Investment (now the Ministry of Planning and Investment).[65]

In the past two years, the national government has attempted to recentralize the political and administrative relationship between the SOEs, their ministry owners, and the national government. Several measures may be cited, namely:

(1) A new uniform legal framework has been established for SOEs. Article 27 of the 1995 Law of State Enterprises[66] reasserted Hanoi's "unified state management" of SOEs with respect to ownership rights, including the allocation of investment capital, the determination of business objectives, and the appointment and dismissal of personnel.

(2) The Prime Minister, with support from the State Planning Committee, has attempted to wean ministries and People's Committees from doing direct business by transferring the diverse business operations of trade departments (starting with Ho Chi Minh City) to a separate corporate group under the administration of a management board on which the trade department has only a minority position.[67] In March 1994, the Prime Minister established economic conglomerates that, in 1995, became the model for 16 newly merged large sectoral SOEs (together labelled Vietnam Incorporated). The general director of each conglomerate or General Corporation is appointed by the Prime Minister. There are now some 80 or more General Corporations, including the Vietnam Rubber Corporation and the Vietnam Steel Corporation. The general department for the management of state investment capital attached

64 T. Vasavakul, "Vietnam's Politics of Administrative Reform," *Singapore Business Times* (27-28 Apr. 1996) 3.

65 Intended as a "single stop shop," the SCCI became known as "the house with many doors." The limited reach of Hanoi compared to the significant power of local People's Committees is summed up in the ancient saying that "the King's order stops at the village gate."

66 Adopted by the National Assembly on 20 Apr. 1995 and proclaimed into effect 30 Apr. 1995.

67 Discussed in Neilson, *supra* note 28 at 54.

to the national Ministry of Finance is to distribute funds and record assets for these conglomerates.[68]

(3) Government Decree 191/CP, which took effect 1 January 1995, attempts to centralize and streamline the FDI project approval process dramatically. According to its terms, most projects must now be appraised by local authorities within 20 days, and a final decision taken by the Ministry of Planning and Investment within 45 days of filing. Large-scale projects deemed high priority are to be appraised directly by the Minister of Planning and Investment and decided by the Prime Minister. Regardless, actual experience confirms that the "hurry up" time limits are rarely met, with bureaucratic blame shared equally by national and local vetting authorities.[69]

These and other national measures serve to underline the first two principal elements of Vietnam's SOE policy: first, to sustain and promote the SOEs as the vanguard instrument of economic development, and second, to draw back to the centre the instruments of political leverage over the management and modernization of strategic industries that are to be dominated by SOEs, sometimes in collaboration with foreign partners.

SOE PRIVATIZATION

Any comprehensive plan for restructuring state enterprise, however, will not include large-scale privatization initiatives. Here again, Vietnam's gradualist approach to economic policy reform will carry the day. In 1993, the national government established the Steering Committee on Enterprise Reform, charging it with the responsibility of reregistering all SOEs, "equitizing" (not "privatizing") some non-strategic SOEs, and creating incentives and regulatory measures that would encourage more efficient SOEs. Under this cautious approach, equitization has been the least visible and largely unimplemented part of the SOE reform policy. Equitization runs counter to the government's heavy support of major industrial SOEs (and their many subsidiaries), not to mention its complementary consolidation of strategic sectoral conglomerates. Other SOEs have effectively avoided equitization by merging their principal assets into joint venture companies with foreign partners.

Although recent steps have been taken by the Ministry of Finance and the Ho Chi Minh City People's Committee to accelerate the pace of equitization, the fact remains that only ten SOEs have been equitized in the

68 See "Vietnam: Trade and Investment," *Far Eastern Economic Review* (26 Oct. 1995) 47 at 50-56 and particularly Circular 61/TC/TCDN, issued by Ministry of Finance (28 July 1995); also "Vietnam Inc. Gathers Its Resources," *Vietnam Investment Review* (15 May 1995) 13.

69 Neilson, *supra* note 30 at 86-99.

past four years, including seven in the south and three in the north.[70] Contradictory government policies, managerial self-interest, employee apprehension, and resistant VCP/bureaucratic alliances will marginalize the government's official commitment to privatization of SOEs for the indefinite future.

THE SOE-ASEAN CONNECTION

Taken together, the 1995 Law on State Enterprises, the Enterprise Grouping rationalizations, and the separate establishment of the General Department for Monitoring State Capital and Assets in State Enterprises[71] constitute significant regulatory reform for the SOE sector. The immediate question is how the SOE framework arrangements will relate, over the next ten years, to the liberalization of trade, marketing, and distribution practices expected of the ASEAN/AFTA contracting states. This is a question that may be similarly addressed to several other ASEAN member economies, particularly Indonesia and Thailand, where SOEs (or private exclusive licence holders) also hold dominant positions of market power in key trading, manufacturing, and distribution sectors.

VIETNAM'S LEGISLATIVE SYSTEM: UNDERSTANDING THE VERTICAL MULTIPLICITY OF ENACTMENTS

In legislative terms, pre-*doi moi* Vietnam (1976-86) was driven by government decrees and directives that were churned out by the VCP, the Council of Ministers, and other central authorities to serve the centrally controlled political economy. The National Assembly met once annually, mainly to rubber-stamp the Party/State combination plans for the ensuing year and legitimize, where necessary, ongoing executive actions.[72] The adoption of the *doi moi* or renovation blueprint by the 1986 Party Congress compelled a concurrent rethinking of the role of legislation (and its administration), if the necessary legal framework for liberalized market regulation and the attraction of foreign investment were to be realized.

The foundational law reform measure was the 1987 Foreign Investment Law. The FIL is undoubtedly a liberal document in terms of its conditions for attracting and protecting foreign direct investment, but like other laws in the Vietnamese system of Soviet-style legislative instruments,[73] it is essentially a broadly phrased document that sets forth only the broad

70 "Equitization Bears Fruits But Still Proceeds Slowly," *Vietnam Law & Legal Forum* (Mar. 1997) 7.

71 *Circular* 61/TC/TCDN, Ministry of Finance (28 July 1995).

72 See M. Sidel, "The Re-emergence of Legal Discourse in Vietnam" (1994) 43 Int'l and Comparative L. Q. 163.

73 Neilson, *supra* note 30 at 125-38.

parameters of FDI regulation. Laws are the legal version of policy manifestos, the product of many compromises within the policy-making councils of the Party and the government and are largely inoperative instruments until they are fleshed out by Decrees or other legislative instruments, including Implementation Instructions to civil servants. Proposed laws that are to be considered by the National Assembly are identified and ranked in the annual Legislation Plans, passed one and two years in advance of the actual introduction of the proposed legislation. Ordinances, on the other hand, are passed by the Standing Committee of the National Assembly when the latter body is not in session. Now the National Assembly meets twice annually, for frenetic sessions lasting a month in each of April and October respectively. The Standing Committee, on the other hand, may meet for up to fifteen days each month during the remaining ten months in a given year. Apart from tax measures, which are reserved to the National Assembly, it is not always evident why some legislative matters end up as laws and others as ordinances. Ordinances have equal effect to laws and are clearly a more expeditious choice in enacting legislation, given the limited sitting time of the National Assembly.

Decrees are the legislative workhorses of the SRV Government, issued by the sponsoring Ministry or equivalent authority pursuant to authorizing language usually found in a law or an ordinance. Then come the directives and circulars, which together flesh out even further the application of regulations identified in the decrees. Therefore – and Vietnam is not unique in this sense – a hierarchy of legislative instruments governs everyone doing business in Vietnam, whether they are citizens or foreign investors. The challenge is to discover at any given time the exact state of the law and how it is being administered. From a nearly moribund legal state, Vietnam in the space of just over ten years has turned itself into a veritable legal factory,[74] with thousands of "legal norm documents" spewing forth each month from what is still a highly bureaucratized administrative system that, we must remember, includes a second level of government in the fifty provinces and three major cities having provincial status.

The Provincial People's Councils produce many enactments that affect national legislative initiatives. Some provincial legislation merely incorporates national standards or implements, on a local basis, national framework legislation. Other provincial enactments complement National Assembly legislation and create, in some cases, additional or unexpected

74 "Vietnam has become a law factory and productivity is increasing. According to one authority, 7,059 legal documents exist at the central level and 54,806 have been issued at the provincial and city level. Of the central documents, 1,607 are in need of amendment and 2,014 in need of repeal. Of the local legal documents, 1,243 need to be amended and 9,985 need to be repealed": "Inside View," *Vietnam Economic Times* (Dec. 1994) 35.

rules for interests caught by the enactments. In other cases, the two levels of legislation do not mesh together and lead to competing or inconsistent interpretation and heavy compliance costs.

The mediation of these competing or overlapping provisions constitutionally rests with the Standing Committee of the National Assembly,[75] but is more often resolved by lower level intergovernmental negotiations or, as a last resort, by the personal intervention of the Prime Minister.

It took five years from the 1987 FIL before the Constitution of 1992 actually legitimated the sharing of state monopolies that supports the FIL and its companion measures.[76] The 1992 Constitution also, for the first time, formally subjected the Party and the government to the rule of law.[77] In this case, that means that both institutions must find their authority in legislation emanating from the National Assembly. Without arguing the point in more detail, suffice it to say that rule of law in this political context is translated as rule by law in which questions of constitutionality, due process, and illegality are not reviewable by an independent judiciary.[78]

The new Law on the Promulgation of Statutory Instruments[79] prescribes in detail the competence, procedure, and order for the drafting, enactment, and promulgation of statutory instruments by competent state authorities. Such authorities include the National Assembly and its Standing Committee, the government, the Prime Minister, ministries and equivalent agencies, the Supreme People's Court, and the Supreme People's Procuracy. The hierarchy of the documents, in terms of their constitutional standing, is confirmed by the new law, and separate provisions are made for required statutory structure, drafting procedures, consultation, and publication.

That said, there is no disputing that Vietnam has produced over the past six to eight years an extraordinary array of commercial legislation of direct consequence for foreign direct investors and those trading with Vietnam. Primary legislation in bankruptcy, land law, advertising, intellectual property, labour, foreign lawyer regulation, taxation, commercial arbitration, and construction law[80] has been promulgated in recent years. A new Civil Code

---

75 1992 Constitution, art. 91.

76 Art. 22 confirmed the demise of the state monopoly over foreign economic relations and foreign investments in Vietnam. The 1987 VIL was clearly in conflict with the then-existing state monopoly provision (art. 21) of the 1980 Constitution.

77 Art. 4 commits the VCP to "operate within the framework of the Constitution and the law," and art. 109 directs the Government to "ensure respect for and compliance with the Constitution and the law."

78 Cf. R. Keith, *China's Struggle for the Rule of Law* (London: St. Martin's Press, 1994) at 19-27.

79 *Law on the Promulgation of Statutory Instruments* (12 Nov. 1996) preceded by Decree No. 60-CP, 7 Oct. 1996, On The Government's Guidance and Inspection Over the People's Councils in the Implementation of Legal Documents of the Higher-Level State Agencies.

80 See generally *supra* note 27.

of more than 850 articles cleared the National Assembly in late 1995.[81] The Ministry of Justice, which did not actually exist between 1957 and 1980, was named as the fourth ranking ministry (after defence, interior, and foreign affairs) in 1992, reflecting its leadership responsibility for spearheading the current program of legal renovation.[82] In reality, at the national level, new legislation arises from the intricate interplay of three expert bodies – the Law Department of the Office of Government, the Office of the National Assembly, and the Ministry of Justice. The importance of a fourth player, the sponsoring Ministry, depends upon the subject matter of the proposed legislation and the amount of discretionary power that is going to be left to the implementing Ministry under the drafting instructions agreed to by the government/National Assembly legislation directors. The VCP has its own law experts who are in regular liaison with their counterpart departments in the government and the Assembly. This is the case with both laws and ordinances, because they are the pathbreaking legislative instruments at the national level.

REGIONALIZING THE VIETNAMESE GOVERNMENT, OR HOW TO COPE WITH ASEAN

An important aspect of Vietnam's new ASEAN membership lies in its impact on the development of an economically literate, English-speaking corps of middle level civil servants in every ministry and national government department.[83] Faced with the English language ASEAN imperative, the need to participate in over 200 ASEAN-organized meetings annually, and the membership implications of numerous ASEAN initiatives, the vertically organized, inward-looking Vietnamese bureaucracy is facing unparalleled challenges of reorganization and retraining.

Prime Minister Vo Van Kiet, in Decision No. 651-TTg (10 October, 1995) recognized the organizational requirements of dealing with ASEAN in the establishment of the National Committee for Coordination of the Activities of Vietnam in ASEAN (National ASEAN Committee).

The National ASEAN Committee has been created to coordinate responsibilities among all ASEAN-related Ministries. The Chairman of the Committee is the Deputy Prime Minister. Other Minister members come from the Office of Government, Foreign Affairs, the State Planning Committee, Trade, and Finance. The Committee's task is to organize and coordinate various ministries and agencies in carrying out Vietnam's ASEAN obligations.[84]

---

81 *Civil Code of Vietnam* (28 Oct. 1995) brought into effect 1 July 1996.
82 *Supra* note 72 at 170-72.
83 "PM sets up ASEAN bodies at all ministries," 7 Business Vietnam (Oct.- Nov. 1995) 6.
84 Decision No. 651-TTg (10 Oct. 1995) of the Prime Minister on Establishment of the National Committee for the Coordination of the Activities of Vietnam in ASEAN,

Separate ministries in turn, have been assigned particular responsibilities for the coordination of Vietnam's participation in ASEAN programs. The Ministry of Trade, for example, is responsible for economic and trade cooperation and the Ministry of Finance for AFTA liaison and commitments.

The Department of Multilateral Trade Policy, attached to the Ministry of Trade (MOT), was established in December 1995 to manage Vietnam's trade policy in regard to both ASEAN and the WTO.[85] Its duties include trade research, the presentation of policy proposals to the MOT, and the drafting of trade agreements.

Apart from AFTA-related legal changes, Vietnam has also become a party to other significant ASEAN-based program initiatives, including

(1) the ASEAN Cooperation Plan on Transboundary Pollution,[86] which covers atmospheric pollution, hazardous waste, and ship borne pollution programs
(2) the ASEAN University Network (AUN), which has been set up by member governments to create regional identity through the promotion of human resources by strengthening the higher education system in the ASEAN region[87] It also aims to promote cooperation and information dissemination among academics in the ASEAN countries
(3) working groups concerned with food security, capital markets development, natural disaster assistance, energy supply and coordination, telecommunications (including Internet regulation), and information on criminal syndicates.[88]

At the Fifth ASEAN Summit held in December 1995 in Bangkok, the ASEAN Leaders adopted the [second] Bangkok Declaration which, *inter alia,*

(1) endorsed a plan to liberalize key service industries such as banking, telecommunications, and tourism to make them more open to intra-ASEAN investments
(2) agreed to implement an ASEAN Framework Agreement on Intellectual Property Cooperation, including the possibility of setting up an ASEAN

Official Gazette (31 Dec. 1995) 27. See also Decision No. 96/TTg Promulgating the Regulations on the Organization and Activities of the National Committee for the Coordination of Vietnam's ASEAN Activities, touched on briefly in "National Committee for Co-ordination of Vietnam's ASEAN Activities" (1996) 5:1 Indochina L. Q. 53 and "International ASEAN Activities" Freshfields: Indochina Notes (Apr. 1996) 5; see also Official Dispatch 6358/VPUB (6 Nov. 1995), *Concerning the Focal Points for Participation in ASEAN Activities.*

85 Decision No. 721-TTg of the Prime Minister (8 Nov. 1995) Official Gazette (15 Feb. 1996) 26.

86 "ASEAN Co-operation Plan on Transboundary Pollution," 11 ASEAN Economic Bulletin 89 (July 1995).

87 "ASEAN University Network Established," ASEAN Update (Jan.-Feb. 1996) 13.

88 "An Outline of ASEAN Cooperation Framework," Business Vietnam (Aug.-Sept. 1995) 10.

patent and trademark system to spur the development of the high technology section in ASEAN

(3) called for the establishment of an ASEAN Free Investment Area (AFIA)

(4) affirmed their commitment to extending to one another preference in trade in services in their acceptance of an ASEAN Framework Agreement on Services "reiterating their commitments to the rules and principles of the General Agreement on Trade and Services (GATS), noting that Article V of GATS permits the liberalizing of trade and services between or among the parties to an economic integration agreement"

(5) "agreed to upgrade ASEAN's human resources by investing and building institutional capacities for education, training, research, science, and technology."[89]

THE ASEAN CHALLENGE TO VIETNAM'S SECOND *DOI MOI* DECADE

The new ASEAN-directed policy initiatives, combined with the timetabled AFTA trade liberalization measures, confirm an increasing regionalization of economic policymaking in Southeast Asia. The accelerating pace of ASEAN Framework Agreements, combined with the hurry-up AFTA tariff reductions, will surely prompt further economic law reforms among the ASEAN member states, including Vietnam.

It is widely accepted, for example, that Vietnam faces serious problems in phasing out its non-tariff barriers. Under the CEPT scheme, ASEAN states are required to eliminate all quantitative restrictions for products under the scheme. Other non-tariff barriers are to be eliminated on a gradual basis within five years of the enjoyment of concessions that apply to these products. Vietnam's difficulty in eliminating quantitative restrictions and other non-tariff barriers rests in the dominant role of its more than 1,250 state enterprises involved in import-export trade. This role far outstrips that of state enterprises in other ASEAN countries. As well, the creation of 80 or more General Corporations raises serious questions about the potential anticompetitive effects of Vietnam's state enterprise policy. The Corporations enjoy substantial advantages over all present and potential competitors in their access to import-export licences, credit, business licences, and preferential taxes. The compatibility of the General Corporations policy with AFTA's scheduled liberalization of trade, marketing, investment, and distribution practices is much in doubt. The same considerations apply to the accession requirements facing Vietnam's bid to join the World Trade Organization.[90]

---

89 See ASEAN Update (Jan.-Feb. 1996) 1-3 (ASEAN Secretariat, Jakarta) and 12 ASEAN Economic Bulletin 409 (Mar. 1996).

90 H. E. Dato Ajit Singh, Secretary-General of ASEAN, Address to the ASEAN-CCI Meeting (Ho Chi Minh City, 21 Aug. 1996), ASEAN Economic Bulletin (Nov. 1996) 275-77; R. Chua, "Vietnam May Be Taking the Wrong Path to Tigerdom by Following the Philippines," *Asian Wall Street Journal Weekly* (28 Oct. 1996) 1.

For these reasons, while the Common Effective Preferential Tariff (CEPT) experience suggests that Vietnam may receive special dispensation in the form of more time to conform with ASEAN-wide legal standards, there is increasing evidence that Vietnam underestimated the scope and potential range of the ASEAN-originated economic policy changes and moreover, that its membership expectations misaligned with the government's political and administrative capacity for internal economic policy reform in *doi moi*'s second decade.[91]

91 "How ASEAN's Newest Member Is Coping," *Singapore Business Times Weekend Edition* (29-30 June 1996) 3; "Hanoi Delays Critical Deal on ASEAN Economic Disputes Resolution," *Bangkok Post Weekly Rev.* (20 Sept. 1996) 13.

Part II: The Civic Sector

4
Parliamentary Supremacy in Canada, Malaysia, and Singapore

Cheryl Crane, Mark Gillen, and Ted L. McDorman

INTRODUCTION

A pillar of British constitutional jurisprudence and practice is parliamentary supremacy: that is, the concept that the enactments of the elected assembly in Westminster are constitutional and, therefore, are not and cannot be determined or declared to be constitutionally invalid.[1] In the United Kingdom, the lack of a clearly identifiable constitutional document against which to assess parliamentary, executive, and other governmental action assures the parliamentary supremacy principle full reign. One important consequence of an unwritten Constitution and parliamentary sovereignty is that the British judiciary has virtually no role in restraining the actions of the elected assembly, or the actions of those to whom the elected assembly has delegated power, provided that the elected body speaks clearly.[2]

Canada, Malaysia, and Singapore share the legal traditions and practices of the United Kingdom, including the concept of parliamentary supremacy. However, unlike the U.K., the three former colonies have documentary constitutions, which outline the structural components of government and the relationships between the governed and the governing.[3] The constitutions

---

1 The classic statement of English parliamentary supremacy or parliamentary sovereignty comes from A. V. Dicey, *Introduction to the Study of the Law of the Constitution*, 10th ed. (London: Macmillan, 1959) at 87-91. A convenient review of Dicey's thinking is provided by E. McWhinney, *Judicial Review*, 4th ed. (Toronto: Univ. of Toronto Press, 1969) at 31-34. See also E. C. S. Wade and A. W. Bradley, *Constitutional and Administrative Law*, 10th ed. (London: Longman, 1985) at 64-75.

2 In fact, British courts have an important role in the restraining of government action. They have long used administrative law concepts, in particular the idea that a public authority may not act outside its powers (*ultra vires*) as a means to exercise control over parliamentary and executive abuse of powers. This use of *ultra vires* is well-explained in W. Wade, *Administrative Law* (Oxford: Clarendon Press, 1988) at 39-48. It remains true, however, that with appropriate clarity British courts can be avoided, despite their ingenuity in finding grounds to constrain parliamentary action.

3 See *The Constitution of the Republic of Singapore*, reproduced in A. P. Blaustein and G. H. Flanz, *Constitutions of the Countries of the World* (Dobbs Ferry, N.Y.: Oceana Publications,

of Canada, Malaysia, and Singapore all contain a provision that establishes *constitutional supremacy* by declaring that laws inconsistent with the Constitution are void or of no force or effect.[4] On its face, constitutional supremacy is inconsistent with parliamentary supremacy, since the effect of constitutional supremacy is that executive action or laws emanating from the legislatures in Canada, Malaysia, and Singapore can be determined to be void or of no force or effect.

Although none of the constitutions of the three former colonies explicitly directs that it is the mandate of the judiciary to determine the constitutional consistency of properly enacted laws, in all three countries the judiciary accepts that this is its role.[5] The judiciary, therefore, can find itself in the position of reconciling the principle of constitutional supremacy with that of parliamentary supremacy. This puts the judiciary in the role of second-guessing the constitutionality of legislation, and of executive and government action.

The questioning of this role of the judiciary as constitutional custodian in Malaysia was the genesis of this chapter. The Malaysian Prime Minister, Datuk Seri Mahathir Mohamed, faced with a court decision that thwarted government action on the grounds of inconsistency with the Malaysian Constitution, posed the following question: "(I)f the British Parliament is supreme, what is wrong if in legislating laws in Malaysia, Parliament is given the same right?"[6] The question recognizes that constitutional supremacy

---

1971, updated by loose-leaf) [hereinafter the *Constitution of Singapore*] and the Federal Constitution of Malaysia, reproduced in Blaustein and Flanz, *ibid.* [hereinafter the *Malaysian Constitution*].

The two principal documents that form Canada's written Constitution are the *Constitution Act, 1867* which was originally enacted as the *British North America Act, 1867*, 30-31 Victoria, c. 3 (U.K.) and was renamed by the *Constitution Act, 1982* which was enacted as Schedule B to the *Canada Act, 1982* (U.K.), c. 11, [hereinafter the *Constitution Act, 1867*] and the *Canadian Charter of Rights and Freedoms*, Part I of the *Constitution Act, 1982* enacted as Schedule B to the *Canada Act 1982* (U.K.), c. 11 [hereinafter the *Charter*].

4 *Constitution of Singapore*, art. 4; *Malaysian Constitution*, art. 4(1); *Constitution Act, 1982*, s. 52(1).

5 The judiciary's authority to evalute the constitutional consistency of legislation or executive or public authority is based on the U.S. Supreme Court decision *Marbury v. Madison*, 1 Cranch 137 (1803). The U.S. Supreme Court asserted that, despite the U.S. Constitution's silence on which body had the authority to undertake constitutional review, it was logical and acceptable that the courts should have this role. Absent other institutions specifically assigned constitutional review functions, courts have successfully asserted this authority in common law countries with written constitutions. For a Singaporean view of this issue, see V. S. Winslow, "The Constitution of the Republic of Singapore," in L. W. Beer, ed., *Constitutional Systems in Late Twentieth Century Asia* (Seattle: Univ. of Washington Press, 1992) at 630-34. Respecting Malaysia, see M. Gillen and T. L. McDorman, "The Removal of the Three Judges of the Supreme Court of Malaysia" (1991) 25 Univ. of British Columbia L. Rev. 171 at 178-79. For a more detailed review of this issue in the United States and Canada, see C. P. Manfredi, *Judicial Power and the Charter* (Toronto: McClellan and Stewart, 1993) at 21-36.

6 S. Aznan, "The Tilt of Power," *Far Eastern Economic Review* (31 Mar. 1988) 15 at 16.

exists in Malaysia, but queries why this should be the case and why parliamentary supremacy should not exist.

The three former colonies have not totally rejected parliamentary supremacy in their respective constitutions. The constitutions of Canada, Malaysia, and Singapore allow for situations where constitutional supremacy must yield to the will of the legislature or executive.[7]

The influence of parliamentary supremacy was dominant in Canada until 1982, when Canada inserted the supremacy clause into the Constitution and adopted the *Canadian Charter of Rights and Freedoms*.[8] Since 1982, constitutional supremacy has been dominant in Canada, as is evident from the increased authority of the judiciary to review the constitutionality of Canadian legislation and government action.[9] By contrast with the recent practices in Canada, despite the clear enunciation of constitutional supremacy in the constitutions of Malaysia and Singapore, parliamentary and executive supremacy, in fact if not in form, has become an important principle of constitutional law and practice in these two countries. In Malaysia in particular, the principle of parliamentary sovereignty can be seen as dominating the concept of constitutional supremacy. The position in Singapore is not as clear as that of Malaysia. Events and cases indicate a tilt towards the parliamentary supremacy principle in Singapore, while recent changes to the Singapore Constitution indicate that constitutional supremacy is in the ascent.

It is the thesis of this chapter that, while parliamentary supremacy is losing its dominant position in Canadian constitutional law and practice, in Malaysia, parliamentary supremacy has supplanted constitutional supremacy in importance. The situation in Singapore, while not as dramatic as in Malaysia, indicates that parliamentary supremacy is an important principle of constitutional law and practice.

The situation in Canada since 1982 is easily demonstrated by the vigour of the courts in dealing with the constitutionality of Canadian legislation and government action in a way that is now comparable with the vigour of United States courts in dealing with their Constitution.[10] However, demonstrating

7 Respecting Malaysia, see *infra* text with notes 64-68; respecting Singapore, see *infra* text with notes 217-36; and respecting Canada, see the discussion of the *Constitution Act, 1982*, s. 33 *infra* text with notes 293-300 and text with notes 311-12.

8 See *infra,* text with notes 293-300, "Patriation, Amendment and Adoption of the Charter."

9 See *infra,* text with notes 311-12, Judicial Review on Division of Powers Issues, and text with notes 313-26, Judicial Review of Charter Issues.

10 A statistical analysis of the changing face of Canadian judicial review under the Charter is provided by F. L. Morton, P. H. Russell, and T. Riddell, "The Canadian Charter of Rights and Freedoms: A Descriptive Analysis of the First Decade, 1982-1992" (1994) 5 Nat. J. of Constitutional Law 1-60. Concerns about American influence on Canadian interpretation and application of constitutional principles are outlined in D. V. Macdougall, "Canadian Legal Identity and American Influences" (1991) 15 Legal

the position of parliamentary supremacy in Malaysia and Singapore is more difficult. Reliance on quantity of constitutional court challenges in Malaysia and Singapore reveals little, although compared with Canada there have been few cases. Instead, what must be explored is the attitude of the executive and legislative branches of government to limitations on their authority that emanate from the Constitution. In both Malaysia and Singapore, several high profile cases and events demonstrate that the attitude of the government towards court interference, even where a court's action is based on constitutional supremacy reasoning, is such that the courts will have received the unmistakeable message that constitutional supremacy is to yield to parliamentary supremacy. In the case of Malaysia, and to a lesser extent Singapore, the legislatures' employment of privative clauses to remove from the courts supervisory jurisdiction over government decision-making and the courts' deference to the will of the legislature and executive clearly indicate an acceptance of parliamentary supremacy.

Constitutional supremacy, particularly as found in its most extreme form in the United States, creates a tyranny of a written, and usually aged, document over the realities and pragmatic needs of modern government. Constitutional supremacy relies on courts to interpret vintage terminology in the light of new circumstances in order to evaluate the constitutional *bona fides* of legislation and government action. Given that the judiciary in Canada, Malaysia, and Singapore are appointed, and once appointed are largely unaccountable for their actions,[11] constitutional supremacy may lead to unelected, unaccountable courts thwarting the will of elected legislatures.[12] Constitutional supremacy can be viewed, therefore, as undemocratic. Parliamentary supremacy is the antidote to the undemocratic practices of constitutional supremacy. Parliament, as the body representing the will of the people as expressed through democratic elections, can be removed from office and laws enacted repealed if the majority wills it. The difficulty with parliamentary supremacy, however, is that the majority may pay little heed to minorities. Constitutional supremacy can, therefore, have an important role in the protection of minorities.

The reconciliation of constitutional and parliamentary supremacy is not the goal of this contribution and neither is "passing judgment" on the emerging practices in Canada, Malaysia, and Singapore regarding their reconciliation of constitutional supremacy with parliamentary sovereignty. This

---

Studies Forum 15-35. A substantive comparison of Canadian-American constitutional jurisprudence can be found in the papers in (1992) 55 Law and Contemporary Problems 1-202.

11 Respecting Malaysia, see *infra* text with notes 51-63, "The Judiciary"; respecting Singapore, see *infra* text with notes 199-215, "The Judiciary"; and respecting Canada, see *infra* text with notes 301-310, "The Judiciary."

12 This paradox of liberal democracies is well described and analyzed in Manfredi, *supra* note 5 at 36-39 and see also 188-211.

contribution will, however, attempt to explain why the three former colonies are dealing with parliamentary supremacy in different ways. The following discussion looks at relevant cases, events, and practices in Malaysia, Singapore, and to a lesser extent Canada to substantiate the thesis that Malaysia and Singapore deal with parliamentary supremacy in a manner different from Canada. The first section looks at the relevant issues country by country. The next section posits several reasons for the divergence in how three countries deal with parliamentary supremacy.

PARLIAMENTARY SUPREMACY AND JUDICIAL REVIEW IN MALAYSIA, SINGAPORE, AND CANADA

Malaysia

Background

Constitutional and Political History[13]

Malaysia achieved independence from Great Britain in 1957 as a federation of nine formerly semi-independent Malay states[14] plus the British Straits Settlements of Penang and Melaka. Sabah and Sarawak joined the Federation in 1963.[15]

The Constitution of Malaysia was based primarily on the work of the Reid Commission established by the British government and chaired by Lord Reid with the explicit task of designing a Constitution for the soon-to-be independent country.[16] The fundamental factor that had to be faced by the constitution-makers was the distinctive racial mix of Malay, Chinese, and Indian.[17] The Chinese and Indian populations were introduced into the Malay peninsula by the British to work in the cities and as labourers in tin mines and on rubber estates.[18] The British deliberately chose not to adopt a policy

---

13 A more extensive constitutional history of Malaysia is provided in e.g. H. P. Lee, *Constitutional Conflicts in Contemporary Malaysia* (Kuala Lumpur: Oxford Univ. Press, 1995) c. 1.

14 The nine formerly independent Malay states were the states of Johore, Kedah, Kelantan, Negeri Sembilan, Pahang, Perak, Perlis, Selangor, and Trenganu. See *Malaysian Constitution*, art. 1(2).

15 See the *Malaysia Act*, Act No. 26 of 1963. Singapore also joined the Federation in 1963 but left the Federation in 1965. See the *Constitution and Malaysia (Singapore Amendment) Act*, 1965, Act No. 31 of 1965.

16 See the terms of reference of the Reid Commission set out in A. Ibrahim and M. P. Jain, "The Constitution of Malaysia and the American Constitutional Influence," in L. W. Beer, ed., *supra* note 5, 507 at 508.

17 According to the 1991 census the population of Malaysia was 18,379,655, consisting of approximately 50% Malay, 10.6% Other (non-Malay) Bumiputera, 28.1% Chinese, 7.9% Indian, and 3.4% others, consisting primarily of aboriginal natives on the peninsula or in Sabah or Sarawak. See *Population and Housing Census of Malaysia 1991: General Report of the Population Census* (Kuala Lumpur: Department of Statistics, 1995) vol. 1, 39-41.

18 See e.g. D. K. Mauzy, "Malaysia," in D. K. Mauzy, ed., *Politics in the ASEAN States* (Kuala Lumpur: Marizan and Sons, 1984) at 147-48.

of integrating the different races.[19] Attempts by the British following the Second World War to create a Malayan Union that would treat the racial groups equally foundered, because the Malays were concerned that they would be dominated both economically and politically by the non-Malays and that their language, religion (Islam), and culture would be compromised.[20] The 1957 Constitution, therefore, attempted to strike a political compromise between the Malays and non-Malays.

Pursuant to the 1957 Constitution, the Malays obtained special rights with respect to language and religion.[21] The Malay Rulers of the states were to remain as nominal heads of their states and retained powers with respect to religion.[22] The non-Malays obtained changes in citizenship laws to ensure they received Malaysian citizenship[23] and thereby avoid becoming peoples without a country, as had happened to Chinese and Indian emigrants in other parts of Southeast Asia.

In the midst of the discussions and debates over the impending independence of Malaysia in the mid-1950s, the distinctive political structure that now exists was formed. The principal characteristics are political parties organized along racial lines and a coalition government. The dominant political party, the United Malays National Organization (UMNO), was formed in the pre-independence period to represent Malays and ensure a federation that provided political balance and protection of Malay language, religion, and culture.[24] The Malaysian Chinese Association (MCA) was formed to represent Chinese interests and the Malaysian Indian Congress (MIC) was formed to represent the interests of the Indian community. UMNO, together with MCA and MIC, formed a coalition (the Barisan Nasional), led by UMNO, which has won a majority of seats in the Malaysian parliament in every general election since independence.[25]

---

19 Indeed, "[t]he immigrants were encouraged to set up their own vernacular schools, newspapers, and associations and to govern their own intra-ethnic affairs, subject only to overall colonial rules of the land. The effect of protection combined with the considerable autonomy accorded the immigrant communities was the creation of a multilingual, multi-cultural, and multi-religious society": see Mauzy, *ibid.* at 147-48.

20 On the Malayan Union generally, see e.g. J. Allen, *The Malayan Union* (Monograph Series No. 10, Southeast Asian Studies, Yale University, 1967); A. Lau, *The Malayan Union Controversy 1942-48* (Singapore: Oxford Univ. Press, 1991). On the concerns of the Malays see e.g. Mauzy, *supra* note 18 at 149; Y. A. M. Raja Azlan Shah, "The Role of Constitutional Rulers in Malaysia," in R. A. Trindade and H. P. Lee, *The Constitution of Malaysia: Further Perspectives and Developments* (Singapore: Oxford Univ. Press, 1978) 76 at 79; and Tunku Abdul Rahman, *Looking Back* (Kuala Lumpur: Pastake Antara, 1981) at 27.

21 See arts. 3(1) and 152 of the *Malaysian Constitution*.

22 See arts. 3(2), 70, 71 and Schedule 8, Part I, ss. 1 and 2 of the *Malaysian Constitution*.

23 See generally Part III, arts. 14-22 of the *Malaysian Constitution*.

24 On the development of the United Malays National Organization (UMNO), see e.g. G. P. Means, *Malaysian Politics*, 2d. ed. (London: Hodder and Stoughton, 1976) at 99-102.

25 The coalition was originally called the Alliance. The name was changed to the Barisan Nasional (or National Front) after the 1969 election. On Malaysian election results

Heavily influencing the political and constitutional experience of Malaysia has been the tension between the races, which manifested itself in riots in May 1969. The riots broke out after non-Malay parties made unexpected gains in the 1969 general election.[26] A state of emergency was declared. Parliament was suspended and the country was governed by a National Operations Council.[27] Following the crisis, the Constitution was amended to, in effect, make it illegal to publicly debate sensitive ethnic issues.[28] The government sought to address the discontent of the Malays by implementing the New Economic Policy, which was intended to bring Malay control of the economy to 30% by 1990 by favouring Malays in government economic policies.[29]

The Constitutional Structure

The Constitution provides for a parliamentary democracy at both the federal level and within the states. The formal structure of the central government is like that found in most Commonwealth countries: a bicameral legislature consisting of an elected House of Representatives and a Senate, which is not directly elected, and a relatively powerless monarch. The Senate

---

from 1955-86, see NSTP Research and Information Services, *Elections in Malaysia: Facts and Figures* (Kuala Lumpur: Balai Berita, 1990). On the 1990 election results see "In Victory, New Tests," *Asiaweek* (2 Nov. 1990) 20-21. On the 1995 election results see "Tidal Waves: Malaysia's Booming Economy Propels Prime Minister Mahathir's National Front Coalition to a Stunning General Election Victory," *Far Eastern Economic Review* (4 May 1995) 14-15.

26 On the 13 May 1969 riots and their aftermath, see e.g. J. P. Ongkili, *Nation Building in Malaysia 1946-1974* (Singapore: Oxford Univ. Press, 1985) at 38-52; Goh Cheng Tek, *The May Thirteenth Incident and Democracy in Malaysia* (Kuala Lumpur: Oxford Univ. Press, 1971); Tunku Abdul Rahman, *May 13: Before and After* (Kuala Lumpur: Utusan Melayu Press, 1969); and F. V. Gagliano, *Communal Violence in Malaysia 1969: The Political Aftermath* (Athens, Ohio: Ohio Univ. Centre for Int'l Studies, 1970).

27 For the Proclamation of the Emergency pursuant to art. 150 of the *Malaysian Constitution* see P. U. (A) 145/69, 15 May 1969. Uncompleted elections in Sabah and Sarawak were suspended by the *Emergency (Essential Powers) Ordinance*, 1969, P.U. (A) 146/69, 15 May 1969. An order dated 15 May 1969 also directed the legislative assemblies of the states not to meet: see P.U. (A) 147/69.

28 *See* the *Sedition Act*, 1948, Laws of Malaysia, Act 15, as amended by P.U. (A) 282/70, ss. 3(1)(f), 3(2)(b),(c). See also the *Constitution (Amendment) Act*, 1971, Laws of Malaysia, Act A30, ss. 2-4 amending arts. 10, 63, and 72 of the Federal Constitution allowing Parliament to pass laws restricting freedom of speech otherwise protected by art. 10 "in the interest of the security of the Federation ... public order or morality" [see the amended version of art. 10(2)(a)] and "prohibiting the questioning of any matter, right ... [or] privilege" set out with respect to citizenship, language rights, or quotas in favour of the Malays [see the amended version of art. 10(4)]. It made members of Parliament and state legislative assemblies subject to charges of sedition in respect of these matters [see arts. 63 and 72 subsequently modified by the *Constitution Amendment Act,* 1993, Laws of Malaysia, Act A848]. It also made amendments to these sections subject to the consent of the Conference of Rulers [see amended art. 159(5)].

29 The New Economic Policy is set out in Government of Malaysia, *Second Malaysia Plan, 1971-75* (Kuala Lumpur: Government Press, 1971) especially paras. 133-56.

consists of two senators elected by each of the 13 state legislative assemblies and 43 senators appointed by the King on the advice of the Cabinet.[30] The federal head of state, the King (Yang di-Pertuan Agong),[31] is selected by the Conference of Rulers (Majlis Raja-Raja), which, for the purpose of the selection of the King, consists of the nine Malay state sultans.[32] The King chosen by the Conference of Rulers remains King for five years.[33] The choice of King has traditionally been rotated among the sultans of each Malay state.[34] On most issues the King acts on the advice of cabinet or cabinet ministers, including the Prime Minister.[35]

The Malaysian Constitution, despite providing for a division of powers between the states and central government, is heavily weighted in favour of the central government: "Matters of local importance remain with the States but it is evident that matters of the first level of government importance like external affairs, defence, internal security, finance, civil law and procedure, and the administration of justice, citizenship, trade, commerce and industry, are within the Federal competence."[36]

The Constitution sets out a number of fundamental liberties.[37] These include the right not to be deprived of life or liberty save in accordance with law,[38] protection against unlawful detention,[39] the right to consult a legal practitioner of the person's own choice,[40] the prohibition of slavery,[41] protection against retrospective criminal law and repeated trials,[42] the right to

---

30 *Malaysian Constitution*, art. 45 and the Seventh Schedule. See also art. 40 with respect to the Yang di-Pertuan Agong acting on the advice of cabinet. Initially, art. 45 called for 16 appointed senators and two senators elected by the legislative assemblies of each of 11 states. Subsequent amendments in 1964 (*Constitution (Amendment) Act, 1964*, Laws of Malaysia, Act No. 19 of 1964), 1965 (*Constitution and Malaysia (Singapore Amendment) Act, 1965*, Laws of Malaysia, Act No. 53 of 1965), and 1978 (*Constitution (Amendment) Act, 1978*, Laws of Malaysia, Act A442) have increased the number of appointed senators to forty-three.

31 *Ibid.* at art. 32(1).

32 *Ibid.* at art. 32(3) and the Fifth Schedule, art. 7.

33 *Ibid.* at art. 32(3).

34 See also the provisions of the Third Schedule, art. 4 of the *Malaysian Constitution*.

35 *Ibid.* at art. 40.

36 Tun Sri Datuk Mohd. Salleh Bin Abas, "Federalism in Malaysia – Changes in the First Twenty Years," in Tun Mohamed Suffian, H. P. Lee, and F. A. Trindade, eds., *The Constitution of Malaysia – Its Development: 1957-1977* (Kuala Lumpur: Oxford Univ. Press, 1978). See generally, A. Ibrahim and A. Joned, *The Malaysian Legal System* (Kuala Lumpur: Dewan Bahasa Pendidikan Malaysia, 1987) at 180-86; for more detail, see B. H. Shafruddin, *The Federal Factor in the Government and Politics of Peninsular Malaysia* (Singapore: Oxford Univ. Press, 1987).

37 Part II of the *Malaysian Constitution*, arts. 5-13.

38 *Ibid.* at art. 5(1).

39 *Ibid.* at art. 5(2) and (4).

40 *Ibid.* at art. 5(3).

41 *Ibid.* at art. 6.

42 *Ibid.* at art. 7

equality before the law and equal protection of the law,[43] protection against discrimination on the basis of religion, race, descent, or place of birth,[44] freedom of speech,[45] rights with respect to education,[46] and the right not to be deprived of property without adequate compensation.[47] Many of these fundamental liberties are, however, constrained in varying degrees.[48] For instance, protection against discrimination is qualified with respect to provisions for the protection, well-being, advancement of, or reservation of a reasonable proportion of suitable positions in the public service to Malays, the aboriginal people of the Malay peninsula, and the natives of Sabah or Sarawak.[49] Freedom of speech, expression, assembly, or association can be constrained "in the interest of the security of the Federation" or "public order or morality."[50]

The Judiciary

At the top of the Malaysian court structure sits the Federal Court ("Mahkameh Persekatuan"),[51] with a president of the Court known as the Chief Justice of the Federal Court.[52] In 1985, this became the undisputed highest court in Malaysia when the possibility of appeal to the Judicial Committee of the Privy Council was removed.[53] Below the Federal Court are the Court of Appeal,[54] and two co-existent High Courts, one for peninsular Malaysia and one for Sabah and Sarawak, each with its own Chief Justice.[55] The Federal Court, Court of Appeal, and High Courts are creatures of the Constitution,[56]

---

43 *Ibid.* at art. 8(1).
44 *Ibid.* at art. 8(2).
45 *Ibid.* at art. 10(1).
46 *Ibid.* at art. 12.
47 *Ibid.* at art. 13.
48 See e.g. H. M. Hashim, "Human Rights in Malaysia" [1978] 1 M.L.J. lxi. See also Ibrahim and Jain, *supra* note 16, 507 at 521-24.
49 *Malaysian Constitution,* arts. 8(2), 8(5)(c), 153, and 160 (definition of "Malay").
50 *Ibid.* at art. 10(2).
51 *Ibid.* at art. 121(2), formerly called the Mahkamah Agong or Supreme Court prior to a constitutional amendment in 1994, *Constitution (Amendment) Act 1994,* Laws of Malaysia Act A885.
52 *Malaysian Constitution,* art. 122. Before a constitutional amendment in 1994, the person holding the highest judicial position in the court was referred to as the Lord President: *Constitution (Amendment) Act 1994,* Laws of Malaysia Act A885.
53 A 1984 constitutional amendment removed the possibility of appeal from Malaysia to the Privy Council: *Constitution (Amendment) (No. 2) Act 1984,* Laws of Malaysia Act A585. The right of appeal to the Privy Council had previously been restricted in 1975 and 1978. See Tan Sri Dato Abdul Hamid Omar, "The Administration of Justice in Malaysia" [1987] Denning L.J. 1 at 11-12. See generally H. Chan Hui Meng, "The Privy Council as Court of Last Resort in Singapore and Malaysia: 1957-1983," in A.J. Harding, ed., *The Common Law in Singapore and Malaysia* (Singapore: Butterworths, 1985) at 75.
54 *Malaysian Constitution,* art. 121(1B), 122A.
55 *Ibid.* at art. 121(1).
56 See *supra* notes 51, 52, 54, and 55.

whereas the non-superior courts, the Magistrates' Courts and Sessions Courts, have been established pursuant to the federal *Courts of Judicature Act, 1964*.[57] Although all the above courts rely on federal law or the Constitution for the delineation of jurisdiction and procedure, they deal with issues of both state and federal law. Dealing specifically with Islamic law matters is the Syariah Court and in Sabah and Sarawak there are native courts. These courts have narrow jurisdictions.[58]

The Malaysian Constitution contains express provisions to secure the independence of individual judges. Judges of the superior courts have security of tenure until the age of 65.[59] A complicated procedure for removal of a sitting superior court judge exists.[60] Where the Prime Minister, or the Chief Justice after consultation with the Prime Minister, recommends to the King that a judge of a superior court ought to be removed because of misbehaviour or inability due to sickness to discharge the functions of judge, the King will appoint a tribunal to investigate the situation. The King may, on the recommendation of the tribunal, remove the judge from office. The tribunal is to consist of not less than five members who hold or have held high judicial office in Malaysia or, if the King deems appropriate, in other parts of the Commonwealth.[61] Another protection for the independence of judges is the constitutional requirement that remuneration and other terms of office of a judge may not be altered to one's disadvantage following appointment.[62] Also, the conduct of a judge can only be discussed in Parliament pursuant to a substantive motion of which notice has been given by a quarter of the members of the House.[63]

Parliamentary Supremacy in Malaysia

That parliamentary supremacy is the dominant constitutional principle in Malaysia is evident in the constraints imposed on judicial review and in the restraint shown by the judiciary with respect to judicial review. The discussion below briefly surveys some of the constraints on judicial review, provides examples of judicial restraint, and suggests some possible explanations for judicial restraint in Malaysia and the apparent trend to increasing judicial restraint.

---

57 *Laws of Malaysia*, Act No. 91. On the Malaysian court structure, see generally Ibrahim and Joned, *supra* note 36 at 269-338 and Abdul Hamid Omar, *supra* note 53 at 6-19.

58 Ibrahim and Joned, *supra* note 36 at 48-50 and 60-71.

59 *Malaysian Constitution*, arts. 125(1) and (9).

60 *Ibid.* at art. 125(3), (4), and (5). On the procedure for the removal of superior court judges in Canada, see P. H. Russell, *The Judiciary in Canada* (Toronto: McGraw-Hill Ryerson, 1987) at 175-81.

61 *Malaysian Constitution*, art. 125(4).

62 *Ibid.* at art. 125(7).

63 *Ibid.* at art. 127.

Constraints on Judicial Review in the Constitution

The Constitution has, from its inception, precluded judicial review of legislation on the grounds that it imposes restrictions on the right to freedom of movement or the right to freedom of speech, assembly, or association.[64] It has also precluded judicial review of legislation intended to deal with subversion where that legislation interferes with liberty of the person, rights to property, freedom of movement, or freedom of speech, assembly, or association.[65] Judicial review of the declaration of an emergency in which, to the satisfaction of the King, security, economic life, or public order are threatened is now also precluded pursuant to a 1981 amendment to the Constitution.[66]

Perhaps the most significant provision of the Constitution with respect to parliamentary supremacy is article 121 which, pursuant to an amendment in 1988, provides that the High Courts and inferior courts of Malaysia only "have such jurisdiction and powers as may be conferred by or under federal law."[67] It has been said of this amendment that "[u]nbeknownst to society, a deft stroke of the parliamentary draftsman's pen and the voice of the mighty majority in the legislature have begun to deal death strokes to judicial independence. There is now nothing but moral conscience to prevent that majority from enacting ordinary statutes, pursuant to this amendment, to seal the fate of the judiciary."[68]

Statutory Constraints on Judicial Review

Two features of Malaysian statutes contribute to the dominance of parliamentary supremacy over judicial review. One is the tendency to give a very broad scope to the discretionary powers of government administrators. The other is the use of broadly drafted privative clauses.

An example of the kind of broad discretionary powers that are often conferred on government administrators is the power of "absolute discretion" given in the *Printing Presses and Publications Act 1984*.[69] The Home Minister (who is the Prime Minister) has an absolute discretion with respect to the granting of a licence for a printing press[70] or a permit to publish a

---

64 *Ibid.* at art. 4(2).

65 *Ibid.* at art. 149. See the discussion in R. Yatim, *Freedom Under Executive Power in Malaysia: A Study of Executive Supremacy* (Kuala Lumpur: Endowment Sdn. Bhd., 1995) at 91-93.

66 Art. 150(8), added by *Constitution (Amendment) Act, 1981*, Laws of Malaysia, Act A514, s. 15(d).

67 *Constitution (Amendment) Act, 1988*, Laws of Malaysia, Act A704, s. 8(b).

68 A. Khalid and Chee Yoke Ling, "Constitutional Law," in A. Krishnan, ed., *Survey of Malaysian Law 1987* (Kuala Lumpur: Malayan L. J., 1989) 78 at 82. See also the discussion in Yatim, *supra* note 65 at 103-105.

69 Laws of Malaysia, Act 301.

70 *Ibid.* at s. 3. A "printing press" is defined in s. 3(2) as "the machine, equipment or article for printing, copying or reproducing any document described in Schedule I."

newspaper.[71] The Home Minister also has an absolute discretion under the Act to prohibit the printing, importation, publishing, or possession of any publication that "is likely to be prejudicial to public order, morality, [or] security."[72] The Act was amended in 1987 to add the words "or is likely to alarm public opinion" to the scope of this discretion.[73]

A second example can be found in the *Internal Security Act, 1960*[74] which provides that, "[i]f the Minister is satisfied that the detention of any person is necessary with a view to preventing him from acting in any manner prejudicial to the security of Malaysia or any part thereof or to the maintenance of essential services therein or to the economic life thereof, he may make an order ... directing that that person be detained for any period not exceeding two years."[75] Similarly broad discretionary powers are provided in the *Dangerous Drugs (Special Preventative Measures) Act 1985*[76] and the *Emergency (Public Order and Prevention of Crime) Ordinance 1969.*[77]

Many statutes in Malaysia also contain broadly drafted privative clauses that, if interpreted liberally, give considerable support to parliamentary supremacy by restraining judicial review. For example, the *Internal Security Act, 1960*[78] which allows for detention without trial for up to 60 days and subsequent detentions for two-year periods on orders of the Home Minister, was amended in 1989 to provide that "[t]here shall be no judicial review in any court of, and no court shall have or exercise any jurisdiction in respect of, any act done or decision made by the [King] or the Minister in the exercise of their discretionary power in accordance with this Act, save in regard to any question on compliance with any procedural requirement in this Act governing such act or decision."[79] For the purposes of the privative clause, judicial review is defined to include applications for mandamus, prohibition, certiorari, declaration, injunction, the writ of habeas corpus, "or

---

Schedule 2 refers to "Letterpress, Lithography, Gravure, Intaglio or any other process of 1,000 impressions per hour or more."

71 *Ibid.* at s. 6. A "newspaper" is defined in s. 2 as "any publication containing news, intelligence, reports of occurrences or any remarks, observations or comments, in relation to such news intelligence or occurrences, or to any other matter of public interest, or any magazine, comic or other forms of periodical printed in any language for sale or free distribution at regular or irregular intervals, but does not include any publication published by or for the Federal or any State Government or the Government of Singapore."

72 *Ibid.* at s. 7(1).

73 *Printing Presses and Publications (Amendment) Act 1987*, Laws of Malaysia, Act A684, s. 3, amending s. 7(1) of the *Printing Presses and Publications Act 1984*.

74 Laws of Malaysia, Act 82.

75 *Ibid.* at s. 8(1).

76 Laws of Malaysia, Act 316, s. 11.

77 P.U.(A) 187/1969, s. 7.

78 *Supra* note 74.

79 *Internal Security (Amendment) Act 1989*, Laws of Malaysia, Act A739, s. 2, adding ss. 8B, 8C, and 8D to the *Internal Security Act 1960*.

any other suit, action or other legal proceedings relating to or arising out of any act done or decision made by the [King] or the Minister in accordance with this Act."[80] Identical privative clauses were also inserted in the *Emergency (Public Order and Prevention of Crime) Ordinance*[81] and the *Dangerous Drugs (Special Preventative Measures) Act 1985*[82] in 1989.

In 1990 a privative clause was also added to the *Societies Act 1966*[83] to discourage judicial review of decisions by political parties with respect to their constitutions, rules, or regulations. According to the added privative clause, such a decision "shall be final and conclusive and such decision shall not be challenged, appealed against, reviewed, quashed or called in question in any court on any ground, and no court shall have jurisdiction to entertain or determine any suit, application, question or proceeding on any ground regarding the validity of such decision."[84]

The previously noted *Printing Presses and Publications Act 1984*,[85] which provides for licensing the use of printing presses and the granting of permits for the publication of newspapers,[86] was amended in 1987 to provide that no person is to be given an opportunity to be heard with respect to an application for a licence or permit, or relating to the revocation or suspension of a licence or permit, under the Act.[87] The Act was further amended in 1987 to provide that "any decision of the Minister to refuse to grant or to revoke or to suspend a licence or permit shall be final and shall not be called in question in any court on any ground whatsoever."[88]

Numerous other acts contain privative clauses that attempt to preclude judicial review. One type of common privative clause provides that the "decision of the Minister shall be final and shall not be questioned in any court of law."[89] This has been held to preclude review on questions of law but not

80 Section 8C of the *Internal Security Act 1960*, added by the *Internal Security (Amendment) Act 1989*, *supra* note 79, s. 2.

81 *Emergency (Public Order and Prevention of Crime) (Amendment) Act 1989*, Laws of Malaysia, Act A740, s. 2, adding ss. 7C to 7E.

82 *Dangerous Drugs (Special Preventative Measures) (Amendment) Act 1989*, Laws of Malaysia, Act A738, s. 2, adding ss. 11C to 11E.

83 Revised 1987, Laws of Malaysia, Act 335.

84 *Societies (Amendment) Act 1990*, Laws of Malaysia, Act A743, s. 2 adding s. 18C to the *Societies Act 1966*.

85 *Supra* note 69.

86 Sections 3, 5, and 6.

87 *Printing Presses and Publications (Amendment) Act 1987*, *supra* note 73, s. 9, adding s. 13B to the *Printing Presses and Publications Act 1984*, *supra* note 69.

88 *Printing Presses and Publications (Amendment) Act 1987*, *supra* note 73, s. 9, adding s. 13A to the *Printing Presses and Publications Act 1984*.

89 See e.g. *Immigration Act 1959-1963*, Revised 1975, Laws of Malaysia, Act 115 of 1975, s. 59A added by *Immigration (Amendment) Act 1989*, Laws of Malaysia, Act A719; *Housing Developers (Control and Licensing) Regulations 1989*, P.U.(A) 58/1989, s. 12; *Malaysian Timber Industry Board (Incorporation) Act, 1973*, Laws of Malaysia, Act 105, s. 18.

to preclude certiorari on questions of jurisdiction.[90] Another type of privative clause found in Malaysian statutes provides that a decision, usually of an administrative board, shall be final.[91] On the basis of the English case, *Re Gilmore*,[92] Malaysian commentators are of the view that this only precludes review on questions of fact but not on questions of law.[93]

Conservative Approach to Judicial Review

The constraints on judicial review provided by constitutional limitations on the scope of judicial review, broad discretionary powers, and privative clauses might be of little significance regarding parliamentary supremacy if the judiciary were to narrowly interpret these constraints. Observers of judicial review in Malaysia have concluded, however, that the Malaysian judiciary has taken a conservative approach to judicial review through a reluctance to invalidate laws on constitutional grounds,[94] interfere with the effect of administrative discretion through the use of prerogative writs,[95] or limit the effect of privative clauses.[96]

---

90 See *Wong Yet Eng v. Chin Cheng Foo*, [1985] 1 M.L.J. 36 (Fed. Ct.).

91 See e.g. *Malaysian Cocoa Board (Incorporation) Act 1988*, Laws of Malaysia, Act 343, s. 12(1); *The Optical Act 1991*, Laws of Malaysia, Act 469, s. 25(5); *Banking and Financial Institutions Act 1989*, Laws of Malaysia, Act 372, s. 117; *The Railway Act 1991*, Laws of Malaysia, Act 463, s. 79(6); *Ports (Privatisation) Act 1990*, Laws of Malaysia, Act 422 of 1990, s. 10(4); *Electricity Supply Act 1990*, Laws of Malaysia, Act 447, s. 18(2); *Malaysian Agricultural Research and Development Institute (Amendment) Act 1990*, Act A757, adding s. 7A(9) to the *Malaysian Agricultural Research and Development Institute Act 1960*, Laws of Malaysia, Act 11. Similar privative clauses are contained in the following Acts: *Bank Pertanian Malaysia (Amendment) Act 1990*, Laws of Malaysia, Act A758; *Federal Agricultural Marketing Authority (Amendment) Act 1990*, Laws of Malaysia, Act A759; *Farmers Organization Authority (Amendment) Act 1990*, Laws of Malaysia, Act A760; *Muda Agricultural Development Authority (Amendment) Act 1990*, Laws of Malaysia, Act A761; *Kemubu Agricultural Development Authority (Amendment) Act 1990*, Laws of Malaysia, Act A762; *Lembuga Kemajuan Ikan Malaysia (Amendment) Act 1990*, Laws of Malaysia, Act A763 and A764.

92 [1957] 1 All E.R. 796.

93 See e.g. Gan Ching Chuan, "Administrative Law," in M. Sirag, ed., *Survey of Malaysian Law 1989* (Kuala Lumpur: Malayan L. J., 1991) at 19; and M.P. Jain, "Administrative Law in Malaysia," in M. B. Hooker, ed., *Malaysian Legal Essays* (Kuala Lumpur: Malayan L. J., 1986) 213 at 255-56.

94 According to Professor Shad S. Faruqi, courts in Malaysia "have shown extreme reluctance to invalidate parliamentary legislation on grounds of constitutionality. Our judges seem to be steeped in the British tradition of parliamentary supremacy which has no legal basis here": S. S. Faruqi, "Role of the Judiciary: The Courts and the Constitution," in Aliran, *Reflections on the Malaysian Constitution* (Penang: Aliran, 1987) at 110.

95 See e.g. H. Chaud, "Two Decades of Administrative Law in Malaysia," in *Developments in Malaysian Law: Essays to Commemorate the Twentieth Anniversary of the Faculty of Law, University of Malaya* (Petaling Jaya: Pelanduk Publications, 1992) 1 at 27-30; C. M. Chinkin, "Abuse of Discretion in Malaysia and Singapore," in Harding, *supra* note 53, 261 at 288. After reviewing the use of various prerogative writs in Malaysia, Professor M. P. Jain concluded that "[o]n the whole, the remedial law in Malaysia, when compared with its counterpart in other common law countries, would appear to be somewhat restrictive. Public power is growing apace in Malaysia as in other countries but

Prerogative Writs and the Conservative Approach to Interfering with the Exercise of Discretion Malaysian courts have adopted the principle applied in other common law jurisdictions that the exercise of discretion must be fair and reasonable.[97] The determination of "fairness" and "reasonableness" gives the court considerable latitude to either intervene or not intervene in the exercise of administrative discretion.[98] Generally, the courts in Malaysia have taken a deferential stance with respect to the exercise of discretion.[99]

In the context of preventative detention, challenges to the exercise of the broad discretion granted by the *Internal Security Act 1960*,[100] the *Dangerous Drugs (Special Preventative Measures) Act 1985*,[101] or the *Emergency (Public Order and Prevention of Crime) Ordinance 1969*[102] have been largely constrained to a showing that the discretion has been exercised in bad faith.[103] It has also been held that the onus of proving bad faith is on the person challenging the exercise of discretion[104] and that this onus "is normally extremely difficult to discharge," evidence of mere suspicion of bad faith not being sufficient to discharge the onus.[105]

The discretion of the Minister to refuse an application for a licence or permit in his absolute discretion under the *Printing Presses and Publications Act 1984*[106] was reviewed in a case involving an application to publish a magazine in the Malay language called *Seruan Aliran*.[107] The High Court granted the application for certiorari and mandamus, but this decision was

---

the remedial law is not keeping pace with this trend": M.P. Jain, "Constitutional Remedies," in Trindade and Lee, *supra* note 20, 157 at 184.

96 See e.g. Gan Ching Chuan, "Private Clauses: Post-*Fire Bricks* Development and Trend" [1991] J. of Malaysian and Comparative L. 109 at 115, 126-27; and Jain, *supra* note 93 at 257-61; and the discussion of *Senator Lau Keng Siong v. Ng Cheng Kiat* [1990] 3 M.L.J. 417 in Gan Ching Chuan, "Administrative Law," in M. Siraj, ed., *Survey of Malaysian Law, 1990* (Kuala Lumpur: Malayan L. J., 1992) 23 at 54.

97 See Chinkin, *supra* note 95 at 274.

98 *Ibid.* See e.g. *Merdeka University Bhd. v. Government of Malaysia*, [1981] 2 M.L.J. 356.

99 Chinkin, *ibid.* at 274-82. C. V. Das, "Constitutional Supremacy, Emergency Powers and Judicial Attitudes" [1983] J. of Malaysian and Comparative L. 69 at 81 and 84; and Jain, *supra* note 95 at 184.

100 *Supra* note 74.

101 *Supra* note 76.

102 *Supra* note 77.

103 *Karam Singh v. Menteri Hal Ehwal Dalam Negeri, Malaysia*, [1969] 2 M.L.J. 129 at 138. On the grounds for judicial review of preventive detention orders, see e.g. Gan Ching Chuan, "Judicial Review of Preventive Detention in Malaysia" [1994] 1 M.L.J. cxiii. Gan Ching Chuan suggests that there is potential for a much broader application of extended *ultra vires* in preventative detention cases.

104 *Ibid.* See also *Yeap Hock Seng v. Minister for Home Affairs*, [1975] 2 M.L.J. 279 at 284. See also Gan Ching Chuan, *supra* note 103 at cxix.

105 *Karam Singh*, *supra* note 103; and *Yeap Hock Seng*, *supra* note 104.

106 *Supra* note 69.

107 *Minister of Home Affairs v. Persatuan Aliran Kesedaran Negara*, [1990] 1 M.L.J. 351 (Supreme Court), reversing [1988] 1 M.L.J. 440 (High Court). Aliran publishes a magazine in English that is often critical of the Malaysian government.

reversed on appeal to the Supreme Court.[108] The Supreme Court concluded that "unless it can be clearly established that the Minister for Home Affairs had in any way exercised his discretion wrongfully, unfairly, dishonestly or in bad faith, the High Court cannot question the discretion of the Minister for Home Affairs."[109] The Supreme Court found no evidence that would justify quashing the decision of the Minister for Home Affairs.

In Malaysia, the law with respect to the granting of relief in the form of mandamus or injunction is set out in the *Specific Relief Act 1950*.[110] For the most part, the Act codifies the common law with respect to these forms of relief.[111] Under s. 44(1) of the Act "[a] Judge may make an order requiring any specific act to be done or forborne, by any person holding a public office." The High Court has ruled that "public office" means an office in any of the public services mentioned in s. 132(1) of the Constitution. [112] The effect of this interpretation of public office is that it prevents an order of mandamus against the government of Malaysia or its ministers.[113] It has been observed that this "greatly limits the efficacy of this method of judicial review in modern public law when the bulk of powers under statutes are conferred on Ministers."[114]

Section 54(d) of the *Specific Relief Act 1950*[115] provides that an injunction cannot be granted to interfere with the public duties of any department of any government in Malaysia. Also the *Government Proceedings Act 1956*[116] precludes an order of injuction or specific relief against the government, allowing instead only for orders declaratory of the rights of the parties.[117] Further, the court cannot order an injunction against an officer of the government if the effect of the order would be to give relief against the government that could not have been obtained in proceedings against the government itself.[118] On this basis, courts have held that injunction or specific performance cannot be obtained against government officials.[119] It has

108 Now the Federal Court. See *supra* notes 51 to 52.

109 [1990] 1 M.L.J. 351 at 355. See also *Liew Ah Kim v. Menteri Hal Ehwal Dalam Negeri*, Rayuan Emula, 24-83-91 Appeal No. 01/92 (unreported), as cited in Rais Yatim, *supra* note 65 at 175, in which the court concluded that the Minister's discretion in the granting of a licence was final and conclusive and the court could not go behind such a subjective determination.

110 Revised 1974, Laws of Malaysia, Act 137 of 1974.

111 See Jain, *supra* note 95 at 172.

112 *Loh Wai Kong v. Government of Malaysia and Ors.*, [1978] 2 M.L.J. 175; [1979] 2 M.L.J. 33.

113 See Jain, *supra* note 95 at 173.

114 *Ibid.*

115 Laws of Malaysia, Act 137 (Revised 1974).

116 Revised 1988, Laws of Malaysia, Act 359 of 1988.

117 *Ibid.* at s. 29. See Jain, "Constitutional Remedies," *supra* note 95 at 175-77.

118 Jain, *ibid.* at 176.

119 Jain, *ibid.*, citing *Ramamoorthy v. Menteri Besar of Selangor*, [1969] 2 M.L.J. 97 (holding that a claim of specific performance could not be obtained against the Menteri Besar

been observed that "[t]he bar on the issue of an injunction against the Government and its officials very much reduces the efficacy of the injunction as a remedy in public law."[120]

Malaysian courts have also taken a restricted approach to the granting of applications for habeas corpus. Habeas corpus applications are provided for by article 5(1) and (2) of the Constitution. Article 5(1) guarantees that no person shall be deprived of liberty save in accordance with law. Article 5(2) provides that, where a complaint is made, the High Court shall order the release of a person who is being unlawfully detained. Section 365 of the *Criminal Procedure Code*[121] also provides that the High Court may, when it thinks fit, order the release of a person alleged to be improperly detained. A number of applications for habeas corpus have been made with respect to preventative detention, but with little success.[122] This is because the words "save in accordance with law," "unlawfully detained," or "illegally or improperly detained" constrain the remedy to the applicable law, which, in the case of preventative detention, depends on the subjective view of the detaining officer.[123] Several cases have held that this subjective satisfaction of the need to detain a person is not subject to judicial review other than on the basis of *mala fides* and thus have generally taken a very restrained approach to the grant of habeas corpus.[124] The courts have been willing to grant habeas corpus in cases where they found some fault in strict compliance with the procedures set out in the legislation for detention.[125] However, as noted below,[126] the government has tended to provide legislative responses to such successful applications for habeas corpus.

---

of a State and that the court could only make an order declaratory of the rights of the parties); *Haji Ismail bin Che Chik v. State Commissioner of Penang*, [1975] 1 M.L.J. 271; and *Nanthakumanan v. Jaffnese Co-operative Housing Society Ltd.*, [1980] 1 M.L.J. 114 (refusing the issue of an injunction against the Registrar of Titles).

120 Jain, *ibid.* at 176-77.

121 Statutes of the Federated Malay States, c. 6, as amended.

122 See Jain, *supra* note 95 at 163; H. F. Rawlings, "Habeas Corpus and Preventative Detention in Malaysia and Singapore" (1983) 25 Mal. L.R. 324.

123 See *Malaysian Constitution*, art. 5(1) and (2) and the *Criminal Procedure Code*, *supra* note 121, s. 365; and see M. P. Jain, *supra* note 95 at 162-64.

124 Jain, *ibid.* at 163. See also Rawlings, *supra* note 122 at 339-41 and Abu Bakar Munir, "Malaysia," in A. Harding and J. Hatchard, *Preventative Detention and Security Law: A Comparative Survey* (Dordrecht: Martinus Nijhoff, 1993) 131 at 144-46. See also *Karam Singh v. Menteri Hal Ehwal Dalam Negeri*, [1969] 2 M.L.J. 129; *Yeap Hock Seng v. Minister of Home Affairs*, [1975] 2 M.L.J. 279; and *Karpal Singh v. Minister of Home Affairs*, [1988] 1 M.L.J. 468.

125 See e.g. *Ex parte Johannes Choeldi and Ors* (1960), 26 M.L.J. 184; *Re Datuk James Wong Kim Min*, [1976] 2 M.L.J. 245 (F.C.); *Re Tan Boon Liat*, [1977] 2 M.L.J. 108; *Minister for Home Affairs v. Karpal Singh (No. 2)*, [1988] 3 M.L.J. 323; *Minister for Home Affairs v. Jamaluddin bin Othmani*, [1989] 1 S.C.R. 311; and *Re Tan Sri Raja Khalid bin Raja Harun*, [1988] 3 M.L.J. 29.

126 See *infra* notes 155 to 162 and the accompanying text.

Conservative Approach to Privative Clauses It has been suggested that Malaysian courts have taken a restrained approach to the judicial review of administrative decisions in the face of privative clauses.[127]

Malaysian courts have nonetheless shown a reluctance to completely abandon their powers of judicial review in the face of broadly worded privative clauses.[128] However, the much broader provisions recently added to the *Internal Security Act 1960*, the *Dangerous Drugs (Special Preventative Measures) Act 1985*, and the *Emergency (Public Order and Prevention of Crime) Ordinance 1969*, noted above, appear to meet Lord Denning's requirement in *Re Gilmore*[129] that in order for a privative clause to completely oust judicial review it must be in "the most clear and explicit words."[130]

Sources of Judicial Conservatism

Educational Background of the Judges The apparent reluctance of judges in Malaysia to engage in judicial review of government action, whether on the basis of the Constitution or in applying principles of administrative law, may in part be due to the training of most judges in Malaysia. Although more lawyers are being trained locally, many of Malaysia's judges were trained in Britain,[131] where, given the lack of a written Constitution, the notion of

---

127 See Gan Ching Chuan, "Privative Clauses," *supra* note 96 at 115, 126-27 and Jain, *supra* note 93 at 257-61. But, to the contrary, see V. Anantaraman, "Judicial Review: The Malaysian Experience" [1994] 1 M.L.J. xliv at lxvii.

The judicial attitude towards privative clauses may have been affected for several years by the decision of the Privy Council in *South East Asian Fire Bricks Sdn. Bhd. v. Non-Metallic Mineral Products Manufacturers Employees Union*, [1980] 2 M.L.J. 165, which was on appeal from Malaysia. In maintaining a distinction between errors of law and errors of jurisdiction the *Fire Bricks* decision was out of step with developments in England at the time, and was also out of step with subsequent developments in England. The courts in Malaysia have subsequently abandoned such an approach. See *Syarikat Kenderaan Melayu Kelantan Bhd. v. Transport Workers' Union*, [1995] 2 M.L.J. 317 at 342 (C.A.); affirmed in *Kumpulan Perangsang Selangor Bhd. v. Zaid bin Hj Mohd Noh*, [1997] 1 M.L.J. 789 at 800 (C.A.), and *Kesultanan Pahang v. Sathask Realty Sdn. Bhd.*, [1997] 2 C.L.J. 723 at 737-39 (C.A.). See also the discussion in V. Anataraman, "Revisionism of the Restructured Judiciary in Malaysian Industrial Relations" [1997] 1 M.L.J. lxxxix, and N. Shanmugam "Deliverance From the Dominance of *Fire Bricks*" [1995] 3 M.L.J. cxxxvii.

The recent change in rhetoric concerning judicial review probably does not make a significant difference in the likelihood of court intervention. Under the *Fire Bricks* approach, the court could intervene by construing an alleged error of the inferior tribunal as an error of jurisdiction, and avoid intervention by construing an alleged error of the inferior tribunal as an error of law. See V. Anataraman, *supra*, demonstrating how courts in Malaysia were able to take either approach. Now the court may decide either to intervene or not on the basis of whether the court found an error of law, an unfair procedure, or an unreasonable decision (*Syarikat Kenderaan Melayu Kelantan Bhd. v. Transport Workers' Union, supra* at 342).

128 See Anantaraman, *supra* note 127 at lv-lvi.

129 *Supra* note 92.

130 *Ibid.* at 801.

parliamentary supremacy may be stronger. However, Malaysian judges, it has been said, appear to be less willing to engage in judicial review than their British counterparts.[132] Thus other factors appear to play a role in the judicial restraint shown by judges in Malaysia.

Tensions between the Government and the Judiciary[133] Through the latter part of the 1980s, there was evidence of a growing tension between the government (in particular the Prime Minister), and the judiciary. In 1985 the Prime Minister had said: "We are very fortunate that our judiciary is straight and honest. We are fortunate that it is independent of the Executive ... We are fortunate in having on the Bench men of high professional competence and high moral integrity."[134] However, events after 1985 led to tensions between the government and the judiciary, with exercises of judicial review leading to immediate legislative responses.

In August 1986, the immigration permits of two *Wall Street Journal* correspondents were cancelled in the wake of reports critical of the government. One of the correspondents challenged the cancellation of his work permit on the basis that it was cancelled without a hearing. The High Court upheld the cancellation of the work permit,[135] but this decision was reversed on appeal by the Supreme Court, which held that a work permit could not be cancelled without a hearing.[136] Shortly after the High Court decision, the Prime Minister stated:

> The judiciary says [to Parliament] "although you passed a law with a certain thing in mind, we think that your mind is wrong, and we want to give our interpretation." If we disagree, the court will say: "We will interpret your disagreement." If we go along we are going to lose our power of legislation. We know exactly what we want to do, but once we do it, it is interpreted in a different way, and we have no means to reinterpret it our way.[137]

---

131 See "Divided at the Bar, United on the Bench," *Far Eastern Economic Review* (21 July 1988) 15.

132 See e.g. Chinkin, *supra* note 95 at 284. See also Jain, *supra* note 93 at 258-60; and Gan Ching Chuan, "Privative Clauses," *supra* note 96 at 112-15.

133 The story of the tensions between the government and the judiciary is also discussed in H. P. Lee, *Constitutional Conflicts in Contemporary Malaysia* (Kuala Lumpur: Oxford Univ. Press, 1995), c. 3 entitled "The Judiciary under Siege."

134 Cited in *Lawyers Committee for Human Rights, Malaysia: Assault on the Judiciary* (New York: Lawyers Committee for Human Rights, 1989) at 17.

135 *J. P. Berthelson v. Director General of Immigration, Malaysia and Ors.*, [1987] 1 M.L.J. 134.

136 *Ibid.* at 137.

137 "I Know How the People Feel," *Time* (24 Nov. 1986) 18.

The Prime Minister also noted that if laws were interpreted contrary to the intentions of Parliament, "then we will have to find a way of producing a law that will have to be interpreted according to our wish."[138]

In 1986, Aliran, the publisher of an English language magazine often critical of the government, sought a licence to publish a Malay language magazine. Shortly after the High Court quashed the decision of the Minister of Home Affairs (who is also the Prime Minister), who had refused to grant the licence to Aliran,[139] the Prime Minister said: "There are black sheep in every group who want to be fiercely independent ... When you want to be fiercely independent, you are simply implying that you'd forget your duty to be just and fair ... You stretch things a bit. You have to prove you can hammer the government."[140]

Events towards the end of 1987 led to arrests under the *Internal Security Act 1960*.[141] These arrests led to applications for habeas corpus.[142] One high profile arrest was that of Karpal Singh, a prominent lawyer and opposition politician. The High Court granted Karpal Singh's application for habeas corpus, finding that his detention order, signed by the Prime Minister, contained a charge that was factually inaccurate and outside the scope of the *Internal Security Act*, and that the cavalier attitude in issuing the detention order amounted to *mala fides*.[143] It was shortly after this case that the Constitution was amended to allow Parliament to limit the jurisdiction of the High Courts and inferior courts. Amendments to the *Internal Security Act* that attempt to preclude judicial review were also forthcoming.

The UMNO Case and the Removal of Three Supreme Court Judges The most significant event affecting the judiciary occurred in the midst of a case involving UMNO, the dominant Malay party in the ruling coalition government. In April 1987 the Prime Minister retained his UMNO party leadership

138 *Ibid.*

139 *Persatuan Aliran Kesedaran Negara v. Minister of Home Affairs*, [1988] 1 M.L.J. 440.

140 See *Malaysian Business* (1 Jan. 1988) as cited in *Malaysia: Assault on the Judiciary, supra* note 134 at 27; and in "A Judicial Shake Up," *Far Eastern Economic Review* (14 Jan. 1988) 27.

141 On the arrests, see Committee Against Repression in the Pacific and Asia, *Tangled Web: Dissent, Deterrence and the 27 October 1987 Crackdown in Malaysia* (Kuala Lumpur: Kong Lee Printers, 1988).

142 For instance, a group of eight persons detained under the *Internal Security Act* petitioned the court for writs of habeas corpus questioning the legality of their detentions. See *Theresa Lim Chin Chin and Ors v. Inspector General of Police*, [1988] 1 M.L.J. 293. The petitions were denied on the basis that in "security cases" the reasons for the arrest need not be disclosed.

143 *Karpal Singh*, [1988] 1 M.L.J. 468 at 473-74.

144 Mahathir retained his party leadership position by a margin of 761 votes to 718. See "The Vital Forty-Three," *Far Eastern Economic Review* (7 May 1987) 12-15; and see the discussion in D. K. Mauzy, "Malaysia in 1987: Decline of 'The Malay Way'" (1988) 28 Asian Survey 213 at 214-16.

by a very narrow margin.[144] The losing faction mounted a court challenge. The challenge led to a decision by the High Court on 4 February 1988 that UMNO was illegally constituted.[145] The decision put in doubt the position of the Prime Minister as the person able to command the support of the House,[146] since the legality of the main party in the ruling coalition and the Prime Minister's position as leader of that party were in doubt. The decision was appealed to the Supreme Court.[147]

The response of the Prime Minister and his UMNO supporters was to set up a new party called UMNO Baru. UMNO Baru managed to obtain the substantial assets of UMNO and allegedly kept the Prime Minister's rivals in the former UMNO party from joining the new party.[148] Once these steps were taken, it was seen to be in the Prime Minister's interest not to have the High Court ruling overturned by the Supreme Court. On 27 May 1988 the Lord President was informed that he was suspended pending a report of a tribunal on his continued fitness to be a judge. Four days earlier, 23 May 1988, the Lord President had set the UMNO case down for consideration before a coram of all nine judges of the Supreme Court.[149] Never before had a case been heard before the full coram of the Supreme Court. Thus the Lord President appeared to think that the case was not straightforward but required the careful consideration of the full bench. This may have made the outcome of the case appear additionally uncertain.[150]

In the events that followed the suspension of the Lord President, five other judges were suspended pending the report of a second tribunal.[151]

---

145 *Mohamed Noor bin Othman and Ors. v. Mohamed Yusoff Jaafar and Ors.*, [1988] 2 M.L.J. 129.

146 Under s. 43(2) of the Malaysian Constitution, the person appointed as Prime Minister must be likely to command the confidence of the majority of members of the House.

147 *Mohamed Noor bin Othman and Ors. v. Haji Mohamed Ismail and Ors.*, [1988] 3 M.L.J. 82; [1988] 2 S.C.R. 219.

148 See e.g. "Old Lamps, New Lamps," *Asiaweek* (13 May 1988) 21; "Legal Battles," *Asiaweek* (29 Apr. 1988) 21; "A Grand Master Move," *Far Eastern Economic Review* (3 Mar. 1988) 14; "A Premium on Loyalty," *Asiaweek* (11 Mar. 1988) 19; "Mine, Yours or Ours?" *Far Eastern Economic Review* (14 Apr. 1988) 31.

149 For a summary of the events leading up to the suspension of the Lord President in 1988, see F. A. Trindade, "The Removal of the Malaysian Judges" (1990) 106 L.Q. Rev. 51; H. P. Lee, "A Fragile Bastion Under Siege – the 1988 Convulsion in the Malaysian Judiciary" (1990) 17 Melbourne Univ. L. Rev. 386; A. J. Harding, "The 1988 Judicial Crisis in Malaysia" (1989) 39 I.C.L.Q. 57; Gillen and McDorman, *supra* note 5 at 182-92; H. P. Lee, *supra* note 133 at 43-77; and Yatim, *supra* note 65 at 305-62.

150 See K. S. Nathan, "Malaysia in 1988: The Politics of Survival" (1989) 39 Asian Survey 129 at 134 suggesting that the case may have threatened the political future of the Prime Minister.

151 The suspension of five additional judges of the Supreme Court and the appointment of a second tribunal occurred as a result of an emergency session of the Supreme Court held contrary to the wishes of the Acting Lord President (and ultimate successor to the suspended Lord President). The emergency session heard an application for

While the judges were suspended, the important UMNO case was heard before five judges, three of whom were temporary replacements for the suspended judges.[152] When the tribunals submitted their reports, the Lord President and two other Supreme Court judges were removed from the bench.

Constraints Imposed in Response to Judicial Activism It was in the midst of the tensions between the judiciary and the Prime Minister, and just before the suspension of the Lord President, that the Constitution was amended to provide that the High Courts and inferior courts would have only such jurisdiction as was vested in them by federal law.[153] In the debates over the amendment, the Prime Minister spoke critically of certain decisions of the judiciary, most notably the case involving the Asian *Wall Street Journal* correspondent, saying that "[we] [the government] go by the law in discharging our duties, likewise the judges should also abide by the law ... that is all we want."[154]

In 1989, in what appeared to be a response to the case involving the Asian *Wall Street Journal* correspondents, the *Immigration Act* was amended to provide that no person, or member of a class of persons, shall be given the opportunity to be heard before the Minister or the Director General of Immigration who makes an order in respect of any matter under the Act or regulations.[155] The 1989 amendments to the Act also made decisions of the Minister or Director General "final" and provided that their decisions "shall not be called into question in any court on any ground whatsoever."[156]

The amendments to the *Societies Act*, noted above, appear also to have been timed to suggest that they were a response to the UMNO case.[157] The tendency of the government to amend legislation in direct response to judicial activism was also clear in the run-up to the UMNO general assembly of 1993. Meetings of some branches were delayed by injunctions. The Prime

---

the temporary stay of the work of the tribunal appointed to inquire into the removal of the Lord President. The application was based on allegations that the members of the tribunal were biased. In particular, it alleged that the chair of the tribunal, the Acting Lord President replacing the Lord President while he was suspended, was biased in that he was the apparent successor to the position of Lord President were the current suspended Lord President ultimately removed. The High Court judge had suspended the hearing into the temporary stay application, made on a Friday, until the following Monday. It was rumoured that the tribunal would be finished its work and would have made its report by the intervening Sunday. These events are reviewed in the items cited *supra* note 149.

152 See e.g. "The End of a Legal Battle," *Asiaweek* (19 Aug. 1988) 19-20; "Judgement Week," *Far Eastern Economic Review* (18 Aug. 1988) 22-23.

153 *See supra* notes 67 to 68 and the accompanying text.

154 As cited in *Malaysia: Assault on the Judiciary, supra* note 134 at 28.

155 *Immigration (Amendment) Act 1989*, Act A719, adding s. 59 to the *Immigration Act.*

156 *Ibid.* adding s. 59A.

157 *See supra* notes 83 to 84 and the accompanying text.

Minister suggested that, if the courts had such powers, the legislation would have to be amended to prevent such interference by courts.[158]

The timing of the 1989 amendments, which added privative clauses to acts providing for preventative detention, suggest that they were in response to successful applications for habeas corpus.[159] Further amendments to the *Dangerous Drugs (Special Preventative Measures) Act 1985* deleted wording that had led to successful applications for habeas corpus in two cases[160] and added a provision retrospectively validating the orders of the sort impugned in the two cases.[161] The spate of new privative clauses appearing in legislation in recent years also suggests that the increased tendency to use such clauses may be linked to the recent tensions between the government and the judiciary.[162]

Conclusion on Parliamentary Supremacy and Judicial Review in Malaysia

A review of a sample of cases between 1980 and 1988 gave an approximately 43% success rate for application for judicial review. A similar review of cases from 1989 to mid-1993 gave an approximately 18% success rate for applications for judicial review. This is consistent with the impression, formed on the anecdotal evidence discussed above, that the Malaysian judiciary is becoming more reluctant to invalidate laws or intervene in administrative decisions. This may be due in part to the British training of many Malaysian judges. However, recent tensions between the government and the judiciary, the removal of three Supreme Court judges, and the government's legislative response to judicial activism may have made Malaysian judges more reticent to exercise judicial review powers. Consequently, parliamentary supremacy in Malaysia appears to dominate and to be growing stronger.[163]

---

158 "Umno to seek legal advice on court rulings," *New Straits Times* (21 Sept. 1993) 2.

159 *See supra* notes 79 to 82 and the accompanying text.

160 *Dangerous Drugs (Special Preventative Measures) (Amendment) Act 1990*, Act A766, amending s. 6 of the Act in response to *Tan Hoom Seng and Anor. v. Minister of Home Affairs and Anor.*, [1990] 1 CLJ 423 and *Poh Chin Kay v. Menteri Hal Ehwal Dalam Negeri, Malaysia and Anor.*, [1990] 2 M.L.J. 297. See Gan Ching Chuan, "Administrative Law," *supra* note 96 at 29.

161 S. 6A(2).

162 *See supra* notes 78 to 88 and 155 to 162 and the accompanying text.

163 A similar conclusion is reached by Yatim, *supra* note 65 at 360, where he says: "The message is clear: Judges are only allowed to interpret the law in the way that the executive had determined through the language passed by Parliament." At 363, he says that "the supremacy of the executive in Malaysia is complete and comprehensively self-sustaining," and (at 364) that "laws have been passed largely to enhance the power of executive government. So extensive and entrenched are the executive powers in the Constitution that the document may aptly be described as the executive's bill of rights rather than that of the citizen."

Singapore

History and Structure of the Constitution

Constitutional and Political History

To a large degree, the constitutional and political history of Singapore has been interwoven with that of Malaysia. For two turbulent years before its 1965 independence, Singapore was a state within the Malaysian Federation. However, with its predominantly Chinese population and perceived different manner of doing things, Singapore was not seen as fitting the developing Malaysian national mosaic.[164] Since independence, Singapore has emerged as the unquestioned economic success of Southeast Asia with a standard of living unmatched in the region.

Former Prime Minister Lee Kuan Yew has been the dominant political actor in Singapore for nearly four decades. In 1959, Lee Kuan Yew and his People's Action Party (PAP) swept to electoral victory and since that time the PAP has both won every election and rigorously fought political opposition.[165] Fuelled by the insecurity at independence of being a small city-state[166] and the security of unquestioned political domination within Singapore, Lee Kuan Yew and the PAP have striven to instill in the population values such as discipline, hard work, honesty, cleanliness, abstention from drugs, and observance of family obligations, all of which are seen as promoting success and efficiency.[167] The Singaporean government has directly and indirectly sought to mould and shape the values and population of Singapore. Two long-time observers concluded that various social and economic actions of the Singaporean government "add up not to totalitarianism but rather to a paternalistic, ordered, and planned approach to society, based on the government's belief that it knows best."[168]

In 1980 the government of Singapore produced a consolidated Constitution of Singapore that, with its subsequent amendments, is deemed to be the authentic text of the Singapore Constitution.[169] Prior to this single-

164 See J. H. Esterline and M. H. Esterline, *"How the Dominoes Fell": Southeast Asia in Perspective* (Lanham, Maryland: Hamilton Press, 1986) at 177-79 and R. S. Milne and D. K. Mauzy, *Singapore: The Legacy of Lee Kuan Yew* (Boulder: Westview Press, 1990) at 57-61.

165 *See Milne and Mauzy, supra* note 164 at 51-76 and 84-91. For a more controversial view of the PAP and political control, see G. Rodan, "Preserving the One-party State in Contemporary Singapore," in K. Hewison, R. Robson, and C. Rodan, eds., *Southeast Asia in the 1990s: Authoritarianism, Democracy and Capitalism* (St. Leonards, Australia: Allen and Unwin, 1993) at 77.

166 Respecting the bleak outlook for Singapore in 1965, see Esterline and Esterline, *supra* note 164 at 179-80 and Milne and Mauzy, *supra* note 164 at 62-64.

167 Milne and Mauzy, *supra* note 164 at 8.

168 *Ibid.* A different perspective is provided in Rodan, *supra* note 165 at 77-108.

169 Winslow, *supra* note 5 at 629 and V. Winslow, "The Constitution and Legal System of Singapore," in C. V. Sison, ed., *Constitutional and Legal Systems of ASEAN Countries* (Manila: Univ. of the Philippines, 1990) at 261.

document Constitution, Singapore relied upon the 1963 Constitution developed for its participation as a state in the Malaysian Federation[170] and, pursuant to the Republic of Singapore Independence Act, 1965,[171] selected provisions of the Malaysian Constitution and modifications necessary to any laws, including the constitutional documents, made by the President.[172] In creating the 1980 document, referred to as the "Reprint," the Attorney-General was authorized[173] to publish a consolidated reprint of the Constitution of Singapore, amalgamating provisions of the Malaysian Constitution as applicable and modifying existing provisions as deemed appropriate.[174] It has been suggested that the Attorney-General's power was so extensive that the Constitution could be and to a limited extent was modified without the approval of the Legislature.[175] Irrespective of these legal niceties, the 1980 Reprint, as amended and updated, is taken to be the principal constitutional document in Singapore.[176]

Outline of the Constitutional Structure

While Singapore shares with Malaysia the heritage of parliamentary democracy based upon the Westminster system, the structure of government in Singapore has always been distinctive, and modifications made in the past few years have moved Singapore further away from both its neighbour and the British model.

The recent changes have involved the Presidency, the head of state in Singapore. Since independence, the President, elected by Parliament, has had a ceremonial role, akin to the role of the monarchy in Malaysia and Canada, exercising power only with the advice of the Cabinet or individual ministers.[177] In early 1991 amendments to the Constitution were approved, although they did not come into effect until 1993, modifying the position of the President.[178] The President is now directly elected by the people of

170 The 1963 Constitution was derived from the 1958 self-rule Constitution. See Winslow, *supra* note 5 at 628-29 and Winslow, *supra* note 169 at 259.

171 Act No. 9 of 1965 (Singapore Statutes, rev. ed. 1985, Part I). Respecting the *Republic of Singapore Independence Act*, see Winslow, *supra* note 169 at 261-62 and K. T. Y. Lee, "The Evolution of Singapore's Modern Constitution: Developments From 1945 to the Present Day" (1989) 1 Singapore Academy of Law J. 1 at 16-20.

172 Winslow, *supra* note 5 at 629 and Winslow, *supra* note 169 at 260-62.

173 The authorization was granted by statute: *Constitution (Amendment) Act, 1979* (Act 10 of 1979), which is now in *Constitution of Singapore*, art. 155.

174 See Winslow, *supra* note 169 at 261 and Lee, *supra* note 171 at 21.

175 *Ibid.* and Lee, *supra* note 171 at 22-23.

176 Respecting the constitutional status of the *Republic of Singapore Independence Act*, see Winslow, *supra* note 169 at 261-62.

177 Respecting the prerogatives of the President, see Winslow, *supra* note 169 at 265-66.

178 See generally on the 1991 constitutional changes regarding the Presidency, K. T. Y. Lee, "The Elected Presidency in Singapore: Constitution of the Republic of Singapore (Amendment Act 1991)" [1991] Singapore J. of Legal Studies 179-94; V. S. Winslow, "Electing the President: The Presidential Elections Act 1991" [1991] Singapore J. of

Singapore[179] for a six-year term.[180] To be a candidate, one must fulfill a detailed list of qualifications,[181] including having held one of a series of listed offices,[182] be "a person of integrity, good character and reputation,"[183] and not be a member of a political party when nominated.[184] One commentator has noted that the exacting qualifications "assumes that Singaporeans are incapable of selecting a suitable President to lead them" and that they ensure that a candidate will be a member of the establishment.[185] The discretionary authority of the President[186] originally extended to a veto regarding certain appointments to public office[187] and the spending of foreign reserves,[188] but changes made in 1996 have restricted the independent action of the President.[189] One commentator summarized as follows:

> [T]he ... new President is a hybrid between a purely constitutional head of state, with limited or no discretion to refuse Cabinet advice, and an executive President. Indeed, he has partial executive powers, in the form of a veto power in certain matters only, but with no power to take the initiative in any action. Also, as President, he will continue to have the executive authority of the State vested in him, and thus the Presidency is not a

---

Legal Studies 476-81 and K. Y. L. Tan and L. Thio, *Constitutional Law in Malaysia and Singapore*, 2d ed. (Singapore: Butterworths Asia, 1997) at 236-42.

179 *Constitution of Singapore*, art. 17(2). In August 1993, Ong Teng Cheong became the first elected President of Singapore.

180 *Ibid.* at art. 20(1).

181 The qualifications are noted in *Constitution of Singapore*, arts. 19(2) and 44(2). Art. 18 creates a Presidential Elections Committee with the mandate to ensure Presidential candidates fulfill the qualifications. For a brief commentary, see Lee, *supra* note 178 at 183-85.

182 *Constitution of Singapore*, art. 19(2). Winslow, *supra* note 5 at 635 refers to this as a "unique" qualification.

183 *Ibid.* at art. 19(2)(e). This is to be determined by the Presidential Elections Committee.

184 *Constitution of Singapore*, art. 19(2)(f). Again Winslow, *supra* note 5 at 636 refers to this as a "unique" qualification and provides an explanation for its inclusion.

185 Lee, *supra* note 178 at 190-91. One opposition member commented that the qualifications were so stringent that no one in his party would qualify as a candidate. N. Balarkrishnan, "One Horse Race," *Far Eastern Economic Review* (17 June 1993) 31.

186 *Constitution of Singapore*, art. 21(1) requires the President to act under the advice of the cabinet. Arts. 21(2) and 22 detail areas over which the President has discretionary authority. For many of these decisions, the President is to consult the Council for Presidential Advisers, art. 21(3). The establishment and role of this Council is set out in arts. 37A-37K. See generally Lee, *supra* note 178 at 187. Changes were made to the Council through *Constitution of the Republic of Singapore (Amendment) Act 1994*, Act No. 5 of 1994.

187 *Constitution of Singapore*, arts. 21(2)(e) and 22.

188 *Ibid.* at art. 21(2)(c) and (d).

189 See *Constitution of the Republic of Singapore (Amendment) Act 1996*, Act No. 41 of 1996. Where the President acts contrary to the advice of the Council of Presidential Advisers, the Parliament, by two-thirds majority, can overrule the decision of the President. See generally Tan and Thio, *supra* note 178 at 142.

separate organ of government, but is rather an institution forming part of the executive, and which exercises a check on another part of the executive, namely the Prime Minister and the Cabinet.[190]

Irrespective of the changing authority of the President, the principal locus of governmental power is the Parliament. Unlike Malaysia, Singapore has only a single legislative body.[191] Popularly elected members control the Parliament,[192] but the Constitution provides for two different categories of nominated members of Parliament, although the numbers in each of the two categories are not to exceed six.[193] The Prime Minister and cabinet are to be drawn from the elected members of Parliament,[194] although the selection of the Prime Minister is within the discretion of the President.[195]

The Fundamental Liberties provisions of the Singapore Constitution, articles 9-15, are drawn from similar provisions within the Malaysian Constitution, with only minor modifications reflecting Singapore's differing social distribution of population.[196] One right in the Malaysian Constitution that is not in the Singaporean Constitution concerns the right to property. The right to property and compensation for expropriation was not accepted in Singapore because of fears of excessive litigation as Singapore's limited territory makes land acquisition for public purposes a necessity.[197] As in Malaysia, there are limitations placed on the listed liberties by law, thus few rights are absolute.[198]

---

190 *Winslow, supra* note 5 at 636. See also L. Thio, "Working Out the Presidency: The Rites of Passage" [1995] Singapore J. of Legal Studies 509-57.

191 See Winslow, *supra* note 5 at 636-39; Winslow, *supra* note 169 at 267-72; and L. Thio, "The Post-Colonial Constitutional Evolution of the Singapore Legislature: A Case Study" [1993] Singapore J. of Legal Studies 80-122.

192 Note L. E. Laine et al., "Principles and Practices of Voting: The Singapore Electoral System" (1996) 17 Singapore L. Rev. 244-321.

193 *Constitution of Singapore,* art. 39(1)(b) creates non-constituency Members of Parliament and art. 39(1)(c) creates nominated Members of Parliament. While the Constitution provides that either category may be up to six, non-constituency members are controlled by the Parliamentary Elections Act (art. 39(1)(b)) and the nominated members by the Presidency (art. 39(1)(c)). Art. 39(2) restricts the voting rights of these two categories of Members of Parliament.

The rational for the non-constituency members arose from concerns over the lack of an opposition in the elected Parliament in the 1980s: see Winslow, *supra* note 169 at 269-70. The creation of nominated members arose from a desire to improve Parliamentary debate, to correct the view that the PAP was closed to alternative viewpoints and to provide room for special expertise from non-politicians. See generally Thio, *supra* note 191 at 97-102.

194 *Ibid.* at art. 25(1), and see generally Winslow, *supra* note 169 at 266-67.

195 *Ibid.* at arts. 25(1) and 21(2)(a).

196 See Winslow, *supra* note 169 at 274-76 and general discussion at 276-79.

197 *Ibid.* at 279.

198 Regarding Singapore generally, see Winslow, *supra* note 169 at 281-82. For a detailed treatment, see Tan and Thio, *supra* note 178, cc. 11, 12.

The Judiciary

During the brief period when Singapore was a state within the Malaysian Federation, the Singapore court system was integrated into the Malaysian judicial system.[199] At independence, Singapore's principal constitutional documents (in particular the 1963 State Constitution) did not contain provisions regarding the judiciary, and Singapore continued to rely on the Malaysian court structure.[200] This was remedied by constitutional change in 1969 with the creation of the Supreme Court and the vesting in this Court of "the judicial power of Singapore."[201]

Constitutional changes and amendments to the *Supreme Court of Judicature Act* in 1993 has created a two-tiered Singapore Supreme Court composed of the High Court and the Court of Appeal.[202] The permanent Appeal Court has a membership that, except in unusual circumstances, does not overlap with the High Court.[203] The creation of the Court of Appeal was a step towards termination of recourse to the Judicial Committee of the Privy Council. In 1994 the relevant provision of the Singapore Constitution was repealed, and there no longer is recourse to the Privy Council from Singapore.[204] In 1994 an addition to the Constitution created a tribunal, composed of three Supreme Court judges, to give opinions of questions referred to it by the President.[205] In April 1995, the first such tribunal rendered its opinion respecting the power of the President and constitutional amendment.[206]

As in Malaysia, despite the lack of a constitutional provision explicitly granting to the Singapore Supreme Courts the jurisdiction to review the

---

199 Briefly described in K. T. Y. Lee, "A Short Legal and Constitutional History of Singapore," in W. Woon, ed., *The Singapore Legal System* (Singapore: Malaya L. Rev., 1989) at 30.

200 Lee, *supra* note 171 at 16, 24.

201 *Constitution of Singapore*, art. 93. See Winslow, *supra* note 5 at 631-32.

202 See generally T. Y. Lin, "Supreme Court of Judicature (Amendment) Act 1993" [1993] Singapore J. of Legal Studies 557-77 and D. Chang and T. Liyin, "Changes in the Supreme Court of Singapore" (1993) 14 Singapore L. Rev. 396.

Singapore has undertaken a number of judicial reforms in an effort to make the system of adversarial adjudication more cost and time efficient. A central thrust of the changes is to give the Courts a more interventionist role in litigation. See J. Pinsler, "Court Practice: Singapore at a Legal Threshold," in *Southeast Asian Affairs 1995* (Singapore: Institute for Southeast Asian Studies) at 309-24.

203 Lin, *ibid.* at 557-63 and Chang and Liyin, *supra* note 202 at 397-401.

204 Art. 100, *Constitution of Singapore* (1992) was repealed by s. 3 of the *Constitution of the Republic of Singapore (Amendment) Act 1994*, Act No. 5 of 1994.

205 *Constitution of the Republic of Singapore (Amendment No. 2) Act 1994*, Act No. 17 of 1994, s. 16. See Thio, *supra* note 190 at 526-28.

206 *Constitutional Reference No. 1 of 1995*, [1995] 2 S.L.R. 201. For an analysis of the decision, see Thio, *supra* note 190 at 528-47; Chan Sek Keong, "Working Out the Presidency: No Passage of Rights – In Defence of the Opinion of the Constitutional Tribunal" [1996] Singapore J. of Legal Studies 1-42; and G. L. Low and Chia Jin Chong Daniel, "Tribunal's Findings on the Powers of the Elected President" (1995) 16 Singapore L. Rev. 212-27.

constitutional validity of government legislation, the existence of the supremacy clause stating that the Constitution is the supreme law and that acts inconsistent with the Constitution are void[207] assures the existence of judicial review.[208]

The Constitution of Singapore contains numerous provisions regarding the maintenance of the independence of the judiciary from interference from the executive or legislature. As in the Malaysian Constitution, in Singapore judges of the Supreme Court have security of tenure until age 65,[209] remuneration cannot be adjusted to the disadvantage of a sitting judge,[210] and restrictions exist on discussing the conduct of judges in Parliament.[211] Appointments to the Supreme Court are to be by the President acting under the advice of the Prime Minister[212] and following consultation with the Chief Justice,[213] although the President has the discretion not to accept the advice of the Prime Minister.[214] The process for removing a sitting judge, including the necessity of a five person tribunal to examine the situation, follows the procedures found in the Malaysian Constitution.[215]

Attitudes and Practices Regarding Parliamentary and Constitutional Supremacy [216]

Singaporean attitudes and practices regarding parliamentary supremacy, the judiciary, and constitutionalism are less obvious than in Malaysia. While the evidence below tilts towards parliamentary supremacy, there is also evidence that there is a shifting attitude towards constitutional supremacy as Singapore contemplates the post-Lee Kuan Yew era. The balance being struck in Singapore between parliamentary and constitutional supremacy is demonstrated by examining the changes made in the amending process, the provisions of the Constitution, which directly provide for parliamentary

---

207 *Constitution of Singapore*, art. 4.

208 For a detailed argument on the existence of judicial review for constitutional compliance, see Winslow, *supra* note 5 at 630-31; Winslow, *supra* note 169 at 284-85; and L. R. Penna, "The Diceyan Perspective of Supremacy and the Constitution of Singapore" (1990) 32 Malaya L. Rev. 207 at 234-35.

209 *Constitution of Singapore*, art. 98(1). Under art. 94(2), an office of a judge cannot be abolished.

210 *Ibid.* at art. 98(8).

211 *Ibid.* at art. 99.

212 *Ibid.* at art. 95(1).

213 *Ibid.* at art. 95(2).

214 *Ibid.* at art. 22(1)(a). Failure of the President to accept the advice of the Prime Minister can be overruled by a two-thirds majority of Parliament: art. 22(2), added in 1996 by the *Constitution of the Republic of Singapore (Amendment) Act 1996*, Act No. 41 of 1996, s. 5.

215 *Ibid.* at art. 98(3),(4), and (5). See the situation in Malaysia *supra* notes 60 to 61 and the accompanying text.

216 This section relies heavily on the work done for the authors by Shannon Craig.

supremacy, the courts' manner of dealing with statutory constraints on judicial review and events in 1987-1988 involving the *Internal Security Act.*

Constraints on Judicial Review in the Constitution

The Singaporean Constitution contains a number of provisions that directly or effectively exclude the opportunity for judicial review of government action. For example, given the authority of the Attorney General to publish a consolidated reprint of the Constitution as the authentic text,[217] a provision in the Constitution denies the opportunity for the judiciary to question that the text produced by the Attorney General is the authentic text.[218] In the recent changes made to the Constitution respecting the role of the Presidency, the decision of the Presidential Elections Committee respecting whether a candidate fulfils the qualifications to run for the Presidency is final and not subject to judicial review.[219]

An explicit constitutional constraint on judicial review, which the Singaporean Courts have undermined to a limited extent through the use of administrative law principles, is section 2 of the Third Schedule to the Constitution, which declares that any decision made by the Minister with regard to citizenship matters is not subject to appeal or review in any court. In *Mohan Singh v. Attorney-General,* the High Court of Singapore recognized that an appeal based on the merits of the case was ousted by section 2, but held that the court retained its supervisory jurisdiction.[220] The exercise of the Minister's discretion was held to be reviewable either on the grounds of bad faith or jurisdictional error. Quoting from the House of Lords decision in *Council of Civil Service Unions and Others v. Ministry for the Civil Service,*[221] the Singapore Court included in jurisdictional error decisions that were based on irrationality, illegality, or procedural impropriety.[222]

On their face, all of the provisions in the Fundamental Liberties part of the Singapore Constitution are without restrictions on judicial review. This can be contrasted with the Malaysian Constitution, which explicitly excludes judicial review of legislation, even where it may interfere with the freedom of movement, speech, assembly, or association.[223] Singaporean fundamental liberties, however, are not without constraints. The Parliament can enact laws respecting the freedoms of speech and expression, assembly,

217 See *supra* text with notes 169-76, "Constitutional and Political History."
218 *Constitution of Singapore,* art. 155(3). This was confirmed in *Heng Kai Kok v. Attorney-General, Singapore,* [1987] 1 M.L.J. 98.
219 *Ibid.* at art. 18(9).
220 [1987] 2 M.L.J. 595.
221 [1984] 3 All E.R. 935 at 950.
222 *Supra* note 220 at 600.
223 *Malaysian Constitution,* art. 4(2). See *supra* "Constitutional Structure," text with notes 37-50.

and association with "such restrictions as it [Parliament] considers necessary or expedient in the interest of the security of Singapore."[224] Singaporean Courts have not interpreted this phraseology,[225] leaving it open to speculation respecting what restrictions may validly be enacted that may infringe freedom of speech, assembly, and association. However, litigation has been influential respecting the constitutional provision that no person shall be deprived of life or personal liberty save in accordance with law.[226] The Privy Council, in a case originating from Singapore, decided that a court could only strike down infringing legislation if it was not in accordance with the "fundamental rules of justice."[227] The issue is one of balancing individual liberty with societal needs or demands for order. *Colin Chan v. P. P.*[228] required the Singapore Court of Appeal to balance religious freedom with compulsory national service. The Court determined that it was not its role to substitute its view over that of the Minister as to whether a threat to national security existed.[229] Reviewing this case in a broader context, one Singapore academic concluded that "judicial decisions in constitutional liberties seem to affirm rather than constrain power" and that there exists a presumption of "judicial deference to the legislature."[230]

Part XII of the Singapore Constitution allows for the temporary suspension of fundamental liberties and other parts of the Constitution in emergency situations. Where the President issues a Proclamation of Emergency, Parliament can, notwithstanding the Constitution, make whatever laws are deemed necessary by reason of the emergency.[231] No law or ordinance enacted in an emergency situation "shall be invalid on the ground of inconsistency with any provision" of the Constitution.[232] The question of the justiciability of an emergency proclamation issued in accordance with article 150 has never come before Singapore courts, but based on the Malaysian case law it appears that the question of whether reasonable grounds existed to proclaim an emergency would not be open to judicial review.[233]

Article 149 of the Constitution allows Parliament to prevent subversion by passing legislation that may infringe upon the liberties guaranteed in

---

224 *Constitution of Singapore*, art. 14(1) and (2).

225 Winslow, *supra* note 5 at 643-44. See also Tan and Thio, *supra* note 178 at 788-89.

226 *Constitution of Singapore*, art. 9(1).

227 *Ong Ah Chuan v. Public Prosecutor*, [1981] 1 M.L.J. 64. See also *Haw Tua Tau v. Public Prosecutor*, [1981] 2 M.L.J. 48. For a commentary, see Winslow, *supra* note 5 at 639-40.

228 [1994] 3 S.L.R. 662.

229 [1994] 3 S.L.R. 662 at 685.

230 L. Thio, "An 'i' for an 'I'? Singapore's Communitarian Model of Constitutional Adjudication" (1997) 27 Hong Kong L. J. 152 at 185. See also L. Thio, "Trends in Constitutional Interpretation: Oppugning Ong, Awakening Arumugam?" [1997] Singapore J. of Legal Studies 240-90.

231 *Constitution of Singapore*, art. 150(4).

232 *Ibid.* at art. 150(5)(a).

233 See *Stephen Kalong Ningkan v. Government of Malaysia*, [1968] 1 M.L.J. 119.

articles 9, 11, 12, 13, and 14.[234] The *Internal Security Act* (*ISA*)[235] was passed pursuant to this power.[236]

Statutory Constraints on Judicial Review

In the general area of administrative law where courts may be called upon to review the wisdom of authority delegated by the legislature or exercised by the executive, Singaporean and Malaysian practices are interwoven.[237] In Singapore as in Malaysia, evidence of attitudes towards the balance between parliamentary and constitutional supremacy can be surmised from judicial approaches to legislative grants of executive discretion and privative or ouster clauses. In general, Singaporean courts have given a broad scope to discretionary powers given to the executive by statute. In this regard, Singapore is similar to Malaysia. However, although the Singapore legislature uses privative or ouster clauses to attempt to insulate administrative and executive decisions from judicial questioning, it does not appear that the practice is as prevalent in Singapore as in Malaysia.

Privative Clauses Singaporean legislators have not employed privative clauses to the same extent as Malaysian legislators, but they do exist.[238] A recent example arises from the Maintenance of Religious Harmony Act, which allows the Minister to make restraining orders against any religious leader whom he "is satisfied" is committing any of a variety of acts that will cause religious disharmony.[239] Orders made by the Minister are to be referred to the Presidential Council for Religious Harmony for recommendation, and all restraining orders require confirmation from the President.[240] Section 18 declares that "all orders and decisions of the President and Minister and recommendations of the Council made pursuant to this Act shall be final and shall not be called in question in any court."[241]

Singaporean courts have not been called upon to deal with judicial review of privative clauses. It can be anticipated that the leading Malaysian and British cases would be relied upon. In the previously noted constitutional

234 Note Tan and Thio, *supra* note 178 at 581-86.

235 Revised Statues of Singapore 1985, c. 143 [hereinafter *ISA*].

236 The availability of judicial review of actions taken pursuant to the *ISA* will be discussed *infra*, text with notes 265-78, "The Internal Security Act: Events of 1987-1989."

237 See generally M. P. Jain, *Administrative Law of Malaysia and Singapore* (Singapore: Malayan Law Journal, 3d ed., 1997).

238 One author has commented that in Singapore there is a "widespread" use of privative clauses. Chinkin, *supra* note 95 at 267.

239 Act No. 26 of 1990, ss. 8,9.

240 See ss. 10-12 and *Constitution of Singapore*, art. 221.

241 For a commentary on this legislation, see V. S. Winslow, "The Separation of Religion and Politics: The Maintenance of Religious Harmony Act 1990" (1990) 32 Malaya L. Rev. 327-31. At 329, the author comments that the s. 18 privative clause may allow for judicial review for errors of law that go to jurisdiction.

case, *Mohan Singh v. Attorney-General*, the Singapore court cited with approval the Malaysian-origin *Fire Bricks* case from the Privy Council.[242]

Privative clauses in Singapore are less in evidence than in Malaysia, but would be treated in the same manner to ensure limited judicial review of administrative and executive decision-making.

Review of Administrative Discretion and Prerogative Writs The *Supreme Court of Judicature Act* grants to Supreme Court judges the authority "to issue to any person or authority directions, orders or writs ... for the enforcement of any of the rights conferred by any written law or for any other purpose."[243] Use of prerogative writs to interfere with the broad statutory discretion has not been commonplace. One of the high profile cases in this area involved the *Newspapers and Printing Presses Act* (*NPPA*) under which the Minister, in his discretion, may issue licences required to own a printing press or print or publish a newspaper.[244] Section 16 of the *NPPA* gives the Minister the power to declare a newspaper published outside Singapore to be engaging in domestic politics with the result that the circulation of that paper can be restricted. In *Dow Jones Publishing Company (Asia) Inc. v. Attorney General*, the Minister's section 16 declaration and the consequent circulation restriction of the Asian *Wall Street Journal* was upheld.[245] The Singapore Court of Appeal declined to overturn the Minister's decision, although the decision apparently was based on the refusal of the *Journal* to allow a reply to a series of articles that questioned the motives of the Singapore government in setting up a second stock exchange.[246]

Judicial review based on the grounds of irrationality, illegality, and procedural impropriety as articulated in the *Council of Civil Service Unions and Others v. Ministry for the Civil Service*[247] is the accepted test in Singapore courts. In numerous cases, the courts have affirmed the view that the judiciary will not question the nature or sufficiency of evidence relied upon by the

---

242 See *Mohan Singh v. Attorney-General, supra* note 220 and the discussion of this case accompanying *supra* notes 220-22.

243 Revised Statutes of Singapore 1985 [hereinafter R.S.S. 1985], c. 322, s. 18(2).

244 See R.S.S. 1985, c. 206, ss. 3, 14 and 15A [hereinafter *NPPA*].

245 [1989] 2 M.L.J. 385.

246 Pursuant to amendments made to the *NPPA* in 1990, a licence is required for the sale of offshore newspapers in Singapore. This provision was used in 1993 to restrict the circulation of *The Economist*. See N. Balakrishna, "Row Over A Sentence," *Far Eastern Economic Review* (12 Aug. 1993) 13 and "A Singapore Saga," *The Economist* (7 Aug. 1993) 34. Under the pre-1990 legislation, numerous foreign publications had their circulations constricted. See generally A. M. Ramchand, "Freedom of the Press: Regulation Under the Newspaper and Printing Presses Act, 1974" (1990) 11 Singapore L. Rev. 130-47 and R. S. Frank et al., "The Decline in the Rule of Law in Malaysia and Singapore, Part II-Singapore" (1991) 46 Record of the Association of the Bar of the City of New York 5 at 73-76.

247 [1984] 3 All E.R. 935 at 950.

Executive in the exercise of discretion.[248] Administrative decisions are upheld, provided they are not so unreasonable that no reasonable person informed of the matter could have come to the decision,[249] or as long as they are fair and within the rules of natural justice.[250]

However, the courts will closely review and even overturn decisions of administrators and boards. For example, in *Wong Kok Chin v. Singapore Society of Accountants*, a decision of the accounting disciplinary committee made pursuant to the *Accountants Act* was quashed as being against the rules of natural justice.[251] In *Re Application of Leo Boh Boey*, the Court determined that the Commissioner of Labour had not properly exercised his discretion and issued a writ of mandamus to direct that the Commissioner was to assess compensation owed to the dependants of a deceased worker.[252] Certiorari was granted in *Re Letter of Request from the Court of New South Wales for the Prosecution of Peter Bazos*, on the grounds that the Minister of Law had exceeded the authorized jurisdiction by delegating power to make an appointment of a magistrate to take evidence for a foreign proceeding.[253]

In *J. B. Jeyaratnam v. Public Prosecutor*, the absolute discretion of the executive to grant licences to hold public meetings pursuant to the *Public Entertainments Act* was questioned.[254] Mr. Jeyaratnam had been refused a licence and complained that his freedom of speech had been infringed. While holding that the licence had not been wrongfully denied, Chan Sek Keong J. commented that, "if the discretion vested in the licensing officer under the Act were absolute and untrammelled, there might be a case for arguing that

---

248 A small sampling of cases includes *Heng Kai Kok v. Attorney General, Singapore*, [1987] 1 M.L.J. 98; *Jacob v. Attorney General*, [1970] 2 M.L.J. 133; *Wong Kim Sang and Anor. v. Attorney-General*, [1982] 1 M.L.J. 176; and *Leong Kum Fatt v. Attorney-General*, [1984] 2 M.L.J. 197. See also Jain, *supra* note 237 at 428-31.

249 See *Re Tai Choi Yu*, [1988] 1 M.L.J. 375; *Re Siah Mooi Guat*, [1988] 3 M.L.J. 448; and *Re Yap Lack Tee George*, [1992] 1 SLR 488.

250 *Tay Eng Chuan v. Professional Engineers Board*, [1982] 1 M.L.J. 249.

251 [1990] 1 M.L.J. 456.

252 [1986] 1 M.L.J. 469.

253 [1989] 3 M.L.J. 408.

254 [1990] 1 M.L.J. 129. This case involving Mr. Jeyaratnam, former secretary-general of the Workers' Party of Singapore and one-time sole opposition Member of Parliament, is one of a series. Most recently, in *Jeyaratnam v. Lee Kuan Yew*, [1992] 2 S.L.R. 310, Senior Minister Lee Kuan Yew was awarded damages for defamation from Mr. Jeyaratnam. The broad legal issues of this case are discussed in M. Hor, "The Freedom of Speech and Defamation" [1992] Singapore J. of Legal Studies 542-56. In a case that went to the Privy Council, *J. B. Jeyaratnam v. Law Society of Singapore*, [1988] 3 M.L.J. 425, the Court found for Mr. Jeyaratnam, overturning the Singapore Courts and ordering his reinstatement to the Singapore Bar. At 434, Lord Bridge on behalf of the Privy Council, commented: "Their Lordships have to record their deep disquiet that by a series of misjudgements the appellant and his co-accused ... have suffered a grievous injustice. They have been fined, imprisoned and publicly disgraced for offences of which they were not guilty. The appellant, [Mr. Jeyaratnam] in addition, had been deprived of his seat in Parliament."

This is the last case that went from Singapore to the Privy Council.

the licensing scheme is unconstitutional, as then the licensing officer would have been vested with arbitrary power to deprive a citizen of his constitutional right to freedom of speech and expression contrary to the objects of article 14(2)."[255] A related case is *Lau Seng Poh v. Controller of Immigration, Singapore*,[256] which involved an application for a writ of habeas corpus respecting a removal and detention order under the *Immigration Act*. The Court found that it could examine the facts and decide whether the decision of the Controller of Immigration was justified. The position of the Government was that a valid and regular order was a complete defence against the writ. Thean J. states that, if this were the case,

> judicial review of the decision of the executive in exercising such a draconian power of removal and detention under the Act would be precluded practically in all cases. Such drastic deprivation of rights of those subject to the Act to have recourse to courts for judicial review cannot have been intended by the legislature and indeed there is nothing in the Act to vouch for such a conclusion.[257]

The court quashed the orders and reversed the findings of the Controller.

Conclusion The above brief survey indicates a judicial robustness for reviewing government administrative decisions, a judicial sensitivity to the role of the courts as a watchdog on government action, a reluctance of legislators to deprive courts and citizens of access to courts by the use of privative clauses, yet a high degree of judicial deference to the will of Parliament and the executive in cases with political echoes such as regarding the *Religious Harmony Act*, the Jeyaratnam prosecution and the newspaper case.

Amending the Constitution

While deference to parliamentary supremacy is evident in the constraints on judicial review in the Constitution and, to a lesser extent, by the judicial attitudes to statutory constraints, the evolution of the procedures for amending the Singapore Constitution evidences a trend towards constitutional supremacy.

At independence, the 1963 State Constitution, the principal constitutional document, required amendments to be passed by a two-thirds majority vote of the Singapore legislature.[258] This was altered soon after independence to the lesser requirement of a simple majority vote of the Parliament.[259] In

255 *Ibid.* at 134.
256 [1985] 2 M.L.J. 350.
257 *Ibid.* at 353.
258 Lee, *supra* note 171 at 16 and Penna, *supra* note 208 at 218.
259 Lee, *supra* note 171 at 16 and Penna, *supra* note 208 at 218. The simple majority requirement allowed for change to take place quickly to meet the uncertain future.

1979, when the Attorney-General was instructed to produce a consolidated Constitution of Singapore, the amendment procedure was also changed. First, the two-thirds majority vote of Parliament was reinstated for virtually all changes to the Constitution.[260] Second, respecting the protection and surrender of sovereignty (Part III), constitutional change could take place only where a two-thirds positive vote was acquired in a national referendum.[261] The 1991 constitutional amendment regarding the redefined Presidency extended the areas where amending the Constitution could require a national referendum to include the office of the presidency, the financial provision of the Singapore Constitution, and the fundamental liberties sections.[262] The President had the discretion to call a referendum. However, these provisions never came into force.[263] New constitutional amendment provisions were adopted in 1996[264] that retain the presidential discretion to call a referendum where change is to be made to the office of the President or to the fundamental liberties section. The ability of the President to withhold consent to a constitutional amendment bill has been restricted. Again, these provisions are not yet in force.

The ease of constitutional amendment before 1991 led to numerous amendments. Now, although constitutional amendments are still numerous, the tightening of the requirements for amending the Constitution (when they come into force) indicates the adoption of an attitude that favours constitutional supremacy.

The Internal Security Act: Events of 1987-89

While it is unwise to draw untestable conclusions from events that are receding into history, the 1987-88 employment of the arrest powers under the *Internal Security Act (ISA)* and the subsequent cases, followed by the

---

260 *Constitution of Singapore*, art. 5(1) and (2). See Lee, *supra* note 171 at 21-23 and Penna, *supra* note 208 at 219. Further changes in 1984 removed all areas from constitutional change by simple majority.

261 *Ibid.* at art. 8(1). See Penna, *supra* note 208 at 220.

262 See generally Lee, *supra* note 178 at 191-92.

263 *The Constitutional Reference, supra* note 206, was provoked by the non-implementation of the amendment process. The question was whether the President could block any bill affecting the office of the President, including a bill designed to change the Constitution, under then art. 22(4), or whether the President could not block a bill designed to change the constitutional authority of the President. The suspended constitutional amendment provision would have applied and forced the President to determine whether a referendum was necessary, but not allowed for blocking of the bill itself. The Tribunal held that the President could not block a constitutional amendment bill since it was clearly the legislative intent that such bills be dealt with pursuant to the suspended Constitutional amendment provisions. For a detailed commentary, see the material cited in *supra* note 206.

264 *Constitution of the Republic of Singapore (Amendment) Act 1996*, Act No. 41 of 1996, ss. 2, 3.

revision of the Act and amendment of the Constitution, provide a window on Singaporean attitudes to parliamentary and constitutional supremacy.

In May-June 1987, 22 individuals were detained pursuant to the *ISA* for alleged involvement in a Marxist conspiracy against the State.[265] All but one of the detainees were released within a short period, but only one was released unconditionally. Eight of the original detainees were re-arrested under the *ISA* in April 1988 following their issuance of a statement alleging physical and mental abuse while in detention and denying their involvement in any Marxist conspiracy.[266] The Singapore Court of Appeal in December 1988, overturning a lower court decision, granted habeas corpus to four of the detainees.[267] The technical flaw seized upon by the Court of Appeal was quickly corrected, and the four successful applicants were re-arrested almost immediately on their release.[268]

The 1988 Court of Appeal decision has been described as one of the most important in the Commonwealth in recent years, not for the technical aspects that resulted in the issuance of the writ of habeas corpus, but because of the Court's statements regarding judicial review of detention orders.[269] Section 8(1) of the *ISA* allowed the Minister of Home Affairs to make a detention order "if the President is satisfied" that a person is acting prejudicially to the interests of Singapore. The Court of Appeal held that the exercise of this discretion was reviewable by the courts and that the standard of review was to be an objective one rather than a subjective one.[270]

---

265 Not surprisingly, the arrests attracted considerable attention in Singapore. The arrests also attracted considerable attention outside Singapore. The 1987 detentions are described in L. L. To, "Singapore in 1987: Setting A New Agenda" (1988), 28 *Asian Survey* 202 at 204-206 and more briefly in Milne and Mauzy, *supra* note 164 at 80-82. See also Frank, *supra* note 246 at 27-31.

More generally respecting Singapore's *Internal Security Act*, see: A. J. Harding, "Singapore," in Harding and Hatchard, *supra* note 124 at 193-208; Yee Chee Wai, Ho Tze Wei Monica, and Seng Kiat Boon Daniel, "Judicial Review of Preventive Detention under the Internal Security Act – A Summary of Developments" (1989) 10 Singapore L. Rev. 66 at 68-77 and Frank, *ibid.* at 22-27.

An insightful analysis comparing preventive detention laws and practices in countries that have common law antecedents is provided by S. Greer, "Preventive Detention and Public Security – Towards A General Model," in Harding and Hatchard, *ibid.* at 23-40. Reading this contribution puts the 1987-89 events in Singapore in an interesting comparative context.

266 See T. J. Bellows, "Singapore in 1988: The Transition Moves Forward" (1989) 29 *Asian Survey* 145 at 147-48 and Frank, *supra* note 246 at 31-33.

267 *Chng Suan Tze v. Minister of Home Affairs*, [1989] 1 M.L.J. 69.

268 Harding, *supra* note 265 at 199.

269 *Ibid.*

270 See *Chng Suan Tze v. Minister of Home Affairs*, [1989] 1 M.L.J. 69 at 77-88. The Court was obviously aware that it was taking a bold step; at 78, the Court stated: "In our judgment, the time has come for us to recognize that the subjective test in respect of ss. 8 and 10 of the *ISA* can no longer be supported."

Harding, *supra* note 265 at 198-203 provides a concise and insightful analysis of the decision. At 198, he notes that in the case "the entire theory of judicial review of

Within two weeks of the Court of Appeal decision, the government of Singapore introduced a bill to alter the *ISA*[271] and to amend the Constitution. [272] The unmistakable goal of both actions was to reverse the decision of the Court of Appeal and restore the law on judicial review of executive actions under the *ISA* to its previous state of non-interference by the judiciary.[273] The changes made to article 149 of the Constitution ensured that no challenges of constitutional *ultra vires* of action taken under the *ISA* can be maintained.[274] The changes to the *ISA* provide that the standard of judicial review that is to apply is that which existed as of 13 July 1971 and, specifically, that no judicial review can be made of actions under the *ISA* except respecting whether procedural requirements have been met.[275] In examining the *ISA* shortly after the revisions were enacted, the Singapore High Court determined that the legislative changes did not conflict with the Constitution and that the subjective test preventing substantial judicial review of the exercise of discretion pursuant to the *ISA* was the prevailing law in Singapore.[276]

The vigour of the Singaporean government's reaction, Constitutional amendment, and restriction on judicial review, to the assertion by the Court of Appeal that executive discretion must be open to scrutiny suggests that parliamentary supremacy remains a core constitutional value in Singapore. On the revised *ISA* and 1989 constitutional amendments, a student writer commented: "The purpose of the amendments is laudable, in that they seek to ensure that the elected representatives of the people, and no one else, are responsible for national security."[277]

Governments naturally feel a reluctance to allow court interference in security matters. Democratic principles direct that elected rather than unelected decision-makers be responsible for fundamental societal choices. The national security context of the government action under the *ISA* may constrain its usefulness as a window on attitudes towards constitutional

---

preventive-detention decisions was overturned with the substitution of an objective for a subjective test of their legality." See also Wai, *supra* note 265 at 77-98 and Sin Boon Ann, "Judges and Administrative Discretion – A Look at Chng Suan Tze v. Minister of Home Affairs and Ors" [1989] 2 M.L.J. ci-cvii. The latter author is highly critical of the Court's decision.

Concerning judicial review of preventive detention more generally, see Greer, *supra* note 265 at 30-36.

271 *Internal Security (Amendment) Act 1989*.

272 *Constitutional Amendment 1989*.

273 Harding, *supra* note 265 at 203.

274 See Wai, *supra* note 265 at 98 and Harding, *supra* note 265 at 203.

275 These legislative changes are described in Harding, *supra* note 265 at 203-204 and Wai, *supra* note 265 at 98-99. See also T. C. Ho, "Judiciary Under Seize?" (1992) 13 Singapore L. Rev. 60 at 73-79.

276 *Teo Soh Lung v. Minister of Home Affairs* [1989] 2 M.L.J. 449. This case is commented upon by Harding, *supra* note 265 at 204-206 and Wai, *supra* note 265 at 99-102.

277 Ho, *supra* note 275 at 79.

and parliamentary supremacy. However, as one authority has noted, the message of non-interference with executive decisions in national security matters has a way of colouring the whole approach to judicial review.[278]

Canada

Constitutional and Political History

Like Malaysia and Singapore, Canada is the product of a colonial past. European legal and political systems arrived with explorers and settlers first from France and later from Britain. After British military victories over France resulted in the cession of the colony of New France to Britain in 1763, Britain asserted ultimate legal and political sovereignty over almost all the territory that is now Canada, with little regard for the claims of the aboriginal peoples. British authority in Canada was then gradually bolstered and consolidated through exploration, trade, and settlement, and particularly by an influx of Loyalist immigrants from the American colonies into eastern Canada immediately following the American Revolution.

In 1867, the *British North America Act*,[279] an act of the British Imperial Parliament, united three of Britain's North American colonies[280] into the federated colony of Canada. This process, known as Confederation, had been spurred in part by fears that the rapidly expanding and rambunctious American Republic might soon turn its expansionism northward. The result was a federal state initially composed of four provinces and a national government. Other provinces and territories were gradually added to the federation until the present constellation of ten provinces and two territories was achieved.[281]

Although Confederation brought with it a very large measure of self-government, it did not bring full independence. Movement towards severing remaining colonial ties with Britain was an evolutionary process that continued into the twentieth century. It culminated in 1931, when passage of

278 Harding, *supra* note 265 at 200.

279 *British North America Act, 1867*, 30 and 31 Victoria, c. 3, renamed the *Constitution Act, 1867* by section 53 of the *Constitution Act, 1982*, being Schedule B to the *Canada Act, 1982*, U.K., 1982, c. 11. The *British North America Act, 1867*, is hereafter cited as the *C.A., 1867*, and the *Constitution Act, 1982*, is hereafter cited as the *C.A., 1982*.

280 New Brunswick, Nova Scotia, and Canada.

281 The four original provinces were Ontario, Quebec, New Brunswick, and Nova Scotia. Provinces were added in the following sequence: Manitoba, 1870; British Columbia, 1871; Prince Edward Island, 1873; Alberta and Saskatchewan 1905; and Newfoundland, 1949. The two existing territories are the Yukon Territory and the Northwest Territories. A third territory, Nunavut, will be carved out of the Northwest Territories no later than 1 April 1999, when the *Nunavet Act*, S.C. 1993, c. 28, is scheduled to come into effect unless it is sooner proclaimed in force by the Governor in Council. The remaining portion of the Northwest Territories is likely to be renamed.

the *Statute of Westminster*[282] formally marked the end of the last significant vestiges of colonial status. Even then, however, several legal ties with Britain were maintained: appeals to the Judicial Committee of the Privy Council in civil matters continued until 1949; the British Parliament retained the formal legal power to amend Canada's constitutional legislation until 1982, when the Constitution of Canada was finally "patriated";[283] and the British Queen is still recognized as the Queen of Canada.

Two themes emerging from Canada's colonial past have been particularly influential in shaping the present legal and political system. First, and perhaps most obviously, Canadian legal and political institutions are directly based on British models. Second, the uneasy relationship between French-speaking and English-speaking Canadians dating from 1763 has remained a pivotal factor in Canadian politics and government. Many of the institutions adopted at Confederation, including federalism itself, reflect a concern with cultural and linguistic dualism and Canadian politics since that time have been marked by periodic revivals of French-Canadian nationalism. Indeed, the most recent revival of strong nationalist sentiment in Quebec acted as a catalyst for the movement that led to patriation of the Constitution in 1982[284] and currently threatens to lead to the separation of Quebec from Canada.

While these historical factors remain significant, more recent developments mingle with them and, in some ways, act as counterweights to them. Two deserve specific mention. First, Canada has always been a nation of immigrants, the numbers of whom soon overwhelmed the aboriginal populations. Over time, however, patterns of immigration have shifted away from European and American sources. This change has generated increasing ethnic, racial, and religious diversity in the population and the corresponding pressures that diversity can entail.[285] To some extent, these

---

282 *Statute of Westminster*, 1931 (U.K.), 22 Geo. V, c. 4.

283 Power to amend Canadian constitutional legislation remained in Britain following the *Statute of Westminster* in 1931 because Canadians could not agree on an amending formula. After 1931, however, Britain could exercise its amending power only upon a request from Canada. "Patriation" is used here to refer to the final termination of all British authority over Canada through the enactment of the *Canada Act, 1982*, *supra* note 279, and the inclusion of domestic amending procedures in the *C.A., 1982*.

284 See *infra*, text with notes 293-300, "Patriation, Amendment, and Adoption of the Charter."

285 For example, in 1901, of a total population of 5,371,315, only about 12% of Canadian residents identified themselves as having origins other than British or French. Approximately 8.5% of the population were characterized as having other European origins, and only about 3% identified themselves as either being of Asiatic (Chinese, Japanese, or other Asiatic) or other origins – e.g. native Indian and Eskimo, negro, other, and not stated categories. Source: Dominion Bureau of Statistics, *Ninth Census of Canada 1951*, Vol. 1, Table 31, Population By Origin for Canada (Ottawa: Queen's Printer, 1953) at 31. In the 1991 census, of a total population of 26,994,040, approximately 69% of the population identified themselves as having British only, French

demographic changes counterbalance the more traditional French-English dynamic, justifying multiculturalism (as opposed to bilingualism and biculturalism) and providing a rationale for protecting individuals against discrimination (as opposed to protecting groups in their enjoyment of collective rights). Second, close ties to Britain have been replaced by close ties to the United States, with which Canada shares military alliances, the world's longest undefended border, and the world's largest trading relationship. While Canadians in the nineteenth century looked to Britain for models, in the twentieth century Canadians have been increasingly influenced by American legal, political, and cultural trends.

Constitutional Structure

Legislative Institutions and Responsible Government

The governmental institutions adopted for the Dominion of Canada in 1867 were based on the Westminster model and operate in accordance with the basic premises of a Cabinet system of responsible government.[286] The federal Parliament consists of three components: the Queen, as represented by the Governor General; a democratically elected House of Commons (currently made up of 282 Members of Parliament); and an appointed Senate.[287] Of these, the House of Commons is unquestionably the most powerful component. The legislative powers of the monarch as exercised through the Governor General are purely formal, confined to the automatic bestowal of Royal assent to bills that have been passed by the House of Commons and Senate.[288] The Senate itself, composed of 104 members appointed by the Governor General on the recommendation of the Prime Minister, as an unelected body, labours under doubts about the legitimacy of its role in a

---

only, British and French, or British and/or French and other origins. Approximately 15% identified themselves as having European origins (other than French or English), and approximately 15% identified themselves in categories other than French, British, or European. Approximately 6% categorized themselves as Asian, Arab, or African; 2% as aboriginal; 0.7% as Caribbean or Latin/Central/South American; 0.8% as black; 2.8% as Canadian; and 3% as "other." Source: Statistics Canada, 1991 Census of Canada, cited in Ministry of Industry and Science, *Canadian Social Trends* No. 30 (Ottawa: Ministry of Industry and Science, 1993) at 19-20.

286 The preamble to the *C.A., 1867* declares that Canada is to have "a Constitution similar in Principle to that of the United Kingdom." The conventions associated with responsible government, including the roles of the Prime Minister, the Premiers, and their Cabinets, are part of the unwritten constitution inherited from Britain.

287 *C.A., 1867*, s. 17.

288 In non-legislative matters, too, the Governor General almost invariably acts only on the advice of the Prime Minister and the Cabinet. The personal prerogatives or reserve powers of the Governor General are extremely limited, and relate primarily to the appointment and dismissal of the Prime Minister and the dissolution of Parliament. Their use is curtailed by constitutional convention and can be resorted to only in exceptional circumstances. See P. Hogg, *Constitutional Law of Canada*, 3d ed. (Scarborough, Ont.: Carswell, 1992) loose-leaf edition at 9-20 to 9-26.

modern democracy. Furthermore, although the Senate was intended to provide for the representation of regional interests,[289] it is generally conceded not to be an effective body for that purpose, largely because senators tend to vote in accordance with party, rather than regional, loyalties. Probably for both these reasons, the Senate has traditionally exercised its extensive legislative powers with great restraint.[290]

The ten provincial legislatures are similarly modelled on the British parliamentary system with the exception that all of them consist of a single elected chamber, termed a Legislative Assembly, with no upper chamber. The Queen is represented in each province by the Lieutenant Governor of the Province, appointed by the Queen on the recommendation of the federal government. As in the case of the Governor General, the powers of the Lieutenant Governor are exercised with restraint and have become almost entirely matters of formality.

Federalism

Federalism is a predominant feature of Canadian constitutional arrangements. Under the *Constitution Acts* 1867-1982, legislative and executive power in Canada is distributed between two levels of government, federal and provincial, both of which exercise extensive, and sometimes overlapping, legislative powers.[291] A key aspect of federalism, Canadian style, is the importance of the provincial governments. Although it is typically claimed that the original framers of the Constitution intended to create a strongly centralized federal system dominated by a powerful central government,[292]

289 *C.A., 1867*, s. 22 provides that there shall be 24 senators appointed from each of four regions: i.e. Ontario, Quebec, the maritime provinces, and the western provinces. In addition, six senators are appointed from Newfoundland and one from each of the Yukon and the Northwest Territories. In 1990, an additional eight senators were appointed under the special provisions of s. 26 of *C.A. 1867*.

290 Technically, under the provisions of the *C.A. 1867*, the Senate enjoys virtually the same legislative powers as the elected body, the House of Commons, except that all money bills must originate in the House. However, in practice, the members of the Senate have accepted a subordinate role to that of the House of Commons. Consequently, the Senate rarely refuses to pass legislation that has been approved by the House of Commons, although it not infrequently may delay passage and move amendments.

291 See *C.A., 1867*, ss. 91 (federal legislative powers) and 92 (provincial legislative powers). The territorial governments in the Yukon and the Northwest Territories are creatures of Parliament, created by federal statute.

292 One of the arguments for creating a strong central government in 1867 was the perceived need for self-defence against possible threats from the United States. Legal indicators commonly pointed to in support of the argument that a highly centralized system was intended in 1867 include: the federal power to reserve and disallow provincial legislation (*C.A. 1867*, s. 90); the federal power to declare works and undertakings to be for the general advantage of Canada, and thus within federal jurisdiction (*C.A. 1867*, s. 92(10)(c)); and the federal residual power (jurisdiction over matters not expressly enumerated in ss. 91 and 92 lies with the federal government per the preamble to s. 91 of *C.A. 1867*).

it is generally conceded that Canada now has one of the more decentralized federal systems in the world.

Provinces have jurisdiction over important subject matters such as health, education, the administration of justice, matters of a local and private nature, and, most importantly, property and civil rights in the province. The latter jurisdiction, in particular, has been interpreted to give provinces control over a broad range of subject matters. Parliament, on the other hand, exercises jurisdiction over matters of national concern such as foreign affairs, defence, international trade, banking and the monetary system, internal trade and commerce, interprovincial transportation and communication undertakings, and the criminal law. It also has a general power to make laws for the "peace, order, and good government of Canada," but this power is largely confined to emergency situations and cannot be freely exercised to oust provincial jurisdiction in ordinary circumstances. It is important to note that Parliament has much broader taxation powers than the provincial governments, a fact that has created the need for co-operative federalism and a variety of revenue-sharing agreements under which federal money is provided to the provinces to assist them in spending on programs within provincial jurisdiction.

Patriation, Amendment, and Adoption of the *Charter*

In 1982, the Canadian legal and political system underwent radical change with the patriation of the Constitution, the adoption of the *Canadian Charter of Rights and Freedoms*,[293] and constitutional recognition of the aboriginal and treaty rights of the aboriginal peoples of Canada.

Patriation brought with it power to amend the Constitution in Canada through a complicated set of procedures.[294] Constitutional amendments relating to the right of a province to certain minimum numbers of seats in the House of Commons, the offices of the Queen, Governor General, and the Lieutenant Governor, the use of the English and French languages in national institutions, the composition of the Supreme Court of Canada, and the amending provisions themselves, require unanimity on the part of the federal Senate and the House of Commons and the ten provincial legislative assemblies.[295] Other amendments can be made through the general amending formula, which requires the approval of the House of Commons, the Senate, and the legislative assemblies of at least two-thirds of the provinces having in the aggregate at least 50% of the population of all the provinces.[296] The political situation in Canada suggests that unanimity, where it is required, will be extremely difficult to obtain, and it is likely that even

293 *Supra* note 3.
294 The amending provisions are set out in ss. 38-49 of *C.A. 1982*.
295 *C.A. 1867*, s. 41.
296 *C.A. 1867*, s. 38(1).

the general amending formula will rarely be invoked successfully.[297] Canada's constitutional arrangements must thus be considered to be relatively rigid.

The *Charter*, adopted as part of the patriation package in 1982, enshrines a sweeping set of individual rights and civil liberties. *Charter* rights fall into seven categories: (1) fundamental freedoms (freedom of religion and conscience, freedom of thought, belief, opinion, and speech, freedom of the press, freedom of peaceful assembly, and freedom of association); (2) democratic rights (the right to vote and to be qualified to be a candidate in federal and provincial elections, annual sittings of the legislature, and elections every five years); (3) mobility rights (the right of citizens and permanent residents to enter and leave Canada, to move from province to province, to reside in any province and to pursue the gaining of a livelihood in any province without being unduly restricted by legal barriers); (4) legal rights (the right to life, liberty, and security of the person and the right not to be deprived thereof except in accordance with the principles of fundamental justice, freedom from unreasonable search and seizure, the right of an accused person to have counsel, to be tried within a reasonable time, and to be presumed innocent, and freedom from retroactive criminal laws, double jeopardy and cruel and unusual punishment); (5) equality rights (the right to be equal before and under the law and to have the equal benefit and protection of the law without discrimination); (6) language rights (the right to use either English or French in national political institutions and federal courts and the right to receive federal government services in either official language); and (7) minority language education rights (minimum guarantees to receive education in either French or English subject to a number of qualifications and a "where numbers warrant" restriction).

The *Charter* is binding on Parliament and provincial legislatures as well as on federal and provincial governments.[298] It applies not only to legislation but also to the exercise of executive or administrative governmental powers, whether they are based on statute or on Crown prerogative, and to the exercise of police powers. However, *Charter* rights are subject to two key

297 Since patriation, a package of relatively minor amendments relating to aboriginal rights has been approved *(Constitution Amendment Proclamation, 1983*, R.S.C. 1985, Appendix II, No. 46). However, two significant initiatives for amendments, the Meech Lake Accord in 1987-90, and the Charlottetown Accord in 1991-92, ultimately failed. See generally P. Monahan, *Meech Lake: The Inside Story* (Toronto: Univ. of Toronto Press, 1991); K. Swinton, "Amending the Canadian Constitution: Lessons from Meech Lake" (1992) 42 U.T.L.J. 139; K. McRoberts and P. Monahan, eds. *The Charlottetown Accord, the Referendum and the Future of Canada* (Toronto: Univ. of Toronto Press, 1993).

298 *Charter*, s. 32. On the interpretation of this provision see generally *Retail, Wholesale and Department Store Union Local 580 et al. v. Dolphin Delivery Ltd.*, [1986] 2 S.C.R. 573; *McKinney v. University of Guelph*, [1990] 3 S.C.R. 229; *Harrison v. University of British Columbia*, [1990] 3 S.C.R. 451; *Douglas/Kwantlen Faculty Assn. v. Douglas College*, [1990] 3 S.C.R. 570; *Lavigne v. O.P.S.E.U.*, [1991] 2 S.C.R. 211.

restrictions. First, section 1 of the *Charter* declares that the rights and freedoms referred to in it are guaranteed "subject to such reasonable limits prescribed by law as can be demonstrably justified in a free and democratic society." This "saving clause" provides scope for governments to justify legislation or government action that, on its face, appears to conflict with or restrict *Charter* rights. Second, section 33 of the *Charter* effects a significant compromise on the constitutional entrenchment of rights. It allows Parliament or a provincial legislature to expressly declare in an enactment that it is to operate notwithstanding a conflict with *Charter* rights.[299] Although the section 33 "override" is likely to be invoked only rarely,[300] section 1 operates as a constant limitation on the otherwise broadly framed *Charter* rights.

The final aspect of the patriation package that deserves special mention is the recognition and affirmation of the aboriginal and treaty rights of the aboriginal peoples of Canada found in section 35 of the *Constitution Act, 1982.* This section is not part of the *Charter*, and thus is not subject to either section 33 or section 1. Although section 35 refers only to "existing" rights, it signifies a new era in the often troubled relationship between aboriginal and non-aboriginal people in Canada and has a legal and political effect that goes beyond symbolism. Since its entrenchment, aboriginal peoples have made significant gains in terms of legal and political recognition of their rights, movement towards settlement of their outstanding land entitlement claims, and inclusion of their representatives in national constitutional reform processes.

The Judiciary

The Canadian court system is primarily structured along provincial lines. Each province has its own hierarchical court system, typically consisting of inferior courts and a superior court of general jurisdiction with both trial and appeal levels. Although these courts are created by provincial statutes

---

299 The sweeping scope of this "override" provision is narrowed somewhat by the fact that it cannot be used in relation to democratic rights, language rights, or minority language education rights, and by the five-year time limit that is placed on such declarations.

300 A blanket invocation of the s. 33 override was used by Quebec in 1982 to minimize the impact of the *Charter* in Quebec on the ground that Quebec had not consented to the patriation package (S.Q. 1982, c. 21). The constitutionality of this attempt to have the s. 33 override apply to all Quebec statutes was considered and upheld by the Supreme Court in *Ford v. Quebec,* [1988] 2 S.C.R. 712. In the period from 1982 to 1985, a notwithstanding clause was also routinely inserted into every new Quebec statute. While this practice stopped in 1985, since that time Quebec governments have not hesitated to insert notwithstanding clauses into Quebec statutes whenever it is deemed to be necessary to protect Quebec legislation from *Charter* review. See generally P. Hogg, *supra* note 288 at 36-2 to 36-4. Outside Quebec, however, the override has been invoked only once, by Saskatchewan. Most Canadian politicians have indicated a strong disinclination to resort to use of the override.

and are funded and administered by the province,[301] the Constitution requires that all superior court judges be appointed and paid by the federal Crown.[302] The Constitution also guarantees that superior court judges hold office during good behaviour until age 75 and are removable by the Governor General only upon joint resolutions of the Senate and the House of Commons.[303] The latter has never occurred.[304]

In addition to the courts in the provinces, two important courts have been created by Parliament: the Supreme Court of Canada and the Federal Court.[305] The Supreme Court of Canada, created by federal statute in 1875,[306] is a general court of appeal with jurisdiction throughout Canada. Since 1949, when appeals to the Judicial Committee of the Privy Council were abolished, it has been the court of last resort in all legal matters and it performs a particularly important role in constitutional adjudication. The jurisdiction of the Federal Court of Canada is limited by statute to matters involving the Federal Crown, judicial review of federal administrative tribunals, and specific federal subject matters.[307]

Although there are only limited constitutional guarantees of judicial independence in Canada's written Constitution,[308] the principle is firmly established in practice and is jealously guarded by the courts. Recent decisions

301 In creating these courts, provinces act pursuant to their jurisdiction under s. 92(14) of *C.A., 1867* to legislate in relation to the administration of justice in the province.

302 See ss. 96-100 of the *Constitution Act, 1867*. In practice, judges of the superior, district, and county courts are appointed by the Governor in Council on the recommendation of the federal Minister of Justice. See P. Russell, *The Judiciary in Canada: The Third Branch of Government* (Toronto: McGraw-Hill Ryerson, 1987) at 112-13.

303 *C.A. 1867*, s. 99.

304 The removal procedure has occasionally been invoked but rendered unnecessary by the resignation of the judge concerned. See generally, Hogg, *supra* note 288 at 7-9. At present, an inquiry and a report by the Canadian Judicial Council recommending removal would undoubtedly be considered a precondition to the exercise of Parliament's removal powers. The Council is established under the *Judges Act*, R.S.C. 1985, c. J-1, Part II, and consists of the Chief Justice of Canada and the Chief and Associate Chief Justices of all of the superior courts in Canada. At the request of the federal Minister of Justice or the Attorney General of any province, the Council may conduct an inquiry into whether a superior court judge should be removed from office because he or she has become incapacitated or disabled from the due execution of the office of a judge for reasons such as age, infirmity, or misconduct.

305 These courts are established under s. 101 of the *C.A. 1867*. Under this authority, Parliament has also legislated to create a court system for the Yukon and the Northwest Territories and a Tax Court to hear income tax appeals.

306 *Supreme and Exchequer Courts Act*, S.C. 1875, c. 11; now, *Supreme Court Act*, R.S.C. 1985, c. S-26. Perhaps surprisingly, the Supreme Court is not expressly entrenched in the Constitution.

307 *Federal Court Act*, R.S.C. 1985, c. F-7, as amended by S.C. 1990, c. 8. Only some of the Federal Court's jurisdiction is exclusive. In many areas, its jurisdiction with respect to matters involving the federal Crown is concurrent with the jurisdiction of the superior courts in the provinces. The Court has both a trial and an appeal division.

308 In addition to the provisions of ss. 96-100 of the *C.A. 1867*, s. 11(d) of the *Charter* bolsters judicial independence by guaranteeing those accused of crimes the right to

of the Supreme Court of Canada have referred to judicial independence as a cardinal constitutional principle having at least three essential conditions: security of tenure, financial security, and institutional independence regarding matters affecting adjudication.[309] Judicial impartiality is also recognized as a fundamental principle, and Canadian judges are expected to remain aloof from the political arena and refrain from public political commentary. In 1981, this principle was allegedly violated by a superior court judge who publicly expressed personal views on certain aspects of the constitutional patriation proposals then being hotly debated by Canadians. His remarks were characterized by an investigative committee of the Canadian Judicial Council as "unwise and inappropriate" and sufficiently serious to warrant a recommendation for removal from office. However, the Council stopped short of making such a recommendation on the ground that this was the first such case in Canada and it was possible that judges may have been under a misapprehension as to the nature of the constraints imposed on them by their office. The judge in question, however, resigned, unrepentant.[310]

Judicial Review of Legislative and Administrative Action

Judicial Review on Division of Powers Issues

The British legal and political traditions imported into Canada included the concept of parliamentary supremacy. However, from the time of Confederation, the principle of federalism and the division of legislative authority between the federal and provincial governments ensured that parliamentary sovereignty would not mean the same thing in Canada as it did in Britain. Whereas in Britain courts had no grounds on which to refuse to apply a statute enacted by Parliament, in Canada the existence of a written constitutional document in the form of an Imperial statute that distributed legislative powers between two levels of government provided a basis for judicial intervention. Despite the absence of any reference to judicial review in the Constitution, Canadian courts took up the task of policing the jurisdictional boundaries between federal and provincial governments shortly after Confederation.[311]

---

be tried "in a fair and public hearing by an independent and impartial tribunal." Section 7 of the *Charter* and the preamble to the *C.A. 1867* have been referred to as other sources for constitutional guarantees of the principle of judicial independence. See e.g. *Reference re Remuneration of Judges*, [1997] S.C.J. No. 75.

309 See e.g. *Valente v. The Queen*, [1985] 2 S.C.R. 673; *Beauregard v. Canada*, [1986] S.C.R. 56; *MacKeigan v. Hickman*, [1989] 2 S.C.R. 796; and *Reference re Remuneration of Judges*, *ibid*.

310 For an abbreviated account of this affair, see F. L. Morton, ed., *Law, Politics and the Judicial Process in Canada*, 2d ed. (Calgary: University of Calgary Press, 1992) at 147-53.

311 The authority of the courts to undertake this role was sanctioned by the Judicial Committee of the Privy Council, which remained the court of last resort for Canadians until appeals to that body were abolished in 1949.

Nevertheless, before the advent of the *Charter*, Parliament and the provincial legislatures were each considered sovereign, provided that they acted within the scope of the legislative powers accorded to them by the Constitution. While judges would not hesitate to strike down and declare inoperative any legislation that contravened the division of powers, they explicitly recognized that the principle of parliamentary sovereignty did not allow them to question the wisdom or policy of legislation that was *intra vires*.[312]

Judicial Review of Charter Issues

In 1982, the entrenchment of the *Charter* greatly enhanced the breadth of judicial review on constitutional grounds and correspondingly reduced the scope of parliamentary supremacy. Section 52 of the *Constitution Act, 1982* proclaims that the Constitution is the "supreme law of Canada" and that laws that are inconsistent with it are of no force or effect. This gives courts a mandate to review laws on substantive grounds for conformity with *Charter* rights and to strike down those that are found wanting. In particular, section 1 of the *Charter* invites courts to wade deeply into the realm of policy and political choices in deciding whether legislation that *prima facie* violates *Charter* rights can nevertheless be justified as a reasonable limitation. It follows that, absent a use of the section 33 legislative override, parliamentary sovereignty gives way to constitutional supremacy in any matter that the *Charter* reaches.[313]

The volume of *Charter* cases alone establishes that diminished parliamentary supremacy and augmented judicial control over both legislative and executive branches of government have become a reality in Canada. Virtually thousands of *Charter* cases have been heard and decided by the courts since the *Charter* came into effect and, within ten years of its enactment,

312 These principles were clearly stated by Dickson J. (as he then was) in *Amax Potash Ltd. v. Government of Saskatchewan*, [1977] 2 S.C.R. 576 at 590, as follows:

> A state, it is said, is sovereign and it is not for the Courts to pass upon the policy or wisdom of legislative will. As a broad statement of principle that is undoubtedly correct, but the general principle must yield to the requisites of the Constitution in a federal state. By it the bounds of sovereignty are defined and supremacy circumscribed. The Courts will not question the wisdom of enactments which, by the terms of the Canadian Constitution are within the competence of the Legislatures, but it is the high duty of this Court to insure that the Legislatures do not transgress the limits of their constitutional mandate and engage in the illegal exercise of power.

313 It would be too soon to write an epitaph for parliamentary supremacy in Canada, however. It is clear that, in cases where neither *Charter* nor division of powers issues apply, parliamentary supremacy continues to be recognized as a basic legal reality. See e.g. *Reference re Canada Assistance Plan*, [1991] 2 S.C.R. 525.

314 In the period from April 1982 to April 1995 the Supreme Court of Canada heard 332 *Charter* cases that amounted to approximately 23% of its total docket. (These statistics were provided by the Legal Services Branch of the Supreme Court of Canada, Ottawa,

over 300 had reached the Supreme Court level.[314] Although the government side wins the majority of these cases,[315] judicial supervision for *Charter* conformity has become a constant in the legal landscape and governments accept the need to legislate and act in such a way as to conform with the judicial expectations of *Charter* compliance.[316]

Furthermore, Canadian judges have been activist under the *Charter*. Any doubts about whether they would react conservatively to their new mandate, and not shed their habits of judicial deference to legislative supremacy, were dispelled soon after the *Charter* came into force. In an early *Charter* case, for example, a justice of the Supreme Court answered those who questioned the legitimacy of unelected and unaccountable judges striking down legislation put in place by a democratically elected legislative body in the following terms:

> This is an argument which was heard countless times prior to the enactment of the *Charter* but which has in truth, for better or for worse, been settled by the very coming into force of the *Constitution Act, 1982*. It ought not to be forgotten that the historic decision to entrench the *Charter* in our Constitution was taken not by the courts but by the elected representatives of the people of Canada. It was those representatives who extended the scope of constitutional adjudication and entrusted the courts with this new and onerous responsibility. Adjudication under the *Charter* must be approached free of any lingering doubts as to its legitimacy.[317]

Judges also rationalized their new responsibilities under the *Charter* by denying that it required them to second guess legislative decisions. In another early *Charter* case,[318] a group of peace activists challenged the federal Cabinet's decision to allow the United States to conduct cruise missile

---

Ontario, and are valid as at 24 April 1995. The Branch also reports that of 291 cases heard by the Supreme Court since 1987, when Legal Services began to break down *Charter* appeals statistics into Civil and Criminal matters, 239 (approximately 82%) involved criminal matters and 52 (approximately 18%) involved civil matters.)

315 A study of Supreme Court of Canada decisions in *Charter* cases during the period 1982-92 found that the *Charter* challenges to legislative or government action were upheld in 33% of them. See F. L. Morton, P. H. Russell, and T. Riddell, "The Canadian Charter of Rights and Freedoms: A Descriptive Analysis of the First Decade, 1982-1992" (1994) 5 N.J.C.L. 1.

316 Canadian governments accept *Charter* rulings by the Supreme Court as unquestionably binding. Apart from Quebec, none have resorted to s. 33 to undo a *Charter* decision of the Supreme Court. The standard practice in the case of legislation found to violate the *Charter* is to either abandon it or redraft it to attempt to comply with the *Charter*. Sometimes, of course, governments are happy to live with a statute being declared inoperative by the courts, especially if the legislation was that of a previous government of different political beliefs.

317 *Reference re s. 94 (2) of the Motor Vehicle Act*, [1985] 2 S.C.R. 486 at 497, Lamer J.

318 *Operation Dismantle v. The Queen*, [1985] 1 S.C.R. 441.

testing on Canadian soil. It was alleged that Cabinet had violated the right of Canadians to "life, liberty, and security of the person," as protected by section 7 of the *Charter*, since the missile testing would increase the threat of nuclear war and make Canada a more likely target for nuclear attack. Although the Supreme Court ultimately held that the statement of claim should be struck out on the ground that it disclosed no reasonable cause of action,[319] the Court nevertheless asserted that because the *Charter* imposed a duty on the executive branch of government to observe *Charter* rights, the Court could, in principle, review Cabinet decisions on foreign policy and defence matters, regardless of whether those decisions were based on legislation or on Crown prerogative. Wilson J. emphasized that judges were not being asked whether the government's defence policy was sound, but whether it violated *Charter* rights. The latter was an appropriate question for judicial review; the former was not.

> [I]f we are to look at the Constitution for an answer to the question whether it is appropriate for the courts to "second guess" the executive on matters of defence, we would conclude it is not appropriate. However, if what we are being asked to do is to decide whether any particular act of the executive violates the rights of the citizens, then it is not only appropriate that we answer the question; it is our obligation under the *Charter* to do so.[320]

Another early sign of judicial confidence in the new role of the courts under the *Charter* was the adoption of a stringent test under section 1 for governments seeking to justify restrictions on *Charter* rights as reasonable limitations. Governments would be able to justify *Charter* infringements only if the objectives of a law were accepted by the courts as sufficiently important to warrant overriding constitutionally protected rights and only if the means chosen to achieve that objective were judged to be proportionate to the ends sought to be achieved. Proportionality in this context would require that the means chosen to achieve the objective be rational, fair, and the least intrusive possible.[321] Strict application of this test would obviously make it difficult for governments to justify *Charter* infringements.

More recently, however, courts appear to have settled into a somewhat more cautious approach to *Charter* cases.[322] This has been particularly

319 The majority held that, even if the facts as alleged were true, it would be impossible to prove a causal link between cruise missile testing and an increased threat to life or security of the person. The issues were not susceptible to being proved by evidence; the political effects of testing could only ever be a matter of speculation.

320 *Supra* note 318 at 472.

321 The standard test, known as the Oakes test, was adopted in *R. v. Oakes*, [1986] 1 S.C.R. 103 at 138-39.

322 A decline in the success rate of *Charter* challenges at the Supreme Court level appears to have begun as early as 1985, along with a growing divergence of opinion of judges

noticeable in civil cases involving social policy choices where the legislature has *prima facie* infringed the *Charter* rights of individuals in acting to protect groups or distribute scarce state-funded benefits. For example, the Supreme Court has upheld legislation that limits freedom of expression by restricting pornography,[323] hate speech,[324] and commercial advertising aimed at children,[325] on the basis that the balance struck by government in protecting the targets of such speech was, in each case, a reasonable one. In cases such as these, where the courts characterize the legislature as having engaged in balancing interests between groups, or between groups and individuals, courts tend to take a more restrained approach to judicial review and to accord greater respect for legislative policy choices. On the other hand, in matters involving criminal law, criminal procedure, or law enforcement, judges appear to be more inclined to remain activist, requiring legislation and police to meet strict judicially-imposed standards.[326]

Non-Charter Review of Administrative Action

Apart from judicial review on constitutional division of powers and *Charter* grounds, superior courts in Canada, following English legal precedent, have long exercised a common law jurisdiction to review administrative and executive decisions on administrative law principles. Judicial review on the grounds of procedural error (breaches of natural justice or of the duty of fairness), jurisdictional errors of law, or abuse of discretionary powers, enabled pre-*Charter* courts to exercise an important degree of control over executive and administrative action, and the importance of this kind of judicial review has not diminished in the post-*Charter* era.[327]

---

on the Court as to the proper approach to *Charter* interpretation. See Morton, Russell, and Riddell, *supra* note 315 at 48.

323 *R. v. Butler*, [1992] 1 S.C.R. 452.

324 *R. v. Keegstra*, [1990] 3 S.C.R. 697.

325 *Irwin Toy v. Quebec*, [1989] 1 S.C.R. 927.

326 The origins of this distinction lie in several Supreme Court decisions in the late 1980s. An early articulation of the proposition occurs in *Irwin Toy, ibid.* at 305, where Dickson C.J. suggested that, in applying the s. 1 "reasonable limits" clause, courts would distinguish between cases where the government was seen to be acting as a mediator between different groups, as opposed to those where the government could be characterized as "the singular antagonist" of the individual whose *Charter* rights had been infringed. In the latter category, typified by infringements of ss. 7-14 (the legal rights sections of the *Charter*), a stricter standard of scrutiny would apply since courts would be better able to determine whether the state had chosen the least drastic means to limit the *Charter* right in question.

327 In fact, judicial review on administrative law principles enjoys a constitutional status of its own. Through the Supreme Court's interpretation of the judicature provisions of the *C.A. 1867*, the right of superior courts to review the decisions of administrators on jurisdictional grounds has attained constitutional status and provincial legislatures are not competent to oust superior courts from review for jurisdictional error. In other words, provincially legislated privative clauses cannot constitutionally operate to preclude all judicial review: *Crevier v. A.G. Quebec*, [1981]

In addition, it is clear that judicial review on administrative law principles can extend to the highest levels of the executive. Cabinet and ministerial decision-making is not, in principle, beyond its reach.[328] Whether judges will interfere in any given case of executive or administrative decision-making, however, will depend on factors such as the nature of the power being exercised, its impact on those that could be affected by its exercise, and the scope of discretion accorded to the decision-maker by either legislation or the prerogative. Furthermore, if the decision in question is found by a court to bear upon the "life, liberty or security of the person" of an individual within Canada, the matter falls under section 7 of the *Charter*, and the decision-maker will be required to meet the constitutionalized standard of acting in accordance with the principles of fundamental justice.[329]

In practice, judges tend to hold administrative decision-makers to strict standards of conduct on all procedural matters. Insofar as interpretations of enabling legislation are concerned, however, Canadian judges often accord administrative decision-makers a significant amount of deference. This is particularly the case if the administrative body is recognized as one that has specialist expertise. Furthermore, Parliament and provincial legislatures often protect administrative decision-making through the use of strongly worded privative clauses. Where this has been done, if the decision is found to be one that the legislature intended to be within the jurisdiction of the decision-maker, the standard for judicial review now sanctioned by the Supreme Court allows courts to interfere only if the decision can be characterized as patently unreasonable.[330] Although this test is a malleable one, it allows administrative decision-makers leeway to make errors of law, as long as they are not "patently unreasonable" ones.

POSSIBLE SOURCES OF THE DIVERGENT TRENDS

Introduction

This section speculates on the apparent trend towards increased parliamentary supremacy in Malaysia, a similar but less clearly defined trend in Singapore, and an opposing trend in Canada toward greater constitutional

---

2 S.C.R. 220. It now appears that this principle applies equally to Parliament so that federally legislated privative clauses are likewise not effective to prevent judicial review on jurisdictional grounds, this being the implication of the decision in *MacMillan-Bloedel Ltd. v. Simpson*, [1995] 4 S.C.R. 725.

328 For example *Attorney General of Canada v. Inuit Tapirisat*, [1980] 2 S.C.R. 735.

329 S. 7 of the *Charter* provides: "Everyone has the right to life, liberty and security of the person and the right not to be deprived thereof except in accordance with the principles of fundamental justice." The principles of fundamental justice have been held to include the common law principles related to natural justice and procedural fairness. See e.g. *Pearlman v. Manitoba Law Society*, [1991] 2 S.C.R. 869.

330 The distinction between errors of law on matters within a decision-maker's jurisdiction, where a privative clause will require the "patently unreasonable" standard of

supremacy. The general question addressed is why parliamentary supremacy has been politically acceptable in Malaysia and Singapore while constitutional supremacy has been politically acceptable in Canada. In other words, what differences in political, social, or cultural circumstances may have led to the apparent trend in Malaysia and Singapore while leading to the opposite trend in Canada?

Strong Government for Development

It has been suggested that developing countries need a strong government with broad powers and strong leadership to maintain political unity and otherwise provide the conditions necessary for economic development. The benefits of political unity and economic development arguably justify the occasional, unfortunate injustices that may occur in the exercise of broad executive and governmental authority.[331] Constraints on parliamentary and executive power through invalidation of government legislation or administrative action could interfere with government efforts to provide political unity and the conditions necessary for economic development.

Substantial growth in Malaysia over the past several years may explain the lack of significant political opposition to expanding executive power at the expense of judicial power. Since 1970, except for a brief period in the early 1980s, Malaysia has had an annual growth in real GNP of between 6% and 8%.[332] Between 1970 and 1980, the real GNP per capita of Malaysians increased by 87.5% and between 1985 and 1990 the real GNP per capita of Malaysians increased by 26.5%.[333] Many Malaysians may believe this increased affluence to be attributable to a strong government and thus may be complacent in the face of increases in executive power. Even if Malaysians are equivocal on whether a strong government is the source of increasing affluence, they may not want to challenge the strength of government for fear that a strong government just might be the source of their increasing affluence. A similar case can be made for Singapore, a country that has developed an even higher per capita GNP despite being confined to a small

---

judicial review, and errors of law in relation to "jurisdiction-limiting" provisions in enabling legislation, is a difficult one. See e.g. *Canadian Union of Public Employees, Local 963 v. New Brunswick Liquor Corporation*, [1979] 2 S.C.R. 227; *Union des employés de service, Local 298 v. Bibeault*, [1988] 2 S.C.R. 1048; *National Corn Growers Association v. Canada (Import Tribunal)*, [1990] 2 S.C.R. 1324.

331 See e.g. Z. Anwar, "Government and Governance in Multi-Racial Malaysia," in J. W. Langford and K. L. Brownsey, eds., *The Changing Shape of Government in the Asia-Pacific Region* (Halifax: The Institute for Research on Public Policy, 1988) at 101.

332 *See the Fourth Malaysia Plan 1981-1985* (Kuala Lumpur: National Printing Dept., 1981) at 11 and *Sixth Malaysia Plan 1991-1995* (Kuala Lumpur: National Printing Dept., 1991) at 18.

333 These figures were derived from figures in the Fourth Malaysia Plan, *ibid.* and the Sixth Malaysia Plan, *ibid.*

land mass without natural resources.[334] The geographic reality of Singapore combined with both its inauspicious commencement as an independent state and insecurity as a small state pressured by its two great neighbours Malaysia and Indonesia has provided to the Singaporean government a continuing rationale for the exercise of unfettered government control, subject to electoral opinion.

The unquestioned economic success of both Malaysia and Singapore are rightly triumphed by the political entities in both countries (UMNO in Malaysia and PAP in Singapore) that have provided stable government for over 30 years. The key political players in both countries warn of economic consequences should the electorate scorn them in favour of untried individuals and policies. The implicit warning extends beyond elections to tampering with the successful economic and social formulas promoted through government laws and actions.

In contrast to Malaysia and Singapore, Canada's growth in GNP and GNP per capita has been much more moderate than that in Malaysia and Singapore for many years.[335] However, Canada has long been a developed country having the undeniable economic benefit of being a neighbour of the United States and having a stable government. Canada's economic development has been gradual and Canada has not found itself in a position of needing to "catch up" in standard of living terms. Economic development policies based on a strong government rationale is of little significance in Canada. Any benefits of economic development that might be brought about by a strong government as found in developing countries are remote to most Canadians, and certainly not sufficient to justify injustices that might be brought about by the exercise of broad governmental powers.

Lack of Political Awareness

Another possible source of the divergent trends might be the differences in the degree of political awareness in Malaysia, Singapore, and Canada. A greater degree of political awareness might be associated with a greater degree of resistance to a concentrated locus of political power in a country. In the context of Malaysia, Singapore, and Canada, this would appear to mean a greater degree of political awareness in Canada.

---

334 Respecting Singapore's economic growth in the 1990s, see Kwok Kian-Woon, "Singapore: Consolidating the New Political Economy," in *Southeast Asian Affairs 1995*, *supra* note 202 at 291-308 and Wong Poh Kam and Ng Chee Yuen, "Singapore: Coping With A Maturing Economy," *Southeast Asian Affairs 1993* (Singapore: Institute for Southeast Asian Studies) at 313-24.

335 The average annual growth rate of real gross domestic product per capita in Canada between 1981 and 1995 was 1.01%. This is based on the gross domestic product per capita at 1986 prices reported in *National Income and Expenditure Accounts: Annual Estimates* (Ottawa: Statistics Canada, 1995) Catalogue 13-201, Table 64 on "Selected Per Person Income and Product Series at Current Prices and at 1986 Prices."

If there is a greater degree of political awareness in Canada, it does not depend on illiteracy or ignorance in Malaysia or Singapore. The people of Malaysia and Singapore are literate and well educated.[336] Newspapers, available in all the main languages in both countries, provide access to information on the issues of the day. The public in both Malaysia and Singapore therefore have access to information about political issues, and the public is capable of assessing that information.

However, a possible inhibition on political awareness in Malaysia and Singapore may stem from a relative lack of access to opposing opinion. Major daily newspapers in Malaysia and Singapore are government controlled.[337]

---

336 In Malaysia from 1970 to 1990 between 21% and 24% of the population has been enrolled in education programs from the primary to post-secondary level. These estimates were derived from the Fourth and Sixth Malaysia plans, *supra* note 332.

The numbers enrolled in university education in Malaysia has also been increasing. In 1970 university enrollment in Malaysia was about 8,000 out of a population of 10.4 million (or about 0.077 per cent). By 1980 university enrollment in Malaysia had increased to 23,000 out of a population of 13,746,000 (or about 0.16 per cent). In the ten-year period 1970-80, the proportion of the population enrolled in university has thus more than doubled. See *Information Malaysia: 1992-93 Yearbook* (Kuala Lumpur: Berita Publishing, 1992) at 74.

Reported literacy rates for Malaysia and Singapore are reasonably high. Figures for 1995 show Singapore with a literacy rate of 91.6% and Malaysia with a literacy rate of 80%. These are relatively high compared to countries such as India (52.1%), Nepal (27%), Nigeria (52.0%), Cambodia (37.8%) and Saudia Arabia (64.1%) and compare favourably to the rate in the U.S. (95.5%). See *Asiaweek* (21 Apr. 1995) 58.

337 Major daily newspapers in Malaysia are said to be either controlled or influenced by parties in the Barisan Nasional, the governing coalition. The *New Straits Times* is said to be in the hands of persons supportive of UMNO, the Malay party in the Barisan Nasional, and *The Star* is said to be effectively controlled by the Malaysian Chinese Association, the Chinese party in the Barisan Nasional. Major Malay and Chinese language dailies are also said to be subject to government control or influence. See S. A. Idid, "Malaysia," in A. Mehra, ed., *Press Systems in Asean States* (Singapore: Asian Mass Communication Research and Information Centre, 1989) 41, esp. at 46-49; E. T. Gomez, *Politics in Business: Umno's Corporate Investments* (Kuala Lumpur: Forum, 1990) 51-106; M. K. Anuar, "The Malaysian 1990 General Election: The Role of the BN Mass Media" (1990) 8(2) Kajian Malaysia 82; "Democracy Games," *Far Eastern Economic Review* (11 Feb. 1993) 20-22; and "Deals: A Triumph for Anwar," *Asiaweek* (20 Jan. 1993) 45. Indeed, commenting on the exposures of excesses of the Rulers during a dispute over the removal of the Rulers' legal immunity, one commentator noted that "what a lot of us tend to forget is that our controlled media only revealed to the public what those at the top wanted us to know, nothing more, nothing less." And, commenting on the cessation of the exposures of the Rulers' excesses when the rulers eventually consented to constitutional amendments, the same commentator said, "[s]o why did the media suddenly shy away from its new found role as champions of the ordinary citizen? Simply because they were obeying instructions." See A. Netto, "Amendments to the Amendments: Some Reflections" (1993) 13(2) *Aliran Monthly* 16 at 17. Milne and Mauzy, *supra* note 164 at 26, comment that in Singapore "control of the press is affected in various ways – through the government's licensing powers, through informal advice (or the anticipation of informal advice), through use of the criminal law ... and through the government's ability to restructure newspaper ownership. See generally *ibid.* at 25-27. See also L. Thio, "Singapore," in R. Haas, ed.,

Others that are not government controlled are subject to licensing requirements. In Malaysia, the print media must obtain their licence from the Home Minister.[338] These licences have been revoked or suspended during alleged crises.[339] *Aliran Monthly*, an English language magazine often critical of the government, was for some time refused a licence to publish in the Malay language, and was thus limited in its access to a substantial portion of the population.[340] The Singapore government's control over newspapers is exercised through the *Newspapers and Printing Presses Act* (*NPPA*), which has been used on several occasions to restrict the circulation of foreign papers and magazines in Singapore.[341] Television and radio are limited and are controlled, directly or indirectly, by persons closely connected to government. In the case of Singapore, however, the BBC is receivable directly on FM radio.

The differences in control over the media may make people in Malaysia and Singapore less politically aware than they are in Canada and perhaps, as a consequence, less likely to challenge an expansion in parliamentary supremacy with a reduction in the potential checks and balances of judicial power.

Cultural Attitudes towards the Judiciary

Part of the reason for the lack of a challenge in Malaysia and Singapore to a reduction in the check on executive power provided by the judiciary may lie in the cultural attitudes of Chinese and Malays to a judicial system styled on the English model. Chinese prefer to solve their disputes without access to the judicial system. A Chinese aphorism describes entering a court of law as akin to entering the mouth of a tiger. To the extent this attitude still prevails among the Chinese in Singapore, it may account for the reluctance of the predominantly Chinese population of Singapore to come to the defence of the judiciary. In Malaysia, a similar attitude among the roughly 35% of the population that is Chinese might lead to a similar result.

The approach of the Malay populations of Malaysia and Singapore to dispute resolution was also quite different before the arrival of the English judicial system.[342] Consequently, the Malay people may also not have a

---

Human Rights and the Media (Kuala Lumpur: Asian Institute for Development Communication, 1996) at 69-79.

338 See the *Printing Presses and Publications Act 1984*, *supra* note 69, ss. 3, 6.

339 See e.g. J. Aznami, "Taming the Guerillas: Press Bans Silence Dissent and Sure to Cow Others," *Far Eastern Economic Review* (12 Nov. 1987) 21-22, discussing the suspension of licences for three major newspapers during a period of alleged crisis.

340 *See Persatuan Aliran Kesedaran Negara v. Minister of Home Affairs*, [1988] 1 M.L.J. 440.

341 See text accompanying notes 244-46.

342 Before the arrival of the British on the Malay peninsula, Malay law was primarily a mixture of Malay customary law and Islamic law. Some indications of the Malay approach to dispute resolution can be found in *The Ninety-nine Laws of Perak*, trans. by

sufficiently deep respect for the English-style judicial system to muster a significant challenge to reduction in judicial power.

In Canada, the values and ideologies of the French and English legal systems imported by the earliest settler/immigrants and imposed on the aboriginal peoples included acceptance of judicial power. English judges, in particular, had long played an exalted role in the interpretation and development of the common law, and the origins of judicial constraints on executive power in England date back to the time of the Glorious Revolution of 1688. Thus, the idea that judges should play an important role in upholding the rule of law and policing executive and administrative actions in order to curb arbitrary exercises of power was a notion that British colonists brought with them and transplanted throughout most of Canada.

Popular acceptance of the notion of judicial authority has also been reinforced in Canada by the growing influence of American cultural and legal norms, which include an emphasis on litigation as a preferred method of dispute resolution and judicial protection of individual rights. In the light of such historical and cultural influences, it is not surprising that most Canadians now seem to be quite comfortable with the idea that judges, acting under the *Charter* in the name of constitutional supremacy and defence of individual rights, should exercise significant powers to curb the actions not only of the executive branch of government, but also of the legislative branch.

Cultural Attitudes towards Government

Chinese and Malay attitudes towards government may also be different from Canadian attitudes. The Chinese have had a long history of being subject to

---

J. Rigby and ed. by R. J. Wilkinson, reprinted from R. J. Wilkinson, ed., *Papers on Malay Subjects*, Law, Part II (1908) 20-56 in M. B. Hocker, ed. *Readings in Malay Adat Laws* (Singapore: Singapore Univ. Press, 1970). Edict 11 provides that it is the duty of a *pengulu* to "resolve perplexities" and "see that justice is done when offences are committed." Edict 11 further provides that the *pengulu* "should study the demeanour of the parties. If a man is guilty his face will show it, his postures will be uneasy, his shuffling will show the state of his mind and his guilt will appear in his speech. The guilty must then be pronounced guilty, the innocent must be declared innocent." Edict 21 provides that when there is litigation between neighbours "such as family disputes or mere verbal wrangling" then "no fines should be imposed; the parties should be warned, if they persist, they may be dealt with according to custom." Edict 22 provides that, "[f]irst, the judge must investigate then make diligent search, then the accused should be confronted with his former misdeeds, then the effects of anger, cajolery and deception should be tried. Then his better feelings should be appealed to. And lastly he should be severely cross-examined." Edict 32 deals with the rules that apply when one person sues another. It provides that the courts should "take no cognizance of cases between children and their parents; otherwise it would be regarded as a piece of tyranny on the part of the *raja* or chief. The case must be amicably settled. Of cases between brothers and sisters, the judge may take cognizance as an arbitrator only. Parents and children, brothers and sisters, share the family fortune and the family repute; if one suffers, all suffer, so they should not sue one another in court."

domination by foreign powers.[343] China has also had a history of hierarchical and centralized forms of government without the institutional checks and balances that are characteristic of Westminster-style parliamentary democracy or the notion of constitutional supremacy.[344] Their inherent acceptance of the rules and values of outsiders not well attuned to local needs or values may have been minimal at best. The Chinese who migrated to Malaysia and Singapore may have brought with them an attitude disposed to paying very little attention to government, as long as it did not interfere in their day-to-day business transactions or customary rituals.

Although the government of Malaysia has imposed requirements on the Chinese with respect to taking on Malay business partners, on the whole the government of Malaysia takes a capitalist, laissez-faire approach to business, and the Chinese have been permitted to carry on their business interests relatively unimpeded. Thus the Chinese in Malaysia, just as in China in the past, may accept a strong executive with little in the way of controls on executive power as an inevitable way of life, and may remain complacent as long as the government maintains its present relatively non-interventionist approach. There may be a similar attitude towards government among the predominantly Chinese population of Singapore where the government generally promotes entrepreneurial activities.[345]

Malays too may have a history of accepting broad executive powers. Before the arrival of the British and the introduction of the English judicial system followed by a Westminster-style bicameral parliamentary system, most Malays had for many centuries lived in a predominantly hierarchical system with strong powers vested in a sultan and enforcement through an administrative system of chiefs and sub-chiefs.[346] They were not familiar

343 For instance, China was subject to foreign domination under the Mongol empire from 1271-1368 (the Yuan dynasty) and under the Manchus from 1644-1912 (the Qing dynasty). See e.g. E. O. Reischauer and J. K. Fairbank, *East Asia: The Great Tradition* (Boston: Houghton Mifflin, 1960) at 243-46, 259-89, 345-95. Parts of China were also subject to substantial influence by western powers in the 19th and early 20th centuries. For instance, parts of China were subject to foreign (chiefly British) administrations. See e.g. R. DeCrespigny, *China This Century*, 2d ed. (Hong Kong: Oxford Univ. Press, 1992); E. E. Moise, *Modern China: A History* (London: Longman, 1980) at 28-50.

344 See e.g. the discussion in L. W. Pye, *Asian Power and Politics: The Cultural Dimensions of Authority* (Cambridge, Mass.: Harvard Univ. Press, 1985) at 182-96. See also the discussion of the examination system and the gentry class in Reischauer and Fairbank, *ibid.* at 304-13 and see Chang Cheng-li, *The Chinese Gentry* (Seattle: Univ. of Washington Press, 1955).

345 While slightly dated, a good review of the role of the Singapore government in economic development is provided by Ou Chin-Hock, "The Role of Government in Economic Development: The Singapore Experience," in L. Chong-Yah and P. J. Lloyd, *Singapore: Resources and Growth* (Singapore: Oxford Univ. Press, 1986) at 221-67.

346 Before the arrival of the Europeans the Malay Sultanates operated through a hierarchical structure in which the Sultan ruled through a series of chiefs and sub-chiefs.

with a system, such as a judicial system, that put constraints on executive power. This experience with strong hierarchical authority may have led to the observation that "[t]he Malay ideal of authority calls for sternness, dignity, and paternalistic concern; but it is also understood that those in authority can easily become angered and do irrational things."[347]

This view of Malay attitudes towards authority suggests that Malays feel they should be cautious not to provoke authority and should stay out of its way as much as possible. In this way, the cultural attitude of Malays toward authority may not be much different from that of the Chinese. They may accept the inevitability of a strong government and simply try to live their lives as best they can in spite of it. Further, many Malays have benefited from either the government's New Economic Policy, designed to increase Malay involvement in the economy, or from the constitutionalized discrimination in favour of Malays in the civil service. These Malays may be reluctant to challenge the government that has provided these benefits.

Canadians have been characterized as being deferential to authority and disposed to support strong governmental power in order to achieve national economic development and an orderly society.[348] Particularly in contrast with Americans, Canadians have been seen as more willing to countenance a broader role for state regulation of individual and corporate activity in the market in order to achieve national economic, social, and cultural objectives.

See e.g. Khoo Kay Kim, "The Traditional Malay Sultanate: Administration," in *Workshop on Malay Sultanates* (Kuala Lumpur, 21-24 Feb. 1987) at 3-4. The Malay Rulers' chiefs and subjects were imbued with a strong sense of unquestioning loyalty to the Ruler. See Zainal Abidin bin Abdul Wahid, "Glimpses of the Malaccan Empire – I," in Zainal Abdul bin Abdul Mahid, ed., *Glimpses of Malaysian History* (Kuala Lumpur: Dewan Bahasa dan Pustaka, 1970) 18 at 20. According to the Malay Annals (Sejarah Melaya), "[t]he qualities required of a ruler's subjects are three in number. Firstly, [he is to be] honourable in all his behaviour; secondly, [he] abides by the commands of the ruler; whether he [the ruler] is tyrannical or not, he [the subject] shall follow his commands; thirdly, he desires mercy from his Lord": see C. C. Brown, *Sejarah Melaya* (Kuala Lumpur: Oxford Univ. Press, 1970). There was no notion of a system of checks and balances between executive, legislative, and judicial power. As one observer has put it, "[i]n a Malay State the Ruler is an absolute Monarch; he is the sole fount of honour, the sole source of justice and the sole repository of the executive and legislative power. There is no distinction between executive and legislative acts such as we know under the English constitutional law": see R. Braddell, *The Legal Status of the Malay States* (Singapore: Malaya Publishing House, 1931) at 12. It has also been said that,"the Malay rulers normally enjoyed an almost absolute power. This power was not merely derived from the fact that he could exercise many rights but the Malay masses themselves accorded the ruler with what could be termed as 'blind loyalty.' Although there were exceptions, generally this was true. The cultural tradition of the Malays played an important role in shaping this attitude": See Zainal Abidin bin Abdul Wahid, *supra* at 19.

347 Pye, *supra* note 344 at 257.

348 See generally G. Grant, *Lament for a Nation* (Toronto: McClelland and Stewart, 1965), and G. Horowitz, "Conservatism, Liberalism and Socialism in Canada: An Interpretation" (1966) 32 Can. J. Econ. and Poli. Sci. 143.

Whereas the American political and legal system emphasized individualism, the pursuit of individual freedom and equality, and the need to limit government through the constitutional protection of individual rights, Canadians were supposedly more concerned with the importance of the community and group identity, the achievement of social order and cohesion, and the need for powerful governments that are constitutionally free to act in pursuit of the common good.[349]

As with all generalizations, the above characterization of Canadian attitudes towards government was undoubtedly never entirely accurate. Nevertheless, it probably does reflect to a significant extent how Canadians (or, at least, Canadian elites) have tended in the past to think about their legal and political system and about how it differs from the American system. Furthermore, pre-*Charter* constitutional arrangements, hallmarked by parliamentary sovereignty offset only by federalism and by minimal constitutional protections for certain linguistic and religious rights of the French and English populations, were consistent with this traditional view of Canadian attitudes towards government.

A key premise of this chapter, however, is that, with the advent of the *Charter*, Canadians abandoned parliamentary supremacy in favour of constitutional supremacy. This shift suggests that the attitudes of Canadians towards the proper role of government may have fundamentally changed, bringing them much closer to those of their American neighbours, and making them more circumspect respecting governmental authority. If so, this would accord with a point made earlier in this chapter to the effect that Canadians have inevitably been increasingly influenced by American cultural and legal norms. However, while there has no doubt been a growth of "rights consciousness" on the part of Canadians, particularly since the *Charter* came into effect,[350] to postulate that its adoption, and the corresponding diminution of parliamentary sovereignty that it entails, can be explained primarily by a growing convergence of Canadian and American attitudes towards government would be too simplistic for two reasons.

First, many international and internal political motivators other than American influences can be pointed to as contributing factors in the adoption of the *Charter*. Canadian developments have been influenced by the international human rights movement following the Second World War,

349 This divergence in national attitudes has sometimes been encapsulated in the observation that Americans, in their Constitution, proclaimed a commitment to "life, liberty, and the pursuit of happiness" while Canadians, in the *C.A. 1867*, less prosaically sought to achieve "peace, order, and good government."

350 See generally A. Cairns, "The Charter: A Political Science Perspective," and F. L. Morton, "The Charter Revolution and the Court Party," in P. Monahan and M. Finkelstein, eds., *The Impact of the Charter on the Public Policy Process* (North York: York University Centre for Public Law and Public Policy, 1993) at 157 and 179 respectively.

the promulgation of international human rights instruments by the United Nations, and the global trend towards the adoption of constitutional rights protections. Internally, the growing strength of Quebec nationalism has acted as an immediate spur to the constitutional reform initiatives of the late 1970s that culminated in patriation in 1982 and, in that context, it is possible to see the *Charter* as designed to be, at least in part, a means to counterbalance Quebec nationalism and broader regional and centrifugal tendencies in Canada by imposing on all governments a set of a nationwide norms that would act as a homogenizing force and a unifying rallying point.[351] Seen in this light, changing popular attitudes about government are only part of a much more complicated story behind the adoption of the *Charter* and the movement away from parliamentary sovereignty.

Second, the *Charter* itself, as various authors have pointed out,[352] is not entirely inconsistent with traditional Canadian attitudes towards government and society. Property rights were explicitly excluded from entrenchment, thus leaving governments freer to engage in economic regulation of the market and redistribution of wealth. Recognition of language rights, aboriginal rights, and multiculturalism harken back to concerns with group, as opposed to individual, rights. Inclusion of the section 33 override ultimately preserves the potential for the exercise of parliamentary sovereignty should it be perceived by governments as necessary. Limitations placed on *Charter* rights by governments can be defended under section 1 as justified in the interests of achieving "a free and democratic society," enabling judges to consider if an appropriate balance has been struck between individual and collective interests in any given case. These factors suggest that, although Canadians in adopting the *Charter* have moved away from parliamentary sovereignty, they have not totally abandoned their historic attitudes towards the proper role of government.

Elite Support for Expanding Judicial Power

One theory that has been advanced for the expansion of judicial power in Canada argues that it favours wealthy elite groups at the expense of "have-not" groups. This theory claims that have-not groups can lobby the government over critical issues *en masse* at a much lower cost than they encounter in addressing the same issues in a court.[353] Also, the judiciary is more likely

351 See generally P. H. Russell, "The Political Purposes of the Canadian Charter of Rights and Freedoms" (1983) 61 Can. Bar Rev. 30.

352 See e.g. P. Monahan, *Politics and the Constitution: the Charter, Federalism and the Supreme Court of Canada* (Toronto: Carswell/Methuen, 1987) at 97-120.

353 The argument that the *Charter* will be used primarily by societal elites for protection of their interests is forcefully put by A. Petter, "The Politics of the Charter" (1986) 8 Supreme Court L.R. 474 at 474-93.

to be cut from the same cloth as the elite group and may thus favour the interests of elite groups.[354]

This theory poses some interesting problems when juxtaposed with the Malaysian and Singaporean situations. Leaving aside for the moment the theories considered above, this theory would seem to suggest that the have-nots have won out in Malaysia and Singapore over the interests of the wealthy elites. Perhaps this is the case, but this is probably not the view of those in Malaysia and Singapore who claim to represent the have-nots. It is also hard to imagine, short of violent revolution (which has not occurred), how the have-nots could have effected such a coup. Perhaps the benefits of a strong judiciary have not yet occurred to the wealthy elites of Malaysia and Singapore. Perhaps instead the strong governments in Malaysia and Singapore, persisting and increasing in strength for the reasons noted above, have been able to resist any fledgling lobbying efforts of have-not groups while lending their helping hand to the wealthy elites, thereby eliminating any need for wealthy elite groups to seek judicial obstructions to the lobbying efforts of the have-nots.

Conclusion

Canada, Malaysia, and Singapore have formally independent judiciaries that, because of the existence of documentary constitutions, can review the constitutional validity of legislation. This judicial review authority places the courts in the position of potentially thwarting the action of the elected legislatures and executives. Hence, the conflict between judicial review and parliamentary supremacy created by the documentary constitution.

The argument herein has been that, in Malaysia and Singapore, parliamentary and executive supremacy is a more prominent principle of constitutional practice than in Canada, where parliamentary supremacy has substantially yielded to judicial review and constitutional supremacy. The situation in Canada is readily evident from the changes to the Constitution made in 1982 and the subsequent action of the judiciary in constitutional cases. Demonstrating the dominance of parliamentary supremacy in Malaysia and Singapore is more difficult. It is not simply a task of reviewing case law. Rather it is necessary to uncover the approach of both the legislative/executive branch of government and the judiciary to parliamentary supremacy and judicial review. In Malaysia, for example, the tilt towards parliamentary supremacy is evinced by both the courts and legislatures in dealing with privative clauses that attempt to foreclose court review of

---

354 See the comments and material cited by J. C. Bakan, "Constitutional Arguments: Interpretation and Legitimacy in Canadian Constitutional Thought" (1989) 27 Osgoode Hall L.J. 123 at 173-78 and M. Mandel, *The Charter of Rights and the Legalization of Politics in Canada* (Toronto: Thompson, 1994) at 46-53.

government action taken pursuant to legislation. In both Malaysia and Singapore, it is suggested that certain high profile cases and events have had the effect of restraining the judiciary from becoming too activist and thus ensuring deference to the will of Parliament. The suggested reasons for the different directions of Canada, Malaysia, and Singapore on parliamentary supremacy and judicial review are differences in political cultures, attitudes, and stage of economic development.

5

Constitutional Change and Continuity in Thailand in the Aftermath of the 1991 Coup*

Ted L. McDorman

INTRODUCTION

A constitution is the fountain of the legal legitimacy of the various organs (courts, executive, and parliament) that exercise state authority. In Western-style constitutional democracies, the political and even moral legitimacy of state authority is intimately tied with the legal legitimacy, i.e. constitutionality, of the exercise of power. For this reason, constitutional documents and practices in many Western countries are accorded almost a religious status of saliency and sanctity.[1] Such is clearly not the case in Thailand.

In Thailand, since the end of the absolute monarchy in 1932, written constitutions have been the foundation of the legal legitimacy of the exercise of state authority. However, a Thai constitution has never been the true basis of the political or moral legitimacy of the exercise of state authority.[2] As one Thai authority has put it, in Thailand there has been an acceptance of constitutional processes and frameworks but not of constitutional ideals and practices.[3] However, changes within Thailand in the

* This chapter draws from the author's previous paper, "The 1991 Constitution of Thailand" (1995) 3 Pacific Rim Law and Policy J. 257-98, and from a presentation made at the November 1993 Symposium on Democratic Directions in Thailand hosted by the University of Victoria, Canada, Centre for Asia-Pacific Initiatives held at the time of the granting of an honorary degree to former Thai Prime Minister Anand Panyarachun.

1 This is particularly so in the United States where there exists a cult of the Constitution that was most evident during the recent (1987) bicentennial of the Constitution of the United States.

2 Traditional government legitimacy in Thailand arose from the ability of the government to perform state ceremonies, maintain law and order, and provide security from external threats. While to this may now be added support by the electorate, one commentator has indicated that "the legitimacy of government is still measured by its capacity to perform basic functions": L. Dhiravegin, *Demi-Democracy: the Evolution of the Thai Political System* (Singapore: Times Academic Press, 1992) at 194-96.

3 K. Wongtrangan, "Executive Power and Constitutionalism in Thailand," in C. V. Sison, ed., *Constitutional and Legal Systems of ASEAN Countries* (Manila: Univ. of the Philippines, 1990) at 289.

last two decades, most particularly in 1991-92, indicate that there is a growing convergence of legal and political legitimacy emanating from the written Constitution.

The events of 1991-92 are of central importance since they are a clear watershed in Thailand's constitutional history. The 1991-92 events[4] included: a military coup in February 1991; the replacement of the 1978 Constitution[5] with an interim constitution;[6] the establishment of a civilian government; the drafting and adoption in December 1991 of a new constitution;[7] an election in March 1992; the military opening fire on protestors in Bangkok;[8] the forced resignation of a Prime Minister; a second interim civilian government; several direct interventions by King Bhumibol Adulyadej; and another election in September 1992 followed by a democratically-elected civilian government taking power.

Despite the coup and the consequent upheaval, the legal and political legitimacy of Thailand's Constitution has been enhanced by the above tangle of events. The focus of this contribution will be on the change and continuity that has occurred in Thailand's constitutional practices as a result of the events of 1991-92 and the adoption of the new Constitution in 1991.

---

4 The events of 1991-92 are described in: S. Maisrikrod, *Thailand's Two General Elections in 1992* (Singapore: Institute of Southeast Asian Studies, 1992); S. Maisrikrod, "Thailand 1992: Repression and Return of Democracy," *Southeast Asian Affairs 1992* (Singapore: Institute for Southeast Asian Studies) at 327-49; C. D. Neher, "Political Succession in Thailand" (1992) 32 Asian Survey at 585-605; S. Bunbongkarn, "Thailand in 1991: Coping with Military Guardianship" (1992) 32 Asian Survey at 131-39; and A. Bhuchongkul, "Thailand 1991: The Return of the Military," *Southeast Asian Affairs 1992, supra* at 313-33.

5 Constitution of the Kingdom of Thailand, 22 Dec. 1978, Royal Thai Government Gazette, vol. 95, Part 146 (in Thai) [hereinafter the 1978 Constitution].

6 The 33-section, 1991 Interim Constitution became Thailand's fourteenth constitutional document since 1932: Constitution for the Kingdom of Thailand, BE 2534, 1 Mar. 1991, Royal Thai Government Gazette, vol. 108, Parts 29, 37, and 40 (in Thai), translated version by International Translations Office, Royal Thai Government Gazette, vol. 45, nos. 1-3 [hereinafter 1991 Interim Constitution].

7 *Constitution of the Kingdom of Thailand*, 9 Dec. 1991, Royal Thai Government Gazette, vol. 108, Part 216 (in Thai), translated version by International Translations Office, Bangkok [hereinafter the 1991 Constitution].

8 Maisrikrod, *Thailand's Two General Elections, supra* note 4 at 26-39 and Maisrikrod, "Thailand 1992," *supra* note 4 at 330-34 provides a compact review and analysis of the May events. See also P. Handley, "People's Wrath," *Far Eastern Economic Review* (28 May 1992) 10-11; P. Handley, "An Uneasy Calm," *Far Eastern Economic Review* (21 May 1992) 10-11; "Thailand, the Generals and the King," *The Economist* (23 May 1992) 35-36; "Uneasy Calm after King Intervenes," *Bangkok Post Weekly Review* (29 May 1992) 1-2; "Thailand Licks Its Wounds," *The Economist* (30 May 1992) 33-34; P. Handley, "Counting the Cost," *Far Eastern Economic Review* (4 June 1992) 10-11; and P. Handley, "Rainbow Coalition," *Far Eastern Economic Review* (4 June 1992) 11-12. The death toll from the violence is uncertain. Fifty-two bodies were recovered but there is a discrepancy between 47 and 163 regarding the number of missing. P. Handley, "Still Missing," *Far Eastern Economic Review* (27 May 1993) 16. An analysis of the military's miscalculation regarding the use of force is provided by Neher, *supra* note 4 at 603-604.

THAILAND'S CONSTITUTIONAL HISTORY

Before 1991

The rich constitutional history of Thailand includes the words and actions of the forward-looking monarchs of the 1800s and early 1900s and the thirteen constitutional documents that were employed between the end of the absolute monarchy in 1932 and the adoption of the new Constitution in 1991.[9] From this rich history it is clear that since 1932 power has only infrequently changed hands pursuant to the dictates of a written constitution. More frequently power has changed hands through extra-constitutional means, the coup d'état.[10] With the 13 constitutions of the post-absolute monarchy period, therefore, must be correlated 12 military coups and 18 elections. The relationship between constitutions, coups, and elections has been described as the cycle of Thai politics: a military coup suspends the old constitution; a new constitution is enacted; elections are held; time passes until a perceived crises leads to another military coup.[11]

The principal reason new constitutions have been part of this cycle has been to legitimate the incoming power holders, inevitably military authorities. Most political commentators have accepted that the role of a written constitution in Thailand has been to legitimate the authority being exercised by the then-dominant political forces.[12] As political forces shift, constitutions have been revoked and rewritten to reflect the new political balance. As one commentator has observed: "[A] new one [constitution] has been written and issued each time a shift in political dominance has taken place and with the primary purpose of protecting the new regime coming into power. Each ruling group has striven to consolidate its

---

9 Concerning Thailand's constitutional history, see in particular: M. S. Shin, *The Constitutions of Thailand* (Washington: Library of Congress, 1981) and P. A. F. Aakesson, M. Bunnag, and R. Bunnag, "The Development of Constitutionalism in Thailand: Some Historical Considerations," in L. W. Beer, ed., *Constitutional Systems in Late Twentieth Century Asia* (Seattle: Univ. of Washington Press, 1992) at 656-706. See also C. Samudavanija, "Thailand: A Stable Semi-democracy," in L. Diamond, J. J. Linz, and S. M. Lipset, eds., *Democracy in Developing Countries: Asia*, vol. 3 (Boulder: Lynne Rienner, 1989) at 305-17, and S. Chantornvong and M. Chenvidyakarn, "Constitutional Rule and the Institutionalization of Leadership and Security in Thailand," in S. Chee, ed., *Leadership and Security in Southeast Asia* (Singapore: Institute of Southeast Asian Studies, 1991) at 144-56. Regarding the existence and content of constitutionalism during the period of the absolute monarchy, *see* Wongtrangan, *supra* note 3 at 287-89.

10 Commenting on the popularity and acceptance of coups d'état in Thailand, Dhiravegin, *supra* note 2 at 150, suggests that coups are a continuation of the traditional Thai political process in which conflict over transfers of power were common. He suggests that coups are "sanctioned by Thai socio-religious values": *ibid.* at 195.

11 See e.g. Samudavanija, *supra* note 9 at 336 and Dhiravegin, *supra* note 2 at 147.

12 Samudavanija, *supra* note 9 at 321.

position and in so doing has changed the rules of the game and published a new constitution."[13] The continual re-creation of written constitutions is also a product of the 1932 overthrow of the absolute monarchy and its promised replacement with constitutional, democratic government.[14] Having usurped power to establish constitutional rule, the military has usually seen it necessary to create a constitution-based government.[15] The number of constitutions and the emphasis put on them have created their own momentum for a new constitution when an old one is suspended. Moreover, a constitutional document that contains elements familiar to foreign interests can assist a new government in obtaining international, and even national, acceptance. This aspect of constitution-making, not unique to Thailand,[16] is a familiar one in Thailand, where much of the modern legal system is viewed by some as having been devised in order to appease, if not please, foreign interests.[17] For all the above reasons, written constitutions have been an integral part of Thai political and legal history.

Special mention must be made of 1973, when Thailand's constitutional history took a dramatic turn. In that year, for the first time, there was a

---

13 Shin, *supra* note 9 at 59.

14 C. Samudavanija and S. Bunbongkarn, "Thailand," in Z. H. Ahmad and H. Crouch, eds., *Military-Civilian Relations in South-East Asia* (Oxford: Oxford Univ. Press, 1985) at 79. This promise was never met. Samudavanija, *supra* note 9 at 307 notes: "it is ironical that soon after the success of the westernized elites in their seizure of power from the monarchy [in 1932], constitutional idealism gradually eroded into formalistic constitutionalism."

15 Chantornvong and Chenvidyakarn, *supra* note 9 at 143.

16 E. McWhinney, *Constitution-Making: Principles, Process, Practice* (Toronto: Univ. of Toronto Press, 1981) at 22 comments that constitution-making in some countries may be "in the nature of a public relations exercise, designed in considerable measure to impress governments and public opinion in foreign countries."

17 Concerning the modernization of Thai law in the 1900s and the influence of non-Thais on this process, see *Thailand Official Yearbook* – 1968 (Bangkok: Gov't of Thailand, 1968) at 254-58; M. B. Hooker, *A Concise Legal History of South-East Asia* (Oxford: Clarendon Press, 1978) at 183-85; M. B. Hooker, "The 'Europeanization' of Siam's Law 1855-1908," in M. B. Hooker, ed., *Laws of South-East Asia: European Laws in South-East Asia*, vol. 2 (Singapore: Butterworths, 1988) at 531-607; P. Kasemsup, "Reception of Law in Thailand – A Buddhist Society," in M. Chiba, ed. *Asian Indigenous Law* (New York: KPI, 1986) at 267-99; and generally A. Petchsiri, *Eastern Importation of Western Criminal Law: Thailand as a Case Study* (Littleton, Colorado: Rothman, 1987). Petchsiri comments at 10:

> Although no conclusive evidence is available to show why Thailand embraced the Western system, two major reasons emerge as apparent basic causes of this change. First, voluntary adoption preserved national autonomy and evaded colonial powers and their claims of extraterritorial jurisdiction. Second, Westernization would help Thailand reach developmental goals such as industrialization, national unification, and social welfare.

The former reason is inevitably given more weight than the latter.

popularly-supported replacement of a military government by a civilian government.[18] Despite the reassertion of military power in 1976,[19] the consequence of 1973 has been that the military has no longer been able to make the Thai public accept a constitution nakedly designed to assure the military dominant power and to restrict the participation of other social forces.[20] This is clear from the 1978 Constitution, which deliberately set out to create power-sharing among competing forces.[21] The political aspects of the written constitutions of Thailand are increasingly subject to pressures outside the control of the dominant political force. This is the major shift that has taken place in 60 years of Thai constitutional history.

The 1978 Constitution had a 13-year lifespan, and many of its provisions are repeated in the 1991 Constitution. The following has been said about the 1978 Constitution: "The longevity of this Constitution is quite remarkable, when considered against the background of turbulent Thai politics, and optimistic political observers believe it could succeed in laying a strong foundation for the establishment of a secure democratic leadership that might become institutionalized eventually."[22]

The 1991 Constitution

When the military overthrew the civilian Thai government and suspended the 1978 Constitution in early 1991, one of its first promises was to establish a new constitution. In exploring national experiences in constitution-making, one authority noted the following "options as to arenas for constitutional drafting and enactment": the expert commission; parliamentary enactment; executive diplomacy; constituent assembly; popular initiative; and the popular referendum to legitimate the new or revised

---

18 See J. J. Wright, Jr., *The Balancing Act: A History of Modern Thailand* (Bangkok: Asia Books, 1991) at 197-211 and more generally, on the 1973 revolution and the 1976 coup, D. Morell and C. Samudavanija, *Political Conflict in Thailand: Reform, Reaction and Revolution* (Cambridge, Mass.: Oelgeschlager, Gunn and Hain, 1981) and Dhiravegin, *supra* note 2 at 173-208. All political and social histories of Thailand contain an extensive commentary on the events of 1973. See e.g. J. L. S. Girling, *Thailand: Society and Politics* (Ithaca, N.Y.: Cornell Univ. Press, 1981) and C. F. Keyes, *Thailand: Buddhist Kingdom as Modern Nation-State* (Boulder: Westview Press, 1987).

19 See Wright, *supra* note 18 at 243-61 and more generally the references in *supra* note 18.

20 Chantornvong and Chenvidyakarn, *supra* note 9 at 153 and Neher, *supra* note 4 at 592.

21 Note Chantornvong and Chenvidyakarn, *supra* note 9 at 156. Dhiravegin, *supra* note 2 at 209 refers to the 1978 Constitution as having created "halfway democracy" as the Constitution sought to blend the newly emerged social forces with the entrenched civil and military bureaucrats. Commenting on the objectives of the 1978 Constitution, one of the participants in the drafting stated that there were two objectives: legitimizing military participation in the political process and regulating political structures to support democratic development. K. Tongdhamazhart, "The Influence of the U.S. Constitution on the Thai Constitution," in K. W. Thompson, ed., *The U.S. Constitution and the Constitutions of Asia* (Boston: Univ. Press of America, 1988) at 56.

22 Chantornvong and Chenvidyakarn, *supra* note 9 at 142.

constitution.[23] The experience of Thailand in 1991 involved the employment of an expert commission, parliamentary (a non-elected one) enactment, assent of the executive, and, to a limited extent, popular opinion.[24] The involvement of the commission, parliament, and executive (the King) were set out in the 1991 Interim Constitution.[25] The participation of the general public was not provided for in the constitutional drafting process, but arose spontaneously as a reaction to the direction the Constitution was taking in the formal process. The role and interest of the public in the constitutional crisis following the 1991 coup is one of the most important aspects of recent constitutional developments in Thailand.

Public protests about the drafting of the 1991 Constitution centred on the perceived overt involvement of the military in the drafting process and, when the draft Constitution became known, about the military's attempt to be centrally involved in the government.[26] As one observer has noted: "(T)he military's attempt to dictate a constitution written in blatantly self-interested terms was thwarted by public opposition that threatened to spread out of control."[27] Following the March 1992 election and the assumption of the Prime Ministership by the principal coup leader, demonstrations erupted in Bangkok and elsewhere in the country against the perceived intent of the military to retain political control. In May 1992 the military moved to quell the protestors with force.[28] The Prime Minister was forced to resign and public pressure brought about constitutional amendments to distance the military further from the levers of power.

With Thailand's extensive experience with written constitutions, it is not surprising that the 1991 model has striking facial similarities to its predecessors. The Chair of the Constitutional Drafting Committee stated that the Committee used the 1978 Constitution as the basis for deliberations.[29] The 1991 and 1978 Constitutions are similarly structured, with 11 chapters and a set of transitory provisions; the title and arrangements of the chapters are virtually the same; and a large percentage of the provisions of the 1978 document have been incorporated with minimal change into the 1991 Constitution.

---

23 McWhinney, *supra* note 16 at 27-41.

24 The process of drafting the 1991 Constitution is detailed in T.L. McDorman, "The 1991 Constitution of Thailand" (1995) 3 Pacific Rim Law and Policy Journal at 273-75.

25 1991 Interim Constitution, ss. 10 and 11, and McDorman, *supra* note 24 at 273-75.

26 A review of the contentious constitutional issues that arose during the drafting of the 1991 Constitution is provided by Neher, *supra* note 4 at 598-99; Bunbongkarn, *supra* note 4 at 136-37; and Bhuchongkul, *supra* note 4 at 319-21.

27 Neher, *supra* note 4 at 599. See generally R. Tasker, "Tactical Compromise," *Far Eastern Economic Review* (5 Dec. 1991) 13; R. Tasker, "General's Charter," *Far Eastern Economic Review* (19 Dec. 1991) 15-16; and B. Tasaneeyavej, "Powerful Given Lesson by Charter Protest," *Bangkok Post Weekly Review* (20 Dec. 1991) at 8.

28 See the material cited in *supra* note 8.

29 "Charter not written with bias: Minister," *Bangkok Post Weekly Review* (10 May 1991) 4.

Of fundamental importance, as between the American constitutional model of a strict division between the legislative and executive levels of government and the British model of the executive being drawn from and directly responsible to the legislature, the 1991 Thai Constitution follows its 1978 predecessor in aligning with the British model, albeit with variations.[30] Pressure had existed to adopt the full separation of powers approach, it being argued that, if legislators could not be in the cabinet (Council of Ministers) separation of powers would reduce vote-buying, a perceived prevalent practice in Thai elections.[31] This view was considered but rejected[32] in favour of the system now in the 1991 Constitution that ministers can be, but are not required to be, from the elected House of Representatives and that the ministers are responsible to the Parliament (House of Representatives and Senate).[33]

FIVE KEY CHARACTERISTICS OF 1990S CONSTITUTIONAL LAW AND PRACTICE IN THAILAND

The Monarchy

The primary characteristic of constitutional law and practice in Thailand is the unquestioned position of the current monarch, King Bhumibol, as the head of state.[34] This is regularly affirmed in the written constitutions.[35] However, the King's authority goes beyond the ceremonial role of a constitutional monarch and the role assigned the monarch by the formal constitution. "It has been overwhelmingly accepted, especially since 1973, that the King remains the final arbiter of a national crisis. The social stability

30 A brief discussion of the American model and the British model as viewed in Thailand can be found in Tongdhamazhart, *supra* note 21 at 56-58.

31 "NPKC Insists on Full Separation of Powers" *Bangkok Post Weekly Review* (22 Mar. 1991) 3 and Maisrikrod, *Thailand's Two General Elections*, *supra* note 4 at 22. The existence and prevalence of vote-buying and the attempts made in the 1992 elections to "clean up" the election process is discussed in Maisrikrod, *ibid.* at 50-53.

32 See esp. the comments of former Parliamentary President Ukrit Mongkolnavin noted in "Meechai: Power Separation Deserves Widespread Debate," *Bangkok Post Weekly Review* (29 Mar. 1991) 3. Numerous division of powers proposals were considered. See N. Chetchotiros and B. Tasaneeyavej, "Constitution Drafters Aim to Satisfy All Sides," *Bangkok Post Weekly Review* (31 May 1991) at 8.

33 See *infra* notes 47-48.

34 Not surprisingly, following the 1932 overthrow of the absolute monarchy, the significance of the royalty was minimized. During the regime of military strongman Sarit Thanarat, the kingship was revitalized as a way of establishing legitimacy for the military government. See Chantornvong and Chenvidyakarn, *supra* note 9 at 151 who conclude: "In the end the monarchy has come to exercise a much more important role in Thai politics than the military leaders originally had planned for." The espousal by the military of their close connection with the monarch has given King Bhumibol a degree of leverage over the military.

35 See s. 3 of the 1991 Constitution and more generally ss. 6-23 (chapter 2). The historic position of the monarch vis-à-vis the Thai people and in the written constitutions is summarized in Shin, *supra* note 9 at 16-30.

of Thailand, despite its periodic coups d'état, can be explained by the existence and positive role of the monarchy."[36]

The King's authority is evidenced by the fact that his approval was sought for the 1991 Interim Constitution,[37] and the acceptance by the major protagonists of his intervention following the bloodshed in the spring of 1992.[38] The full extent of the King's authority is unclear, but his constitutional position of representing the interests of the general Thai population is increasingly accepted. King Bhumibol is clearly one of the pillars of the Thai Constitution, irrespective of the content of the written constitution.

Civilian/Military Power-Sharing

There is little doubt that historically the military has been the dominant political player in Thailand. In the words of one commentator:

> [T]he political supremacy of the military has been an outstanding feature in the modern Thai political system since 1932. An absence of strong participatory political institutions and a lack of legitimacy on the part of civilian regimes enable the politicized military to seize power and establish an authoritarian regime without much difficulty. Its organizational complexity and adaptability, prestige, wealth, and control of the mass media are important political resources for control over all other political institutions, including the cabinet, the National Assembly and, to a lesser extent, political parties.[39]

Regarding civilian and military relations and the Thai Constitution, one commentator has observed that "the most important aspect of a Thai constitution is not the provision and protection of civil and political liberties, but the extent to which it allows the elected House of Representatives to participate in the political process."[40]

Critical to the role of the elected legislative body in the political process is its relationship with the executive branch of government. The executive level of government, the Council of Ministers set out in chapter 7 of the 1991 Constitution, is the most powerful of the three traditional levels of government – executive, legislative, and judicial.[41] Under the 1991 Constitution,

---

36 Samudavanija, *supra* note 9 at 337-38.

37 Note R. Tasker, "Post-Coup Worries," *Far Eastern Economic Review* (14 Mar. 1991) 13.

38 Maisrikrod, *Thailand's Two General Elections*, *supra* note 4 at 33; Neher, *supra* note 4 at 604; Maisrikrod, "Thailand 1992," *supra* note 4 at 331 and 334; "King Gives Advice to Help End Crisis," *Bangkok Post Weekly Review* (29 May 1992) 20; and C. Owens, "Deliberate Actions of Thai Royal Family Follow Precedent Set During 1973 Crisis," *Asian Wall Street Journal* (Weekly) (25 May 1992) 3.

39 Samudavanija and Bunbongkarn, *supra* note 14 at 114.

40 Samudavanija, *supra* note 9 at 321.

41 Wongtrangan, *supra* note 3 at 294-96 provides an explanation for the dominance of the executive in the Thai government.

the Council of Ministers has the primary responsibility for the initiation of legislation,[42] the sole responsibility for money bills,[43] and the authority to issue emergency and executive decrees.[44] The Council of Ministers clearly dominates the legislative branch of government. The executive is, however, responsible to the legislative branch, which can control the executive through non-confidence motions.[45]

The public protests of 1991-92 were focused upon the increased role that the military was trying to acquire in the new constitutional order, particularly in the executive.[46] The areas of concern to the public and the principal indicators of the relationship between the military and civilian politicians are (1) the relationship between the elected House of Representatives and the appointed Senate; (2) whether the Prime Minister must be from the House of Representatives; and (3) whether the Prime Minister and other ministers may be military officers.

On the latter two points the civilian authorities have come out ahead of the military. Although not stipulated by the 1991 Constitution, an amendment made in 1992 in response to public pressure *requires* that the Prime Minister be a member of the elected House of Representatives.[47] Other ministers need not be members of the House of Representatives but, as in the

---

42 1991 Constitution, s. 137, para. 1. See generally on the legislative process under the 1991 Constitution, McDorman, *supra* note 24 at 281-85.

43 1991 Constitution, s. 137, para. 1.

44 1991 Constitution, s. 172, para. 1 and s. 174, para. 1. All Emergency or Executive Decrees and Royal Proclamations must be considered by Parliament at the first opportunity and either formally accepted as laws or rejected. See 1991 Constitution, s. 172, paras. 3, 5, 6, and 7. In the case of an emergency decree rejected by the House of Representatives, the decree ceases to have the force of law, although this does not affect the legality of any action taken while the decree was in effect: 1991 Constitution, s. 172, para. 3. S. 172, para. 4 indicates that in the case of a rejected executive decree the pre-existing law comes back into effect.

The operation of Section 172 came under scrutiny in the aftermath of the May 1992 crackdown. By emergency decree, an amnesty was granted to all those involved in the bloodshed including those who ordered the use of force. Emergency Decree on Amnesty for Offenders in the 17-20 May 1992 Incident, 23 May 1992, *Royal Thai Government Gazette*, vol. 109, Part 63 (in Thai). Details of this decree are noted in "Tribunal Discusses Amnesty Decree," *Bangkok Post Weekly Review* (5 June 1992) 3. Although the House of Representatives overwhelmingly rejected acceptance of the Amnesty Decree, the amnesty granted by the decree is considered to still be valid. This was the finding of the Constitutional Judicial Council (Constitutional Tribunal) which examined the constitutionality and legal effect of the Amnesty Decree. "Tribunal Rules in Support of May Amnesty," *Bangkok Post Weekly Review* (20 Nov. 1992) 3 and P. Handley, "Amnesty Upheld," *Far Eastern Economic Review* (26 Nov. 1992) 18. The work of the Constitutional Tribunal is discussed *infra* notes 79-84.

45 Described in detail below, see text accompanying *infra* notes 59-61.

46 See the references in *supra* note 26.

47 Amendment of the Constitution of the Kingdom of Thailand No. 4 (10 Sept. 1992), *Royal Thai Government Gazette*, vol. 109, Part 95 (in Thai). See Neher, *supra* note 4 at 604 and "Amendments Sail through 2 Readings," *Bangkok Post Weekly Review* (5 June 1992) 3. The amendment came into force following the Sept. 1992 election.

case of the Prime Minister, a minister is *not* to be a government (or military) official.[48] Hence, the civilian politicians have the upper hand over the military regarding the executive.

The 1991 Constitution calls for the appointment by the King of 270 senators, *without* the qualification they not be a government or military official.[49] Although the Constitution does not indicate who is to advise the King on Senate appointments, this is the Prime Minister's function.[50] However, the first group of senators to be appointed under the 1991 Constitution were appointed pursuant to section 217, part of the transition chapter, which directs that the King is to be advised on these selections by the President of the National Peace-Keeping Council (the 1991 coup leaders).[51] These senators are to be in office for four years before the Senate-appointment provisions of the 1991 Constitution become operational.[52] Pursuant to the Constitution, on the March 1992 election day, 270 senators were appointed by the King. Of the 270 senators, 154 were military or police officers and 116 were civilians. The number of civilians in the Senate is greater than in the pre-coup Senate (116 to 105) and only 51 people retained their Senate positions.[53]

The 1991 Constitution directs that the elected House of Representatives is to have 360 members.[54] The creation of election areas or constituencies is to be by province with the total Thai population divided by 360 and the provinces assigned the number of representatives their population dictates,[55] with each province entitled to at least one representative.[56] A voter is to

48 1991 Constitution, s. 162. The restriction on a minister from simultaneously being a military or government official was one of the significant tension points in the drafting of the Constitution.

49 1991 Constitution, ss. 94 and 97.

50 The issue of who would advise the King on Senate appointments was, not surprisingly, a controversial issue in the drafting of the 1991 Constitution. The Drafting Committee's original text created a nine-person Constitutional Committee charged with the task of nominating 1,350 senatorial candidates who would among themselves select the 270 senators. B. Tasaneeyavej, "Charter Draft Attacked as Political 'Time Bomb,'" *Bangkok Post Weekly Review* (9 Aug. 1991) 8. This proposal was scrapped following heavy criticism. It was accepted that regarding Senate appointments the King was to be advised by the Prime Minister. "Panel Unveils Controversial Draft Charter," *Bangkok Post Weekly Review* (22 Nov. 1991) 1 and see "Charter Panel Still Undecided on Many Key Issues" *Bangkok Post Weekly Review* (8 Nov. 1991) 3.

51 The National Peace-Keeping Council was the military leadership of the 1991 coup. The NPKC was recognized as a constitutional entity in Section 18 of the Interim Constitution. The Interim Constitution ceased to be effective with the March 1992 election and the NPKC was officially disbanded at that time. See 1991 Constitution, s. 216.

52 1991 Constitution, s. 217, para. 3.

53 "Economic Giants Get Some Clout in 'Traditional' Senate," *Bangkok Post Weekly Review* (3 Apr. 1992) 3.

54 1991 Constitution, s. 99, para. 1.

55 *Ibid.* at s. 100, para. 1.

56 *Ibid.* at s. 100, para. 1.

directly elect representatives by secret ballot.[57] Candidates for the House of Representatives must *not* be military or government officials and must be members of a political party that has at least 120 candidates in the election.[58]

The key to the balance between the legislative and executive levels of government, as well as between the elected House of Representatives and the non-elected Senate, is the ability to use and control non-confidence motions.[59] An individual minister or the entire Council of Ministers must step aside if a non-confidence motion is approved.[60] Following an amendment made to the Constitution in June 1992, the non-confidence apparatus is totally within the hands of the elected House of Representatives.[61] Thus, as between the House of Representatives and Senate, the House is clearly the dominant body, and it is to the elected House that the Council of Ministers is directly responsible.

While this brief review indicates that the civilian politicians of the elected House of Representatives have a clear advantage over the military and the Senate, care must be taken with this conclusion. While not an issue of constitutional law, it is important to recognize that many civilian politicians are either recently retired military officers or have very close ties with the

---

57 *Ibid.* at s. 102, para. 1. At one stage in the drafting of the 1991 Constitution, direct voting for candidates was to have been replaced with party slate voting, where the voter would choose parties rather than individuals. The party slate voting system was withdrawn following massive criticism. The party slate voting system was initially in the 1978 Constitution, but was removed and replaced by a direct voting system by Constitutional Amendment in 1985. Note Samudavanija, *supra* note 9 at 326.

The party slate voting system was strongly favoured by certain political parties and some vocal members of the military establishment, since it was seen as favouring well-financed and high profile candidates. See S. Kasitipradit, "Power Play on the Charter Chessboard," *Bangkok Post Weekly Review* (13 Sept. 1991) 8 and R. Tasker, "The Power Game," *Far Eastern Economic Review* (19 Sept. 1991) 12. The party slate voting system was rejected because of the possible undue influence of big money. See B. Tasaneeyavej, "Senators to Have More Clout in New Charter," *Bangkok Post Weekly Review* (5 July 1991) 3 and N. Chetchotiros and B. Tasaneeyavej, "Constitution Drafters Aim to Satisfy All Sides," *Bangkok Post Weekly Review* (31 May 1991) 8.

58 1991 Constitution, ss. 105(3), 106, and 107(9).

59 The term non-confidence is not specifically used in the translation of s. 150 of the 1991 Constitution, although it is used in s. 137 of the 1978 Constitution, the model for the 1991 provision.

60 1991 Constitution, ss. 168(1) and 169(5).

61 1991 Constitution, s. 221, repealed by Amendment of the Constitution of the Kingdom of Thailand, Nos. 1-3, 29 June 1992, *Royal Thai Government Gazette*, vol. 109, Part 72 (in Thai), translated version by International Translations Office, Bangkok. See generally Neher, *supra* note 4 at 604; Maisrikrod, *Thailand's Two General Elections*, *supra* note 4 at 34; and "Amendments Sail through 2 Readings," *Bangkok Post Weekly Review* (5 June 1992) 3. What the June 1992 amendment did was repeal a provision in the Transition chapter which allowed the Senate, for the first four years following the adoption of the 1991 Constitution, to participate in and vote on non-confidence motions.

Thai military elite.[62] The first of Thailand's two general elections in 1992 resulted in a coalition majority that was supportive of the military's influence in civilian government, in fact the coalition selected the coup leader to be Prime Minister, and, even after the May 1992 bloodshed and resignation of the disgraced military Prime Minister, the so-called anti-military politicians only narrowly formed a majority after the September 1992 election.[63] Moreover, the Senate, the traditional home of pro-military opinion, retains an important role in the enactment of legislation and in the constitutional amendment process.[64]

The Judiciary

By tradition the Thai King was the final arbitrator of disputes. The courts have inherited both the role of decision-maker and the prestige of being an agent of the monarch.[65] In 1908 the court structure was established in its current form, with the adoption of a professional judiciary and, more importantly, an independence from political and bureaucratic interference.[66] As one commentator has noted, despite political change in this century, "the centralized judicial system emerged intact from the political mould in which it was formed, with a permanent shape and legitimacy of its own."[67] This legitimacy and independence of the judiciary has been credited by another commentator as being a factor in assuring that authoritarian leaders in Thailand have not exercised their power in an unduly repressive manner.[68] In the past, interference with the independence of the judiciary, even during periods of military rule, led to wide-scale protests and ultimate removal of the offending measure.[69]

---

62 See Maisrikrod, *Thailand's Two General Elections*, *supra* note 4 at 6-20 where the main political parties in Thailand are profiled.

63 Concerning the elections, see Maisrikrod, *ibid.* 21-25 and 40-49. More generally on these events see the material cited in *supra* note 4.

64 See generally McDorman, *supra* note 24 at 278-79 and 282-83.

65 For a brief history of the judiciary in Thailand, see *Thailand Official Yearbook* – 1968, *supra* note 17 at 262-67. See also D. M. Engel, *Code and Custom in a Thai Provincial Court* (Tucson: Univ. of Arizona Press, 1978) at 18-24 and D. M. Engel, *Law and Kingship in Thailand during the Reign of King Chulalongkorn* (Ann Arbor: Univ. of Michigan, 1975) at 59-93.

66 *Thailand Official Yearbook* – 1968, *supra* note 17 at 265-66.

67 Engel, *Code And Custom*, *supra* note 65 at 25.

68 Samudavanija, *supra* note 9 at 337: "An independent and long-standing judiciary is another institution that has always been safeguarding the encroachment of civil liberties. It is an autonomous body not subjected to the control of the military and the bureaucracy, but has its own independent recruitment and appointment procedures."

69 For example, in late 1972, the military-led National Executive Council under Field Marshall Thanom Kittikachorn, decreed that the Minister of Justice would become more involved in the administration of the judiciary. This was seen as an attack on the independence of the judiciary and, following wide-scale protests, the decree was withdrawn. See R. H. Hickling, "Recent Constitutional and Legal Developments in Thailand" (1973) 3 Hong Kong L.J. 215 at 219-22. It should also be noted that s. 29 of the

The principal mechanism for maintaining the arms-length relationship between the judiciary and executive levels of government has been the Judicial Service Commission.[70] The Judicial Service Commission is constitutionally charged with the responsibility for appointing, promoting, penalizing, and dismissing judges.[71] The 1991 Constitution further protects judicial independence by preventing political officials from being judges,[72] prohibiting the establishment of special courts to replace existing courts to hear specific cases,[73] prohibiting the enactment of a law to deprive a court of its jurisdiction for any specific case,[74] and explicitly stating that judges shall be independent in deliberating on cases.[75]

While the 1991 Thai Constitution reaffirms judicial independence, the 1991 Constitution also reaffirms the disability of the courts to pronounce on the constitutionality of government measures.[76] In short, Thai courts do not have the authority to judicially review the constitutionality of government action. However, in a potential landmark decision in March 1993, the Thai Supreme Court found as unconstitutional an order issued by the coup leaders.[77] The Supreme Court based its jurisdiction to constitutionally review the measure on "general legal principles under which the courts have the authority to decide if any particular laws are constitutional or not in relation to cases under deliberation."[78]

Under the 1991 Constitution, the avenue that exists for the review of the constitutionality of a government measure is the Constitutional Judicial Council, better known as the Constitutional Tribunal.[79] When the

---

1991 Interim Thai Constitution explicitly protected the independence of the judiciary. See also the perceived attack on the judiciary in 1992, *infra* note 70.

70 The Judicial Service Commission has 12 members, 4 elected by senior judges, 4 elected by retired judges, and 4 ex-officio members including the President of the Supreme Court who assumes the Chair. Concerning the Judicial Service Commission, see M. Bunnag and P. A. F. Aakesson, "The Legal System of Thailand," in K. R. Redden, ed., *Modern Legal Systems Cyclopedia* (Buffalo: Hein, 1987) at 340.18-340.19 and *Thailand Official Yearbook* – 1968, *supra* note 17 at 271-72.

The Judicial Service Commission was recently at the centre of a political storm regarding its domination by a particular political faction. An attempt was made by the government to replace the 12-member Commission with a 28-member Commission. The move was perceived as an assault on the independence of the judiciary, and the House of Representatives rejected the alterations to the Commission.

See McDorman, *supra* note 24 at 286-88 for a review of the issues and events.

71 1991 Constitution, s. 193.

72 *Ibid.* at s. 191.

73 *Ibid.* at s. 188.

74 *Ibid.* at s. 189.

75 *Ibid.* at s. 190.

76 *Ibid.* at s. 206, para. 1, replicates s. 191, para. 1 of the 1978 Constitution.

77 N. Chetchotiros and D. Rojanalak, "Assets Seizure Ruling Opens Pandora's Box," *Bangkok Post* (2 Apr. 1993) 4, and see text accompanying notes 120-26.

78 *Ibid.*

79 The body is called the Constitution Judicial Council in the translated 1991 Constitution: see chapter 10 of the 1991 Constitution, and the Constitution Judiciary Commission

constitutionality of a government measure is raised, a court is to suspend the case and refer the constitutional issue to the Constitutional Tribunal for decision.[80] The Constitutional Tribunal can also be requested to review the constitutionality of a bill by the Prime Minister[81] or by the House of Representatives or Senate, if one-fifth of the members of the two Houses request review of a bill.[82] As well, the Constitutional Tribunal can be requested to interpret the Constitution by the Council of Ministers or pursuant to a resolution of either the House of Representatives or the Senate.[83] The final explicit constitutionality function that the Constitutional Tribunal can be asked to perform is to determine whether a regulation regarding the conducting of business in either the House of Representatives or Senate is consistent with the Constitution.[84]

In the aftermath of a series of decisions by the Constitutional Tribunal upholding the constitutional validity of the Amnesty Decree issued by the Prime Minister following the May 1992 bloodshed,[85] there have been questions about the political impartiality of the Tribunal and whether the Tribunal is the appropriate body to deal with constitutional issues. These questions have been given increased saliency by the Thai Supreme Court's willingness to find one of the orders issued by the coup leaders as unconstitutional.[86]

Rights of Citizens

It has been an axiom of Thai history that the dominant political force will not exercise its authority to unduly repress the freedoms of the Thai people. Historically, there is little experience in Thailand of *wide-scale* social,

---

in Amendment of the Constitution of the Kingdom of Thailand (No. 1), 29 June 1992, *supra* note 61; but in the 1978 Constitution and in the press it is called the Constitutional Tribunal. The Constitutional Tribunal is inspired by the Conseil Constitutionnel of France.

The Constitutional Tribunal, as established by the 1991 Constitution has ten members: the President of the Parliament (the Speaker of the House of Representatives); President of the Senate; President of the Dika Court (the Supreme Court of Thailand); the Chief of the Department of Public Prosecutions; and six appointed persons, three appointed by the House of Representatives and three appointed by the Senate. The six appointees are to be qualified in jurisprudence or political science, are not to be members of Parliament or government (military) officials, and are to hold their position for four years. The composition of the Tribunal indicates its political, rather than legal, function.

80 1991 Constitution, s. 206, para. 1.

81 *Ibid.* at s. 205, para. 1(2).

82 *Ibid.* at s. 205, para. 1(1).

83 *Ibid.* at s. 207.

84 *Ibid.* at s. 155.

85 The work of the Constitutional Tribunal on this issue is referred to at *supra* note 44. A fuller account can be found in McDorman, *supra* note 24 at 289-93.

86 See *infra* notes 120-26. See also "Battle Shapes Up Over Key Charter Changes," *Bangkok Post Weekly Review* (23 Apr. 1993) 4.

economic, religious, or political repression,[87] even in times of dictatorial military rule.[88]

> It should be pointed out that Thai authoritarianism is not very repressive. Authoritarian regimes that attempted to be too repressive usually met with strong opposition from various sections of society.
>
> The existence of countervailing forces such as an independent judiciary, a free press, and some favourable social conditions such as relatively little class antagonism or ethnic or religious cleavage are necessary but not sufficient conditions for a viable democracy in Thailand. These conditions do serve as important factors in preventing an authoritarian regime from becoming extreme in its rule.[89]

While Thais respect political power, they do not value political power exercised indiscriminately.[90] Hence, there has existed a tolerance for a degree of non-conformity and an unwillingness to accept interference with the Thai population's freedoms. Reasonable dissent, freedom of the press,[91] freedom of religion,[92] economic freedom, and social freedoms, many of which ex-

---

87 There are a number of exceptions to this bold statement, with the most obvious being the position of women in Thai society. See generally D. Tantiwiramanond and S. Pandey, "The Status and Role of Thai Women in the Pre-Modern Period: A Historical and Cultural Perspective" (1987) 2 *Sojourn: Social Issues In Southeast Asia* 125-49.

88 The Sarit regime, from 1958-63, was unquestionably one of absolute rule with little tolerance for political dissent. Yet, the regime did not exercise its authority totally arbitrarily and did seem to have as a goal the enhancing of the economic lives of the citizenry. Sarit was viewed as a benevolent patriarchal ruler and "was accepted by the general population." See Dhiravegin, *supra* note 2 at 159-65.

89 Samudavanija, *supra* note 9 at 337.

90 Dhiravegin, *supra* note 2 at 151 comments: "The exercise of power is seen as being more effective than going through a long process of bargaining." He goes on to note that "[p]ower is not used as an *ultima ratio* but as part of the process of getting things done."

91 It is generally acknowledged that Thailand has the freest print media in Southeast Asia. See generally P. Chirasopone, "Thailand," in A. Mehra, ed., *Press Systems in Asean States* (Singapore: Asian Mass Communication Research and Information Centre, 1989) at 91-100. While the print media have been beyond direct government control for some time, the broadcast media have been directly government controlled. This is now in the process of being changed. See "New Television Licences Herald Era of Access," *Bangkok Post Weekly Review* (7 Aug. 1992) 3 and "Cabinet Agrees to Overhaul Broadcasting Control Body," *Bangkok Post Weekly Review* (4 Sept. 1992) 20.

The attempt by the military to censor the print media in the spring of 1992 was largely unsuccessful. Maisrikrod, *Thailand's Two General Elections*, *supra* note 4 at 53-54 and 29 and P. Handley, "Press and Pirates," *Far Eastern Economic Review* (11 June 1992) 10-11.

92 The state religion in Thailand is Buddhism with the government involved in the Sangha. See P. A. Jackson, *Buddhism, Legitimation, and Conflict* (Singapore: Institute of Southeast Asian Studies, 1989) at 63-93. For an interesting and provocative assessment of the relationship between the Thai state and Buddhism, see J. Taylor, "Buddhist Revitalization, Modernization, and Social Change in Contemporary Thailand" (1993) 8 *Sojourn:*

isted to some degree before formal constitutional government,[93] have generally been respected irrespective of a written constitution and appear to be widely accepted despite occasional violations. Political and labour freedoms have been less in evidence than the others.[94]

Three chapters of the 1991 Constitution relate to the citizens of Thailand. These are: Chapter 3, "Rights and Freedoms of the Thai People"; chapter 4, "Responsibilities of the Thai People"; and chapter 5, "State Policy." The latter only indirectly deals with the Thai citizenry as it sets out guidelines for state action.[95] Chapter 5 is careful to include the provision that none of the objectives contained in it give rise to a right to sue the state.[96]

Some of the responsibilities placed on the Thai people by chapter 4 of the 1991 Constitution are to exercise the right to vote,[97] comply with the law,[98] pay tax as prescribed by law,[99] and conserve natural resources and the environment as prescribed by law.[100]

Social Issues In Southeast Asia 62-91. However, acceptance of other religions has deep roots in Thailand and a substantial Muslim population exists in Southern Thailand. See Keyes, *supra* note 18 at 126-35.

Within the state-supported Sangha, there have been issues of defrocking and excommunication. See C. Satyawadhna, "The Defrocking of Phra Bodhiraksa: A Case Study of Human Rights Violations in Thailand," in J. Girling, ed., *Human Rights In The Asia-Pacific Region* (Canberra: Australian Nat. Univ., 1991) at 75-91. See also Jackson, *supra* at 159-198. Generally, regarding religious freedom in Thailand in its legal context, see Aakesson, Bunnag, and Bunnag, *supra* note 9 at 674-75.

93 Concerning the abolition of slavery, right to a fair and speedy trial, right to legal aid, right to free speech, right to education, and the right of protection from acts of corrupt officials, see Aakesson, Bunnag, and Bunnag, *supra* note 9 at 670-79.

94 Labour unions have been a frequent target of military repression. Following the Feb. 1991 coup, the military junta announced its intent to remove the legal recognition of state enterprise unions. R. Tasker, "Ready and Waiting," *Far Eastern Economic Review* (28 Mar. 1991) 9. Reportedly, this move by the military junta was viewed with favour in Thailand. Despite promises by the civilian government to restore the union rights of state enterprise employees, there has been delay on this issue. See G. Fairclough, "Back to Work," *Far Eastern Economic Review* (5 Nov. 1992) 21-22. See generally K. A. Doelman, "Thailand's State Enterprise Labor Relations Act: Denying Public Employees the Right of Association and the Right to Organize and Bargain Collectively" (1993) 2 Pacific Rim L. and Policy Jour. 63-96.

95 Among other things, chapter 5 of the 1991 Constitution sets out that the state is to maintain, promote and develop equality between the sexes; maintain the environment and protect against pollution; provide social welfare, and assist and provide social welfare to the aged and disabled; protect labourers, especially women and children, and provide for fair wages; promote standard public health and provide health assistance to the poor free of charge; let farmers have possession of lands through land reform, allocation, or other means; preserve and maintain the arts and culture of the nation; promote understanding of and belief in the kingship democratic system; and support the private sector to play its role in the economy.

96 1991 Constitution, s. 59.

97 *Ibid.* at s. 51.

98 *Ibid.* at s. 54.

99 *Ibid.* at s. 55.

100 *Ibid.* at s. 58

The constitutional rights of the Thai people, which are set out in chapter 3,[101] include most of the universally recognized rights, such as:

- equality under and equal protection of the law[102]
- freedom of religion[103]
- presumption of innocence in criminal cases[104]
- freedom from arbitrary arrest, detention, or search[105]
- freedom of speech, including freedom of the press[106]
- freedom of assembly[107]
- freedom of association[108]
- freedom of movement within Thailand[109]
- the right to sue government officials[110]
- the right of criminally accused indigents to legal aid[111]
- the right to property[112]
- the right to conduct business or engage in the occupation of choice.[113]

---

101 A brief history of the rights of Thai people in the various constitutions is provided in Shin, *supra* note 9 at 40-51. Aakesson, Bunnag, and Bunnag, *supra* note 9 at 670 comment that "a number of rights and privileges enjoyed by the Thai people now ... are guaranteed by the Constitution. However, many such rights have their roots and beginnings in the days of the early absolute monarchs." They go on, at 670-80, to discuss many of those rights.

102 1991 Constitution, s. 25. Section 4 affirms that all Thai people are equally protected under the Constitution. Concerning the position of women in Thailand, see the materials cited in *supra* note 87.

103 *Ibid.* at s. 27, para. 1. The right is qualified by the requirement that religious beliefs are not to be in conflict with one's duty as a citizen or be against the peace, order, or morals of the people. See also the text and materials noted in *supra* note 92.

104 *Ibid.* at s. 29.

105 *Ibid.* at s. 30. Arrest, detention, or searches may be conducted in accordance with the law.

106 *Ibid.* at s. 37, para. 1. S. 37, para. 2 provides that restrictions on freedom of speech may be employed under provisions of national security law, to maintain peace, order, and public morality, and to protect the freedom, honour, and good names of individuals. Regarding freedom of the press, see the materials noted in *supra* note 91.

107 *Ibid.* at s. 39, para. 1. Paragraph 2 provides that limitations on this freedom may exist under special laws regarding public meetings, to protect use of public places, or during times of emergency or martial law.

108 *Ibid.* at s. 40, para. 1. Para. 2, however, indicates that the establishment, operation, or dissolution of associations, unions, federations, and cooperatives shall be in accordance with the law.

109 *Ibid.* at s. 43, para. 1. Paragraph 2 provides that limitations on this freedom may be imposed by laws for public security, laws for peace, order, or public welfare, or laws of town planning.

110 1991 Constitution, s. 46. Concerning the history of this right, see Aakesson, Bunnag, and Bunnag, *supra* note 9 at 678-79.

111 *Ibid.* at s. 31. See generally K. Kittayarak, "Toward Equal Justice: The Right to Counsel in Thailand" (1989-90) 6 Chulalongkorn L. Rev. 98-125.

112 *Ibid.* at s. 35, para. 1. This paragraph also indicates that the limitation of property rights shall be in accordance with law. S. 36 deals specifically with expropriation.

113 *Ibid.* at s. 48, para. 1. This is a new provision not found in previous Thai constitutions. See "New Charter to Protect Rights," *Bangkok Post Weekly Review* (21 June

Many of the provisions recognizing the above rights also severely limit these rights by indicating that they exist except where laws otherwise exist.[114] One commentator has noted that "[t]o grant a right yet immediately qualify that its exercise must be 'in accordance with the provisions of the law' is to create ambiguity, leaving that 'right' subject to interpretations of transient governmental majorities."[115] Moreover, section 49 of the 1991 Constitution provides a broad limitation on the use of the rights provisions of the Constitution, stating that "[p]ersons may not exercise the rights and freedoms as prescribed under this Chapter against the country, religion, the King, and the Constitution."

Finally, there is no direct avenue for judicial review on constitutionality questions except through the Constitutional Tribunal. Thus, it can be argued that there is no effective means for the enforcement of rights or, since the Constitutional Tribunal can only determine constitutionality of legislation, of obtaining a remedy.[116] All of the above has been summarized by another authority as follows:

> While, theoretically, the constitution is the highest law of the land, the constitution limits its own power by stating that citizens have political and civil liberties "except where laws otherwise so stipulate." Thus laws, executive decrees, etc. have precedence over constitutional rights and liberties. Such laws limiting rights and freedoms are framed in terms of national security, public order, public morality. Seldom, if ever, is a law challenged on the basis of unconstitutionality. Even if a constitutional issue were to be raised, it would not be decided by an independent judiciary but by a Constitutional Tribunal.[117]

Coups and Law

Mention must be made of a constitutional practice that has existed because of the extraconstitutional means by which power has so frequently changed hands in Thailand. Courts and subsequent governments have accepted that, regardless of the illegality of the acquisition of authority, once a usurping authority is in an unquestioned position of power, any legislative action that it takes is legally effective.[118] This practice makes it unnecessary to re-

---

1991) 1. The numerous limitations on the new right are noted in 1991 Constitution, s. 48, para. 2.

114 See the limitations noted above in notes 103, 105-109, 112-13.

115 V. Engkagul, "Recognition of Human Rights under Thai Laws," in H. M. Scoble and L. S. Wiseberg, eds., *Access to Justice: The Struggle for Human Rights in Southeast Asia* (London: Zed Books, 1985) at 99.

116 *Ibid.* at 100.

117 Samudavanija, *supra* note 9 at 321.

118 Engkagul, *supra* note 115 at 99: "Contemporary Thai jurisprudence has now recognized the legitimacy of the military mechanisms that have toppled previous lawful

enact laws made before a new constitution comes into force and, moreover, is a pragmatic recognition of political reality unencumbered by legal formalism.[119] Sections 222 and 223 of the 1991 Constitution specifically direct that laws, notifications, and orders issued under the Interim Constitution are valid under the 1991 Constitution. To a constitutional purist, however, such a practice recognizes the legitimacy of the illegal means of acquiring power and an acceptance of might as right.

This pragmatic practice of acceptance of coups has been brought into question by the March 1993 ruling of the Thai Supreme Court that an order issued by the National Peace-Keeping Council (the coup leaders) in February 1991[120] was inconsistent with Thai constitutional practices.[121] The Supreme Court did not strike down the offending law because of the illegality of the seizure of power, but because they found the law to be inconsistent with the relevant provisions of the 1991 Interim Constitution.[122] The Supreme Court rejected the argument that section 32 of the Interim Constitution, which provided that all orders of the National Peace-Keeping Council

governments. According to the precedent established by the present Supreme Court of Thailand, the (military) leader of any coup d'état who successfully takes over power from the lawful government is deemed the supreme ruler of the government. Therefore, any decrees or commands issued by him during his rule are now regarded as of equal status to the lawful actions of the Parliament. In the past 50 years in Thailand there have been numerous successful coups and revolutions, yet all legislation enacted by means of revolutionary decrees are considered valid laws. There is no doubt that almost all of these decrees, etc., were enacted in contradiction to the ideology of human rights; nonetheless, in the context of the current Thai Constitution, all are regarded as valid, as integral parts of the provisions of the laws."

119 The problem of courts dealing with actions by successful coup-makers has been dealt with in British Commonwealth jurisprudence. The result has been that "judges ultimately accorded recognition to the revolutionary government's decrees on the grounds of public necessity": S. Guest, "Revolution and the Position of the Judiciary" [1980] Public Law 168 at 169.

120 Announcement of the National Peace-Keeping Council No. 26, re: Attachment and Freezing of Property, 25 Feb. 1991, Royal Thai Government Gazette, vol. 108, Part 34, Special Issue (in Thai), translated version by Bangkok Business and Secretarial Office Limited. The effect of this order was to freeze the assets of members of the pre-coup civilian government whom it was felt had become unusually rich through corrupt practices. A seven-member Property Examination Committee was established to evaluate whether property had been improperly acquired. See generally Bhuchongkul, *supra* note 4 at 321-22.

121 The details of the decision are discussed by Chetchotiros and Rojanalak, *supra* note 77.

122 The Supreme Court determined that the Property Examination Committee established by NPKC Order No. 26, *supra* note 120, exercised a judicial function that was reserved by ss. 3 and 29 of the Interim Constitution for the Courts and hence that the establishment and actions of the Property Examination Committee were unconstitutional. Chetchotiros and Rojanalak, *supra* note 77.

123 About this aspect of the decision, Chetchotiros and Rojanalak, *supra* note 77 at 4 comment: "[i]n fact, the Supreme Court in the past had upheld the legality of all orders issued by coupmakers and until last week, this line of traditional interpretation on constitutionality of such orders [s. 32 of the Interim Constitution] had been prevailing."

were legally valid, insulated the order from constitutional attack.[123] The narrow basis of the Court's findings of unconstitutionality combined with the particular facts that gave the Supreme Court jurisdiction to examine the relevant order,[124] and the uncertainty over the legality of the Supreme Court's jurisdiction to pronounce on the constitutionality of laws[125] raises doubts whether the case can either be used to challenge other orders issued by the coup-makers[126] or has wider implications in Thai constitutional practices. The decision is either a bold step in undermining the legitimacy conferred upon coup-makers by Thai practices, or an anomaly that will be circumvented as being inconsistent with the pragmatism necessary to maintain a coherent legal system faced with abrupt, illegal changes of government.

CONCLUSION: CHANGE AND CONTINUITY

From 1978 to 1991, Thailand was slowly proceeding along a path of Thai-style democracy with the governing power structure becoming ever more distant from the control and influence of the military. The 1978 Constitution was seen as providing a workable framework for an evolution to an increasingly democratic and responsible civilian government. Despite coup attempts in the 1980s,[127] the 1978 Constitution and the government had not been usurped. This situation led to a conviction that legal and political legitimacy were increasingly linked together with the 1978 Constitution.

The events of 1991-92 shattered the complacency within Thailand that successful military coups were a thing of the past. Moreover, these events demonstrated that the military still believed that it had the legitimacy not

124 NPKC Order No. 26, *supra* note 120, was amended in late 1991 to allow for a review of a finding of the Property Examination Committee by the entire Supreme Court of Thailand, thus bypassing the lower courts. The curious political circumstances of this amendment is noted by Bhuchongkul, *supra* note 4 at 322. In late 1991 and early 1992, the Property Examination Committee found that ten individuals had acquired assets in an improper manner. These individuals appealed to the Supreme Court to review and reverse the findings.

125 S. 206, para. 1 of the 1991 Constitution reserves to a Constitutional Tribunal the exclusive jurisdiction to pronounce on the constitutionality of government action. See *supra* text accompanying notes 76-84. However, the 1991 Interim Constitution did not establish a Constitutional Tribunal. S. 31 left the question of constitutionality of law or action to be decided by the appointed National Legislative Assembly. The Thai Supreme Court decided that NPKC Order No. 26 had to be assessed pursuant to the 1991 Interim Constitution and that since, by 1992, the appointed National Legislative Assembly no longer existed, the issue of constitutionality fell to be determined by the Supreme Court. Moreover, as Chetchotiros and Rojanalak, *supra* note 77 at 4 observe: "the Supreme Court judges referred to general legal principles under which the courts have the authority to decide if any particular laws are constitutional or not in relation to cases under deliberation."

126 See Chetchotiros and Rojanalak, supra note 77.

127 See Wright, *supra* note 18 at 262-64, 271-73, and 283-87.

only to seize power where it believed the government to be out of control, but also to gain necessary support to remain an active participant in day-to-day government. It is the latter point on which the Thai military miscalculated. Faced with a turning point in constitutional development between reorganizing the Constitution to appease the military and thus stepping back from the further development of democracy and using the painful events of 1991-92 as an opportunity to enhance the legitimating role of the Constitution, public pressure ensured the choice of further democratization. The 1991-92 events, therefore, must be seen as a "blip" in the path that commenced with the 1978 Constitution towards a constitutionally-based, democratic political system.

The constitutional law and practices in Thailand in the aftermath of the 1991 coup represent *a continuity* of large parts of the law and practices found in the 1978 Constitution, *a continuation* of the democratization trends of the 1980s, and *a change* that enhances the importance of and respect for the Thai Constitution as the source of legal and political legitimacy.

The *continuity* is clear from a comparison of the 1978 and 1991 Constitutions. As noted, significant parts of the new Constitution replicate its 1978 predecessor. The citizen's rights and judicial provisions, for example, are little changed. The fundamental structure of government with the executive responsible to the Parliament have been retained, despite an attempt to introduce the American model of separation of the legislative and executive levels of government.[128] The constitutional role of the monarchy has been left unaltered.

What is described above as a *continuation* is simultaneously a continuity of the evolution of Thailand along a path of democratization as exemplified by constitutional changes that occurred in 1991-92. The continuity is that ministers, including the Prime Minister, must not be military officers. The change is that the Prime Minister now must be a member of the elected House of Representatives. Achieving this continuity and change came only after direct pressure from the public and from forces opposed to conspicuous military involvement in the government. Pressure to increase the power of the Senate vis-à-vis the House of Representatives was also repulsed, ensuring a continuation of pre-1991 practices.

The *changes* that took place in 1991-92, which will be of critical importance in the future of Thailand's constitutional law and practices, involved the role of the public and the courts. First, the Supreme Court of Thailand in its ruling that an order by the coup-makers was unconstitutional may signal the end to a legal tolerance for coups. Even if this is too broad an interpretation to place on the decision, the willingness of the Thai Supreme

128 See *supra* notes 30-32.

Court to rely on general principles regarding constitutional behaviour and the Court's role in supervising the Constitution indicate a possible awakening of judicial power in Thailand. The Court may be leading or merely reflecting public opinion in an intolerance for unconstitutional behaviour.

The most significant change, however, was the public's direct involvement in constitution-making. A Thai observer once summarized the public's concern about the Constitution as follows: "The Thai public has not been observed to defend its constitution vigorously."[129] This is patently no longer accurate. Public opinion and protest were exerted successfully to ensure that a more democratic constitutional document was produced in 1991 and 1992 than the one envisioned by the military. The public viewed the constitutional discussions as being of critical importance. Clearly constitutional law and practices in Thailand will never be the same now that the public demands that legal and political legitimacy be derived from the Constitution.

It would be premature to pronounce that Thailand has a stable, democratic constitutional framework that is the fountain of both legal and political legitimacy. However, the trend of Thai constitutional law and practice is in the direction of fusion. Paradoxically, the coup of 1991 and the bloodshed of 1992 have enhanced, rather than reversed, the progression of Thai-style democracy.

POSTSCRIPT: THE 1997 THAI CONSTITUTION[130]

Introduction

The reverberation of the military coup of 1991 and the use of force in 1992 continues in Thai politics and constitutional development. In early 1995, substantial revisions were made to the 1991 Constitution,[131] and in late 1997, following an extensive drafting process, Thailand adopted a new Constitution. The principal concerns of Thai constitutional construction in 1997 have been institutional: trying to decrease the role of money-politics (vote

---

129 Wongtrangan, *supra* note 3 at 293.

130 The 1997 Constitution of the Kingdom of Thailand was approved in October 1997 as this book was in its final editing stages. As noted below, until the final debates within the Thai Parliament it was not clear that a new Charter would be adopted. At the time of writing there was no complete or official English translation of the 1997 Constitution. The *Nation*, a daily newspaper in Bangkok, produced an English translation of most of the draft Constitution submitted to Parliament. References in this postscript are to this translated version. The author thanks the staff at the library of Tilleke and Gibbins, Bangkok for their assistance during a hurried trip to Bangkok. Any errors, omissions, or misinterpretations, however, are solely the responsibility of the author.

131 Constitution of the Kingdom of Thailand (Amendment No. 5), 10 Feb. 1995, translated version by International Translations Office, Royal Thai Government Gazette, vol. 49, no. 13. For a brief commentary on the 1995 changes, see S. Sucharitkul, "Thailand" (1995) *Asia-Pacific Constitutional Yearbook* 315 at 323-28.

buying)[132] in national elections; trying to decrease the opportunity for corruption, cronyism, and self-interested political deal-making by politicians; and establishing a balance of civilian-military relations that enhances constitutionalism and civilian rule. These three concerns are inextricably interlinked: less vote buying should lead to less need for corruption, which should lead to better decision-making and elected officials of high integrity, which should reduce the military's perceived role as national stabilizer.

The proposed Constitution delivered by the drafting committee to Parliament in the summer of 1997 attempted to strike at the heart of money-politics. Not surprisingly, Parliament was reluctant to endorse the new Charter. The final debates in Parliament took place amidst "palpable tension in the air" with one observer noting that "Thailand came close to the brink of civil unrest over the Charter during the lengthy parliamentary debate."[133] Tension over the proposed Charter was heightened by the demand for political leadership at the onset of the economic reversal in Thailand. The Thai military is credited with ensuring that the politicians did not detour or scuttle the constitutional reform package.[134]

Key Characteristics of Constitutional Law and Practice in Thailand

The Monarchy

The 1997 Constitution does not change the power or authority of the monarch.

Civilian/Military Power-Sharing

The 1997 Constitution seeks to firmly establish the civilian authorities as the dominant political partner with the military. Institutionally this has been accomplished by dismantling the appointed Senate, traditionally a bastion of pro-military forces, and creating a directly elected Senate. Thailand will now have twin elected bodies, each with independent authority, and while the House of Representatives is the more powerful body, both levels of Parliament will be required to cooperate.

Under the 1997 Constitution, the Prime Minister must be from the House of Representatives, although upon becoming Prime Minister he or she must resign from the House. This qualification of the Prime Minister has long been a pivotal issue in the Thai polity. Other cabinet members do not have to be from Parliament, although any that are must also resign their seats.

---

132 The phenomenon of vote buying in Thai elections is described and discussed in W. A. Callahan and D. McCargo, "Vote-Buying in Thailand's Northeast: The July 1995 General Election" (1996) 36 Asian Survey 376 at 376-80.

133 M. Vatikiotis, "People's Putsch," *Far Eastern Economic Review* (18 Sept. 1997) 15.

134 *Ibid.* at 14.

The 1997 Constitution attempts to go beyond changing the furniture of government and deals directly with building the legitimacy of elected politicians to govern. Money-politics is the targeted scourge. The 1997 Constitution creates an independent Election Commission to oversee the electoral process and a National Counter Corruption Commission (NCCC) to investigate corruption. In order to counter corruption, it is constitutionally required that political office-holders disclose their assets and debts to the NCCC both on taking and leaving office. Moreover, the revelation must be made public where the office is in Parliament or cabinet. Also related to public confidence in politicians is the requirement that, unless he or she has already been either a senator or member of Parliament, a newly elected parliamentarian must have a bachelor's degree.

The Judiciary

The 1997 Constitution has made a number of changes to the administration of courts and has created the Administrative Court. Although not an important concern, there has also been an enhancement of the legitimacy and the independence of the judiciary.

Of interest is an apparent significant expansion of the role of the Thai courts within section 28 of the 1997 Constitution. Paragraph 2 of section 28 states: "Individuals whose rights and liberties as prescribed in this Constitution are offended can use the constitutional provisions to bring their cases to the courts." When tied with section 29, which directs that liberties can only be restricted consistent with the Constitution, Thai citizens may now be able to use the courts to directly challenge government actions which arguably infringe their constitutionally-protected rights. Sections 28 and 29 appear to create a constitutional judicial review authority for Thai courts.

Rights of Citizens

The 1997 Constitution is acknowledged as having expanded both the nature of individual rights protected and the way in which those rights are to be protected. A significant change is that noted above in section 29, where constitutional liberties are only to be restricted by laws consistent with the Constitution, replacing the previous approach that a liberty existed except where a law otherwise directed.[135] An important institutional change is the creation of the National Human Rights Commission with the mandate of monitoring human rights violations and regularly reporting to Parliament. One commentator concluded that the 1997 Constitution "gives more to the people than any other charter in Thai history."[136]

---

135 See above text accompanying footnotes 114 and 115.

136 T. Thongpao, "Charter Promotes Rights," *Bangkok Post* (12 Oct. 1997) 6.

Change and Continuity

The 1997 Constitution is as noted for its changes from, as well as its continuity with, past Thai constitutional practices. The continuity with Thai constitutionalism since 1978 is demonstrated in the increasing importance of the written Constitution as the source of legitimation for the exercise of authority,[137] and the increased acceptance of civilian rule over military power. Further evidence of continuity is the increased reliance on direct democracy as the path for governing Thailand.

The most significant change associated with the 1991 Constitution, the public's direct involvement in constitution-making, was continued in the drafting and adoption of the 1997 Constitution. First, the drafting process directly involved the Thai public, and the public responded directly. It is estimated that nearly a million people attended the various debates and open forum discussions organized by those responsible for drafting the Constitution.[138] Second, as already noted, the final debates in Parliament galvanized public attention in such a way as to force the hand of reluctant politicians to accept the 1997 Constitution.

The significant changes arising from the 1997 Constitution are twofold: institutional and aspirational. The goal of the 1997 Constitution is to change the way in which politics, particularly elections, are conducted and to inspire public confidence in public officials. Institutionally, a number of changes arise under the 1997 Constitution: for example, an elected senate, a National Counter Corruption Commission, and a National Human Rights Commission.

---

137 J. Ockley, "Thai Society and Patterns of Political Leadership" (1996) 36 Asian Survey 345 at 354-55 reveals that there has been a shift in the style of Thai leaders towards respect for law and process rather than exercise of raw power. Thus, constitutionalism is of increasing importance.

138 Editorial, "Politicians Seem to Fear Full Financial Disclosure," *The [Bangkok] Nation* (20 Aug. 1997) 5.

6
The 1992 Vietnamese Constitution: Economic Reform, Political Continuity

Joanna Harrington, Ted L. McDorman, and William A. W. Neilson

INTRODUCTION

Most states feel compelled to have written constitutions. This is as evident in Southeast Asia as elsewhere in the world. In the midst of the 1991 military coup in Thailand, one of the first promises by the coup leaders was that a new constitution would be quickly adopted.[1] Myanmar, in the grips of strict military rule since 1990, has been moving towards the development of a new constitutional document.[2] The Philippines revised its constitution following the "people power" success of Corazon Aquino in 1986.[3] Both Laos and Cambodia have adopted new constitutional documents within the past few years.[4] The other countries of the region, Brunei, Indonesia, Malaysia, and Singapore, have written constitutions that are over 30 years old. Finally, Vietnam adopted what is effectively a new constitution in 1992.[5]

---

1 S. Bunbongkarn, "Thailand in 1991: Coping with Military Guardianship" (1992) 32 Asian Survey 131 at 133. See generally T. L. McDorman, "The 1991 Constitution of Thailand" (1995) 3 Pacific Rim Law and Policy Journal 257-98 and T. L. McDorman, "Constitutional Change and Continuity in Thailand in the Aftermath of the 1991 Coup" (c. 5 in this volume).

2 See J. M. Diller, "Constitutional Reform in a Repressive State: The Case of Burma" (1994) 33 Asian Survey 39 and R. H. Taylor, "Myanmar: New, but Different?" in *Southeast Asian Affairs 1995* (Singapore: Institute for Southeast Asian Studies) 241 at 244-45.

3 See D. Wurfel, *Filipino Politics: Development and Decay* (Quezon City: Ateneo de Manila University Press, 1988) at 297-311. More specifically, see E. M. Fernando and E. Quisumbing-Fernando, "The 1987 Constitution of the Philippines: The Impact of American Constitutionalism Revisited," in L. W. Beer, ed., *Constitutional Systems in Late Twentieth Century Asia* (Seattle: Univ. of Washington, 1992) at 571-613.

4 Respecting the 1991 Constitution of Laos, see M. Stuart-Fox, "The Constitution of the Lao People's Democratic Republic" (1991) 17 Rev. of Socialist Law 299-317. Respecting Cambodia's new constitution, see generally W. Shawcross, *Cambodia's New Deal* (Washington: Carnegie Endowment for International Peace, 1994) 106 and F. Frost, "Cambodia: From UNTAC to Royal Government," in *Southeast Asian Affairs 1994* (Singapore: Institute for Southeast Asian Studies) 79 at 87-88.

5 The 1992 Constitution was enacted by the National Assembly 15 Apr. 1992 and promulgated on 18 Apr. 1992: "National Assembly Passes Constitution," *Voice of Vietnam*

A written constitution is usually seen as the most important public law document and cornerstone of the civic sector of a legal system. The reasons why most states view a written constitution as essential are varied. One reason is that there exists an international community expectation that independent states will have formal constitutions. It is not surprising, therefore, that, as part of Myanmar's hoped for re-emergence and re-acceptance on the world stage, a new constitutional document is being prepared. The international community expectation that a state will have a written constitution also leads to foreign expectations as to what will be contained in the formal constitution. A second reason why states engage in establishing written constitutions is to legitimize the action and status of governments. The legitimacy sought by a government for its actions and the exercise of authority is not only from within a country but also from without. Hence, written constitutions are designed for both internal and external purposes and, as a consequence, are influenced both by internal and external considerations and expectations. The experience in Thailand with its 1991 Constitution was primarily motivated by legitimation concerns. A third reason why a written constitution is important is that it can be used as an aspirational statement of governing or societal principles. Governments may find it useful to have their principal public law document express ideals. This may be of particular importance in states where national unity is a major concern. The Indonesian Constitution appears to be motivated in part by these concerns.[6] A fourth reason why a written constitution is important is that it can outline the relationship between the governing and the governed and establish constraints and restraints on the exercise of governmental authority. This aspect of a written constitution is most graphically demonstrated in U.S. constitutional experience. Within Southeast Asia, the Constitutions of both Malaysia and Singapore can be viewed as creating constraints on the exercise of government authority.[7]

Vietnam's recent experience with the revision of its written constitution arose from its need to assure the world community (in particular its partners in the Association of Southeast Asian Nations (ASEAN)), that Vietnam is fully embracing open-market economic reform. Moreover, the revised Constitution was necessary to provide legitimacy for the internal changes

---

(Hanoi) (15 Apr. 1992), reprinted in Foreign Broadcast Information Service, East Asia Series [hereinafter FBIS-EAS], 15 Apr. 1992, 057; "Papers Hail Promulgation of New Constitution," *Voice of Vietnam (Hanoi)* (18 Apr. 1992), in FBIS-EAS, 28 Apr. 1992, 049. For an English version of the 1992 Constitution, see A. P. Blaustein and G. H. Flanz, eds., *Constitutions of the Countries of the World* (New York: Oceana Publications, 1992), Supplemental Volume.

6 See P. Wahjono, "Democracy in Indonesia: Pancasilia Democracy," in Beer, *supra* note 3 at 462-66.

7 See M. C. Crane, M. Gillen, and T. L. McDorman, "Parliamentary Supremacy in Canada, Malaysia, and Singapore" (c. 4 in this volume).

being made to facilitate economic reform. Hence, legitimation and international community expectation were the principal motivators for the renewal of Vietnam's written constitution. These motivations for change to the economic provisions of Vietnam's Constitution did not lead to significant change in the political provisions of the 1992 Constitution. In the political realm, while the revised Constitution rearranges the exercise of governmental authority through new and redesigned institutions, the ultimate power of the Vietnamese Communist Party is unaffected. Vietnam has shown little sensitivity to external factors both historic (the collapse of world-wide communism) and macropolitical (liberal democratic principles) in the rearranged political institutions.

Vietnam's experience with constitutional revision must also take into account the socialist ideology that has dominated its post-Second World War history and the perceived role that constitutions play in a socialist legal system. Constitutions in a socialist legal framework "are not intended to serve as permanent documents reflecting the timeless political and philosophical values of a given society."[8] They do not seek to regulate relations between state and society, nor do they have a determinative legal function. The primary purpose of a constitution in a socialist state is "to chart the progress of that society as it evolves through stages of growth to a final state of classless communism."[9] At each stage of revolution, a new constitution is developed to establish the policies of that stage, to motivate the populace, and to set forth the objectives to be achieved in preparation for the next stage. As M. Beresford explains "stability in the (socialist) Constitution and unconditional adherence to its provisions are therefore not considered necessary, or even desirable, goals."[10]

Vietnam's 1992 Constitution is an attempt to interweave internal and external considerations and expectations and produce a document that provides governmental legitimacy at home and abroad respecting economic change without undermining the authoritarianism of the Vietnamese Communist Party. Vietnam's constitutional revision raises a host of questions. Are the economic changes signalled by the 1992 Constitution of a permanent nature or, consistent with socialist constitutions, will they be altered when new circumstances exist or a new socialist stage reached? Does the 1992 Constitution represent a break with Vietnam's socialist legal system traditions? Can Vietnam's political leaders encourage open-market economic

---

8 W. J. Duiker, "The Constitutional System of the Socialist Republic of Vietnam," in Beer, *supra* note 3 at 331.

9 *Ibid.* Concerning changes in the Soviet Constitution, see W. E. Butler, *Soviet Law* (London: Butterworths, 1983) at 137-38 and for the People's Republic of China (PRC), see W. C. Jones, "The Constitution of the People's Republic of China," in Beer, *supra* note 3 at 60-74.

10 M. Beresford, *Vietnam, Politics, Economics and Society* (New York: Pinter, 1988) at 98-99.

reform while continuing to constrain open-market political reform? Does the 1992 Constitution involve more than rhetoric and aspiration?

The purpose of this chapter is to examine the 1992 Constitution of Vietnam in the context of internal and external considerations and expectations. The starting point is the historical context from which the 1992 Constitution sprang. The content of the 1992 Constitution will be outlined under the separate headings of economic provisions and political provisions. In the concluding section, Vietnam's 1992 Constitution will be placed in the comparative setting of its Southeast Asian neighbours – in particular, Brunei, Indonesia, Malaysia, the Philippines, Singapore, and Thailand.

VIETNAM'S CONSTITUTIONAL HISTORY

Overlaying the constitutional history of Vietnam, which traces its roots to the declaration of Vietnam's independence from France in 1945, is socialist legal ideology and the role that written constitutions are seen as playing within a socialist legal framework.[11] Consistent with constitutional practice in socialist states,[12] Vietnam has had four written constitutions since 1945: the first in 1946, the second in 1960, the third in 1980, and the most recent in 1992.[13]

The 1946 Constitution, adopted by the National Assembly of the then-named Democratic Republic of Vietnam[14] on the eve of renewed hostilities with the French colonial regime based in southern Vietnam, was drafted with the intent of building a Vietnamese "united front" to secure independence from colonial rule. Hence, its provisions were designed to appeal to a broad spectrum of Vietnamese society.[15] Democratic freedoms

11 Respecting socialist law as a distinct legal system, see R. David and J. E. C. Brierley, *Major Legal Systems in the World Today,* 3rd ed. (London: Stevens and Sons, 1985) at 155-306.

12 A concise comparison of Anglo-American and Soviet attitudes to constitutions is provided in Butler, *supra* note 9 at 135-36.

13 English language versions of the 1960 and 1980 Constitutions are reprinted in Blaustein, *supra* note 5, Historic Constitutions Volume. The 1946 Constitution is included in appendix 1 of B. B. Fall, *The Viet-Minh Regime: Government and Administration in the Democratic Republic of Vietnam* (New York: Institute of Pacific Relations, 1956) at 156-64. For a Vietnamese analysis of the three constitutions, see Pham Van Bach and Vu Dinh Hoe, "The Three Successive Constitutions of Vietnam" (1984) 1 Int'l Rev. of Contemporary Law 105.

Some commentators refer to Vietnam's second Constitution as the 1959 Constitution. For clarification, Vietnam's second Constitution was enacted 31 Dec. 1959 and promulgated 1 Jan. 1960. See B. B. Fall, "North Viet-Nam's Constitution and Government" (1960) 33 Pacific Affairs 282 at 284.

14 Despite legislative approval from the National Assembly, the 1946 Constitution was never officially promulgated. Duiker, *supra* note 8 at 359 n. 3 and R. F. Turner, *Vietnamese Communism: Its Origins and Development* (Stanford: Hoover Institution Press, 1975) at 64.

15 Duiker, *supra* note 8 at 331.

were promised[16] and the sanctity of private property guaranteed.[17] In fact, the 1946 Constitution gave a generally "western democratic" impression to the reader, in that it did not deal in economic theories and did not make use of stereotyped communist phrases such as the "working people" or the "victory of the dictatorship of the proletariat."[18]

While the preamble to the 1946 Constitution stated that the country was "entering a new phase,"[19] no reference was made to the ultimate goal of transforming Vietnam into a communist state. At this stage of the Vietnamese revolution, and with southern Vietnam under foreign control, nationalist interests took precedence over class interests and socialist dogma.

After the French defeat at Dien Bien Phu in 1954, Vietnam was formally divided into the two separate zones of North and South.[20] The separation was described in the Geneva Peace Accord as provisional, and national elections were scheduled for 1956. When it became apparent that the elections would not be held, North Vietnam set about drafting a new constitution.[21] This new constitution was to combine the desire to create a socialist society in the North[22] with the hope of soliciting southern support for reunification.[23] The new constitution, which took three years to draft, was promulgated on January 1, 1960.

The 1960 Constitution was a radical departure from the 1946 Constitution.[24] Unlike its predecessor, the 1960 Constitution expressly dealt with economic theories and directly incorporated communist phrases and dogma.[25] Article 9, for example, announced that North Vietnam was "advancing step by step from people's democracy to socialism." The 1960 Constitution described the various functions of the state's executive, legislative,

---

16 For example, the 1946 Constitution provided for freedom of speech, press, and assembly: R. J. Cima, *Vietnam: A Country Study* (Washington: U.S. Govt. Printing Office, 1989) at 204.

17 Art. 12 of the 1946 Constitution stated: "The right to private property is guaranteed." See Bach and Hoe, *supra* note 13 at 107.

18 B. B. Fall, "Constitution-Writing in a Communist State: The New Constitution of North Viet-Nam" (1960) 6 Howard L.J. 157 at 159 (quotes in original).

19 Bach and Hoe, *supra* note 13 at 106.

20 For further details on the First Indochina War and the Geneva Peace Accord, see generally Cima, *supra* note 16 at 54-60.

21 Beresford, *supra* note 10 at 100. The fact that South Vietnam became a Republic by popular referendum in 1955 may also have been a motivating factor. Fall, *supra* note 18 at 158.

22 Some steps had already been taken. Land reform was completed and the majority of peasants had been placed in low-level collectives. See Duiker, *supra* note 8 at 331 and Beresford, *supra* note 10 at 100.

23 In its preamble, the 1960 Constitution described itself as "a Constitution for the building of socialism in North Vietnam and for the struggle for the reunification of the country and the completion of the Popular Democratic National Revolution."

24 For a full discussion of the 1960 Constitution, see generally B. B. Fall, "North Viet-Nam's New Draft Constitution" (1959) 32 Pacific Affairs 178, and notes 34 and 39.

25 Fall, *ibid.* at 178.

and judicial bodies; however, the all-important role of the Communist Party,[26] with the Party having the final authority on all matters, [27] was not mentioned in the body of the Constitution. Perhaps the reason for the omission was, as W. J. Duiker suggests, that "the regime wished to avoid alienating moderate elements in the South at the opening of what would eventually become known as the Vietnam War."[28]

With the withdrawal of the United States and the reunification of North and South in 1975,[29] Vietnam created a new constitution to reflect yet another stage in its development. The task of redrafting the constitution was completed in 1980.[30] Vietnam's goal of becoming a socialist regime by the end of the 1980s was reflected throughout the 1980 Constitution. Moreover, unlike the 1960 Constitution, the 1980 Constitution expressly recognized the pivotal, political authority of the Vietnamese Communist Party.[31] In article 4, the Party was described as the "only force leading the state and society, and the main factor determining all successes of the Vietnamese revolution."

Constitutional change has come easily to Vietnam and has reflected the perceived needs of the state in the face of changed external and internal circumstances. The flexible role of a written constitution in a socialist legal structure has encouraged Vietnam to undertake regular revision. The difference with the 1992 Constitution is that Vietnam is attempting to signal to the world community that it is undertaking economic change. The goals of the 1992 Constitution appear to be in contrast to the posturing found in Vietnam's previous Constitutions and more generally found in constitutions in socialist legal systems.

THE MOTIVATION AND MECHANISM OF CONSTITUTIONAL CHANGE

The Economic Motivation

In the 1980s Vietnam was one of the poorest countries in the world. The country endured high unemployment, inadequate food production, and soaring inflation.[32] Low labour productivity, the under-use of resources and

26 The party was called the Vietnamese Workers' Party at that time.

27 Cima, *supra* note 16 at 205.

28 Duiker, *supra* note 8 at 332.

29 For an account of the origins of American involvement in Vietnam, see generally S. Karnow, *Vietnam: A History* (New York: Viking Press, 1983).

30 For a discussion of the redrafting process and the contents of the 1980 Constitution, see Duiker, *supra* note 8 and Beresford, *supra* note 10 at 102-14.

31 Curiously, no reference is made either to the 1980 Constitution or to its express recognition of the role of the Vietnamese Communist Party in O. Weggel, "The Vietnamese Communist Party and Its Status Under Law," in D. A. Loeber et al., eds., *Ruling Communist Parties and Their Status Under Law* (Boston: Martinus Nijhoff, 1986) at 411-19.

32 See generally R. J. Cima, "Vietnam's Economic Reform: Approaching the 1990s" (1989) 24 Asian Survey 786 ff.

a cumbersome state bureaucracy hampered production in both the agricultural and industrial sectors. In addition, sustained involvement in regional military conflicts diverted necessary resources from improving the economic and industrial infrastructure.[33]

The failings of Vietnam's centrally planned economy were publicly acknowledged by the Vietnamese Communist Party at its Sixth Party Congress in December 1986.[34] Following this meeting, Vietnam embarked on a program of economic reform or *doi moi*.[35] *Doi moi* literally means "new change" or "new thinking," but is most frequently translated as renovation.[36] Under *doi moi*, the Party has implemented market-oriented measures designed to improve agricultural production, increase the availability of consumer goods, promote exports, and reduce inflation.[37] Farmers have been given the right to withdraw from collectives and farm families are permitted to lease land.[38] A renewed foreign investment law was enacted in 1987,[39] and private corporations were legitimized in 1988.[40] The Party leadership realized that "while socialism remained an ideal, the benefits of market economics and individual initiative were essential if Vietnam was to resolve its dire economic problems."[41] At the Seventh Party Congress in 1991, the Vietnamese Communist Party reiterated its commitment to socialism, but placed

---

33 One authority estimated that the Vietnamese army absorbed 30% to 50% of Vietnam's annual national budget. D. M. Finkelstein, "Vietnam: A Revolution in Crisis" (1987) 27 Asian Survey 973 at 983.

34 R. A. Scalapino, *The Last Leninists: The Uncertain Future of Asia's Communist States* (Washington: Center for Strategic and International Studies, 1992) at 30.

35 For a discussion of the political reforms that have accompanied *doi moi*, see generally: C.A. Thayer, "The Challenges Facing Vietnamese Communism," in K. S. Sandhu, ed., *Southeast Asian Studies 1992* (Singapore: Institute of Southeast Asian Studies, 1992) 349-64 and G. Porter, "The Politics of 'Renovation' in Vietnam" (1990) 39 Problems of Communism 72-88. On *doi moi* generally, see also W. S. Turley and M. Selden, eds., *Reinventing Vietnamese Socialism: Doi Moi in Comparative Perspective* (Boulder, Col.: Westview Press, 1993).

36 See D. Tonkin, "Whither Vietnam?" (1992) 23 Asian Affairs 295 at 296 and C. A. Thayer, "Political Reform in Vietnam" (1993) 70 Current Affairs Bulletin 22 at 22. Some authors interpret *doi moi* to mean "renewal": Cima, *supra* note 32 at 789.

37 Scalapino, *supra* note 34 at 31.

38 *Ibid.*

39 Vietnam's revised *Law on Foreign Investment* was promulgated 29 Dec. 1987. The new law permitted foreign businesses and investors to operate in Vietnam via joint state-private ventures and via wholly foreign-owned corporations. See generally Van Vu Nguyen, "Foreign Investment in Vietnam Through Business Cooperation Contracts" (1994) 28 Int'l Lawyer 133; J. Gillespie, "Foreign Investment in SR Vietnam Revisited" (1990) 18 Int'l Business Lawyer 416; W. G. Vause, "Doing Business with Vietnam – Prospects and Concerns for the 1990s" (1989) 4 Florida Int'l L.J. 231; C. Ngo, "Foreign Investment Promotion: Thailand a Model for Economic Development in Vietnam" (1992) 16 Hastings Int'l and Comparative L. Rev. 67 at 71-85 and W. A. W. Neilson, *Vietnam Investment Manual* (Hong Kong: Asia Law and Practice, 1995).

40 Scalapino, *supra* note 34 at 31.

41 Tonkin, *supra* note 36 at 296.

renewed emphasis on the need to establish a market-centred economy as a necessary transitional step to socialism.[42] *Doi moi* was pursued with increased vigour.

Changes to the 1980 Constitution were seen as necessary to ensure the success of the Vietnamese economic renovation policies. As explained by Vo Chi Cong, a key Party adviser and the chair of Vietnam's Constitutional Amendment Committee:

> After more than ten years of implementing the 1980 Constitution ... it was found that some stipulations of the 1980 Constitution, especially those of the economic system, were not consistent with the law on production relations and the capability and nature of the production force ... For this reason, we were unable to release all production forces and develop all the potential of society. Moreover, during the 1980s, our nation was hit hard by a prolonged socioeconomic crisis.[43]

The Process of Revision

According to Vo Chi Cong, the National Assembly intended to "revise" the 1980 Constitution, rather than redraft a new Constitution.[44] He emphasized that "the continuity and successiveness of the Vietnamese Constitutions, particularly between the 1980 Constitution and the amended one, must be respected and thoroughly understood."[45] However, the 1992 Constitution so significantly changes the content of the previous 1980 Constitution as to be a new document. As noted by Levien Do, only 12 of the 1992 Constitution's 147 articles remain unrevised from the 1980 Constitution.[46]

The process of revising the 1980 Constitution began in 1988,[47] but as with *doi moi* the revision process was only pushed in earnest after the Vietnamese Communist Party's Seventh Party Congress in 1991.[48] Four key principles guided the revision.[49] First and foremost, the Party was to remain as

---

42 Scalapino, *supra* note 34 at 32-33. For a complete discussion of the developments in Vietnam in 1991, see D. Pike, "Vietnam in 1991: The Turning Point" (1992) 32 Asian Survey 74. See also W. A. W. Neilson, "Vietnam's Economic Law Transformation within the ASEAN Community" (c. 3 in this volume).

43 "Vo Chi Cong Discusses New Constitution," *Voice of Vietnam (Hanoi)* (2 Jan. 1992) in FBIS-EAS, 10 Jan. 1992, 066.

44 "Vo Chi Cong Article Views Revised Constitution" Vietnam News Agency (Hanoi) (4 Jan. 1992) in FBIS-EAS, 6 Jan. 1992, 074.

45 "Vo Chi Cong Discusses," *supra* note 43 at 066.

46 Levien Do, "Vietnam's Revised Constitution: Impact on Foreign Investment," in C. A. Thayer and D. G. Marr, eds., *Vietnam and the Rule of Law* (Canberra: Australian Nat. Univ., 1993) at 116. However, Do submits that "judging by the proportion of unchanged or revised articles compared to the number of newly introduced ones, the Constitution appears essentially to be a re-draft of the 1980 Constitution."

47 D. R. Avery, "Vietnam in 1992: Win Some; Lose Some" (1993) 33 Asian Survey 67 at 68.

48 *Ibid.* and see Pike, *supra* note 42.

the leading force in the state and society. Second, the political system was to remain unilocular,[50] with no separation of powers among the executive, legislative, and judicial branches. Third, Vietnam was to remain a socialist democracy, and fourth, the new Constitution was to reflect the Party's commitment to economic renovation.

The revision process involved four drafts[51] and a seemingly high level of public participation.[52] The draft constitutional documents were prepared by the Constitutional Amendment Committee, which had been established by the National Assembly in 1989 and was comprised of senior Party and government officials.[53] The first draft was submitted to high and middle-ranking Party officials in May 1991, followed by a second draft presented to the National Assembly in July.[54] This draft was also submitted to the Party's Central Committee[55] to ensure endorsement at the highest political levels.[56] A third draft was circulated for public comment in January 1992, with the final draft going to the National Assembly for approval in April 1992. After three weeks of debate in the National Assembly, the revised 1992 Constitution was adopted unanimously.[57]

THE ECONOMIC PROVISIONS IN THE 1992 CONSTITUTION

Fundamental change is evident in the constitutional provisions regarding Vietnam's economy. Seven new articles have been added to the chapter on

49 "Vo Chi Cong on Constitutional Amendments," Vietnam News Agency (Hanoi) (29 July 1991) in FBIS-EAS, 29 July 1991, 071.

50 Unilocular is the term used in Pike's interpretation of Vo Chi Cong's statement. Pike, *supra* note 42 at 77.

51 The only substantial difference between the four drafts was the elimination of the Council of State. The Council was included in the first draft, but dropped from the final version. The Council of State was, in effect, the collective presidency of Vietnam. "Dropping of State Council from Constitution Urged," *Voice of Vietnam (Hanoi)* (6 Feb. 1992), in FBIS-EAS, 12 Feb. 1992, 070.

52 For example, 1.4 million suggestions were reportedly made by citizens in Hanoi. "People Contribute to Draft Constitution," *Voice of Vietnam (Hanoi)* (6 Mar. 1992), in FBIS-EAS, 11 Mar. 1992, 067. D. R. Avery suggests the public debate was orchestrated: Avery, *supra* note 47 at 68; but R. H. H. Khng suggests that "the publicized debates were, in parts, substantive enough to show that it was not entirely a managed affair." R. H. H. Khng, "The 1992 Revised Constitution of Vietnam: Background and Scope of Changes" (1992) 14 Contemporary Southeast Asia 221 at 228.

53 "Vo Chi Cong Discusses," *supra* note 43 at 066. In addition to chairing the Constitutional Amendment Committee, Vo Chi Cong was an adviser to the Party's Central Committee and chair of the Council of State.

54 Khng, *supra* note 52 at 222 and "Vo Chi Cong Discusses," *supra* note 43 at 066.

55 Political power in the Vietnamese Communist Party is formally vested in the Central Committee, a body elected by the National Party Congress. The real decision-making body of the Central Committee is the Political Bureau or "Politburo," which is composed of the Party's highest ranking members: Cima, *supra* note 16 at 196.

56 "Vo Chi Cong Discusses," *supra* note 43 at 066.

57 "National Assembly Passes Constitution," *supra* note 5 at 057.

the economic system and all previous provisions in the 1980 Constitution on economic matters have been revised.[58] Under article 15, Vietnam has affirmed its support for the development of a multi-sectoral, commodity economy based on market principles. It also recognizes that this new economic structure depends on three systems of ownership: state ownership,[59] collective ownership, and private ownership. This differs from the 1980 Constitution, which only recognized the first two types of ownership.[60] These changes are subject to two qualifications. The 1992 Constitution stipulates that state and collective ownership must remain as the core of Vietnam's economic structure, and that greater economic diversity must be based on "state management and socialist orientations."[61] Thus, the private sector economy exists to complement or supplement the socialist public sector economy, with the state ultimately exercising supervision and control over the private economy.

Vietnam's new Constitution attempts to signal a relaxation of state interference in production and business. Pursuant to article 21, "individual and private capitalist economies may choose their own forms of production and business and may set up trade businesses without any limit on the scope and areas of operations." The qualification, also in article 21, is that the businesses must be "beneficial to the nation and the people."

The economic chapter in Vietnam's 1992 Constitution reaffirms the desire to increase the receipt of foreign aid and investment. The Constitution specifically encourages foreign organizations and individuals to invest capital and technology in Vietnam and extends an explicit invitation for investment from overseas Vietnamese.[62] In return, article 25 of the Constitution promises to "guarantee the right of ownership of the legitimate capital, property and other interests of foreign organizations and individuals." It further stipulates that "business enterprises with foreign invested capital shall not be subject to nationalization."

Respecting the critical issue of land ownership,[63] Vietnam has, within the socialist construct, instituted a measure of reform. As in other socialist legal

58 Khng, *supra* note 52 at 223.

59 This is described in art. 15 as "ownership by the entire people."

60 See 1980 Constitution, art. 20.

61 1992 Constitution, art. 15.

62 1992 Constitution, art. 25. On foreign investment generally in Vietnam, see *supra* note 39 and Neilson, *supra* note 42. For more information on overseas Vietnamese investment, see M. Hiebert, "Wooing Them Home: Overseas Vietnamese Cautious About Investment," *Far Eastern Economic Review* (23 Jan. 1992) 18.

63 Given that 75% of Vietnamese are farmers, the question of land use is of prime importance. M. Hiebert, "The New Charter: Economic Freedom Offset by Party's Political Role," *Far Eastern Economic Review* (30 Apr. 1992) 20. On land law generally in Vietnam, see Nguyen Qui Binh, "Real Estate Laws in Vietnam," in Thayer and Marr, *supra* note 46 at 148-50. Regarding land-use rights and transfers in Vietnam, see Gillespie, *supra* note 39 at 338-43 and 350-55.

systems, individuals in Vietnam do not have the right to own, sell, or inherit land.[64] Article 17 of the 1992 Constitution affirms that land will continue to be "under the ownership of the entire people." However, the Constitution provides a compromise in article 18 through the allotment of land by the state for use on a "stabilized and long-term basis." It is this right of land use, rather than the land itself, that can be transferred by sale or inheritance.[65] In addition, the 1992 Constitution prohibits "the nationalization of legal property" and provides for the payment of compensation based on market values if property is expropriated for state purposes.[66]

The alterations in Vietnam's economic structure are a clear sign of change; however, given the numerous qualifications, foreign investors and others should not interpret the 1992 Constitution as an unequivocal abandonment of economic socialism.

THE POLITICAL PROVISIONS IN THE 1992 CONSTITUTION

The Communist Party of Vietnam

In contrast to developments in eastern Europe and the former Soviet Union, and more like its Chinese neighbour, the Vietnamese Communist Party appears determined to retain its monopoly on political power. Several commentators have suggested that Vietnam's refusal to initiate fundamental political reforms is precisely because of the recent events in the former communist countries.[67] Vietnam fears that a weakening of Party hegemony will lead to instability.

64 Generally on property in socialist legal systems, see E. B. Pashukanis, "A Course on Soviet Economic Law," in P. Beirne and R. Sharlet, eds., *Pashukanis: Selected Writings on Marxism and Law* (Toronto: Academic Press, 1980) at 320-35. See also Butler, *supra* note 9 at 169-71.

65 According to M. Hiebert, "some of the most heated debates in the assembly centred on the question of farmers bequeathing land, which remains the property of the state, to their children. Many delegates wanted to include the right of inheritance but, following last minute pressure from the party, the assembly voted to allow farmers only to 'transfer the right to use land,' which can include the right of inheritance." "The New Charter," *supra* note 63. According to Ngo Ba Thanh, the former head of the Judicial Committee of the National Assembly, "a more comprehensive leasehold system of land usage is likely to be introduced, which might allow the buying and selling of land leases, the inheritance of land use by immediate descendants and eventually the use of leasehold as a mortgage": Ngo Ba Thanh, "The 1992 Constitution and the Rule of Law," in Thayer and Marr, *supra* note 46 at 92. For an assessment of the 1993 *Land Law* effect on rural property, see R. L. Prosterman and T. Hanstad, *Agrarian Reform in Vietnam and the 1993 Land Law* (Seattle: Rural Development Institute Monograph #13 on Foreign Aid and Development, Jan. 1994).

A similar compromise was adopted by the People's Republic of China in 1988 when it amended art. 10 of its 1982 Constitution to allow transfers of the right to the use of land. See Jones, *supra* note 9 at 74.

66 1992 Constitution, art. 23. "Legal property" is undefined.

67 M. Hiebert, "Rewriting the Future: Party's Latest Draft Political Report Criticised," *Far Eastern Economic Review* (7 Mar. 1991) 28; Tonkin, *supra* note 36 at 297 and B. Womack,

During the Party's 1991 meeting, General Secretary Nguyen Van Linh, the leading advocate of *doi moi*,[68] vigorously opposed political pluralism and the development of a multiparty opposition system. Linh argued that "to accept the multiparty system of opposition is to create conditions for the reactionary forces of revenge within the country and from abroad to rear their heads immediately and legally to operate against the homeland, the people and the regime. Our people definitely reject this."[69]

This was not rejected by *all* people. Requests were made by some Vietnamese citizens for a hint of political pluralism to be included in the 1992 Constitution.[70] In the end, the Party's position prevailed and the 1992 Constitution does not provide encouragement for a multiparty political system. However, there has been a slight modification in the constitutional description of the role of the Vietnamese Communist Party. Article 4 states that the Party is the "leading force of the state and society" rather than the "only force leading the state and society" which was the wording in the 1980 Constitution. However, this article must be read within the context of the Constitution's preamble, which provides an unequivocal summation of the party-state relationship: "the Party is the leader, the people the master, the state the manager."

Article 4 also provides that "all Party organizations operate within the framework of the Constitution and the law."[71] A similar provision existed in

---

"Reform in Vietnam: Backwards Towards the Future" (1992) 27 Government and Opposition 177 at 185.

68 C. A. Joiner, "The Vietnam Communist Party Strives to Remain the Only Force" (1990) 30 Asian Survey 1053 at 1055.

69 As cited in Scalapino, *supra* note 34 at 59. A slightly different translation is included in Womack, *supra* note 67 at 177-78. On pluralism, see also G. Porter, *Vietnam: The Politics of Bureaucratic Socialism* (Ithaca, N.Y.: Cornell University Press, 1993) at 96-100. The Vietnamese Communist Party's rejection of pluralism or even power sharing is hardly surprising. Even less so, given the following description of the Party's power by Weggel, *supra* note 31 at 416:

> In modern Vietnam the state is managed in a remarkably unparticipatory way. There is neither formal opposition to check the Party leadership nor a second chamber to screen its proposals. Neither is there a federal Constitutional Court nor an Administrative Court to rap its knuckles, nor any notion of separation of powers. There are no election campaigns, and leading politicians generally are spared any embarrassment by citizens' initiatives. Party policy is never criticized by the press; on the contrary, even the press is at the constant disposal of the VCP as a device for purveying all kinds of justifications.

70 The debate over pluralism was publicly acknowledged by Vo Tran Chi, a member of the Politburo, presumably acting with the Party's approval, in an interview with *Saigon Ghai*: "Vo Tran Chi on Democratic State," *Saigon Ghai* (Ho Chi Minh City) (15 Feb. 1992) 1 at 5; in FBIS-EAS, 17 Mar. 1992, 055.

71 An attempt to amend art. 4 to read "all party organizations *and members* operate within the framework of the constitution and the law" was unsuccessful: Khng, *supra* note 52 at 226 and M. Hiebert, "Cutting Red Tape: Review of Constitution to Streamline Government," *Far Eastern Economic Review* (22 Aug. 1991) 11.

the Soviet Union's 1977 Constitution without precluding rule by Party fiat.[72] The Soviet provision meant that Party members were to guide, rather than administer, state affairs.[73] The explanation of the provision in Vietnam's 1992 Constitution is similar. According to Politburo member Vo Tran Chi, article 4 means that "the Party leads the legislative branch by its guidelines and resolutions and through its politically prestigious organizations and members."[74]

Several commentators have suggested that, under the revised Constitution, the Vietnamese Communist Party will continue to guide state policy, but will no longer interfere in the day-to-day administration of the government.[75]

STATE INSTITUTIONS AND STRUCTURE

While the Communist Party remains as the unquestioned source of ultimate decision-making, the 1992 Constitution has redesigned the formal political and institutional structure of government in Vietnam. The four key institutions are the National Assembly, the Standing Committee, the Prime Minister, and the President. The latter three institutions are either new or substantially redesigned under the 1992 Constitution. The administrative and executive structure of the 1980 Constitution resulted in many Party officials holding dual or overlapping positions within the central government apparatus. This situation led to an uncertain division of responsibilities and a paralysis in state policy-making.[76] The 1992 Constitution attempted to streamline the central decision-making process, clarify the chains of command, and reduce bureaucratic overlap.

The National Assembly

The National Assembly is Vietnam's supreme legislative body,[77] responsible for the enactment and observance of the Constitution and law.[78] According

72 The Soviet provision read: "All Party organizations shall function within the framework of the Constitution of the U.S.S.R." See J. N. Hazard, "The Common Core of Marxian Socialist Constitutions" (1982) 19 San Diego L. Rev. 297 at 307.

73 See M. Lesage, *La Constitution de L'USSR, 7 October 1977: Texte et Commentaries* 31 (1978), as cited in Hazard, *supra* note 72 at 307.

74 Vo Tran Chi, *supra* note 70 at 055.

75 The New Charter, *supra* note 63 at 20 and Avery, *supra* note 47 at 68.

76 *Ibid.*

77 Under art. 83 of the 1992 Constitution, the National Assembly "is the people's highest representative agency," "the highest organ of state power," and "the sole legislative and constitutional agency."

78 Under art. 84(1) of the 1992 Constitution, the National Assembly has the power to "draw up and amend the Constitution, make and amend laws, and decide on law-building programs." Under art. 84(2), the Assembly has the power "to exercise the supreme right of supervision over the observance of the Constitution, the laws and National Assembly resolutions." Under art. 84(9), the Assembly has the power "to

to article 83, the National Assembly "is the sole constitutional and legislative agency. It decides the fundamental foreign and domestic policies; the socioeconomic, national defence, and security tasks; the main organizational and operational principles of the state machinery; and the social relations and activities of the citizens."[79]

In addition, the National Assembly has the power to exercise its "supreme right of supervision over all operations of the state,"[80] including the power to elect, dismiss, and impeach the President, Prime Minister, and Chief Justice of Vietnam.[81]

Before the 1992 Constitution, the National Assembly met once a year, sometimes for only a few weeks at a time, reflecting its limited responsibilities for law-making. Its primary raison d'être was, and remains, to provide legitimacy for government policy pronouncements and increasingly to provide a public forum for calling government ministers to account, in the broadest sense, for the performance of their public duties.

In the July 20, 1997 national elections, 450 deputies from 663 candidates were elected to the tenth National Assembly in multi-member constituencies from each of the 61 provinces, which include four provincial status cities (Hanoi, Ho Chi Minh City, Haiphong, and Da Nang).[82] Party and state agencies nominated 141 of the deputies while 40 members were elected from the 53 ethnic minority groups living in Vietnam.[83] The election was conducted under the new Electoral Law, which set the new voting age at 18. The Law underwent nine drafts and substantial debate in the National Assembly meeting in April 1997. Efforts by the Central Committee of the Vietnam Fatherland Front (the "mass organization" responsible for nominating candidates) to more closely control the nomination of candidates and the election campaign itself were rebuffed by the deputies.[84] One-third of the members are full-time representatives (chosen by the Standing Committee

abrogate those documents of the President of state, the National Assembly's Standing Committee, the government, the Prime Minister, the People's Supreme Court and the Supreme People's Organ of Control, which are at variance with the Constitution, the law, and the National Assembly resolutions."

79 Do, *supra* note 46 at 117. With respect to government organization, the National Assembly can define the powers of state bodies, establish or dissolve ministries, and assess the performance of the government and ministers. With respect to policy-making, the Assembly can define the state plan, create taxes, and control foreign policy. With respect to leadership control, the Assembly can appoint the President and Prime Minister, supervise the provincial people's committees and abrogate decisions of state organizations that are inconsistent with the Constitution, enacted laws, and Assembly resolutions.

80 1992 Constitution, art. 83.

81 *Ibid.* at art. 84(7).

82 Vietnam Law and Legal Forum, July 1997, 8.

83 Ibid. May 1997, 9.

84 "The National Assembly," *Vietnam Economic Times* (July 1997) 14-15; "Fresh Faces Shine in New Assembly," *Vietnam Investment Review* (11 Aug. 1997) 10.

of the National Assembly), based in Hanoi. The remaining members are part-time, often with one or more posts in their constituency with provincial people's councils, social organizations, etc. The Assembly meets twice annually,[85] in April and October, to debate and pass new laws, receive performance reports from government ministers, approve legislation plans for both itself and the Standing Committee, and adopt resolutions directing the government to implement "urgent tasks" before the next session of the National Assembly. The members are increasingly prepared to call upon ministers to account for their actions, to probe budget statements and, occasionally, to suggest amendments to proposed legislation.[86] In another recent example, the deputies rejected the Prime Minister's nomination of the incumbent governor of the Central Bank to remain in his post.[87]

The 1992 Constitution does little to diminish the predominant role of the Communist Party in Vietnam's legislature and polity. Since 1945, the National Assembly has served as a rubber-stamp body for decisions previously made by the highest organs of the only legally recognized political party.[88] As explained by W. J. Duiker, "[p]arty control was established at the start, through the electoral process. While deputies to the National Assembly ... were elected on the basis of universal suffrage, with voting equal, direct and secret, in practice the elections were controlled by the Party."[89]

Following the adoption of the 1992 Constitution, a new election law was passed to allow independent candidates to contest National Assembly elections. According to press reports,[90] 44 people tried to run as independent candidates, but only two survived the complex candidate screening process controlled by the Party-dominated, Vietnam Fatherland Front, which managed the elections.[91] The election campaign reportedly "was

85 Art. 86 states that extraordinary sessions of the National Assembly may be convened at the request of the National Assembly Standing Committee, the President, the Prime Minister or at least one third of the total number of National Assembly deputies. According to D. R. Avery, efforts to have the Assembly meet more often failed to gain enough support in the constitutional amendment process. Avery, *supra* note 47 at 69.

86 See A. Schwarz, "Vietnam: Nation Builders – Assembly Lays Foundation for Rule of Law" *Far Eastern Economic Review* (16 Nov. 1995) 22.

87 "Gone, Not Forgotten," *Far Eastern Economic Review* (20 Nov. 1997) 12, noting that "Vietnam's National Assembly may have been able to remove Cao Si Kiem from his post as Governor of Vietnam's Central Bank, but it can't vote him out of his Communist Party position," noting that "Kiem remains Head of the Party Commission responsible for banking."

88 Duiker, *supra* note 8 at 338.

89 *Ibid.*

90 See M. Hiebert, "Letting Off Steam," *Far Eastern Economic Review* (30 July 1992) 10.

91 As noted by C. A. Thayer, "mass organizations and other groups at national, provincial and local levels were intimately and intensely involved in the process to select suitable qualified candidates, and the personal lives and backgrounds of potential candidates came under close scrutiny. Potential candidates were required to win majority support in their workplace and in their place of residence in order to qualify for selection."

tightly controlled and excited little interest"[92] and resulted in a National Assembly dominated by Party members.[93]

Elections remain carefully managed. In the July 1997 election, for example, the Fatherland Front approved a list of 39 names from which Ho Chi Minh city voters chose 25 deputies. Of these candidates, 32 were locally nominated and seven were centrally selected. Of the 32 local nominations, two were so-called "independent" or non-party candidates, who were selected by the Front from a list of 22 independents. There is no real election campaign. The new Electoral Law only allows candidates to talk to the voters in meetings organized by the Fatherland Front.[94]

According to some observers the National Assembly "has become an increasingly important platform ... for (deputies) to criticise unpopular policies and incompetent or corrupt officials."[95] But, given the aims of *doi moi*, criticism of incompetence, corruption, and other detriments to Vietnam's economic success would not be discouraged. More telling is the fact that deputies have not criticized the central role or leadership of the Communist Party.

The Standing Committee[96]

The Standing Committee is the permanent body of the National Assembly, the operative legislative body when the National Assembly is not in session,[97] and in day-to-day political terms acts as the cabinet or executive of the National Assembly. Despite its importance, the membership and precise role of the Standing Committee is not clear in the Constitution. No equivalent body to the Standing Committee existed under the 1980 Constitution.

The Standing Committee consists of 13 members, including its chair, the President of the National Assembly. The other members of this powerful legislative and executive body include the chairs of the eight National

---

Thayer, *supra* note 36 at 25. But, as explained by M. Hiebert, the "complex screening procedure gives the ruling communist party many different ways of blocking a candidate who might give the country's leaders a hard time." M. Hiebert, "Election Strategy: No Threat to Communist Party Rule in July Polls," *Far Eastern Economic Review* (9 July 1992) 21.

92 Avery, *supra* note 47 at 69.

93 Over 92% of the deputies elected were Party members. The remaining 8% were "approved" by the Party. All of the 60 members of the Party's Central Committee who stood for election, including nine members of the Politburo, were elected: Thayer, *supra* note 36 at 25.

94 "The National Assembly," *Vietnam Economic Times* (July 1997) 15.

95 Hiebert, *supra* note 91 at 21.

96 The information in this section is based upon personal interviews conducted in Hanoi by W. A. W. Neilson with members of the Law Department of the Office of the National Assembly in May 1995. See Neilson, *supra* note 39 at 125-38 and 283-84. The law-making and supervisory powers of the Standing Committee were recently codified in the *Law on the Promulgation of Legal Documents*, 24 Official Gazette 11 (31 Jan. 1997).

97 1992 Constitution, arts. 91 and 92.

Assembly Committees and the Director or Secretary General of the Office of the National Assembly. Members of the Standing Committee are not permitted to hold positions in the Government, unlike other delegates of the National Assembly. Nomination of Standing Committee members is controlled by the VCP, replicating the Party's control over the selection of ministers and equivalent authorities to the Office of Government (Cabinet).

In its law-making capacity, the Standing Committee promulgates ordinances on a vast range of legislative issues. The actual topics for law-making are approved annually by the National Assembly, based upon a list of proposed legislation (laws and ordinances) prepared by the Standing Committee in consultation with the Office of Government. Ordinances are equal in force to laws. The Standing Committee meets approximately fifteen days per month during the ten months each year that the National Assembly is not in session. As legislative gatekeeper for the Assembly, the Standing Committee reviews and presents draft laws to the Assembly at each session.

Eight line Committees of the National Assembly report to the Standing Committee and are responsible for reviewing legislative proposals and monitoring the activities of government ministries and agencies. The chair of each permanent committee sits on the Standing Committee. Their line responsibilities are borne out by their titles – the Committees for Law, Budget and Economics, Social Affairs, Culture Education and Youth, Science Technology and Environment, Defence and Security, Foreign Relations and Ethnic Minorities. For all intents and purposes, these permanent committees are run by their chairs, working with staff attached to mirror departments of the Office of the National Assembly, including staff in the Office of the Deputies Delegation based in each province. These full-time staff (close to 500 in total), working closely with committee chairs (who together constitute the majority membership of the Standing Committee), guarantee strong central control over the National Assembly's exercise of its nominally independent constitutional responsibilities.

The Prime Minister

In the 1992 Constitution, Vietnam adopted a cabinet-style government headed by a Prime Minister elected by the National Assembly.[98] The ministers of the government are chosen by the Prime Minister and subject to

98 Before 1992, the highest executive and administrative body in Vietnam was the Council of Ministers. The Council was a powerful, albeit cumbersome, entity comprised of a chair, several vice-chairs, and the heads of the various government ministries, as well as the heads of a host of government agencies that duplicated and supervised the activities of the ministries. Members of the Council were elected by and accountable to the National Assembly, and, by law, most members served simultaneously as deputies in the National Assembly: *The Law on the Organization of the Council of Ministers* of 1981, as cited in Duiker, *supra* note 8 at 340.

ratification by the National Assembly.[99] The Constitution directs that ministers are not to be National Assembly deputies.[100] The Prime Minister and ministers collectively form what is termed the "government" in the Vietnamese Constitution.[101] The government is responsible to the National Assembly. According to article 109 of the 1992 Constitution, the task of the government is to "exercise unified managerial control over the implementation of political, economic, cultural, social, national defence, security, and foreign affairs of the state" and to "ensure the effectiveness of the state machinery from the central down to the grassroots level."

On paper, the Prime Minister appears to have effective control over the governing of Vietnam. The Prime Minister has the authority to select ministers and dismiss the chairs and vice-chairs of the local people's committees that govern the provinces and cities.[102] Moreover, the Prime Minister has the power to rescind decisions, directives, and circulars of both ministers and local people's committees.[103] With these powers, the Prime Minister ostensibly can ensure that all economic reform initiatives sponsored by the central government are fully supported by Vietnam's ministers and local government.[104]

The President

After witnessing the dismantling of the Soviet Union and the Soviet Communist Party by powerful individuals such as Gorbachev and Yeltsin, Vietnam's constitutional reformers had concerns about giving too much power to a single individual.[105] Consequently, the 1992 Constitution recreates the office of President to offset the powers of the newly-established position of Prime Minister. Under both the 1946 and 1960 Constitutions, the office of President accommodated the powerful and symbolic figure of Ho Chi Minh.[106] Following Ho's death in 1969, the presidency devolved into a ceremonial office and in 1980 was replaced with a collective executive body called the Council of State.[107] Under the 1992 Constitution, the

---

99 1992 Constitution, art. 114(2).

100 *Ibid.* at art. 110.

101 *Ibid.* at arts. 109, 110.

102 1992 Constitution, art. 114(3). Local government in Vietnam is the responsibility of popularly elected people's councils. The people's committees are the party-dominated executive bodies of the councils.

103 1992 Constitution, art. 114(4).

104 According to Levien Do, these powers are likely the result of "anecdotal evidence that in recent years certain investment projects supported at the national level did not proceed due to a lack of enthusiasm or cooperation by local governments": Do, *supra* note 46 at 120.

105 Khng, *supra* note 52 at 227 and Thayer, *supra* note 36 at 24.

106 Duiker, *supra* note 8 at 340.

107 1980 Constitution, art. 98.

Council of State has vanished and the presidency has re-emerged as a political institution.

Pursuant to articles 102 and 103 of the 1992 Constitution, the President is to be elected by the National Assembly and serve as the head of state and the commander-in-chief of the armed forces. The President's power derives from the capacity to recommend to the National Assembly the election, and more importantly, the removal of the vice-president, the Prime Minister and the Chief Justice of the Supreme People's Court.[108]

The Judiciary

Given that one of the key principles guiding the revision of the 1992 Constitution was that there was to be no separation of power among the executive, legislative, and judicial branches,[109] and the emphasis in the revision on economic reform, it is not surprising that Vietnam's judicial system has remained largely unchanged under the 1992 Constitution. The judiciary remains a hierarchical and centralized system consisting of the Supreme People's Court in Hanoi, local people's courts at each administrative level, and several military tribunals.

The National Assembly, through article 127 of the Constitution, has the power to create special tribunals at its discretion. It is uncertain, however, whether the National Assembly can establish a specialized court or dispute tribunal apart from the Supreme People's Court system.[110] Strict constructionists and VCP conservatives argue against the proposition. The debate reached the floor of the National Assembly in December 1993 in the passage of the Law on the Organization of the People's Courts, which added the economic courts as the third division of the people's court system, in addition to the criminal courts and civil courts.[111] The Minister of Justice, as one of the sponsors of the proposed legislation, had originally indicated a readiness to establish the economic courts separate from the people's court system, apparently to give greater assurance to foreign investors and other commercial litigants of the announced independence and impartiality of the new specialized court. The Chief Judge of the Supreme People's Court,

108 1992 Constitution, art. 103(3).

109 "Vo Chi Cong on Constitutional Amendments," Vietnam News Agency (Hanoi) (29 July 1991) in FBIS-EAS, 29 July 1991, 071.

110 Under the Constitution, the Supreme People's Court is to supervise the special tribunals, unless the National Assembly decides otherwise. However, in practice, the supervisory authority of the Supreme People's Court is partly reduced by the administrative control exercised by the Ministry of Justice over the activities of the judiciary: M. Sidel, "The Re-Emergence of Legal Discourse in Vietnam" (1994) 43 Int'l and Comparative L. Quarterly 163 at 170.

111 *Law Amending the Law on the Organization of the People's Court*, 28 Dec. 1993, followed by the *Ordinance on the Procedures for Handling Economic Cases* (Standing Committee), 1 July 1994.

who is a member of the National Assembly,[112] and his supporters on the Law Committee and the Standing Committee of the National Assembly prevailed, so that the economic court is now included as a branch or division of the people's court system.

In July 1996, a system of administrative courts, also tied to the people's court system, came into operation. These courts were charged with the hearing of appeals against regulatory or administrative decisions by government officials. A right of appeal has been given to citizens and economic parties, including foreign invested enterprises, to test the legality of specified licensing and permit approval rulings by local officials.[113] Since Vietnamese courts are not authorized to review fundamental questions of legality or constitutionality, it is expected that the review jurisdiction of these courts will extend only to issues of consistency and administrative fairness.

Under previous Vietnamese constitutions, judges and jurors were elected for terms of office that corresponded to that of the electing state organ. For example, judges of the Supreme People's Court were elected by the deputies of the National Assembly and served a term equal to that of the National Assembly.[114] The 1992 Constitution makes no mention of the election of judges. Article 128 states that "the systems of appointment, dismissal and demotion; the office term of judges; the electoral system and term of office of people's jurors of the people's courts at all levels will be defined by law." According to the former head of the National Assembly's Judicial Committee, the appointment of judges will "ensure (the) selection of competent professional judges having high prestige and credibility."[115] However, the new Constitution does provide for the election by the National Assembly of Vietnam's highest judicial officer, the Chief Justice of the Supreme People's Court.[116]

The 1992 Constitution provides for political supervision over the judiciary. Under article 135, judges of the local people's courts are "responsible and accountable" to the local people's councils and the judges of the Supreme People's Court are "responsible and accountable" to the National Assembly and the Standing Committee.

In countries following a socialist legal model, the judiciary's primary function is to serve the interests of the state in the transition to socialism.[117]

---

112 1995 Constitution, arts. 128 and 135.

113 "Court Gives Forum for Public Complaint," *Vietnam Investment Review* (8-14 July 1996) 1. It is noted, however, that "the court requires the people first file a formal complaint to the organization with whom they have a grievance and ... if the organization does not reply, the administrative court will not hear the case."

114 Beresford, *supra* note 10 at 114.

115 Ngo Ba Thanh, *supra* note 65 at 112.

116 1992 Constitution, art. 84(7).

117 Duiker, *supra* note 8 at 347.

Courts form an integral, unseparated part of the political-state apparatus. Consistent with this rationale, there continues to be no independent judicial review and no separation of executive, legislative, and judicial powers under Vietnam's 1992 Constitution.

Lack of Leadership Change

The structure of Vietnam's governing apparatus has been reorganized by the 1992 Constitution. Cumbersome collective bodies have been replaced by individuals, such as the Prime Minister, in order to establish clearer lines of authority and accountability. However, the restructuring may be more apparent than real. In September 1992, the National Assembly met to pass a number of laws defining the organization and duties of the government and to elect the new leadership. The elected leadership "turned out to be less 'new' than anticipated."[118] Both the size and the membership of the cabinet government was largely unchanged from its predecessor. Only two of the approved nineteen ministers were new,[119] and all but four were members of the Party's Central Committee.[120]

Calculated gradual change also characterized the new leadership accepted by the National Assembly in late September 1997 following the July elections. In keeping with the very cautious Vietnamese practice, the deputies met first behind closed doors to receive the results of the Communist Party's 170-member Central Committee's deliberations on key government personnel changes. The Committee's collective mind in turn had been focused by the views of the 18-member Politburo, which has its own "inner five," the Standing Board. As one observer dryly noted "a little democracy stretches a long way in Vietnam."[121] The new Assembly validated the VCP's choices of new Prime Minister Vo Van Kiet and President Tran Duc Luong. It is expected that Lieutenant General Le Kah Phieu will succeed Do Muoi over the next year as the Party's general-secretary to become "first among equals" in the triumvirate that dominates Vietnam's political system. For its part, the Assembly is part of a gradual change process which, like the political succession, is being managed with infinite care by a Party that intends to refurbish State institutions without surrendering the commanding heights.

CONCLUSION

Historically, Vietnam has followed the precepts of a socialist legal system with a written constitution designed primarily for internal and external propaganda purposes. The 1980 Constitution, with its overtly socialist economic

118 Avery, *supra* note 47 at 69.
119 *Ibid.*
120 Thayer, *supra* note 36 at 26.
121 P. Alford, "Changing of the Old Guard," *The Australian* (18 Sept. 1997).

orientation, was seen as inconsistent with the open-market economy desired by Vietnam to improve living standards. Vietnam is attempting, through the revisions contained in the 1992 Constitution, to both legitimize economic reform within Vietnam and signal to the outside world that the reforms being undertaken involve fundamental changes to the Vietnamese legal system. However, the changes in investment and commercial laws were not seen as sufficient to demonstrate that Vietnam was indeed stepping away from its socialist economic ideology. The cornerstone of the civic sector, the written constitution, had to be altered to reflect the apparent economic realignment taking place in Vietnam.

The changes in governing institutions that occurred in the 1992 Constitution have also been motivated by economic concerns. Legislative and executive authority has been streamlined with the goal of improving economic decision-making efficiency. However, the institutional changes do little to dilute the ultimate political authority of the Communist Party of Vietnam.

The primary external audience for Vietnam is its partners in ASEAN. Since Vietnam was one of ASEAN's newest members, it was seen as important for it to replace socialist economic ideology with open-market conceptions in order to achieve a better fit with the economic policies followed by other ASEAN states.

The economic motivation for Vietnam's revision of its written Constitution makes Vietnam unique within ASEAN. None of the other states has undertaken constitutional revision for economic reasons. Thailand and the Philippines have adopted new constitutional documents within the past decade as a result of internal political upheaval unrelated to economic issues. Malaysia and Singapore have retained the same basic constitutional instruments since independence, although amendment has been constant. These amendments have led to significant change in the constitutions of the two countries, but none of the alterations has been motivated by economic considerations. Brunei and Indonesia have had stable, unchanged constitutions for several decades.

While Vietnam's ascribing to economic reform was important for ASEAN states, political reform within Vietnam was not as important. Within ASEAN a full range of political and governing structures exists. There is a monarchical authority with limited restraint in Brunei,[122] a long-serving constitutional monarch in Thailand[123] and a rotating monarchy with limited independent authority in Malaysia.[124] The Philippines and Indonesia have

122 See A. Ibrahim and V. S. Winslow, "Constitution and Monarchy in Brunei," in Beer, *supra* note 3 at 365-72.

123 See McDorman, "The 1991 Constitution of Thailand," *supra* note 1 at 268.

124 See M. R. Gillen, "The Malay Rulers Loss of Immunity" (1995) 29 Univ. of British Columbia L. Rev. 163-97.

presidential executive governments. In Indonesia and Thailand the military plays both an official and unofficial role in the political process.[125] In Singapore, which has a president with limited powers, the principal political power is located, as in Malaysia, in the elected legislature and the office of Prime Minister.[126] Given this array of governing structures and the changed regional security situation in Southeast Asia, the Vietnamese Communist Party's retention of ultimate authority under the 1992 Constitution is not of great concern within ASEAN.

There is a significant variation among the ASEAN states as to the role played by the written constitution in the reality of the exercise of governmental authority and the relationship between the governed and the governing. One way to explore the operational effect or reality of a written constitution in a state is to examine the way in which the written constitution is used and referred to by four stakeholder groups that have a direct interest in constitutionalism: that is, (1) the political players that make up the effective government of a state; (2) other political players, either the opposition or competing political factions; (3) the judiciary, which may be called upon to deal with constitutional questions; and (4) the general population, which may demand constitutional behaviour from political elites.

In Canada, the written constitution is used as the legitimation of government action. The written constitution defines the limits of acceptable action with the result that all political players, the courts, and the general population view the written constitution as a document that constrains and restrains governmental power. This restraining or constraining aspect of the written constitution is the defining feature of constitutionalism in Canada. Similarly, in Singapore and Malaysia, the written constitution has an important restraining aspect, which has led the relevant governments to make constitutional change where the constraint was felt to be inappropriate.[127] In Thailand, the constraining aspect of the 1991 Constitution is not clearly evident. However, opposition and competing political factions and the general Thai population, particularly the urban elite in Bangkok, are increasingly demanding that those exercising power be cognizant of the limitations on authority in the Constitution.[128] This restraining or constraining aspect of a written constitution has been absent from Vietnam's experience. It does not appear that the 1992 Constitution changes this situation.

125 Respecting Indonesia, see Ngandani, "Leadership and Security in Indonesia: The Institutional Role of ABRI," in S. Chee, ed., *Leadership and Security in Southeast Asia* (Singapore: Institute of Southeast Asian Studies, 1991) at 26-52. Respecting Thailand, see Chai-anan Samudavanija and Suchit Bunbongkran, "Thailand," in Z. Haji Ahmad and H. Crouch, eds, *Military-Civilian Relations in Southeast Asia* (Singapore: Institute of Southeast Asian Studies, 1985) at 78 ff.

126 See generally Crane et al., *supra* note 7.

127 *Ibid.*

128 See McDorman, "The 1991 Constitution of Thailand," *supra* note 1 at 296-98.

The purpose of the 1992 Constitution of Vietnam is to legitimize governmental actions necessary to reinforce transformation of the country into an open-market economy. There is no intent that the Vietnamese Constitution is to operate as a constraint or restraint on governmental activity. Neither non-political elites (an opposition), the judiciary, nor the general population are expected to use the Constitution as a basis to suggest that there be a limit on governmental action. The conclusion is that, unlike the situation in many of Vietnam's ASEAN partners, the 1992 Constitution will not have a constraining or restraining effect on government action either directly or indirectly.

Fitting Vietnam's 1992 Constitution into the ASEAN constitutional mosaic finds Vietnam with a written constitution that remains important for rhetorical purposes and for the operational purposes of the political authorities, but without effect as a significant constraint on governmental or Party actions. This situation results from Vietnam's socialist traditions respecting the role of a constitution in a legal system and from the unshared authority exercised by the Vietnamese Communist Party.

Part III: The Behavioural Sector

7

Legal Regulation of Mental Disorder: Looking East and West

Gerry Ferguson, in collaboration with
*Molly Cheang (Malaysia), Thamrong Dasananjali (Thailand), Dadang Hawari (Indonesia), Kok Lee Peng (Singapore), and Stephan Salzberg (Japan and Taiwan)**

INTRODUCTION

This chapter is dedicated to an examination and comparison of the legal regulation of mental disorder in Western countries, principally Canada, and in east and southeast Asian countries, principally Japan, Taiwan, Thailand, Malaysia, Singapore, and Indonesia. The perception and definition of mental disorder and responses to it are shaped by both similarities and differences culturally, socially, medically, and legally in each of the countries under study. This book and this chapter focus on legal development in the sense of how legal norms and institutions are consciously created or adapted to deal with a wide array of human activities. It is essential to examine mental disorder in its broadest social context if one is to identify and evaluate the range of internal and external factors that facilitate or obstruct the creation or adaptation of legal rules and systems to regulate mental disorder. This chapter is a blend of the law and development and the law and society approaches to comparative law as described in the introduction to this book.

A law and society approach to comparative legal studies often suffers from two methodological weaknesses. First, there is frequently a paucity of available written material (at least in English) which analyzes legally or sociologically the topic under study in the "foreign" country. Second, the would-be comparative author, who is usually from a Western country, often lacks in-depth knowledge or experience about how the specific subject and the legal system operate in practice in the Asian countries under study. In an attempt to ameliorate these difficulties, this chapter was prepared through the collaborative efforts of the principal author and five regional experts.

* Although the collaborators provided invaluable information for the writing of this chapter, the views expressed in this chapter are the sole responsibility of Professor Ferguson, not the collaborators. Professor Ferguson would also like to thank Peter Brady, Jeff Joudrey, and Tanya Scharbach for their valuable research assistance and the Canada-ASEAN Centre in Singapore for its financial support of this research project.

The regional experts provided the principal author with written materials on mental disorder and its regulation in their respective countries. In addition, the principal author and the regional experts held a three day workshop to discuss these written materials with a view to clarifying for the principal author how mental disorder is actually dealt with in each country.

Mental disorder falls within the behavioural sector of the legal system. The behavioural sector deals with personal and interpersonal aspects of human behaviour to a greater extent than the economic and civic sectors, and for this reason it touches upon some of the most fundamental values within society. Significant aspects of conduct within the behavioural sphere are in fact regulated outside the formal legal system by social conventions, religious practices, or cultural taboos operating through institutions such as the family, schools, and community or other social organizations. Because the behavioural sector is in part rooted in fundamental religious and cultural beliefs and practices, there is greater room for diversity in the way in which legal systems in the countries under study respond to mental disorder than might be the case in either the economic and civic sectors.

An analysis of the extent to which Western laws and Western medicine have been imposed upon, adopted by, or have influenced Eastern laws and Eastern medicine in regard to mental disorder is a central theme in this chapter. That process of imposition, adoption, or influence should not be viewed as a black and white snapshot frozen in time but rather as a rich and varied tapestry of changing scenes. The nature and extent of the adoption and influence varies with each country depending on a number of factors. It is different in regard to medicine than it has been in regard to law. And the nature and pattern of adoption have been somewhat different in criminal law than in civil law.

The following section deals with some of the historical and cultural similarities and differences in the perception and treatment of mental disorder in the East and the West. The legal regimes in the East and the West that deal with mental disorder in both criminal and civil law are then compared. The final section contains a few concluding comments on the adoption or imposition of Western laws in Asia.

HISTORICAL AND CULTURAL OVERVIEW OF MENTAL DISORDER: EAST AND WEST

Introduction

There are many points of interesting comparison both historically and culturally between Eastern and Western approaches to mental disorder. First, and most obvious, is the belief that mental disorder can be caused by spirit or demon possession or by other supernatural forces. Although that belief system has been largely displaced in the West by secular medical views, such beliefs are still very much alive today in large segments of the population in Asian countries. Second, to the extent that symptoms of mental disorder were sometimes treated as a medical problem, there is a striking resemblance between early Western medical theories based upon Greek, Hippocratic theories of humeral medicine and Eastern theories of humeral medicine based upon traditional Indian Ayurvedic medical theories. The notion of keeping the various bodily elements in balance that was central to both theories also has some similarities to the notion of balance found in the ancient Chinese medical concepts of yin and yang. Third, the West's reliance on jails and private confinement of the mentally disordered, usually under inhumane conditions, also had its counterparts in some Asian countries. And when insane asylums were introduced in the West and East, these asylums or mental hospitals either began or often ended up as places of secure confinement and custody rather than places of medical or psychiatric treatment. Fourth, in the West, medicine was captured in the nineteenth and twentieth centuries by science, with the result that traditional folk conceptions of illness and disease were denigrated and largely dismissed. However, modern Western medicine was adopted in Asia (perhaps with the exception of Japan) only by foreign settlers and a small, elite group within the indigenous population. Thus indigenous folk medicine has continued in the past two centuries to be practised by most indigenous people in the East. Fifth, for a variety of reasons, Western medicine and psychiatry is slowly being imported into Eastern countries and is being practised for the most part alongside traditional folk medicine. Finally, both East and West have in recent decades moved increasingly to a broader medical, social, and psychological conception of mental health and to a public health, community-based model of treatment. These points of comparison will be pursued in more detail below.

Mental Disorder and the Supernatural

The West

The history of the treatment of mental illness in the West is at one and the same time both sad and fascinating.[1] In medieval times, there was a general belief that a person's feelings, ambitions, and accomplishments were subject to supernatural or divine control. The suggestions by Renaissance humanists in the sixteenth century that such matters were subject to control by one's own mind rather than control by supernatural powers was not widely accepted.[2] In general, the predominant belief was that mental

1 For a more detailed overview of this history, see F. G. Alexander and S. T. Selesnick, *The History of Psychiatry: An Evaluation of Psychiatric Thought and Practice from Prehistoric Times to the Present* (New York: Harper & Row, 1966) c. 3-5 and A. Deutsch, *The Mentally Ill in America*, 2d ed. (New York: Columbia Univ. Press, 1949).

2 Alexander, *ibid*. at 102-103.

disorders were caused by the influence of the stars or demons.[3] The response to, or treatment of, mental disorders was naturally premised on assumptions as to its causes. For minor symptoms of mental illness thought to be caused by the stars, diagnosis and treatment were based on astrology, palmistry,[4] and other magical techniques. More severe symptoms of mental illness were often thought to be the result of demonic possession.[5] Persons displaying these symptoms were either treated by exorcists, or accused of being witches (hosts of the devil), interrogated by ecclesiastics, and, if found to be a witch, burnt at the stake. The intensity of the witch-hunts reached a fevered pitch in the 1600s.[6] The belief in demonic possession was supported by theological beliefs, in particular the principle of dualism that Deutsch explains in the following manner:

> To its exponents the world was seen as a huge battle-ground over which two antagonistic powers, good and evil, light and darkness, God and Satan, were engaged in a struggle for mastery. It was quite consistent with the anthropomorphic conception of the universe to believe that the immortal souls of men were the chief prizes sought in this cosmic conflict. Everywhere Satan and his infernal demons were at work striving to gain possession of human souls by every ruse possible. Just as the theology of the time surrounded God with choirs of angels, so did it credit Satan with legions of devils and imps, who lurked in every chimney and corner watching for an opportunity to jump into human bodies in unguarded moments and "possess" them.[7]

The witch-hunts were not only directed at the mentally ill, but also at dissident persons or classes of persons whose political or religious disaffections were seen as a threat to the Church and the State.[8] The Church also had a concern about the extent of sexual activity and abuse engaged in by the supposedly celibate clergy. Its response to this crisis was to characterize women as the cause of men's licentiousness and as such to assume that they might be carriers of the devil. Any behaviour by women that was considered lewd was confirmation of this theory. In such a belief system,

---

3 Insanity was often attributed to changes of the moon and hence the word "lunatic" was used to describe the insane.

4 By studying the palms of a person's hands, it was believed that future events could be predicted and that a person's character and personality could be determined.

5 Deutsch, *supra* note 1 at 16-17. Helpful explanations are provided by historians to explain how belief in demonical possession captured the medieval mind to an extent unknown before.

6 It is reported that hundreds of thousands of women and children were burnt at the stake (Alexander, *supra* note 1 at 99 and Deutsch, *supra* note 1 at 18). Not all were mentally ill, but a significant number certainly were. See e.g. Deutsch, *supra* note 1 at 21.

7 Deutsch, *supra* note 1 at 16-17.

8 *Ibid.* at 21.

psychotic women who voiced their sexual fantasies or sacrilegious beliefs were especially vulnerable to being characterized as possessed by the devil.[9] During this period, mental illness was seldom treated as a medical disease, but when it was, it was analyzed and treated within the context of the Hippocratic doctrine of the four humours.

While leaps in scientific knowledge of the physical universe were being made in the seventeenth century, little advance was being made in better understanding the workings of the body or the mind.[10] In the eighteenth century, while many advances were being made in the development of Western medicine, these advances largely bypassed the field of mental illness. Notwithstanding this, there were still increasingly strong, adverse reactions by philosophers, social reformers, and physicians against superstitious beliefs in witchcraft and demon possession.[11] Such beliefs were increasingly scorned as unscientific. As a result, witchcraft began to disappear in the 1700s. The laws against witchcraft were repealed in England in 1736 but persecution of the insane who were suspected of practising witchcraft and sorcery did not immediately cease.[12]

The East

Unlike the relative simplicity of the Western, Judeo-Christian belief in the duality of God and the devil, many Asian countries had and still have a rich multiplicity of religious and philosophical belief systems that shape their conception of the nature of mental illness. These belief systems include Confucianism, Buddhism, Taoism, Shintoism, Hinduism, Islam, and ancestor worship. More than one belief system is normally operative in each country. For example, in Singapore, the population is 77.6% Chinese, the majority of whom are Buddhist or atheist, while 14.2% of the population are Malay who are generally Muslim, and 7.1% of the population are Indian and mostly Hindu.[13] Malaysia's population is composed of the same three races, but in different proportions: 59% Malay, 32% Chinese, and 9% Indian. In Indonesia, 87% of the population are Muslim with the rest being Hindu, Buddhist, animist, or Christian. In Thailand, 95% of the population are Buddhist. In Taiwan, most people are of Chinese origin and 93% practise a mixture of Buddhism, Confucianism, and Taoism. In Japan, where 99% of the population is Japanese, Confucianism has shaped Japan's national ideology and social behaviour, while Shintoism is observed by 96% of the Japanese and 76% also observe their own form of Buddhism.

9 Alexander, *supra* note 1 at 96-97.
10 *Ibid.* at 124-43.
11 *Ibid.* at 23.
12 *Ibid.*
13 *Singapore Facts and Pictures, 1993* (Singapore: Ministry of Information and the Arts, 1993) at 3.

In Singapore, Chinese beliefs regarding mental illness are influenced by "Singapore Buddhism,"[14] an amalgamation of ancestor worship, shenism, Taoism, and Buddhism. It includes a belief that there are two planes of existence – a mortal one of present day existence and a supernatural one populated by deities and spirits.[15] These planes interact, and the latter plane can cause mental disorder by one of two methods: either directly by making the person mentally disordered, or by possession of a person who then acquires the characteristics of the deity. Two common deities are the Monkey God and Tua Pek Kong (Grand Uncle God); usually such gods are masculine.[16] Offences such as making a wrong utterance, defiling the deity's abode, or omissions such as failing to give thanks, or even simply being in the wrong place at the wrong time, can cause deities to inflict mental disorder. The Chinese also believe in the Hungry Ghost month, the month of the seventh moon (August), when all the deities are released temporarily from the underworld. The spirits roam at night and a person who encounters such ghosts, or accidentally steps on an offering, might experience bad luck in the form of mental illness.[17] There is also a belief that mental illness may arise because of violations of taboos or neglect of rituals and obligations. Treatment corresponding to this belief system is carried out by a shaman or religious figure who acts as a medium with the spirit world and conveys the message back from the spirit world as to the nature of the problem or taboo violation.[18] There is also a common belief in charms.[19] Western drugs and medicines

14 L. P. Kok, "Historical, Cultural and Legal Overview of Mental Disorder" (Paper presented at Canada-ASEAN Workshop on Mental Disorder, Victoria, Canada, 27-29 May 1993, [unpublished], citing V. Wee, "Buddhism in Singapore," in R. Hassna, ed., *Singapore: Society in Transition* (Oxford: Oxford Univ. Press, 1976) at 155-88. See also W. F. Tsoi & L. P. Kok, "Mental Disorders in Singapore," in T. Y. Lin, W. S. Tseng, and E. K. Yeh, eds., *Chinese Societies and Mental Health* (Hong Kong: Oxford Univ. Press, 1995) at 266-78; L. P. Kok, W. F. Tsoi, "Culture and Mental Illness in Singapore," in I. Al-Issa, ed., *Handbook of Culture and Mental Illness: An International Perspective* (Madison, Conn.: Int'l Univ. Press, 1995) at 159-67; H. B. M. Murphy, "Culture and Mental Disorder in Singapore," in M. K. Opler, ed., *Culture and Mental Health* (New York: Macmillan, 1955).

15 Kok, *supra* note 14.

16 *Ibid.*

17 *Ibid.*, citing C. S. Wong, *A Cycle of Chinese Festivities* (Singapore: Malaysia Publishing House, 1967).

18 Kok, *ibid.*

19 It is believed that magic of this sort can cause mental disorder. A cure is sought by visiting a more powerful medium or magician. Mediums from Thailand are believed to be the strongest, although charms from Japan are also considered strong. The relative strength of the medium is more important than ethnicity, and so a powerful Malaysian medium might be able to undo the work of a less powerful Thai medium. Typically mediums will use water or powder to curse or cure, and there is a belief in the influence and balancing of the four elements: earth, air, fire, and water. Little spirits raised in jars by mediums are said to be especially powerful when used against enemies (Kok, *supra* note 14).

20 Another explanation for the origin of mental disorder is a lack of love or unrequited love, especially when the person suffering from mental disorder is young. The treatment

are assumed to be of no avail for these supernatural forces.[20] As a general rule, older, Chinese Singaporeans are more culturally attached to their traditional Chinese roots and customs and tend to believe in supernatural explanations more than the younger, more educated, and more Westernized generation. One interesting exception to that is the rise in fundamentalist, charismatic Christian beliefs among young Chinese college students, a small number of whom believe among other things that mental illness is a visitation by Satan and his devils (e.g. the schizophrenia devil). These evil forces must be exorcised by faith healing sessions that may involve trances and speaking in tongues.[21]

Malays who live in Singapore have both animistic and Islamic beliefs.[22] The original animistic beliefs centred around spirits and supernatural forces. Spirits were able to assume living forms, had feelings, and could eat or drink. Any part of nature, including animals, trees, plants, mountains, and rocks, could harbour spirits. Ghosts of the departed could bring illness and afflictions, particularly the ghosts of those who died by suicide and those who were murdered.[23]

Singaporeans of Indian origin also have beliefs that are similar to both Chinese and Malay beliefs, in that they believe that mental illness can be caused by spirits. One such spirit is the snake spirit. A second is Kali, the goddess of war, who causes violent, aggressive, and destructive sorts of behaviour in the mentally disordered. The Monkey spirit is common to all three races, and when it possesses a person, that person takes on the characteristics of a monkey.[24] Treatment of such conditions is typically sought through traditional healers or from the temples. If a patient is unable to travel to a temple, he or she may be visited by a traditional healer, and charms, amulets, and holy water may be used to effect a cure. In addition, Indians may purchase holy ashes for healing purposes.[25]

In Malaysia, like Singapore, belief in mental illness by large segments of the population revolves around cultural traditions and beliefs concerning spirits.[26] Perceived causes of mental illness include: moral transgressions; supernatural agencies (*gila laban antu*); being misled by spirits; failure to

---

is relatively straightforward: a marriage is arranged as soon as possible (Kok, *supra* note 14).

21 Kok, *supra* note 14.

22 *Ibid.*, citing: Hj Mohtar b Md Dom, *Traditions and Taboos* (Kuala Lumpur: Federal Publication, 1977); Hj Mohtar b Md Dom, *Malay Superstitions and Beliefs* (Kuala Lumpur: Federal Publication, 1979); Hj Mohtar b Md Dom, *The Bomoh and the Hantu* (Kuala Lumpur: Federal Publication, 1979).

23 *Ibid.*

24 *Ibid.*

25 *Ibid.*

26 M. Cheang, "Historical and Cultural Overview of Mental Disorder" (Paper Presented at Canada-ASEAN Workshop on Mental Disorder, Victoria, Canada, 27-29 May 1993) [unpublished].

fulfil spiritual commands; trespassing (walking over spirit offerings); spell-castings; breaching taboos (such as a male walking under a woman's undergarments hung out to dry); frustrated love; and the breaking of customs such as changing from one religion to another.[27]

Some of these beliefs are common to all races in Malaysia, although there tends to be a distinction between the rural and urban populations. The rural populations are much more likely to hold superstitious beliefs than are urban populations. Notwithstanding official efforts to ensure that Muslim Malays abandon animist or magical practices, it appears that such practices and beliefs still persist. Even when Western-style medical treatment is available, Malays are more resistant to seeking Western treatment, while Indians are proportionally over-represented in seeking such treatment.[28]

About 90% of those who seek treatment from hospitals have previously sought the assistance of traditional healers, bomohs, sinsehs, or bobo hizans. It is only when these sources fail that a person is brought to a modern medical facility.[29] Delays are longest when the person has consulted a bomoh, and in general this prolongation of the disorder before seeking other remedies can make curative therapy more difficult. The tendency to seek traditional cures first indicates the pervasiveness of magico-religious beliefs in Malaysian society, and the relation of such beliefs to views on the causation of mental illness. Economic growth and rapid social changes have affected and will continue to affect the mental life, structure, and functioning of individuals, family, and society as a whole. Attitudes towards mental health care are still influenced by local customs and superstitions, and the general public tends to lump all forms of mental disorder under the single label of "madness."[30]

In Indonesia, along with the animism that is indigenous to Indonesia, early Indian merchants introduced Hinduism and Buddhism.[31] However, outside Bali, there is presently little Hindu influence left. In the ninth century, Islam was introduced from Saudi Arabia. In the seventeenth century, Portuguese and Spanish traders and Dutch settlers came to Indonesia, bringing

---

27 *Ibid.*

28 *Ibid.*

29 *Ibid.*

30 *Ibid.*

31 D. Hawari, "Comments on Historical and Cultural Aspects of Mental Disorder in Indonesia" (Paper presented at Canada-ASEAN Workshop on Mental Disorder, Victoria, Canada, 27-29 May 1993) [unpublished] citing D. Hawari, "Psychiatry and Mental Health of Indonesia in Facing the Future: Past, Present and Future Direction," Inaugural Speech, Faculty of Medicine, University of Indonesia, Jakarta, 28 Apr. 1993 [unpublished]; R. K. Setyonegoro, "Native/Traditional Healing Practices" (1982) XV(2) DJIWA (Indonesian Psychiatric Quarterly) 57; E. Bahar et al., "The Role of Traditional Healers on Child and Adolescent Psychiatric Cases in Palembang" (1982) XV(2) DJIWA 63; D. H. Idries "Some Socio-Cultural Aspects of Psychiatry in Indonesia" (1971) IV(4) DJIWA 111.

with them the influence of Christianity.[32] Today the vast majority of the population is Muslim.[33] Native conceptions of mental health, especially among the Javanese, are based on occult explanations such as punishment for misdeeds or simply fate. There is also the belief that one can be punished for the acts of other family members. Occult forces are believed by the Javanese to be especially strong on Tuesdays and Fridays. Magic force (*guna-guna*) is said to influence love, to cause men to become mute, aggressive, talk irrelevantly, etc., or cause a women to undress and run around naked.[34] Water is used in ceremonies and there is also use of talismans and charms. All stratas of society continue to hold magico-religious beliefs despite the national philosophy of Pancasila with its first principle: Believe in One Supreme God.[35] There is a mixture of religious and mystical beliefs in which there is a hierarchy of mystical powers, and where an increase in mystical powers can cause psychiatric disturbances.

The description given to some mental illnesses reflects sociocultural influences. For example, *koro* is described as a kind of phobia in which the patient suffers from a fear that his penis will disappear into his bowels, or that her breasts will become smaller and her labia sucked into her bowels. This disorder appears suddenly and may last for several days. *Latah* is a condition where the patient suffers from symptoms of echolalia, echopraxia, and coprolalia. These symptoms cannot be controlled by the patient. *Amok* describes a disorder where a patient suddenly becomes aggressive and may even commit murder, and following the incident the patient has amnesia. *Voodoo* is the term used to describe a situation where the patient dies without any discernible organic cause. Such a death is usually evoked by breaking a taboo, or if the patient feels that a spell has been put on him or her. Death may also occur as a result of deep fear.[36]

It is legal to practise occultism when not directly in conflict with the law, but there is some control over group activities by an official government

---

32 Hawari, *supra* note 31, citing Idries at 114.

33 *Ibid.* However, in Bali, 93% of the population are Hindu. Balinese Hindus believe in a supreme god, in the eternal nature of the soul, and in multiple reincarnation until achieving the perfect life, which is then rewarded by final unity with God. Mental and physical activities, including mental illness, are functions of the soul and every action has rewards or consequences. Balinese believe that their present behaviour is in part caused by their actions in past lives, and that mental illness can be caused by physical factors or by supernatural forces (i.e. spirit possession or a curse of an ancestor or the gods). Interestingly, the Balinese consider mental illness caused by supernatural forces to be curable and not a matter of family shame or stigma, whereas mental illness thought to be caused by physical factors is considered genetic, incurable, and a matter of family disgrace. See generally L. K. Suryani, "Cultural Factors, Religious Beliefs, and Mental Illness in Bali: Indonesia," in Al-Issa, *supra* note 14 at 203-13.

34 Hawari, *supra* note 31, citing Idries at 113.

35 *Ibid.*

36 *Ibid.*, citing Idries at 113.

agency, the PAKEM (Pengawas aliran kepertjajaan dalam masjarakat). This agency visits the places where groups practise their mysticism and evaluates their activities.[37]

In Thailand, Higginbotham has suggested that there are at least four major traditional explanations for mental illness in addition to three other popular conceptions.[38] The first traditional explanation is based on humeral imbalance derived from traditional Indian Ayurvedic medical beliefs. The second traditional explanation is that mental illness may arise from spirit possession. Although spirit possession by the many Hindu spirits is generally desirable, *phii* spirits are believed to cause physical and mental illness. Risk of possession is said to increase in persons who have violated local customs or taboos. A third traditional cause is "soul loss" and the fourth belief relates to sin or karma. According to Buddhist teachings, persons acquire merits and demerits according to their actions. The balance of one's merits determines one's future life form when reincarnated. Mental retardation or other congenital defects can be attributed to bad karma in a previous life.[39] Mental illnesses such as anxiety disorders or depression (evidenced in stomach pains, listlessness, etc.) will often be viewed as physical disorders. As such, these ailments will be treated by traditional herbalist medical healers. Other disorders will be popularly attributed to the overwhelming burdens life sometimes throws in one's way – accidents, deaths, natural disasters. A third popular conception is the belief that violation of certain moral taboos (e.g., masturbation, homosexuality, or perhaps adultery) may be the cause of mental illness.[40]

As in other Asian countries, resort to Western medicine and psychiatry will vary depending on a person's educational level and whether that person lives in an urban or rural area. Western psychiatry is often a last resort and, when resorted to, there is a client expectation that the mode of treatment will be drugs, not some form of psychotherapy (which is more likely to be practised by Buddhist monks in their own way).[41] In one study of a *koro* epidemic in Northern Thailand, 70% sought help from local healers, 5% went untreated, while 20% sought help from their local hospitals.[42]

In Japan, explanations for mental disorders are not oriented to the human spirit world, but rather to possession by animal spirits. Often this is a benign spirit such as the fox spirit. Water cures are available in some temples, but there is comparatively little folk treatment of mental disorder. The

37 *Ibid.*

38 H. Higginbotham, *Third World Challenge to Psychiatry: Culture Accommodation and Mental Health Care* (Honolulu: Univ. of Hawaii Press, 1984) c. 5, "Mental Health System in Thailand" at 201-204.

39 *Ibid.*

40 *Ibid.*

41 *Ibid.* at 204-205.

42 *Ibid.* at 206.

near total displacement of indigenous folk treatment with Western medical practices in Japan in the 1800s and 1900s is atypical of the experience in the other Eastern countries under study.[43]

In Taiwan, popular beliefs about mental illness follow both secular and sacred lines. The etiology of various disorders is often attributed to the balance of polar opposites in the body. The concepts of hot/cold and yin/yang are used in explaining the origins of a mental disorder. Disorder causality is classified as lying "within the body" or "outside the body." "Inside the body" disorders may be dealt with by Chinese or Western physicians, whereas "outside the body" sickness involves supernatural forces and must be dealt with by practitioners of sacred healing.[44] The family holds a pre-eminent position in the lives of its members. When a family member becomes ill, the family operates as a "health management" team, assuming responsibility for choosing and implementing the treatment most suited to the ill member's condition. Outsiders will be consulted only after intrafamilial resources prove ineffective. Even then, the family retains the discretion to choose whom to consult, when to comply with instructions, and when to change practitioners.[45] Interestingly, the stigma associated with mental illness resides more with the family of the mentally ill person than the mentally ill person. This situation is a consequence of popular moral and religious beliefs that ascribe "madness" to incorrect life within the family and misdeeds by one's ancestors, respectively. It is the family that is shamed, more than the ill member, by the label of mental illness.[46] Due to the stigma that attaches to mental illness, if a family must take the radical step of bringing its ill member to a Western-style psychiatrist, they may reject and abandon the member to institutional confinement. In addition, the family will often seek to have the mental illness treated as a biological problem, so as to avoid implicating or disgracing the family or its ancestors.

Mental Disorder and Natural Forces

In both the East and the West (at least before the establishment of modern biomedical sciences), the explanations and theories of physical illness were premised on a belief that illness arose when certain basic body elements –

---

43 See further discussion of this point in the text *infra* preceding note 121. See also J. Pelzel, "Comments on Traditional and Modern Medical Systems in East Asia," in A. Kleinman et al., eds., *Culture and Healing in Asian Societies* (Cambridge, Mass.: Scheatman, 1978); see also discussion in text *infra* at notes 80-88.

44 Higginbotham, *supra* note 38 at 93. For a series of recent articles on mental health issues in Taiwan, see T. Y. Lin, W. S. Tseng, and E. K. Yeh, eds., *Chinese Societies and Mental Health*, *supra* note 14.

45 *Ibid.*

46 K. M. Lin, "Traditional Chinese Medical Beliefs and Their Relevance for Mental Illness and Psychiatry," in A. Kleinman and T. Y. Lin, eds., *Mental and Abnormal Behaviour in Chinese Culture* (Dordrecht: D. Reidel, 1981).

Hippocratic humours in the West and *dosha* (Indian) or yin and yang (Chinese) in the East – were not in balance.

The West

In the 1700s, medical beliefs in the causes of mental illness were still based primarily on ancient physiological speculations such as the Greek, Hippocratic doctrine of the four humours:

> This theory stated that the four basic elements (fire, earth, water and air) represented four basic qualities (heat, dryness, moisture and cold). The four humours of the body were blood, phlegm, yellow bile and black bile. They were found in the heart, brain, liver and spleen. An imbalance of these humours was considered to be the basic cause of disease and one could cure the disease by using drugs that had qualities opposite to the four fundamental qualities – heat, dryness, moisture and cold.[47]

The four humours had their associated qualities: blood (hot and moist), phlegm (cold and moist), black bile, also called melancholy (cold and dry), and yellow bile or choler (hot and dry).[48] A person was believed to be in a healthy state when these four substances were in correct proportion to one another. A person's temperament was shaped by these substances: the *sanguine* were ruddy, cheerful, and optimistic; the *phlegmatic* were calm, composed, sluggish, and apathetic; the *melancholic* were depressed and sad; and the *bilious* were choleric and ill-tempered. Medical diagnosis involved a determination of which humour or humours were excessive or deficient and then treatment of the imbalance by techniques such as bloodletting, purgatives, dietary treatments, dousing in ice-cold water, blistering of the forehead, and the spinning-chair treatment.[49] The fact that Hippocratic humeral medicine no longer held any credence for physical diseases but was still readily accepted as an explanation for mental illness in the 1700s shows the extent to which advances in medical science had bypassed the area of mental illness.

The East

Indian Ayurvedic medicine dates back at least several centuries before the birth of Christianity. Foster and Anderson describe it as follows:

---

47 Alexander, *supra* note 1 at 52-53.

48 G. Foster and B. Anderson, *Medical Anthropology* (New York: John Wiley, 1978) at 56.

49 *Ibid.* at 57-58. The spinning chair treatment was used by those who believed that diseases "arose out of 'disordered motions' of the nervous tissue of the body and that the rotating chair would correct the disharmony." Another theory supporting the use of this treatment was the belief "that congested blood in the brain produced mental illness and that this condition would be relieved by rotary movement" (Alexander, *supra* note 1 at 147-48).

> According to Ayurvedic theory, the universe is composed of the same four elements recognized by the Greeks (earth, water, fire, air), plus a fifth, ether. The arrangement of these elements in the body, each of which possesses five "subtle" and five "material" forms, is a microcosm of the universe. The human body also has three humours, or *dosha* (hence the term *tridosha* theory): phlegm, or mucus; bile, or gall; and wind, or flatulence. Good health exists when the three dosha are in equilibrium; ill health manifests itself when one or more of the dosha are not functioning properly. The dosha also are associated with age and the seasons: phlegm with youth and the growing season, bile with middle age and the rainy season, and wind with old age and cold and dry weather. The similarities shared by Ayurvedic medicine and humeral pathology point to significant interrelationships between the two systems. Yet the historical record is such that mutual influences are difficult to prove until fairly late in time. Beginning early in the twentieth century, Ayurveda has become more and more important among Indian nationalists as a symbol of the antiquity and greatness of Indian civilization.[50]

While humeral medicine has disappeared in Western medicine (although aspects of it can still be seen in current Western folk medicine), Indian Ayurvedic medicine is taught and practised broadly in India and other Asian countries.[51]

Practitioners of traditional Chinese medicine began to turn to naturalistic explanations of health and illness about the same time as the Greeks and Indians.[52] The dual forces of yin and yang lie behind all natural phenomena including the functioning of the body. The proper balance of yin and yang in the body is essential to good health.[53] Yin and yang are endowed with innumerable qualities, summarized by Foster and Anderson as follows:

> Thus, yang represents heaven, sun, fire, heat, dryness, light, the male principle, the exterior, the right side, life, high, noble, good, beautiful, virtue, order, joy, wealth – in short, all positive elements. Yin represents the opposite: earth, moon, water, cold, dampness, darkness, the female principle, the interior, the left side, death, low, ignoble, bad, ugly, vice, confusion, and poverty – in short, all negative elements. Because of its heat, excessive yang causes fever; because of its coldness, excessive yin produces chills. Diseases believed caused by external forces are yang diseases, and those believed caused by internal forces are yin diseases. Yet yin and yang have

50 *Ibid.*
51 *Ibid.* at 62.
52 *Ibid.* at 63.
53 *Ibid.*

always been conceived as a single entity combining, in any being or situation, both positive and negative elements.[54]

Many of the principles of traditional Chinese medicine are adhered to and practised today among those of Chinese origin in various Asian countries.

The Confinement Response

The West

Apart for the above-noted medical practices, the mentally ill in England in the 1700s were usually dealt with in one of three ways. The less seriously mentally ill were cared for by family or allowed to wander at large, in which case they were frequently the subject of scorn, ridicule, and beatings.[55] More seriously ill, psychotic persons were sometimes interned in a special public hospital called Bethlem or Bedlam. The accommodation consisted of filthy, dark, dungeon-like cells where patients were often chained, naked, and subjected to physical and verbal abuse by their keepers. The food was abominable and the medical regimen, when it existed at all, consisted of emetics, purgatives, bloodletting, and other bizarre treatments.[56] The "dangerously" mentally ill who were not accommodated in Bedlam were treated to similar conditions in local jails and prisons. A third alternative, often for chronic but less violent persons, was confinement in private madhouses that flourished in England in the eighteenth century and into the nineteenth century.[57] Although the adverse conditions in England's private madhouses have sometimes been exaggerated and sensationalized, it is no exaggeration to say that conditions were quite inadequate and often cruel and inhumane.[58]

Although mental illness in the latter half of the 1700s was no longer widely assumed to be a matter of demonic possession, the treatment of the insane was still very inhumane. Alexander and Selesnick suggest that this treatment can only be understood when three other factors are taken into account: namely, "the almost complete ignorance of the nature of mental illness, the deeply felt dread of the insane, and finally, the belief then current that mental disease is incurable."[59]

It was against this backdrop of inhumane treatment of the insane that the "moral treatment" movement was born. The images of Philippe Pinel releasing patients in 1793 from their chains at the Bicêtre in Paris and of William Tuke, the English Quaker, establishing a moral treatment regime at

54 *Ibid.*
55 Alexander, *supra* note 1 at 154.
56 *Ibid.* at 154-56.
57 See generally W. Parry-Jones, *The Trade in Lunacy: A Study of Private Madhouses in England in the Eighteenth and Nineteenth Centuries* (London: Routledge and K. Paul, 1972).
58 *Ibid.*
59 Alexander, *supra* note 1 at 154.

his celebrated "Retreat" at York, England in 1792, have acted as the dominant symbols of this shift from inhumane confinement to humane confinement and treatment of the insane.[60]

As originally designed by the Quaker layman, William Tuke, moral treatment was not equated with medical treatment. Rather it was the use of compassion and kindness, in a strictly controlled environment, designed to relieve patients' fears, to distract them from their morbid preoccupations, to induce in them self-respect and to encourage them to exercise self-control over their passions.[61] For this, a new institution was required – an institution that could act as a retreat or "asylum" for them. Its location, its architecture, and its programs of work, play, and prayer were designed to exert positive moral influences on those unfortunate patients whose powers of moral reasoning were lost or diminished.[62] Although the operation of these asylums was not the exclusive prerogative of the medical profession in the first half of the nineteenth century, the medical profession did manage to wrest control of most asylums from the hands of lay superintendents in the second half of the century.[63] In 1844, thirteen medical superintendents of insane asylums in the United States formed the American Association of Medical Superintendents. That Association subsequently evolved into the American Psychiatric Association. Thus the insane asylum in the second half of the eighteenth century became the breeding ground for the new medical discipline called psychiatry.[64]

In Canada, signs of the moral treatment movement began to appear in the 1830s in the Maritimes and Ontario. No separate facilities for the insane existed, except in Quebec, until this period. As a result, the destitute insane were confined in horrible conditions in poorhouses or local jails, often chained and left to lie in filthy, unlit cells.[65] The first, true attempt to establish a

---

60 It has been said that, "when Philippe Pinel took over the administration of the Bicêtre in 1793, he himself was considered mad by his contemporaries – for he released the patients from their chains, opened their windows, fed them nourishing food, and treated them with kindness." Alexander, *supra* note 1 at 154. And it has also been noted that "to the surprise of the public, when the insane were housed, clothed, and treated as humans they responded accordingly. Inmates who were thought to be hopeless cases were able to return to the community, although it is not clear how they fared after release": J. I. Williams, K. M. Kopinak, and W. D. Moynagh, "Mental Health and Illness in Canada," in C. Boydell, C. Grindstaff, and P. Whitehead, eds., *Deviant Behaviour and Societal Reaction* (Toronto: Holt, Rinehart, and Winston, 1972) at 400.

61 D. Francis, "The Development of the Lunatic Asylum in the Maritime Provinces" (1976) 6 Acadiensis 23.

62 *Ibid.* at 30-33.

63 A. Scull, "The Discovery of the Asylum Revisited: Lunacy Reform in the New American Republic," in A. Scull, ed., *Madhouses, Mad-Doctors and Madmen* (London: Athlone Press, 1981) c. 6.

64 *Ibid.*

65 R. Splane, *Social Welfare in Ontario, 1791-1893: Study of Public Welfare Administration* (Toronto: Univ. of Toronto Press, 1965) at 69 and 203; see also Williams, *supra* 60 at 400.

moral treatment asylum in Canada did not take place until 1848 in St. John, New Brunswick.[66] Others were opened in Toronto in 1850, in Kingston in 1856, in Halifax in 1859, and in London in 1870.[67] However these asylums were never large enough to house all the mentally ill, and many insane persons were still confined under appalling conditions in local jails.[68] In addition, it was not unusual for mentally ill persons to be convicted of crimes and sentenced to imprisonment. These persons were subjected to the same strict prison regime that applied to sane prisoners, but, since they lacked the self-control to adhere to the rules of prison life, they were repeatedly punished by severe whippings.[69]

Although the campaign to establish moral treatment and insane asylums was usually promoted on the basis of claims of humane treatment and the assumed curative potential of moral treatment, these claims often went unfulfilled due to inadequate facilities, a shortage of money, chronic overcrowding, and untrained and poorly supervised staff. In addition, in the latter half of the nineteenth century, with insane asylums being controlled by medical superintendents, the psychological components of moral treatment were pushed aside in favour of a more physiological approach.[70] During this period there was extensive study in the medical sciences of human anatomy. In particular, neurology assumed a position of considerable importance, with efforts to equate emotional disorder with specific neurological conditions.[71] Psychiatry entered into a sterile period of data gathering, and it was not until the end of the century that Freud introduced a new dynamic psychological element into the understanding of mental illness.[72] Although advances were made in the classification of mental illnesses during this period, it was not without its costs. Once an illness was classified, if it happened to be in a classification that was considered untreatable, the mentally ill person "became a case number awaiting the ultimate fate of deterioration. Custodial care, even though it was humane, did not change the nihilistic attitude of the staff caring for the unfortunate victim."[73]

In the United States, insane asylums that had been attempting to operate on the humane principles of moral treatment were beginning to slip badly

66 Francis, *supra* note 61 at 23.

67 Splane, *supra* note 65 at 204, and Francis, *ibid.* See also V. E. Appleton, "Psychiatry in Canada a Century Ago" (1967) 12 Canadian Psychiatric Ass'n J. 345.

68 Williams, *supra* note 60 at 400.

69 J. Beattie, *Attitudes Towards Crime and Punishment in Upper Canada, 1830-1850: A Documentary Study* (Toronto: Centre of Criminology, Univ. of Toronto, 1977) 15-35; and A. Edmison, "Some Aspects of Nineteenth-Century Canadian Prisons," in W. McGrath, ed., *Crime and Its Treatment in Canada*, 2d ed. (Toronto: Macmillan, 1976) at 347.

70 Alexander, *supra* note 1 at 190-91.

71 *Ibid.* at 196-214.

72 *Ibid.* at 191.

73 *Ibid.* at 212-13.

by the 1870s. As the population increased, overcrowding occurred.[74] The comforts and meaningful work of former years disappeared; they were replaced by a state of destructive idleness: "The mental hospital degenerated into the 'snake pit'; its motto became, 'Abandon hope, all ye who enter here.'"[75] This change naturally resulted in long-term confinement, since there was little hope for recovery. Fear of the potential abuse of inappropriate long-term confinement precipitated a strong lobby by some reformers for strict commitment laws and protection of patients' rights.[76]

In Canada, the decline in moral treatment was not as rapid and did not fully occur until the early 1900s. But when it arrived, its collapse under the weight of overcrowding and under-financing was just as complete. Insane asylums continued to grow in size. To keep costs down, staff were kept to a minimum and custodial care rather than active treatment was the norm.[77] Treatment such as seclusion rooms, hydrotherapy, straitjackets, electric shock therapy and lobotomies were used more for the purpose of controlling, managing, and restraining overactive or violent patients than as curative devices.[78] Once admitted, patients often remained until their death. Friends and family were urged to forget these lost, unrecoverable persons.[79]

The East

As pointed out above, the common response in the West to serious forms of mental disorder, especially if the disordered person was seen as violent or dangerous, was to confine that individual in jail, in a private madhouse, or in an insane asylum or mental hospital. In jails and private madhouses the primary objective was custody, not treatment, and although treatment was the stated objective in asylums and mental hospitals, in practice they frequently offered little more than custody. Similar responses, historically and currently, can be seen in the East.

In Japan, from about 1700 onwards, primary responsibility for the mentally ill fell on the family of the mentally ill person. The immediate community, however, would bear joint responsibility for violations of public order

---

74 R. Slovenko, "Criminal Justice Procedures in Civil Commitment" (1977) 24 Wayne L. Rev. 1 at 2.

75 *Ibid.* at 3.

76 *Ibid.* at 3; N. Kittrie, *The Right to Be Different: Deviance and Enforced Therapy* (Baltimore: Johns Hopkins, 1971) at 64-65.

77 For an account of the British Columbia history, see R. G Foulkes, "From Asylum to Community: A Century of Mental Health Services in British Columbia," in R. G. Foulkes, *Special Report: Psychiatry at the Crossroads: A Review* (Health Security for British Columbians Project) (Victoria, B.C.: Dept. of Health, 1974); Splane, *supra* note 65 at 53, 38-39, 49, 203-207; D. G. McKerracher, *Trends in Psychiatric Care* (A Study for the Royal Commission on Health Services) (Ottawa: Queen's Printer, 1966) at 6-7.

78 Williams, *supra* note 60 at 401-402.

79 *Ibid.*

resulting from acts of the mentally ill.[80] Public policy regarding the mentally ill was dominated by public security; those who were deemed a threat were isolated and confined. The most common form of confinement was private imprisonment by the family in a locked, generally barred cell or cage inside or near the family home.[81] Official permission was required for such imprisonment upon a formal request by the family complete with documentation attesting to the person's madness. Officials were to make an inspection of the cell and the person to be confined.[82] The same procedures were required for discharge. These minimal safeguards proved to be inadequate to prevent abuse of the system.[83]

The only other option to home confinement, apart from treatment at a few shrines and temples where local monks had acquired a reputation for alleviating or curing mental illness through prayer and bathing regimens,[84] was detention in prison. In addition, if the mentally ill person's condition had deteriorated to the point that proper supervision in regular prisons was impossible, that person was sent, along with underage criminals and other criminals who were extremely ill, to special detention centres maintained by members of a taboo class called *hinin* ("non-persons").[85] Conditions of home confinement and of prison were very grim.[86]

The first public mental hospital was not established until 1874 during the Meiji era (1868-1912). Private home confinement remained the dominant means of handling the mentally ill. However, by 1930, half the mentally ill were housed in private hospitals, which acted as a substitute for the lack of public mental hospitals.[87] Private home confinement was abolished in 1950, and private hospitals ended up housing up to 85% of the mentally ill. Conditions in private hospitals, which were subject to minimal government standards and inspections, were so bad (beatings, occasional deaths, indefinite detention in locked wards with little or no right to communicate with the outside world, poor food and living conditions) that national and international pressure forced Japan to alter its mental health system and laws in 1987.[88]

In China, at least from 1750 onward, when a man became mad, the law required his family to notify officials and to keep him under physical

80 S. M. Salzberg, "Japan's New Mental Health Law: More Light Shed on Dark Places?" (1991) 14 Int'l J. of Law and Psychiatry 137 at 144, citing J. Russell, *The Descendants of Susano* (Ph.D. dissertation, Harvard, 1988) at 36.

81 *Ibid.* at 145.

82 *Ibid.*

83 *Ibid.* at 144-49.

84 *Ibid.* at 145.

85 *Ibid.*

86 *Ibid.* at 147.

87 *Ibid.* at 147, n. 58.

88 *Ibid.* at 138-44.

restraint in a secluded and secure apartment (cage). The officials themselves were to apply the fetters. Women who went mad were seen as less dangerous and did not need to be fettered in a secure apartment; the family was merely required to keep such women under their control. Relatives were severely punished (by beating) for failure to keep a mad person secure. Release of a mad person was to occur only after officials had been notified and verified for themselves that the person's madness had disappeared. Where the family of a mad man had no appropriate apartment to seclude him, the local officials were supposed to secure him in jail.[89]

There has been little or no discussion in the literature of the nature and extent of confinement of the mentally disordered in Taiwan prior to the development of modern psychiatry in Taiwan commencing about 1945. Higginbotham notes that at the end of the Second World War, the few Japanese psychiatrists who were in Taiwan were repatriated, leaving a psychiatric system "devoid of personnel and consisting of no more than a few buildings housing unattended psychotics."[90] Since caring for the mentally ill is the principal responsibility of the family in Taiwan, there must have been a certain degree of family confinement, although I have not found any discussion of its nature or extent, or how it may have compared to that same practice in Japan.[91] Being of Chinese origin, the Taiwanese may well have followed Chinese practices in this regard.

As noted previously, principal responsibility for caring for the mentally ill falls upon the family in Taiwan. Since mental illness is often attributed to incorrect living within the family or misdeeds by one's ancestors, mental illness can be a source of great shame, guilt, disgrace, and stigma for the family. Thus the family will often not seek help from anyone. Tolerance for disturbed behaviour within the family is quite high. When help is sought, it may often be from a traditional herbalist healer on the assumption that the cause is physical. If that fails, the problem may be placed in the hands of local shamans.[92] Resort to Western psychiatric hospitals or services is less

89 G. MacCormack, "The Legal Treatment of Insane Persons in Late Imperial China" (1992) 13 (3) J. of Legal History 251 at 252-53.

90 "The Mental Health System of Taiwan," in Higginbotham, *supra* note 38, c. 3 at 53.

91 For example, there is no mention of private or public confinement of the mentally ill in early Taiwan by Higginbotham, *supra* note 90. See also Salzberg, "Taiwan's Mental Health Law" (1992) 15 Int'l J. of Law and Psych. 43; E. Ahern, "Sacred and Secular Medicine in a Taiwan Village: A Study of Cosmological Disorders," in Kleinman, *supra* note 43, c. 2; E. Ahern, "Chinese-Style and Western-Style Doctors in Northern Taiwan," in Kleinman, *supra* note 43, c. 5; W. S. Tseng, "Traditional and Modern Psychiatric Care in Taiwan," in Kleinman, *supra* note 43, c. 16; A. Kleinman, "Comparisons of Practitioner-Patient Interactions in Taiwan: The Cultural Construction of Clinical Reality," *ibid.* c. 17.

92 Salzberg, *supra* note 91 at 45-47; Higginbotham, *supra* note 90; W. S. Tseng, *supra* note 91; Kleinman, *supra* note 91; Ahern, *supra* note 91; W. S. Tseng, "Folk Psychotherapy in Taiwan," in I. W. P. Lebra, ed., *Culture Bound Syndromes, Ethnopsychiatry and Alternate*

frequent and often a last resort.[93] When Dr. Lin did his famous epidemiological survey in Taiwan between 1946 and 1948, he found that 10.8 individuals out of every 1000 required some psychiatric attention, but that 95% of them had no contact with any modern treatment.[94] By 1975, there were three mental hospitals (with a total of 2600 beds) and a 150 bed specialized psychiatric centre, which operates in a similar fashion to modern Western mental hospitals. In addition, there were 3800 psychiatric beds in military hospitals and 1800 beds in 60 small private hospitals. The military beds are primarily used for long-term chronic cases and are largely custodial. Apart from a few elite private hospitals, the owners of private hospitals are paid a pittance by the government to care for the impoverished mentally ill. Conditions in these hospitals are bleak, treatment is minimal, and confinement may be for life. They function more like prisons or warehouses than hospitals.[95]

Higginbotham has observed that in the earlier years of the colonization of Asia (that is, the 1700s and early 1800s), the British, Portuguese, and Dutch incarcerated disturbed individuals in jails, alongside common criminals, just as they did in their own countries.[96] It was also necessary for indigenous families to bind or chain mentally disturbed relatives who were in need of control and did not respond to traditional medical or shamanistic remedies.[97] Dr. Sangsingkeo of Thailand reports that, if the insane person remained hysterical, that person might even be beaten unconscious.[98] This process of family chaining or binding continued long after the establishment of insane asylums, especially in remoter areas of Thailand.[99] Indeed, even today, the odd case of family binding is reported.[100]

As the new institutional structure known as the insane asylum developed in Europe in the early and mid-1800s, that same institution was also introduced into some Asian countries. Some lunatic asylums appeared in Asia earlier than in Canada. In 1829, a lunatic asylum was established in Penang (now part of Malaysia) for the Chinese, Portuguese, and Indian

---

Therapies (Honolulu: Univ. of Hawaii Press, 1976) at 164; Y. Y. Li, "Shamanism in Taiwan: An Anthropological Inquiry," in Lebra, *ibid.* c. 13.

93 Higginbotham, *supra* note 90; and Salzberg, *supra* note 91. For a series of recent articles on mental health issues in Taiwan, see T. Y. Lin, W. S. Tseng, and E. K. Yeh, eds., *Chinese Societies and Mental Health*, *supra* note 14.

94 Higginbotham, *supra* note 90.

95 Higginbotham, *supra* note 90; Kleinman, *supra* note 91 at 333-34.

96 Higginbotham, *supra* note 38 at 2.

97 P. Sangsingkeo, "Thailand," in J. G. Howells, ed., *World History of Psychiatry* (New York: Brunner/Mazel, 1975) at 651.

98 *Ibid.*

99 *Ibid.*

100 One such case was reported in the *Bangkok Post* between 1993 and 1995, although I cannot now locate the specific date of that report.

communities.[101] In 1841, a 30 bed "Insane Hospital" was established in Singapore. In 1862 it moved to a new site with a 100 bed capacity and was renamed "Lunatic Asylum." In 1887, a "New Lunatic Asylum" was built with 250 male and 50 female beds.[102] Indeed, Singapore had a higher psychiatric bed ratio at this time than Canada or the United States.[103] In Thailand, the first Western hospital (Siriraj Hospital) opened in 1889, and in that same year the first mental hospital of sorts opened when 30 psychotic patients were brought to an old building of a nobleman in Klong Sarn, Thonburi, across the river from Bangkok.[104] In 1912, a new hospital for the insane was built (later called Somdej Chaopraya Mental Hospital), designed by a British architect and administered by a British physician.[105] The first mental hospital in Indonesia was established in Bogor in 1882 by the Dutch colonial government. A second mental hospital was built in 1902 in Lawang with a 1000 bed capacity.[106] In Indonesia, the mentally ill were kept at home if possible because of the stigma attached to being hospitalized.

In general, these Asian insane asylums suffered from the same defects that plagued many of their Western counterparts: they were overcrowded, understaffed, largely custodial rather than treatment-oriented, and often operated under cruel and inhumane conditions.[107] For example, when the first hospital for the insane was opened in Thailand in 1889, it was clearly for the purpose of segregating and confining psychotic patients who could not be kept with other hospital patients. Imprisonment and chaining was the primary objective, although occasionally there was some treatment in the form of herbs and magic.[108] By 1910 there were 296 patients (32 of whom were female) at the insane asylum. The asylum superintendent had "a rather primitive medical education,"[109] although the asylum was under the overall administration of Dr. Hyde, the British physician who was in charge of

---

101 Higginbotham, *supra* note 38 at 3.

102 Kok, *supra* note 14 at 29(b).

103 Higginbotham, *supra* note 38 at 3. In 1861, Singapore had a 100-bed asylum for a population of 82,000.

104 T. Dasananjali, information presented at the Canada-ASEAN Mental Disorder Workshop, Victoria, Canada, 27-29 May 1993 [unpublished]; Higginbotham, *supra* note 38 at 157; Sangsingkeo, *supra* note 97 at 651-52.

105 *Ibid.*

106 D. Hawari, "Psychiatry and Mental Health of Indonesia in Facing the Future," *supra* note 31 at 1-2. The Dutch colonial government sent two doctors, Bauer and Smit, to several European countries to conduct a study on the development of a mental hospital.

107 See e.g. T. H. Woon, "A History of Psychiatry in Peninsula Malaysia, 1830-1975" (1978) 32 Medical J. of Malaysia 258-63; N. Buhrich, "Psychiatry in Peninsula Malaysia" (1980) 14 Australian and New Zealand J. of Psychiatry 299-303; Higginbotham, *supra* note 90 at 3-4; S. L. Varma and M. Z. Axhar, "Psychiatry Coming of Age in Malaysia" (1992) 1 J. of Mental Health 369-70.

108 Sangsingkeo, *supra* note 97 at 652.

109 *Ibid.*

medical health in Bangkok. In 1910, Dr. Hyde reported on the conditions at the hospital in the following words:

> [T]here are 264 male patients and 32 female. Out of these, 54 patients are dangerous and may attack at any time. These are kept separately. But due to shortage of room some of them have to be kept together and often fight each other. Some are chained to the floor like fierce animals. Some of the rooms need repairs badly and cannot be kept clean. This accounts for the diarrhea and dysentery suffered by the patients. This hospital is shamefully falling apart. It is quite apparent that the government should do something to improve it. I myself cannot find stronger words to show how humiliated and disgusted I am.[110]

These conditions are reminiscent of the conditions that existed at many other insane asylums in both the East and the West.

When the new asylum was built in Thailand in 1912, it was placed under the superintendence of a British physician, Dr. Cathew. Food and accommodation were improved, chaining was abolished, and an effort was made to run it as a Western hospital. Still, the rooms resembled jail cells, surrounded with bars.[111] Dr. Cathew was influenced in his running of the hospital by the methods of Dr. Connolly and others in the moral treatment movement.[112]

The Influence of Modern Western Medicine

Modern Western medicine, which largely developed over the past three centuries, has been adopted comprehensively in the West. It has virtually displaced all previous supernatural and traditional folk conceptions of illness and disease. With the Cartesian separation of body and mind clearly in place, Western medicine focused on the physical and the observable, on the natural, not the supernatural, on the body, not the soul or spirit. The earlier conceptions that mental illness was caused by spirit possession or other supernatural forces were castigated as unscientific, false, and unworthy of further respect.[113] When Western colonizers came upon somewhat similar indigenous beliefs and practices in regard to illness in Eastern countries, they characterized these practices as unscientific and uncivilized. These indigenous beliefs and practices confirmed their own ethnocentric view that

110 *Ibid.*

111 *Ibid.* at 653. Dr. Dasananjali, *supra* note 104, reports that the hospital was at first called "madhouse – Rong Kon Sia Chalit" or "red-roofed hospital – Rang Kha Doeng" because of the red roof of the hospital, which was similar to buildings commonly seen in England.

112 *Ibid.*

113 See e.g. Alexander, *supra* note 1 and Deutsch, *supra* note 1.

Western countries were far superior in both economic and industrial development as well as scientific knowledge.

The West: Canada

Before European explorers, traders, and settlers arrived in North America, the indigenous or aboriginal inhabitants (Inuit and North American Indians) had a rich culture of folk medicine based on natural and supernatural beliefs. Medicine men, shamans, and other healers attended to illnesses of various sorts.[114] In the 1700s, Britain and France began to colonize and settle Canada extensively. The aboriginal population of Canada was relatively small and widely spread out across Canada. This population, particularly the Indian population, was drastically reduced by wars with the Anglo-European settlers and by deadly Western diseases for which their bodies had no immune system resistance. The aboriginals who did survive the wars and diseases were shoved off their land and isolated on reserves. They were generally portrayed by Anglo-Europeans as wild savages (which, of course, justified savage treatment of them). Their indigenous beliefs and practices were not properly understood and in any event were seen as uncivilized superstitions by the Anglo-European settlers.[115] Thus Canada became a country composed almost exclusively of Anglo-European settlers,[116] who completely adopted Western science and medicine. Indigenous, aboriginal medical or spiritual practices nearly died out. If they were practised at all, it was in private by small groups of isolated aboriginals who were generally perceived as being outside mainstream Canada.

The East

In Asia, on the other hand, the Western colonizers, although they exercised varying degrees of economic and legal power, did not constitute a large proportion of the population. In other words, the Anglo-Europeans remained a minority; they did not displace the indigenous population as occurred in North America. Thus the adoption of Western medical practices has never been anything close to complete in these Eastern countries, except perhaps in Japan. In most Eastern countries, indigenous folk medicine and Western medicine co-exist largely as two separate systems with some interaction between them. In many parts of Asia, folk medicine is resorted to far more frequently than Western medicine. For example, studies in peninsular Malaysia as late as the 1970s and 1980s have shown that up to 90% of persons

---

114 E. Margetts, "Canada: Indian and Eskimo Medicine, with Notes on the Early History of Psychiatry among French and British Colonists," in Howells, *supra* note 97 at 400.

115 *Ibid.*

116 Today the aboriginal population stands at 3% to 5% of the total Canadian population: Statistics Canada, *Ethnic Origins: The Nation* (Ottawa: Industry Science and Technology, Canada, 1993).

who seek treatment at Western-style hospitals have previously sought the assistance of traditional healers.[117] Dr. Suwanlert of Thailand, and many other Asian psychiatrists, have pioneered in the diagnosis and treatment of "spirit possession" cases amongst the indigenous population.[118] They do so by inquiring into and accepting the patient's belief system, and then using their Western medical and psychological techniques in a way that is not incompatible with the patient's indigenous beliefs.[119] Many psychiatrists and mental hospitals do not object to, or occasionally may even encourage, patients to continue visiting traditional healers.[120]

Apart from the fact that European settlers remained a small minority in Asian countries, there are other factors that explain why Western medicine was only partially adopted in most Asian countries. First, Western medicine, and the physiological assumptions underlying it, were foreign to most Eastern conceptions of physical or mental illness. Second, Western medicine was not widely used; it was restricted to the small group of Anglo-European settlers in each country and a few elite indigenous people. Third, reliance on Western medicine, which required substantial educational training and economic resources for hospitals and equipment, was naturally limited by each country's economic ability to provide it.

In spite of these factors, there was a rapid disappearance of indigenous medical beliefs and practices in Japan during the late 1800s and into the 1900s. Prior to the Meiji Restoration of 1868, the Japanese medical belief system was a combination of native Japanese and imported Chinese elements. But after 1868, Japan moved rapidly to adopt a wholly Western system of medical beliefs and practices, with few remnants of prior indigenous practices. Pelzel points to a few factors in an effort to explain so radical a change in Japanese medicine. The importation of Western medicine was only one part of a massive restructuring of Japanese society after 1868. During this era, there was a greater intellectual curiosity in Japan than elsewhere to examine Western ideas of anatomy and physiology and to adopt Western technologies. Pelzel suggests that Japan saw the adoption

117 Cheang, *supra* note 26. In Dr. Suwanlert's study of 62 cases of *phii pob* spirit possession in two Northern Thai villages, only 10 were admitted by relatives for treatment at Srithunya Hospital because shamans could not drive the spirits off: S. Suwanlert, "*Phii Pob*: Spirit Possession in Rural Thailand," in Lebra, *supra* note 92, c. 6. And in a study of a *koro* epidemic in Northern Thailand, only 20% sought help from their local hospital: Higginbotham, *supra* note 38 at 206. In Bali, Suryani found that 76% of patients treated at a psychiatric hospital had been seen by traditional healers before being referred to the psychiatric hospital: Suryani, *supra* note 33 at 207-208.

118 Dr. Suwanlert's approach is summarized in Higginbotham, *supra* note 38 at 204.

119 Higginbotham, *supra* note 38 at 203-210.

120 *Ibid.* Suryani, *supra* note 33 at 208 reports that 80% of Balinese patients and families continued to follow traditional healing rituals during psychiatric hospitalization and after discharge.

of Western technology, including Western medicine, as a necessary part of Japan's quest to excel as a society.[121]

It is interesting to observe that the West's original ethnocentric view as to the lack of value of indigenous folk therapies is beginning to change. In Western countries, there is a growing scepticism as to the appropriateness and efficacy of Western medicine as the sole answer to physical and mental disorders. More and more Westerners are turning to alternative therapies that are practised in a holistic fashion. Eastern countries are being looked to as an example and a model of how folk therapies can be effective and how the Western and Eastern systems can operate together.

Eastern Adoption of Western Psychiatry: A Continuing Process

Although the utility of Western psychiatry clearly has some cultural limitations in Asian countries, there is nonetheless a continuing and, in most cases, an increasing tendency for Asian countries to import and rely upon Western psychiatry, albeit not exclusively. As Higginbotham has pointed out, national independence (generally after the Second World War) did not end the pattern of colonial psychiatry that had been established in the East.[122] He points to several factors that have led to the continued adoption of Western medicine and psychiatry. The first factor relates to the process of modernization or industrialization that has been occurring in Asia since the Second World War. This process has involved requests for foreign aid from Western states in regard to technology, education, and health care. Foreign aid for health care has generally involved the exportation of Western medicine to the East. Second, it is widely assumed that modernization has created a new layer and level of psychological stress and social disorder (in the form of more crime, more suicides etc.).[123] Since this stress is a Western-created problem, it seemed natural that some Asian countries would turn to a Western-created solution to deal with the adverse impact of modernization.

Third, although mental disorders may be defined and perceived in a cultural context, a strong body of evidence indicates that the same mental disorders exist worldwide, particularly severe, chronic disorders such as schizophrenia.[124] There is a further corollary belief in the cross-cultural efficacy of Western treatment methods, especially physiological treatments such

121 Pelzel, *supra* note 43 at 265-70.

122 Higginbotham, *supra* note 38 at 4.

123 This point was emphasized by Dr. Kok for Singapore, Professor Cheang for Malaysia, Dr. Hawari for Indonesia, and Dr. Thamrong Dasananjali for Thailand at the Canada-Asean Workshop, Victoria, Canada, 27-29 May 1993. See also Higginbotham, *supra* note 38 at 6 for a reference to some of the extensive literature on this point.

124 Higginbotham, *supra* note 38 at 9-13.

as drug therapy and ECT. In short, if a treatment is effective in the West, there is a strong assumption it should also be effective in the East. A bit of perverse irony to this ethnocentric belief has arisen in follow-up studies of schizophrenic patients in developing countries who have, in fact, had better results with Western treatment methods than schizophrenics in developed countries. These interesting results are now assumed to relate to the fact that Western treatment methods are augmented by stronger family and community support systems in the East than in the West,[125] and lend support to the thesis that psychiatric illness and treatment occur on a biological, psychological, and social level and involve an interaction among each.[126]

There are a number of mechanisms whereby Western psychiatry has been transferred to the East. First, a significant number of the leading mental health professionals in Asian countries have received graduate, specialized training in Western countries and have attempted to put that training into effect in their own countries. Second, as part of foreign aid plans, Western psychiatrists and mental health experts have been used as expert consultants, on both short and long-term visits, to set in place Western models of mental health care. Likewise, regional training programs and workshops on Western medical techniques have been frequently sponsored by Western mental health sponsors for Asian participants. Finally, international collaborative research projects involving Western and Eastern partners have provided another conduit for the importation of Western ideas and techniques.[127]

Convergence towards a Community Health Model

In both the East and the West one can observe a shift in the last half of this century from traditional Western psychiatry, which has emphasized institutionalization and biomedical treatment, to a more multi-disciplinary approach that encourages an integration of psychological, social, and biological factors in a more holistic, community based approach.

The West

It was not until the 1950s that a discernible change in policy occurred in Canada. As a consequence of the number of mental health casualties of the Second World War, the Canadian government began in 1948 to support mental health facilities in a significant financial way. Hospital construction grants were made to increase the number of available beds and other grants

125 See Higginbotham, *supra* note 38 at 10-13 for a reference to some of the findings on the universal nature of mental disorders and the cross-cultural outcomes of some forms of treatment.

126 D. A. Moltz, "Bipolar Disorder and the Family: An Integrative Model" (1993) 32 Family Process 409.

127 These mechanisms are discussed in Higginbotham, *supra* note 38 at 13-18.

were made to upgrade mental health services.[128] Smaller, short-term psychiatric hospitals were built and psychiatric units appeared in general hospitals. Treatment, not custody, was the primary objective. However, much of the care in the large mental hospitals still remained custodial.[129] The rediscovery in England and the United States in the 1940s of some of the ideals of moral treatment, under a new and revised rubric called "therapeutic community," did not take hold in the large Canadian mental hospitals.[130]

In conjunction with the establishment of new psychiatric units, the single, most important event during this period occurred in the mid-1950s with the introduction of anti-depressant and anti-psychotic drugs. These "miracle drugs" revolutionized psychiatric treatment by controlling and stabilizing patient behaviour, thereby reducing the use of physical restraints and creating new opportunities for professional counselling and treatment.[131] In addition, patients could be released after much shorter periods of treatment. Today confinement in mental hospitals is shorter and more humane than it once was, but the quality of life and treatment within mental hospitals is still not all that it could be.[132]

In conjunction with, or perhaps because of, the new drug therapies, a significant shift in emphasis to community mental health began to occur in the early 1960s. The population of psychiatric hospitals has been gradually reduced to a third and a quarter of its former size.[133] To be effective, however, community mental health must develop a complete and integrated service from prevention through to aftercare. Although substantial progress has been made, Canada has not yet reached a stage of complete and full integration.[134] The trend to de-institutionalization in favour of lo-

128 A. Richman, *Psychiatric Care in Canada: Extent and Results* (A Study for the Royal Commission on Health Services) (Ottawa: Queen's Printer, 1964) at 34-35 and 42-43. See also Williams, *supra* note 60 at 402-403.

129 Williams, *supra* note 60 at 403.

130 McKerracher, *supra* note 77 at 150-51 and 235; Williams, *supra* note 60 at 403.

131 Williams, *supra* note 60 at 403.

132 R. G. Foulkes, *Health Security for British Columbians* (Victoria: Report to the Minister of Health, B.C., 1973) at IV-C-12-5; British Columbia Ombudsman, Public Report No. 33, *Listening: A Review of Riverview Hospital* (Victoria, B.C.: Ombudsman Office, 1994) c. 5 and 6.

133 For example, in Ontario the in-patient population of provincial psychiatric hospitals dropped from 15,921 in 1963 to 4,255 in 1978: Debates Legislature of Ontario, 11 Apr. 1978 at 1443. The bed size at British Columbia's largest and only major mental hospital fell from 4,306 beds in 1956 to 1,853 beds in 1976, to 1,306 beds in 1985, and to 907 beds in 1991: *Report of the British Columbia Royal Commission on Health Care and Costs* (Victoria, B.C.: Queen's Printer, 1991) at C-77. Likewise, the population in the California state hospitals dropped from 37,000 in 1967 to 6,300 in 1976. It has been estimated that the mental hospital population in the United States dropped in the 1970s from 900,000 to 190,000. See Slovenko, *supra* note 74 at 5, n-23.

134 *Report of the British Columbia Royal Commission on Health Care and Costs*, *supra* at C-73 to C-84. With reduced rates of psychiatric hospitalization, the burden of treating mental

cal community care is still continuing in Canada, although there is evidence of an unfortunate shift back to re-institutionalizing the mentally ill in the United States.[135]

Although pursuit of a complete and integrated system of community mental health services is desirable, official government policies to downsize mental hospitals and provide alternative community mental health treatment must be examined cautiously. First, community mental health services are not without their own unique social burdens.[136] Second, there is a real danger of governments closing or downsizing large mental hospitals, but not directing all the savings from such downsizing into alternative community health services. Third, with a decreasing sense of community in large urban centres, with an unwillingness to accept those who are different, and with minimal community resources, the official government shift to community mental health can easily become a new disguise for the continued neglect and abuse of persons with mental illness.[137]

---

illness has fallen more heavily on family physicians who are not well trained for that job. In 1997, the Canadian Psychiatric Association and the College of Family Physicians of Canada announced plans to create a national program for "shared care" of mentally ill persons by family doctors and psychiatrists, including expanded training for family doctors in mental health care and ready access to psychiatrists for those family physicians who need immediate expert advice. See J. Coutts, "Doctors' Groups Propose 'Shared Care' for Mentally Ill," *The [Toronto] Globe and Mail* (15 Oct. 1997) A11.

135 J. Q. LaFond and M. L. Durham, in *Back to the Asylum: The Future of Mental Health Law and Policy in the United States* (New York: Oxford Univ. Press, 1992) at 159 argue that, in the neo-conservative era of the 1990s, the mentally ill are at serious risk of being singled out and treated especially harshly because of the anxiety over crime in general. LaFond and Durham also note (at 169-70) that the mentally ill in many U.S. cities are either forcibly removed from the streets to overcrowded, shabby, and unsafe shelters or coercively dumped into crowded and understaffed state hospitals.

136 Williams, *supra* note 60 at 407, summarizing the findings from studies in England by D. Mechanic, *Mental Health and Social Policy* (Englewood Cliffs, N.J.: Prentice-Hall, 1969) to the effect that: the patient's illness was harmful to the health of the relative; children were adversely affected; it was financially costly to provide support services in the home; leisure time activities were restricted; relatives were unable to have visitors at home; the relatives of community patients reflected more anxiety than relatives of hospitalized patients; the community patients received more superficial treatment than did hospitalized patients; and lastly, it appears that birth rates for the mentally ill women increased substantially.

137 This concern has materialized in some parts of the United States where studies have shown that large numbers of mental hospital patients have been released back into the community without adequate, alternative resources to assist them. They have been abandoned in the community and left to fend for themselves: Slovenko, *supra* note 74 at 36; D. Bazelon, Foreword to K. Donaldson, *Insanity Inside Out* (New York: Crown, 1976) at x-xi; R. J. Isaac, *Madness in the Streets: How Psychiatry and the Law Abandoned the Mentally Ill* (New York: Free Press, 1990). In Canada, the same concerns have also materialized. As noted in an editorial,"Have We Abandoned the Mentally Ill?" *The [Toronto] Globe and Mail* (17 Nov. 1997) A20, for many mentally ill people in Canada today, "the community" means "a dank rooming house, a crowded hostel or a windswept street corner." See also S. Davis, "The Trouble with Closing the Asylums," *The [Toronto] Globe and Mail* (18 Mar. 1996) A13.

The East

The community mental health model in Asian countries is characterized by the following four features: (1) emphasis on primary prevention; (2) training of paraprofessionals; (3) extension of professional resources through consultation and education activities; and (4) mobilization of community resources to maintain the patient outside the hospital.[138]

In some respects the implementation of a community health model has been easier in the East than the West. Because the structure of traditional Western psychiatric institutions in Asian countries is not as large as in the West, the task of shifting resources is not as difficult. In addition, scarce medical and psychiatric resources in some Asian countries have made the delivery of these services on a public health model unavoidable. For example, modern Western psychiatry was not introduced into Taiwan in any systematic way until 1945. Dr. Lin, who received his medical training in Japan and graduate training in the United States, returned to Taiwan and set about establishing a three-part, 25-year plan to establish a national mental health program for Taiwan.[139] In devising a plan, he was not constrained by the existence of a system of custodial mental hospitals that Western colonizers had left in some other Southeast Asian countries.[140] Dr. Lin was an adherent to social psychiatry, and his plan was to integrate mental health services into general public health services, to be dispensed through general hospitals, health stations, clinics, and even schools. Psychiatric services were to be offered as much as possible in a non-custodial context. The implementation of Dr. Lin's plans were retarded and frustrated by the fact that, until the mid-1980s, mental health received the lowest priority of all the government health initiatives and programs.[141]

The delivery of mental health services on a public health, community-based model is also official government policy in Indonesia[142] and Thailand.[143] In Malaysia, community mental health care is becoming an important component of the national mental health program, which is still in its early stages. One component of this plan is the training in mental health care of general physicians who will deliver these services through the rural, general health care system in Malaysia.[144] Because Singapore is in effect a city state, services are largely concentrated in one institution, Woodbridge Hospital, but there are also a number of smaller psychiatric units in other medical facilities as well as out-patient treatment clinics in

138 Higginbotham, *supra* note 38 at 23.
139 *Ibid.*; and Salzberg, *supra* note 90.
140 *Ibid.* at 53.
141 *Ibid.* at 53-55; and Salzberg, *supra* note 90 at 43-44.
142 Hawari, *supra* note 31.
143 Dasananjali, *supra* note 104.
144 Varma, *supra* note 107 at 370.

various parts of Singapore.[145] In Japan, to a greater extent than other Asian countries, psychiatric services have been concentrated on in-patient, custodial care in private hospitals. This system was severely criticized and resulted in a new law and health care delivery plan in 1987. There is a new emphasis on social rehabilitation and new intermediate community-care centres, but a fundamental shift from an extensive custodial structure to a community-based model will not come easily in Japan.[146]

MENTAL DISORDER AND CRIMINAL LAW

The Adoption or Imposition of Western Criminal Law

The laws and procedures for dealing with mentally disordered persons who come into conflict with the criminal law are strikingly similar in the countries under study. This should be no surprise since nineteenth-century Western criminal law was either adopted or imposed on each of the countries under study and these countries have, for the most part, allowed these "western" criminal laws to continue in force ever since.

Prior to its independence in 1867, Canada was a British colony and as such it adopted British criminal law, which law was codified in 1892 in the first Canadian *Criminal Code*. With some significant amendments, that code still remains in force today. British criminal law was also adopted in the British colonies of Malaysia and Singapore. The penal codes of Malaysia and Singapore (originally the Straits Settlements) were enacted in 1871 and were closely modelled after the Indian *Penal Code* of 1860.[147] The Indian *Penal Code* was initially drafted by Lord Macaulay in 1837 for the then British colony of India and was primarily based on general principles of British criminal law with valuable assistance also being derived from the French *Penal Code*.[148]

In the late nineteenth century, Thailand, which was then known as Siam, "voluntarily" adopted Western laws as a deliberate move to lessen the chances of direct colonization by England, France, or other European states and to also put an end to these foreign states' claim of extraterritorial jurisdiction.[149]

---

145 Kok, *supra* note 14.

146 Salzberg, *supra* note 80 at 166-67.

147 G. Ferguson, "The Insanity Defence in Canada, Malaysia and Singapore: A Tale of Two Codes," [1990] J. of Malaysian and Comparative L. 1. Although largely similar, there are also some notable differences between the Indian and the Malaysian and Singapore Penal Codes. See e.g. M. Cheang, "The Insanity Defence in Singapore" (1985) 14 Anglo-American L. Rev. at 260 n. 5.

148 Indian *Penal Code*, Introduction at 6-7, reprinted in (1837-38) Vol. 41, British Sessional Papers at 468-69.

149 A. Petchsiri, *Eastern Importation of Western Criminal Law: Thailand as a Case Study* (Littleton, Colorado: Rothman, 1987) at 30. Extraterritorial jurisdiction was a situation in which more powerful foreign states insisted that their law apply to legal disputes involving their nationals, even though the disputes arose or took place in the

Beginning in 1895, Thailand appointed foreign legal advisers of different nationalities – French, British, Belgian, Japanese, and American – to help "westernize" the law and administer it.[150] In 1897, a commission was established to draft a penal code. That commission's draft was submitted to M. George Padoux, the legislative adviser and French consul, who headed up a second drafting commission in 1904. The Padoux Commission produced a draft which became the Thai *Penal Code* of 1907. Although it was largely drafted by Padoux and his French assistants, Padoux indicated that the code was influenced by at least eight, foreign, Western-style penal codes including the French *Penal Code* of 1810, the Indian *Penal Code* of 1860, the Dutch *Penal Code* of 1881, the Italian *Penal Code* of 1889 and the draft Japanese *Penal Code* of 1903. The code was drafted in English and later translated into Thai.[151] Although the Thai *Penal Code* has undergone a number of significant changes since 1908, including a recodification in 1956, it still remains essentially a "western" code.[152]

The first significant foreign influences on the Japanese legal system derived from early imperial Chinese laws and institutions during the seventh and eighth centuries.[153] The second wave of foreign influence occurred in the mid-nineteenth century when European states, with trade and commerce in mind, forced the opening of Japan to the West. The Tokugawa regime of the previous 200 years collapsed and a form of imperial rule was restored under the Meiji regime (1868-1912).[154] As in Thailand, the leaders of the Meiji government viewed the adoption of Western law as a mechanism to stave off direct colonization and to put an end to the extraterritorial jurisdiction of foreign states in Japan.[155]

---

second country. For example, if a British subject was involved in a criminal or civil dispute, the case would be tried by a British consular court applying British law: Petchsiri, *ibid.* at 27. See also V. Muntarbhorn, "Human Rights in Thailand," in L. Palmier, ed., *State and Law in Eastern Asia* (Aldershot, England: Dartmouth Publishing, 1996) at 105-106.

150 Petchsiri, *ibid.* at 37.

151 Petchsiri, *ibid.* at 82-84. See also A. Petchsiri, "A Short History of Thai Criminal Law Since the Nineteenth Century" (1986) 28 Malaya L. Rev. 134.

152 Petchsiri, *ibid.* at 66-72.

153 J. Haley, *Authority Without Power: Law and the Japanese Paradox* (Oxford: Oxford Univ. Press, 1991) at 17-32; G. Koshi, *The Japanese Legal Advisor: Crimes and Punishments* (Rutland, Vermont: Charles E. Tuttle, 1970) at 39-41; H. Oda, *Japanese Law* (London: Butterworths, 1992) at 14-24.

154 Haley, *ibid.* at 67-80.

155 *Ibid.* at 68. The process of westernizing the legal system began with the translating of foreign law codes, especially French and German codes, the use of foreign legal advisers, and the gradual, piecemeal supplanting of traditional laws and institutions with western ones while a broader general code or statute was being drafted. *Ibid.* at 70. See also Takayanagi, *infra* note 157 at 18-20; Oda, *supra* note 153 at 26-27; A. J. G. M. Sanders, "The Reception of Western Law in Japan" (1995) 28 Comparative and Int'l L.J. of S. Africa 280.

In 1875, Japan set up a court system patterned along French lines.[156] In 1880, a penal code was enacted. It was drafted by a French legal adviser and was modelled after, but not identical to the French *Penal Code* of 1810 and its subsequent amendments.[157] Over the next 25 years, Japanese students of criminal law who went abroad generally studied in Germany. This had the effect of increasing respect for German law and legal theory at the expense of French law.[158] In 1907, a new penal code was enacted along German lines. This code, with some significant amendments, remains in force today.[159] A set of regulations for criminal procedure using the French semi-inquisitorial system was also adopted in 1880. These regulations were slightly revised and re-enacted as the first *Code of Criminal Procedure* in 1890.[160] The 1890 Code was replaced in 1920 by a new *Code of Criminal Procedure*. The 1920 code relied heavily on German procedures but still retained much of its French origins as well.[161] The post-Second World War allied occupation of Japan resulted in a new constitution that guaranteed individual rights and freedoms to all citizens, including criminal suspects, along Anglo-American lines. This in turn necessitated the reform of existing laws to conform to the provisions of the new Constitution. In 1948, a new *Code of Criminal Procedure* was adopted. It abandoned some of the features of the Franco-German inquisitorial procedure and adopted a number of significant features of the Anglo-American accusatorial form of criminal procedure.[162] As Haley notes, "Japan's formal system of criminal justice is therefore somewhat of a hybrid. It combines basic features of continental European, especially German law and practice with elements of American law, particularly the procedural protections."[163]

In Indonesia, with a culturally diverse population spread across a large archipelago, the Dutch colonial powers adopted a system of legal pluralism whereby Indonesian inhabitants were divided into population groups, based primarily on racial origin, with each group having what amounted to its own legal system.[164] Dutch civil law applied to Europeans while local customary law – adat law – applied to the other groups.[165] Only in recent

156 *Ibid.* at 69.

157 K. Takayanagi, "A Century of Innovation: The Development of Japanese Law, 1868-1961," in A. von Mehren, ed., *Law in Japan: The Legal Order in a Changing Society* (Cambridge: Harvard Univ. Press, 1963) at 15-17; Oda, *supra* note 153 at 388-89.

158 *Ibid.* at 17-18. See also Y. Noda, *Introduction to Japanese Law,* trans. A. Angel (Tokyo: Univ. of Tokyo Press, 1966) at 207-208.

159 *Ibid.*

160 Noda, *supra* note 158 at 209-10; Takayanagi, *supra* note 157 at 19-21; S. Dando, *Japanese Criminal Procedure,* trans. B. J. George (South Hackensack, N.J.: Rothman, 1965) at 14-16.

161 *Supra* note 160.

162 Noda, *supra* note 158 at 210-11; Takayanagi, *supra* note 157 at 23; and Dando, *supra* note 160 at 17-18.

163 Haley, *supra* note 153 at 126.

decades has there been a concerted effort in Indonesia to introduce uniform laws in regard to civil or private law matters.[166] However, in criminal law, uniformity was achieved much earlier. In 1915, an Indonesian *Penal Code* was drafted and it came into effect 1 January 1918.[167] In fact, it has been suggested that the separate and distinct criminal regulations that had been in force for the different population groups before that time were in fact substantially similar since at least the 1870s, and therefore the 1918 Code unified in law what already existed in fact.[168] In any event, the 1918 Code bore a close resemblance to the Dutch *Penal Code* of 1881, which was itself influenced by the French *Penal Code*.[169] The 1918 Code was amended following the Declaration of Independence in 1946, and this Code remains in force today.[170] A *Code of Criminal Procedure* was first produced in 1848, revised in 1941 and a new *Code of Criminal Procedure* was promulgated in 1981.[171]

In Taiwan, the *Penal Code* of the Republic of China, which went through a major revision in 1935 and additional amendments in 1954, is in force.[172]

Informal Diversion from the Criminal Justice System

Sometimes criminal behaviour is not reported to the police. Non-reporting of some crimes is a practice common to all the countries under study. It may occur for a variety of reasons. In some cases, the victim may, for example, be too ashamed to report a sexual offence or may not want the anxiety or inconvenience of being a witness at trial. In other cases, such as those involving domestic assaults or theft by employees, the criminal conduct may be viewed as a private or family matter, rather than as a matter for the

---

164 S. Gautama and R. Hornick, *An Introduction to Indonesian Law: Unity in Diversity* (South Hackensack, N.J.: Rothman, 1974) at 1; M. B. Hooker, *A Concise Legal History of South-East Asia* (Oxford: Clarendon Press, 1978) at 187-213.

165 *Ibid.*

166 Hooker, *supra* note 164 at 212-13.

167 Gautama, *supra* note 164 at 14. Notwithstanding the existence of a national criminal code, local judges still apply local adat criminal law from time to time where it conflicts with the Code: *Ibid.* at 14.

168 *Ibid.* at 14. Before that time, Dutch criminal law applied to Europeans and *adat* criminal law applied to natives. See M. B. Hooker, *Legal Pluralism: An Introduction to Colonial and Neo-Colonial Laws* (Oxford: Clarendon Press, 1975) at 254-55.

169 D. C. Fokkema et al. (eds.), *Introduction to Dutch Law for Foreign Lawyers* (Deventer, Netherlands: Kluwer, 1978) at 298-99.

170 Gautama, *supra* note 164 at 14. For more detail, see B. S. Han, *An Outline of the Recent History of Indonesian Criminal Law* (Koninklijk Instituut voor Taal-Land-en Volkenkunde, S-Gravenhage, Netherlands: Martinus Nijhoff, 1961).

171 J.'t Hart, "Aspects of Criminal Justice," in H. Thoolen, ed., *Indonesia and the Rule of Law: Twenty Years of "New Order" Government* (A study prepared by the International Commission of Jurists) (London: Frances Pinter, 1987) at 166-67.

172 C. Kim, "Asian Criminal Law: A Comparison with Proposed Federal Criminal Code" (1972-73) 14 S. Texas L.J. 43.

criminal justice system. Similarly, when a mentally disordered person engages in certain forms of criminal behaviour, family, friends, or neighbours may consider the invocation of the criminal justice system to be an inappropriate response. For example, many persons who are voluntarily or involuntarily committed to a mental hospital (especially those who are committed on the basis of being a danger to others) may well have committed a criminal assault on friends or family either by threats or actual use of force. But friends or family will not necessarily consider such assaults to be within the domain of the criminal law. Informal diversion of the person to the mental health system will often be a more useful or effective response. Since the criminal law system is a blunt, expensive, and often ineffective mechanism for receiving treatment or for achieving peace, order, and public safety, it should be used only when other alternative responses are unavailable or inappropriate. It is worth noting that in Malaysia (and Singapore), section 13 of the *Code of Criminal Procedure* requires every person to report information to the police concerning the commission of certain serious offences including treason, unlawful assembly, riot, culpable homicide, kidnapping, extortion, robbery, and arson, but not offences such as assault, rape, theft, or other related property offences.

Formal Diversion from the Criminal Justice System

In some incidents, the police may become involved either because they are witnesses to the criminal incident or because of complaints from other persons. When the police do intervene, they must assess the situation and decide whether formally to invoke the criminal justice system. Depending on all the circumstances, including the seriousness of the incident, the police may exercise their discretion not to invoke the criminal justice system. Instead they may direct the suspect into the mental health system.

In British Columbia, a police officer is authorized to take a person into custody and to convey that person directly to a physician where that person "is acting in a manner likely to endanger his or her own safety or that of others and is apparently suffering from mental disorder."[173] The mental health

173 *Mental Health Act,* R.S.B.C. 1996, c. 288, s. 28 states that a person may be admitted to a mental health facility on an emergency basis for up to 72 hours upon the certificate of one physician who is satisfied that the person is mentally disordered and in need of care, supervision, or control for his or her own protection or welfare or for the protection of others. The physician need not be psychiatrically trained. At the end of the 72 hour period, the person must be discharged or committed under the regular committal procedure (a certificate of two physicians indicating that the person is mentally disordered and needs psychiatric hospitalization). S. 28(6) authorizes the director of the mental health facility to detain such persons, to examine them, and to treat them for their condition during the 72 hour period. For discussion of similar provisions in other Canadian provinces, see M. Schiffer, *Mental Disorder and the Criminal Trial Process* (Toronto: Butterworths, 1978) at 10-16. See also R. G. Fox and P. G. Erickson,

legislation in Singapore and Malaysia, following earlier English legislation,[174] also authorizes the police to bring a person before a medical officer or directly to a mental hospital if the person is mentally disordered and wandering at large or is dangerous by reason of mental disorder.[175] The medical officer can sign a Form 1, which authorizes that person's detention and treatment for 72 hours, and if a second medical officer examines the person and is of the opinion that further detention and treatment is required, then

---

Apparently Suffering from Mental Disorder: An Examination of the Exercise of Police Power under s. 10 of the Mental Health Act of Ontario (Toronto: Centre of Criminology, University of Toronto, 1972).

174 See T. Fahy, J. Dunn, and D. Bermingham, "Police Admissions to London Mental Hospitals – Patient Profiles and Police Attitudes," in F. Koenraadt and M. Zeegers, eds., *Trends in Law and Mental Health* (Arnhem, Netherlands: Gouda Quint, 1988), in which the authors state, at 378-79:

> [In England] The Madhouse Act (1774) introduced medical certification of insanity as a condition of detention in a private mental hospital and the doctor's role in assessing the requirement for compulsory admission expanded in the nineteenth century.
>
> Despite the increased influence of doctors in disposal of the mentally ill, nineteenth and twentieth century laws continued to include provisions for police constables to remove mentally disordered persons from public places. The 1890 Lunacy Act authorised police officers to convey the mentally disordered to a workhouse without consultation with psychiatrists. This provision is the predecessor of Section 136 of the 1959 Mental Health Act which restricted the police to intervene only when the person was in a public place. This power remained virtually unchanged in the 1983 Mental Health Act, where Section 136 is defined as follows:
>
> (1) If a constable finds in a place to which the public have access a person who appears to him to be suffering from mental disorder and to be in need of care or control, the constable may, if he thinks it necessary to do so in the interests of that person or for the safety or protection of other persons, remove that person to a place of safety within the meaning of Section 135 above.
>
> (2) A person removed to a place of safety under this section may be detained there for a period not exceeding 72 hours for the purpose of enabling him to be examined by an Approved Social Worker and of making any necessary arrangements for his treatment and care.

175 In Malaysia, s. 34 of the *Mental Health Disorders Ordinance, 1952*, as amended, states:

> 34.(1) It shall be the duty of every police officer to apprehend all persons found wandering at large whom such police officer has reason to suspect to be mentally disordered or dangerous by reason of mental disorder and to bring such person before a medical officer.
>
> (2) It shall be the duty of every police officer not below the rank of Sergeant to apprehend any person wherever found whom he has reason to suspect to be dangerous by reason of mental disorder and to bring such person before a medical officer.

A similar provision is included in Singapore's *Mental Disorders and Treatment Act 1985*. The original Singapore legislation was amended in 1942 to authorize the police to bring a mentally disordered person to a medical officer who could detain that person for 72 hours and a 1957 amendment authorized the police to apprehend a person and take him or her directly to a mental hospital (where the person could be admitted for up to one month under a Form 2 certificate). See Kok, *supra* note 14.

the person can be detained for a period of one month (under Form 2), and thereafter on a yearly basis if necessary (under Form 3).[176] Although legislation in the other countries under study does not specifically refer to this police power, police officers can proceed in this manner as part of their general discretion in keeping the peace.[177]

In Thailand, the police have the discretion to take such persons directly to hospital rather than to the police station for the laying of charges. This is most likely to occur when the offence is a minor one and the alleged offender's behaviour is bizarre. Alternatively the police may conduct an investigation, including contacting the alleged offender's relatives, before deciding how to deal with the suspect. While conducting an inquiry, an inquiry official (who may be a senior police officer) may suspend the inquiry and order a medical examination where the alleged offender appears to be of unsound mind and unable to put up a defence, and if the alleged offender is of unsound mind the inquiry official may send that person to a mental hospital.[178]

In Singapore and Malaysia, the police will either exercise their discretion not to charge and convey the person directly to a mental hospital or alternatively will decide that criminal charges are appropriate and take the suspect to a police station for processing of charges which will eventually lead to the accused appearing in court. In Malaysia (and Singapore), sections 110 and 120 of the *Code of Criminal Procedure* generally anticipate that the police will investigate and send a report to the Public Prosecutor unless there are insufficient grounds for proceeding or unless the offence is of a character that the Public Prosecutor has directed need not be reported to them. In

---

176 Kok, *supra* note 14.

177 In Canada, Malaysia, and Singapore, broad police and prosecutorial power has always existed under the English common law system. In Japan, Haley, *supra* note 153 at 126 notes that "the most striking departure from German and other European practice ... is the extent of discretion enjoyed by police, prosecutor, and judge alike." Under the German system, the police and prosecutor have very limited discretion. The German system is often referred to as a system of mandatory prosecutions, which means that the prosecutor must submit all cases to a court if the criminal investigation has revealed a suspicion of guilt. The court then has the authority to decide whether the matter should proceed to trial or not. See B. J. George, "Discretionary Authority of Public Prosecutors in Japan" (1984) 17 *Law and Japan* at 47-48. However, Japan, Thailand, and Indonesia have all departed from the European model of judicial control over charging by giving the police and prosecutor a wide measure of discretion in regard to not laying charges.

178 Thailand *Code of Criminal Procedure*, s. 14. See also note 225 *infra*, in which T. Dasananjali notes that two-thirds of insane, convicted killers at one Thai mental hospital were referred there by the police. On the other hand, see Muntarbhorn, *supra* note 149 at 128-30, who argues that the wide discretion given to the police in the Thai criminal law system has enormous implications for abuse of powers, especially if police are badly paid and seek to manipulate the discretion conferred on them for their own ends.

Indonesia, if a suspect shows signs of mental disorder, the police, under their legal duty to investigate, will try to interview that person, then attempt to contact the person's family to determine whether there is any previous history of mental disorder. If there is a past history of mental disorder, the police will convey the individual directly to a mental hospital, when they consider that to be appropriate. Otherwise the person will be conveyed to the police station for the processing of criminal charges.

In each country, if an individual is conveyed to the police station, a superior officer at the police station may once again exercise his or her discretion as to what to do with the individual. The individual may be released into the custody of family or relatives without any charges being laid, or charges may be laid, or the person may simply be held overnight for further observation. In some larger cities where resources permit, a physician may also come to the police station to assess the individual before that individual appears in court. If the accused is held in custody by the police, the accused will normally be required to be brought before a magistrate or justice of the peace within a relatively short period of time.[179] The court will then be responsible for deciding whether further action should be taken in regard to the accused's mental state.

Although the police in each country have the discretion to officially divert such persons from the criminal justice system by not laying charges and conveying them to mental health facilities for psychiatric assistance, statistics on the frequency of such practices are not readily available. The decision to divert to the mental health system rather than to invoke the criminal justice system will be influenced by the seriousness of the criminal incident, the nature of the accused's mental disorder, the availability of mental health services for such persons, and the general attitude of the

---

179 For example, in Canada, Malaysia, and Singapore, when the police arrest a person, that person must be brought before a judge without unreasonable delay and in any event within 24 hours (Canadian *Criminal Code*, s. 503; *Malaysian Criminal Procedure Code*, ss. 28, 42, and 117). In Japan the police may detain a suspect for 48 hours and the prosecutor may detain the suspect for an additional 24 hours before petitioning the court for an order for further detention of the suspect: See F. Bennett Jr., "Pre-Trial Detention in Japan" (1990) 23 *Law in Japan: An Annual* at 67. In Thailand, an arrested person may be kept in police custody for 48 hours (which may be extended to 7 days if necessary to complete the investigation) before being brought before a court. If more time is required to complete the inquiry, the prosecutor or inquiry official must apply to the court for a warrant authorizing further detention (Thai *Code of Criminal Procedure*, s. 87). For a description of Thai criminal procedure, see P. Kovilaikook, "The Legal System of Thailand," in ASEAN Law Association, *ASEAN Legal Systems*, *infra* note 242 at 406-408 and 416-19. In Indonesia, *Law No. 8/1981 on Criminal Procedure* specifies the maximum length of duration of detention at each stage of the criminal process – investigation, prosecution, and trial. Initial detention by an investigator can be for 20 days, and that can be extended by a public prosecutor for 40 more days: J.'t Hart, *supra* note 171 at 175.

police as to the appropriateness of diverting certain cases to the mental health system. In Canada, police officers seem quite reluctant to exercise their discretionary powers to divert the mentally disordered. In general, they prefer to lay charges and pass the decision on to the prosecutor or courts.[180] The same appears to be the case in Singapore and Malaysia, whereas police diversion seems to occur more often in Japan and perhaps in Thailand.[181]

In Japan the police discretion not to lay charges is quite broad and is used extensively, especially in regard to "minor crimes." For example, in 1978, 21% of suspects who could have been charged with criminal offences were instead released without charges being laid pursuant to article 246 of the *Code of Criminal Procedure,* which authorizes the police to close "simple" cases that have been specifically designated as such by the public prosecutor. Statistics suggest that between 1975 and 1980, countrywide, the police disposed of nearly 18% of all criminal code offences (excluding criminal code traffic offences) without charges. In the city of Tokyo itself, it has been estimated that the police dispose of up to 40% of minor cases without referring them to the prosecutor's office for a further decision as to prosecution.[182]

The most frequently encountered cases disposed of by the police without further reference to the prosecutor's office are assaults, thefts, fraud, embezzlement, and gambling.[183] These referrals are made because these offences are considered less serious offences, suspects have shown remorse, restitution has been made, or victims have expressed forgiveness.[184] How many occur because of the person's mental disorder is not known.

In common with the police, prosecutors in all the countries under study have a wide discretion not to lay or proceed with criminal charges. Again,

180 Schiffer, *supra* note 173 at 16.

181 In Thailand, one study reported that 23% of forensic psychiatric examinations were instituted by the police while approximately 70% were made by the court: T. Dasananjali, "The Characteristics of Psychiatric Referrals from Police" (1986), 15(1) Thailand Jour. of Forensic Science 23-30. The police referrals for psychiatric examination involved many instances of violent crimes as well as some less serious property crimes.

182 Haley, *supra* note 153 at 126. In regard to the prosecutor's discretion and independence from the judiciary, see George, *supra* note 177 at 49-50 and M. Goodman, "The Exercise and Control of Prosecutorial Discretion in Japan" (1986) 5 Pacific Basin L.J. 16. In regard to the police discretion not to proceed with criminal charges and the relationship between the police and the prosecutor, see George, *supra* note 177 at 50-54. For further discussion of the police discretion to dispose of cases without referral to the prosecutor's office, in accordance with a set of criteria that are normally promulgated by the prosecutor's office in regard to less serious crimes where the accused is not considered especially dangerous, see N. Araki, "The Flow of Criminal Cases in the Japanese Criminal Justice System" (1985) 31 Crime and Delinquency 601 at 609-10.

183 George, *supra* note 177 at 51 n. 94.

184 *Ibid.* and Haley, *supra* note 153 at 129.

the fact that a person is mentally disordered may be one factor that will influence the prosecutor not to lay or proceed with criminal charges.[185] In Canada, Singapore, and Malaysia, the prosecutor's discretion is not specified in the codes of criminal procedure but is derived from the British common law tradition of prosecutorial discretion. In Japan and Thailand, this discretion is formally recognized in their codes of criminal procedure. In Thailand, the prosecutor has the power to issue a non-prosecution order,[186] and in Japan the prosecutor may order a suspension of prosecution (kiso yüyo) "in which as a formal matter the decision whether or not to file an accusatory instrument is held in abeyance, pending a suspect's future behaviour."[187] The suspension is in effect until the normal limitation period for institution of criminal charges has expired. This period may be five, ten, or fifteen years depending on the seriousness of the offence.[188]

The Japanese practice of prosecutorial suspension of prosecution is guided in general by the factors mentioned in section 248 of the Japanese *Code of Criminal Procedure* which states: "If, after considering the character, age and situation of the offender, the gravity of the offence, the circumstances under which the offence was committed, and the conditions subsequent to the commission of the offence, prosecution is deemed unnecessary, the prosecution may not be instituted." Suspension of prosecutions are used in up to 10% of all criminal cases, including serious as well as minor cases.[189] For

185 In all countries under study, once the police have transferred a case to the prosecutor's office, the police have no further role to play in deciding whether criminal charges will proceed. The decision lies within the sole discretion of the prosecutor. As mentioned earlier, this is not subject to judicial oversight or review as occurs under western European systems, such as in Germany.

186 Under the Thai *Code of Criminal Procedure*, ordinary police officers have the power to conduct investigations in criminal cases (s. 17), while certain senior police officers (inquiry officials) are authorized to conduct inquiries. No criminal charges are laid without an inquiry (s. 120). In some circumstances, the inquiry officer may refrain from holding an inquiry (s. 122) or may settle the case (ss. 37-38), if the offender voluntarily agrees to pay a fine or compensation to the injured party in an amount set by the inquiry official. If an inquiry is conducted, the officer will send the inquiry file to the prosecutor with a recommendation as to whether a prosecution or non-prosecution order should be made (s. 141). The prosecutor will then decide whether "to close the inquiry" by issuing a non-prosecution order, or issue a prosecution order and prefer a charge against the alleged offender (s. 143).

187 Japanese *Code of Criminal Procedure*, s. 248. The procedure of suspension of prosecution is distinct from the situation where charges are not laid because of lack of evidence or death of the alleged offender etc, or from situations where charges are laid but later withdrawn. See Araki, *supra* note 182 at 615 and George, *supra* note 177 at 56-60.

188 Japanese *Code of Criminal Procedure*, s. 250. George, *supra* note 177 at 59-60.

189 Haley, *supra* note 153 at 128. Haley notes further (at 129):

> by almost any standard criminal justice in Japan is extraordinarily lenient. Large numbers of offenders identified by the police are never reported as suspects by the procuracy. Of those reported, most are convictable. Yet the vast majority are

example, in 1982, 1072 homicides were prosecuted in Japan but there were an additional 75 homicides in which prosecution was suspended, often on the basis that the alleged offender was thought to be insane.[190] In this respect there is a significant difference between Canadian and Japanese practice.

In Canada, on a serious charge such as murder, the prosecutor would almost always prefer a charge and allow the court to decide at trial whether the accused is unfit to stand trial or not guilty on account of insanity. In Japan, in cases where insanity may be an issue, the prosecutor will have the suspect examined by a psychiatrist, and if the psychiatrist is of the view that the suspect is insane, the prosecutor may report the suspect to the governor of the prefecture (district or province) instead of instituting a prosecution. The governor may arrange for the suspect's commitment to a mental hospital under the *Mental Health Act*.[191]

> allowed to take advantage of summary proceedings that result in minor fines equivalent to a few hundred dollars. For many others, prosecution is routinely suspended. Even though prosecution of those that remain seems tantamount to conviction in ordinary trials, sentences are generally suspended in more than half of all cases. Except for detention during police interrogation, few offenders, it appears, ever see the inside of a jail.

Prevailing societal values in Japan encourage confession and repentance. Those who confess and show remorse are rewarded with a lenient response in terms of non-prosecution or a more lenient sentence if prosecution proceeds. However Haley notes (*ibid.* at 135) that:

> for whatever reason, Western societies failed to develop institutional props for implementing such moral commands. Instead the legal institutions and processes of Western law reflect and reinforce societal demands for retribution and revenge ... In the United States punishment is favored as the primary response to crime. In Japan compensation is considered far more important ... the Japanese may well prefer compensation because their system works. Americans, on the other hand, may seek punishment because theirs does not.

190 Araki, *supra* note 182 at 617. To the same effect, see Y. Satsumi and S. Oda, "Mentally Ill Offenders Referred for Psychiatric Examination in Japan" (1995) 18 Int'l J. of Law and Psychiatry 323.

191 Salzberg, *supra* note 80 at 149-50 explains that one form of involuntary commitment known as "hospital measures" existed under the old 1950 *Mental Hygiene Law* and is continued under the new *Mental Health Law, 1987*. Salzberg explains this commitment procedure in the following words:

> It is initiated by a request to the prefectural governor from a member of the general public seeking an examination of and necessary protection (*hogo*) for a person who is or who is suspected to be mentally disordered or by a report to the governor from the medical superintendent of a mental hospital, a police officer, public prosecutor, head of a probation office, or of any correctional institution.
>
> Having received such a request or report, or on his own initiative, the governor must order the person concerned examined by a physician certified by the [Ministry of Health and Welfare] for the performance of certain medical tasks provided in the Law. If upon that examination, the person is deemed to be a mentally disordered person and likely to cause injury to himself or others by reason of that mental disorder unless hospitalized, the governor may commit that person to a prefectural or designated hospital.

Remands for Psychiatric Examination

The codes of criminal procedure in all the countries under study anticipate the need under certain circumstances to have a medical or psychiatric examination of the accused's mental state. Such an examination may provide essential information in deciding whether the accused is mentally fit to stand trial, or whether the accused should be relieved from criminal responsibility because he or she was insane at the time of the offence. Such an examination may also provide useful information for sentencing or disposition purposes.

The criminal procedure provisions in the various countries under study (including those in the Canadian *Criminal Code* until its 1992 amendments) share many common features. To begin, legal provisions concerning remands for psychiatric examination are brief and (surprisingly) lacking in detail. This may be attributed to many factors: (1) for the most part, the provisions were drafted a long time ago when medical and especially psychiatric resources were either scarce or non-existent; and (2) there may be less concern for legal safeguards when procedures involving a deprivation of liberty are carried out by doctors or psychiatrists whose apparent purpose is to act benevolently in the patients' best interests, as opposed to procedures carried out by police or prosecutors in regard to their law enforcement duties. This latter attitude has undergone a radical change in Western countries since the 1960s, but less so in Asian countries. Growing scepticism about psychiatry and its coercive use in both criminal and civil law contexts has become part of the increasing preoccupation (some might say fetish) of the West in regard to individual rights and freedoms. This emphasis in the West on individual rights and legalism can be clearly seen at work in the 1992 amendments to the mental disorder provisions of the Canadian *Criminal Code*.

The following comments can be made concerning the remand provisions in the Asian countries and in Canada before 1992. First, the purposes for

---

> Once hospitalized the patient is to be examined by two or more certified physicians who must each agree with the initial diagnosis, that the patient is likely to injure himself or others by reason of his mental disorder unless placed under involuntary hospitalization measures.
>
> Procedures for this type of involuntary hospitalization are essentially the same under both the old and new Laws. The 1950 Law, however, established no criteria to be followed in determining whether a person is likely to injure oneself or others by reason of mental disorder unless hospitalized. Such criteria have now been promulgated by regulation under the 1988 Law.

In recent years, commitments under this procedure have dropped from 30% of commitments in 1970 to 6% in 1987: Salzberg, *ibid.* See also Araki, *supra* note 182 at 615 n. 12; J. Takeuchi, *Introduction to the Preparatory Draft for the Revised Penal Code of Japan, 1961* (American Series of Foreign Penal Codes, No. 8) (Littleton, Colorado: F. B. Rothman, 1964) at 14.

ordering a psychiatric remand may not be specified at all, as in the case of the Japanese *Code of Criminal Procedure,*[192] or may be expressly but perhaps unintentionally confined only to examinations for fitness to stand trial and may not refer to the power to remand for observation to assess whether the accused was insane at the time of the offence. The latter situation occurs in the criminal procedure codes in Thailand,[193] Malaysia, Singapore,[194] and Canada (before 1992).[195] Second, the provisions in the Japanese, Thai,

---

192 Japanese *Code of Criminal Procedure*, art. 167: "When expert evidence is required in respect to the mental or physical condition of the accused, a court (by writ of confinement) may, if necessary, confine the accused in a hospital or other proper place for a fixed period ... A court may, if necessary, extend or shorten the period of confinement."

See also the Japanese *Rules of Criminal Procedure*, art. 130-2: "The writ of confinement for expert evidence shall contain ... the place where to detain him, the period of confinement, the purpose of taking expert evidence." Japan does not have special forensic psychiatric units as in Canada and the United States. Initial psychiatric assessments of accused persons are normally done in detention centres, but when medical tests or a formal assessment is required, a court can order that the accused be examined in a hospital. A brief pre-trial examination can normally be conducted in seven to ten days while a formal psychiatric examination may take three months: Satsumi and Oda, *supra* note 190.

193 Thailand *Code of Criminal Procedure*, s. 14: "Whilst holding an inquiry, preliminary examination or trial, if there is reason to believe that the alleged offender or accused is of unsound mind and is unable to put up a defence, the inquiry official or the court, as the case may be, shall instruct a medical officer to examine such person. After the examination, the medical officer shall be summoned to make a statement or testify as to the result of the examination."

194 The provisions in the Singapore and Malaysian Codes of Criminal Procedure are nearly identical, although there are some small differences. The relevant provisions may be summarized as follows:

(1) If a judge or magistrate holding a trial or inquiry has reason to suspect that the accused person is of unsound mind and consequently incapable of making his defence, the judge or magistrate shall investigate the issues (which investigation may but need not involve the opinion of a medical officer) [Singapore, s. 307(1) and (2); Malaysia, s. 342(1) and (2)].

(2) If after this investigation the judge or magistrate is not satisfied that the suspect is capable of making his defence, the judge or magistrate may remand the person for 30 days for observation in any mental hospital [Singapore, s. 307(3); Malaysia, s. 342(3)].

(3) At any stage of any proceedings before trial, the public prosecutor may order that an accused person whom he suspects to be of unsound mind be sent to a mental hospital for observation for a period not exceeding one month [Singapore, s. 307(5); Malaysia, s. 342(5)].

(4) The medical superintendent may request a further remand of two months if necessary to form his opinion as to the accused's state of mind. The judge or prosecutor [in Malaysia, but not in Singapore], as the case may be, may order the accused person to be detained for a further period not exceeding two months [Singapore, s. 307(5); Malaysia, s. 342(5)].

(5) If the medical superintendent certifies that the accused is of sound mind and capable of making his defence, the judge or magistrate shall, *unless satisfied to the contrary*, proceed with the trial or inquiry; if the medical superintendent certifies that the accused is of unsound mind and incapable of making his defence, the judge or

Malaysian, Singaporean, and Canadian codes refer to an examination by a medical officer with no requirement that the medical officer be trained in psychiatry. This was understandable at the time when most of these provisions were enacted, since there were very few trained psychiatrists, especially in the Asian countries.

Third, the provision in the Thai and Japanese codes authorizes an examination of the accused, while the Singapore, Malaysian and pre-1992 Canadian codes refer to detaining the accused for observation. Apart from observation or examination, none of these codes specifically states that the accused may also be treated involuntarily if necessary for his/her mental illness. In practice, such treatment will be given when necessary even though the legal authority for such treatment is not specified.[196]

Fourth, the period for which an accused is remanded into custody for the purpose of conducting a mental examination may be longer than necessary to accomplish the assigned task. The Thai and Japanese codes do not specify any time limit on the length of medical examination. The Singaporean, Malaysian, and pre-1992 Canadian codes specify a period of up to 30 days, which may be extended to 60 or 90 days if deemed necessary. The same 30 to 90 day time periods also apply in Indonesia. A medical examination for the purposes of determining whether an accused is fit to stand trial can normally be completed in a matter of a few hours or a few days, whereas an examination for the purposes of the insanity defence may take much longer. However, it is highly questionable whether the practice of ordering 30 day remands should be the standard practice for fitness remands. It should also be noted that the codes in Japan, Thailand, Malaysia, Singapore, and pre-1992 Canada assume that remands will be in custody at a mental hospital. The codes do not direct a court to consider, on a case by case basis, the feasibility or appropriateness of "out-patient" psychiatric examinations.

---

magistrate shall, if satisfied of the fact, find accordingly and postpone the inquiry or trial [Singapore, s. 308(1); Malaysia, s. 343(1)]. [The words emphasized above appear only in the Singapore code. This means that the medical opinion that the accused's mind is "sound" is conclusive in Malaysia without the court exercising its own independent judgment on the matter.]

(6) If the trial or inquiry is postponed, the judge or magistrate may release the accused into the care of an appropriate person upon sufficient security if the offence is bailable. If the offence is not bailable the accused will be remanded to a mental hospital for safe custody to await the pleasure of the ruler of the state (or minister in Singapore) [Singapore, s. 309; Malaysia, s. 344].

195 Canadian *Criminal Code*, s. 537(1)(b) and (2)-(4) and s. 615(2),(3) (prior to 1992).

196 M. Cheang, "Fitness to Plead in Singapore and Malaysia" (1988) 17 Anglo-American L. Rev. 209 at 220. It should be noted that, although s. 309 of the Singapore *Code of Criminal Procedure* authorizes a psychiatric remand "for observation" and not treatment, Form 5, which is the Magistrate's order for detention, specifies that the person be detained "for care and treatment."

Fifth, in some countries, including Thailand and Canada, the power to order a psychiatric remand is given only to a judge or magistrate. In Japan, the prosecutor may divert a suspect to the prefectural governor who can arrange for a medical examination, but in Malaysia and Singapore the Public Prosecutor has the power at any time before trial to order that an accused person be remanded to a mental hospital for observation.[197]

In Canada, the 1992 amendments to the *Criminal Code* concerning mental disorder involved the following changes:

(1) the various purposes for ordering a psychiatric remand are now specified in the Code

(2) the Code specifically states that psychiatric remands are for assessment and observation and not for treatment (any treatment that may occur would have to be done with the accused's consent or under the provisions of the *Mental Health Act*)

(3) assessments to determine whether an accused is unfit to stand trial shall be for no more than five days, excluding holidays and travel time, whereas assessment orders for other purposes (e.g., insanity defence, sentencing, etc.) shall not normally exceed 30 days

(4) the Code now creates a presumption against in-custody orders; a judge shall not order an in-custody assessment unless custody is necessary to conduct the medical assessment or custody is otherwise justified under the normal bail provisions of the Code; notwithstanding this new provision, in practice most remands are still in custody, since out-patient facilities are limited and not always suitable for such assessment

(5) before 1992, there were no provisions in the *Criminal Code* dealing with the admissibility at trial of statements made by the accused to psychiatrists or staff during a psychiatric remand. Canadian courts exhibited some uncertainty and disagreement as to the admissibility of such statements. As a result, defence counsel sometimes advised an accused to remain silent during a psychiatric examination, or at least to avoid making any statements that might incriminate the accused. The 1992 amendments now provide that statements made by an accused during the course of a psychiatric assessment are admissible at a fitness hearing, but not at trial without the accused's consent, unless the accused puts his/her capacity for criminal intent into issue, or the accused's testimony at trial is inconsistent with something the accused said during the psychiatric assessment.

Unfitness to Stand Trial

The legal provisions dealing with accused persons who are unfit to stand

197 *Supra* note 191 and note 194, para. 3. In Indonesia, the prosecutor's only power seems to be to seek a civil commitment of the accused: *infra* note 198.

trial are in many respects very similar to one another in the countries under study. And, like the legal provisions dealing with psychiatric remands, these provisions are short on detail, as the following discussion illustrates.

Definition

In general, the concept of being unfit to stand trial is inadequately defined in all the codes. To start, it should be noted that, in Indonesia, the *Code of Criminal Procedure* does not seem to deal at all with situations where the accused, before or during a trial, becomes incapable of conducting his/her defence due to mental illness. However the State Law on Prosecutors does give the prosecutor the power to seek a civil commitment of the accused in a mental hospital.[198]

In Japan, section 314 of the *Criminal Procedure Code* states that, after hearing the opinion of the public prosecutor, defence counsel, and a medical expert, the trial shall be stayed "if the accused is in a state of insanity" and shall remain stayed "during the continuance of such state." The Japanese Code does not define the expression "a state of insanity" and, more surprisingly, does not even mention that the state of insanity must be of such a nature as to render the accused incapable of defending him/her self. In reality, fitness to stand trial is rarely assessed by Japanese courts, since prosecutors often divert such cases before they get to court.

In Thailand, section 14 of the *Code of Criminal Procedure* states that where "the alleged offender or accused is of unsound mind and is unable to put up a defence," the inquiry official or court shall suspend the proceedings until that person recovers. The same language – "unsound mind" and "incapable of making his defence" – is used in the Singapore (section 307) and Malaysian (section 342) Codes of Criminal Procedure. And the language used in the pre-1992 Canadian *Criminal Code*[199] is "incapable of conducting his defence on account of insanity." In none of these codes are the expressions "unsound mind" or "insanity" or "incapable of conducting his defence" defined. Nor do the codes specify that the expressions "unsound mind" or "insanity" have one meaning for the purposes of the "fitness to stand trial" test and a very different meaning for the "criminally responsible" test. These matters of definition have been left up to the courts in each country. By and large, the courts have given a very broad meaning to the expressions

---

198 M. Reksodiputro, "Exclusion of Punishment in the Indonesian Criminal Justice System: A Discussion of Article 44 of the Criminal Code" (Paper delivered at the *Symposium on Juridical Aspects of Mentally Ill Patients*, Jakarta, Indonesia, 23 Nov. 1993) [unpublished].

199 The 1992 amendments to the Canadian *Criminal Code* have changed the word "insanity" to "mental disorder" and also specify that mental disorder means "disease of the mind." But the courts have still been left the task to define "disease of the mind" for the purposes of the fitness rule and the insanity defence.

"unsoundness of mind" or "insanity" for the purposes of the fitness rule.[200] The courts' conception of the criteria for determining whether a person is fit or unfit are also fairly similar. In general these criteria include the ability to understand the nature of the proceedings and to participate in them (that is, to understand the evidence and protect one's rights).[201] In the 1992 amendments to the Canadian *Criminal Code*, a definition of "unfit to stand trial" has been expressly included.[202]

Quantum and Burden of Proof

The pre-1992 Canadian *Criminal Code* did not specify the quantum of proof required to find an accused person unfit, nor did it specify which party (prosecution, accused, or judge) bore the onus of proof. This same situation prevails in the Codes of the other countries under study. In the absence of express legislative provisions, courts in Canada, Malaysia, and Singapore have followed English common law, which presumes that accused persons are sane and therefore places the burden of proving unfitness on a balance of probabilities on the person who alleges unfitness (whether that be the defence or prosecution or judge).[203]

---

200 Dando, *supra* note 160 at 117 nn. 5 and 6; Cheang, *supra* note 196 at 212-13; Schiffer, *supra* note 173 at 65.

201 For example, the Japanese Supreme Court has defined fitness as "the capacity to understand the significance of a given procedural act ... and to protect one's own rights." Dando, *supra* note 160 at 117 n. 6. In Singapore, Malaysia, and Canada the courts have relied upon definitions set down in English cases such as *R. v. Roberts*, [1953] 2 All E.R. 340, [1954] 2 Q.B. 329, in which the courts have referred to factors such as the ability to: (1) understand the nature of the charges against him/her and the possible consequences of a conviction. The understanding required is only what an ordinary person would understand; (2) appreciate what an oath is and the penalty for lying under oath; (3) understand the difference between guilty and not guilty; (4) know who the participants in the trial proceeding are; (5) concentrate, participate, instruct, and receive instructions from counsel. With respect to the requirement of instructing counsel, certainly it is not expected of the accused to give detailed instructions to counsel as to how to conduct his/her defence. What it amounts to, is whether he/she is able to tell counsel his/her version of the facts; (6) to answer to the charge against him/her; (7) to challenge witnesses.

202 Canadian *Criminal Code*, as amended 1992, s. 2 states that "unfit to stand trial" means "unable on account of mental disorder to conduct a defence at any stage of the proceedings before a verdict is rendered or to instruct counsel to do so, and, in particular, unable on account of mental disorder to (a) understand the nature or object of the proceedings, (b) understand the possible consequences of the proceedings, or (c) communicate with counsel."

203 Cheang, *supra* note 196 at 217-20; Schiffer, *supra* note 173 at 73-76. S. 672.22 of the 1992 amendments to the Canadian *Criminal Code* now expressly states that "an accused is presumed fit to stand trial unless the court is satisfied on the balance of probabilities that the accused is unfit to stand trial." And s. 672.32 states that once a court finds that an accused is unfit, the burden of proof that the accused has subsequently become fit to stand trial is on the party who asserts it and is discharged by proof on the balance of probabilities.

Right to Assigned Counsel

The Japanese and Canadian codes specifically state that where an accused person is suspected of being insane, defence counsel shall be assigned to that person.[204] This safeguard is not expressly provided for in the other codes, although it may be possible in some countries for a court to exercise an inherent jurisdiction to appoint counsel where it is deemed necessary in the interests of justice. However, it should be noted that legal representation is less frequent in Asian countries than in Canada, where the per capita size of the legal profession is much larger and the availability of free legal aid is much greater.

Procedures to Try the Issue of Fitness

All the codes under study are silent on the procedures that should be used in trying the issue of whether an accused is unfit to stand trial. The appropriate procedures are left up to the inquiry official or judge, as the case may be.

Postponing the Issue of Fitness

In Thailand, Malaysia, and Singapore,[205] the codes of criminal procedure do not have a provision similar to s. 615(5) of the pre-1992 Canadian *Criminal Code*, which grants the court the power to postpone the inquiry into the accused's fitness until the end of the case for the prosecution.[206] If the prosecutor has not proven the accused guilty at this stage, the trial judge may acquit the accused without trying the issue of the accused's fitness to stand trial. Section 314(1) of the Japanese *Code of Criminal Procedure* also specifies that the issue of fitness need not be tried in cases where there are "obvious reasons" for entering an acquittal or a dismissal of prosecution.

Disposition of Persons Found Unfit for Trial

The provisions for disposition of unfit persons in the various codes are lacking in detail and in safeguards for the rights of the unfit. The Japanese and Indonesian penal codes are silent on what a court should do with an accused person who has been found unfit, although presumably the court could instigate a civil commitment process. According to the Thai *Code of Criminal Procedure*, where an inquiry official or the court is of the opinion that an alleged offender or accused is unfit, the inquiry official or court has

204 Japanese *Code of Criminal Procedure*, art. 37(4); Canadian *Criminal Code*, s. 672.24.

205 See e.g. Cheang, *supra* note 196 at 211.

206 The power to postpone the trial of the fitness issue has been expanded further in s. 672.25 of the 1992 amendments to the Canadian *Criminal Code* to allow postponement up until the time for the opening of the case for the defence or "on motion of the accused, any later time that the court may direct."

the discretion to commit that person to a lunatic asylum, or to release the unfit accused to any other person willing to take charge of the accused.[207] In the pre-1992 Canadian *Criminal Code*, a court had no discretion to release an unfit accused; the matter of confinement in a mental hospital or release was left to the unreviewable discretion of the lieutenant governor of the province.[208] In Malaysia and Singapore, the court has a discretion in the case of bailable offences to release an unfit person into the care of family or friends, but in non-bailable offences the court must commit the unfit person pending an order of the ruler of the state (in Malaysia) or the minister (in Singapore).[209]

The major problem with the above disposition provisions is that they authorize, under the criminal law power, the indefinite commitment of unfit persons who have not yet been convicted of any crime. Their period of commitment may far exceed in length any sentence of imprisonment that they would have received even if they were found guilty. The length of commitment is in the discretion of a senior representative of the state (for example, the ruler, the minister, or the lieutenant governor) who may be advised periodically (usually every six or twelve months) by a review board or a board of visitors as to the need for continued detention of the unfit person. But the review board's or visitor's opinion is advice only and need not be followed by the ruler, minister, or lieutenant governor.

The 1992 Canadian *Criminal Code* amendments have tried to respond to these concerns:

(1) by requiring the court (or review board) to release the accused "if the accused is not a significant threat to the safety of the public," or to otherwise make the least onerous and least restrictive disposition[210]
(2) by making review board decisions binding rather than advisory, and by allowing judicial review of review board decisions;[211]
(3) by instituting regular reviews[212]
(4) by requiring the state (at least every 2 years) to convince a court that the state still has "sufficient evidence to put the accused on trial"[213]

---

207 Thai *Code of Criminal Procedure*, s. 14.

208 Canadian *Criminal Code*, ss. 614-617.

209 Malaysian *Code of Criminal Procedure*, s. 344; Singapore *Code of Criminal Procedure*, s. 309.

210 Canadian *Criminal Code*, s. 672.54. In *Winko v. B.C. (Forensic Psychiatric Institute)* (1996), 112 C.C.C. (3d) 31 (B.C.C.A.) and *R. v. Lepage* (1997), 119 C.C.C. (3d) 193 (Ont. C.A.), the courts have held that this provision, which authorizes an insane acquittee's detention if he or she is a significant threat to the safety of the public, does not violate that person's fundamental rights and freedoms under the *Canadian Charter of Rights and Freedoms*.

211 *Ibid.* at ss. 672.47-672.53 and 672.72-672.80.

212 *Ibid.* at ss. 672.81-672.85.

213 *Ibid.* at s. 672.33.

(5) by putting a cap on the length of time an unfit person may be confined; the time varies with the seriousness of the offence. Unfortunately this "capping" provision has not yet been proclaimed.[214]

The Insanity Defence

The penal codes, in all countries under study, include a provision on the insanity defence. These provisions vary somewhat in language, but they are all the product in one way or another of the creation and development of the insanity defence in Western criminal law during the past two centuries. That creation and development has been accompanied, at least in Western countries, by a vigorous legal, medical, and public debate on the subject. The debate has included concerns about the nature, scope, rationale, and definition of the insanity defence, about the role of medical and psychiatric experts in establishing the defence, and about the disposition of persons who have committed crimes while insane. In light of the very large literature that exists on the topic (at least in Western countries), only a few comparative comments will be made on the subject here.

The Scope of the Defence

Whether they follow it exactly or not, the legal provisions on the insanity defence in the countries under study have been greatly influenced by the famous case of *M'Naghten* decided in England in 1843.[215] The *M'Naghten* rules restrict the insanity defence to a medical model involving a high level of cognitive impairment. The essential elements of the *M'Naghten* test require proof that at the time of the alleged offence the accused (1) was suffering from a disease of the mind and (2) this disease caused a defect of reason to the extent that the accused person (a) did not know the nature and quality of his/her act, or (b) if he/she did know the nature and quality of the act, did not know that it was wrong. The meaning of the key words in the above test – "disease of the mind," "defect of reason," "know," "nature and quality," "wrong" – have been the subject of extensive judicial scrutiny and immense academic debate. But even with a liberal interpretation, the test is still a fairly restrictive one since it incorporates only cognitive impairment. The test has been criticized by many commentators for not including within its scope volitional impairment (inability to control one's conduct) and affective impairment (impairment of emotions, feelings, etc.). Some jurisdictions have recognized these latter components through legislative or judicial expansion of the *M'Naghten* test.

Where do the countries under study stand in regard to the scope of the insanity defence? The insanity defence provisions in the penal codes of

---

214 *Ibid.* at s. 672.64.

215 (1843) 8 E.R. 718.

Canada,[216] Malaysia, and Singapore[217] have been strongly influenced by the *M'Naghten* test, particularly in restricting the test solely to cognitive impairment. However, the language used in the codes is not identical to the language used in the *M'Naghten* test. There has been an unfortunate tendency by courts in Canada, Malaysia, and Singapore to ignore the precise wording in their own penal provisions and to apply English principles and precedents concerning the *M'Naghten* test as if they were in all respects identical to *M'Naghten*. This tendency has disappeared in Canada in the past 20 years, but it still seems to linger in Malaysia and Singapore.[218] One may expect to see it increasingly disappear in the latter two countries as they continue to distance themselves from the effects of colonial rule.

The Japanese *Penal Code*, enacted in 1907, and the Taiwan *Criminal Code* followed the model in the French *Penal Code* where insanity is recognized as a defence but not defined.[219] Although the insanity defence has not been frequently litigated or judicially defined in Japan, the courts there have apparently recognized both cognitive impairment and volitional impairment as part of the insanity defence.[220] The Indonesian *Penal Code*, which came into force in 1918, follows the original Dutch *Penal Code* provision, which restricts the insanity defence to a defect or disorder of the intellectual faculties.[221] Thus the test is only cognitive in its scope. There

216 S. 16 (1) of the Canadian *Criminal Code* states: "No person is criminally responsible for an act committed or an omission made while suffering from a mental disorder that rendered the person incapable of appreciating the nature and quality of the act, or that he is doing what is either wrong or contrary to law."

217 S. 84 of the Malaysian and Singapore Penal Codes are the same and state: "Nothing is an offence which is done by a person who, at the time of doing it, by reason of unsoundness of mind, is incapable of knowing the nature of the act or omission or of knowing that it was wrong."

218 Ferguson, *supra* note 147 at 4-7.

219 Art. 39 of the Japanese *Penal Code* states (under "Insanity: Weak-mindedness"): "An act of an insane person is not punishable ... Punishment shall be reduced for acts of weak-minded persons." S. 19 of the Taiwan *Criminal Code* provides that an accused cannot be convicted of an offence if insane at the time of the offence.

220 Takeuchi, *supra* note 191 at 6 and 8, suggests that the insanity defence in the Preparatory Draft for the *Revised Penal Code* of Japan, 1961 is primarily derived from the insanity test as developed by the courts under the existing art. 39. Art. 14 of the Draft Penal Code proposed to define the insanity defence along the lines of the American Law Institute Model Penal Code so that mental incapacity either "to discriminate as to the propriety of his conduct" [cognitive incapacity] or "to act according to such discrimination" [volitional incapacity] are both included within the scope of the insanity defence.

221 Reksodiputro, *supra* note 198 at 2. In 1925, the Dutch introduced a law on psychopaths and changed the expression "intellectual faculties" to "mental faculties" in their definition of the insanity defence. However that change was not made to the Indonesian *Penal Code*.

222 Reksodiputro, *ibid.*, states that there are not many cases in which the Indonesian courts have agreed to an insanity defence. He states that he was only able to find three cases in the past six or seven years.

has been very little use and even less judicial discussion of the insanity defence in Indonesia.[222]

In contrast to the other codes, the Thai *Penal Code*, which was first enacted in 1907, appears to have followed the German *Penal Code* model, which recognized both cognitive incapacity and volitional incapacity as part of the insanity defence.[223] As in other Asian countries, there are virtually no judicial interpretations of the insanity defence.[224] Notwithstanding this judicial silence, one study at a Thai mental hospital reported that 18.5% of convicted murderers over a ten-year period (1970-1980) were insane.[225] Two-thirds of those persons were referred to the mental hospital by the police. Most of these persons suffered from paranoia (that is, delusions and/or hallucinations).[226]

In summary, it can be said that apart from Thailand, and perhaps Japan, the legal definition of the insanity defence in the countries under study is restricted to instances of severe cognitive impairment. However, it is not clear that the inclusion of volitional impairment in the insanity defence in Thailand, and perhaps Japan, has resulted in a wider application of the defence in practice. In the first place, it appears that most persons who successfully rely upon the insanity defence in Thailand and Japan are in fact suffering from cognitive impairments (delusions or hallucinations). Second, several studies in the United States have indicated that differences in the exact wording of the defence (that may include or exclude volitional impairment) may not be very significant in the ultimate decision whether the accused is found to be insane or not.[227]

---

223 The drafters of the Thai *Penal Code* of 1907 do not cite the German *Penal Code* as one of the foreign codes they relied upon, so it is quite possible that their decision to include both cognitive and volitional incapacity within the scope of the insanity test may have come from some source other than the German *Penal Code*. The German *Penal Code* was quite influential in the drafting of other European Codes and the Japanese *Penal Code* of 1907. In any event, s. 46 of the 1907 Thai *Penal Code* states: "A person shall not be punished for any act done by him if at the time it is done he is prevented either by defective mental power or by any disease effecting his mind from appreciating the nature or illegality of his act, or from controlling his own conduct."

The insanity defence is now found in s. 65 of the Thai *Penal Code* as revised in 1956. S. 65 continues to include both cognitive and volitional incapacity within the definition of insanity. See e.g. T. Dasananjali et al., "Criminal Law Review on the Concept of Dangerousness" (1981) 64(5) J. Med. Assn. Thailand 236.

224 This observation was made in 1992 in a conversation with Professor Apirat Petchsiri, Faculty of Law, Chulalongkorn University, Bangkok, Thailand.

225 T. Dasananjali, "Insane Murderer" (1986) 38 Siriraj Hosp. Gaz. 347-51.

226 *Ibid.*

227 See G. Ferguson, "A Critique of Proposals to Reform the Insanity Defence" (1989) 14 Queen's L.J. 135 at 143 (1989); Petrila, "The Insanity Defense and Other Mental Health Dispositions in Missouri" (1982) 5 Int'l J. of Law and Psychiatry 81; G. H. Morris, *The Insanity Defense: A Blueprint for Legislative Reform* (Lexington, Mass: Lexington Books, 1975) at 23-24; R. J. Simon, *The Jury and the Defense of Insanity* (Boston: Little, Brown, 1967) c. 10.

Another consideration in assessing each country's approach to mental disorder as a defence is whether that country recognizes a defence of diminished responsibility due to mental disorder short of insanity. Canada,[228] Malaysia, and Indonesia do not. However in its 1956 recodification, Thailand added a diminished responsibility provision to its penal code by stating that, if a person is only partially able to appreciate or control his conduct due to mental disorder, the accused will be convicted but the punishment may be reduced. A similar provision, but drafted in a vague and inadequate form, exists in the Japanese Code.[229] Clear revisions to that section were proposed in the Draft *Penal Code* for Japan in 1961, but that code was never enacted.[230] In 1961, Singapore enacted a diminished responsibility defence quite different than the one in Thailand and Japan. The Singapore provision is based on the limited concept of diminished responsibility, which was enacted in England by section 2(1) of the *Homicide Act*, 1957. It applies only to persons who are charged with murder and whose mental responsibility was substantially impaired by an abnormality of the mind short of insanity.[231] If successful, the accused is acquitted of murder and convicted instead of the lesser offence of culpable homicide not amounting to murder (or in England, of manslaughter) and normally sentenced to prison (with the hope that psychiatric treatment will be provided there).[232] Although originally intended to supplement the insanity defence, there is some concern in England that it has a tendency to displace the insanity defence in

---

228 In Canada, the defence of no *mens rea* due to mental disorder short of insanity has been used to reduce murder to manslaughter and in that sense it could be likened to the defence of diminished responsibility. However, it will normally not work for a person who knows what he or she is doing, but cannot resist it, since that person will have *mens rea*. See D. Stuart, *Canadian Criminal Law: A Treatise*, 3d ed. (Toronto: Carswell, 1995) at 366-70.

229 Japanese *Penal Code*, art. 39(2) provides: "Punishment shall be reduced for acts of weak-minded persons." Weak-minded persons are not defined, but are obviously intended to be persons who are, in some unspecified fashion, mentally disordered but not insane.

230 Art. 15 (2) of the *Preparatory Draft Penal Code* for Japan provides: "Punishment for acts of a person whose capacity as set out in paragraph (1) [the insanity defence] is markedly diminished as the result of mental disorder may be reduced."

231 The Singapore *Penal Code*, s. 300, Exception 7, provides: "Culpable homicide is not murder if the offender was suffering from such abnormality of mind (whether arising from a condition of arrested or retarded development of mind or any inherent causes or induced by disease or injury) as substantially impaired his mental responsibility for his acts and omissions in causing the death or being a party to causing the death." See also M. Cheang, "Diminished Responsibility under Singapore Law (An Evaluation)" [1990] J. of Malayan and Comparative Law 29; L. P. Kok, M. Cheang, and K. T. Chee, "Diminished Responsibility: The Position in Singapore" (1987) 16 Anglo-American L. Rev. 268.

232 L. P. Kok, M. Cheang, and K. T. Chee, *Diminished Responsibility with Special Reference to Singapore* (Singapore: Singapore Univ. Press, 1990) at 23, 34, and 156.

murder cases.[233] This does not seem to be the case in Singapore, at least not completely.[234]

The Role of Forensic Experts

Due to its medical-legal nature, the insanity defence invites interaction between the legal profession and the medical profession, and in so doing creates the possibility of disputes and conflict between them. While the issue of what an accused's mental state is or was may be a matter for medical expertise, the issue of whether an accused is or ought to be held criminally responsible and punished is a matter of moral and legal judgment for the courts.

There is a tendency in all the countries under study for the legal profession and the courts to allow these legal-psychiatric decisions to be made in effect by the medical-psychiatric profession. This tendency is more prevalent in some countries than others. For example, in Indonesia, psychiatric reports to the courts on fitness and insanity are typically very short; they are often written using medical/psychiatric terminology, which is different from legal terminology; they are conclusory rather than explanatory; and they do not necessarily address the issues or criteria the courts must apply in arriving at a decision on fitness or insanity.[235]

In Canada and other Western countries such as England and the United States, the tendency to hand over these medico-legal determinations to medical or psychiatric experts has substantially diminished in the past 30 years. This trend might be attributed to the more aggressive nature of the adversary system that operates in these countries, the increased concern with accused persons' legal and civil rights, and a growing scepticism about the accuracy and objectivity of psychiatric opinions.

Disposition of Persons Found Insane

In Malaysia, Singapore, and Canada, the provisions for disposition of persons who are found insane at the time of committing a crime are generally

---

233 See e.g. N. Walker, *Crime and Insanity in England* (Edinburgh: Edinburgh Univ. Press, 1968) at 161; S. Dell, "Diminished Responsibility Reconsidered" [1982] Crim. L. Rev. 809.

234 See e.g. the list of persons suffering from schizophrenia who are found insane rather than in a state of diminished responsibility cited by Kok, *supra* note 232 at 37-40.

235 See Reksodiputro, *supra* note 198 at 6, where the author states that in the three insanity cases that he was able to find, the psychiatric opinions and the medical concepts, not the legal concepts, were the determining factor in the court's decisions as to the accused's insanity. See also the paper on psychiatric reports by W. Darmabrata "Pemeriksaan Psikiatrik Tersangka Gangguan Jiwa" at the *Symposium on Juridical Aspects of Mentally Ill Patients* (Jakarta, Indonesia: 23 Nov. 1993) [unpublished]. In Japan, the rate of agreement between psychiatric experts and the court is no less than 88%: Satsumi and Oda, *supra* note 190.

the same as the disposition provisions for persons who are found unfit to stand trial.[236] In Japan, the Code is silent, since the accused is released unless a civil commitment procedure is initiated.[237] Likewise, in Indonesia, the Code is silent but the court has the power to commit such a person to a mental hospital for up to one year.[238] Presumably continued confinement beyond one year would have to be authorized by a civil commitment process. In Thailand, section 48 of the *Penal Code* authorizes a court, in cases where insanity or diminished responsibility have been established, to order that person "to be put under restraint in hospital" if that person's release would not be safe for the public. The order may be revoked at any time by the court. In Taiwan, section 87 of the *Criminal Code* authorizes a judge to commit a person who has been acquitted of an offence by reason of insanity to a hospital, if there is sufficient evidence that hospitalization is required, and considering the seriousness of the offence and the likelihood of repetition.

In Canada, before the 1992 *Criminal Code* amendments, concerns were raised about the indefinite length of commitment of persons found not guilty on account of insanity and the fact that the release of those insane persons was in the sole discretion of the Lieutenant Governor (who was advised by a review board but not legally bound to follow the review board's recommendations). In addition, the Lieutenant Governor's decision not to release an insane person, even if the review board recommended release, was not reviewable by the courts. In Canada, there was an additional concern that, in insanity cases that had received a lot of publicity, the decision not to release a person might be more influenced by political fear of arousing public criticism of the government than by medical factors as to whether the insane person was now cured and no longer a threat to the community. It would be interesting to discover if similar concerns exist in any of the other countries under study.

---

236 *Supra* notes 208 and 209. The Canadian provisions were altered in 1992 as noted earlier between notes 210 and 214, *supra*. See s. 348 of the *Malaysian Penal Code* which states:

> (1) Whenever the finding states that the accused person committed the act alleged, the Court before which the trial has been held shall, if such act would, but for incapacity found, have constituted an offence, order such person to be kept in safe custody in such place and manner as the Court thinks fit and shall report the case for the orders of the Ruler of the State in which the trial is held: provided that if the Court concerned is a Magistrate's Court, the Magistrate may in his discretion, if he considers that the offence charged is not of a serious nature and that such person can safely be released without danger of his doing injury to himself or any other person, caution and discharge him.
>
> (2) The Ruler may order such person to be confined in a mental hospital during the pleasure of the Ruler of the State.

237 Takeuchi, *supra* note 191 at 14.

238 Reksodiputro, *supra* note 198.

MENTAL DISORDER AND CIVIL LAW

An Overview of Western Influence on Asian Mental Health Laws

In general, modern Western laws on the civil aspects of mental disorder have had limited impact in Asia. That impact varies with each country. On the one hand there is Thailand, which has not yet considered it necessary to enact a mental health law, although there has been some consideration of doing so in recent years.[239] Similarly, Taiwan had no mental health law before the enactment of its first such law in 1990.[240] In Indonesia, the Dutch colonial government issued an *Ordinance on the Mentally Ill* in 1897, which governed the establishment of state mental hospitals. After independence, that ordinance was superseded by the 1966 *Mental Health Act*,[241] which has in turn been superseded by the 1992 *Health Act*. But these Indonesian laws on mental health have not and do not reflect the Western preoccupation with issues such as the legal criteria for involuntary commitment to and release from mental hospitals, the right to refuse treatment, and other patients' rights issues that have been debated and litigated in some Western countries.[242] The 1992 Indonesian *Health Act* has only a few provisions specifically related to the mentally ill,[243] although the Health Ministry is apparently preparing a more detailed *Mental Health Regulation* to fill in some of the details.

Japan's mental health system has evolved in the past 100 years into a system of large scale confinement of mental patients, 85% of whom were

---

239 Dasananjali, *supra* note 104.

240 Salzberg, *supra* note 91.

241 S. O. Gardjito, "Country Report – Indonesia," in D. B. Lubis, ed., *ASEAN Federation for Psychiatry and Mental Health Reports and Directory* (Jakarta: AFPMH Secretariat, Dept. of Psychiatry, Univ. of Indonesia, 1983) at 9-13. Hawari, *supra* note 31.

242 Herkutanto, "Aspek Mediko Legal Pada Gangguan Jiwa" (Paper delivered at the *Symposium on Juridical Aspects of Mentally Ill Patients*, Jakarta, Indonesia, 23 Nov. 1993 [unpublished]. S. Hartono, in "The Legal System of Indonesia – Historical Overview," in ASEAN Law Association, *ASEAN Legal Systems* (Singapore: Butterworths Asia, 1995) at 18 notes that Indonesia attempted between 1950 and 1959 to imitate the liberal democratic governments of European states but soon concluded that this liberal system of government did not support Indonesian social values represented in the five principles of *Pancasila* in the Preamble to the 1945 Constitution. A. B. Nasutin, "Democracy's Struggle in Indonesia," in L. Palmier, ed., *State and Law in East Asia, supra* note 149, argues that the notion of the "integrated state" that prevails under the Indonesian legal and constitutional structure emphasizes national goals of unity, integrity, and stability at the expense of individual interests and rights. Since the state and the people constitute a unity, government leaders are assumed to be acting in the best interest of all the people in situations where it may appear to the western eye that civil rights are being inhibited or limited. Similarly, the judiciary is under the control of the executive to a much greater extent than in western countries and thus courts are less likely to render decisions that favour individual rights over government interests.

243 Herkutanto, *ibid.*

confined until recently in private hospitals under extremely poor conditions and with little or no administrative or legal safeguards. A series of public scandals involving the abuse and deaths of mental patients attracted national attention for more than a two-year period between 1984 and 1986. These scandals also prompted international pressure and resulted in an investigation of and report on Japan's mental health system by the International Commission of Jurists. As a consequence of this national and international pressure, the Japanese government issued a new *Mental Health Law* in 1987 with the stated purpose of "promoting the protection of the human rights of mentally ill patients."[244] Although the 1988 Law does not include all the due process safeguards found in some of the more modern Western mental health laws, it certainly is a significant step in that direction.[245]

Taiwan's first *Mental Health Law* came into force in 1990, but, unlike the Japanese law, it was not created as a reaction to any national and international pressure concerning human rights abuses of mental patients.[246] The new law reflects the Taiwanese government's policy decision to give mental health and disorder a higher priority than it previously had. The law attempts to fashion a modern, community-based mental health care system for Taiwan. The Taiwanese architects of the new system have been influenced but not driven by mental health care trends in the West. One purpose of the new law is to impose a legal duty on the "caretaker" of a mentally ill person to obtain medical treatment for, and assist in the hospitalization of severely ill patients. This new legal obligation is designed to end the current Taiwanese pattern of long delays in seeking, or even total avoidance of, hospitalization and modern psychiatric treatments. At the other end of the spectrum, the mental health laws of Malaysia and Singapore have been in place for over 100 years and are modelled after the mental health laws of England.[247]

Mental Health Legislation in Canada

The Uniform Mental Health Act

With ten provinces and two territorial governments having their separate mental health acts, it is difficult to generalize about mental health legislation in Canada. In addition, many provinces have recently amended or are

244 Salzberg, *supra* note 80 at 144 n. 36.

245 *Ibid.*

246 Two tragic incidents in Taipei in the mid-1980s in which two seriously disordered schizophrenic persons caused serious injury to 20 students in one case and death to a high government official by his spouse in the second case prompted the government to move more quickly on its plans to enact a new law: Salzberg, *supra* note 91 at 51.

247 Kok, *supra* note 14. It is worth observing that some commentators have noted that the common law (i.e. judge made law) in Singapore has not continued to develop or

in the process of amending this legislation. The *Uniform Mental Health Act* was prepared in 1987 by provincial and territorial representatives. This Act was not an actual piece of legislation but was designed to serve as a model to guide amendments to various provincial and territorial mental health laws so that those laws would conform with the individual rights that are protected in the *Canadian Charter of Rights and Freedoms*. Many provinces have undertaken an examination of their mental health legislation, and amendments have been made by some provinces. Among other issues, those amendments have addressed the following:

- the definition or re-definition of mental disorder (e.g. in Alberta and Manitoba)
- the criteria for involuntary admission for psychiatric assessment and procedures for involuntary admission. For example, Manitoba now has a staggered, two-certificate system in which the first certificate, signed by a general practitioner, allows assessment for up to 72 hours, and the second certificate, signed by a psychiatrist, permits admission for up to 20 days.
- the issue of patients' rights. For example, in Ontario, patients have, with few exceptions, the right to view their clinical records.

Other issues that have been or are being discussed include consent to treatment and the appointment of a decision-making authority for those individuals who need to receive treatment as involuntary patients. Saskatchewan has instituted a system of automatic appeals to review panels (e.g. with respect to detention and treatment within a facility). Patient advocate/advisory services have also been developed (e.g. in Alberta and Ontario). Patient advisers can offer assistance and advice to involuntary patients in psychiatric facilities, and can ensure that these individuals are aware of their rights throughout treatment.[248]

British Columbia's Mental Health Act: Background

The last major revision of the British Columbia *Mental Health Act* was in 1964. There is widespread agreement that the existing Act is inadequate and inappropriate. Between 1992 and 1994, British Columbia conducted a major review of its Act under a project known as The British Columbia Mental Health Act Review. Unfortunately this Review group became

---

grow as it has in England and other western common law countries: A. Harding, "Smart Laws in Singapore," in L. Palmier, ed., *State and Law in East Asia*, *supra* note 149 at 90, citing A. B. L. Phang, *The Development of Singapore Law: Historical and Socio-Legal Perspectives* (Singapore: Butterworths, 1990).

248 *Mental Health Services in Canada* (Ottawa: Health and Welfare Canada, 1990) at 173-74.

gridlocked between those advocating greater legal safeguards for involuntary admission, discharge, and treatment of mental patients (the "legal process model") and those favouring a (paternalistic) medical model,[249] under which commitment, discharge, and treatment decisions would be made by psychiatrists acting according to their assessment of the best interests of the patient and in accordance with sound medical practices.

The current British Columbia *Mental Health Act* reflects the type of mental health legislation that was prevalent in Canada in the 1960s. The British Columbia Mental Health Act Review describes this type of legislation as follows:

> The mental health legislation of the 1960s, in Canada, provided for involuntary admission on the basis of very broad and vaguely worded criteria. These criteria allowed mentally ill persons who were deemed unable to care for themselves to be admitted to mental health facilities and treated for their own "welfare," "protection," "safety," the welfare of others or welfare of the community. These criteria are related to parens patriae, but of course include the stricter criteria necessary for the exercise of police powers.
>
> Historically, persons with mental illness in institutions have been considered incapable of making any decisions. The fact that an individual required institutionalization was sufficient proof that the person was not able to make decisions for him/herself. As a result, most mental health legislation did not address the question of consent and treatment in institutions. It was assumed that the patient should receive whatever the physician or the director decided was the course of treatment.[250]

Comparison of Eastern and Western Mental Health Legislation

In this section, I will compare a number of key issues in mental health legislation in Eastern and Western countries. In regard to Western countries, I will use the mental health legislation in British Columbia, Canada, as my primary example. As noted above, the British Columbia legislation, which has not been substantially altered since the early 1960s, is in serious need of reform. Such reform now appears imminent.[251] The issues that will be examined and compared include the following:

---

249 I. Grant, in "Mental Health Law and the Courts" (1991) 29 Osgoode Hall L.J. 747 at 749-50, describes the paternalistic model.

250 Mental Health Act Review, *Issues and Options Paper* (Victoria B.C.: Ministry of Health, 1991) at 4.

251 Bill 22, *Mental Health Amendment Act*, 1998, was introduced into the B.C. Legislature in May 1998 and is expected to be passed by the Legislature by July 1998. Bill 22,

- legal criteria for civil commitment
- review processes for discharge from involuntary commitment
- legal provisions on consent to treatment and the right to refuse treatment
- disclosure of psychiatric information to the patient and/or family
- role of family members.

Criteria for Civil Commitment

Voluntary Commitment

It should be noted that a significant effort has been made in the past 50 years in many Western countries and some Asian countries to ensure that the majority of patients in mental hospitals are admitted voluntarily, not involuntarily. The mental health laws of British Columbia, Singapore, and Malaysia provide for voluntary or informal admission and the majority of patients are admitted on that basis. In Japan, until the 1987 *Mental Health Law*, there was no legal provision for voluntary admission. Over 90% were admitted, at least theoretically, on an involuntary basis upon the application of their guardian or caregiver supported by the opinion of one physician (not necessarily a specialist). A small percentage were admitted upon their own request and their hospitalization could be terminated by them at their will. In Taiwan, the 1990 *Mental Health Law* deals only with involuntary commitment. In Thailand, there is no mental health law; a statutory basis for civil commitment could be found in the *Civil Code* guardianship provisions, but this is not resorted to in practice. In Thailand, admissions are called voluntary, but this refers to voluntary committal by the patient's family, not the patient. The patient is discharged at the physician's discretion or upon the request of the family.

Involuntary Commitment

Canada (British Columbia) The British Columbia *Mental Health Act* provides for short-term (emergency) and long-term involuntary commitment. Short-term commitment may be initiated by a police officer who has observed or received information that a person is acting in a manner likely to endanger the safety of that person or others, and is apparently suffering from a

---

which is more paternalistic than rights-oriented, replaces the term "mentally ill person" with the newly defined term "mentally disordered person"; expands the criteria for involuntary commitment; permits involuntary admission for up to 72 hours on the basis of one medical certificate; authorizes non-consensual treatment of involuntary patients; and allows for the re-committal of patients who stop taking their prescribed medication after their temporary release from hospital.

mental disorder.[252] The person is brought to a physician (not necessarily a psychiatrist), and if the physician is satisfied that the person is mentally disordered and in need of care, supervision, or control for his own protection or the protection of others, the person may be taken to a mental health facility and held there for up to 72 hours.[253]

A judge may also order short-term admission on application from any person having good reason to believe that the person in question is mentally disordered or is dangerous to be at large. If the judge is satisfied that the above is true and that formal procedures would result in dangerous delay, the judge may issue a warrant to apprehend the person and place him/her in a mental health facility.[254] Emergency admission may be effected on the basis of a medical certificate by one physician rather than the two normally required.[255] Certification is the same as that discussed below under long-term admission. This procedure is intended to deal particularly with isolated geographical regions where a second physician may not be readily available. Detention and forced treatment for up to 72 hours may be effected.

Long-term admission is made on the basis of certificates provided by two physicians that must indicate the following. First, it must be noted that the physician has examined the person and believes him or her to be mentally ill, as defined in the Act (that is, "suffering from a disorder of the mind that seriously impairs his ability to react appropriately to his environment or to associate with others"), accompanied by the reasons for that opinion. In addition, there must be a statement that the person requires both medical treatment in a mental health facility, and requires care, supervision, and control in a mental health facility for his own protection or that of others.[256]

A person may initially be detained for a period of up to one month. The first renewal may be for one month, the second for three months. After that, renewal of authority to detain is required every six months.[257] Renewal is based upon the report of a physician who has examined the patient and determined that further detention and treatment is necessary. This renewal procedure is in addition to review by the mental health panel discussed below.

Japan Under the 1950 *Mental Hygiene Law*, an estimated 92.6% of admissions were involuntary civil commitments. While the Law required a

252 R.S.B.C. 1996, c. 288, s. 28. See also S. Salzberg, *Conference Briefing Papers for the International Conference on Mental Health Law* in Taipei, Taiwan, 1-3 June 1992 [unpublished] at 16.

253 *Ibid.*, s. 28.

254 *Ibid.*; forced treatment may be applied during the 72 hour period.

255 *Ibid.*, s. 27.

256 *Ibid.*, s. 22.

257 *Ibid.*, ss. 23 and 24.

person to be likely to injure him/herself or others unless hospitalized, it did not provide criteria by which this was to be determined.[258] Consent was possible from the person responsible (*hogogimusha*) in conjunction with the opinion of the superintendent of the mental hospital, despite a lack of consent from the person to be institutionalized; all that needed to be determined was that the person was mentally disordered. The latter term lacked clear definition and included persons who were psychotic due to intoxication and mentally retarded persons.[259]

Under the 1987 *Mental Health Law*, long-term involuntary (from the patient's perspective) committal can be done pursuant to the order of a prefectural governor, or with the consent of a specified family member. When prefectural or local health authorities receive a report that a person is or is suspected to be mentally disordered, they must have that person examined by a qualified psychiatric specialist.[260] If the person is deemed to be mentally disordered and likely to cause injury to himself or others unless hospitalized, the person may be committed to a designated mental hospital.[261]

The other option requires that a specialist physician, upon examination of the person, determines that the person is mentally disordered and in need of hospitalization for medical treatment and protection. The patient may then be admitted with the consent of a specified family member, whether the patient consents or not.[262] Where there is no available family member, consent can be given instead by a municipal official. Only since 1987 have there been admission standards for compulsory admission, but the purposes of "protection or medical treatment" do not have distinct parameters for application.

Criteria for making a determination under governor's orders have now been established under regulations. The primary issue is whether the mentally disordered person is likely to commit acts that pose a threat to life or limb of him/herself or actions posing a threat to the life, body, chastity, reputation, or property of others.[263] The regulations list symptoms that indicate that the person may be deemed likely to attempt acts, such as suicide, that injure his own life or limb, or "actions posing a threat to the life, body, chastity, reputation, or property (etc.) of others or to protected

258 Salzberg, *supra* note 80 at 149-50.

259 *Ibid.* at 151.

260 Salzberg, *supra* note 252 at 18.

261 *Ibid.*

262 *Ibid.* For this reason I have placed this type of consent under the involuntary heading, although technically it is considered voluntary in Japan. Professor Salzberg notes that family consent implies a lack of objection from the specified family member, and given the strong social norm towards politeness, such objections are highly unlikely. Thus, it is possible that a person might still be institutionalized despite having expressly denied consent and the family having misgivings.

263 *Ibid.*

legal interests of society (*shakaiteki hoeki*), such as murder, injury, assault, problematic sexual behaviour, slander, destruction of property, robbery, intimidation, theft, fraud, arson, playing with fire, etc."[264] The regulation says that generally the acts causing harm to others should be of a nature and degree that are the concern of criminal law.[265]

There are a number of forms of short-term admission. One allows a person who, based upon the diagnosis of one specialist physician, would meet the criteria under a governor's order to be held for up to 72 hours without corroborating diagnoses when usual procedures are not possible. Another allows 72 hour emergency hospitalization, without the consent of the specified family member, when a specialist physician has found the person to be mentally disordered and failure to immediately hospitalize would be a clear threat to the person's medical treatment and protection.[266] There is also provision for further observation for up to three weeks, with consent of the specified family member.[267]

Taiwan Only "severely ill" persons are subject to involuntary hospitalization. Such hospitalization is to occur only when an initial diagnosis and confirming diagnoses by at least two specialist physicians determine that a severely ill person who is clearly likely to injure himself or others, or has engaged in injurious behaviour, requires full-time hospitalization. Short-term admission for evaluation is not to exceed seven days. The person may be compelled, if he/she will not voluntarily submit to further treatment, to remain in the hospital for another 30 days upon the evaluation of another specialist physician that full-time in-patient treatment is necessary. At the end of that time, if two specialist physicians deem that continued in-patient treatment is necessary, and the person will not voluntarily submit, hospitalization can be compelled for a further six months, with the same renewal procedures required at succeeding six month intervals.[268]

The 1990 *Mental Health Law* also establishes the requirement that the hospital may not keep hospitalized, without reason, a patient whose condition has moderated or been cured, and for whom in-patient treatment is

---

264 Salzberg, *supra* note 80 at 150.

265 *Ibid.* Professor Salzberg notes that antisocial behaviour (*fuzoku hanteki kodo*), eating or drinking at a restaurant without paying (*musen inshoku*), and riding public transportation without paying (*muchin josha*) are categories of problematic behaviour on the diagnosis form for hospitalization, citing Ministry of Health and Welfare circular No. 16, 13 May 1988, Form No. 18, in Zenshiryo at 157.

266 Salzberg, *supra* note 252 at 18.

267 *Ibid.*

268 *Ibid.* at 17. See also Salzberg, *supra* note 91 at 57.

no longer necessary. This requirement effectively amounts to a duty to discharge. This duty to discharge is combined with a duty on the part of the caretaker of a severely ill person to receive the discharged patient and assist in the patient's continuing care and treatment.

Singapore and Malaysia Singapore and Malaysia have similar provisions. In Singapore, the *Mental Disorders and Treatment Act* provides for compulsory or involuntary admissions of patients as follows:

(i) A person of unsound mind shall be apprehended by the police if he or she is believed to be dangerous to himself or others by reason of a mental disorder, and shall be brought:
   (a) to any medical officer who may then arrange for him or her to be sent to a mental hospital; or
   (b) directly to a mental hospital.

(ii) A medical practitioner may send any mentally disordered person who requires psychiatric treatment to a mental hospital.

(iii) In addition relatives may bring such a person to a hospital for admission. The admitting medical officer may detain a person only if he or she is found to be suffering from a mental disorder which warrants detention and it is necessary to do so in the interest of that person's health, safety, or for the protection of others.

   The medical officer, by signing Form 1 may detain a person for 72 hours. In Form 1 the words "be admitted for treatment of suspected mental illness" are used. This term "mental illness" is not defined but presumably means a mild or major mental illness.

   Within 72 hours, if another medical officer examines him or her and is of the opinion that further detention is required, that officer may extend the period of detention for a period of one month, by signing a Form 2.

   Further detention up to a year is authorized under Form 3. Form 3 requires that two medical officers, one of whom is a psychiatrist, separately examines the patient and be satisfied that he or she requires further treatment. The facts indicating unsoundness of mind have to be entered onto Form 3.

(iv) The court may also order a mentally disordered patient to be committed. Under section 25 of the Act, persons found by a court to be of unsound mind and incapable of managing themselves and their affairs may be sent by the court to a mental hospital for suitable custody.

Thailand As already noted, mental hospital admissions are called voluntary, but this refers to the voluntary committal by the patient's family, not the patient. As Higginbotham has noted:

Thailand operates on an informal system (Curran and Harding 1977). The hospital medical officer makes the decision to admit except on those occasions when the patient is sent on a court order. Only one physician is required to do the certification and length of stay is indefinite. Appeals, periodic review, and discharge procedures are neither specified nor required under this informal system. In many cases, however, patients are voluntary or brought in by family members who can be as adamant about release as they were about admission.[269]

Indonesia Article 26 of the 1992 *Indonesian Health Act* provides as follows:

> (1) Persons suffering from mental disorders who may cause a disturbance to public safety and order are obligated to be treated and cared for at mental health care facilities or other health care facilities.
>
> (2) The treatment and care of persons suffering from mental disorders may be undertaken at the request of a husband or wife, a guardian (*wali*), a family member, or at the initiative of a public official responsible for safety and order in the local area or a judge in cases when suspicion arises that the party involved suffers from a mental disorder.

Article 84 provides that anyone who obstructs a mentally disordered person from obtaining treatment or care under Article 26(1) *supra* is guilty of a criminal offence punishable by up to one year imprisonment and/or a fine of 15 million rupiah. Article 26 of the *Indonesian Health Act* is clearly much broader than the involuntary commitment provisions in Canada, Japan, Malaysia, or Singapore.

As a practical matter, it should be observed that there has traditionally been less of a concern for large-scale abuse of involuntary civil commitment to mental hospitals in some Asian countries like Indonesia and Thailand because of the relative scarcity of psychiatric beds in these countries. The following Table sets out the number of psychiatric beds per 100,000 population and the number of psychiatrists per 100,000 population. The number of psychiatric beds in Canada has been significantly reduced (perhaps by as much as one-third to one-half) in the past 20 years as part of the shift to community mental health. As the Table demonstrates, psychiatric bed space is very scarce in Indonesia and fairly scarce in Thailand.

---

269 Higginbotham, *supra* note 38 at 191.

270 *Mental Health Act*, R.S.B.C. 1996, c. 288, s. 25.

271 *Ibid.*

272 *Ibid.* at s. 25(3).

273 *Ibid.* at s. 25(5). The three persons are a chair appointed by the government, a psychiatrist appointed by and on the staff of the mental health facility where the patient is being detained, and a person appointed by the patient. The patient's appointee may

Table 1

Psychiatric beds and psychiatrists (1992-93)

Country	Psychiatric beds per 100,000 population	Psychiatrists per 100,000 population
Japan	274	7.1
Canada	107	11.1
Singapore	100	2.0
Taiwan	64	1.0
Malaysia	32	.5
Thailand	14	.5
Indonesia	4	.2

Review Processes for Discharge from Involuntary Commitment

Canada (British Columbia)

The British Columbia *Mental Health Act* provides for review of detention by a review panel.[270] Application can be made by or on behalf of any involuntary patient and this right is available during every detention period, that is, one during the first month of detention, one in the second month, one during the next three months, and thereafter one during each six month period.[271] It is possible that a person might have more than one review during a period. The chair of the review panel has the discretion to shorten the time period between reviews in the best interests of the patient or to consider newly available information.[272] Therefore, this right to a review during each period of detention should be considered a minimum. However, there is no provision for automatic review – the patient or someone on the patient's behalf must apply for the review.

A review panel consists of three members.[273] The patient has the right to be represented by a lawyer or agent who may call witnesses or make submissions on the patient's behalf before the panel. The chair is required to give the patient at least two full days' notice of the review hearing. The panel is entitled to all information and records relevant to the hearing. Hearings are generally held in private. While patients are usually present, they may be excluded if the chair believes that exclusion would be in their best interests.[274] Likewise, the panel may withhold some of the information from the patient if its members believe that it would be distressing to the patient. Despite having some resemblance to adversarial court procedures,

---

not be a member of the patient's family. When the patient does not indicate an appointee, the director of the hospital may appoint someone with a knowledge of the patient's circumstances.

274 Salzberg, *supra* note 252 at 58.

the hearing does not apply any strict rules of evidence.[275] Commonly a social worker will prepare and submit a report which outlines the patient's history, available community resources, and the social worker's recommendations.

The Act provides no standard upon which the panel is to base its decision. The criteria are wholly within the discretion of the panel. Because the panel is not required to give reasons for its decision, it is difficult to know what criteria are applied in any particular case. The panel makes its decision, which must be in writing, to discharge or to continue detention within 48 hours of the hearing's conclusion. Usually a decision is made at the time of the hearing.

The decision may be challenged in court on the basis of an alleged error of law, but given the vague and discretionary aspects of the Act and regulations, and the general deference of the courts to expert panels, a successful challenge is extremely difficult.[276] Judicial review of detention is also available without reference to the review board on application from the patient, or anyone who believes that there is insufficient cause for admission or detention.[277]

The Office of the Ombudsman is also available for review of the treatment of patients by mental health officials. The concept of the ombudsman is originally of Scandinavian origin and spread to the Commonwealth countries via New Zealand, France, Germany, and the United Kingdom. It is presently enjoying widespread popularity, especially in Europe, where 80 countries currently have an ombudsman. A review can be made of the actions and decisions of all government employees and officials. The jurisdiction of the Ombudsman's Office extends to all government bodies, including mental hospitals, prisons, and educational facilities.[278]

---

275 *Ibid.*

276 *Ibid.* at 59. See also Grant, *supra* note 249.

277 *Mental Health Act*, s. 33. The petition may be made before admission to seek prohibition of admission or after admission for discharge from detention. The petition is heard in private rather than in open court and evidence is usually by affidavit, although judges normally interview the persons concerned if they are present. The critical determination is whether, at the time the petition is made to the court (and not the time of original detention), the detention can be justified. The onus is on the patient or the patient's representative to show that on the balance of probabilities detention is not justified. The courts require a lower threshold for justification than is required to impose detention initially. The court will find continued detention justified if the person is mentally disordered and *either* requires medical treatment *or* needs care, supervision, or control for his or her own protection or the protection of others. To be detained in the first instance, *both* of these conditions must obtain. Such proceedings are not common and successful challenges are rare. Given delays of up to two months in this type of hearing and the courts' characteristic deference to psychiatric expertise, most patients and their advocates do not choose to employ this method of review.

278 Although the office is a public body and accountable to the Legislature, one of its essential features is independence from the government, which allows it to conduct

While previously the British Columbia Ombudsman's Office waited for referrals, it has now become more active and can investigate and make recommendations on its own initiative. In this more active role it is typically acting on behalf of persons who are institutionalized and unable to act on their own behalf. The power to investigate, supplemented with the power to obtain documents and interview persons, is backed by criminal sanctions for non-cooperation. While these powers are broad, the results of the Ombudsman's investigations take the form of recommendations. Each year the Ombudsman publishes an Annual Report Card on government bodies. While this may not appear to be a forceful result, the fact that Canada is a representative democracy with a very active media results in the recommendations carrying a great deal of sway with politicians. The Report Card is respected by politicians and government officials out of a fear of bad publicity.[279]

One area that generates activity for the Ombudsman's Office is the detention of persons under 16 who have not consented to their detention, although their guardians have. There exists a recognition that youth are often conduct-oriented and their problems may not be a mental disorder *per se,* and that as a result they may be channelled into inappropriate streams of services. Another place where the Ombudsman is active is in providing an effective channel for the patient's input into shaping the policy and procedures of public institutions.[280]

---

non-biased investigations of government bodies. The Ombudsman has a fixed term of office, is independent, and has a high profile to guarantee fair service for citizens by the government. In addition, the Ombudsman has staff to aid in investigations. Currently there are 50 full-time staff in British Columbia's Ombudsman's Office, 40 of whom are full-time investigators with master's degrees.

279 The office of the Ombudsman has a good reputation for independence and impartiality, which is necessary for the cooperation of both potential complainants and government officials. While people often fear retribution for complaining to the institution in which they reside, the Ombudsman is seen as a safe body with which to lodge a complaint. Usually the Ombudsman initially recommends internal review systems, but may either participate in such reviews or may impose jurisdiction if necessary.

In 1992 there were 16,000 complainants, 11,000 of which were investigated. All cases in the past six years have been satisfactorily resolved. In two-thirds of these cases the problem between the complainant and the government body has been the result of miscommunication, which the Ombudsman's Office has corrected. Within this framework, 40% of those who have reviews or appeals regarding detention are discharged, often for technical errors of formality. The Ombudsman's Office is sensitive to the fact that at times the due process model is in conflict with the real needs of the patients, and acts accordingly. There are very few complaints regarding the review process of the Ombudsman.

280 In the context of mental disability, the activities of the office of the Ombudsman have resulted in investigations into the problem of suicides, and recommendations regarding the design of facilities; investigations of the malfeasance of security officials; recommendations that sheriffs and police officers receive proper training regarding the mentally disordered, so that such people are not mistreated while in their

Japan

There is no review for voluntary patients. Ostensibly the Psychiatric Review Boards (PRBs) established under the 1987 *Mental Health Law*, one of which has been established in each prefecture, are the primary bodies that protect patients' rights. The PRB consists of five to fifteen members appointed by the prefectural governor.[281] Its primary function is the review of periodic reports on involuntary patients and consideration of requests for discharge or improved physical treatment. The PRB operates as a five-person panel.[282]

The necessity for hospitalization is subject to review by the PRB. While there are elaborate procedures in place,[283] there is strong reason to suspect that this will not be particularly efficacious. From approximately 106,000 reviews of committed persons, only 11 were freed.[284] This figure can be compared to British Columbia, where 20-50% of patients are released after review.[285] Although the review board has the form of a Western model, which is based on concern for the liberty of the patient, due to Japan's different cultural context, this formal commitment to patients' liberty rights is not followed in practice.

Under the 1987 *Mental Health Law*, periodic reports based upon the examination of a certified psychiatrist must be submitted to the prefectural authorities once every six months for patients admitted involuntarily under a governor's order, and every twelve months for patients admitted with the consent of their *hogogimusha*.[286] In exercising its mandatory review function with respect to periodic reports, the panel normally conducts only a review of report documents transmitted by the hospital. Only in cases where the panel deems it necessary will the panel request that the governor exercise his extraordinary powers to request reports or conduct on-site investigations or medical examinations, and provide the information so obtained.[287]

---

custody; monitoring of solitary confinement to ensure that it is used for control (when necessary) and not as a means of punishment; recommendations that the review procedure be deinstitutionalized; and recommendations that service in the community be made available with protection from widespread abuse and discomfiture during the reintegration phase.

281 Salzberg, *supra* note 252 at 59-60.

282 The panels consist of three psychiatrists, one person knowledgeable and experienced in law, and another person knowledgeable and experienced in a relevant field.

283 Salzberg, *supra* note 80 at 160-62.

284 This figure was produced by Professor Salzberg during discussions at the Canada-ASEAN Mental Disorder Workshop, Victoria, Canada, 27-29 May 1993.

285 These statistics are based on discussions with persons knowledgeable about the review board process. The number of people released in Canada fluctuates; at the moment this relatively high rate probably reflects current policy of treatment on an out-patient basis, but may fall in the future with increasingly conservative views regarding the perception of public safety.

286 Salzberg, *supra* note 252 at 60.

287 *Ibid*. Where it is deemed "especially necessary," the panel may hear the opinion of the hospital superintendent, the patient, or others. When this occurs, however, there is

The other mandatory review function of the PRB concerns requests to the prefectural governor made by any involuntarily admitted patient or *hogogimusha* that the patient be discharged or that necessary measures be taken to improve the patient's treatment with respect to physical and behavioural restraints. In reviewing these requests, the PRB panel reviews pertinent documentation and considers the opinions of the patient, the person making the request (if different), the hospital superintendent or others. If the patient is to have a representative with respect to review of the request, the representative must be a lawyer.[288] Those opinions that the panel will consider are to be collected before the panel meeting, either through interviews or written submissions, by one or more of the panel members, one of whom must be a psychiatrist.[289]

Taiwan

Involuntary hospitalization must be renewed after the initial 30 day period, and thereafter every six months through re-examination and certification by two specialists. Under the Taiwan *Mental Health Law*, there is no judicial or other review of involuntary hospitalization. The primary recourse for protecting the rights of patients is through written complaints lodged with health authorities at any governmental level.[290] These complaints are to be initially received and reviewed by the Mental Illness Prevention Deliberation Committees, which are established under the law at every governmental level. At the central level the body is concerned with overall planning and policy-making, as well as the protection of patients' rights. Local committees are charged with developing research regarding the prevention of mental illness, and hearing and taking action upon complaints raised by or on behalf of ill persons.[291]

The Law also addresses the problems of the past associated with the standards and supervision of private sector mental health care. The level of care

---

no requirement that the opinions be presented at a hearing or before the entire panel or the patient. Before a panel decides that further hospitalization is appropriate, it must hear the opinion of the hospital superintendent.

288 Salzberg, *ibid.* at 60, notes that given the small number of lawyers in Japan and their relative unavailability for matters such as this, this requirement is somewhat onerous.

289 *Ibid.* at 60. At the review session, which is closed to the public, the requester, hospital superintendent, and others deemed appropriate by the panel may make oral submissions. If deemed unnecessary, the panel need not consider these opinions. The patient may also be excluded from the opportunity to appear before and address the panel when it deems it unnecessary, because the patient's views have already been made known to the panel. The PRB is to make the results of its review, achieved by a majority vote, known to the governor who in turn informs the requester of the results and, when the PRB so recommends, it is to order the discharge or improvement of the patient's physical treatment.

290 *Ibid.* at 59.

291 *Ibid.* at 59.

in these institutions was generally very low, and the government structure of compensation for the poor meant that private hospitals primarily served as long-term holding facilities for the chronically ill. Social assistance was barely sufficient to provide rudimentary subsistence, let alone adequate psychiatric care. The new Law provides for rules and guidelines to be set forth by the central health authorities for the establishment and operation of rehabilitation and guidance institutions. In addition, standards are to be set for approved methods of treatment and rehabilitation for both public and private institutions. Sanctions, including fines, suspension of operations, or revocation of licences, are available for institutions that violate the prescribed guidelines.[292]

Singapore and Malaysia

A visitor system based on the former English model is maintained under the *Mental Disorders and Treatment Act* in Singapore and the *Mental Disorder Ordinance* in Malaysia. The system is virtually identical in both countries. What follows is a description of the Singapore system. Each mental hospital is to have a board of visitors of not fewer than twelve visitors, six of whom are medical officers (defined as registered practitioners in the service of the government) appointed by the Minister of Health. The qualifications of the other six members are not specified in the legislation, but they are usually appointed from a wide range of related professional groups such as legal officers, justices of the peace, psychologists, medical social workers, and nurses.[293] The visitors constitute the only formal review mechanism under the law. They have the formal responsibility for reviewing patients detained pursuant to the first instance certification by two physicians and for determining whether those patients require detention for another period of twelve months.[294]

Based on their interview of the patient and the report of the psychiatrist, the visitors can apply to a magistrate for an order of further detention if they are satisfied that the patient should be further detained for care and treatment. They have the authority to discharge such patients before the twelve month period is up.[295] The majority of in-patients are informal or on the 72 hour detention order and these patients do not come within the ambit of the visitors' review power.[296] The bulk of the work done by the visitors is on the review of mentally abnormal offenders remanded to the hospital through court orders under the *Code of Criminal Procedure*.

---

292 Salzberg, *supra* note 91 at 54.

293 Kok, *supra* note 14. For Malaysia, see *Mental Disorder Ordinance, 1952*, s. 32.

294 *Ibid.*

295 Singapore *Mental Disorders and Treatment Act*, s. 39.

296 Kok, *supra* note 14.

Any patient on long-term detention must be visited at least once every six months by at least two visitors. These visitors must make a special report to the Minister of Law as to the state of mind of persons who were admitted to hospital by an order of the court.[297] If the visitors certify that in their judgment the patient may be discharged without danger of doing injury to himself or others, the Minister of Law may thereupon order that person to be discharged. Otherwise they may report that the person should remain in detention. The patient is interviewed at the visitors' review and his or her relatives may be present if they wish. The visitors have access to all of the patient's records and the latest report on his or her mental state and progress by the treating psychiatrist.[298]

Section 30 of the *Mental Disorders and Treatment Act* provides that two or more visitors shall at least every month together inspect every part of the mental hospital (in particular, this inspection involves review of appropriate case files). The visitors also have the power to enter and inspect any part of the hospital at any time. At the regular review meeting in the hospital the visitors may make general comments or recommendations on the management and conditions of the hospital and its patients. Such comments are recorded in a book, which is forwarded to the Director of Medical Services. There is also a human rights commission but it is rarely used. More often people write to newspapers, and this action seems to have some influence. Newspapers do not investigate individual cases the way an ombudsman's office in Canada would, but they do serve as a means to draw public attention to unbecoming conduct or abuses.

Thailand

In Thailand there is no formal guarantee of review; it is all a matter of the psychiatrist's discretion. A patient may be returned to a family upon request or with their consent. This reflects a strong trust in the professionalism of psychiatrists, who generally enjoy a good reputation.[299]

Indonesia

In Indonesia as in Thailand, review and release are within the discretion of the physician and family. There is a complaint box in the hospital and the medical association has a review body of its own. The self-regulating medical profession does make use of its powers and takes its role seriously. There have been approximately 130 "disbarments" of physicians in Indonesia.[300]

---

297 *Ibid.*

298 *Ibid.*

299 Higginbotham, *supra* note 268; information also provided by Dr. Thamrong Dasananjali during Canada-ASEAN Workshop discussions, *supra* note 283.

300 Information provided by Dr. Dadang Hawari during Canada-ASEAN Workshop discussions, *ibid.*

Consent to Treatment

Canada (British Columbia)

For voluntary patients in British Columbia, the legal rules derive from the common law developed with respect to medical treatment generally. Consent must be given for the specific treatment actually administered; "blanket consent" to all treatments is not legally sufficient. Consent must be voluntary. Consent must be informed – that is, the patient must understand the nature of the proposed treatment, as well as any risks associated with it. The patient must be competent to give consent and capable of weighing the relative risks and benefits and making a decision on that basis. If a patient is not competent, a court may appoint a guardian who may give substitute consent.[301]

For persons admitted involuntarily, there are effectively no requirements for consent to treatment. The director of a mental health facility may sign consent to treatment forms.[302] A patient may give consent if deemed capable, and a physician certifies the patient was capable of understanding the nature of the authorization signed.

Japan

"Informed consent" is not a concept that is legally recognized in Japan. The family accepts the burden of the mentally disordered family member until it is no longer able to cope. As well as having the primary responsibility to care for that person, the family has the right to consent on behalf of the person. The 1987 *Mental Health Law,* which reformed the previous system, contains no provision concerning consent to medical treatment. Although Psychiatric Review Boards were created, their mandate extends only to physical interventions (bodily restraints, isolation, etc.), and to questions of detention, but does not extend to psychiatric treatment *per se*. Also, because the general law concerning informed consent in the doctor-patient relationship has not yet developed the sorts of principles that are found in Western jurisprudence, there is no principle of informed consent that could be applied in a psychiatric context.[303]

Taiwan

Although there is no general right to refuse treatment, certain treatments cannot be administered without safeguards. While such procedures as

---

301 See Salzberg, *supra* note 252 at 29; although it is not legally sufficient, some doctors apparently rely on the substitute consent of a family member even without the formal appointment of a guardian.

302 R.S.B.C. 1996, c. 288, s. 31. This section may not withstand judicial scrutiny under the *Canadian Charter of Rights and Freedoms,* especially where a person may be involuntarily committed but is competent to give consent to treatment.

303 Salzberg, *supra* notes 252 and 91 at 57 and 61.

psychosurgery and long-term out-patient hormone implantation may only be carried out by psychiatric teaching hospitals and require review by a board composed of persons with medical skills, legal specialists, and social workers, the consent of the patient is not required by law.[304] Other procedures such as electro-convulsive therapy (ECT) and "clinical research not involving bodily experimentation" require the written consent of the patient. This usually means that consent must be obtained from the spouse or closest relative. In addition, there must be a written notice by a specialist physician as to the necessity of the procedure.[305] On the consent form, the patient is to be informed of the purpose and the means employed, anticipated results and possible side-effects, alternative treatments and the fact that the patient may withdraw consent at any time.

If the patient lacks the capacity to consent, ECT and clinical research not involving bodily experimentation may be carried out with the substitute consent of the patient's legally designated representative, spouse, or closest relative and the written opinion of at least one other specialized physician that the treatment is necessary. If the substitute consent has not or cannot be obtained, the treatment may be carried out on the basis of the written opinions of two other specialized physicians that the treatment is necessary.[306]

Singapore and Malaysia

The provisions governing general consent, which may include consent to medical treatment, are in sections 87-92 of the *Penal Code*. These provisions relate to penal liability and state that consent may be express or implied. It should be voluntary and not given through coercion, fear of injury, or a misconception of fact. The person consenting should be able to understand the nature and consequence of what is consented to. The person must also be of a certain age.[307]

By law a person is not considered competent to consent when, because of unsoundness of mind as a result of mental illness,[308] or through intoxication by alcohol, medication, or drugs,[309] or by reason of having a mental age below 12 (that is, those who are mentally retarded),[310] the person is

304 *Ibid.* at 30.
305 Salzberg, *supra* note 91 at 60.
306 Salzberg, *supra* note 252 at 30.
307 Kok, *supra* note 14, notes that here there is some ambiguity, because s. 87 of the Singapore *Penal Code* indicates that the person should be above 18 while s. 90 states that the person should not be below 12. These are not mutually exclusive, but it does create some uncertainty about persons between the ages of 12 and 18. The provisions are identical in the Malaysian *Penal Code*.
308 *Ibid.* citing s. 84.
309 *Ibid.* citing s. 85.
310 *Ibid.* citing s. 83.

unable to understand the nature and consequence of what he/she consents to. The civil law regarding informed consent does not state specifically how much information a patient should be given, but in general it should include knowledge of the purpose of the treatment, possible danger, and risks and benefits. The issue of informed consent has not been raised in Singapore courts, but if it did one would expect English jurisprudence to be very influential.[311] In practice, if a subject is unable to consent due to unsoundness of mind, then the family has to give consent. If family members are not available and the procedure is deemed necessary to prevent death or grievous hurt, or to cure a grievous hurt or infirmity, then the doctor in charge can give consent and proceed. If it is not an emergency but the family is unavailable, then the opinion of another independent psychiatrist is necessary.

Written consent is not required for psychopharmacological treatment. Consent is implied if the patient does not refuse treatment. Also, a guardian's consent is not necessary. Such treatments can be given to involuntary patients. If an informal patient refuses treatment where "treatment is warranted and detention necessary in the interests of the patient's health, safety and protection of others," that person can be made into an involuntary patient and treated.[312]

Thailand and Indonesia

The only legal provisions on consent in Thailand and Indonesia are in the penal codes dealing with assault which involves the non-consensual touching of another person. In general, the patient, or where a patient is unable, a family member, may be requested to consent to treatment. However, physicians are assumed to have the authority to treat patients without consent when such treatment is considered necessary, for example to prevent suicide. Physicians who fail to treat under such circumstances may be liable to claims of unethical practice under the medical discipline laws.[313]

Degree of Disclosure to Patient and/or Family

Canada (British Columbia)

The Minister of Health can gain access to any information, but this power is exercised very rarely. Usually physician billing is a source of record keeping.

---

311 *Ibid.*, where Kok notes that the standard test is likely to be the *Bolam* principle for negligence, which provides that a doctor is not guilty of negligence if he or she has acted in accordance with a practice accepted as proper by a responsible body of medical persons skilled in that particular practice. See *Bolam v. Friern Hospital Management Committee*, [1957] 2 All E.R. 118. For more details regarding the general law of informed consent, see L. P. Kok, M. Cheang, and K. T. Chee, "Consent for Electro-Convulsive Therapy in Singapore" (1992) 21 Anglo-American L. Rev. 485.

312 *Ibid.*

313 Information provided by Dr. Thamrong Dasananjali and Dr. Dadang Hawari during Canada-ASEAN Workshop discussions, *supra* note 284.

Statistical information is reported but without disclosing the identities of those it reflects. There is a professional ethical duty of confidentiality, although to date there has been no successful suit for a breach of confidentiality. In the past few years patients have acquired general control over access to their records.[314]

A patient can block records being transferred to other hospitals, but in practice doctors often disclose to other doctors for practical reasons. Although it has not yet been decided, it is likely that doctor-doctor disclosure for medical purposes would be justified in law. Another problem revolves around the liability of physicians for non-disclosure to persons who might be injured by dangerous patients. It is not fair to hold doctors liable for breach of confidentiality if they disclose, and leave them liable in negligence if they do not.

Japan and Taiwan

Neither the Japanese nor Taiwanese statutes deal specifically with confidentiality. To find a legislative basis for this issue, one would need to examine the general public administration legislation. In Japan a doctor may disclose "with good reason," but because this phrase has not yet been judicially interpreted it is difficult to say what might be included within its bounds. In practice, disclosure of conditions or cures is very rare. There is a possible conflict of interest here, because doctors often dispense medication and so stand to make additional profits when they assign prescriptions. This situation may result in the danger of over-medication or needless medicating. To give an idea of the strength of the tendency towards silence, in the realm of physical medicine only 20% of terminal patients are informed of their condition. Medicine is very much a stronghold of private enterprise and business in Japan.[315]

Although it is mandatory in Japan to file reports to the government regarding individual patients, these are deemed public and not private records. These records are subject to central registration, but one may question to what purpose. Japan allocates very little in the way of resources to the review of these documents. This general laxness is reflected in other areas as well. While there are 230 hospitals testing for the AIDS virus, only one social worker serves as a counsellor for all of these hospitals.[316] Whatever the purpose may be for filing centrally registered reports on the condition of people in mental institutions, it is not for the benefit of those who are being treated. Since it is very difficult to gain access to these records, there is no

---

314 *McInerney v. MacDonald*, [1992] 2 S.C.R. 138, a case involving patients' rights of access to medical records. But see discussion in text at note 324.

315 Salzberg, *supra* notes 80 and 91.

316 S. Salzberg, "The Japanese Response to Aids" (1991) 9 Boston Univ. Int'l L.J. 243.

private recourse against abuses of doctors to support malpractice suits, due to the difficulty of obtaining evidence.

Singapore and Malaysia

Records in these jurisdictions are hospital property to which the courts can gain access. Patients or relatives themselves do not, however, have an automatic right of access, although they can request the right to see reports. Employers cannot gain access to records without the consent of the patient and the family unless the patient is a government employee who is being investigated. Other government divisions cannot gain access to the records of those who are not their employees. Reports filed for payment purposes that do not include the sort of detail that would be informative of the condition of the patient may be made available. Similarly, general reports are also filed in the form of statistical information. Courts may subpoena records, and both the police and courts can obtain records as a matter of right. Where families are involved in the treatment and management of patients (usually in-patients), disclosures of the patient's condition(s) will be made routinely to the family unless specifically objected to by the patient.

Thailand

In Thailand, if a person has had a serious mental disorder for three years it is grounds for divorce, and a person with such a disorder cannot be a beneficiary of a will; consequently, disclosure has broad legal significance. While a doctor may disclose to family members against a patient's will, very rarely will a patient forbid disclosure to the family. Disclosure is limited by a physician's ethical obligation of confidentiality and potential legal liability. Doctors cannot disclose a patient's medical history or condition to a patient's legal opponent, but may be required to disclose such information to a court. If medical reports need to be sent to schools or employers, this action is usually taken with the express or implied consent of the patient. In addition, the explanation given will be tailored to the education of the seeker and the degree to which he/she is able to understand the relevant conceptions. If an out-patient card is released, it will be stamped "of no legal import"; in order to receive a letter with legal force, a separate letter must be requested. Patients often forbid disclosure of their personal medical information to companies. There is a mandatory requirement to submit a report on every hospital admission for the purposes of centralized statistics-keeping.[317]

317 Dr. Thamrong Dasananjali, *supra* note 311. Muntarbhorn, *supra* note 149 at 121-22, has observed that there is in general no guaranteed access in Thailand to government information and little legal protection for the privacy of citizens' individual data kept by the government, although an *Official Information Bill* has been proposed in Thailand to alter that situation.

Indonesia

The ethical obligations of the Indonesian medical association include the confidentiality of patient information. Only a judge can order the disclosure of information. There is a great deal of caution in disclosing information to a patient or family member, since it is believed that such information might upset a patient or aggravate his/her condition. Since the stigma surrounding mental disorder might generate further psychological difficulty, tact is employed, and the information is often disclosed in "watered down" terms. There is also the possibility that family members may misuse such information. For example, evidence that a person is suffering from a mental disorder may influence divorce or inheritance proceedings, and may result in lawsuits as a backlash to the disclosure. Disclosure is available, but it is on a "good cause" basis and subject to a gloss or translation from the doctor.[318]

Further, since the costs of physical ills are reimbursed by many companies' health programs while the costs related to mental illnesses are not, doctors often diplomatically designate psychological illnesses as organic to allow recovery under these plans.[319] This practice is in part justified by the fact that Indonesian physicians do not employ the sharp dichotomy between mind and body that is common to the West.

Role of Family Members

Canada (British Columbia)

The family has little or no express legal role within the provisions of British Columbia's *Mental Health Act*. There is a provision allowing the director of a mental health facility to release on leave a detained patient for designated purposes, and for stipulated periods of time, on conditions specified by the director, to the care of relatives or others capable of assuming responsibility for his or her care.[320] A guardian can request the informal admission of a minor.[321] Females who are to be admitted require accompaniment by a near relative or a female person between the time of request for admission and the time of admission.[322] There are provisions for advising, in writing, the next of kin of the rights of a patient who has been involuntarily admitted.[323]

There is currently a movement towards providing for greater inclusion of

---

318 Dr. Dadang Hawari, *supra* note 313.

319 In such a case the psychiatrist would use "M.D." instead of "psychiatrist" so that undue suspicion would not be raised.

320 *Mental Health Act*, R.S.B.C. 1996, c. 288, s. 37.

321 *Ibid.* s. 20.

322 *Ibid.* s. 19.

323 *Ibid.* s. 34.

the family and community in providing mental health services to those in need.[324] This aspect of community mental health services is somewhat complicated by the pervasiveness of patients' rights in Canada. As a patient has a right to know who has requested their committal to a mental institution, family members are sometimes reluctant to admit those in need of help, for fear of estranging them and irrevocably damaging relations. With the improvement of medical science, there has been an increase in the possibility of a cure. The hope of a cure reduces the stigma generally attached to mental disorder and leads to the probability that someday the person will be released. More attention needs to be paid to ensuring that psychiatric commitment initiated by family members does not irreparably sever the family-patient relationship.[325]

Japan

There is an emphasis in Japan on the family's responsibility for its members. This emphasis is reflected in the traditional approach in which the family protects society at large by removing a mentally ill family member from the public. Home detention was not prohibited until the 1950 Law. Nonetheless, the predominant mode of admission to hospital under the 1950 Law was by substitute consent (that is, the consent of a designated family member, or *hogogimusha*), and a finding by the superintendent of the psychiatric hospital that the person required hospitalization for medical treatment and protection.[326]

The basic premise of substitute consent in this form is that the family can and should make important medical decisions for an ill member. This is consonant with the relationship between the family and its members generally, and with the relationship among the patient, family, physician, and institution with respect to important medical decisions. Substitute consent is also common with physical ailments, even of the life-threatening variety, where patients themselves are usually not informed of their condition.[327] The ranking of priority for the choosing of the *hogogimusha* is the person's guardian, spouse, person exercising parental authority, or the person responsible for support under the *Civil Code*.[328]

The issue of substitute consent is significant when one considers that the vast majority of mental hospitals (89%) are private businesses that stand to

324 See e.g. the move made by Friends of Schizophrenia regarding confidentiality in the doctor-patient relationship that has excluded family.

325 To date there appears to have been very little study of this problem.

326 Salzberg, *supra* note 252 at 39; the preference for this type of admission was indicated by administrative directives suggesting that, even where the patient himself was willing to be hospitalized, the consent of the family member should be obtained and the admission should be considered as the "consent" form of admission.

327 *Ibid.* at 39.

328 *Ibid.* at 39-40.

profit from admitting these unwilling patients. Also, due to the stigma surrounding mental disability, when a patient is committed, his/her membership in the family often comes to an end. While it is a difficult decision to abandon a relative, once the person is committed, the family will generally cease to care for that person. These factors combine to paint a picture in which a person may be easily committed to a private mental hospital, and once there, neither family nor state would check to see that the patient would be well cared for.

Further, family consent is often implied from a lack of objection. Considering Japan's premium on politeness, seldom does a family object to a person's admission (although they may be reluctant to bring the family member to psychiatric facilities in the first place due to a recognition of the consequences). The general view that autonomy is subordinated to the "nurturance and security afforded by one's group, and especially one's family" even extends to the common practice of using substitute consent for medical decisions. Generally, even terminal conditions are disclosed to the family but not to the patients themselves.[329]

Involuntary admissions have been on a decline in recent years – a mere 6.4% as of June 1987 – but this is somewhat illusory, since the vast majority are voluntary but with substitute consent.[330] Substitute consent continues to exist under the 1987 *Mental Health Law* due to its basic cultural acceptability and despite widespread comment and criticism from both doctors and lawyers.[331] While essentially the same, the new law reduces the possibility of abuse by adding some procedural safeguards. The initial examination to determine if a person is "mentally disordered" must be done by a physician certified under the 1987 *Mental Health Law*, referred to as a Designated Physician (*shitei'i*).[332] Even though the name has changed from "consent" to "admission for treatment and protection," and the requirement has been added that it be a specialist physician who conducts the examination to determine whether hospitalization is necessary, the threshold for these admissions is still considerably lower than that required for admission pursuant to a governor's order (the other form of "compulsory" admission).[333]

In addition to giving consent to hospitalization for treatment and protection, the *hogogimusha* must ensure that the mentally disordered person receives medical treatment, give supervision so that the person does not harm himself or others, protect the financial interests of that person, and receive the hospitalized patient upon discharge. Responsible family members also

---

329 Salzberg, *supra* note 80 at 153.

330 *Ibid.* at 150-51.

331 *Ibid.* at 153-54.

332 *Ibid.* at 154.

333 Salzberg, *supra* note 252 at 39.

have the right to request that a psychiatric review board review the detention or physical treatment of a patient who has been hospitalized.[334]

Taiwan

Traditionally the family has played a major role in caring for a mentally ill family member. One of the prime objectives of the 1990 *Mental Health Law* was to establish medical care, against competing forms of traditional treatment, as the main response to mental illness.[335] In an attempt to transform the role of the family, the previous moral or practical responsibility for care has been converted into a legal duty to care for an ill member of the family. The onus now lies on the family to seek modern psychiatric facilities. The ill person's legally designated representative, spouse, or family member has a duty to get medical attention for that person. For severely ill persons, a so-called "caretaker" is to be put in place. The caretaker is chosen from among the following, beginning with the first option and moving down the list: legal guardian, spouse, parent, or family member (who need not be related, but merely cohabiting with the severely ill person). The caretaker's duties include ensuring that the ill person receives medical treatment, assisting in hospitalization, and preventing the person from doing harm to self or others.[336]

The *Mental Health Law* attempts to enforce the duties with respect to both ill and severely ill persons by imposing legal and monetary liability on a family that does not bring its ill member to modern psychiatric facilities.[337] The law further aims to encourage families to seek psychiatric or other medical intervention early in the course of the person's illness by imposing liability on the caretaker for any injury to the rights or interests of others caused by a failure to get medical assistance for the person concerned. There is a standard of reasonable care that limits this liability.[338] Under the *Mental Health Law*, no one is specifically charged with enforcing the liability that arises for failure to carry out the above described duties. It could be that the liability regime will be enforced by private litigation or negotiations, by government administrative procedures, or by the imposition of criminal liability.[339]

After the patient's discharge, the caretaker is to assist in that person's continuing receipt of out-patient treatment, community rehabilitation, at-home treatment and educational training or employment guidance. However, the *Mental Health Law* does not expressly impose liability upon the caretaker for

---

334 *Ibid.* at 40.
335 *Ibid.* at 37.
336 Salzberg, *supra* note 91 at 55.
337 Salzberg, *supra* note 251 at 38.
338 *Ibid.*
339 Salzberg, *supra* note 91 at 56.

violation of these continuing duties.[340] The legislators also anticipated that the caretaker or the family generally may not be willing to accommodate the patient upon discharge from hospital. Therefore the law provides that the caretaker may, for purposes of medical treatment, rehabilitation, educational training, or occupational guidance, place restrictions, without threats or use of force, on the place where the severely ill person may reside.[341]

While the law does not provide for substitute consent with respect to compulsory hospitalization, a patient's legally designated representative, spouse, or close relative may give substitute consent for certain treatment procedures.[342]

Apart from the formal apparatus of law, the family continues to play a major role in psychiatric admissions. In most cases hospitals will not accept even voluntary admissions (which are not regulated by statute) without another person, usually a relative, accepting responsibility as guarantor. In some hospitals it is the family member and not the patient who is deemed to apply for admission to the hospital. The guarantor is made to sign an agreement accepting the financial and legal responsibility for the patient while releasing the hospital staff from liability with respect to the patient.[343]

Singapore and Malaysia

One of the striking features in an Asian society like Singapore is that the patient is very seldom alone during admission; usually one or more family members are with the person.[344] The deep integration with the family often means that family members have an influential input in decisions regarding medical matters. An important factor contributing to the system of family consent is the belief that those who are mentally ill may not be the best judge of what is in their best interests and are not capable of making decisions. It is felt that only those with minds unaffected by a mental disorder are able to think clearly and weigh the pros and cons of treatment.[345] Further, the family knows the person concerned most intimately, and is in the best position to help with these sorts of decisions.

The role of the family may also arise in relation to issues of consent to treatment. In practice, if a patient is unable to consent, invasive treatments and procedures considered necessary would require the consent of relatives or (if the relatives were unavailable), an independent psychiatrist.[346]

---

340 *Ibid.* at 56.
341 *Ibid.* at 59.
342 Salzberg, *supra* note 252 at 38.
343 *Ibid.* at 39.
344 Kok, *supra* note 14.
345 *Ibid.*
346 *Ibid.*

Thailand and Indonesia

The family plays the same pivotal role in regard to mentally disordered persons in Thailand and Indonesia as it does in other Asian countries such as Singapore and Malaysia.

CONCLUSION: THE ADOPTION AND IMPOSITION OF WESTERN LAWS IN ASIA

Western law, like Western medicine and psychiatry, has been adopted and imposed in Asian countries at varying rates and in varying degrees. The adoption of Western law occurred earlier and was more complete in regard to criminal law than it was in regard to civil laws dealing with mental disorder. The adoption of Western criminal law was an important priority for the Western states that exerted colonial power over Asian countries. They were anxious to ensure that a familiar, Western form of criminal law applied in those countries. Such laws would provide a means of social control if necessary and a measure of comfort and security to foreigners living in and trading with these Eastern countries. Also, the imposition of a familiar system of civil law on these Eastern countries, at least as it related to trade and commerce, was an important priority for the Western colonizers. Some areas of civil law were clearly more important than others. Issues that were more of a behavioural nature (such as family or religious matters) could be more safely left to indigenous practices, since those issues did not clearly affect trade and commerce. For this reason, there was no perceived urgency to adopt Western laws in regard to mental disorder, at least in the civil law context.

Another factor that explains the slower adoption of Western laws dealing with the civil aspects of mental disorder is the fact that the legal regulation of mental disorder in the West was itself a relatively low priority and was still in its infancy when those Western countries began to exert their power over Asia in the latter half of the nineteenth century.

Finally, a significant difference in the legal cultures of East and West also explains the somewhat limited extent to which Western laws dealing with mental disorder have influenced Eastern laws on the same subject. The difference in the legal cultures has at least two significant aspects: the centrality of law and the primacy of individual rights over group interests in Western countries.

In regard to the first point, law occupies a central position in Western states. It is used in the West as a primary instrument for controlling and regulating a wide range of social activities and as a basis for mediating or adjudicating disputes. Laws, courts, and lawyers are plentiful; some would say too plentiful. There is a strong tradition of independence of judges and lawyers from government control. This feature fosters public confidence in the fairness of the judicial system as a mechanism for dispute resolution. In

Asian countries law has a much lower priority in regulating social activities. Social control is achieved through less formal mechanisms – for example, instilling group obligations and isolating those from the group who do not conform. Laws, lawyers, and courts are far fewer than in the West. Often laws do not provide any remedy for social concerns or injuries. And even if the law does provide a remedy, the law may be a last resort since it may be viewed as a shameful acknowledgment by the parties of the breakdown in social relations and their inability to resolve the matter on their own.[347]

Second, Western legal tradition, dating back to the Roman law adage "where there is a right, there is a remedy," is based on a system of rights and remedies, whereas the Eastern Confucian tradition of law is premised on duties, not rights.[348] And in the context of rights, Western liberal democratic thought over the past 200 years has increasingly emphasized the preeminence of individual rights over group rights, whereas political and ideological tradition in the East has generally placed group and community interests above individual interests. The Western pre-occupation with individual rights is especially evident in the development of international human rights instruments since the Second World War. Western efforts to impose these rights, and the instruments for their enforcement, on other countries with different legal traditions has understandably met with some opposition and resentment.

In suggesting that the centrality of law and the primacy of individual rights over group rights are features that distinguish the legal systems of the West from those of the East, I do not mean to imply that these features are uniform within all Eastern or Western legal systems. There is too much diversity in the ideological, political, religious, and cultural traditions of each country to expect any such uniformity. Just as there are significant differences between Western legal systems such as those of Canada and Germany, there are significant differences between Eastern legal systems such as those of Japan and Thailand. For example, Japan is more litigious and legalistic than China or Thailand.[349] And Japan, following Chinese tradition on this point, has a more "positivist" or secular view of law than a country like Thailand, which has been influenced by Indo-European systems that view law more as a set of moral commands from a deistic source,

347 J. Haley, "Law and Society in Contemporary Japan: American Perspectives" (1984) 17 Law in Japan 1; J. Haley, *Authority Without Power: Law and Japanese Paradox* (Oxford: Oxford Univ. Press, 1991).

348 Haley (1991), *supra* note 347 at 10-11; A. Petchsiri, *Eastern Importation of Western Criminal Law: Thailand as a Case Study* at 79-80 and 93-121 (Littleton, Colorado: F. B. Rothman, 1987). For example, China and Japan are influenced by traditional Confucian concepts, involving a duty-centred system and a hierarchical system in which every individual is contingent on another. Such a system is deeply incompatible with western legal notions of individualism. See also note 242, *supra*.

349 Haley, *ibid.* at 3.

be it Judeo-Christian, Hindu, or Islamic.[350] And the colonial history and experience of Malaysia and Singapore seem to have generated more ingrained Western legal systems than those of Thailand and Indonesia. However, notwithstanding the substantial differences among Asian countries, the centrality of law and the West's preference for individual over group rights does help to explain the limited adoption in Asia of Western civil laws dealing with mental disorder.

350 *Ibid.* at 24.

8

Whores, Soiled Doves, or Working Women? Law, Society, and the Sex Trade in Australia, Canada, and Thailand

John P. S. McLaren

INTRODUCTION

This chapter investigates the relationship between law, culture, and morality in the specific context of the treatment of the sex trade in three countries – Thailand, Australia, and Canada. Although this subject matter touches upon and overlaps with the transactional and civic themes examined elsewhere in this volume, it falls primarily within the behavioural sector outlined in the Introduction. The behaviour in this instance comprises conduct that is deeply embedded in the human experience – the purchase and sale of sexual services (commonly described as prostitution). Prostitution is behaviour propelled by a powerful combination of demand for sexual stimulation and excitement on the one hand, and for a means of livelihood on the other, which has sensual as well as social and economic impulses and explanations. This form of conduct has met with variable responses ranging from social approbation to social revulsion, both across and within human communities. Accordingly, its moral status has more often than not been ambiguous and the question of what to do about it is highly contested. As the introductory chapter implies, the context is not one that is easily accommodated within the confines of more conventional legal analysis and critique.

This study relating specifically to human behaviour can be expected to be closely influenced by culture across both time and place. There is thus a concern in what follows to consider how far the social realities of prostitution are contingent – that is, moulded by specific cultural assumptions and values in the three countries. Based on anthropological, sociological, and historical literature, as well as interviews, the chapter examines the socio-legal significance of prostitution in each society. In particular it considers: (1) the social impulses that explain the sex trade; (2) the various forms that the sex trade has taken; (3) the political economy of prostitution (the societal, political, and economic status of the trade); (4) the normative order and commercial sex, especially how far and in what ways it has been condoned, tolerated, condemned, and controlled and, to the extent that it has been marked as deviant, the relative roles of community morality, institutional religion, and the legal system and its agents in dealing with it; (5) the effectiveness of the normative order in controlling sex for sale – that is, the extent to which the values or policies embodied in customary, religious, or legal proscriptions constrain this behaviour and translate into community or official action when transgressions or offences occur.

The choice of the three countries reflects a desire both to illustrate differences in the socio-legal status of the sex trade between Western and Eastern societies, and to demonstrate that, even within the same cultural milieu – the European settler experience as it played out in Australia and Canada – there have been and still are variations in approach and ideology that reflect the idiosyncrasies of local political, social, and economic experience.

While the study analyses the impact of cultural difference in the construction of the sex trade, it is also sensitive to the fact that there may be commonalities in both social attitudes and practices within the three societies examined that allow for more general conclusions on the place and role of prostitution across cultures. Despite cultural differences, complex hierarchical societies may exhibit common understandings of the relative roles of constituent groups – for example, those constructed around gender, class, and race. The assessment of common themes is also important in this study, because the focus is, on the one hand, on two western European ex-colonial settler communities that inherited to a significant degree the social, economic, and legal culture of the colonial power, and, on the other, an ancient Asian state that has more recently experienced the superimposing of Western economic imperatives and social values with their individualistic presuppositions on a society geared much more closely to communitarian values and a rural, subsistence economy. A central feature of the study is to show how these broader structural and cultural changes have resulted in the importation of Western commercial organization into the sex trade itself and of Western social and legal notions in fashioning normative and institutional responses to it. At the same time, attention is directed to the issue of how far these developments have been reconciled or are at odds with traditional values and their normative consequences in Thai society. The evolution of a society that blends elements of traditional and imported culture also raises questions about the relevance of models to Thailand of control and regulation tried in Western countries such as Australia and Canada.

The comparisons and contrasts investigated here also have broader international significance in the sense that there has been and is a transnational sex trade whereby workers, customers, and organizers move across national boundaries to secure jobs and to stimulate and service demand. This reality has exercised both the League of Nations and the United Nations, which have sought over the years to secure adherence by national governments to legal principles and proscriptions, often based on Western precedents, to battle the trade in all its aspects. In recent decades emphasis in the international campaign has shifted to those parts of the trade that involve juvenile prostitution and the securing of specific domestic legislation in states from which exploiters come, rendering them and their commercial sponsors subject to prosecution at home. There are now linkages that reflect an understanding that these are not matters confined to the borders of any one state, and that collaborative effort is needed if significant progress is to be made in dealing with this most troublesome aspect of the trade.

There are, of course, inherent dangers in a person from one culture seeking to divine and understand the cultural dynamics of other societies. Intellectual colonialism is quite as real as physical colonialism, as Edward Said has so eloquently argued.[1] In approaching the topic I have attempted to compensate for any cultural biases I may have by consulting, especially in Thailand, with local people involved in research on and work with those in the sex trade. My thanks are due to them for being so generous with their time and so detailed and frank in the insights they provided.[2] Several Australian contacts were also most helpful in providing insights into the realities of the sex trade in that country and in explaining the differences in political and social discourse, and how they have played out in the law.[3] In the final analysis, it is abundantly evident that there is little to be confident about in the attempts of Western societies to control or regulate the sex trade by law, and that it is very difficult to take a holier-than-thou position

---

1 E. Said, *Orientalism* (New York: Vintage Books, 1979).

2 Dr. Supanya Lamsam, at that time Senior Planning Officer, Planning, Evaluation and International Affairs Bureau, Population and Community Development Assoc.; Dr. Phanna Waikakul, Assistant Program Director, Women's Economic and Leadership Development Program, National Commission on Women's Affairs; Dr. Sombat Thanprasertsuk, Epidemiology Section, Division of AIDS, Department of Communicable Disease Control, Ministry of Public Health; Dr. Malee Pruekpongsawalee, Faculty of Law, Thammasat University; Khun Siriporn Skrobanek, General Secretary, Foundation for Women; Justice Vicha Mahakun, Deputy Chief Justice of the Region I, Bangkok; Professor Apirat Petchsiri, Vice Dean of Academic Affairs, Faculty of Law, Chulalongkorn University; Dr. Surichai Wun'Gaeo, Director, Centre for Social Development Studies, Chulalongkorn University; Dr. Chakrapand Wongburanavart, Dean, Faculty of Social Sciences, Chiang Mai University; Dr. Sidthinat Prabudhanitisarn, Associate Dean for Academic Affairs and Foreign Relations, Faculty of Social Sciences, Chiang Mai University; Police Colonel Montri Pongtadsirikul, Chiang Mai Detachment, Thai National Police; Dr. Chayan Vaddhanaphuti, Director, Social Research Institute, Chiang Mai University; Dr. Virada Somswasdi, Associate Professor, Head of the Women's Studies Centre, Chiang Mai University.

3 Those consulted included: Professor Marcia Neave, Faculty of Law, Monash University; Dr. Barbara Sullivan, School of Government, University of Queensland, Visiting Fellow, RSSS, Australian National University; Ms. Christine Harcourt, Reasearch Officer at the Sydney Sexual Health Centre, Sydney Hospital, formerly Research Officer with the NSW Select Committee of the Legislative Assembly upon Prostitution.

in assessing the comparative record of communities in other parts of the world.

THE CULTURAL CONSTRUCTION OF PROSTITUTION, WEST AND EAST

The Sex Trade in Western Europe

The social practice of women providing sexual services to men for money is, as Richard Posner has recently noted, an old, if not an ancient one in Western societies.[4] It was, however, a form of economic activity that was invariably surrounded by intellectual, emotional, and moral ambiguity, at one and the same time applauded, condemned, manipulated, and despised. Providing sex for money was not, in other words, just like any other trade. Although there was over the long haul general acceptance that prostitution was inevitable (a necessary evil), because it provided a sexual safety valve for men whose libidinous urges might otherwise be directed at virtuous women, it was also seen as dangerous because it threatened the social, and later with the emergence of knowledge about venereal disease, the physical body. The pseudo-medical discourse, which appropriated terms such as contamination, pollution, and leprous to describe the adverse effects of prostitution, reflects these anxieties, and explains the depiction of female prostitutes as depraved, debauched, abnormal, and above all else, whores.

Conflicting with, but at the same time feeding off this visceral discourse was that of Christian morality, which drew in part on the biblical teaching of the New Testament and Jesus' forgiveness of sexual sinners, in particular the whore-like figure of Mary Magdalen.[5] In this view even the most degenerate prostitute was redeemable and capable of working to the glory of God. It followed that confirmed and God-fearing Christians had an obligation to bring prostitutes to virtue and the Christian life. And yet there was also the Pauline tradition within Christendom, which associated "female" with the body as opposed to the mind and spirit, and characterized women as potential temptresses and sources of moral pollution. In this mindset the figure of "whore" was a metaphor for everything that a virtuous, God-fearing woman should not be. This theology fed easily into the determinist discourse of women born to sin, and was capable of supporting variously both toleration and cruel repression.[6]

Whatever the theoretical justifications for or arguments against venal sex in Western societies, social historians have shown that it was practised widely

---

4 R. Posner, *Sex and Reason* (Cambridge, Mass.: Harvard University Press, 1992) at 130-33.

5 V. Bullough, *The History of Prostitution* (New York: University Books, 1964) at 57-68; N. Roberts, *Whores in History: Prostitution in Western Society* (London: Grafton, 1993) at 57.

6 G. Parker, "The Legal Regulation of Sexual Activity and the Protection of Females" (1983) 21 Osgoode Hall L. J. 187 at 188-90; Roberts, *supra* note 5 at 57-64.

in a variety of social contexts and forms. These ranged from the notorious activities of the courtesans of monarchs and aristocrats tied by law and the Christian religion to monogamous relationships, to the more secretive world of the women of supposedly celibate priests and the armies of women who plied their business to service a bachelor population frustrated by late marriage, married men whose sexual needs were not being accommodated within the nuptial state, and artificially constructed all-male communities such as armies and navies.[7]

From the same sources we also know of the institutionalization of prostitution in *bagnios* and brothels throughout Europe, either as a profitable sideline of religion or government, or by way of private enterprise. The "stews" in Southwark, which escaped the unpredictable crusading zeal of Henry VIII because they operated on land owned by the Bishop of Winchester, responded to the demands of the sexual economy, as did the private brothels run several centuries later by Mother Wells, a target of the campaign of those fraternal Bow Street magistrates, Henry and John Fielding, to clean up the metropolis.[8]

As these two examples demonstrate, the ambiguous status of the sex trade meant that it was exposed from time to time to crusades, personal or organized, principled or pragmatic, to close it down or limit its availability. Before the Reformation, these campaigns seem to have been directed more towards controlling competition from the private sector with state or church-sanctioned brothels, rather than reflective of moral disgust.[9] After the Reformation, especially in countries that felt to one degree or another the heavy hand of puritanism and later, evangelical Christianity, the objective of reformers was outright suppression of the trade.[10] More generally, through the Middle Ages into the early modern period, while venal sex was more tolerated than repressed, it always occupied an uncertain terrain in terms of the law. In England in particular, facets of prostitution-related conduct could be caught by the criminal law within the tensile offences of common nuisance and vagrancy, as well as by a range of more generic petty crimes.[11] There was enough proscriptive law for moral entrepreneurs and busybodies

7 Bullough, *supra* note 5 at 107-58; Roberts, *supra* note 5 at 82-186.

8 Roberts, *supra* note 5 at 117-18 details the status of the Southwark stews. E. Bristow, *Vice and Vigilance: Purity Movements in Britain Since 1700* (Dublin: Gill and Macmillan, 1977) at 59 mentions the career of Mother Needham.

9 Roberts, *ibid.* at 95.

10 Bristow, *supra* note 8 at 14-31.

11 See W. Russell, *A Treatise on Crimes and Misdemeanours*, Vol. I (New York: Garland Publishing, 1979, reprint of 4th Edition, 1865) at 449-51; W. Hawkins, *A Treatise of Pleas of the Crown*, Bk. I (London: Professional Books, 1973, reprint of 1716 Edition) at 196 on Common Nuisance; L. Radzinowicz, *A History of English Criminal Law and Its Administration from 1750* (London: Stevens and Sons, 1956, 1968) vol. 2, at 18-20; vol. 4, at 14-25 on vagrancy.

to make life uncomfortable for the women in the trade, when and for as long as they so desired. The whore provided a convenient metaphor for what was wrong with a society that had strayed far from religious teachings (especially those of the Pauline tradition), and a crowning example of the need for rigid adherence to a religious and legal regime of gender relations that emphasized the unlimited power of husbands over wives and fathers over daughters. The common law, which emphasized the merging of the wife's identity in that of the husband and viewed women in proprietary terms, was more than ready to oblige.[12]

The historical evidence in the West also indicates that despite the general disdain shown towards the public face of prostitution and its uncertain legal status, prostitutes were capable of resistance to protect their interests and turf. Roberts chronicles the rebellions of the whores of Toulouse in the fourteenth and fifteenth centuries, and the formation of prostitutes' guilds in both Paris and Avignon (in the latter city under the patronage of Queen Joanna of Naples, the owner of the official brothel).[13] There is also support in the work of social historians for the claim that even in Protestant countries, despite the attempts of religious authorities, legislators, and judges to scare or dictate compliance with moral and legal codes, significant segments of the population took a more relaxed approach to sex and sexuality. Indeed, in England before the nineteenth century, the evidence suggests that sex relations and their negotiation owed more to local custom than they did to the strictures of the clergy and the formalities of the law.[14]

Sex for Purchase and Sale in Asia

Venal sex was not confined to the Western European world in the pre-modern period. Sexual services for money were available in patriarchal communities in Asia, in which political, religious, and social power was reposed in men.[15] Women were subject to male needs and dictates in sexual matters. It does not seem to have mattered what religious and legal tradition was followed, women were on earth to do men's bidding and subject to their formal control. This was true in the context of the family, as it was in the broader community. Culture and religious tradition, however, often decreed that the construction of sexual relations was different to that in the Christian West. In Islamic, Hindu, Buddhist, and Confucian tradition, sex as a human activity was, more often than not, celebrated. Moreover, within all

---

12 W. Blackstone, *Commentaries on the Laws of England, Book I* (Oxford: Clarendon Press, 1765, reprint by Legal Classics Library, 1983) at 430-31.

13 Roberts, *supra* note 5 at 97-99.

14 J. Gillis, *For Better, For Worse: British Marriages, 1600 to the Present* (Oxford: Oxford Univ. Press, 1985) at 9-128.

15 Bullough, *supra* note 5 at 69-103.

these traditions polygyny was practised to a greater or lesser degree.[16] It was to an extent legally approved, which meant that a man's access to more than one woman, as a wife or concubine, was acceptable. In wealthy families the existence of servant and slave girls in the household who had little or no rights provided an even larger pool of women with whom the male members of the family could find sexual satisfaction. The reality of plural sexual relationships was recognized in law or custom in practices of the sale and pledging of daughters by wealthy families seeking politically and socially advantageous unions, and poor families desirous of finding financial sponsors for their female children.[17] As in the West, however, law and religion did not always dictate what people actually did. In some communities at least monogamy was the norm, and within those communities tradition and custom, not to mention lack of privacy, meant that it was those normative orders that actually controlled people's lives, most of the time.[18]

Prostitution did exist in these societies, because there was invariably an unmet male need for sexual excitement. For those outside the charmed circle of the elite, maintaining multiple wives and concubines was often not feasible. Wealthy and powerful men travelled and sought companionship while away from home. As well, from time to time they had both sensual and strategic reasons for not seeking sexual pleasure within the household. More generally, males who were organized into armies, navies, and labour details or were leading transient lifestyles also created a demand for casual sexual relations that was met by prostitutes. Each society had its institutions catering to this range of sexual desires.[19]

Nevertheless, the more relaxed attitude towards sex in these societies did not mean that women could expect understanding if they showed sexual independence, because virtuous womanhood was highly prized by men. The adulteress came in for particularly harsh punishment. Divorce was more difficult for women than it was for men. Furthermore, while prostitutes were often tolerated and free of formal legal proscription, they were also the target of religious and moral opprobrium. Viewed as driven by bodily and

---

16 Bullough notes that within Hindu communities monogamy was the norm, although polygyny was practised in wealthy families as a means of ensuring that the lineage was continued where the first wife did not bear children: *ibid.* at 88-89.

17 On the detail of sale and pledge in traditional Chinese society, see S. Gronewold, *Beautiful Merchandise: Prostitution in China 1860-1936* (New York: Haworth Press, 1982) at 1-4.

18 Where the other religious traditions were in the ascendancy, cultural norms on marriage often differed depending on the community in question. Thus a Christian community in a Moslem country where polygyny was practised by the religious and cultural majority would practise monogamy. Even where the vast majority of a population adhered to a religious tradition in which polygyny was lawful, such as Buddhists in Thailand, many would feel constrained by local custom, not to mention economic realities, to practice monogamy.

19 For China, see Gronewold, *supra* note 17 at 4-25.

material desire and as the source of pollution (in particular because of menstruation), women clearly had to work hard to earn the title of "virtuous." If a woman lost it, it was because she had allowed her natural impulses to submerge virtuous instincts, or because she was inherently aberrant in her character and desires. The result was that she was marked, if not as a matter of law, then as a matter of morality, as fallen, unclean, or undeserving.

Gender Relations and Prostitution in Traditional Thailand

What we know of the social history of Thailand reflects several of the general themes evident in the construction of Asiatic attitudes towards sex and gender, as well as some peculiarities deriving from its own particular cultural experience.

The royal law, as it appears in the major compilation known as the Law of the Three Seals of 1805, leaves no doubt about the subservience of women to men.[20] Females were treated as property, subject to the physical chastisement of father or husband, and could be given in marriage, sold, or pledged by their masters at will.[21] Women were expected to be loyal to only one man. Mutilation or the death penalty attended adultery by a female spouse. By contrast a husband was entitled by law to have multiple wives, both to satisfy his desires and to strengthen the bonds of patronage and connection that defined his status. The 1805 code set out the number of wives allowed to aristocrats as four (one for service to the King; a second by arranged marriage; a third at the husband's choice; and a slave wife as a fourth).[22] The King, it seems, was not bound by this limitation. This institutionalization of patriarchy drew strength from the Brahminical interpretations of kingship, status, and masculine power that were part of the religious heritage of the Thai state.

Despite evidence that the Lord Buddha recognized the equality of women and men in seeking enlightenment, and accepted the important role of female religious communities, his teachings were interpreted by his Brahminical followers to stress male superiority in both the religious and political spheres, leaving women to the material and domestic realms.[23] Although Buddhism lacks the widespread institutionalized judgmentalism associated with much traditional Christian reflection on prostitution, some

---

20 On the traditional Thai law, see M. B. Hooker, *A Concise Legal History of South-East Asia* (Oxford: Clarendon Press, 1978) at 25-32.

21 K. Rayankorn, ed., "Women and the Law in Thailand," in *Women's Legal Position in Thailand* (Chiang Mai: Women's Studies Program, Chiang Mai Univ., 1991) at 20; K. Thitsa, *Providence and Prostitution: Image and Reality for Women in Buddhist Thailand* (London: Change International Reports, 1980) at 5-7.

22 D. Tantiwiramond and S. Pandey, "The Status and Role of Thai Women in the Pre-Modern Period: A Historical and Cultural Perspective" (1987) 2 Sojourn 124 at 135.

23 C. Kabilsingh, *Thai Women in Buddhism* (Berkeley: Parallax Press, 1991) at 13-35.

Buddhist interpretations of the female role and status have clearly marginalized women. This has been achieved by preaching that they are born to suffering, that they are sources of physical and thus ritual pollution, and that they have suffered a decline in merit for transgressions in former lives by being born female.[24] In consequence guilt has lain heavy on some women, and they have felt as a particular burden the need to do merit to improve their *kharma* (spiritual status) in future incarnations.

Like the situation in Western societies, the dictates of the law and religion have never told the whole truth about gender relations in Thailand. Outside the ranks of the elite in Thai society, it seems as though life and sexuality were governed much more by local custom and reverence for ancestors than by the prescriptions of royal edicts or scholarly interpretations of the faith. Relationships between the sexes were monogamous and what were clearly strong bonds of obligation associated with marriage and family union related to concerns about offending ancestral spirits.[25] Matrilineal transmission practices, the matrilocal residence of young married couples, family economies in which all shared, and the power associated with female ancestral figures (in particular in Northern Thailand) all contributed to a social reality in which gender relations were probably far less polarized than either religion or law would suggest.[26]

Determining the existence of widespread prostitution in Thailand before the nineteenth century is problematic, since there is little or no available documentary evidence bearing on the issue. Speculative comments are made by some Thais that prostitution came to Thailand with foreigners, in particular Chinese workers and settlers. While foreign communities, including Western ones, would almost certainly have generated a demand for prostitutes in the past as well as in the present, it would be wrong to conclude that there was no indigenous "trade."[27] To some extent, practices and customs within Thai society may have worked against this form of sex for sale. In its higher echelons polygyny was both condoned and widely practised. This reality and the unimpeded access of the *paterfamilias* to servants and slaves may have reduced the need to find sexual playmates elsewhere, except perhaps when travel or household politics seemed to demand it. Among

24 Thitsa, *supra* note 21 at 16-18; Kabilsingh, *ibid.* at 22-35.

25 A. Turton, "Matrilineal Descent Groups and Spirit Cults of the Thai-Yuan in Northern Thailand" (1972) 60 J. of the Siam Society 217.

26 B. Yoddumnern-Attig, "Thai Family Structure and Organization: Changing Roles and Duties in Historical Perspective," in B. Yoddumnern-Attig et al., eds., *Changing Roles and Statuses of Women in Thailand* (Nahkonpathom: Institute for Population and Social Research, Mahidol University, 1992) at 8, 14-16, 22-23; A. Soonthorndhada, "Domestic Role Behaviour, Expectations and Adaptations: Past to Present," *ibid.* at 64-69; Thitsa, *supra* note 21 at 7-9.

27 S. De La Loubere, *A New Historical Relation of the Kingdom of Siam* (London: Oxford Univ. Press, 1969 reprint of 1693 original).

the majority of the population the cultural constraints of custom and spirit worship and the lack of mobility may well have militated against it while on home turf. However, it has been suggested that the all-male communities formed by service in the military or in the annual corvées demanded by the king or the nobility created a demand for prostitutes and a resulting supply.[28] Unless Thai males were abnormally abstinent, it is difficult to suppose that they did not seek and were not provided with sexual release in such circumstances.[29] There seems to have been no formal law relating to the practice of prostitution, which suggests that to the extent it existed it was tolerated.

Cultural Variables and Commonalities in Commercial Sex

Before the nineteenth century, prostitution and its treatment in both Europe and Asia reflected in part the particular cultural milieu in which sex for purchase and sale operated. The practice was thus contingent upon attitudes towards sexuality and how gender relations were constructed in terms of their political, social, religious, economic, and, in turn, legal significance. However, it is also apparent that there were more transcendent influences at work that made for definite parallels in the social treatment of venal sex across cultures. Dominating the construction of prostitution was the tradition and practice of patriarchy, which seems to have been present in all complex hierarchical societies and invariably to have coloured social responses to this form of behaviour. Patriarchy and the inconsistencies it has generated explain the widespread phenomenon of prostitution being both condemned and tolerated in the same society. While the male holders of power insisted on treating women as politically and socially inferior, to be controlled by law and religion but, where necessary, available to satisfy men's sexual needs and desire, there was little enthusiasm for legal or other normative panaceas that might thwart and penalize those impulses.

THE RECONSTRUCTION OF GENDER RELATIONS AND COMMERCIAL SEX IN THE MODERN ERA IN AUSTRALIA AND CANADA

Introduction

The period from 1800 to the mid-twentieth century represents a period of major changes in thinking and practices regarding sex and sexuality in Western societies. As a consequence, these issues have been elevated to the

---

28 M. Muecke, "Mother Sold Food, Daughter Sells Her Body: The Cultural Continuity of Prostitution" (1992) 35 Social Science Medicine 891 at 892, quoting from S. Skrobanek, *The Transnational Sex-ploitation of Thai Women* (M.S. thesis, Institute of Social Studies, The Hague, 1983). On the corvée system, see Tantiwiramond and Pandey, *supra* note 22 at 134.

29 For a recent journalistic source that indicates a long indigenous history of prostitution in Thailand, see "Foreigners 'Blamed' for Sex Problems," *Bangkok Post* (25 Dec. 1994).

level of major social and often political concern and discourse,[30] leading to a greater degree of intrusiveness and manipulation of people's lives and values. Especially in English-speaking, Protestant countries, advocates of moral cleansing and regeneration have often taken the initiative in vigorously attacking contemporary mores and an apparent growth in sexual promiscuity, and pressing for campaigns to stop a headlong slide into an abyss of immorality.[31] Although the call to fashion a more virtuous community has often been inspired by women organizing as distinctive social agents and claiming their own share in policy-making and reordering society, until recently it has been the voice of maternalism rather than radicalism that has held centre stage. Moreover, when women have attempted to bring their own more sensitive insights and strategies to bear, they have often been thwarted or co-opted by male-dominated groups with the political clout to work change. The outcome has in some instances been a reworking of patriarchal discourse and assumptions, leading to a greater acceptance of the concept of "separate spheres" in which women are the caregivers and moral managers, and the resulting idealization and stereotyping of women as both virtuous and asexual.[32] Under this reconstruction of the female *persona* and psyche, the whore or "fallen woman" has become an even more troublesome figure – a person to be pitied, redeemed, or excoriated, but never to be allowed her own voice or personality.[33] In legal terms, this view has led to the implementation of more extensive and harsher criminal law provisions, allegedly designed to protect girls and women from sexual predators, and the development of regimes and institutions for the resocialization of "fallen women" and the protection of girls at risk. The reality, however, has been quite different. Law enforcers have rarely shared the apocalyptic and instrumental assumptions of the reformers. Their agenda has varied during the period from continued tolerance of prostitution, through ill-fated experiments with formal regulation of prostitute communities, to a compromise form of informal regulation that uses the tools of the criminal law and its public *persona* in a highly discretionary way to exercise a form of remote control over the trade. By mixing selective enforcement with toleration and establishing unwritten rules about boundaries and limits and the implications of transgressing them, the police in most English-speaking common

30 M. Foucault, *The History of Sexuality, Vol. 1: An Introduction*, trans. R. Hurley (New York: Vintage Books, 1980); J. Weeks, *Sex, Politics and Society: The Regulation of Sexuality Since 1800* (London: Longman, 1981).

31 Bristow, *supra* note 8.

32 C. Ball, "Female Sexual Ideologies in Mid to Late Nineteenth Century Canada" (1986) 1 Can. J. of Women and the Law 324.

33 E. Trudgill, *Madonnas and Magdalenes: The Origin and Development of Victorian Social Attitudes* (London: Heinneman, 1976); F. Mort, *Dangerous Sexualities: Medico-Moral Politics in England Since 1830* (London: Routledge, Kegan and Paul, 1987).

law countries have sought to leave the practitioners of commercialized sex (especially the women) in a legal twilight zone, never sure of their legal status and when the police may strike next.[34] The power that attends discretionary law enforcement has not infrequently tempted police officers to exploit the system for their own benefit. One of the main sites of graft in policing has been the morality or vice squad.[35]

The control over prostitution exercised by the police in Western countries benefited for several decades in the first half of this century by the medicalization of prostitution at the hands of both public health doctors and psychiatrists. In legal terms this translated into draconian provisions related to sexually transmitted diseases (STDs), and the use of mental health and child welfare legislation to get control of the so-called "feeble minded," a group into which many prostitutes were seen as falling.[36] The institutionalization of prostitutes and girls "at risk" has also proven problematic because of the moral and professional stereotyping that has been the mark of these experiments, and the understandable resistance to which it has given rise among the "deviant" populations.[37]

As we shall see, in more recent decades counter-discourses about the sex trade have emerged, reflecting both civil libertarian and feminist concerns that the law has vacillated between treating prostitutes as highly deviant and calculating on the one hand and childlike idiots on the other. Moreover, the argument goes, whatever the stance of the law in formal terms, the institutional and ideological imperatives of law enforcement have invariably victimized prostitutes, while largely ignoring the males creating and managing demand for paid sexual services. Some of these critiques, especially those from feminist discourse that has included or been affected by the views and opinions of sex trade workers themselves, have emphasized that for many women this is a job like any other designed to keep

34 See A. Reiss, "Consequences of Compliance and Deterrence Models of Law Enforcement for the Exercise of Police Discretion" (1984) 47 Law and Contemporary Problems 83; J. Skolnick, *Justice without Trial*, 2d ed. (New York: Wiley, 1975); G. Marquis, "Power from the Street: The Canadian Municipal Police," in R. C. Macleod and D. Schneiderman eds., *Police Powers in Canada: The Evolution and Practise of Authority* (Toronto: Univ. of Toronto Press, 1997) at 24.

35 For a classic example from recent Australian police history, see P. Dickie, *The Road to Fitzgerald* (St. Lucia, Queensland: Univ. of Queensland Press, 1988) detailing corruption in the Queensland police over four decades, and M. Finnane, "The Fitzgerald Commission: Law, Politics and State Corruption in Queensland" (1988) 47 Aust. J. of Public Administration 332.

36 J. Cassel, *The Secret Plague: Venereal Disease in Canada 1838-1939* (Toronto: Univ. of Toronto Press, 1987); S. Buckley and J. Dickin McGinnis, "Venereal Disease and Public Health Reform in Canada" (1982) 63 Can. Historical Rev. 337.

37 C. Backhouse, "Nineteenth Century Prostitution Law: Reflection of a Discriminatory Society" (1985) 18 Social History 387; C. Strange, "'The Criminal and Fallen of Their Sex': The Establishment of Canada's First Women's Prison, 1874-1901" (1985) 1 Can. J. of Women and the Law 79.

body and soul together and to provide support for families. It follows that prostitution should be treated like other work and subject to commercial regulation and health and welfare benefits that are associated with paid employment generally.[38]

Thailand has not been left untouched by these developments. The progressive penetration of the traditional economy and social structures by Western colonialism and commercial expansionism has resulted in increasing pressure on successive Thai governments to adopt Western social and moral values, and to ensure the process by introducing Western constitutional institutions and law, especially criminal, family, and administrative law, to replace traditional law and custom. As Apirat Petchsiri has convincingly shown, although Thailand was never colonized by a European power in the formal sense, it was clearly within the sphere of influence of several. The price for remaining at least nominally free was to adopt European governmental practices and civil, commercial, and criminal law, and to outlaw practices that offended the sensibilities of Western governments and their citizens or threatened to compromise their best interests.[39] Pressure to conform to avoid the older colonial option has, during the twentieth century, been replaced by equally persuasive forces preaching the benefits of economic development and the need to placate the moral values of the international community. The result of this increasing identification of Thailand with Western priorities and agendas in the area of prostitution has been, on the one hand, the enhanced commercialization of the practice, and on the other its reification as a form of conduct that the law has an important interest in labelling and controlling. As the record in Western countries shows, the sexual economy is inherently unruly and tensile, and law an instrument of dubious efficacy in dealing with it. Because both the economics and regulation of prostitution in contemporary Thailand reflect imported value systems and depend upon administrative and legal regimes that are to an extent alien and unstable, the problems identified with social and legal policy towards the sex trade in the West are magnified and distorted in this Asian community. However, as in the West, some contemporary voices are taking issue with the contradictory assumptions and influences that have affected the law and social policy in this area. Front and centre are feminist scholars and activists, human rights experts, and the representatives of non-governmental organizations (NGOs) concerned with poverty and public health who decry the partial application of the law, the oppressive power over the lives of women and children that it condones, and the

38 A leading example of this sort of analysis and critique is R. Perkins, *Working Girls: Prostitutes, Their Life and Social Control* (Canberra: Australian Institute of Criminology, 1991).

39 A. Petchsiri, *Eastern Importation of Western Criminal Law: Thailand as a Case Study* (Littleton, Colorado: Rothman, 1987) at 17-64.

failure of the political and legal system to provide basic protections to those who work in the sex trade.[40]

Law, the State, and Prostitution in Australia and Canada to 1860

Both the Australian and Canadian colonies inherited the pre-industrial criminal law of England, including the vague, catch-all offences of common nuisance and vagrancy.[41] Social conditions, however, were not congenial to any serious attempts to enforce this law against parties engaged in prostitution. In New South Wales and later Tasmania, which were convict colonies, the gross imbalance in the relative numbers of males and females worked against any serious attempt to proscribe sex for sale. (In 1800, men counted for 80% of the population over 12 years of age: 61 years later there were still 38% more men than women in Australia.)[42] So did the fact that the female convict population included former prostitutes and that women offenders who were not prostitutes either were or were assumed to be sexually available in ways that belied any concern for protecting female virtue.[43] The authorities were either not interested in applying English criminal law, or, if they were, quickly recognized the futility of doing so in any systematic way.

In the free Canadian colonies (after the early years in which gender imbalance and transitory populations made a mockery of attempts to enforce the law against prostitution), Nova Scotia, New Brunswick, and later Upper and Lower Canada enacted legislation designed to make brothel-keeping and street-walking explicit species of vagrancy.[44] This legislative effort formally imitated British legislation. However, despite occasional flurries of enforcement activity, usually in the wake of outcries of moral indignation

---

40 Rayankorn, *supra* note 21; Thitsa, *supra* note 21.

41 On common nuisance, see *supra* note 11. On the evolution of vagrancy laws, see J. Phillips, "Poverty, Unemployment and the Administration of the Criminal Law: Vagrancy Laws in Halifax, 1864-1890," in P. Girard and J. Phillips, eds., *Essays in the History of Canadian Law, Vol. III, Nova Scotia* (Toronto: Osgoode Society, 1990) 128 at 129. On the adoption of English vagrancy law relating to prostitution in Canada, see Backhouse, *supra* note 37 at 388-90.

42 B. Sullivan, *The Politics of Sex: Prostitution and Pornography in Australia since 1945* (Cambridge: Cambridge Univ. Press, 1997) at 17.

43 See P. Robson, "The First Forty Years," in J. Mackinolty and H. Radi, eds., *In Pursuit of Justice: Australian Women and the Law 1788-1979* (Sydney: Hale and Iremonger, 1979) at 1. For a somewhat different take on the role of women in these penal colonies, see K. Daniels, "Prostitution in Tasmania during the Transition from Penal Settlement to 'Civilized' Society," in K. Daniels, ed., *So Much Hard Work: Women and Prostitution in Australian History* (Sydney: Fontana Books, 1984) at 15.

44 See e.g. *An Act to Authorize the Erection and Provide for the Maintenance of a House of Industry* (1837), 7 Wm. IV, c. 24 (Upper Canada). *An Act for the More Speedy and Effectual Punishment of Persons Keeping Disorderly Houses* (1829), 9 and 10 Geo. IV, c. 8 (New Brunswick); *An Act for Punishing Rogues, Vagabonds, and Other Idle and Disorderly Persons* (1774), 14 Geo. III, c. 4 (Nova Scotia).

from respectable citizens, official lassitude quickly set in and sex for sale was basically tolerated.[45] This reflected both the prevailing establishment view that prostitution was inevitable and necessary to protect virtuous females in communities – for instance, ports, garrison towns, and bush camps – in which there was a surfeit of unattached males, and the institutional reality that there was no system of professional policing that could have initiated or sustained long-term, orchestrated campaigns of law enforcement against sexual vice.

Only with the emergence of more stable communities populated by free settlers and middle class families with economic and emotional investment in the area or region, did prostitution come into focus, along with other forms of "immoral" and "anti-social" behaviour, as requiring special social and legal attention. This occurred earlier, it seems, in Canada than in Australia, a mark perhaps of a different chronology and pace of settlement and divergent immigrant pools, as well as the continuation of the transportation of convicts to Australia well into the middle decades of the nineteenth century.[46] Front and centre in the construction of vice as socially corrosive in Canada was evangelical religion, which combined with embryonic feminism and strains of utilitarian reformism to fight it.[47] The initial target of attention considered to be at the heart of all moral degradation was alcohol. In this, as with other sources of social anxiety, the rhetoric in Canada normally flowed from the United States, and the social and legal responses from Britain.[48] Concerns about vice were also generally ethnocentric. Fugitives, such as the black population of Nova Scotia, or immigrants, especially the clannish and "unruly" Irish Roman Catholics, were alleged to be its most frequent practitioners.[49] The earliest impulses of moral reformers were that education and sermonizing were the keys to creating a virtuous

---

45 See T. B. Aikens, *History of Halifax City* (Halifax: Nova Scotia Historical Society, 1895) at 158; E. Guillet, *The Pioneer Farmer and Backwoodsman*, Vol. 1 (Toronto: Ontario Publishing, 1963) at 146; J.-P. Wallot, "Religion and French Canadian Mores in the Early Nineteenth Century" (1971) 52 Can. Historical Rev. 51.

46 On the law and prostitution in the first free colony in Australia founded in 1836, see S. Horan, "'More sinned against than sinning'? Prostitution in South Australia, 1836-1914," in Daniels, *supra* note 43 at 87-126.

47 See H. Graff, "'Pauperism, Misery and Vice': Illiteracy and Criminality in the Nineteenth Century" (1977) 11 J. of Social History 245.

48 See e.g. M. Garland and J. Talman, "Pioneer Drinking Habits and the Rise of Temperance Agitation in Upper Canada Prior to 1840" (1931) 27 Ontario Historical Society Papers 341; J. Clemens, "Taste Not; Touch Not: A Study of the Social Assumptions of the Temperance Movement in Canada West Between 1839 and 1859" (1972) 64 Ontario History 142.

49 On this phenomenon of blaming the "Other" for immorality, see J. Fingard, *The Dark Side of Life in Victorian Halifax* (Halifax: Pottersfield Press, 1989), on Afro-Nova Scotians; J. Weaver, "Crime, Public Order, and Repression: The Gore District in Upheaval, 1832-1851" (1986) 78 Ontario History 175 at 186-94, on the Irish.

nation.[50] Initially, there was no campaign to reform the existing law on prostitution, with its rationale in public order. However, pressure was exerted in some communities, most notably those with stable institutional infrastructures and professional police forces, for it to be actually enforced. In Canada, Toronto was to take the lead.[51] To the extent that new law was constructed to fight sexual vice, it was embodied in the bylaws of the new municipal corporations – a sign that prostitution in the mid-nineteenth century was viewed very much as a local, and not as a provincial or national problem.[52]

Regulation by Contagious Diseases Legislation: Queensland, Tasmania, and the Canadas

Ironically, it was not the moral reformers who initially campaigned for new law to control prostitution, but an alliance of establishment political and military interests, on the one hand, and public health physicians, on the other. The ideological rationale for what was known in British imperial practice as contagious diseases legislation was laid by British physician and venereologist, William Acton.[53] Acton was strongly of the view that sexuality was biologically gendered in the sense that men were by nature sexually active and aggressive, while most women were asexual. It followed that it was difficult, if impossible, for men, especially those without education, to sublimate their sexual urges.[54] Accordingly, if respectable women were to be safe, then that safety could only be guaranteed if there were other sexual outlets for hypersexual men. Biology and environment seem to have come to the rescue by providing a class of women with aberrational sexual impulses, ready to provide these services – prostitutes and "fallen women" more generally.[55] There was unfortunately a medical price for this irresistible male sexual urge and the bifurcation of female sexuality – the existence and transmission of venereal diseases (VD). As a public health doctor, Acton, while recognizing the inevitability of the sex trade and well aware of the absence of cure for VD, believed that it was possible by the regulation of prostitutes to minimize the risks associated with their spread.[56] In this view,

---

50 Graff, *supra* note 47.

51 N. Rogers, "Serving Toronto the Good: The Development of the City Police Force 1834-84," in V. Russell, ed., *Forging a Consensus: Historical Essays on Toronto* (Toronto: Univ. of Toronto Press, 1984) 116.

52 G. Marquis, "The Contours of Urban Justice, 1830-1875" (1987) 15 Urban History Rev. 269 at 270-72.

53 W. Acton, *Prostitution Considered in its Moral, Social and Sanitary Aspects, in London and in other Large Cities: with Proposals for the Mitigation and Prevention of its Attendant Evils* (London: MacGibbon and Kee, 1968, edited version of 1857 original).

54 *Ibid.* at 114-18.

55 *Ibid.* at 118-20.

56 *Ibid.* at 138-70.

not surprisingly, he was influenced by the system of regulated brothels (*maisons de tolerance*) in France.[57]

The implementation of regulated prostitution in the British Empire was closely associated with reform of the armed services and anxiety about the high incidence of venereal disease amongst Queen Victoria's fighting men.[58] Concern about the sensibilities of male partners at being subject to compulsory medical inspection led to the establishment of contagious disease legislation first in Britain and then in several Australian and Canadian colonies and non-white territories such as India and Singapore that made women the target of the law.[59] Rather than establishing a regulated brothel system, the legislation vested in the police powers to question, arrest, and consign for compulsory examination in hospitals women picked up on the streets under suspicion of being prostitutes with infection. If found to have contracted a venereal disease, they were subject to detention in hospital until pronounced cured or safe to release.

Interestingly, the social impact of this legislation varied within the imperial system, reflecting perhaps differing degrees of political and social maturity, and, in particular, divergent experience with female activism. The successful campaign led by Josephine Butler and others for the repeal of the *Contagious Diseases Act* in Britain as repressive of and discriminatory towards poor women and sanctioning "state regulation of vice" was not emulated in Australia or Canada. In the former, legislation enacted in Queensland (1868) and Tasmania (1879), apparently to meet the Royal Navy's fear about the spread of infection in the fleet, generated little or no resistance and remained in force until the early twentieth century.[60] Kay Daniels has suggested that, in the case of Tasmania, one explanation for the legislation's acceptance and durability was the lack of a political alliance of resistance in the colony, such as that between middle-class women and working-class

---

57 On French prostitution and its control in the nineteenth century, see A. Corbin, *Women for Hire: Prostitution and Sexuality in France after 1850,* trans. A. Sheridan (Cambridge, Mass.: Harvard Univ. Press, 1990).

58 J. Walkowitz, *Prostitution and Victorian Society: Women, Class and the State* (Cambridge: Cambridge Univ. Press, 1980) at 73; R. Davenport-Hines, *Sex, Death and Punishment: Attitudes to Sex and Sexuality in Britain since the Renaissance* (London: Fontana Press, 1990) at 166-67.

59 The parent legislation was *An Act for the Prevention of Contagious Diseases at Certain Naval and Military Stations* (1864), 27 and 28 Vict., c. 85 (England). On its application in India, see Davenport-Hines, *ibid.* at 175-80, and in Singapore, J. Warren, "Prostitution and the Politics of Venereal Disease, 1870-98" (1990) 21 J. of Southeast Asian Studies 360.

60 *Suppression of Contagious Diseases Act* (1868), 31 Vict., c. 30 (Queensland); *Contagious Diseases Act* (1879), 42 Vict., c. 36 (Tasmania). On the Queensland legislation, see R. Evans, "'Soiled Doves': Prostitution in Colonial Queensland," in Daniels, *supra* note 43 at 141; on Tasmania, see Daniels, "Prostitution in Tasmania," *supra* note 43 at 57-86.

men in Britain.[61] In Upper and Lower Canada, however, the legislation was allowed to lapse in 1870 after only five years. This was probably not the result of any principled objection to it (although such arguments were voiced in certain quarters), but rather the absence of the medical facilities and police capacity to make it work. Although contagious diseases legislation was dropped, repealed, or died out in the white empire and was in that sense a failed experiment, it had a much more durable consequence. It embedded the notion in public policy circles as well as in middle class culture of the street or public prostitute as inherently different and deviant – that is, the quintessential whore.

Moral Reform Movements in Canada and Australia and the Battle against Sexual Exploiters

The ill-fated experiment with medical-moral regulation of prostitution gave way to an ostensibly more successful campaign for changes to and expansion of the criminal law to deal with it. The pressure for further and harsher criminalization of prostitution-related activity in Australia and Canada was a product of a set of anxieties in the late Victorian and Edwardian English-speaking world associated with perceived adverse changes in both the conditions of life and values in modern Western society. Particularly worrisome for the middle class were expanding industrialization and urbanization, increases in female employment opportunities, a decline in the importance and solidity of the family and its values, and enhanced immigration numbers.[62] The traditional verities associated with church, hearth, and honest male labour seemed to count for less and less. As a result, youth was increasingly exposed to moral corruption. Girls who lacked adequate familial guidance or were rebellious and those with a naivety born of life in middle class families were thought to be at risk from vicious forces beyond their control, while boys generally were believed to be subject to irresistible temptations to engage in a series of vices, including premarital sex. It was a period during which in both Canada and Australia the "child saving" movement got under way, and the framework for child welfare legislation was laid.[63] Particular targets of these systems and susceptible to being removed from their

61 Daniels, "Prostitution in Tasmania," *supra* note 43 at 77-9.

62 See e.g. J. Walkowitz, *City of Dreadful Delight: Narratives of Sexual Danger in Late-Victorian London* (Chicago: Univ. of Chicago Press, 1992); C. Bacchi, *Liberation Deferred: The Ideas of English-Canadian Suffragists, 1877-1918* (Toronto: Univ. of Toronto Press, 1983); C. Strange, *Toronto's Girl Problem: The Perils and Pleasures of the City 1880-1930* (Toronto: Univ. of Toronto Press, 1995); M. Connelly, *The Response to Prostitution in the Progressive Era* (Chapel Hill: Univ. of North Carolina Press, 1980); F. Grittner, *White Slavery: Myth, Ideology and American Law* (New York: Garland Press, 1990).

63 A. Jones and L. Rutman, *In the Children's Aid: J. J. Kelso and Child Welfare in Ontario* (Toronto: Univ. of Toronto Press, 1981); N. Sutherland, *Children in English-Canadian Society: Framing the Twentieth Century Consensus* (Toronto: Univ. of Toronto Press, 1976).

communities and relatives and placed in care or reformatories were children from "bad" family backgrounds, including those whose mothers were prostitutes.[64]

The era was one in which the criminal law was expanded and increasingly invoked to provide the primary ammunition in the fight against commercial sex. In Canada the initial inspiration came from W. T. Stead, the father of yellow journalism in Britain, who spearheaded the moral campaign in that country for more criminal law to protect girls and young women.[65] The framers of the *Criminal Code* were induced by a disciple of Stead, the Montreal moral reformer, D. A. Watt, to include a series of provisions proscribing the activities of male sexual predators.[66] The result was a messy amalgam of an old vagrancy-type law directed against streetwalking and the activities of brothels, a new nuisance crime of keeping a common bawdy house, and procuring, pimping, seduction, and abduction offences.[67] Throughout the 1890s, Watt and two major women's groups, the National Council of Women (NCW) and the Women's Christian Temperance Union (WCTU), continued to press for more extensive changes to the law and to complain of the relaxed attitude of the police to enforcement.[68]

The resolve of Canadian reformers was to sharpen in the first decade of the new century as a result of connections with the British-led anti-white-slavery movement. Those crusaders had "discovered" that the tentacles of an international trade in women reached into western Europe and North America. It was also occurring to the reformers in Canada that police in many communities were effectively tolerating prostitution.[69] These revelations were to convince social purity reformers, especially the male leaders of campaigns for moral renewal in the Methodist and Presbyterian churches, that a coalition of effort, similar to that already in place to fight for total prohibition of liquor and Sunday observance, was necessary if the law against venal sex was to be strengthened and vigorously enforced.[70] In due course

64 Backhouse, *supra* note 37 at 415-18.

65 See R. Shults, *Crusader in Babylon: W. T. Stead and the Pall Mall Gazette* (Lincoln: Univ. of Nebraska Press, 1972).

66 See G. Parker, "The Origins of the Canadian Criminal Code," in D. Flaherty, ed., *Essays in the History of Canadian Law*, vol. I (Toronto: Osgoode Society, 1981) 249 at 268-69, and Parker, *supra* note 6 at 217-26. For Watt's agenda, see D. Watt, *Moral Legislation: A Statement Prepared for the Information of the Senate* (Montreal: Gazette Printing Co., 1890).

67 Canadian *Criminal Code*, S.C. 1892, c. 29, ss. 181-187, 190, 198, 282, 283, 574.

68 See e.g. N.A.C., RG 13, Department of Justice Files, 86-87/084, Box 27, File 63\1894, letter from Watt to Deputy Minister of Justice, 28 June 1895; Provincial Archives of Ontario (PAO), Canadian W.C.T.U., Report of Ninth Convention, Toronto, 1896, 58-60; N.A.C. Aberdeen Papers, MG 28 I 25, vol. 68, File #2, letter from Lady Ishbel Aberdeen to A. R. Dickey, Minister of Justice, 28 Feb. 1896.

69 J. McLaren, "White Slavers: The Reform of Canada's Prostitution Laws and Patterns of Enforcement, 1900-1920" (1987) 8 Criminal Justice History 53 at 70-77.

70 *Ibid.* at 77-84.

they were to draw into the campaign the NCW and the WCTU. The campaign was assisted in political circles by earlier legislation in both the United States and Great Britain directed specifically at the scourge of "white slavery."[71] The results of pressure from the coalition were amendments to the *Criminal Code* in 1913, which extended the list of exploitative offences (especially relating to brothels and procuring) and strengthened penalties, and evidence of greater police activity to target the trade.[72] Contrary to the assumptions of the reformers, however, much of the law enforcement activity was directed at prostitutes and small brothels, rather than at the insidious and calculating conspiracies supposedly exploiting them.[73] At the level of official discourse, however, the reformers *had* scored a victory in the sense that a middle class script combining exhortation to personal renewal by prostitutes and "fallen women" through moral education and the penalization of exploiters was to dominate the construction of the criminal law and statements of public policy for decades to come.[74]

A similar moral uplift campaign in Australia between 1890 and 1920, supported by equivalent reform interests, resulted in the explicit criminalization of various types of prostitution-related conduct – soliciting, brothel keeping, and living on the avails – in most states.[75] The discourse that supported these steps was not, however, uncontested. Within the Labour Party in Australian politics there was vigorous opposition to making prostitution a focus of the criminal justice system – a result, as Barbara Sullivan has persuasively argued, of client-centred concerns among working class males. This may well explain why in Queensland, in which Labour was the government for most of the first half of the present century, there was official resistance to criminalization, and concentration on public health legislation and police discretion to regulate the sex trade.[76] Even in Western Australia where standard criminal law proscriptions existed, Australian "digger" culture was

---

71 On the campaign behind and the enactment of the *White Slave Traffic Act*, otherwise known as the *Mann Act*, 36 Stat. U.S., c. 395 (1910), see David J. Langum, *Crossing Over the Line: Legislating Morality and the Mann Act* (Chicago: Univ. of Chicago Press, 1994) at 15-47. The British campaign leading to the *Criminal Law Amendment Act* (1912), 2 and 3 Geo. 5, c. 20 is canvassed by Bristow, *supra* note 8 at 189-91.

72 *Criminal Code Amendment Act,* S.C. 1913, c. 13, ss. 9-11, 23, 29; McLaren, *supra* note 69 at 85-87.

73 *Ibid.* at 87-101.

74 J. McLaren and J. Lowman, "Enforcing Canada's Prostitution Laws, 1892-1920: Rhetoric and Practice," in M. Friedland, ed., *Securing Compliance: Seven Case Studies* (Toronto: Univ. of Toronto Press, 1990) 21 at 68.

75 Sullivan, *supra* note 42 at 23-25. See *Police Offences Act*, 1908 Stat. N.S.W., No. 12, ss. 4-6; *Police Act*, 1892 Stat. W.A., No. 17, ss. 57, 65, as am. 1902 Stat. W.A., No. 31, ss. 7, 8; *Police Offences Act*, 1890 Stat. Vict., No. 1126, ss. 30, 40 and 1891 Stat. Vict. No. 1241, s. 7, as am. 1907 Stat. Vict., No. 2093, ss. 4-6.

76 Sullivan, *ibid.* at 26-27. See *Health Act*, 1911 Stat. Queensland, No. 26. which prohibited soliciting and pimping but focused more on continuing the regime

strong enough to support tolerated zones for prostitution in Perth and the mining community of Kalgoorlie.[77]

War, Venereal Disease, and the Medicalization of Prostitution

In both Canada and Australia, the First World War was to generate a new set of anxieties about prostitution, its connections with venereal disease, and high levels of infection among servicemen. By this juncture far more was known medically about the pathology of various STDs, and the medical profession was again pressing for law that would facilitate regulation and now, with the discovery of Salvarsen, possible cure.[78] As the historical record shows there is nothing like hostilities, when the national welfare is apparently at peril, to accentuate fears about debilitating disease and the conduct that allegedly produces it.[79]

Remarkably, given the rather different nature of discourse about the sex trade in Canada and Australia during these years, and the relative dominance of reformist argumentation in the former, the legal responses to the new peril were similar. In both countries, with the notable exception of South Australia, where more traditional feminist arguments about the "double standard" were able to nip such initiatives in the bud, remedial legislation focused on health regulation and control, with the prostitute or fallen woman as the target of medical and police attention.[80] However, there was a difference in the form of debate in the two countries. In Canada, perhaps because of the formation of a moral coalition in which male reformers predominated, a variety of reform interests, including mainline or "maternal" feminists lined up behind the draconian regimes being developed.[81] This was an era in North America in which both science and its younger cousin social science were widely accepted as providing the key to further progress

---

earlier established by the *Contagious Diseases Act*, 1868 Stat. Queensland, No. 40, to detain and treat prostitutes who had VD. Although brothel keeping was an indictable offence under the *Criminal Code*, there was no summary offence for owning, letting, or keeping premises for purposes of prostitution until 1931 (*Vagrants, Gaming and Other Offences Act*, 1931 Stat. Queensland No. 27, ss. 8, 9).

77 Sullivan, *ibid.* at 24-25. See also R. Davidson, "'Dealing with the Social Evil': Prostitution and the Police in Perth and on the Eastern Goldfields, 1895-1925," in Daniels, *supra* note 43 at 162.

78 Cassel, *supra* note 36 at 101-21.

79 *Ibid.* at 112-44.

80 Buckley and Dickin McGinnis, *supra* note 36; J. Smart, "The Great War and the 'Scarlet Scourge': Debates about Venereal Disease in Melbourne during World War I," in J. Smart and T. Wood, eds., *An Anzac Muster: War and Society in Australia and New Zealand 1914-18 and 1939-45*, Monash Publications in History, no. 15 (Clayton, Vict.: Monash Univ. Press, 1992) at 58.

81 Buckley and Dickin McGinnis, *ibid.* at 341-42.

and the solution to a whole range of societal problems.[82] In Australia, as Judith Smart has shown, the issue of whether there should be a legislative response to venereal disease in the armed forces and what form it should take was vigorously argued. Feminist organizations such as the Women's Political Association in Victoria, which took a stand against the oppression of poor women and the dangers of medical tyranny, lined up against the medical profession and the representatives of party politics, including Labour women, who were persuaded of the medical imperatives for the control of contagion and thus of the need for regulation.[83] In the outcome it was the latter alliances that were to win the day.

Informal Regulation of Prostitution in Canada and Australia: The Interwar Years

In both Canada and Australia, prostitution and the sex trade ceased to be issues of burning public debate and policy between 1920 and the advent of the Second World War. The application and mediation of both social and legal policy during this period were largely in the hands of the police. Police practices ranged from widespread tolerance to an informal system of regulation secured by discretionary invocation of the criminal law at periodic intervals, enough to impress those in the trade, especially the prostitutes, as to who was in charge, and to satisfy the middle class that the police had the situation under control. Since the approach of the constabulary was that of preserving public order, prostitution tended to take place behind closed doors, under the control of madams and male managers with whom the guardians of the law had at least tacit understandings about raids, charges, and penalties. In both countries, although perhaps more so in Australia, male vice czars and powerful madams exercised some internal control over the trade. These arrangements between the police and the operators and managers of commercial sex establishments encouraged graft and corruption among the law enforcers. Roberta Perkins reports that wholesale police payoffs were part of the cost of doing business in the trade in New South Wales.[84] In some Canadian cities, Vancouver and Montreal being the most notorious examples, periodic scandals involving the vice squad, and on more than one occasion a Chief of Police, demonstrated how fragile was the line

82 See e.g. A. McLaren, *Our Own Master Race: Eugenics in Canada 1885-1945* (Toronto: McClelland and Stewart, 1990); Connelly, *supra* note 62.

83 Smart, *supra* note 80; J. Smart, "Feminists, Labour Women and Venereal Disease in Early Twentieth-Century Melbourne" (1992) 15 Australian Feminist Studies 25.

84 R. Perkins, "Working Girls in 'Wowserville': Prostitute Women in Sydney since 1945," in R. Kennedy, ed., *Australian Welfare, Historical Sociology* (Melbourne: Macmillan, 1989) 362 at 366-67.

85 See G. Marquis, "Vancouver Vice: The Police and Negotiation of Morality, 1904-1935," in H. Foster and J. McLaren, eds., *Essays in the History of Canadian Law, Vol. 6, British*

between discretionary control and co-option into the values of the sub-culture in question.[85]

Wartime Anxieties in Canada and Australia

Predictably the outbreak of the Second World War was to regenerate anxieties about venereal disease subverting the national interest and reducing the capacity of fighting men in both Canada and Australia. Again public health advocates spoke out about the need for tight regulation and vigorous law enforcement. In an article by the Medical Officer of Health for Vancouver, sexually transmitted diseases were likened to a "fifth column" within the community that, if not excised, would do the work of the Germans and Japanese for them.[86] War measures legislation was used in several Canadian communities with a military or naval presence, as well as in some Australian states, to make life very tough for prostitutes.[87] The danger to the health and welfare of servicemen was cited as the reason for these and other oppressive initiatives.[88] Interestingly, however, in Canada the level of prosecutions for prostitution-related offences decreased significantly during the Second World War. This may have been less the result of a downturn in police activity than their reliance on the powers granted to them to channel prostitutes into public health regimes.[89] In Australia, despite bleating in respectable society about the need to preserve the moral fibre of the country and the health of its forces, the reality of an influx of American and other allied servicemen created an enhanced demand for sexual services – a demand largely provided by women not attached to brothels or pimps who worked the bars and hotels – the so-called "good-time girls."[90]

Columbia and the Yukon (Toronto: Osgoode Society, 1995) 242 at 252-61; J. Swan, *A Century of Service: The Vancouver Police, 1886-1986* (Vancouver: Vancouver Police Historical Society and Centennial Museum, 1986) at 20; A. Levesque, *La Norme et Les Deviants: Des Femmes au Québec: Pendant L'Entre-Deux-Guerres* (Montreal: Les éditions du remue menages, 1989) at 139-61.

86 D. Williams, "The Suppression of Commercialized Prostitution in the City of Vancouver" (1941) 27 J. of Social Hygiene 364.

87 B. Sullivan, *Australian Politics and the Sex Industry* (Ph.D. thesis, School of Government, Univ. of Queensland, 1993) at 26. The state where the authorities were most vigorous was Queensland, where, as we have seen, a health regime of long standing was in existence, and which was the only state with a lock hospital operative. See also M. Murnane and K. Daniels, "Prostitutes as 'Purveyors of Disease': Venereal Disease Legislation in Tasmania, 1868-1945" (1979) 5 Hecate: A Women's Interdisciplinary Journal 5 at 15-19.

88 In New South Wales, the government passed the *Disorderly Houses Act*, 1943 Stat. N.S.W., No. 6, ss. 3, 7-10, 13 giving the police powers to close down such establishments to protect American servicemen from falling prey to chicanery and swindling – see R. Perkins, *Working Girls: Prostitutes, Their Life and Social Control* (Canberra: Australian Institute of Criminology, 1991) at 130-31.

89 G. Marquis, *Policing Canada's Century: A History of the Canadian Association of Chiefs of Police* (Toronto: Osgoode Society, 1993) at 206-208.

90 Perkins, *supra* note 88 at 367.

The Quiet Decade in the Sex Trade in Canada and Australia, 1945-55

The decade following the Second World War was a relatively quiet period in terms of police activity against the sex trade in both Canada and Australia. For a while the demand side slipped back to pre-war levels. In Sydney, Perkins reports, brothel and street prostitution re-emerged as the predominant forms for the delivery of sexual services, although the control over the brothel trade had largely slipped from the hands of the old-style madams.[91] By the early 1950s, however, new sources of business emerged from the arrival of unattached or unattended immigrant men who were arriving on Australian shores in increasing numbers.[92]

In both countries the police in the main continued their policy of informal regulation and containment by selective use of the criminal law. Law enforcers seem generally to have been less active than during the previous decade of peace. The figures for prosecutions and convictions across Canada were significantly lower than in the 1930s, and Sullivan notes a similar phenomenon in Australia.[93] This is probably explained by several factors in addition to the return to civilian normality: a renewed sense among police ranks that the trade was again under control; a decrease in public concern about the health dangers in prostitution with the application of penicillin to cure venereal diseases; and the redirection of law enforcement energies to other deviant activity (in Canada, for instance, this was a period during which the pursuit of heroin traffickers and users heated up).[94] The revelations from the inquiry into the stewardship of Chief Mulligan of the Vancouver Police in 1955,[95] and evidence laid before the recent Fitzgerald Commission into police corruption in Queensland over decades[96] provide clear evidence that control of the trade, with its attendant temptations to graft, lay at the core of police strategy during this period. At the level of public policy the prostitute continued to be the centre of attention, characterized variously as aberrant (especially in Australia), vulnerable, or both, although there was little in the way of amendment to the criminal law.[97] To the extent that the authorities were consumed by excessive worry, it seems to have been in relation to what was seen as a troubling increase in prosecutions and convictions for male homosexual activity, including prostitution.[98]

---

91 *Ibid.* at 368-69.
92 *Ibid.* at 369.
93 Sullivan, *supra* note 42 at 47.
94 *Ibid.* at 46-47.
95 Swan, *supra* note 85 at 82.
96 Dickie, *supra* note 35.
97 Sullivan, *supra* note 42 at 50-51.
98 *Ibid.* at 54-56.

Public and Private Sex in the English-Speaking World: Enter Sir John!

Interestingly, patterns of legal control in Canada and Australia were to diverge during the next 20 years, although the impact on the sex trade and on prostitutes in particular was remarkably similar. After the relatively dormant first decade of the post-war years, renewed activity developed on the law enforcement front after 1955. At the level of criminal justice policy, this activity seems, in part, to have resulted from the response of the white common law world to the recommendations of the British *Report of the Committee on Homosexual Offences and Prostitution*, associated with its chair, Sir John Wolfenden.[99] The central premise of the report – that sexual conduct in private by consenting adults should be put beyond the reach of the criminal law, while public manifestations of immoral conduct, especially by prostitutes who were labelled by the report as dangerous, corrupt people, were its legitimate targets – struck a responsive chord with legislators in several Australian states.[100] In Victoria and New South Wales, for example, street prostitution offences were reformulated in due course to provide the police with power to arrest and charge where there was mere suspicion of an intent to solicit, and in theory at least to catch actual or potential customers and "curb crawlers."[101] As pimps and other exploiters of prostitutes, especially those from recent migrant populations, were increasingly viewed with distaste, laws against living on the avails were beefed up.[102] In New South Wales, disorderly house legislation was amended to provide the police with greater powers to close down establishments known as locations for "habitual prostitution," including houses or rooms containing a solo operator.[103] In other states, such as Queensland and Western Australia, pressure on the trade to the extent that it was considered necessary came from police practice.[104] As might be expected, the result of this flurry of law reform and enforcement activity was an increase in the targeting of prostitutes by the police.

In Canada there were no changes in the law relating to prostitution, not even that dealing with street prostitution. This inaction at the parliamentary level may well have reflected the reach of the old "Vag C" offence,

---

99 U.K. Cmnd. 247, H.M.S.O., 1957. Sullivan, *ibid.* at 80-85.

100 Sullivan, *supra* note 42 at 85-111.

101 For Victoria, see *Police Offences Act*, 1952 Stat. Vict., No. 6069, s. 28(6), as am. 1957 Stat. Vict., No. 6124, s. 2 (male clients and curb crawlers were only added in 1967 by the *Summary Offences Act*, 1967 Stat. Vict., No. 7635); for New South Wales, see the *Vagrancy, Disorderly Houses and Other Acts (Amendment) Act*, 1968 Stat. N.S.W., No. 32, s. 2.

102 See Victoria's amendments to the *Crimes Act* in 1961 in the *Prostitution Act*, 1961 Stat. Vict., No. 6766, s. 2.

103 *Vagrancy, Disorderly Houses and Other Acts (Amendment) Act*, 1968 Stat. N.S.W., No. 32, s. 2.

104 Sullivan, *supra* note 42 at 106-109.

which tied police powers of arrest and charge to the failure of a "common prostitute" or "night walker" to give a good account of herself.[105] The police were the effective judges of whether a woman fell within one of the two categories of street prostitutes mentioned, and there was no requirement of actual or attempted soliciting. That provision served police control purposes more than adequately, especially if political or community heat required instant resolution. In Canada then, to the extent that the *Wolfenden Report* had purchase, it was in the realm of enforcement rather than law reform.

Changes in the Law on Prostitution in Canada and Australia since 1970: The Prostitute as Working Woman?

Since 1970 the pattern of criminal law reform on prostitution in Canada and Australia has reflected mixed messages. Throughout this period, new voices have been added to the debate about what, if anything, should be done about the sex trade, and a few tentative and limited steps towards experimenting with new approaches have been taken.

The dominant discourse of the previous 15 years, which had emphasized the bad character of the prostitute population, has been increasingly challenged. Opposition has come from the ranks of civil libertarians, whose representatives have argued that consensual sexual conduct should be outside the reach and moral judgments of the criminal law, and by feminist opinion, which, while not always at one on how to deal with prostitution as a social phenomenon, has advocated decriminalization of the activities of prostitutes who, they quite rightly judge, were and continue to be the primary targets of law enforcement activity.[106] Ranged against these forces and their discourses there has been (1) a loose alliance of community groups from areas allegedly blighted by street prostitution preaching "anywhere but here" and advocating general suppression; (2) religious groups (predominantly evangelical, but not exclusively so), predicting the imminent revival of Sodom and Gomorrah everywhere; and (3) police forces anxious to retain the mixture of power and discretion that had for so long allowed them to manipulate the system and preserve a modicum of order, thereby maintaining the trust of their middle class masters.[107]

In Canada the trenchant observation in the *Report of the Royal Commission on the Status of Women* in 1970 that there was no warrant for a status offence such as streetwalking, which was directed exclusively at the female party in an actual or apprehended transaction for paid sexual services and therefore entirely discriminatory, did not go unheeded.[108] Parliament went

105 *Criminal Code*, S.C. 1953-54, c. 51, s. 164(c).
106 McLaren and Lowman, *supra* note 74 at 66-68; Sullivan, *supra* note 42 at 139-43.
107 McLaren and Lowman, *ibid.* at 68; Perkins, *supra* note 38 at 133-39.
108 *Report of the Royal Commission on the Status of Women in Canada* (Ottawa: Queen's Printer, 1970) at 369-75.

so far as to repeal the former "Vag C" offence in 1972. It was replaced with a gender neutral offence of soliciting in a public place "for purposes of prostitution."[109] This change, which initially seems to have been accepted by the nation's police forces, was hotly contested by some of them after 1978, when the Supreme Court of Canada in *R. v. Hutt* interpreted the soliciting provision as requiring an element of "importuning," meaning "to solicit pressingly or persistently."[110] Police and community griping, as well as civil libertarian and feminist angst, induced the federal Liberal Minister of Justice, Mark MacGuigan, to establish in 1983 the *Special Committee on Pornography and Prostitution* to study the state of the law and practice and make recommendations. Although the Fraser Committee advocated moves towards partial decriminalization, especially of the law related to brothel keeping and pimping, the Tory government of Brian Mulroney seized its most conservative recommendation, a soliciting provision with a minimalist importuning requirement, and converted it into the notorious "wink and nod" provision that now constitutes s. 213 of the *Criminal Code*.[111]

The Canadian government was moved to act more resolutely on the issues of child prostitution and sexual abuse. In those areas, a number of new exploitative offences were added to the *Code*, following the recommendations of the 1984 *Report of the Committee on Sexual Offences Against Children and Youth* (the *Badgely Committee*).[112] Effectively, this is where the law in Canada stands today – a messy amalgam of old and new provisions reflecting different outbreaks of social anxiety, changing sexual values, and discourses that come nowhere near resolving the basic ambiguity surrounding prostitution as a social practice.[113] Enforcement continues to be highly discretionary, ranging from inertia in the case of several of the exploitative offences (the police argument being that it is difficult to secure convictions), to selective enforcement of others, especially the soliciting provision.

---

109 *Criminal Code Amendment Act*, S.C. 1972, c. C-13, ss. 12, 15.

110 *Hutt v. The Queen* (1978), 38 C.C.C. (2d) 418 (S.C.C.). See McLaren and Lowman, *supra* note 74 at 67.

111 For the report's recommendations on adult prostitution, see the *Report of the Special Committee on Pornography and Prostitution*, vol. 2 (Ottawa: Canadian Government Publishing Centre, 1985) at 511-58. The recommendation on street soliciting is dealt with at 538-43. It advocated the inclusion of a nuisance offence in then s. 171 of the *Criminal Code*, entitled "Disorderly Conduct, Indecent Exhibition, Loitering, Soliciting." The offence would have required at least one advance or attempt at importuning for conviction. The legislated provision (*Criminal Code Amendment Act*, S.C. 1985, c. C-50, s. 1 (now s. 213 of the *Code*) makes it sufficient that the accused has communicated or attempted to communicate in any manner "for the purposes of engaging in prostitution or of obtaining sexual services."

112 *Report of the Committee on Sexual Offences Against Children and Youths* (Ottawa: Canadian Government Publishing Centre, 1984). The offences added to the *Criminal Code* in the wake of the report include sexual interference (s. 151), invitation to sexual touching (s. 152), and sexual exploitation (s. 153).

113 McLaren and Lowman, *supra* note 74 at 68-75.

Notwithstanding the formal gender neutrality of the law, female prostitutes are the major target of police activity for solicitation offences. To the extent that the sex trade is regulated, it is through the incidental application of business licensing provisions and general economic regulation to enterprises such as massage parlours and escort services, rather than through any conscious effort to ensure the safety and dictate the working conditions of those who work in these establishments.[114]

Discussions have recently taken place between federal and provincial representatives with a view to securing further legislative changes relating to prostitution.[115] These discussions have included debate on partial decriminalization and the enactment of regulatory regimes over parts of the sex trade. What has emerged to date has been agreement on the need to get tough with the exploiters of child prostitution. In Bill C-27, which came into force in May 1997, it is an offence for Canadian citizens or residents to commit sexual offences against children outside the country. Living on the avails of a prostitute under 18 years of age or that the accused believed to be under that age, and compelling that person to engage in prostitution or using or threatening violence on that person carries a minimum of 5 years and a maximum of 14 years in jail. Moreover, employing the sexual services of one under 18 years of age brings a sentence of not less than 5 years in jail.[116] Separate and apart from the legislation, it is also proposed that special steps be taken to develop the enforcement and support services in communities that will make prosecution more feasible and successful.[117]

In Australia, civil libertarian and feminist objections to the construction of the criminal law relating to prostitution has had some purchase in legislative changes in two states, New South Wales and Victoria. Feminist opinion in Australia was and is divided on the practice of prostitution. It ranges from the characterization of prostitution as an unacceptable feature of a patriarchal culture to its being a business like any other in a capitalist economy whose workers are exploited and require the full protection of the law in terms of working conditions and benefits. Feminists, however, have

114 For an excellent critique of the failure of the present law relating to prostitution and the need to change the focus of the law to serve the economic and public health needs of the women involved, see F. Shaver, "The Regulation of Prostitution: Avoiding the Morality Traps" (1994) 9 Can. J. of Law and Society 123.

115 The ongoing consultation process is described as "Dealing with Prostitution in Canada," in Department of Justice Press Release, 18 Apr. 1996, Backgrounder at 1.

116 Bill C-27, S.C. 1997, c. 16, ss. 1, 2(3), 2(4). The bill also makes amendments to some of the existing clauses on procuring. These seem to be designed to deal more easily with the practice of inveigling women and girls, including those from outside Canada, into brothels (s. 2(1), (2)). The ability of the system to hear evidence from complainants and witnesses in safe circumstances is also enhanced by these proposals (s. 6).

117 *Supra* note 115.

118 Sullivan, *supra* note 42 at 164-66 and 203.

been at one in deprecating criminal law provisions that, in practice, if not in theory, victimize sex workers.[118] As Barbara Sullivan has noted, prostitutes and other sex workers who began to organize collectively in the late 1980s and in the 1990s have themselves become more active as a voice to be heard in the debate on prostitution and its treatment by the law. Sex worker organizations, she reports, are active in all the capital cities, as well as in regional areas. In some states they have received financial support from government to promote safe sex. These groups have been in the forefront in Australia of advocating decriminalization of prostitution.[119]

The Labour government of Neville Wran in New South Wales proved to be sympathetic to civil libertarian and feminist critiques of the law. Its legislative response in 1979 was to decriminalize the offence of soliciting in or near a public place and to remove the offence of being a reputed prostitute on premises habitually used for prostitution.[120] This imaginative attempt at law reform was bitterly contested by the Opposition, church, community, and business groups, and not least the police, who were able to point to an apparent increase in soliciting and its spread into other neighbourhoods.[121] There is, however, evidence that the New South Wales police, like their counterparts in several Canadian municipalities after the *Hutt* decision, adopted a calculated policy of refusing to enforce the law against offensive conduct in public places, in order to turn the legislative clock back to the sort of provisions that maintained their control over street prostitution, or more correctly street prostitutes.[122] The political heat generated by this powerful alliance of police and community activism was ultimately strong enough to persuade the Labour government to backtrack to the point of outlawing soliciting in public places close to dwellings, schools, churches, and hospitals in 1982.[123] Despite the *Report of the Select Committee of the Legislative Assembly*, 1986 which advocated educational strategies for combating prostitution and management initiatives as the way to control the brothel trade, these proposals were ignored by the Wran government and its successor, the Liberal-National government of Nick Greiner, elected into office in 1988.[124] Indeed, further amendments to the law have shrunk the space in

---

119 *Ibid.* at 202.

120 *Ibid.* at 180-82; Perkins, *supra* note 38 at 139-44. For the legislation, see the *Prostitution Act*, 1979 Stat. N.S.W., No. 71. Both Sullivan and Perkins argue that the motives for these changes were mixed, embodying not only feminist and libertarian concerns, but also a "managerial" concern about lack of deterrence and the cost of enforcement under the traditional system.

121 Sullivan, *ibid.* at 182-83; Perkins, *supra* note 38 at 144-45.

122 See S. Egger and M. Findlay, "The Politics of Police Discretion," in M. Findlay and R. Hogg, eds., *Understanding Crime and Criminal Justice* (Sydney: Law Book Co., 1988) at 209.

123 This was achieved by the *Prostitution (Amendment) Act*, 1983, Stat. N.S.W., No. 12, s. 3.

124 Sullivan, *supra* note 42 at 184-85; Perkins, *supra* note 38 at 144-49.

which soliciting can take place and actually proscribed the act of prostitution if it occurs in public, although making both parties to the transaction potentially liable. The advertising for the services of prostitutes has also been banned.[125]

In New South Wales, partial decriminalization of soliciting has provided some room for the street trade in well-established stroll areas such as King's Cross in Sydney, although there is still tension in other neighbourhoods that feel invaded by it. By and large, brothels continued their business unimpeded, especially in the cities, although the prospect of charges under the *Disorderly House Act* continued to hang over these enterprises. As a result of major exposures of police corruption associated with prostitution in the state in the Wood Royal Commission report of 1995, which was linked to the exercise of police discretion under the *DHA*, the Labour government of Robert Carr amended the Act, providing a process whereby complaints against disorderly brothels could be brought by municipal councils before the Land and Environment Court. Unless a brothel is the subject of a complaint, it seems that it may continue to operate lawfully. Living on the avails no longer extends to those engaged in a legitimate commercial relationship with a prostitute, although new penalties for inducing another to commit an act of prostitution or surrender the proceeds of prostitution were introduced in the same amending legislation.[126]

A second and more durable experiment was the decision of the Liberal government in Victoria to move the control of brothels in the state from the criminal to the land use planning law in the early 1980s, a reflection of developing sentiment that sexual relations between consenting adults should be removed from the purview of the criminal justice system. Legislation to fully operationalize this plan was put in place by the Labour government of John Cain in 1985 while awaiting the report of a Commission of Inquiry into Prostitution by Marcia Neave of the University of Melbourne.[127] The report proceeded from a strong feminist position that prostitution is an undesirable practice that has its roots in female economic and social deprivation and male sexual prerogative in patriarchal societies.[128] Strategies accordingly needed to be developed to change the culture of gender relations that has supported and continues to support it. At the same time, Neave recognized that the social and economic initiatives required were long-term

125 This was secured through the *Summary Offences Act*, 1988 Stat. N.S.W., No. 25, ss. 14-21, which resulted in a large increase in the number of convictions for soliciting: see Perkins, *supra* note 38 at 153-54; Sullivan, *ibid.* at 216.

126 Sullivan, *ibid.* at 216-17.

127 *Ibid.* at 185-89. The legislation is the *Planning (Brothels) Act*, 1984 Stat. Vict., No. 19904.

128 *Inquiry into Prostitution. Final Report* (Melbourne: Queens Printer, 1985). See also M. Neave, "The Failure of Prostitution Law Reform" (1988) 21 Australian and New Zealand Journal of Criminology 202.

in scale and effect, and that prostitution is a practice that will not disappear overnight. She reached the common sense conclusion that, in the shorter term, decriminalization of prostitution-related activity was needed, except where the prevention of harm to prostitutes or the suppression of genuine sources of nuisance was the objective of offences. A corollary of such a step was, she argued, that the sex trade had to be managed more effectively and with an eye to protecting the workers in it. The government in Melbourne responded positively to many of the recommendations of the commissioner, but left untouched the provisions relating to street prostitution, where she had advocated partial decriminalization.[129] Nor were steps undertaken to relax the definition of a common bawdy house to make it possible for small groups of women to operate brothels on their own account without having to find the money for the stiff licence fees to qualify as owners of legalized brothels. Since the government also did not proclaim several of the provisions of the *Prostitution Regulation Act* of 1986, no adequate steps have been taken to control the management of large brothels, which is, of course, where the money is.

The Liberal government of Jeff Kennett elected in 1992 has sought to address some of these issues by establishing a Prostitution Control Board with power to monitor the system and the players in it, to refer matters of occupational health and safety to the appropriate agencies, and to launch education programs about prostitution and its dangers. Also under the *Prostitution Control Act*, solo or dual operators of brothels may now acquire licences to run brothels and thus avoid the high registration fees charged to larger establishments, although they still need to secure municipal planning approval. Higher penalties were introduced for street prostitution, although in an interesting twist the fine for clients is twice that for prostitutes. Offensive behaviour towards prostitutes in public places has also been made an offence. Under the new Act a series of regulations with safe sex practices and sex worker safety as their object have been promulgated.[130]

Sullivan suggests that it is too early to assess the effects of these changes. They do not deal with the reluctance of municipalities to issue planning permits to brothels, nor do they remove the legal disabilities of prostitutes operating out of their own homes, who are still liable to prosecution. As a result, it likely that a sizeable illegal brothel trade will continue to operate, as well as street prostitution. Furthermore, as street soliciting is still proscribed by the State's criminal law, now with enhanced penalties, prostitutes will likely remain the primary targets of police attention. Local

---

129 The changes were set out in the *Prostitution Regulation Act*, 1986 Stat. Vict., No. 124, although not all the provisions were proclaimed.

130 Sullivan, *supra* note 42 at 213-15, and the *Prostitution Control Act*, 1994 Stat. Vict., No. 102.

governments were not given the discretion to enact limited decriminalization of prostitution in their jurisdictions, despite the fact that one, St. Kilda in Melbourne, has expressed some interest in moving in this direction.[131]

Ironically enough it is Queensland, which for so long relied on a tolerated sex trade and health regulation, that has been in the forefront of criminalizing and prosecuting prostitution-related conduct.[132] There is evidently a backlash among state politicians against the systemic corruption and graft that attended the old system and was exposed by the Fitzgerald Inquiry into organized crime and police corruption. These people have no stomach for decriminalization with controls.[133] Tougher penalties were introduced by the new *Prostitution Act* for procuring, even of adults. Advertising prostitution services is now an offence, as is knowingly participating in their provision – a change that threatens all those who facilitate contact between those seeking and those providing sexual services. A found-in offence has been added. Penalties for street soliciting have been increased, although the offence has been made gender-neutral. On a less draconian note, solo operators from homes or rented accommodation are protected from prosecution for providing sexual services, as long as their operations are orderly – an exemption, it seems, designed to permit small-scale prostitution. The law does provide for the institution of health education and retraining programs, and the state government has invested quite heavily in these. Sullivan doubts whether they can offset the harsher legal sanctions and greater dangers to sex workers created by other segments of the same legislation.[134]

For the rest of the states, the longstanding system of selectively enforced criminal law used as an unofficial system of regulation and control applies, much as it does in Canada.[135]

Outside the states, both the Northern Territory and Australian Capital Territory have embarked on interesting new experiments with the control of the sex trade. In the former, the government has opted to license and

---

131 *Ibid.* at 215. For Professor Neave's critique of the earlier legislative changes, see Neave, *supra* note 128 at 209-12 and M. Neave, "Prostitution Laws in Australia – Past History and Current Trends" (Faculty of Law, Univ. of Melbourne, 1994) [unpublished] at 16-22.

132 Sullivan, *supra* note 42 at 208-12; Neave, *ibid.* at 8-12. See *Prostitution Amendment Act*, 1992 Stat. Queensland, No. 15. This tack was taken by the government of Queensland, despite the rather more enlightened approach in the report of its Criminal Justice Commission, *Regulating Morality? An Inquiry into Prostitution in Queensland* (Brisbane: Criminal Justice Commission, 1991) at 21-34.

133 See M. Vann, "The Goss Position" (1993) 18 Alternative L.J. 38.

134 Sullivan, *supra* note 42 at 211-12.

135 Neave, *supra* note 131 at 4-7. See also Neave, Table 1: Laws Criminalizing Prostitution-related Activities, and Table 2: Laws Punishing Prostitutes and Clients (Western Australia; South Australia; and Tasmania).

136 *Ibid.* at 22-25; Sullivan, *supra* note 42 at 212-13. See *Prostitution Regulation Act*, 1992 Stat. N.T., No. 64.

regulate escort services, while continuing to proscribe brothels and street soliciting.[136] Living on the avails has ceased to be an offence unless a child is involved or an adult forced or duped into the trade by a pimp. Registration and regulation is carried out by the Escort Agency Licensing Board and a system of certification of employees of agencies administered by the Commissioner of Police. As Marcia Neave has observed, the legislation is highly selective in its choice of sex trade workers to be regulated. Moreover, it does far more in providing safe access by male residents and tourists to sexual services than it does for the autonomy and safety of the workers, who are still subject to police discretion, as well as being forced to operate in settings involving serious risk of personal danger.[137]

The Australian Capital Territory (ACT) has gone much further by repealing entirely the old offences of brothel-keeping, living on the earnings of prostitution, and non-coercive procuring, although tough new penalties were introduced for engaging in child prostitution and a $2000 fine is visited upon those engaged in public soliciting.[138] Both those opening brothels and setting up escort agencies have to register their businesses with the Registrar of Brothels. The establishments may be inspected, and prostitutes are subject to compulsory medical examinations. Brothels are limited to prescribed locations, except for those operated by single prostitutes. The two satellite communities prescribed, Fyshwyck and Mitchell,[139] are commercial and light industrial areas separated from other communities by green space; this separation may account for the political palatability of this the most radical of the Australian experiments with prostitution regulation. The legislation is remarkable in that it also seeks to minimize the health risks associated with commercial sex by placing legal responsibilities, a safe sex obligation on owners, workers, and clients to ensure that safe sex is practised.[140] According to Sullivan, reports suggest that the system works well. A consultative committee representing the sex trade and its workers, as well as AIDS organizations, government agencies, and the police provide ongoing review and a channel of communication to the Attorney General. There are few illegal brothels and little street soliciting, although there are likely a large number of solo workers who are unregistered.[141]

---

137 Neave, *ibid.* at 25. Based on her research, Professor Neave is of the view that women working for escort agencies are typically in greater danger than those working in brothels. Sullivan agrees, although she argues that as far as the legislation goes it provides a zone of legality, and that, because of the formality of licensing, it may reduce police corruption: *ibid.* at 213.

138 Neave, *ibid.* at 25-28. Also *Prostitution Consequential Amendments Act*, 1992, Stat. A.C.T. No. 65, and Sullivan, *ibid.* at 205-208.

139 *Prostitution Regulations, Subordinate Law No 19*, 1993 A.C.T.

140 Neave, *supra* note 131 at 27-28.

141 Sullivan, *supra* note 42 at 207.

The Commonwealth parliament for its part has been moved to pass legislation seeking to deal with the Australian citizens and residents who engage in the sexual exploitation of children in other countries, most notably in Asia. Under the *Crimes (Child Sex Tourism) Amendment Act* of 1994, prosecutions may be brought in Australia for sexual intercourse or conduct with underage persons or inducing a child to engage in sexual conduct committed outside the country.[142] It is also an offence to benefit from or to encourage conduct proscribed under the legislation – a provision designed to get at those who organize sex tours.[143] Despite problems associated with acquiring evidence from extraterritorial sources, prosecutions have been launched and succeeded under this legislation, and pedophile activity exposed in the Australian diplomatic service.[144]

The story of the socio-legal status of the sex trade in Canada and Australia is marked by an ill-ordered and ill-administered sequence of experiments in criminal and regulatory law designed to control or even suppress the trade. Few of these initiatives worked entirely as anticipated, and some were clear failures. As has so often been the case with law reform in this area of activity, the law has evolved as an ill-ordered collage of provisions reflecting very different social and moral assumptions about prostitution and lacking any serious attempt to reconcile old and new, conservative and progressive. Even the same legislative initiative may have internal inconsistencies in policy and law within it.

In recent decades, the comfortable assumption of middle class society that sexual vice is under control in Canada and Australia has been undermined by new examples of the sex trade relocating to take advantage of business opportunity and to dodge police pressure. At the same time there have emerged counter-discourses, in particular those of civil liberties groups, feminists, and sex trade workers themselves, seeking to redefine prostitution in social and economic terms. It is now being more openly and vigorously argued that prostitution is gainful employment that is entitled to the same respect as other work and should be subject to statutory employment safety and health regimes.[145] Australia, with its plurality of jurisdictions in matters of criminal law and administrative regulation, is providing a testing ground for these reformist ideas, and in the case of the ACT has gone a

142 *Crimes (Child Sex Tourism) Amendment Act*, 1994 Stat. Australia, No. 105, s. 3.

143 *Ibid.* There is also a series of provisions dealing with the taking of evidence from the foreign source.

144 See "Paedophile Jailed on Sex Tourism Charge," *South China Morning Post* (4 May 1996) and "An Undiplomatic Scandal," *South China Morning Post* (27 Apr. 1996).

145 See Shaver, *supra* note 114; J. Dickin McGinnis, "Whores and Worthies: Feminism and Prostitution" (1994) 9 Can. J. of Law and Society 105; L. Bell, ed., *Good Girls, Bad Girls: Sex Trade Workers and Feminists Face to Face* (Toronto: The Women's Press, 1987); Perkins, *supra* note 38.

significant distance down the road towards a regulatory regime that treats the sex trade as a business and its workers as entitled to the general protection of employment safety and health regimes. To date Canada is proving far less imaginative at the level of both ideas and action. Both countries have begun to recognize the international dimensions of the sex trade and the extent to which their nationals are involved as sponsors and participants.[146]

THE RECONSTRUCTION OF GENDER RELATIONS AND COMMERCIAL SEX IN MODERN THAILAND

Introduction

The evolution of the law relating to the sex trade in Thailand since the first decade of this century has clearly been influenced by the types of developments, experiments, and models in Western countries already outlined here. Thailand has followed a similar, although not identical, process of experiment as some Western countries, with regulatory and proscriptive legal regimes to deal with prostitution. These regimes have been imported into Thailand as the result of pressure from individual Western countries or the international community. Accordingly, in addition to the apparently ubiquitous challenge that faces many countries in attempting to constrain behaviour that is widely characterized as unruly and marginal, Thailand has had the further difficulty of adapting the law developed to a society in transition. Thai society is evolving from a family and community-based rural subsistence economy governed by local custom and traditional religion to a modern, capitalist, consumer economy, in which a much greater premium is placed on individualism and social freedom and the legal protection of individual rights. Both tradition and progress claim the hearts and minds of many Thais. These conflicting pulls are reflected in the evolution of the law on prostitution, and how it has been and is applied in practice.[147]

Importing Health Regulation into Thailand

The first decade of the present century marks the first occasion when Thai law directly addressed the issue of what to do about the sex trade. During the reign of King Rama IV (Mongkut, 1851-68) the law of marital status had been reformed to allow a woman to resist a marriage arranged by her parents, or sale by her husband.[148] Like other reform legislation of this type, it

146 For an Australian example of the advocacy behind this movement, see E. Evatt and J. Millbank, "Child Prostitution and Tourism," in *Reform* (Summer 1993) 18.

147 C. Sethaput and B. Yoddumnern-Attig, "Occupational Role Behaviours Over Time," in B. Yoddumnern-Attig et al., *supra* note 26 at 80-91.

148 V. Somswasdi, "Women in the Constitution of Thailand: A Far-Fetched Hope for Equality," in *Women's Legal Position in Thailand*, *supra* note 21 at 7. K. Thitsa, *supra* note 21 at 5, writes that the powers of sale, pawn, or gift exercisable by a husband over a wife

is likely that it was prompted by royal concern to placate Western sensibilities and to reduce the opportunities for colonial intervention.[149] It is doubtful that it had much effect in actually changing social practices.

The first legislation directed specifically against prostitution reflected public health concerns and, in particular, an apparent growth in the incidence of venereal disease in the general population. This may well have been connected to the abolition of slavery in 1905, when former women slaves were drawn into the sex trade.[150] King Rama V (Chulalongkorn) proclaimed the *Law for the Prevention of Venereal Disease*, based on an earlier draft penned by a Western doctor, H. Campbell Highet.[151] Owing much to models of venereal disease regulation from both continental Europe and the British Empire, the preamble made it clear that prostitutes were viewed as the source of contagion.[152] Both they and premises used for prostitution were required to be registered. Rules about how the trade was plied were set down and medical examination was made compulsory for all prostitutes. If found to be diseased, a woman was banned from work, forced to hand over her permit, and to subject herself to medical attention. The permit would be returned only if she secured a favourable medical report. There was at that time no attempt to provide special medical care for women who were infected.

Reflecting a theme that has since become commonplace in the regulation and even criminalization of prostitution activity in Thailand, the law proved ineffective after a brief flurry of administrative monitoring and enforcement activity.[153] The women resisted attempts to compel examination. Moreover, governmental resolve was blunted because it received revenue from opium sold in brothels. As a consequence, the law began to draw press criticism for its ineffectiveness. The unsatisfactory state of the law and its enforcement were also the target of attacks by Thai feminists annoyed at the lack of any effective strategy to prevent the spread of venereal disease,

---

allowed by the *Law of the Three Seals*, 1805 lasted into the reign of Rama V (1882-1902).

149 Under the Bowring Treaty of 1855, Britain acquired special extra-territorial and commercial rights in Thailand. K. Thitsa, *supra* note 148 at 4, indicates that the latter effectively became a client state of that imperial power until after the Second World War.

150 S. D. Bamber, K. J. Hewison, and P. J. Underwood, "A History of Sexually Transmitted Diseases in Thailand: Policy and Politics" (1993) 69 Genitourin Med. 148 at 149.

151 *Ibid.* The authors indicate that by the early years of the present century the figures available through western-style hospitals and Thai army records point to a high incidence of VD among elements of Bangkok's population and the armed forces.

152 *Ibid.* Part of the preamble to the statute read: "some women are suffering from diseases which could be transmitted to the men who have relations with them. As there are no doctors to examine them and treat their diseases these are likely to keep spreading until they become a great danger to mankind."

153 *Ibid.* at 149-50.

who advocated the closing down of brothels, which they felt were both tolerated and unregulated.[154]

Thailand, the League of Nations, and Trafficking in Women

The 1920s and 1930s were largely a period of drift in terms of socio-legal policy towards prostitution.[155] The law of 1908 remained on the books, and licences were requested and issued. However, many prostitutes and brothels chose to work outside the system. Anxieties were voiced especially in the 1930s that venereal disease infection was on the rise, especially in Bangkok. In 1930 the first serious steps were taken to put into place hospital treatment for sexually transmitted diseases and to mount health education programs.[156]

On the law reform front, one change occurred that introduced criminal penalties for some forms of sexual exploitation. The *Trafficking in Women and Girls Act* was introduced in 1928 to satisfy League of Nations policies on the suppression of female sexual slavery.[157] This statute made it an offence to bring women or girls into the country for the purposes of prostitution. The law was directed primarily against exploiters, although the women or girls could be sent to a rehabilitation centre for an extended period if a judge so ordered. It is unlikely that it was enforced with any enthusiasm. That Thailand was generally subject to pressure from the League is evident in the criticism the government received from that body for its failure to raise the age of consent to sexual intercourse above twelve years, something that it said was impossible to do.[158] In none of the legal expedients taken in Thailand before 1940 was there any evidence of sensitivity to indigenous culture and the character of traditional gender relationships. Laws were passed based on external models without any consideration of whether they fit local social and economic circumstances. In practice they seem to have been largely ignored, leaving it to the market as manipulated by the police for their own benefit to reign supreme. Despite episodic discussion about the need to further medicalize the regulation of prostitution, the war and the Japanese occupation scotched proposed legislative initiatives to that

154 *Ibid.* at 150. The authors note an article carried in 1922 in *Nari Sapada*, a women's magazine, criticizing the law and its application as useless from a public health point of view, and unfair to the women involved in the trade. The piece advocated the closing down of the brothels or their serious medical regulation.

155 *Ibid.* at 149-50.

156 *Ibid.* at 150. The Control Unit to Reduce Venereal Diseases was established at the Bang Rak Hospital in Bangkok in 1930, after a visit by one of the royal princes to other countries to observe their STD control systems.

157 See Asia Watch and the Women's Rights Project, *A Modern Form of Slavery: Trafficking of Burmese Women and Girls in Brothels in Thailand* (New York: Human Rights Watch, 1993) at 21-22.

158 Bamber, Hewison, and Underwood, *supra* note 150 at 150.

end.[159] Only in the wake of the war, and a perceived connection between occupation by allied soldiers and a dearth of medicinal drugs combined with an increase in sexually transmitted diseases, did anxieties recur.

Western Hegemony and the Contradictions of Socio-Legal Policy on the Sex Trade in Cold War Thailand

The period from the late 1950s on in Thailand was marked by significant legislative activity in relation to prostitution. During those decades, a range of prostitution-related activities of various sorts were criminalized for the first time, while establishments that catered to an increasing demand for commercial sex were able to legitimate themselves by choosing to become licensed "entertainment places."[160]

The uneasy coexistence of a system of criminal and regulatory law governing the sex trade reflects the continuing and now more complex influence of external forces on the country and the readiness of Thai authorities to respond positively to social and economic pressures from the West. This was a period of widespread political and military instability in Southeast Asia that did not leave Thailand untouched. The dominant political and military elements, often the same cast of characters, committed Thailand to the Western, primarily the American, cause in the region, and were usually only too willing to dance to the tune of the Western piper.[161] With the stationing of and furlough for American troops in Thailand, a significant external demand for sexual services from military personnel was introduced into the country from the early 1960s until most of the troops left at the end of the Vietnam War. This caused a boom in the sex trade, especially in Bangkok and the resort town of Pattaya.[162] It would be wrong, however, to suggest that domestic considerations were irrelevant.

If life in pre-modern Thailand was marked by a division in gender relations and sexual practices between the elite and the vast bulk of the population, particularly those residing in rural areas, in the decades after 1960 that division was to become truly blurred. The effect of a Westernizing consumer market economy, and the resulting withering of the traditional subsistence agricultural economy, together with attendant changes in social institutions and practices, was a significant trend towards the dominance of materialism and impersonal urban values in people's lifestyles.[163] A demand for sexual services among Thai men was, of course, developing long before

159 *Ibid.* at 150-51.
160 *Ibid.* at 151-52.
161 Thitsa, *supra* note 21 at 7-8.
162 *Ibid.* at 15-16. See also P. Levan, "Curtailing Thailand's Child Prostitution through an International Conscience" (1994) 9 Amer. Univ. J. of Int'l Law and Policy 869 at 879-81.
163 Thitsa, *supra* note 21 at 10-13.

this period. However, this period marks the culmination of a gradual diffusion of the values of the male aristocracy and professional and business elite through the male population at large. The old patriarchal preserve of freedom in taking wives and concubines and exploiting servants and slaves has been effectively transformed, I would argue, into a more widespread culture of Thai men seeking sexual satisfaction both before and outside marriage, and so creating an expanding demand for commercial sex that is quick, cheap, and casual.[164]

There has been no problem in servicing that demand. The social and economic dislocation that has increasingly impoverished families close to the margin in rural areas has led to a movement of young females with limited educational attainment to the city to find jobs to help support their parents and younger siblings.[165] Increasingly, the sex trade, with its higher economic rewards, has attracted more and more of these young migrants.

If, then, there have been pressures from outside the country for a reconfiguration of the law relating to the sex trade in Thailand, there have also been internal pressures. To complicate matters, both external and internal demands for change have been inconsistent in their vision of what the law should be called upon to do. The result is a complex of legal provisions that defy rational explanation but are rooted in the contradictions and strains of modern Thai political and social development.

The traditional relaxed attitude towards prostitution came to a formal end with the enactment in 1960 by the government of Field Marshal Sarit Thanarat of the *Suppression of Prostitution Act*.[166] This comprehensive attempt to criminalize prostitution was prompted by the passage of the *United Nations Convention on Discrimination Against Women* in that same year. Under this document, states undertook to abolish regulated prostitution and to substitute criminal law sanctions, directed in particular against the sexual exploiters of women and children. The rightist Sarit regime was concerned both to improve the country's morals and its international reputation.[167]

164 Sethaput and Yoddumnern-Attig, *supra* note 147 at 89-90. See also Levan, *supra* note 162 at 877-79. Thitsa, *ibid.* at 7, notes that polgyny and concubinage still exist in Thailand in the practice of men taking minor wives, for status purposes among the rich and for economic support among the poor.

165 Thitsa, *supra* note 21 at 8-13; Levan, *supra* note 162 at 872-77; S. Kriengkraipetch and L. Smith, *Value Conflicts in Thai Society: Agonies of Change Seen in Short Stories* (Bangkok: Social Research Institute, Chulalongkorn Univ., 1992) at 5-16, 127-48; K. Archavanitkul and N. Havanon, *Situation, Opportunities and Problems Encountered by Young Girls in Thai Society* (Nakhonpathom: Institute for Population and Social Research, Mahidol Univ., 1990).

166 Asia Watch, *supra* note 157 at 22-24.

167 *Ibid.* at 22. The study notes, quoting from S. Hantrakul, "Thai Women: Male Chauvinism à la Thai," *The [Bangkok] Nation* (16 Nov. 1992) that this did not prevent the Field Marshal from taking more than 100 minor wives himself. Like most autocrats, he held the morals of others in doubt, not his own.

The provisions of the Act and the existing *Penal Code* ostensibly were designed to suppress the trade and at the same time to direct prostitutes to rehabilitation programs. The new law and changes to the *Penal Code* adopted earlier in 1956 gave Thailand a complex of substantive provisions proscribing prostitution-related activity that were already well ensconced in the criminal law of Canada and Australia – namely, brothel keeping, procuring, living on the avails, soliciting, child prostitution, and statutory rape.[168] In only one particular did this law make formal concessions to traditional Thai values, and that was in the case of rape of a victim over thirteen years of age where the perpetrator was not in a position of trust. The offence is compoundable by the payment of compensation to the girl and her kin.[169]

Despite the ostensible intention to criminalize the conduct of sexual exploiters, the legislation also included elements of the double standard of sexual conduct. Nowhere were customers of prostitutes penalized except where the female was underage.[170] Moreover, the reforms targeted prostitutes in its provisions for their involuntary rehabilitation in so-called "assistance centres." A convicted prostitute might be sent to such a facility for up to 12 months to undergo treatment for STDs and skills training to aid her reform. There was no equivalent provision for male parties convicted under the legislation.

Any hope that this new legal regime might effectively impinge upon the sex trade faded with the Thai government's response to the expansion of that trade in 1960s, particularly in Bangkok and Pattaya, to service the new source of demand, American servicemen stationed in the country. In 1966 the *Entertainment Places Act* was passed.[171] This legislation regulates night clubs, dance halls, bars, and places for "baths, massage or steam baths which have women to attend male customers." These establishments are required to obtain operating licences from the local police authorities. Employment of or admission to such a place of a person under 18 years of age is proscribed. Women employees are not allowed to dwell on the premises. The latter provision gives the impression that brothels and their operations are not covered and remain subject to the criminal law. However, the general

---

168 On the *Penal Code* provisions, see Asia Watch, *supra* note 157 at 25-26. It proscribes procurement (with higher penalties than those in the *Suppression of Prostitution Act*), the abduction and seduction of women and girls, and rape.

169 D. Engel, *Code and Custom in a Thai Provincial Court: The Interaction of Formal and Informal Systems of Justice* (Tucson: Univ. of Arizona Press) at 108.

170 For a critique of the skewed focus of the legislation, as well as its imprecision at points, see Asia Watch, *supra* note 157 at 23-24.

171 *Ibid.* at 24-26. In 1967, one year after the passage of the Act, an agreement was reached between the Thai government and the U.S. military to allow American service personnel to take "rest and recreation" leave in Thailand. In that year it was estimated that $5 million was spent on R and R by American troops in Thailand. This rose to $20 million by 1970: see Thanh Dam Truing, *Sex, Money and Morality: Prostitution and Tourism in Southeast Asia* (London: Zed Books, 1990) at 161.

thrust of the legislation is that it was designed to legitimate operations where sexual services are provided, although outwardly dedicated to other recreational or entertainment functions.

The sex trade, rather than suffering a decline because of criminalization, was to undergo exponential growth. The driving forces were foreign military business, domestic demand and supply encouraged by dislocation in social values, and the painful restructuring of an economy being drawn inexorably into the web of Western military and political imperatives. This swelling of the trade was cynically condoned by Thai governments desiring to placate a military ally and an important foreign aid source.

A Wasteland: The Law, Police, and the Sex Trade in Contemporary Thailand

In Thailand, the complex legal regime described earlier, involving health regulation, suppression of trafficking in girls and women, criminal proscription, and the regulation of places of entertainment remains in place. The sex trade has continued to grow, fuelled by enhanced demand from domestic sources in which visits to the brothel are a form of diversion for groups of young men out on the town and for solo users seeking sexual excitement outside the matrimonial home, and by a burgeoning sex tourist trade organized by tour companies offering vacations with sexual services supplied by beautiful compliant girls and women in exotic surroundings.[172] To these temporary users should be added the *farangs* residing permanently or temporarily in Thailand who are attracted to longer-term sexual possibilities with Asian women (or for that matter men). A proportion of both groups of foreign users are attracted to sex with children.[173]

Generating and managing the supply of girls and women to service the sex trade has become increasingly institutionalized and sophisticated, with agents operating throughout the country inducing families to allow their female teenagers to take jobs in the cities – especially Bangkok or Chiang Mai – or the resort communities in the south, such as Phuket.[174] These offers, which are supported by cash payments (in fact loans), are often dressed up to look like employment opportunities in the recreational or entertainment industries. In a consumer economy in which those families

---

172 Thitsa, *supra* note 21 at 13-16; Levan, *supra* note 162 at 882-85; M. Muecke, supra note 28 at 894-95. Several years ago the Thai Public Health Ministry released figures showing that 75% of Thai men sleep with prostitutes and 44% pay for their first sexual experience: "Foreigners 'Blamed' for Sex Problems," *supra* note 29.

173 On the relationships between Thai prostitutes and *farangs*, see E. Cohen, "Love-lorn *Farangs*: The Correspondence between Foreign Men and Thai Girls" (1986) 59 Anthropological Quarterly 115; E. Cohen, "Sensuality and Venality in Bangkok: The Dynamics of Cross-Cultural Mapping of Prostitution" (1987) 8 Deviant Behaviour 223.

174 Archavanitkul and Havanon, *supra* note 165 at 24-25.

at or below the economic margin find it hard to survive while being barraged by the need to have the latest gadgetry, this is tempting stuff. It is clear that some families in rural areas where older children or those of relatives or friends are already working in the sex trade know full well what their daughters will be doing. For children raised in a culture in which there is still a strong, felt obligation to support older generations and younger siblings, there is no question of where their duty lies.[175]

Unlike boys, who after leaving school have access to temples as novitiates or helpers and to continue their education, girls have no opportunities open to them.[176] They are, as a consequence, the ones pressured to go away to find a job. Even if their initial experience is in a job outside the sex trade, the financial rewards associated with the latter will inevitably draw them into it. Thai Buddhism continues by and large to ignore the problem and to leave prostitutes to work out their own sacred and secular salvation within the traditional confines of gender roles and the system of doing merit.[177]

The sex trade also has international dimensions in that an increasing number of Thai girls and women are being induced to take up jobs in both Asian and Western countries where they are often illegal entrants and powerless to resist the exploitation to which they are subject.[178] By the same token, as Asia Watch and the Women's Rights Project have recently reported, there is a flourishing trade in girls and women brought in from outside Thailand, especially from Burma, to feed demand within.[179] Like their Thai sisters who go overseas, these females are mercilessly exploited, sometimes serving as sexual slaves, because they have absolutely no bargaining power with the authorities in the host country.

Because of the inner contradictions in the legal regime that applies to prostitution in Thailand, there has been more or less open season for the sex trade to flourish.[180] Many police officers have been able to benefit financially from it, and politicians and bureaucrats have often proven resistant to attempts to reform it. Until recently, it was considered unexceptional for those in government to advocate publicly the preservation and even expansion of the trade to enhance tourism.[181] Only when some exploitative outrage or tragedy has come to light have those in government responded,

175 See the short story, "The Fifth Train Trip" and commentary in Kriegkraipetch and Smith, *supra* note 165 at 128-34.

176 Archavanikutul and Havanon, *supra* note 165 at 8-20.

177 Muecke, *supra* note 172 at 893-94; Thitsa, *supra* note 21 at 16-18 and 20-22.

178 Thitsa, *ibid.* at 14. See also C. Goldberg, "From Thai Grocery Store to a New York Brothel," *Bangkok Post Weekly Rev.* (12 Sept. 1995), a report on a Thai girl, Na, induced to go to New York, only to find herself in a brothel.

179 For a harrowing account of the exploitation of Burmese women and girls in Thailand, see Asia Watch, *supra* note 157.

180 *Ibid.* at 26-28.

181 Levan, *supra* note 162 at 882-84; Muecke, *supra* note 172 at 896-97.

and even then the energy of politicians and officialdom has been short-lived.[182] The twilight zone of illegality/legality produced by the co-existence of criminal and regulatory law has ensured that the legal status of sex trade outlets and the individuals who run and work in them is ambiguous. As their legal status is dictated by the police and depends on the exercise of police discretion, this system is rife with opportunities for graft and corruption. Segments of the Thai police have not been at all shy in exploiting the financial potential of the situation, largely through demands for protection money from the operators and inmates of sexual service establishments.[183] There is also clear evidence of the complicity of individual police officers and immigration officials in the cross border trade in girls and women.[184]

The manipulation of the sex trade in Thailand has increasingly met with criticism from human rights experts, feminist scholars and activists, and the representatives of non-governmental organizations working with the poor and disadvantaged. Nevertheless, until recently there has been little will in governmental circles to engage in anything other than rhetoric and cosmetic gestures about reforming the law. What has shaken the complacency of politicians, bureaucrats, and even business leaders, however, has been the growing realization that Thailand is facing an incipient AIDS epidemic that promises to subvert the recent economic advances that have made it one of the Asian miracle economies.[185] After an initial knee-jerk reaction that sought to associate the AIDS problem with prostitutes and to advocate quarantining them, public health authorities have now turned to education in safe sex as likely to be more productive of change.[186] In this, the authorities have been clearly embarrassed by non-governmental organizations such as the Population Development Association led by Khun Mechai, which has been preaching condom use in a very public way.[187]

Less evident has been the development of true political will to remedy the structural problems afflicting the law and law enforcement. The heady political changes of the early 1990s produced statements of resolve to reform the law so that child prostitution would be vigorously suppressed,

---

182 Asia Watch, *supra* note 157 at 27, quoting from Professor V. Muntarbhorn, "A Scourge in our Midst," *Bangkok Post* (13 Nov. 1992).

183 *Ibid.* at 28, in which it is estimated that police officers can earn between $120-200 a month in protection money. See also G. Fairclough, "Duty Calls: Serving the Public Doesn't Come Easy to Thai Police," *Far Eastern Economic Review* (1 Dec. 1994) at 28.

184 Asia Watch, *ibid.* at 75-82.

185 Bamber, Hewison, and Underwood, *supra* note 150 at 152-53.

186 *Ibid.* at 153-55. See also W. Boonchalaksi and P. Guest, *AIDS and Children: Prospects for the Year 2000* (Institute for Population and Social Research, Mahidol Univ., IPSR Publication No. 168, July 1993); T. Brown and P. Xenos, *AIDS in Asia: The Gathering Storm* (East-West Center, Asia Pacific Issues, Analysis No. 16, Aug. 1994) at 11-12.

187 Bamber, Hewison, and Underwood, *ibid.* at 153. The switch in government policy on AIDS was assisted by the fact that Mechai served as a minister in the interim government of Anand Panyarachan from Feb. 1991 to Mar. 1992.

while non-coercive adult prostitution would be decriminalized.[188] These proposals of the Anand Panyarachan government unfortunately never took legislative form before the political hiatus of 1992. The regime of Chuan Leekpai, in power from 1992 to 1995, proved to be long on words and short on action, despite growing criticism from inside and outside the country about child prostitution and the public health dangers associated with it.[189] There was little evidence that a stated resolve to end child prostitution and enforce child labour laws produced anything substantial in the way of results.

Recently the Thai parliament has passed legislation that seeks to deal more resolutely with the serious problem of child prostitution in that country. The *Prostitution Prevention and Suppression Bill* amended in 1993 and again in 1996 puts in place much harsher penalties for those engaged in the sexual exploitation of children of both sexes and those operating vice services.[190] Jail terms ranging from two to twenty years have been included, depending on the age of the child and the degree or responsibility and trust vested in the offender. In a significant departure from previous legislation and reflecting pressure from NGOs, women's groups, and social welfare organizations, the Act establishes an Occupations Protection and Development Committee "to map out preventative policies, protective mechanisms and measures to equip former prostitutes with the skills to enter other occupations and improve their lives."[191]

THE SEX TRADE IN AUSTRALIA, CANADA, AND THAILAND: TRENDS AND CONNECTIONS

Two important aspects of contemporary legal research are the assessment of the cultural and ideological factors that condition how law is constructed and applied, and an evaluation of how far the law in action reflects the theoretical and pragmatic suppositions of those who framed it. Nowhere are these characteristics of the research enterprise more pertinent than in assessing the formation and working out of law that seeks to address social practices that are the objects, often contemporaneously, of both censure and approval within human communities.

In Western societies, sexual conduct that transcends the boundaries of what is thought to be respectable or conventional has always occupied contested terrain. Prostitution and its legal treatment have been particularly susceptible to changes in social judgment; they have reflected different views

188 Asia Watch, *supra* note 157 at 30-37.

189 *Ibid.* at 3-7.

190 See *Bangkok Post Weekly Review* (5 Apr. 1996) 2.

191 *Ibid.* The Committee is chaired by the Labour and Social Welfare permanent secretary and comprises eleven senior officials and seven experts, five of whom must be from NGOs.

within the community of prostitution as being corrosive, cathartic, or conventional behaviour.

This chapter shows how those different meanings have influenced social and legal attitudes to the sex trade in two settler countries, increasingly populated by European immigrants, but with somewhat different patterns of colonial development and ethnic concentration. The pattern of social evaluation of and legal response to prostitution has at times shown significant similarities between Canada and Australia. Both experienced a general movement from effective toleration to experiments with regulated prostitution and from there to a criminal law regime that was converted by the police at street level into an instrument of unofficial regulation of the trade. This process of evolution was the product of the competing pulls of social and moral reformers intent on reconstituting these countries as virtuous communities, and police officials much more concerned with the day-to-day business of detecting and prosecuting crime and keeping order who did not see prostitution as high among their operational priorities. The law enforcers were, of course, realists enough to be ready and willing to enforce the law when it counted, in order to placate middle class sensibilities. In both nations, too, largely as a result of wartime anxieties, the sex trade was medicalized to provide significant power to public health officials to prosecute or detain those suspected of spreading or carrying sexually transmitted diseases. However, the history also suggests that there are sufficient cultural variables between Canada and Australia that some differences in attitude and policy are evident between the two countries.

In Australia, there has been historically greater resistance to the notion that the criminal law is the preferred vehicle for dealing with prostitution. This resistance reflects a powerful working class culture that has opposed wholesale criminalization of this form of conduct for reasons of simple self-interest. For working class men who wanted access to prostitutes, the criminal law was potentially constricting. Moreover, it did nothing to deal with the public health risks associated with commercial sex. Regulation and management of the trade were, in this view, more likely to achieve the dual goals of accessibility and safety, than the doubtful and less direct impact of the criminal law.

Scepticism about the value of the criminal law in controlling the sex trade has also had greater purchase in Australia than in Canada in more recent decades, when the legal system's biased treatment of prostitutes has fallen under attack from civil libertarians, feminists, and sex trade workers. While Canadian politicians seem to have adopted the view that there is a moral bottom line, represented by the complex of offences in the *Criminal Code*, below which they cannot go on pain of political excommunication, some Australian politicians have shown a capacity for experimentation with new legal approaches to the sex trade. In the most radical of these experiments, the traditional concerns with labour and health risks have been given a totally new twist by the building-in of employment safeguards for sex workers.

None of this is to suggest that either Australia or Canada has yet found durable and comprehensive approaches to reducing the incidence of prostitution. There is still a lack of creative thought about economic, social, and educational policies that address the privation, physical abuse, and mental and emotional neglect that induce many girls and women to enter the trade, while accommodating its practice in more humane ways. In communities in both countries, prostitutes are largely powerless and subject to the capricious exercise of police discretion, which often leaves them wondering from day to day whether they will be the focus of police and prosecutorial attention. The so-called "prostitution problem" is also chased around, especially in Canada, as ordinary citizens voice their objections to its presence in their neighbourhood. In most Australian states and across Canada, the police remain the effective social and legal managers of the trade in the sense of establishing the ground rules by which it is regulated, practised, and disciplined. This situation frees the rest of the population, and especially the politicians, from direct responsibility for what happens and from anything approaching creative thought. It is high time that the focus of attention shifted to improving the conditions under which prostitutes work and to developing strategies and applying resources to alleviate the social and economic conditions that encourage young people to prostitute themselves, and the adult male population to seek them out.

If prostitution remains to one degree or another in social and legal limbo in Australia and Canada, its status in Thailand borders on the surreal. In the first place, the undeniable growth of the sex trade has been fuelled by political, social, and economic changes over which the vast majority of citizens have little say, let alone control. The demand for sexual services for money reflects in part the fast-paced development of an urban-generated, Westernized consumer economy, which has created a predictable migration of people, dislodged by the demise of the traditional subsistence economy, from country to city. The consumer economy has also spawned and sustained an expanding urban middle class and placed a premium on acquisitive urges among the population generally. In the sexual economy, the result has been a steady increase in the desire of Thai males for access to prostitutes for recreation and relief. Complementing this and reflective of the same forces has been the emergence of a sex trade to meet the desires of foreigners. Sex tourism has become embedded so firmly in economic discourse and strategizing that it continues to operate, if rather more circumspectly than previously. The same social and economic choices that have influenced demand also explain the growth in the supply of sex workers, although here the story is one of individuals and families seeking to survive the dislocation caused by the new order rather than capitalizing on it by choice.

Superimposed on these socioeconomic realities is a contradictory set of legal regimes and provisions, largely constructed to placate inconsistent moral and economic pressures from outside. That the result is a highly manipulative and self-serving regulatory regime cynically worked by the police, in which girls and women are often exploited by everyone in sight, enjoying no rights to protection from violence, coercion, and disease, should perhaps be a surprise to no one. In the first place, the complex of legal provisions in place has little or no reference to either cultural tradition or change in Thailand. To the extent that it reflects anything, it reflects the bloodless demands of the market and the individual graft that often attends market economics. Although, as this study has hopefully shown, there are definite commonalities in the sexual culture of the two Western countries and Thailand, especially in the power of patriarchy to order women's lives according to male scripts, there have been and are still cultural variables. The most important is the relative importance of both the extended family and kin groups in rural Thai society. While these broader and more pervasive reference points may have faded in urban areas, they still exercise a strong pull in the country and go far to explain the strong sense of obligation that both female and male children feel towards their elders and the welfare of their families. It would be difficult to claim that significant numbers of girls and women in Australia and Canada in the sex trade are there to support parents and siblings out of a sense of duty. In fact, in many cases quite the reverse is true; entry into prostitution reflects a desire for detachment and freedom from parental and familial constraints. In Thailand the law as recently practised may, as a police colonel in Chiang Mai tried to persuade me, recognize this reality by allowing room for females to contribute to the family economy. It does nothing to provide them with the protection of health and personal dignity, and still less to afford them employment benefits. Those who employ girls and women to provide sexual services operate with the profit motive firmly in mind, calculating what little they need to do for economic reasons to keep their workers serviceable. The more vulnerable the girls and women are in legal and social terms, the greater the exploitation, since they are dispensable. There is always a new supply of workers among "illegals" in Thailand or those brought in directly from Myanmar, Laos, and even China.

Although it is important to recognize the cultural particularities, it is clear that a combination of patriarchy and the commodification of sexual services within a broader market economy have been and continue to be an impediment to the adoption of more imaginative and humane policies towards the sex trade in all three countries. One may rue the direction and pace of events in Thailand, but it is unlikely that the clock will be turned back to a simpler, more tranquil cultural environment. But that is not to preach inaction. What is required is the development of policies and strategies that recognize both the cultural realities and the pattern of social and economic change that have followed in the wake of modern Thai political history.

The recent changes to the law in Thailand under the *Prostitution Prevention and Suppression Bill* clearly represent a step in the right direction. The joinder of enhanced criminal law provisions directed against the sexual exploiters of children (1993) with sections which seek proactive solutions to the economic and social roots of prostitution (1996) is a creative step. However, based on a record of past inertia there is ample room for scepticism. The legislation will not succeed in its purpose unless attended by the development of the political will to take control of the situation, and a genuine commitment to make the structural and institutional changes that will support the growth of a non-exploitative system. Politicians and bureaucrats need to disabuse themselves of the belief that they can merely "imagine" the problem of child prostitution away.[192] The government has to recognize that job opportunities are needed for young Thais that provide a realistic alternative to the financial lure of the sex trade. Moreover, the Thai police must be thoroughly reformed and paid the sorts of salaries that reduce temptations to graft.

In Thailand, as in the West, prostitution is a practice that seems to paralyze the imagination of decision makers and their ability to see its connection with patriarchy and social and economic deprivation. In short, the authorities in Thailand have been myopic on the issue of prostitution. As a result, it has been left to social critics and NGOs to undertake the demanding work of both visioning and working out a brighter future for girls and women, whether inside or outside the sex trade. Although there has not been to date the emergence of prostitutes' collectives in Thailand lobbying for change, one NGO, "Empower," has taken the initiative in working with sex trade workers to improve their communication and life skills.[193] Meanwhile, female academics, for instance those at the Women's Centre at Chiang Mai University, have shown imagination and courage in working with women at the grass roots level in village communities, with a view to providing counselling and assistance to families and girls who are the targets of sex trade agents.[194] For their part, women activists (for example, those working

192 For a critique of the wishful thinking of politicians and bureaucrats in relation to the sex trade in Thailand, see the editorial, "Tough Laws Alone Won't Save Sex Slaves," *Bangkok Post* (11 Feb. 1994) at 6, and C. Vanaspong, "Prostitution: New Law Won't Help," *Bangkok Post Weekly Rev.* (19 Apr. 1996) at 7. On imagining the problem and its dimensions, see the *Bangkok Post* (4 Feb. 1994) at 20. The *New York Times* had reported a figure of two million prostitutes in Thailand, including 800,000 children. Thai officials reacted strongly to that as a gross overestimate. While rejecting the low estimate of 60,000 made by the Public Welfare Department, the Joint Public/Private Committee on Social Affairs finally agreed to put the number around 100,000.

193 Meeting with Ms. Jackie Pollock of the Empower group in Chiang Mai, January 1994.

194 Interview with Professor Virada Somswasdi, Head of the Women's Studies Centre at Chiang Mai University, Jan. 1994.

through the *Foundation for Women*) have sought to organize politically to press for resolute action on both the national and international fronts.[195] It is to be hoped that, if the proposed legislation on child prostitution is passed and a structure put in place to begin to combat the social and economic roots of the sex trade, both the NGOs with experience in the field and local communities will be listened to and involved in the process of securing change.[196] Only in this way it is likely that strategies will emerge that reflect Thai cultural traditions and grass roots commitment.

Finally, it has to be recognized that the internationalization of the sex trade in recent decades has produced patterns of movement of both users and suppliers between Western and Asian countries. Subsequently, these countries are faced with a common problem, and are increasingly challenged to take both national and international steps to suppress the sex trade's most noxious exploitative practices. As indicated above, Western countries such as Australia and Canada have passed or are contemplating legislation making it a criminal offence in their domestic criminal law to engage in the sexual exploitation and abuse of children in other countries. These steps, which may be more symbolic than practical, considering evidential difficulties attending prosecution for offences committed elsewhere, are only part of a broader strategy needed to combat international female and child slavery.[197] Using both obligations under international conventions that are designed to protect women and children from sexual exploitation, and domestic law, both host and supply countries need to cooperate to control and regulate the sex trade more effectively and to police and prosecute child prostitution more vigorously. At the same time, they must persuade themselves of the value of directing significant resources to dealing assertively with the social and economic conditions that feed the sex trade. In all of this effort, the voices of those who work in the trade and the NGOs and communities who work with and for them need to be listened to as never before.

Several recent developments at an international level suggest that countries that receive and supply children and women for the sex trade are willing to support in principle initiatives to suppress the international trafficking in children. The International Labour Office (ILO) issued a report in 1996

195 See *Recommendations to Combat International Traffic in Women* (Bangkok: Foundation for Women, 1995) at 26-39.

196 For an interesting and instructive example of interaction between international and national NGOs and Thai village communities, see the account of the International Workshop on International Migration and Traffic in Women, Chiang Mai, 17-21 Oct. 1994 in *Voices of Thai Women*, No. 12, Dec. 1994 at 9-13.

197 See Levan, *supra* note 162 at 907-12; D. Hodgson, "Combatting the Organized Sexual Exploitation of Asian Children: Recent Developments and Prospects" (1995) 9 Int'l J. of Law and the Family 23.

on child labour that targeted child prostitution, among other forms of exploitation, for elimination.[198] Even more significant are the developments arising from the World Congress Against Commercial Sexual Exploitation of Children, held in Stockholm in August 1996. This congress sought to build on a series of international agreements and conventions in the *Convention on the Rights of the Child*, 1989. The Agenda of Action from the Congress includes (1) giving high priority to action against commercial sexual exploitation of children, with adequate resources to support them; (2) the criminalization of commercial and non-commercial sexual exploitation of children and condemnation of the exploiters, while ensuring that the child victims are not penalized; (3) co-operation between law enforcement agencies; (4) ensuring through education, social mobilization, and development activities that parents are helped to fulfil their responsibilities in protecting their children; and (5) enhancing the role of popular participation in preventing and eliminating the commercial sexual exploitation of children.[199] What action follows remains to be seen.

198 International Labour Office, *Child Labour: Targetting the Intolerable* (Geneva: ILO, 1996), Report VI(1).

199 World Congress Against Commercial Sexual Exploitation of the Child, General Rapporteur Professor Vitit Muntarbhorn, *Report of the Congress* (1996).

Part IV: Cross-Sectoral Contexts

9 Environmental Law as "Sacred Text": Western Values and Southeast Asian Prospects

Douglas M. Johnston

INTRODUCTION

There can be no doubt that environmental concerns have priority status in the 1990s. It is difficult to imagine any event or collective change of heart or mind that could result in the relegation of these concerns. The concept of sustainability, derived as it is from the older goals of conservation and rational management, comes close to encapsulating the ethos of our time.

Because of its ethical and social significance, environmental law is an instrument of public policy[1] that can be deployed in a wide variety of situations. In the theory of comparative law, it has, at least potentially, operational implications in civic, transactional, and behavioural sectors of any legal system. From the civic perspective, one of the major issues of public policy is the allocation of responsibilities for resource management and environmental protection among the various levels, organs, and agencies of government. In transactional contexts, existing policies and practices in trade, industry, investment, finance, and property-holding are subject to increasingly insistent demands for modification in light of environmental concerns. Even at the level of interpersonal and institutional behaviour, officially promoted environmental awareness is beginning to affect almost everyone's perceptions and expectations related to hazard, waste, efficiency, respect, balance, and restraint in human affairs. Environmental law has to be characterized as "trisectoral," just as it has to be approached as a component of the cross-disciplinary field of environmental policy and management.

---

1 Lawyers who might normally shrink from the general proposition that law should be treated as an instrument of public policy seem not to object to the instrumentalist theory of law as applied to the particular area of environmental law. Acceptance seems to be due to three principal factors. First, the area is seen to be new despite the scattered existence of rather general antecedent principles of relevance to environmental protection in property, tort, criminal law, international law, and other fields of law. Second, the development of modern environmental law is chiefly the province of the

Because environmental law is being developed rapidly in most legal systems, in response to ethical demands from outside as well as inside each national system, this area of legal development has to be seen as a reflection of the phenomenon of transnationalization of law. Arguably the ethical foundation of environmental law serves to pull this area of legal development in the direction of "sacred text." What is examined in this essay is whether these external, chiefly Western, influences are likely to shape Southeast Asian legal developments into conformity with Western legal systems.

THE GLOBALIZATION OF ENVIRONMENTAL LAW

The Transnationalization of Law

Law in general tended, in earlier times, to develop within the framework of national and subnational jurisdictions. The civil law, originating in the domestic context of the Roman republic, took almost 2000 years to become a cross-jurisdictional system adaptable to a variety of national needs and cultural values.[2] Likewise, the common law had over 500 years to take root in its native English soil before the tasks of transplantation had to be dealt with throughout the British Empire.[3] As we know, the 70-year history of

legislature, despite the mounting volume of environmental lawsuits in the more litigious legal cultures. Third, most contributions to environmental policy development that assume statutory form at the national level are widely publicized as derivatives from international diplomacy and the political arena. Few, if any, areas of law are more closely scrutinized by the general public, and therefore less likely to be converted into a wholly technical area under the control of an elite within the legal profession.

2 Roman law might be said to have developed over a period of 2,200 years, from the foundation of the city of Rome (traditionally fixed to the year 753 B.C.) through the fall of the Western Roman Empire in A.D. 476 until the demise of the Eastern Empire in 1453. However, Roman legal development began with the promulgation of the Twelve Tables in 451 B.C. and ended with the publication of the Justinian Code in A.D. 533, more than 50 years after the fall of the Western Empire. It is commonly agreed that Rome did not impose its own law on the provinces by force, but rather that it was accepted by traders as a matter of necessity. The "rediscovery" of Roman law, which in the Dark Ages had largely retreated to the monastery under the guise of canon law, took place in the late 11th century, when Roman law as such was made an object of scholarship at Bologna and other centres of learning in northern Italy. There a school of "glossators" emerged, dedicated to the task of reconstructing Justinian's Code through a 200-year succession of annotations. In the 14th century it fell to the "postglossators" or "commentators" to effect a liaison between the revived Roman law and the "living laws" of the Italian cities in light of the practical needs of the day. The separate civil law systems of Europe that evolved between the 15th century and the era of national codifications in the 18th and 19th centuries were all derived in part from the mosaic of Roman law, Germanic law, canon law, and local custom known as the *jus commune*, which cohered conceptually on the basis of updated and widely accepted principles derived from the old Roman law.

3 The Norman Conquest of England in 1066 effectively ended the supremacy of the old Saxon laws, which lingered on only at the local level. As a new but indigenous tradition, the common law evolved steadily on the basis of Norman custom brought over by the conquerors, who resisted any attempt by the clergy to incorporate the corpus of the

communism was too short to reveal how long it would have taken the transnational system of socialist law to jell around the values and institutions of the Soviet Union.[4] The history of all three of these major Western legal "families," across very different time-lines, shows a similar trend to separate national development.

The need for legal uniformity in the commercial world gave rise to the law merchant in early times.[5] Yet it was not until the late nineteenth century that the established pattern of separate national legal development, within these three international families, was seen to obstruct, or at least complicate, the creation of goods and services, effective property relationships, efficient communication and exchange, and other transactional purposes, and thus to create the need for "solutions" through efforts to produce uniformity, codification, integration, harmonization, and other modes of convergence.[6] As for the civic and behavioural sectors of legal systems, little

---

Roman *jus civile*. Later attempts to introduce Roman law to England, even as late as the 16th century, when the Roman civilization was becoming the model for enlightenment, were beaten back in theory, although unacknowledged Roman influences persisted in practice. The export of the common law dates from the early settlements of the late 16th century. It is normal to distinguish the voluntary reception of Roman law with the involuntary "imposition" of the common law during the colonial period, which has been characterized as "legal acculturation."

4 At the time of the Bolshevik Revolution in 1917, Russia was the inheritor of the Romano-German legal tradition. Ostensibly, much of this tradition was replaced by a new system of norms based on the principles of Marxist-Leninist ideology, a system that extended to the 14 other countries of Eastern Europe and other regions that had embraced the Marxist-Leninist system of government by the 1950s. Some jurists have maintained that, despite these fundamental changes of substantive law, the conceptual apparatus and methodology remained essentially those of the civil law tradition. Socialist scholars, however, always maintained that socialist law was a separate system with a common core, distinguished from others by such features as the dominance of state ownership of the factors of production, the supremacy of the proletariat, the leadership role of the Communist Party, and the denial of any distinction between the public and private sector. Whether the distinctiveness of socialist law would have prevailed over its civil law antecedents will presumably never be known.

5 From the early 11th century, one can trace the emergence of a consensus among the merchants of medieval Europe that they needed a common system of rules, separate from the ordinary laws that varied from place to place, to provide the certainty and uniformity essential to stable commercial relations and equitable settlement of trade disputes. Foreign traders were often subject to confiscations and other types of harassment if one of their compatriots had defaulted in a transaction. What was needed was a system whereby traders of different nationalities could negotiate contracts and relationships that would be recognized and protected throughout the merchant community. Gradually a system of rules evolved in such a way that they could be applied in special courts conducted at the numerous trade fairs held throughout Europe, where local and foreign merchants met to transact business.

6 The first systematic effort to induce juridical convergence, outside the framework of the canon law, the law merchant, and the cognate sectors of banking and insurance, was based on the strategy of codification, which began to surface in the Scandinavian countries in the 18th century, many decades before the appearance of the Code Napoleon in 1804. Despite subsequent attempts to romanticize this famous Code as an innovative

success could be expected in achieving the convergence of legal systems until the Charter and machinery of the United Nations were available to promote and facilitate this function of international organizations.[7]

Today it is commonly understood that virtually all areas of law are subject increasingly to the forces of transnationalization. Even though international society is still very far short of the goal of a single world legal order, or even of agreement on the desirability of such a future, most legal development since the end of the Second World War, especially in the transactional sector, seems to provide evidence of an apparently irreversible trend toward convergence of national legal systems.[8]

The phenomenon of juridical transnationalization is now so familiar to most lawyers that it no longer has the power to startle or astonish. Yet, given the flux of social values caught up in many areas of law reform and legal development, perhaps we should at least be mildly surprised that the convergence of law has proceeded as swiftly as it has. After all, the past 50-year period of world history has been marked by frequent threats to the goal of international solidarity, and even to the more modest objective of reducing international tensions. More recently, the value of cultural diversity has seemed likely to slow down the pace of imitation, especially in civic and behavioural sectors of the law.[9] Yet the trend to transnationalization continues.

---

breakthrough, it seems rather to have been "a re-working of Roman law, ancient customs, and ancient maxims": J. Gordley, "Myths of the French Civil Code" (1994) 42 Amer. J. Compar. L. 459 at 505. The unification-of-laws movement began a century later, early in the 20th century, and more modern efforts at integration and harmonization did not begin to attract attention until the integration of Western Europe took permanent institutional form under the Treaty of Rome in the late 1950s. Apart from *ad hoc* arbitration, there was no apparatus in place for the systematic application of public international law until the early 1920s, when the Permanent Court of International Justice at The Hague began to settle international disputes by resort to common legal principles.

7 The purposes of the UN Charter, as affirmed in the preamble, include war prevention, furtherance of human rights, respect for justice and legal obligations, and promotion of "social progress and better standards of life in larger freedom." As described more formally in art. 1, the purposes of the United Nations are fourfold: (1) the maintenance of international peace and security; (2) the strengthening of universal peace through the development of interstate cooperation; (3) the solution of economic, social, cultural, and humanitarian problems; and (4) the promotion of human rights and the fundamental freedoms of individuals. Although there is no specific reference to the convergence of legal systems, it might be regarded as implied by the theme of interstate cooperation, which is the dominant motif of this "sacred text" of the organized world community (or interstate system).

8 For an early prediction of the acceleration of this trend, see R. St. J. Macdonald, G. L. Morris, and D. M. Johnston, "The New Lawyer in a Transnational World" (1975) 25 Univ. of Toronto L.J. 343.

9 During the Cold War era, political opposition to the universalist claims of the Universal Declaration of Human Rights (1948) and the International Covenant on Political and Civil Rights (1966) was ascribed to the dominance within the UN system of the

The Convergence of Environmental Regimes: Four Models

Why is there an apparent trend to the convergence of legal systems? Is it more apparent than real? Why is it more apparent in some areas or sectors than in others? Can we discern an emerging ideology of value assimilation? If so, what are its causes and effects, and what can be projected for the next century? Is the apparent globalization of environmental law a special case, or is it the harbinger of things to come in other areas of the law? These difficult questions seem to call for hypotheses.

First, it might be argued that an area like environmental law, unlike almost any other legal area, must be scientific in the sense that it should be based on scientific truths. That is, it may be perceived as an instrument of environmental management, which in turn is designed to reflect and implement the best scientific understanding of nature and of human impacts upon it.[10] If this understanding changes, with new discoveries, then the law should also change in the light of the best available knowledge. If environmental law is conceived as the institutional reflector of scientific truths, based on such tenets as the need for sustainability and a precautionary approach to potentially harmful activities,[11] then logically, at no time should

---

capitalist states, whose cultures pivoted on the pre-eminence of individual autonomy rather than on communal harmony. Opposition to this Covenant, which was based very largely on the Universal Declaration, delayed its entry into force until 1976. Many non-socialist states of the developing world shared these resentments, but it is only recently, since the end of the Cold War, that the cultural origins of their reluctance to ratify have become apparent in the western world. It is easier now to be sympathetic to cultural sensitivity than it was then to be sympathetic to ideological hostility!

10 Several recent environmental treaties negotiated at the global level have been designed in accordance with near-consensus or majority opinion in the relevant sector of the scientific community: e.g., the 1986 Convention on the Protection of the Ozone Layer, the 1992 Convention on Biological Diversity, and the 1992 United Nations Framework Convention on Climate Change. In none of these cases is the scientific rationale free from dissent on the part of many qualified scientists, especially in the case of climate change, but normative development is under way notwithstanding in all three contexts. On the overriding of dissent within the scientific community, see J. M. Bewers, "The Declining Influence of Science on Marine Environmental Policy" (1995) 10 Chem. and Ecol. 9.

11 Virtually no responsible natural scientist seems to dispute the general proposition that the harvesting of renewable natural resources should be kept within the apparent limits of sustainability, but a few have questioned the logic of certain kinds of sustainable development policies. Few would deny the need for sensible precautions in the planning, design, and execution of development projects and other initiatives that might possibly cause harm to the environment, but scientific and other expert opinions vary widely on how to interpret and apply the counsel of caution inherent in the adjective "precautionary," and many disagree strongly that it should be elevated to the level of a legal principle. See D. Bodansky, "Scientific Uncertainty and Precautionary Principle" (1991) 33 Environment 4; D. L. VanderZwaag, *CEPA and the Precautionary Principle/Approach* (Ottawa: Ministry of Supply and Services, 1994); and G. J. Hewison, "The Precautionary Approach to Fisheries Management: An Environmental Perspective," in K. L. Matics and T. L. McDorman, eds., *Summary and Selected Papers of the SEAPOL Tri-Regional Conference* (Bangkok: SEAPOL, 1995) at 123.

there be any gross incompatibility between the environmental laws and procedures of one country and those of others. At most there should be only relatively minor differences due to differences in data sets and in the interpretation placed on the data within the scientific community.[12] By this model, scientists and lawyers must have a close collaborative relationship, and the latter should acquire the work style of the former, sharing information and ideas globally on a virtually continuous basis and constantly striving to reduce or avoid basic discrepancies among legal systems in the environmental field.

Second, environmental law could be said to reflect a set of universal values. Taking this position, many specialists in environmental law, especially international environmental law, have advocated that legal development in this area should be promoted in much the same fashion as human rights.[13] The analogy with human rights may not, however, serve environmental law as well as hoped, if it creates an ideology of *entitlement* unbalanced against the equally important, or even more relevant, concept of *responsibility*.[14]

---

12 However, because most scientific research is still conducted in the developed countries, developing countries are sometimes suspicious of claims or demands that purport to be based on scientific findings. The argument that all science is wholly objective, value-free, and culturally neutral is difficult to accept, even if the claim is limited to the physical sciences. Within the natural or life sciences, it is usually agreed to be arbitrary to treat nature as detached from the human presence, and of course human impacts vary enormously. Above all, differences in the interpretation of scientific data can very often be attributed to differences in cultural perception.

13 On the pros and cons of this analogy, see D. Shelton, "Human Rights, Environmental Rights, and the Right to Environment" (1991), 28 Stanford J. Int'l L. 103. In the theory of international law, an unbridgeable dichotomy has always existed between *treaty law*, which rests firmly on formal acts of consent by sovereign actors (with the right to withhold consent), but is not universal, and *customary law*, which is presumed to be universally binding but is not necessarily the product of consent, except by legal fiction. For a recent summary of the treaty-custom relationship, see H. E. Chodosh, "An Interpretive Theory of International Law: The Distinction between Treaty and Customary Law" (1995) 28 Vand. J. Int'l. L. 973 at 975-81. On the need for a third conceptual source of international law, see H. E. Chodosh, "Neither Treaty nor Custom: The Emergence of Declarative International Law" (1991) 26 Texas Int'l. L.J. 87. Some scholars have called boldly for a solution by recognition of a class of norms that would derive validity from the governing construct of global interdependence: e.g., "universal law" (e.g. J. Charney, "Universal International Law" (1993) 87 Amer. J. Int'l L. 529) or "world law" (e.g. H. J. Berman, "World Law" (1995) 18 Ford. Int'l L.J. 1617). Fundamental principles of international environmental law, such as sustainability, might be put forward as belonging to Chodosh's third declaratory source of norms, if widely perceived as based on "universal values."

14 Both the 1972 Stockholm Conference on the Human Environment and the 1992 Rio Conference on Environment and Development were framed around the concept of human responsibility, whereas many general law-making conferences such as the Third UN Conference on the Law of the Sea (UNCLOS III) are mostly – but not entirely – framed around the concept of state entitlement. The tension between these two, very different, kinds of orientation raises questions about the risk of collision between two divergent mind-sets in the interstate system: D. M. Johnston, "UNCLOS III and UNCED:

Moreover, some would object to the primacy of *human* rights within the holistic framework of the entire planetary environment.[15] Furthermore, at a time when the value of cultural diversity is being conceded more legitimacy than it once was within the field of human rights,[16] this suggested analogy might seem to call into question the goal of universality in the environmental field. The irony might be that, if compromises had to be made with the ethic of cultural relativism, the "universal values" approach to environmental law might end up with less universality than the "scientific truths" approach.

Third, a very different, operational argument can be presented for a "uniform standards" approach to environmental law, on the ground that the continuance of highly differential environmental standards in different national governmental systems is the surest way to defeat any collective effort to protect the environment.[17] This approach might seem to take some

---

A Collision of Mind Sets?" in L. K. Kriwoken et al., eds., *Oceans Law and Policy in the Post-UNCED Era: Australian and Canadian Perspectives* (London, etc.: Kluwer Law Int'l, 1996) 11-24. Some environmentalists argue that environmental responsibility – or indeed human responsibility in an even larger sense – is unattainable within the existing system of nation-states that pivots on the potentially irresponsible concept of sovereignty. P. M. Mische, "Ecological Security and the Need to Reconceptualize Sovereignty" (1989) 14 Alternatives 389.

15 Advocates for nature conservation generally are anxious not to proceed on the basis of a separation between nature and the human experience, and at Rio they succeeded in dropping the Stockholm concept of the "human environment." Advocates of animal rights are, of course, particularly adamant in their hostility to the traditional assumption of human prerogative.

16 In recent years, the debate between absolutism and universalism with cultural variations has divided the human rights community. See e.g. P. Alston, "The Best Interests Principles: Towards a Reconciliation of Culture and Human Rights" (1994) 8 Int'l J.L. and Fam. 1. For a strong traditional argument, see C. C. Joyner and J. C. Dettling, "Bridging the Cultural Chasm: Cultural Relativism and the Future of International Law" (1993) 20 Calif. W. Int'l L.J. 275, which was intended as a response to recent western efforts to "deconstruct" western claims to universality, especially in the context of human rights. Specialists in the fields of cultural studies and Asian studies have challenged the western conception of "orientalism" as based on the imperialist assumption of the west as the "core" of human civilization and of the Orient (and other non-western cultures) as the "periphery." By this view, the west is taken as the norm, the point of reference by which all other cultures are to be measured. For a challenge, see E. Said, *Orientalism* (Harmondsworth, U.K.: Peregrine Books, 1985).

17 This was a crucial assumption in the negotiations on ship-generated marine pollution control issues at UNCLOS III, and continues to govern diplomatic efforts to negotiate further conventions in the marine pollution sector. See e.g. B. H. Oxman, "The Duty to Respect Generally Accepted International Standards" (1991) 24 N.Y.U.J. Int'l. L. and Policy 109. However, international standards are notoriously difficult to determine in the absence of widely accepted standard-setting instruments, and in some areas, such as land-based marine pollution, negotiation to this end seems unlikely to succeed in the near future. In these cases it may be more realistic to seek agreement on minimum standards. See generally A. O. Adede, "The Minimum Standards in a World of Disparities," in R. St. J. Macdonald and D. M. Johnston, eds., *The Structure and Process of International Law: Essays in Legal Philosophy, Doctrine and Theory* (Dordrecht: Martinus Nijhoff

of the truth-based or value-based rhetoric out of the field of environmental law, making the plea for convergence on the ground of institutional effectiveness. This approach assumes the attainability of uniform standards among government systems by placing faith in global or general treaty-making, the techniques of national or regional implementation, the psychology of inducement to comply, and the ethic of capacity-building.[18] Since absolute uniformity of standards is utopian in a real world of gross disparities, this approach to the goal of convergence depends also on a generous tolerance of government systems that simply cannot reach the level of "reasonable" or "substantial," much less that of "full" or "strict," compliance with globally negotiated standards.[19] Most might believe that the goal of a level playing field in the environmental area of law is likely to remain elusive, giving rise to frequent resentment and occasional conflict among nations.[20]

Publishers, 1983, 1986) at 1001-26. However, the concept of minimum standards seems less useful in the technical-industrial context of ship-generated marine pollution than in broader, socioeconomic contexts such as land-based marine pollution, air pollution, or river pollution.

18 Treaty implementation, compliance inducement, and capacity-building have become building-blocks for a new conceptual approach to the making and maintenance of negotiated instruments. For a full-scale development of this argument, see D. M. Johnston, *Consent and Commitment in the World Community: An Analysis and Classification of Negotiated Instruments* (Irvington, N.Y.: Transnational Publishers, 1997).

19 It is, of course, one of the purposes of capacity-building, in a given context, to raise the beneficiary state's capacity from a very low level of treaty compliance capability to a higher level, reasonable if not substantial, and perhaps eventually from the level of substantial compliance to that of full or strict compliance, as the beneficiary state begins to match the capacity of the most developed states. At present it seems useful to regard signatories to complex and demanding global treaties, such as the 1982 UN Convention on the Law of the Sea, as distributed across a spectrum ranging from "minimal response" to "maximal response." Asymmetrical standards or differential obligations seem necessary to induce widespread acceptance of an international regulatory regime despite the "lowest common denominator" problem. For reservations about this approach, see G. Handl, "Environmental Security and Global Change: The Challenge to International Law," in W. Lang et al., eds., *Environmental Protection and International Law* (London: Graham and Trotman, 1991) at 64-66. In Southeast Asia, the "differential obligations" or "common but differentiated" approach would require a classification to be made of different levels of national economic development within ASEAN. For a suggested re-classification of the "third world," see K. P. Magyar, "Classifying the International Political Economy: A Third World Proto-Theory" (1995) 16 Third World Q. 703.

20 Recent trade-and-environment concerns have required negotiators to apply their skills to the drafting of nuanced language that calls for an open international economic system and cautions against unilateral environmental actions that constitute unjustifiable discrimination. For example, art. 3(5) of the 1992 UN Framework Convention on Climate Change prescribes: "Measures taken to combat climate change, including unilateral ones, should not constitute a means of arbitrary or unjustifiable discrimination or a disguised restriction on international trade." Similar language may be found in ch. 39 of Agenda 21, which was adopted at UNCED at the same time as the above Convention. The question of the relationship between trade and environment was also addressed at Rio in Principle 12 of the Declaration on Environment and Development

Finally, the less heroic position might be taken that most national legal systems will tend to converge over time simply as a matter of practical convenience. The history of comparative law shows that it is often fairly easy to persuade states belonging to different legal families to copy one another. A high degree of technical legal skill has gone into the art of such persuasion, especially since the 1920s, in a variety of juridical settings.[21] These efforts have tended to be most successful either when the topic is so technical as to be of little interest or concern to non-technicians, or when the subject-matter is commonly viewed as requiring convergence in order to reduce the prospect of unnecessary and mutually harmful conflicts, as in the sector of transactional law.[22] This "practical convenience" hypothesis of convergence would seem to require that emphasis be given to the technical aspects of environmental law, or even that it be made more technical than it has to be for ethical reasons in order to reduce opposition to convergence initiatives on cultural, ideological, religious, or other social grounds.[23]

---

and in two paragraphs of the non-legally binding Authoritative Statement of Principles for a Global Consensus on the Management, Conservation and Sustainable Development of All Types of Forests: A. O. Adede, ed., *International Law Digest: Instruments for International Responses to Problems of Environment and Development, 1972-1992* (Amsterdam: Elsevier Science Publishers, 1993) at 167-68, 483, and 491.

21 The official sponsorship of unification of laws began in 1926 with the establishment of the International Institute for the Unification of Private Law, which is now, under the United Nations, known as UNIDROIT. Reference should also be made to the non-official but state-supported Hague Conference on Private international Law, which has been active in the unification of private international law since 1895. On its most recent accomplishment, see E. F. Scoles, "The Hague Convention on Succession" (1994) 42 Amer. J. Compar. L. 85.

22 However, it must be noted that many negotiations that result in the successful completion of conventions in highly technical areas of law often fail to be rewarded through the widespread ratification of such instruments.

23 Treaty-making strategy in the environmental field is constrained to some extent by the nature of the problems that have to be dealt with: for example, the problem of sewage discharge, one of the principal causes of land-based marine pollution, could be dealt with at a technical level under a treaty devoted to the setting of international standards, but anything close to substantial compliance with a sophisticted, high-technology, treaty regime would be prohibitively expensive to the least developed countries. There is no prospect that international development programs could cover the costs of effective sewage treatment systems around the world in addition to all the other priority needs that have to be met; and the least developed countries cannot be expected to make major economic sacrifices in other areas in order to curb environmentally harmful practices that are deeply ingrained in their way of life. Guidelines rather than legal standards might be a more appropriate approach, designed for incorporation into educational, public awareness, and technical training programs in the least developed (and most populous) countries, and the hope for implementation of such guidelines rests with technological innovations that may reduce the costs of compliance. On the other hand, in the context of ship-generated marine pollution, oil-rich and major port states might be expected to devote a reasonable proportion of their revenues to whatever technological improvements might be necessary to enable them to comply substantially or fully with stringent and legally binding technical standards approved at the global level.

The Global Dimension of Environmental Law

As an area of special interest and expertise, environmental policy/legislation is less than 40 years old. It was built on the basis of earlier concerns with public health and natural resource and wildlife management in the late nineteenth century,[24] but it is unlikely to have attained its present status and prominence without the widespread alarm over nuclear and chemical hazards through the late 1940s and 1950s, and without general acceptance of the need to deal firmly with a proliferation of pollution problems, which quickened in pace throughout the 1960s.

By the late 1960s, the United Nations was persuaded by a group of concerned states, spearheaded by Sweden and Canada, to treat these sectorally defined issues together as a single, global eco-problem. No fewer than four years of preparation went into the documents finally endorsed at the UN Conference on the Human Environment held at Stockholm in 1972. After much discussion, and a fair amount of dissension between developed and developing countries, the delegates at Stockholm agreed to adopt the Stockholm Declaration on the Human Environment and a comprehensive Action Plan.[25] The normative structure of Stockholm was to set the parameters of United Nations mega-conference diplomacy for the next two decades.[26]

Many of the governments participating at Stockholm had realized the permanence and acuteness of environmental issues and taken the step of establishing their own national environmental ministry or department before meeting at the global level in 1972. Most other governments followed suit shortly thereafter. Although local environmental problems continue to receive a lot of public attention at the local level, the shaping of environmental law almost everywhere since 1972 has been chiefly influenced by international, rather than national, priorities and concepts. Indeed it seems possible to assert that the area of environmental law and policy, like that of human rights, has a *global* significance that transcends the national, drawing most of its ideas and energies from a worldwide network of natural

---

24 Public health legislation began to emerge in the mid-19th century. Concepts of legally sanctioned conservation and preservation took root in statutory form in fishery, forestry, park, and river protection laws in the 1880s and 1890s. For a history, see J. McCormick, *The Global Environmental Movement*, 2nd ed. (Chichester, U.K.: John Wiley and Sons, 1995). General precepts or principles of international law, such as good faith, *sic utere*, good neighbourliness, abuse of rights, and the Harmon doctrine, which all evolved before the end of the 19th century, can, of course, be regarded as relevant to the development of international environmental law in a doctrinal sense, but not as the foundational expression of environmental policy.

25 For the text of the Stockholm Declaration, see P. W. Birnie and A. Boyle, eds., *Basic Documents on International Law and the Environment* (Oxford: Oxford Univ. Press, 1992) at 1-8. For an analysis of the text, see L. B. Sohn, "The Stockholm Declaration on the Human Environment" (1973) 14 Harv. Int'l. L.J. 423.

26 D. M. Johnston, "The Heritage of Political Thought in International Law," in Macdonald and Johnston, *supra* note 17 at 200-201.

scientists and environmentally concerned citizens as well as from the diplomatic arena of the nation-state system.[27] The impact of global consciousness on the development of environmental law and policy was dramatically displayed between the publication of the Brundtland Commission report on the global environment in 1986[28] and the conclusion of the UN Conference on Environment and Development (UNCED) held at Rio in 1992. With extraordinary rapidity, the much publicized concept of sustainability and related policies, favouring precautionary and integrated environmental policy and management, have acquired an unprecedented centrality in the terminology of the diplomatic arena at regional and other sub-global, as well as global, levels.[29] At least on the face of things, national environmental law around the world will be profoundly affected by these concepts and by the instruments adopted at UNCED.

Yet even in the context of environmental law it must be expected that globalization will encounter resistance at the national level. In Southeast Asia, for example, Prime Minister Mahathir of Malaysia has frequently questioned the moral fitness of the West to maintain a world leadership role,[30]

---

27 The implications of the transnational ethical community's involvement in the making and maintenance of negotiated instruments are discussed at length in Johnston, *supra* note 18 at 246-48.

28 World Commission on Environment and Development, *Our Common Future* (Oxford: Oxford Univ. Press, 1987).

29 For a Southeast Asian review of these and other emergent principles, see Foo Kim Boon, "The Rio Declaration and Its Influence on International Environmental Law" [1992] Singapore J. Leg. Studies 347. In 1995, several important instruments made use of these UNCED/Brundtland concepts. For example, the Global Programme of Action for the Protection of the Marine Environment from Land-Based Activities, adopted at a UNEP conference held at Washington, D.C. in November 1995, refers frequently to such objectives as the integration of marine environment protection into "relevant general environmental, social, and economic development policies" and the need for "preventive, precautionary and anticipatory approaches" to protection of the marine environment (see, e.g., Part 1, Introduction, section C, para. 9). The use of the term "precautionary" was strenuously negotiated at the UN Conference on Straddling Fish Stocks and Highly Migratory Species. In the final Agreement for the Implementation of the Provisions of the United Nations Convention on the Law of the Sea of 10 Dec. 1982, relating to the Conservation and Management of Straddling Fish Stocks and Highly Migratory Fish Stocks, the "precautionary approach" is the subject of lengthy treatment in art. 6. Para. 2 provides: "States shall be more cautious when information is uncertain, unreliable or inadequate. The absence of adequate scientific information shall not be used as a reason for postponing or failing to take conservation and management measures." Detailed provisions follow in succeeding paragraphs of art. 6 and Annex II. For an earlier succinct summary of the range of meanings attributed to the term "precautionary principle," see C. Tinker, "Responsibility for Biological Diversity Conservation under International Law" (1995) 28 Vanderbilt J. Transn'l. L. 777 at 792-800. On the potential juridical contribution of UNCED, see P. H. Sand, "UNCED and the Development of International Environmental Law" (1992) 3 *Yearbook of International Environmental Law* 3.

30 For example, in a lecture given in Singapore in 1989, Prime Minister Mahathir underlined the importance of Japan and China, rather than that of the United States and

and Senior Minister Lee Kuan Yew of Singapore has rejected the presumed but unproven universality of Western value concepts such as democracy and human rights.[31] These and other challenges to the West raise questions about the efficacy of future global initiatives that are perceived to be Western in origin and orientation, and not least about the strategy needed to make the environmental commitments of the world community amenable to incorporation in the legal systems and cultures of non-Western countries.

ENVIRONMENTAL LAW AS "SACRED TEXT"

The Transnational Ethical Community

The phenomenon of transnationalization extends far beyond the legal community to what might be described as an "ethical community": that is, to an increasingly interlinked, global network of individuals and organizations sharing a commitment to certain values. Widespread sharing of values was severely curtailed as long as the transmission of ideas depended on

---

Europe, in the future of ASEAN. At the end of the "Seventy Years War" (i.e. between communism and capitalism), he saw the United States, like the Soviet Union, as having paid a high price, "as evidenced by massive deficits and *erosion of its leadership position*" [emphasis added]: Mahathir Bin Mohamad, "Regionalism, Globalism and Spheres of Influence: ASEAN and the Challenge of Change into the 21st Century" (Singapore: Institute of Southeast Asian Studies, Singapore Lecture Series 1989) at 11. In his writings, Prime Minister Mahathir makes it clear that he views British success in the imperial period as due to the obsession of the ruling class with self-discipline, reflected even in their rules of attire. The weakness of the east in that period is attributed to its lack of discipline. After the Second World War, the loss of the colonies and the wealth that went with them led to "a radical change in the western psyche ... [This] change ... did not occur all at once. It began gradually. But as time passed it became faster. Finally all the old values were cast aside, with no definite values to take their place": Mohathir Bin Mohamad, *The Challenge* (Selangor: Pelanduk Publications, 1986) at 46. However, the west continues to exert disproportionate pressure on the east through control of the press, whereby "the Western world is able to shape and control the Eastern mind": *ibid.* at 51. The western model of civilization today consists of good and bad. The east "must decide for itself which aspects can be emulated and to what extent practised": *ibid.* at 55.

31 See e.g. Lee's speech given in Tokyo in November 1992: Lee Kuan Yew, "Democracy, Human Rights, and the Realities," in *Speeches: A Bimonthly Selection of Ministerial Speeches* (Singapore: Ministry of Information, 1992), vol. 16, no. 6 at 37. Lee Kuan Yew's scepticism about the west's fitness for world leadership seems related to his strong faith in Confucian, rather than "Asian," values, but, like Mahathir's, it is rationalized by reference to the virtues of social discipline and the work ethic. See M. Hill and Lian Kwen Fee, *The Politics of Nation Building and Citizenship in Singapore* (London: Routledge, 1995) at 207-209. Much of Lee's earlier admiration for the west's achievement was perhaps due to its apparent ability to develop a high standard of living through economic policies based on the work ethic rather than to his own "ideology of pragmatism." However, his loss of admiration for the west may be attributable both to its eventual commitment to state welfarism at whatever cost and to the loosening of its social discipline. For background to the development of Lee's political thought, see *ibid.* at 188-219.

the spoken word. Great codes of religious faith and aspiration laid down lines of continuity between different generations and cultures, but for thousands of years the maintenance and reinforcement of shared religious ideas depended on the talents of a small elite of writers and preachers. However, the technology of modern communication since the invention of the radio, the telephone, and the computer has transformed many millions of ordinary citizens into highly literate transmitters of value demands as well as receivers of ideas, information, and beliefs.

What has now come into place, especially in Western countries, is a highly-educated and strong-minded "civil society," committed in different ways to influencing the decision-making processes of national governments and the inter-state system.[32] The concerns of these non-governmental groups, associations, coalitions, and organizations range over a wide variety of contemporary issues: the control of nuclear and other weapons of mass destruction; nuclear energy; chemical threats to the environment; protection of wildlife, habitat and wilderness areas; promotion of animal rights and animal welfare; furtherance of political and civil rights; strengthening of democracy; suppression and punishment of genocide, torture, and other forms of barbarism; opposition to discrimination of all kinds; defence of the rights of women, children, and other disadvantaged classes; development of native, indigenous and minority rights; protection of refugees; and dozens of other causes.[33] Despite the fragmentation of issues represented among these groups,

---

32 The 18th century concept of "civil society" (or "civic society") has been been the subject of intensive and extensive debate, east and west, since its rediscovery in the 1980s. Much of the debate pivots on the role of the middle class (or middle class values) in modern political development, on the limitations on state power in open, critical, and chronically dissatisfied political cultures, and on the relationship between special and general interest. Civil society has been described as consisting of "autonomous institutions not run by the state, which act as agents of the will of the people," and reference is made to "an open society in which such institutions as political parties, trade unions, independent industrial enterprises, social movements (an example being ecology groups), free churches, liberal professions, and autonomous universities all operate on the assumption that no one group possesses an infallible social blueprint. Out of the 'creative chaos' of competition between them arises the free environment of an open society": Hill and Fee, *supra* at 221-22. It is said that the individualist ethos of western civilization determines that civil society is perceived as being in opposition to the state, whereas the communitarian ethos of non-western civilizations determines that the state and civil society must be perceived as complementary: *ibid.* at 222-23. On the trend to a "non-liberal communitarian democracy" in Singapore, see Chua Beng-Huat, *Communitarian Ideology and Democracy in Singapore* (London: Routledge, 1995) at 184-202. Needless to say, the idea of a fundamental split between individualistic and communitarian cultures is incompatible with the concept of world leadership and limits the potentiality of a convergence among legal systems. On the western concept of civil society, see G. Almond and S. Verba, *The Civic Culture* (London: Sage, 1989).

33 These non-governmental organizations (NGOs) had their historical origin in the philanthropic and voluntary organizations that began to spring up in the mid to late 19th century. However, NGOs were excluded from the globalizing Hague Conferences of 1899 and 1907, and enjoyed only a limited consultative status under the League: L.

what may be regarded as the cement holding these citizens together as a collective social force, as a super-coalition, is the ethical nature of all these concerns. To that extent, the many millions involved in these different organizations might be regarded as constituting a single, if only loosely related, transboundary ethical community of potentially global dimensions, which opens up the prospect of global governance.[34] Nowhere is this phenomenon of a transnational ethical community of greater potential impact than in the environmental field, where the "bottom up" non-governmental organization (NGO) approach now purports to complement the "top down" approach of the interstate system.[35]

Gordenker and T. G. Weiss, "Pluralising Global Governance: Analytical Approaches and Dimensions" (1995) 16 Third World Q. 357 at 362. Their status and influence within the UN system have grown immeasurably in recent years, especially since the Stockholm Conference in 1972. Today the World Bank, UNDP, UNEP, and other global agencies deal with thousands of international NGOs around the world within the framework of various programs and projects. It has been estimated by the Union of International Associations that the global network in 1993 included over 16,000 "recognisable NGOs that operate in three or more countries and draw their finances from sources in more than one country": *ibid.* at 357. The total number keeps mounting. In addition, most governments are influenced in varying degrees, and in different ways, by an even larger number of local NGOs that may be as many as 50,000, according to the UNDP's *Human Development Report 1994*. On the penetration by these associations into the interstate system, see P. Spiro, "New Global Communities: Non-governmental Organizations and International Decision-Making Institutions" (1995) 18 Washington Q. 48.

34 Since legal writing "overlooks or understates the richness of NGO activity or politics" (Gordenker and Weiss, *ibid.* at 358), it might be noted that the NGO phenomenon overlaps with other manifestations of global governance such as the independent sector, the volunteer sector, civic society, grassroots organizations, social change organizations, and non-state actors. From the umbrella concept of NGOs as used by most political scientists, one tends to exclude profit-making enterprises, criminal associations, insurgents and terrorists, churches in their strictly religious function, transnational political parties, and mass communications media: *ibid.* at 359. Their current impact on intergovernmental organizations is immense and immeasurable. "In their own ways NGOs and ... IGOs grope, sometimes cooperatively, sometimes competitively, sometimes in parallel, towards a modicum of 'global governance.' We define global governance as efforts to bring more orderly and reliable responses to social and political issues that go beyond the capacities of states to address individually. Like the NGO universe, global governance implies an absence of central authority and the need for collaboration or cooperation among governments and others who seek to encourage common practices and goals in addressing global issues": *ibid.* at 357. For a recent development of the concept, see Commission on Global Governance, *Our Global Neighbourhood* (Oxford: Oxford Univ. Press, 1995).

35 It was at the Stockholm Conference on the Human Environment in 1972 that the NGO phenomenon first assumed global significance within the world of professional diplomacy. It has grown exponentially since then. By the final preparatory session for UNCED in 1992 no fewer than 1,421 NGOs had been accredited in addition to those already accredited through ECOSOC in accordance with art. 71 of the UN Charter. K. Conca, "Greening the United Nations: Environmental Organizations and the U.N. System" (1995) 16 Third World Q. 441 at 449. By mid 1995, 550 NGOs had already been accredited by the post-Rio Commission on Sustainable Development: *ibid.* at

The "Sacred Text" Tradition

As the phrase implies, the concept that certain texts acquire the status of sacredness – that of the sacrosanct – has its roots in the history of religions. To protect the texts most pivotal to the maintenance of a particular faith, most religions were compelled to present their scriptures as the revealed or semi-revealed word of God, and therefore beyond the realm of human authority to challenge or amend.[36] Small elites of the scholarly and devout were accepted as authorized to defend these scriptures from revisionist interpretation by rivals, as from defilement by pagans and apostates. By and large, controversy over interpretation of sacred text was the privilege of the anointed few with access to monastic truths.[37]

Ultimately the rise of secular universities would put religious sacred text on the defensive. But the Western secular community of scholars was to elevate its own tradition of sacred text, building on the most revered writings in ethics and political philosophy, including the seminal works of the

---

452. See T. Princen, "NGOS: Creating a Niche in Environmental Diplomacy," in M. Finger and T. Princen, eds., *Environmental NGOs in World Politics: Linking the Local and the Global* (New York: Routledge, 1994); and J. Fisher, *The Road from Rio: Sustainable Development and the Nongovernmental Movement in the Third World* (Westport, Conn.: Praeger, 1993). On the phenomenon in Southeast Asia, see B. Eccleston and D. Potter, "Environmental NGOs and Different Political Contexts in South-East Asia: Malaysia, Indonesia and Vietnam," in M. L. G. Parnwell and R. L. Bryant, eds., *Environmental Change in South-East Asia: People, Politics and Sustainable Development* (London: Routledge, 1996) at 49-66.

36 Sacred text, or holy writ, was originally believed to possess spiritual or magical powers or to be the medium through which divine reality and authority were revealed. Most of the early religious scriptures were originally in oral form and were passed down through memorization, and no doubt embellishment, for many generations before conversion to written form. Some scriptural traditions, such as the Hindu and Buddhist, made distinctions in the degree of sacredness to be imputed to different texts (e.g., the distinction between canonical and semi-canonical). Other traditions, such as the classical Taoist and Confucian, produced texts that were accorded canonical status and profound reverence despite the absence of a tradition of divine revelation. The Jewish canon, known to Christians as the Old Testament, did not receive rabbinical approval until the Yavnen synod of A.D. 90.

37 The possibility of a sacred text tradition depended partly on the physical materials available for the preservation of the written word, but also on psycho-cultural attitude. The existence of clay tablets among the earliest civilizations created the physical opportunity for book-based authority, but the spoken word prevailed. The Egyptian papyrus roll, adopted by the Greeks and passed on to the Romans, was much more fragile, and the Greeks were not especially adamant on the preservation of text. The alphabet that they developed was used chiefly as an instrument of verbal communication. Indeed, even during the golden age of Athens in the 5th century B.C, books were by and large lightly regarded as avenues of learning by what was essentially an oral culture. The reverence for sacred writings in the western world seems to have its origins in Judaism, but with the arrival of Christianity and the addition of the New Testament to the Jewish scriptures, the history of sacred text reached a new plateau. For centuries after A.D. 100, the greatest book writers in the western world were all Christian scholars, such as St. Augustine, St. Jerome, Tertullius, and Origen. Secular writing did not have its revival until the rise of the universities in the 12th century.

ancient Greeks, who fashioned the value goals of democracy, freedom, liberty, justice, and equality, and fixed them permanently at the centre of modern political and social thought.[38] With the opening up of the human spirit in the seventeenth and eighteenth centuries, these goals became entitlements that acquired the status of constitutional guarantees, and ultimately the sanction of popular will, in receptive political cultures. At this stage of constitutional development, the written bill of rights tradition became the special responsibility of a judicial guardian, albeit a mechanism monitored and conditioned by society at large.[39]

Another strand of secular "sacred text" tradition was begun, but not completed, in the early treatises of international law. Hugo Grotius and his natural law contemporaries and successors drew upon the first two strands, the religious and the political, to weave a more complicated fabric of ethical principles and supportive norms that purported to provide a civilizational foundation for the emerging law of nations.[40] Conceived in part as a natural law constraint on the will of sovereign princes and modern sovereign states, this project could not be fully carried through, because of the invincible necessity to make compromises with positivist philosophy and the fact of

---

38 This accumulation of western ideas and ideals, building for two millennia on the foundation of Hellenism, reached a potentially world-transforming stature in the Age of Reason in Europe. By then the western world had acquired an impressive frame of inquiry for addressing fundamental political and ethical issues through a succession of great books by seminal thinkers such as Thomas Hobbes (1588-1679), John Locke (1632-1704), Baron Montesquieu (1689-1755), David Hume (1711-76), and Jean-Jacques Rousseau (1712-78). Though no one work was to achieve the status attained by Confucius in Chinese civilization, western civilization had acquired through revered texts an apparently irreversible mind-set of civic ideals.

39 The infrequency of amendments to the U.S. Constitution over a 200-year period encourages the view of that instrument as a dramatic example of sacred text, subject to changes introduced chiefly through the interpretive skills of the "temple" of judges and the "invisible college" of scholars. The sacredness of the U.S. constitution might also seem to be reinforced by the widespread imitation of much of its bill-of-rights language around the world, even in countries that have not proved truly receptive to such ideas. However, there has always been much argument among American scholars on the true nature of constitutionalism in U.S. society. One scholar, e.g., defines it as "an experiment in self-government" and offers four distinct models pivoting on construction, maintenance, growth, and community: P. W. Kahn, *Legitimacy and History: Self-Government in American Constitutional Theory* (New Haven, Conn.: Yale University Press, 1992) at 5-9. According to a favourite view of things, a "social contract" underlies the famous document, but many U.S. scholars have emphasized the flexibility of the U.S. Constitution, seen as "the result of compromises among people who disagreed radically ... The framers dealt in expediency, leaving principled resolution to future development": *ibid.* at 77. At the extreme, it has been argued that the U.S. constitution should be seen as an "evolving unwritten constitution": *ibid.* at 65.

40 The voluminous literature on the works of Hugo Grotius offers a diversity of scholarly opinion on their lasting significance in the history of international law, and of international relations generally. What has endured is the general belief that the writings of Grotius provided the "foundation" of the natural law tradition in international law.

power-holding.[41] So the classics of international law, conceived as an emergent ethical system, never quite achieved the level of sacred text.

With the ethical deficiencies of classical international law cruelly revealed after the agonies of the First World War, a fresh start was made to provide sacred text in the form of the Covenant of the League of Nations, and after the Covenant's "implosion," in that of the UN Charter. Here at last it seemed that idealism was married to a pragmatic system of power-holding, so that international law as the servant of the nation-state system, might nonetheless go forward on a firm, and legally unchallengeable, foundation of ethical principles and globally shared values.[42] Especially within the newly articulated framework of human rights, natural law protection of universal values seemed beyond the power of denial by recalcitrant states, and an impressive system of human rights instruments was to evolve over the following decades, derived essentially from the "sacred texts" of the formally nonbinding Universal Declaration of Human Rights and the binding twin Covenants that followed.[43] Over the years, the global and foundational credentials of these documents have been challenged on cultural as well as ideological grounds. The demise of communism seems to have taken some of the ideology out of the controversy, and the number of states formally committed to these sacred texts continues to mount. On the other hand, progress is reported in the elite-driven but cross-cultural effort to establish, by way of corrective, a counterpart sacred text in the form of a non-binding Declaration of Human Responsibilities.

---

41 In the general view, international law was inherently flawed as an ethical system because of its coupling with the nation-state system, a mutually convenient arrangement based on reciprocal recognition of the sovereignty residing in each other's nation-state. From this perspective, modern diplomacy can be viewed as a sophisticated exercise in interest-based pragmatism contrived to circumvent this political reality, and international law thus as an instrument of diplomacy.

42 In the orthodox theory of UN law, the responsibilities imposed by the Charter on the member states, other than those involving the application of enforcement measures under Chapter 8, do not "authorize the United Nations to intervene in matters which are essentially within the domestic jurisdiction of any State or ... require the Members to submit such matters to settlement under the present Charter": UN Charter, art. 2 (7).

43 The 1948 Universal Declaration of Human Rights was followed in 1966 by the International Covenant on Civil and Political Rights and the International Covenant on Economic, Social and Cultural Rights. The first has been seen to reflect the individualistic civic values of western liberal democracies, and the second as concessions to collectivist systems and communitarian cultures. The human rights law that has evolved from the UN Charter, and from these sacred texts, can be viewed in two different ways: either as the late 20th century institutionalization and legitimization of the neo-Grotian tradition of natural law, designed specifically to constrain sovereign states, or as a *de novo* empirical search for commonly shared or shareable human values derived from all major cultures. The first interpretation assumes universality, the second attempts to create it.

It is against this background of four "sacred text" traditions that modern environmental law should be seen to be evolving, fuelled by more modern ethical imperatives and driven by an infinitely broader spectrum of citizen-participants. So many groups and individuals are willing to take initiatives, focusing on so many issues, that the international environmental movement may break up into a leaderless, quasi-anarchic condition more quickly than has happened with the earlier ethical tradition. Yet environmental ethicists, faced with the prospect of division and cultural variation, may be expected to demand that law provide a "sacred text" that would possess moral authority so strong as to withstand the normal erosion of time.

The Environmental Quest for "Sacred Text"

The quest for "sacred text" by the environmental movement has already begun at the global level. Because of the underlying logic of ecological interdependence, the need for holistic understanding, and the emphasis on an integrated approach to environmental problem-solving, it may seem obvious to environmentalists that the text sought after must have universal credentials and consist of widely accepted norms.

As to credentials, conflicting evidence is provided by legal history on the question whether it matters if the desired text does not possess the form of a technically binding instrument. The science of international law is still a hospitable home to disciplinarians who insist on the importance of form and formalities in the making of negotiated commitments.[44] It is assumed that states (and other actors expected to be influenced) will accept such commitments at a higher level of intensity if the instrument is endowed with the status of a legally binding treaty. Such a view makes sense, especially if reliance has to be placed on litigational or other adjudicative procedures for purposes of implementation. But how much has the Universal Declaration of Human Rights lost credence in the eye of adjudicators simply because of its non-binding character? If its status is truly a fatal flaw, then we should expect to find a very conspicuous judicial preference for the binding Covenants over the non-binding Declaration. The truth seems to be that, in practice, the requirements of strictly legal logic do not prevail in the case of an instrument that is accepted as having the psychocultural aura of sacred text. Sentiment, it seems, not form, prevails.

However, the environmental quest for sacred text might be more successful than the quest for a standard bill of rights if the scientific truths, universal values, and global standards to which the instrument is addressed are enshrined in a legally binding form. The success of the current attempt to

44 For a general defence of legal formalism, see E. J. Weinrib, "Legal Formalism: On the Immanent Rationality of Law" (1988) 97 Yale L.J. 949. For a critique of the formalism inherent in the law of treaties, see Johnston, *supra* note 18, passim.

secure universal acceptance of an instrument in that form might be considered the best evidence of whether a "sacred text" attitude is likely to be cultivated.[45]

As to the matter of acceptance, safety lies in generality. As with a bill-of-rights instrument, a religious text, or indeed the Charter of the United Nations or the Universal Declaration of Human Rights, the devil of resistance can be fought off by avoiding detail and specificity. Normally this is the only way to articulate the most important values and standards, whose effectuation must be entrusted to judicial, administrative, and other mechanisms, and to academic and social institutions. Most would agree that no one country or region has so far found the optimal balance between these mechanisms and institutions to effectuate a "sacred text" in the field of environmental law and policy. An attractive case can be made for the establishment of a specialized environmental tribunal, for example, but like many attractive arguments it quickly runs into a barrage of practical considerations, not least the objection that the special text should precede the special machinery of interpretation and application.[46]

ENVIRONMENTAL LAW TRENDS IN SOUTHEAST ASIA

Introduction

The above-described ideas may strike the non-Western reader as being the product of Western thought. Even if they are read, as intended, as postulates and not demands, the concepts of a transnational ethical community and of sacred text might be viewed in non-Western cultural mosaic regions, such as Southeast Asia, as irrelevant to the real tasks of legal development in the region, or even as threatening to the cultural autonomy of its various parts.

---

45 For an attempt to put the key environmental principles and concepts of UNCED into draft treaty form, see N. A. Robinson, *International Covenant on Environment and Development* (Gland: IUCN, 1995).

46 This objection can be countered by the proposal that environmental litigation could be undertaken by a specialized chamber of the existing International Court of Justice (ICJ) in The Hague. For a recent discussion, see E. Valencia-Ospina, "The International Court of Justice and International Environmental Law" (1994) 2 *Asian Yearbook of International Law* 1. The idea that specialized areas of international law should be dealt with by specialized tribunals, and not by a general court of law, was supported by many delegations at the Third UN Conference on the Law of the Sea (UNCLOS) and resulted in a dispute settlement system pivoting on the principle of maximal choice. Those states favouring a specialized tribunal may choose to refer their disputes arising out of the UNCLOS III Convention to the new International Tribunal on the Law of the Sea, which came into existence in 1996. Certain disputes affecting the marine environment might, therefore, go to the Tribunal, others to the ICJ and still others to *ad hoc* arbitration or other kinds of third party machinery. It might be suggested that the non-existence of a specialized global tribunal for international environmental disputes generally forces trade-and-environment disputes into dispute settlement tribunals that reflect a trade law mind-set.

The position can be taken that, although many law reform activists in the environmental field clearly regard themselves as ethically motivated, this does not necessarily make the case for treating the entire area of environmental law as essentially ethical in significance. Resistance to the "sacred text" hypothesis might be offered on philosophical as well as technical grounds.[47] Perhaps all that can be argued is that the kind of conceptualization offered here is more likely to be supported in the West than in other legal cultures. There may even be evidence of a widely shared non-Western cultural distaste for elevating law – and therefore lawyers and legislators – to the level of ethical or spiritual authority, whether for environmental or any other secular purpose. Legalism of this exalted kind may not be easily exportable.

On the other side of this argument, there is an abundance of counter-evidence. Respect for secular authority is deeply established in many non-Western societies, not least in many Southeast Asian societies. Sometimes the tradition holds because of continuing reverence for the monarchy as the symbol of public morality, as in Japan, or for an exceptionally dedicated monarch, as in Thailand. Imperial or royal patronage of a nation-wide movement in these two countries for an environmental sacred text would probably win the day over moderate political or technical reservations in these two countries. Strong political leaders in countries like Singapore and Malaysia would also, it seems, be likely to succeed in stamping their environmental laws with special ethical significance, provided they can convince the electorate that it enjoys the protection of an incorruptible public service.

In Southeast Asia, it appears that the problem lies not so much in the concept of sacred text in the field of environmental law as in the perception that public morality must not be subject to external foreign or non-governmental influences. Influences seen to be both foreign and non-governmental would seem to have little chance of success, especially if they are presented as moral imperatives under the rubric of universal principles of entitlement or responsibility. A sacred text tradition must presumably be shown to be of indigenous origin, or shown to be universally accepted as based on universal values.

---

47 For example, philosophical (or ideological) objection can be taken to the notion that any text, which is bound to be couched in indeterminate language, should be accorded sacred status. Such a characterization might be likely to create rigidities that would retard healthy legal development, and possibly advance the *status quo* interests reflected in the text against other interests that may be more deserving of legal protection. At the technical level, paramountcy of one text over others gives precedence to constitutional or public law thinking over private law thinking, placing a premium on abstractionist reasoning that is less likely to become precise than the technical logic of private law doctrine.

What, then, is the evidence that such a tradition is emerging in Southeast Asia in the environmental field?

The Pre-Stockholm Period

In Southeast Asia, like other regions of the world, modern environmental law, dating essentially from the 1960s, had little to build on that could be described as a design for environmental protection. Most of the legal framework already in place in these countries was at best environmentally neutral or at worst an obstruction to environmental purposes to the extent it elevated the prerogatives of ownership or possession or otherwise reflected a *laissez faire* policy in support of unchecked economic enterprise. By the late 1960s it was evident, almost everywhere, that national environmental law would have to be the work of the enlightened legislator.

By this time, at the birth of modern environmental law, most of Southeast Asia had achieved the status of independence; and five countries – Indonesia, Malaysia, the Philippines, Singapore, and Thailand – had come together to form the loose consultative system of ASEAN. In the late 1960s, the legal framework of each of these countries – like that of most other countries – was virtually an environmental vacuum. Relevant legislation existed mostly in a few scattered sectors such as fisheries, agriculture, forestry, plant disease control, public health, water quality, and, in some cases, air pollution. It was still too early for any national vision of environmental needs to provide a stimulus for a reappraisal of these old, mostly colonial, statutory provisions, much less for the establishment of a systematic regime for the environment as a whole. Accordingly, all five of these legal systems were readily amenable to global influences such as the Stockholm Conference on the Human Environment, for which elaborate preparations were under way in 1968, and to the efforts of ASEAN to promote the goal of environmental protection throughout the region.

In the pre-Stockholm years, the ASEAN member states shared the common priority of developing a modern industrialized economy, and in the late 1960s and early 1970s relatively little attention was paid to nature conservation. However, each of the five original ASEAN countries had its own legal framework and a more or less distinctive legal heritage.

Singapore

In Singapore, a territory of less than 650 square kilometres,[48] the degradation of the once rich terrestrial ecosystem, consisting of primary rain forests, secondary forests, mangrove swamps, and marshland, and an equally

48 One source estimates the land area of Singapore (including its offshore islands) to be approximately 626 sq. km. Another suggests 641.1 sq. km. See K. L. Koh, "Singapore" in IUCN, *Legislation for Implementation of the ASEAN Agreement on Conservation*

rich coastal marine ecosystem, began in the colonial era of the nineteenth century, when most of the forest lands were cleared for crop cultivation and other purposes.[49] Upon attaining independence in 1965, Singapore did, of course, inherit a certain amount of colonial legislation in fisheries, forestry, land use, and other contexts. This included the *Planning Act*, whereby land zoning under a Master Plan had been introduced in 1958, providing for buffer zones of gardens and other green spaces. But since Singapore was scheduled for rapid industrialization in the 1960s, many of the existing nature reserves, mangroves, and wetlands were to be bulldozed or reclaimed for development outside the protective framework of the Master Plan. With only a few exceptions, such as the preservation of the colonial Bukit Timah nature reserve,[50] Singapore's environmental effort during the first, highly pollutive, phase of its industrial revolution, down to the late 1970s, was virtually limited to the area of public health.[51]

Malaysia

For geographical reasons, Malaysia, on achieving independence in 1957, had reason to preserve more than Singapore of the corpus of sectoral environmental legislation inherited from the colonial period. For example, the 1920 *Waters Enactment Act* (Act 418) was designed to control the pollution of all rivers and streams throughout the Malay peninsula,[52] the 1952 *Merchant Shipping Ordinance* to govern marine pollution by vessels,[53] the 1952 *Poisons Ordinance* to regulate the use of toxic substances,[54] and the 1953

---

of Nature and Natural Resources, Country Reports (Bonn: IUCN Environmental Law Programme, 1994) [hereinafter "IUCN, *Legislation*"] at 135. It is possible that the first estimate excludes, but the latter includes, two islands whose sovereignty is in dispute between Singapore and Malaysia. Incrementally, the true figure goes up as more and more land is reclaimed from the sea. Singapore's small land area has given it an extremely high level of density of population, which in turn has necessitated comprehensive planning for development: L. S. Chia, "Planning and Environmental Management in Singapore," in C. MacAndrews and L. S. Chia, eds., *Developing Economies and the Environment: The Southeast Asian Experience* (Singapore: McGraw-Hill, 1979) at 201-206.

49 Koh, *supra* note 48 at 136.

50 *Ibid.* On the early history of Singapore's nature reserves, see L. H. Lye, "Wildlife Protection Laws in Singapore" [1991] Singapore J. Leg. Studies 287 at 291-94.

51 Public health received a high priority in Singapore throughout the colonial period, leading to successful programs in ditch clearance, the control of disease-bearing insects, and the construction of efficient "monsoon drains": Chia, *supra* note 48 at 229-30. The *Environmental Public Health Act* of 1968 was the first statutory instrument to be enacted in Singapore specifically for the protection of the environment. It was at the introduction of this statute in 1968 that the government first declared its objective of transforming Singapore into a "green garden city," and only two years later when the first anti-pollution unit was set up in the Prime Minister's office: Koh, *supra* note 48 at 137.

52 S. Thanarajasingam, "Malaysia," in IUCN, *Legislation, supra* note 48 at 71.

53 *Ibid.* at 65.

54 *Ibid.* at 76.

Animals Ordinance to control the spread of animal disease and prevent cruelty to animals.[55] In most matters Sabah and Sarawak inherited their own environmental ordinances, separate from these originally prescribed for the peninsula. Like Singapore, Malaysia moved to land use control as part of its industrialization strategy in the 1960s, using a three-fold classification for agriculture, construction, and industry, under its *National Land Code* of 1965 (Act 56).[56] However, unlike Singapore, Malaysia is a large federal state with a complicated relationship between federal and state authority, which has resulted in a basic weakness in several areas of environmental legislation.[57] In issues related to lands, mines, and forests, from which revenues are assigned to the states, the states usually have little incentive to relinquish control to the federal government or to acquiesce in the application of federal legislation to other environmental topics on the State List. Subject in some cases to this difficulty of exercising federal enforcement powers, post-independence environmental legislation in the pre-Stockholm years included enactments in forestry management,[58] wildlife protection,[59] offshore hydrocarbon development,[60] and land conservation.[61]

55 *Ibid.* at 69.

56 *Ibid.* at 80-81.

57 In the view of most Malaysian lawyers, supremacy lies with the Constitution, not Parliament. Under art. 74 of the Malaysian federal constitution, the division of legislative powers between federal and state levels of government is effected by means of an allocation among three lists (the Federal, State, and Concurrent lists), which are found in the Ninth Schedule. Many areas of environmental responsibility are found in the Federal List, and art. 76(1) gives further power to Parliament, authorizing federal legislation with respect to matters enumerated in the State List, for the purposes of implementing international covenants, for promoting uniformity of legislation, and if so requested by a state. However, List II, which enumerates the legislative powers of the states, includes land, agriculture, forestry, local government, and riverine fishing; and List III, which enumerates matters coming under concurrent jurisdiction, includes protection of wildlife, town and country planning, national parks, drainage, and irrigation. As to the conflicts inherent in concurrent jurisdiction, federal paramountcy seems assured by art. 75: "if any state law is inconsistent with a federal law, the federal law shall prevail, and the state law shall, to the extent of the inconsistency, be void." In practice, however, political considerations have constrained Parliament's exercise of its preponderant authority, and in any event, as a matter of constitutional law, the states of Sabah and Sarawak are accorded special exemptions under the *Malaysia Act* of 1963. Thanarajasingam, *supra* note 52 at 58-60. For suggestions on how to resolve these constitutional difficulties, in view of the urgency of environmental issues in Malaysia to-day, see Thanarajasingam, *supra* note 52 at 60.

58 In the colonial period, there was no attempt to rationalize Malayan forestry laws. The British were interested in mining, but not timber, possibly because "logs from African colonies were of better quality, cheaper, and easier to transport to Great Britain": Nik Abdul Rashid, "The Environmental Law in Malaysia," in I. Kato et al., eds., *Environmental Law and Policy in the Pacific Basin Area* (Tokyo: Univ. of Tokyo Press, 1981) at 13. At the beginning of federation, forest management was perceived to be a local regulatory issue that should be assigned to the State List: Thanarajasingam, *supra* note 52 at 69-70.

Thailand

In common with Malaysia and Singapore, Thailand in the 1950s and 1960s devoted itself chiefly to national economic development goals, which encouraged more intensive uses of natural resources for industry and larger scale agriculture. The Civil and Commercial Codes of Thailand buttressed the rights of private property owners, providing a legal rationale for virtually unregulated development despite numerous statutes concerned with land, forest, water, wildlife, fisheries, and mineral resources.[62] Under the *National Council on Economic and Social Development Act* of 1959, top priority was given to a succession of five-year plans within a framework that did not explicitly include environmental considerations under the definition of socioeconomic development, although public health and "other social welfare" might appear to do so.[63] Despite the lack of an overall environmental protection policy, Thailand acquired an accumulation of statutory provisions that together might have been reasonably effective if they had been vigorously enforced.[64] Water quality management concerns had to contend with high priority irrigation projects under statutes going back to the 1940s,[65] and the closest that Thailand came – or has still come – to direct water and air pollution control measures was through the public nuisance provisions of the 1941 *Public Health Act*.[66]

Indonesia

Environmentalists in Indonesia, unlike those in Singapore, Malaysia, and Thailand, have been able to invoke constitutional language in support of the general cause of environmental protection. At the highest level of

---

59 Under the 1972 *Protection of Wildlife Act* (Act 76), species are protected in accordance with the degree to which they are threatened or endangered: Thanarajasingam, *supra* note 52 at 69.

60 Conservation provisions were included in the 1966 *Continental Shelf Act* and the 1966 *Petroleum Mining Act*: Thanarajasingam, *supra* note 52 at 68.

61 The 1960 *Land Conservation Act* provided for the conservation of hill land and the protection of soil from erosion and siltation. However, it has rarely been enforced at the state level: Thanarajasingam, *supra* note 52 at 71. See also Nik Abdul Rashid, *supra* note 58 at 13.

62 P. Tasneeyanond and D. Nifose, "Thailand," in IUCN *Legislation, supra* note 48 at 226-29. Conservation provisions were included, e.g., in the *Fishery Act* of 1947 and the *Wild Animals Protection and Reserves Act* of 1961: *ibid.* at 209.

63 *Ibid.* at 207-208.

64 For example, control over the loss of vegetation cover, the conservation of forests, and the establishment of protected areas were provided for in the *Forest Act* of 1961, the *National Forest Reserves Act* of 1960, and the *Minerals Act* of 1967, as well as the two statutes cited in note 62, *supra*. See *ibid.* at 213-17.

65 See e.g. the *Irrigation Act* of 1941, the *Royal Irrigation Act* of 1942, and the *Ditches and Dykes Act* of 1962.

66 Tasneeyanond and Nifose, *supra* note 62 at 224-26.

abstraction, the five basic principles constituting the official state philosophy or ideology of Indonesia – the *Pancasila* enshrined in the preamble to the Constitution of 1945 – obligate the new state to protect "the whole of the Indonesian people and their entire native country," a holistic concept generally agreed to encompass the country's resources, both human and non-human, and the natural environment.[67] No enactment in Southeast Asia comes closer to assuming the status of environmental "sacred text." This is underlined by the more specific language of article 33(3) of the Constitution, which provides that "[l]and and water and the natural resources therein shall be controlled by the State and shall be utilized for the greatest welfare of the people."[68] This apparent commitment to an overall policy of environmental integrity has, of course, exposed Indonesian environmental legislation to critical scrutiny. The latter was particularly directed at early sectoral legislation of the pre-Stockholm period, such as the land use planning prescriptions of the *Agrarian Basic Provisions* (Act No. 5 of 1960),[69] the forest management procedures of the *Basic Provisions for Forestry* (Act No. 5 of 1967), the *Government Regulation on Forestry Planning* (No. 33 of 1970),[70] and the restoration requirements of the *Basic Provisions for Mining* (Act No. 11 of 1967).[71]

---

67 K. Hardjasoemantri, "Indonesia," in IUCN, *Legislation, supra* note 48 at 18. The *Pancasila* preamble, which invokes belief in God, love of humanity, national unity, consensus, and social justice, has been described as the Grundnorm or *Rechtsidee* of the Indonesian legal system. Although in the form of a preamble to the 1945 (and current) Constitution, it is ranked ahead of the Constitution itself as the "main and most important source of Indonesian national law." It is paramount: "any law or regulation is expected to conform to this philosophy in its details": ASEAN Law Foundation, "The Legal System of Indonesia," in *ASEAN Legal Systems* (Singapore: Butterworths Asia, 1995) at 23. The language of the *Pancasila* is so general that it lends itself to a holistic "environmental" interpretation.

68 Hardjasoemantri, *ibid.* at 43.

69 *Ibid.* at 39-40. The 1960 Basic Agrarian Law was a bold effort at land reform. It gave the state an overriding authority over access to resources, which came into conflict with traditional land tenure patterns. The resistance to this land reform initiative was so intense that no formal measure to implement the 1960 Law was adopted until 1982, with the enactment of Statute No. 4 of that year, the Basic Stipulation for the Management of the Living Environment (i.e. *Environmental Management Act*). For a study of the traditional system, see, generally, H. Slaats and K. Portier, *Traditional Decision-Making and Law Institutions and Processes in an Indonesian Context* (Yogyakarta: Gadjah Madja Univ. Press, 1992).

70 Hardjasoemantri, *supra* note 67 at 35-36.

71 *Ibid.* at 37. Regulatory pollution control powers have continued to reside in Indonesian sectoral agencies, such as Industry, Agriculture, Transport, Mines, Public Health, Public Works, Energy, and Electricity: Jaafar Abu Bakar and M. J. Valencia, "Marine Pollution: National Responses and Transnational Issues," in G. Kent and M. J. Valencia, eds., *Marine Policy in Southeast Asia* (Berkeley, Calif.: Univ. of California Press, 1985) at 281.

The Philippines

Today there is a clear commitment to the environment in the 1987 Constitution of the Philippines,[72] but in the pre-Stockholm period environmental policy was reflected only in scattered sectoral enactments. Some of these are very old, such as the 1916 *Act for the Protection of Game and Fish* (Act 2590), which is still the principal vehicle for the protection of wildlife, and various land resource statutes.[73] The Philippines is a country top-heavy with enactments.[74] According to one local critic, however, the new statutes are often as inadequate as the old ones, due to "poor draftsmanship, ambiguity, loopholes, inability to foresee all or most of the situations that ought to be covered by the law, possible gaps in enforcement, unrealistic provisions, or inadequacy to cope with the situations that the laws seek to respond to."[75] Needless to say, these basic deficiencies are by no means specific to the Philippines and are in no way curable merely by reason of legal advances at the global and regional levels, only by effective programs in capacity building.[76]

Global Influences, 1972-92

Introduction

The 20-year period from 1972 to 1992 was a highly formative era in the history of environmental law. It began with the convening of the immensely ambitious UN Conference on the Human Environment at Stockholm in June 1972 and reached its climax in the gathering of an even more heroic mega-conference, the UN Conference on Environment and Development (UNCED, or the "Earth Summit"), which was held at Rio in June 1992.[77] In

---

72 Art. 2, s. 16, of the 1987 Constitution of the Philippines requires that "[t]he State shall protect and advance the right of the people to a balanced and healthy ecology in accord with the rhythm and harmony of nature." The vagueness of this commitment is compensated for by less rhetorical provisions applying to sustainable development goals in the articles on agrarian reform, natural resources, economy, and "national patrimony." See S. S. Tolentino, "Philippines," in IUCN, *Legislation, supra* note 48 at 94-95.

73 Tolentino, *ibid.* at 101-102. See e.g. the *Land Registration Act* of 1902 (Act 496), the *Public Land Act* of 1934 (CA 141), and the *Mining Act* of 1936 (CA 937): *ibid.* at 117. See also R. M. Lesaca, "Pollution Control in the Philippines," in MacAndrews and Chia, *supra* note 48 at 237.

74 Allegedly as many as 16,000 statutes have been enacted since the year 1900, consisting of republic acts enacted by Congress, presidential decrees, executive orders, "batas," and various other kinds of regulations. No less than 27 codes are in force, including the *Philippines Environment Code*: ASEAN Law Foundation, "The Legal System of the Philippines," in *ASEAN Legal Systems, supra* note 67 at 184.

75 Tolentino, *supra* note 72 at 96.

76 Mr. Tolentino, the author of this criticism, has himself played an important role in the development of a capacity-building project co-sponsored by IUCN and the National University of Singapore, which is designed to benefit all countries of Southeast Asia and some countries beyond.

77 On the legal develoment implications of UNCED, see Sand, *supra* note 29.

the intervening two decades, a generation of environmentalists grew up – intellectually, politically, and institutionally – constituting a formidable coalition of non-governmental associations, which is now so huge in numbers and capability that it might be viewed in the 1990s as the core of the "transnational ethical community."[78]

Even without the urging of the increasingly globalized environmental movement, the bureaucracies that form the operational core of the interstate system would have had to respond to a diplomatic event as momentous as the Stockholm Conference. By ushering in the era of mega-conference diplomacy, with its own scale, rhythm, and ethos, it was much too important and potentially creative to be ignored, despite its lack of focus as a law-making initiative.[79] The non-binding Stockholm Declaration on the Human Environment[80] was seen from the beginning to belong to the growing family of globally influential policy development instruments in declaratory form. Even if viewed as an example of "elite consensus" within the transnational bureaucratic community, the Declaration was also an effort at political compromise within a context still sensitized by continuing tensions between developed and developing countries.[81] Perhaps even more important as a long-term influence on the new order of global conference diplomacy, the Stockholm Action Plan provided an intellectual blueprint – not least a "mindset" – for all future diplomatic initiatives conceived at the global level for the systematic treatment of highly complex problems.

The ASEAN countries of Southeast Asia were not centrally involved in the negotiation of either the Declaration or the Action Plan endorsed at Stockholm,[82] but their orientation to the tasks of environmental law development was as profoundly affected by these instruments as was the orientation of any other region of the world. This external influence is reflected especially in four sectors of Stockholm concern: marine pollution control, air

---

78 See Section III, A, *supra*, "The Transnational Ethical Community."

79 On the suggested deficiencies of Stockholm, see note 140 *infra*.

80 For an analysis, see Sohn, *supra* note 25.

81 The chief dilemma at Stockholm was how to reconcile the traditional concept of state sovereignty with the modern need to emphasize the responsibility of states to preserve the environment. At that time, this responsibility was seen by most developing countries to rest primarily with the industrially developed states, which had caused most of the pollution, and the former were reluctant to let environmental concerns add to the costs of development, which was the highest of all priorities. Accordingly, there was no willingness on their part to accept any legal document that could be interpreted as a limitation on the emergent "right to development." "Environment" was still regarded chiefly as a pollution problem, and therefore as a cost allocation issue.

82 It should be recalled that in the late 1960s, when preparations were under way for Stockholm, most of the ASEAN countries were still in the early years of independence; flat-out development was the order of the day; and none of the countries of the region had reached the stage of confidence building that allowed them to balance out competing considerations along the lines of the still-emerging concept of sustainable development.

and water quality, environmental impact assessment and monitoring, and nature conservation.

Singapore

Like many other countries around the world, Singapore moved quickly after the Stockholm Conference to create a Ministry of Environment, an agency put together with former units of the Ministry of Health and Ministry of National Development concerned with public health and pollution, respectively.[83] Nineteen years after its formation, the Minister of Environment felt emboldened to claim that the Ministry had "succeeded in attaining most of its long-term targets."[84]

As the busiest port in the world,[85] Singapore has given high priority to the protection of the marine environment and to the management of the Straits of Malacca and Singapore, including its own coastal waters. In 1973, in the year following the Stockholm Conference and in accordance with its recommendations, the existing treaty rules and procedures for the control of vessel-based marine pollution were consolidated and developed in the 1973 International Convention for the Prevention of Pollution from Ships, as later modified by the Protocol adopted by the 1978 International Conference on Tanker Safety and Pollution Prevention (commonly referred to as MARPOL 73/78). In conformity with its usual practice, Singapore delayed ratification of this major global treaty until it had completed consultations with all interested sectors of industry and brought its administrative standards, practices, and procedures into line with the Convention. Finally, in 1990, the Singapore legislature enacted the requisite implementing statute, the *Prevention of Pollution of the Sea Act*, which came into effect to prevent operational discharge and otherwise minimize pollution by all ships using Singapore waters, mirroring the six main parts of MARPOL. The result of

---

83 The mandate of the Singapore Ministry of Environment is very broad and includes the following: industrial water regulation, drainage, solid waste management, waste minimization and recycling, resource conservation, public cleansing, abatement of insanitary conditions and public health nuisances, quarantine and epidemiology, environmental health education and training, environmental monitoring and management, air and water pollution control, control of environmentally hazardous chemicals and waste, transboundary and global environmental issues, and environmental strategies and research: Koh, *supra* note 48 at 137. Broad as it is, it does not explicitly include marine pollution control, which seems to have been conceded to the Port of Singapore Authority (now the Maritime and Port Authority of Singapore).

84 Quoted by Koh, *supra* note 48 at 138. For a recent overview of environmental programs in Singapore, see L. C. C. Koe and M. A. Aziz, "Environmental Protection Programmes," in G. L. Ooi, ed., *Environment and the City: Sharing Singapore's Experience and Future Challenges* (Singapore: Institute of Policy Studies, 1995) at 200-20.

85 This claim is based on total tonnage handled, which was estimated in the early 1990s to be close to 600 million gross tonnes. Sometimes there are as many as 700 vessels in the port of Singapore: Koh, *supra* note 48 at 172.

the commitments accepted under this treaty is that Singapore has brought into place the highest international standards in most sectors of vessel-based marine pollution control.[86] This was achieved, in the 1972-92 period, not only through the implementation of MARPOL, the most all-encompassing treaty in the field, but also through Singapore's acceptance of other major shipping conventions, such as the 1966 International Convention on Loadlines, the 1969 International Convention on Civil Liability for Oil Pollution Damage, the 1972 Convention on the International Regulations for Preventing Collisions at Sea, and the 1974 International Convention on Safety of Life at Sea.[87]

Singapore obtains most of its water from neighbouring Johor, the southernmost state of Western Malaysia, supplemented by supplies from its own reservoirs, which are administered by the Public Utilities Board of Singapore. The water is chemically treated within the Guidelines for Drinking Water Quality of the World Health Organization. During the 1972-92 period, the successful completion of a ten-year project saw the return of aquatic life to the previously filthy Singapore River and Kallang Basin. The pollution of freshwater areas is controlled under the *Water Pollution Control and Drainage Act*, and less directly under the *Sand and Granite Quarries Act.*[88] As to air pollution, it was clear in the 1960s, as the urbanization of Singapore began to accelerate, that the test of public nuisance was an inadequate control mechanism. In 1972, the year of Stockholm, the Singapore *Clean Air Act* came into force, its provisions focusing on industrial and trade premises and other "scheduled premises." In 1975, the Act was extended to construction sites, and in 1980 the schedule was amended to provide for stricter controls over facilities used for the storage of toxic or volatile substances that contribute to air impurity.[89] Exhaust emissions by vehicles were brought under control by the *Road Traffic Act*, in accordance with ECE Regulation 83 annexed to the UN Agreement Concerning the Adoption of Uniform Conditions of Approval and Reciprocal Recognition of Approval for Motor Vehicle Equipment and Parts, and also in conformity with Japanese and U.S. safety regulations.[90] Both traffic and vehicular restrictions in Singapore are now almost certainly among the most stringent in the world.

---

86 These provisions are found mostly in regulations such as: Prevention of Pollution of the Sea (Oil) Regulations: Prevention of Pollution of the Sea (Noxious Liquid Substances in Bulk) Regulations; Prevention of Pollution of the Sea (Reporting of Pollution Incidents) Regulations; Prevention of Pollution of the Sea (Reception Facilities) Regulations: K. B. Foo, "Control of Pollution in Singapore" (1993) 5 Sing. Acad. L.J. 81 at 97.

87 Foo, *supra* note 86 at 96-99.

88 Koh, *supra* note 48 at 160-61.

89 *Ibid.* at 161-66. See also Foo, *supra* note 86 at 90-92.

90 *Ibid.* at 92.

On the face of things, however, Singapore's record of compliance with global standards is marred by its lack of legislation requiring completion of an *environmental impact assessment* (EIA) procedure before the approval of projects that might have adverse impacts.[91] No such EIA provision is in the *Planning Act*. The Central Building Plan Unit of the Pollution Control Department *may* – and apparently in practice often does – conduct its own internal environmental impact assessment, but local critics are dissatisfied with a system that is discretionary and non-transparent. In their own defence, the Singapore authorities have argued over the years that most projects in Singapore are not large enough to justify the economic cost of a mandatory procedure.[92]

Singaporean compliance with global norms and standards extends to some other contexts within the field of nature conservation.[93] In response to Stockholm recommendations, Singapore set up a system for daily monitoring of air pollution throughout the island to ensure that air quality is maintained in conformity with international standards,[94] but the monitoring of wildlife has apparently not been so effective or diligent.[95] To the extent one can discern international standards in the field of land use planning, Singapore's

---

91 C. Briffett and Malone-Lee Lai Choo, "The Case for Environmental Impact Assessment in Singapore" (Paper presented at conference on "Infrastructure: Impact on Development and Environment," Singapore, Institute of Engineers, May 1992) [unpublished]. This increasingly familiar requirement has its origin in the 1969 U.S. *National Environmental Policy Act* (NEP), which requires U.S. federal agencies to demonstrate they have carried out an assessment by publishing an environmental impact statement (EIS), describing in detail probable negative impacts. Recommendations for environmental monitoring and assessment were contained in the 1972 Stockholm Action Plan, but the call for mandatory EIA procedures has been resisted in many countries because of the increased initial cost thereby imposed on development projects.

92 Koh, *supra* note 48 at 181-83.

93 In some usages, the term "nature conservation" (or "conservation of nature and natural resources") is virtually coextensive with "environmental protection." As first used, in the late 1940s at the birth of the International Union for Conservation of Nature and Natural Resources (IUCN, now renamed the World Conservation Union), the term had a narrow connotation, focused chiefly on wildlife, but it tends now to assume a wider meaning, so as to include resource management and even all sectors of pollution control. In various recent charters, a broad approach has been adopted. In the 1985 ASEAN Agreement on the Conservation of Nature and Natural Resources, signed in Kuala Lumpur, the concept encompasses development planning, conservation of species and ecosystems (species, vegetation cover, forest resources, soil, and air), conservation of ecological processes (environmental degradation and pollution), and environmental planning (land use planning, protected areas, and impact assessment).

94 Koh, *supra* note 48 at 169.

95 For a description of legislation since 1884, see Lye, *supra* note 50. The extent of protection afforded depends on the location of the wildlife. The maximum protection is given in nature reserves and national parks, where even insect life is protected and the mere possession of trapping equipment is an offence. Elsewhere, all wild animals and all birds except the house crow are protected, but not invertebrates. Enforcement of these laws varies, and their efficacy depends ultimately on public education and awareness: Lye, *supra* note 50 at 318-19.

record of compliance seems better than that of most countries. Credit should be given to its enlightened policy of interspersing carefully planned green areas among designated industrial and public housing zones, even though this policy is a product of the non-statutory Concept Plan, first introduced in 1971 and revised by the Urban Redevelopment Authority in 1991, rather than the product of the Master Plan, which has been revised every five years since 1958 under the *Planning Act*.[96] In the case of protected areas, called for internationally since the Stockholm Conference, Singapore by 1992 had two national parks, five nature reserves, and twelve catchment area parks, and the 1992 Master Plan for the Conservation of Nature in Singapore envisages the designation of 28 additional sites with protected status.[97]

Malaysia

The impact of the Stockholm Conference on Malaysia was first evidenced in 1974 with the enactment of the *Environmental Quality Act*, which created the Department of Environment and gave it a broad environmental mandate that applied to the whole of the country, subject, as it is, to the constitutional exemptions accorded to Sabah and Sarawak and to the considerable powers vested in local authorities under the *Local Government Act* of 1976.[98] These enactments were followed by the Third Malaysia Plan (1976-80) that, unlike its two predecessors, incorporated the goal of sound environmental management into the official strategy of national economic development, as recommended at Stockholm. To achieve the optimal balance between development and environment, the Third Malaysia Plan assigned priorities to three areas: pollution control, comprehensive land use planning, and integrated project planning.[99]

In the area of pollution control, however, progress has been retarded by the inability of the central government to ensure local enforcement of its various regulations under the *Environmental Quality Act*. For example, the Environmental Quality (Sewage and Industrial Effluents) Regulations of 1979 prohibit the discharge of effluents containing certain substances into any inland waters, but the control of pollution of streams in local authority areas is subject to municipal enforcement under the *Local Government Act*, and enforcement has been virtually non-existent in most of these areas.[100] Similar efforts to control the discharge of effluents from commercial premises ("trade effluents") under the *Street Drainage and Building Act* of 1974 have been ineffective, because they require the prior written permission of the

96 Koh, *supra* note 48 at 175-78.
97 *Ibid.* at 178-81.
98 Thanarajasingam, *supra* note 52 at 59-60.
99 *Ibid.* at 61.
100 *Ibid.* at 72.

local authority.[101] The problem of automotive air emissions, on the other hand, remains unsolved chiefly because of the overlap of ministerial enforcement mandates at the national level: that is, between the Department of Road Transport, which has powers under the Motor Vehicle Control of Smoke and Gas Emissions Rules of 1977, and the Department of Environment, which has enforcement powers under the 1985 amendments to the *Environmental Quality Act*.[102] The regulation of toxic and other hazardous substances in Malaysia is inadequate, because it is still within the sole province of the old 1952 *Poisons Ordinance*, which cannot cope with the rapidly expanding array of industrial chemicals.[103] More success has been achieved under the *Environmental Quality Act* in the non-traditional pollution control sectors of air quality, noise, rivers, and coastal waters.[104]

Another important advance after Stockholm was in the area of land use planning. In 1976 the *Town and Country Planning Act* highlighted environmental protection as an essential aspect of the local planning process, requiring local planning bodies to secure the approval of planning committees at the state level and provide for some degree of public participation, including public hearings in the case of draft local plans. Initially, between 1981 and 1985, the Malaysian Department of Environment experimented with a guidelines system of informal environmental impact assessment procedures, but with the amendment of the *Environmental Quality Act* in 1985, Malaysia, unlike Singapore, adopted a policy of mandatory EIA's for 19 prescribed activities.[105] However, this system, which was put into place in 1988, has been disappointing to local environmentalists.[106]

Post-Stockholm legislation in the area *of* nature conservation, on the other hand, has been impressively voluminous, and the recently developed National Conservation Strategy provides a blueprint for future ecological guidance within the administrative structure of the national government. A national parks system was created under the *National Parks Act* of 1980 (Act 226), but this statute does not apply to Sabah and Sarawak, nor to the states of Kelanban, Pahang, and Terengganu. Nor does the system include three of the country's most important parks, which are still under much less effective management regimes at the state level.[107] However, Malaysian compliance with global and regional environmental standards is reflected in the adoption of 11 ASEAN heritage sites, which were selected through technical collaboration with UNEP.[108]

101 *Ibid.*
102 *Ibid.* at 75.
103 *Ibid.* at 76.
104 *Ibid.* at 78-80.
105 *Ibid.* at 61.
106 *Ibid.* at 81.
107 *Ibid.* at 81-82.
108 *Ibid.* at 82.

Thailand

As a result of the Stockholm concept of sustainable development, the Thai constitution adopted in 1978 provided, in section 65, that the state has the responsibility to "maintain environmental balance."[109] The primary statute, enacted three years before environmental protection policy secured constitutional status, is the *National Environmental Quality Act*, which (1) established the National Environmental Board (NEB), with authority to recommend environmental quality standards to government agencies with statutory powers to prescribe them; (2) provided for the implementation of an environmental impact assessment program; and (3) granted emergency powers to the Prime Minister in the event of an environmental crisis.[110] In 1981 Cabinet approval was given to environmental policy guidelines under the 1975 Act (National Policies and Measures on Environmental Development), which were incorporated into the Fifth National Economic and Social Development Plan of 1981-86. Similar guidelines have also been included in the Sixth and Seventh National Plans developed by the National Economic and Social Development Board, which came into existence in 1987.[111] The Sixth Plan underlined that the "conflict between utilizing and conserving national resources must be contained in order to facilitate both further use and future conservation of the environment."[112]

Despite this high-level commitment, implementation efforts in many sectors have led to frustration. In the context of fisheries, for example, numerous fish conservation and habitat protection restrictions adopted under the old *Fishery Act* of 1947 and the *Wild Animals Protection and Reserves Act* of 1961, and several royal decrees, have failed to protect these resources from severe overexploitation. These domestic failures to implement conservation laws have been aggravated by increased pressure on Thai stocks resulting from new legal barriers against historic Thai fishing in waters off the coast of neighbouring countries, such as Malaysia, Myanmar, Cambodia, and Vietnam.[113] In consequence, the groundfish fishery of the Gulf of Thailand has virtually collapsed.[114]

---

109 Tasneeyanond and Nifose, *supra* note 62 at 204.

110 *Ibid.* at 205.

111 *Ibid.* at 205-207.

112 *Ibid.* at 208.

113 *Ibid.* at 209-12. In the 1990s, Thailand's fishing disputes with its neighbours had become one of the most publicized and emotional issues in Thai foreign relations, because of the number and increasing severity of violent clashes. For a broader view of fishery problems in the region, see D. Y. Coulter, "South China Sea Fisheries: Count Down to Calamity" (1996) 17 Contemp. S.E. Asia 371.

114 In February 1996 the Thai government announced the decision to make a serious effort to rehabilitate these stocks with a view to the eventual resumption of harvesting within the limits of sustainability. For an overview of fishery depletion problems in the region at large, see D. Menasveta, "Fisheries Management in the Exclusive Economic Zones of Southeast Asia Before and After Rio and Prospects for Regional

The problem of deforestation due to the expansion of croplands was first recognized in the Third Plan (1972-76), which advocated crop diversification programs as a partial solution, but no clear strategy for resolving such disputes was offered, and it was not until 1986 that the Thai Cabinet created the National Forest Policy Board with the mandate to develop a national forest policy. The resulting plan has been controversial: only 15% of total land area would be reserved for conservation forests (viz., forests, national parks, wildlife sanctuaries, and high-grade watersheds), whereas 25% would be allotted to economic forests (viz., forested areas suitable for agriculture and deteriorated forests available to the private sector for reforestation). The implementation of economic forest policy has been subjected to particularly heavy criticism.[115]

Problems continue to plague Thai efforts to develop effective pollution controls. Throughout most of the country, due to the lack of sewage disposal management controls (which are the responsibility of the Ministry of the Interior), waste water from households and commercial buildings in congested areas is discharged directly into both inland and coastal waters.[116] On the other hand, the Thai government has spent considerable funds in recent years on marine water quality research in the Gulf of Thailand, focusing on the coastal waters around the mouths of the Chao Phrya and other rivers. Also disappointing to Thai environmentalists is the relative ineffectiveness of the government's "selective projects" approach to its ostensibly mandatory EIA policy, which is generally construed as toothless as well as arbitrary.[117]

Indonesia

Almost immediately after the Stockholm Conference, the commitment to the environment inherent in the Indonesian constitution and the *Pancasila* was reinforced by the general outline of national environmental policy promulgated by the People's Consultative Assembly in the *Garis-garis Besar Negara* (GBHN or Guidelines of State Policy). The policy outline was adopted in these words: "[i]n the implementation of development, Indonesia's natural resources should be rationally utilized. The exploitation of these natural

---

Cooperation," in Koh Kheng Lian et al., eds., *Sustainable Development of Coastal and Ocean Areas in Southeast Asia: Post-Rio Perspectives* (Singapore: SEAPOL and Nat. Univ. of Singapore, 1995) [hereinafter *Post-Rio Perspectives*] at 98, and E. L. Miles, "Comments," *ibid.* at 135. See also D. Menasveta, "Fishery Management Needs and Prospects in the Gulf of Thailand" (1997) (Paper presented to the First SEAPOL Meeting of Experts on the Gulf of Thailand, Hua Hin, Thailand Oct. 1997) [to be published].

115 Tasneeyanond and Nifose, *supra* note 62 at 213-17. On the role of the Thai media, see Ubonrat Siriyuvasak, "Environmental Discourses in the Thai Media" (1994) 2:2 Thailand Environ. Inst. Q. Environ. J. 27-37. On the relationship between deforestation and agricultural development in Thailand, see L. Lohman, "Freedom to Plant: Indonesia and Thailand in a Globalizing Pulp and Paper Industry," in Parnwell and Bryant, *supra* note 35 at 23-48.

resources should not destroy the human environment and should be executed by a comprehensive policy which takes into account the needs of future generations."[118] Every five-year GBHN since then has retained this pledge. Like many other countries after Stockholm, Indonesia took the important step of enacting an overall environmental statute that took a holistic, cross-sectoral approach to environmental protection policy: Law No. 4 of 1982, the *Environmental Management Act* (EMA).[119] Between 1982 and 1992 Indonesia enacted no fewer than 19 statutes and regulations based on the principles and objectives of the 1982 Act, and began to review existing legislation in various sectors, such as agriculture, forestry, mining, water management, and pesticide control.[120]

Among the important new enactments was the 1990 *Act on Conservation of Living Natural Resources* (Act No. 5 of 1990) (LRCA). Linked with the general environmental commitment in the Constitution and in the GBHN, this statute contained Stockholm-based provisions on life-support systems, biological diversity, sanctuaries, preservation of species, sustainable use of living natural resources and their ecosystems, and conservation areas. Further, it prescribed modes of public participation, dealt with the delegation of responsibilities, and provided penalties for environmental offences.[121]

Project planning since the enactment of the EMA of 1982 has been subject to the requirement for an environmental impact assessment. Early planning of most types of development effort or activity must include "a consideration of its major impact on the living environment, both physical and non-physical, including socio-cultural,"[122] through an Environmental

---

116 Tasneeyanond and Nifose, *supra* note 62 at 220.

117 *Ibid.* at 230-32.

118 Quoted at Hardjasoemantri, *supra* note 67 at 19.

119 The EMA sets out the general principles of environmental law to be applied in the implementation of the GBHN. These include a mandatory EIA provision in Principle 6 ("Every development plan which could or would have a significant impact on the environment must be reported to the government, accompanied by an analysis of those impacts in accordance with government regulations"). Principle 8 provides for the punishment of polluters by the obligation to compensate victims and to bear the cost of restoring the environment. Under Principle 9, certain polluters "stipulated in implementing legislation" are to be subject to "strict liability in tort," and under Principle 10 others may be subject to imprisonment for up to 10 years and/or to a fine up to Rp. 100,000.

120 Hardjasoemantri, *supra* note 67 at 22. All of these laws have been found to be inadequate or ineffective. See e.g. L. Potter, "Environmental and Social Aspects of Timber Exploitation in Kalimantan, 1967-89," in J. Hardjono, ed., *Indonesia: Resources, Ecology and Environment* (Singapore: Oxford Univ. Press, 1991) at 177-211; and L. Potter, "The Onslaught on the Forests in South-East Asia," in H. Brookfield and Y. Bryon, eds., *South-East Asia's Environmental Future: The Search for Sustainability* (Kuala Lumpur: Oxford Univ. Press, 1993) at 103-23. See also comments on the latter critique, *ibid.* at 124-28.

121 Hardjasoemantri, *supra* note 67 at 23-24.

122 *Ibid.* at 46.

Information Presentation (PIL) so that an assessment can be made whether an Environmental Impact Analysis Document (ANDAL) should be prepared. Projects that may have significant impact on the environment (Category III) or are certain to have such an impact (Category IV) are required to be scrutinized under the ANDAL procedure.[123] Local critics, however, are less than satisfied with the efficacy of this legislation.[124]

Dissatisfaction with the Indonesian government's efforts to deal with its environmental problems has become more widely apparent as a result of the exceptional "seasonal haze" problem, which has received world-wide notoriety. There is now a widespread impression in the international community that Indonesia's environmental control policy and legislation is seriously inadequate, especially as applied to the remote rural areas that make up the bulk of this huge territory. Recovery from this loss of environmental reputation, coinciding with a loss of economic confidence, will take years of transparent efforts to give greater operational significance to existing environmental laws, not least those designed to regulate land-clearing practices. The environmental and economic injuries inflicted on neighbouring countries such as Malaysia, Brunei, and Singapore as a result of Indonesian land clearing have been enormous, and place an additional burden on ASEAN's capacity for relaxing tensions among member states.[125]

The Philippines

Five years after the Stockholm Conference, a framework law was promulgated

---

123 *Ibid.* at 47.

124 The Governmental Regulation No. 29 of 1986 made it obligatory for an environmental impact assessment to accompany proposals for a wide range of projects that might have adverse environmental impacts. But this regulation, like others in the environmental sector, has been difficult to enforce for the following reasons: too many exceptions and dispensations; the difficulty of monitoring and measuring the extent of environmental threats; the overlapping competences of various government agencies; and uncertainty about the appropriate authority to decide whether a proposed undertaking is environmentally acceptable.

125 For a highly favourable Vietnamese assessment of ASEAN's record in dispute management, see Hoang Ann Tuan, "ASEAN Dispute Management: Implications for Vietnam and an Expanded ASEAN" (1996) 18 Contemp. S.E. Asia 61. Since ASEAN originally was designed primarily as a security arrangement, it is relevant to note the current trend to view threats to security much more broadly than before. See e.g. G. Prins, ed., *Threats Without Enemies: Facing Environmental Insecurity* (London: Earthscan Publications, 1993); S. M. Lynne-Jones and S. E. Miller, eds., *Global Dangers: Changing Dimensions of International Security* (Cambridge, Mass.: M.I.T. Press, 1995); and G. Blake et al., eds., *International Boundaries and Environmental Security: Frameworks for Regional Cooperation* (London: Kluwer Law Int'l, 1997). Some environmentalist writers have gone so far as to challenge the traditional concept of sovereignty. See e.g. Mische, *supra* note 14. Such radical rethinking seems unlikely to have much influence on the membership of ASEAN, but the 1997 haze crisis may provide further stimulation to internal confidence-building as a non-confrontational dispute management strategy for the region.

by Presidential Decree: the Philippine Environment Policy (PD 1151). This policy was complemented by the accompanying Environment Code (PD 1152), which sets out management policies and quality standards for the environment as a whole, not merely for the various sectors of pollution, and introduces an EIA system.[126] Included also are provisions on air quality management, water quality management, land use management, natural resources management and conservation, use and conservation of surface and ground water, and waste management, as well as on population-environment balance and preservation of the cultural heritage. Under a different decree (PD 1121), the National Environmental Protection Council (NEPC) was established, and under an Executive Order (EO 192) the Department of Environment and Natural Resources (DENR). Conflicts between these two agencies have been common, requiring resolution by memoranda of understanding and other administrative processes. On the whole, the result has been a series of frustrating delays in deciding questions of agency jurisdiction and further complicated by DENR's mandate to facilitate the process of decentralization of government as a matter of overriding state policy.[127] As in other large countries, the municipal level of authority has been entrusted with certain areas of environmental control, such as solid waste management, while responsibilities in cognate areas such as the management of toxic and other hazardous wastes are vested in national government by virtue of a 1990 *Republic Act of Congress* (RA 6969).[128]

---

126 Tolentino, *supra* note 72 at 95. The Philippine EIA system requires private establishments and government agencies to submit an environment impact statement (EIS) for every action, project, or undertaking planned by them that may significantly affect the quality of the environment. However, PD No. 1586 (1978) limits coverage by specifying that only "environmentally critical" projects will automatically fall within its purview. Proclamation No. 2146 (1981) identifies three types of environmentally critical projects, i.e., heavy industry projects, resource extraction projects, and infrastructure projects such as dams, power plants, reclamation works, and roads and bridges: ASEAN Law Foundation, *supra* note 67 at 200-202.

127 Tolentino, *ibid.* at 95. Decentralization, it is hoped, will lead to improvements in the much-criticized performance of the Philippine bureaucracy. See generally L. Carino, "Unrequited Love, Impossible Dreams, Unfulfilled Hopes: The Performance Problems of the Philippine Bureaucracy" (1992) 31 Phil. Econ. J. 92. Decentralization is, however, only part of the need for civil service reform. In a recent World Bank study of environmental management problems in Indonesia, it was suggested that a fully developed reform strategy should be based on "an assessment of the implications of the changing role of government, as a result of deregulation and structural change, for administrative structures and the size, skill mix, and composition of the civil service." World Bank, *Indonesia: Sustaining Development* (Washington: World Bank, 1994) at 149. As part of the reform, it was argued, the size of the Indonesian bureaucracy must be reduced drastically to make a higher level of remuneration possible, and thereby a higher level of competence and efficiency. It seems likely that the same prescription could be applied to the Philippines, and indeed many other third world countries with inflated and poorly paid bureaucracies.

128 Tolentino, *supra* note 72 at 96.

Under an Executive Order (EO 192), DENR in 1987 initiated the formulation of the Philippine Strategy for Sustainable Development (PSSD), which identified enforcement as the key problem in ensuring that development is regulated so as to minimize harm to the environment and depletion of resources. This conceptual framework set sustainable development objectives over a wide range of environmental concerns, but lacks official status until it is endorsed by an executive order of the president in the form of an action program. The NEPC was intended to provide overall coordination of environmental and developmental planning by national agencies, but its failure to accomplish this led to its demise and replacement by the Aquino government with a new system of decentralized administration involving DENR in environmental matters. Decentralization of government has given further impetus to the huge environmental NGO community of the Philippines, which extends into virtually all rural areas of this far-flung archipelago.[129]

The national Constitution deals explicitly with wildlife protection and other aspects of natural resource management, including the management of marine living resources in the extensive archipelago waters, territorial sea, and exclusive economic zone areas under the national jurisdiction of the Philippines.[130] But wildlife legislation, which goes back as far as 1916, is relatively ineffective because of a lack of public awareness of the need for such controls. Even as written, the laws fail to require an inter-agency review of development projects likely to have an impact on wildlife habitat areas.[131] In other contexts, as noted, presidential decrees of 1977 (PD 1151) and 1978 (PD 1586) obligate project proponents to submit an environmental impact statement (EIS), but as in many other developing countries, the implementation of this requirement has proved to be beyond the present capacity of the government system, despite constant monitoring by the NGO system of governance.[132] NGOs may have an especially important role in the management of protected areas and wildlife outside the system of national parks, which was set up in 1932 and is badly outdated.[133]

More modern and more sophisticated is the legislation in the area of pollution control, which has been brought under DENR's jurisdiction, chiefly by virtue of *Republic Act* 3931, as amended by PD 983. Yet here, too, this impressive body of statutes and regulations is often inadequate because of the scarcity of funds, qualified personnel, and the appropriate technical information.[134]

---

129 *Ibid.* at 98.
130 *Ibid.* at 99-100.
131 *Ibid.* at 102.
132 *Ibid.* at 121-23.
133 *Ibid.* at 117-21.
134 *Ibid.* at 114-15.

The Impact of Rio

Global Significance

The 1992 Earth Summit was so bold and comprehensive in its reach that it raised the world's expectations to new heights, dangerously close perhaps to the level of unattainability. Yet UNCED has caught the attention of policy-makers at global, regional, national, and even subnational levels of authority. In particular its action plan, Agenda 21, has been widely accepted, despite its non-binding form, as the definitive interstate blueprint for environmental policy development for the 1990s, and perhaps for well into the first decade of the twenty-first century. The countries of Southeast Asia, like those elsewhere, have little operational choice but to grant this document a special significance as the authoritative source of virtually all contemporary, sophisticated, mainstream thinking about the environmental goals and strategies prescribed for adoption throughout the world community.

In many circles outside the world of government, Agenda 21 seems to have been accorded an even higher degree of reverence that brings it close to "sacred text" status. To environmental NGOs, which make up a substantial and politically influential segment of the transnational ethical community, the Rio action plan has become the "green bible," and is being held up as the touchstone of environmental wisdom and integrity in numerous contexts of policy development.

In many countries, especially but not exclusively in the West, public pressure has forced governments to regard themselves as bound by the commitments inherent in Agenda 21 almost as if they are the functional equivalent of formal treaty obligations. It may be premature to suggest that Agenda 21 is perceived as having a constitutional status that places it above the level of ordinary treaties, but recent developments indicate that in the arena of environmental conference diplomacy it enjoys virtually the same degree of respect as relevant global conventions.[135] In numerous contexts one now sees references to the need for the implementation of Agenda 21[136] in much

---

135 For example, the Global Programme of Action for the Protection of the Marine Environment from Land-Based Activities adopted at a UNEP conference held in Washington, D.C., Nov. 1995, affirms, in para. 15 of its executive summary, that the Programme "reflects the fact that States face a growing number of *commitments* flowing from Agenda 21 and related conventions" [emphasis added]. For an extended analysis of the trend to non-binding instruments in the diplomatic arena, see Johnston, *supra* note 18.

136 The references to Agenda 21 in the ASEAN Strategic Plan of Action on the Environment (1994-98) vary. In para. 5 of the executive summary, the assumption of a non-binding instrument is implicit in the language, which acknowledges the "need to respond to specific *recommendations* of Agenda 21 requiring priority action in ASEAN" [emphasis added]. On the other hand, para. 43 of the Plan itself uses stronger language in its description of Agenda 21: "It reflects a global consensus and political *commitment* at the highest level in the government on development and environment

the same way as one invokes the need for the implementation of a fundamental convention, like the UN Convention on the Law of the Sea, or of important (and potentially expensive) environmental treaties, such as the biodiversity and climate change treaties that came out of UNCED.

What evidence is there that the countries of Southeast Asia have begun to implement Agenda 21? For the purpose of this chapter, it may be sufficient to review a few examples of Southeast Asian sensitivity to Rio concerns before and after the Conference and of apparent efforts to comply with Rio concepts and prescriptions.

Orientation of Sustainable Development Strategy

As noted above, several countries of Southeast Asia had responded long before Rio to the World Conservation Strategy, launched in 1980 by IUCN, UNEP and the World Wildlife Fund, with their own national conservation strategies. These instruments of national policy were framed around the Stockholm governing concept of human responsibility to "protect and improve the environment for present and future generations,"[137] but still exhibiting to some extent the sectoral approach to environmental protection that was later to be subjected to challenge by the Brundtland Commission and at UNCED,[138] and of course representing the statist orientation that was now under assault by more radical ecologists.[139] Those countries that are disposed to use these pre-Rio conservation policy documents as the blueprint for national environmental policy-making in the post-Rio period, without updatings in the light of Agenda 21, may be likely to enact environmental legislation that is seen outside the region, and especially in the West, to reflect the Stockholm rather than the Rio mindset, resulting conceivably in divergence rather than convergence of legal systems.[140] To the extent that

---

cooperation and is intended to serve as the *basis for global partnership*. Its successful implementation rests with the governments" [emphasis added].

137 (Stockholm) Declaration of the UN Conference on the Human Environment, Principle 1.

138 The holistic, "anti-sectoral" approach to environmental policy is associated chiefly with the Brundtland Commission and UNCED, but it has its origins in the Stockholm Action Plan, which made the case for ecological understanding. To some extent the holistic perspective is inherent in Principle 13 of the Stockholm Declaration, which called for states to "adopt an integrated and coordinated approach to their development planning so as to ensure that development is compatible with the need to protect and improve the human environment for the benefit of their population."

139 Some environmental extremists take the position that the effective protection of nature is impossible under the constraints inherent in the interstate system, such as the artificial system of jurisdictional entitlements that has evolved within the statist framework of classical and neo-classical international law. To them, effective environmental action depends on the mobilization of smaller-scale "communities" and "neighbourhoods" that are presumed to live more closely to ecological realities.

140 See generally J. Carew-Reid et al., *Strategies for National Sustainable Development: A Handbook for their Planning and Implementation* (London: Earthscan Publications, 1994).

political pragmatism carried weight at Rio, as at Stockholm, requiring a balance between development and environment to be re-articulated, the Brundtland concept of "sustainable development" triumphed in fact as well as name as the dominant motif within the arena in the late 1980s and early 1990s. Since then, however, it has become increasingly common outside the arena, at least in the West, to refer rather to the overriding concept of "sustainability" as a social goal without direct or explicit reference to the need for a balance between competing considerations. The emergence of this, chiefly Western and essentially ethical, intergovernmental demand seems certain to subject the more pragmatic environmental policy and legislation of most Southeast Asian countries to criticism from non-governmental associations outside the region, and it remains to be seen how far Western governments will be pulled along by these demands of Western "civic society."

Causes of Environmental Degradation

One of the major differences between Stockholm and Rio is in the ideology of environmentalism. In the preparations for Stockholm, the mainstream concern was to present the case for environmental protection without seeming to threaten economic development objectives, which had the highest priority in nation-building throughout developing countries. In the preparations for Rio, 20 years later, it was agreed to project the view of environmental degradation as a consequence of poverty and related socioeconomic

---

Some radical environmentalists have criticized these national conservation strategies, which have been developed in over 50 countries, as "shallow." See e.g. D. Fernandes, "The Shaky Ground of Sustainable Tourism" (1994), 2:4 Thailand Environ. Inst. Q. Environ. J. 4 at 19. The differences between the Stockholm and Rio mindsets might be described by reference to the following seven contemporary critiques. First, from the Rio perspective, Stockholm reflects an anthropocentric, not a totalistic, orientation to the environment. Second, Stockholm is seen by many environmental critics to be too pragmatic, to the extent it is essentially concerned with securing the language of political compromise between "right to development" and "right to environment" rhetoric, rather than with articulating the need for a restructured view of the world and the human presence in it. Third, Stockholm is viewed by some as unduly rationalistic, in the sense that it proceeds on the basis of uncritical faith in scientific findings. Fourth, the Stockholm approach is characterized as preventive but insufficiently precautionary, permitting risks of harm to the environment to mount until compelling evidence is available to justify prohibition, termination, or strict regulation of the harmful activity. Fifth, Stockholm reflects a unicausal ideology in the sense it fails to recognize the linkages between environmental degradation, poverty, exploitation, and social injustice. Sixth, it is statist, assuming that effective responses to these problems depend almost entirely on official sophistication within government and between governments, and failing to appreciate roles that must be assumed by non-governmental initiatives at all levels of civic society. Finally, Stockholm might perhaps be judged by some to have conceded too much to the conservationist philosophy, which in most resource management contexts accepts the legitimacy of human use, and to have conceded too little to the preservationist philosophy, which pivots on the adverse consequences of human impact.

deprivations.[141] Environmental measures reflecting a policy that seems indifferent to these causes or aggravations of the problem can be expected to become the target of ideological criticism. This type of criticism might be vilified in the relatively intolerant political cultures of Southeast Asia as unacceptably oppositionist in the political (leftist) or cultural (foreign) sense.

Integration of Responses

Following the Brundtland blueprint, Agenda 21 seems to place unprecedented strain on systems of national government, all of which are structured around the idea of sectoral mandates and responsibilities.[142] Even those more-or-less unitary Southeast Asian systems that are spared the further complications of power-sharing inherent in federal or quasi-federal structures[143] have generally been unable to prevent a huge gap opening up

---

141 To attribute environmental degradation to poverty is to deflect the search for causes to the causes of poverty. Among economists there has been much debate on the causes of poverty at national and other levels. It is agreed only that it can be attributed to a variety of contributory factors and that therefore there cannot be any one approach to its elimination or even reduction. Accordingly, it can be argued that environmental problems cannot be treated effectively without a systematic effort to meet basic human needs. See e.g. B. E. Moon, *The Political Economy of Basic Human Needs* (Ithaca, N.Y.: Cornell Univ. Press, 1991). Opinions vary on the question whether resource scarcity can be so severe in extreme cases as to prevent escape from poverty, or whether inherent capacity or ingenuity can always find a way to successful adaptation, if not to affluence. T. Homer-Dixon, "The Ingenuity Gap: Can Poor Countries Adapt to Resource Scarcity?" (1995), 21 Population and Development Rev. 587. This is, of course, a key question, not least in environmental issue contexts, for development agencies and other funding institutions. In the World Bank, for example, it is generally assumed that economic growth facilitates but does not guarantee improvements in environmental quality. Because one does not necessarily lead to the other, many believe that it is ethically appropriate for institutions like the World Bank to impose environmental conditions on large-scale project assistance grants sought by impoverished countries, even though the conditionality of aid is resisted on principle by many developing nations. In the meantime, the World Bank devotes an increasing proportion of its funds to environmental protection and improvement projects. In 1993 the Bank committed over $2 billion to such projects, a 30-fold increase over such lending in 1989: International Bank for Reconstruction and Development (IBRD), *The World Bank and the Environment: Fiscal 1993* (Washington, D.C.: The World Bank, 1993) at 2. For an earlier criticism of the Bank's environmental policy, see C. Conroy and M. Litvinoff, eds., *The Greening of Aid: Sustainable Livelihoods in Practice* (London: Earthscan Publications, 1985). See also M. Seda, "Global Environmental Concerns and Priorities," in M. Seda, ed., *Environmental Management in ASEAN: Perspectives on Critical Regional Issues* (Singapore: Institute of Southeast Asian Studies, 1993).

142 By this reasoning, officials may be creating environmental expectations at the level of global diplomacy that cannot be met within the structure of bureaucracy at the level of national government.

143 None of the ten countries of Southeast Asia is truly federal in the structural sense of power-division stipulated by state constitutions in such countries as Australia, Canada, Germany, and the United States. By reason of the overriding authority of central government, the constitutional system of Malaysia (and arguably that of Indonesia) might be characterized as quasi-federal. The broader concept of power-

between promise and delivery in the field of environmental legislation. If the goal of inter-agency consultation (or coordination) was the corrective called for by Stockholm, the goal of integration is the cure prescribed by Rio.[144] It might be, ironically, that the least developed bureaucratic systems of Southeast Asia have a better chance of being structured around the Rio concept of integration than the most developed systems of the region have of being restructured to that end.[145]

Modes of Planning

Agenda 21 envisages a linkage between socioeconomic planning and

---

sharing extends to various modes of decentralization that are not constitutionally prescribed, such as those emerging in Thailand, the Philippines, and Vietnam.

144 Despite the frequent use of the adjective "integrated" applied to strategies of development, planning, and management, Brundtland and UNCED could not afford to seem to be instructing complex multi-level government systems on how to design and implement environmental policy and legislation. For example, in the context of coastal zone management they added the adjective "integrated" as if to emphasize the need for close and systematic collaboration, not merely coordination, between different levels of government, in conformity with the original rationale of coastal zone management within the federal system of the United States; but the meaning of "integrated" has had to be left open to interpretation. In addition to integration in this administrative sense, one might invoke the need for *conceptual* integration in the sense of holistic (i.e., totalistic or cross-sectoral) understanding of nature as the basis of all environmental management policy; for *diplomatic* integration in the sense of regional co-operation as the negotiated basis of interstate policy and management; and for *communal* integration in the sense of intranational collaboration between the central authority, the local community, and other stakeholders. See e.g. Chua Thia Eng, "Marine Pollution Developments Since UNCLOS III and Prospects for Regional Cooperation," in *Post-Rio Perspectives, supra* note 114 at 167-70, and D. M. Johnston, "Agenda 21 and UNCLOS," *ibid.* at 1-17.

145 In a single-party, dominant-party, or elitist system of government such as those of Vietnam, Singapore, Brunei, Malaysia, and Indonesia, a nationwide system of power-holding at the local level ought, theoretically, to permit a higher degree of policy coherence and policy implementation than in a fragmented political system such as those of Thailand and the Philippines. In varying degrees, all of the former might be regarded, at least potentially, as systems conducive to effective "top-down" environmental strategy to the extent that loyal power holders are in place at the local level, creating the conditions of integration. In countries like Thailand and the Philippines, it might be argued, a balance between "bottom-up" and "top-down" strategies seems not merely desirable but absolutely essential, given the relative ineffectiveness of central government at the local level. On a day-to-day basis, it is presumed to be bureaucracy that provides the intermediary between central government and the local community, but in Thailand and the Philippines, and indeed elsewhere, the national government bureaucracy is heavily concentrated in the capital and other major cities and strongly resistant to decentralization, even when promoted by the government of the day, as in the Philippines and, to some extent, Thailand. In the case of assistance-dependent countries like Vietnam and Cambodia, it seems more likely that the restructuring of government, with a view to the goal of integrated environmental policy and management, can be effected despite the strong bureaucratic preference for central control. The World Bank, it should be noted, has recently prepared guidelines for integrated coastal zone management: IBRD, *supra* note 141 at 49.

environmental protection, and seems to throw out a challenge to innovative thinking. In Singapore, as in other countries, planning has gone forward on two levels, the legal and the conceptual, in the hope of ensuring that legally sanctioned, short-term and medium-term project development plans are consistent with long-term objectives.[146] Long-term planning needs to be based on a "vision," such as Lee Kuan Yew's vision of Singapore as the "garden city,"[147] and it must be hoped that comparable creativity can be brought to the more difficult problem of planning faced by the larger economies of the region. One kind of experiment under way in several of the other ASEAN countries is in the use of municipal authorities, local communities, indigenous folk groups, and nongovernmental associations in the design, evaluation, implementation, and monitoring of national plans or appropriate components.[148]

Guiding Norms

Part of the Brundtland and UNCED exercises was devoted to the identification of governing constructs in the form of environmental principles, criteria, and other norms, such as the concept of sustainable development or sustainability,[149] the polluter-pays principle,[150] the preventive or precautionary approach,[151] and the requirements for integrated response and

146 Chia, *supra* note 48 at 209-13.

147 See Lee Sing Kong, "Concept of the Garden City," in Ooi, *supra* note 84 at 129-47; and K. L. Koh, "The Garden City and Beyond: The Legal Framework," *ibid.* at 148-70.

148 In Southeast Asia, is environmentalism an essentially middle-class, urban phenomenon, a genuine grassroots movement, or something more complex? One western observer of the environmental NGO scene in Thailand distinguishes nine categories of interest groups: P. Hirsch, "Where Are the Roots of Thailand Environmentalism?" (1994) 2:2 Thailand Environ. Inst. Q. Environ. J. 5 at 12-14. In the city-state of Singapore there seems to be less potential scope for NGOs: K. Mekani and H. G. Stengel, "The Role of NGOs and Near-NGOs," in Ooi, *supra* note 84 at 282-312.

149 Agenda 21 carries the Brundtland concept of sustainable development further by applying the adjective "sustainable" to the process of planning and management over a wide range of environmentally relevant contexts. The current concept, in the expanded form as "sustainability," is increasingly articulated as a basic norm of government or governance affecting anything that might become scarce. Johnston, *supra* note 144 at 18-19. See also note 11, *supra*, on the status of the new principle of sustainability. Both "sustainable development" and "sustainability" carry so much ambiguity that they have limited effect in countries that have already committed themselves to conservation objectives. Because of the vagueness of "sustainable development," it has been suggested that donor governments are free to choose to fund those kinds of environmental protection activities that best meet their overall aid profile.

150 This principle, which originated in Western Europe, requires that the sector of the economy, if identifiable, that constitutes the source of pollution must be legally responsible for the costs involved, whether through remedial research and development, alternative technology, training, product substitution, clean-up, compensation, or otherwise. This has given rise to innovative ideas on how to use economic, rather than legal, instruments as the chief means of attaining costly environmental

environmental impact assessment (EIA).[152] Whereas none of the countries of the Southeast Asian region has had any apparent difficulty in deploying the UN rhetoric of sustainability, these countries have had to react more carefully to the consequences of the polluter-pays principle, the precautionary principle, and the EIA requirement, which can be regarded as threatening to overall development strategy, and to the concept of integration, which can be construed as likely to reduce the autonomy of powerful sectors of bureaucracy.

Contexts of Special Interest or Concern

The reaction of each country to Rio depends, of course, on what it views to be its special interest or concern. In the case of Singapore, which uniquely in the world is a state with an exclusively urban (and increasingly affluent) environment, it has been possible to concentrate on the "greening" issues highlighted in Agenda 21 without the risk of collision with other priorities that arise from the needs of impoverished and remote rural areas.[153] For other, less favourably placed, countries of the region with runaway urbanization, in such areas as Greater Bangkok, Jakarta, or Manila, the problems of city congestion and traffic density have created horrendous problems in air and noise pollution that aggravate the difficulties associated with the planning of city transportation systems.[154] Most of the countries of the region

---

objectives. On its suggested application to water pollution, see e.g. Qwanrudee Limvorapi-tak, "Polluter Pays Principle: Application of Water Pollution Charges" (1994) 2:3 Thailand Environ. Inst. Q. Environ. J. at 38-50. The polluter-pays principle is more rigorously applied in Singapore than in the other countries of the region to the problem of controlling air and water pollution, as befits an economy that has virtually attained the status of a developed economy. J. Hui, "Environmental Policy and Green Planning," in Ooi, *supra* note 84 at 16. On the application of economic instruments to the problem of waste management in Singapore, see Lo Tuck Leong and E. Quah, "Management of Non-Hazardous Solid Waste," in Ooi, *supra* note 84 at 221-43. When legal responsibility is placed squarely on identifiable polluters, it is relatively easy and simple for governments to conduct regular spot checks at the factory level as part of an enforcement program in the classical, top-down, regulatory manner: Hui, *supra* at 17-18.

151 See *supra* note 11.

152 See Section IV, D, 4, *supra,* "Integration of Responses." See also note 91 *supra*. In Southeast Asian countries where the EIA requirement is incorporated into legislation, the requirement is "toothless" in the absence of enforcement machinery or the political will to use it. For a Thai critique, see [Editorial], "The Role of EIA in Thailand: A Toothless Tool to Protect the Environment" (1994) 25 Thai Development (newsletter on development and the NGO movement) at 25-28.

153 However, some of Singapore's experience, such as its success in cleaning up the Singapore Ri, may be relevant to non-urban environmental policy in other countries of the region. On this success, see J. Hui, "Environmental Policy and Green Planning," in Ooi, *supra* note 84, 13 at 18-19.

154 Compare N. Boontherawara et al., "Traffic Crisis and Air Pollution in Bangkok" (1994) 2:3 Thailand Environ. Inst. Q. Environ. J. at 38-50, with the Singapore experience reported in A. P. G. Menon, "Transport and the Environment," in Ooi, *supra* note 84 at 171-84.

have also had to accept the inevitability of assigning priority to tourism as a sector of rapid economic development and a source of foreign revenues, usually with inadequate consideration of the environmental impacts. Brundtland and UNCED warnings, and recommended experiments in "ecotourism" may be likely to have an effect in areas where large investments have not yet been made in environmentally harmful modes of tourism development,[155] and related recreational initiatives catering to the affluent urban middle classes.[156] As noted above, much criticism, both national and international, has been directed at forestry management policies and practices in the region. Southeast Asian objections, voiced chiefly by Malaysia, had much to do with blocking the effort to produce a Rio treaty on deforestation.[157] Perhaps the priority most widely shared among the ASEAN members, including its newcomer Vietnam, is coastal management and related concerns such as marine pollution control.[158]

---

155 Tourism development is a popular target of environmental critics, and yet it is difficult to measure the costs and benefits involved within this industry, precisely because they reach so deeply into society, both tangibly and intangibly. The proposal for ecotourism, designed around international interests in wildlife and wilderness, has ironically complicated the issue by focusing tourism development on parks and other protected areas that are the most deserving of special protection. For a moderate view, see Surachet Chettamart and Dachanee Emphandu, "The Tourism Industry and Sustainable Development in Thailand" (1994) 2:4 Thailand Environ. Inst. Q. Environ. J. at 39-46. Eco-tourism is often linked with national parks and other wildlife areas, but a recent study of national parks in Indonesia suggests that they have not yet contributed to the cause of conservation: J. Cochrane, "The Sustainability of Ecotourism in Indonesia: Fact and Fiction," in Parnwell and Bryant, *supra* note 35 at 227-59. For a more radical view, see Fernandes, *supra* note 140.

156 Golf, or rather golf course development and maintenance, is seen (along with skiing or ski resort development and maintenance) to be the chief threat to the environment caused by the affluent middle class appetite for new recreational facilities. Golf is a resource-hungry sport that consumes large areas of land, most of which tends to be agricultural or forest land. Golf course development in rural areas tends to reduce, not increase, the local sources of employment, resulting in better paid jobs for a smaller number of people. Golf course maintenance requires large amounts of water. It has been estimated that the average Thai golf course consumes 6,500 cubic metres of water daily, equal to the total daily needs of 6,000 Bangkok residents. In addition, a golf course involves heavy use of artificial chemical fertilizers, pesticides, fungicides, soil-improving agents, coagulants, and artificial colouring agents – all of which tend, in excessive concentration, to harm the natural environment: A. Pleumarom, "Sport and Environment: Thailand's Golf Boom Renewed" (1994) 2:4 Thailand Environ. Inst. Q. Environ. J. at 47-61. Concern over the environmental impacts of golf course development and maintenance has been expressed in most countries of the region, including Singapore where the Nature Society (Singapore) has raised objection to the proposed golf course at Lower Pierce Reservoir. Apparently as a result of this concern, the Singapore planning authorities have delayed the startup of this project.

157 Opposition by developing countries, led by Malaysia, forced UNCED organizers to abandon the original attempt to conclude a treaty on deforestation. The alternative fallback, a document containing non-binding guidelines that pertained to all types of forests, not just tropical rain-forests, was acceptable as less intrusive in a "reserved domain" that remains subject to national sovereignty.

Local Authority and Community Roles

Not least in the context of forest management, the Thai government in particular has responded to the Brundtland call for imagination in the use of local authorities in environmental planning, management, and monitoring, although nervous about the challenge posed by a non-governmental political confrontation movement funded and led by urban middle-class activist elites, both indigenous and foreign.[159] In Thailand and other countries of the region, the issue of large dams has also been of intense concern to affected local communities and a target for activist NGOs.[160] Confrontations of this kind are of even greater concern if they involve indigenous communities outside the ethnic mainstream of the country.[161]

Role of the Business Community

Also in response to Agenda 21, Southeast Asian countries have made a special effort to involve their business communities in the development of environmental policies and guidelines designed to regulate industrial and

---

158 For a recent overview, see E. D. Gomez, "Coastal Zone Management and Ecosystem Protection: Prospects for Cooperation in Southeast Asia," in *Post-Rio Perspectives, supra* note 114 at 191-220, and A. T. White, "Comments," *ibid.* at 207-20. For recommendations supported by many of the region's leading ocean policy specialists, see "Report and Recommendations," *ibid.* at 225-27. Improvements in this area involve implementation of the 1982 UN Convention on the Law of the Sea. See L. A. Kimball, "The United Nations Convention on the Law of the Sea: A Framework for Marine Conservation," in IUCN, *The Law of the Sea: Priorities and Responsibilities in Implementing the Convention* (Gland: IUCN, 1995) at 1-119. Regional priorities might include the establishment of "marine protected areas": G. Kelleher and R. Kenchington, *Guidelines for Establishing Marine Protected Areas* (Gland: IUCN, 1932). For an earlier study of the region's marine environment problems, see D. M. Johnston, *Environmental Management in the South China Sea: Legal and Institutional Developments* (Honolulu: East-West Center, 1982).

159 As part of its overall strategy of decentralization, the Thai government has allotted a role in forest management to subdistrict councils called *tambons*, though only in areas designated as community forests, and not yet to the more extensive areas of reserved forests: A. Pantasen, "Decentralization, the Tambon Council, and Community Forest Management" (1994) 2:2 Thailand Environ. Inst. Q. Environ. J. at 38-50. More generally, see Hirsch, *supra* note 148. For a counterpart study of this trend in the Philippines, see G. C. Braganza, "Philippine Community-Based Forest Management: Option for Sustainable Development," in Parnwell and Bryant, *supra* note 35 at 311-29.

160 For a global view see D. Hubbel, "Environmental and Social Impacts of Large Dams: Experience from Around the World" (1994) 25 Thai Development 20-24. For several years the Thai environmental movement has focused much of its energy on dam construction (and deforestation) issues, such as the completed Pak Moon and proposed Kaeng Sua Ten projects. The latter has been delayed by three environmental assessments, the last two initiated because of NGO criticism of the predecessor: see "Editorial," *supra* note 152 at 25. The third, commissioned by the World Bank and expanded to include a review of the impacts of tourism and recreation in the region of the dam, was apparently the first to be made available for public scrutiny.

161 For this kind of criticism applied to the 1990 Conceptual Framework of the Philippine Strategy for Sustainable Development, see Fernandes, *supra* note 140 at 21.

commercial enterprises. Effective leadership of this kind has been provided by prominent Asians such as former Prime Minister Anand of Thailand,[162] former Foreign Minister Mochtar Kusuma Atmadja of Indonesia,[163] and Ambassador Tommy Koh of Singapore.[164]

Need for Environmental Education and Training

It seems to have been accepted in Southeast Asia that a special effort must be made to raise environmental awareness at all levels of formal and public education, as recommended in Agenda 21. Since there is a regular forum for the ASEAN Ministers of Education, this particular area of policy has benefited from a degree of regional promotion and consultation.[165] Similarly, the need for specialized environmental training has been acknowledged through programs organized by both government agencies and non-governmental institutions.

ASEAN as Facilitator

In the field of environmental policy and legislation, many of the critical tasks to be addressed by the countries of Southeast Asia require action at the regional level. The Association of Southeast Asian Nations (ASEAN) is the most obvious, and perhaps potentially the most significant, mechanism to facilitate regional cooperation in this field, albeit complemented by the work of other regional bodies.[166] Given the consultative, rather than directive or regulatory, nature of ASEAN, it is wise not to overstate what can be accomplished under such auspices, but on the face of things the present ASEAN mandate, though chiefly economic in orientation, is broad enough to include, among other objectives, at least the following three kinds of regional

---

162 Former Prime Minister Anand chairs the Thailand Business Council for Sustainable Development.

163 Former Foreign Minister Mochtar has taken a prominent role in organizing conferences dealing with problems of the marine environment, especially under the auspices of the Southeast Asian Programme on Ocean Law, Policy and Management (SEAPOL).

164 Ambassador Koh has accepted a number of leadership roles in the environmental field in association with such organizations as APEC, SEAPOL, the Nature Conservancy, the Institute of Policy Studies, and the Asia Pacific Centre for Environmental Law (APCEL) at the National University of Singapore.

165 See Southeast Asian Ministers of Education Organization (1996) 3:2 *SEAMEO Forum*. See also V. R. Savage, "Eco-Education in Singapore," in Ooi, *supra* note 84 at 313-30.

166 Reference should also be made to the law-related efforts of global intergovernmental bodies with Southeast Asian programs such as the United Nations Environment Programme (UNEP) in Bangkok and the International Maritime Organization (IMO) in Manila; to the principal UN regional body with a developmental mandate, the Economic and Social Commission for the Asia-Pacific Region (ESCAP); to the "hybrid" IUCN which is now developing law-related projects in Southeast Asia; and to non-governmental networks such as SEAPOL, which has organized many law-of-the-sea conferences and programs throughout the region since 1981.

initiatives: (1) the facilitation of implementation efforts by the member states to bring their environmental policies, legislation, and administrative practices into reasonable or substantial compliance with global commitments negotiated and incurred through acceptance of treaty or treaty-like instruments; (2) the development and promotion of regional norms (policies, principles, standards, or guidelines) designed to shape national environmental policies, legislation, and administrative practices; and (3) the harmonization of different but potentially compatible national policies, laws, regulations, and administrative practices. The weight given to these three roles will no doubt vary with the sector of environmental policy at stake and what are perceived to be the central issues in a given context.

ASEAN itself was born in 1967, the year when the world was just beginning to gear up for the Stockholm Conference on the Human Environment (1972), the preliminary phase of the Third UN Conference on the Law of the Sea (1968-1973), and important marine pollution treaties such as the London Dumping Convention (1972) and MARPOL (1973). The impact of Stockholm on the ASEAN region as a whole is reflected in the ASEAN Environment Programme I (1978-82),[167] the ASEAN Environment Programme II(1983-87),[168] and the ASEAN Environment Programme III (1988-92).[169] The influence of Rio is apparent in the ASEAN Strategic Plan of Action on the Environment (1994-98).[170]

In the first phase of the ASEAN Sub-Regional Environment Programme (ASEP I), six priority program areas were identified for the purposes of regional cooperation: (1) environmental management (including environmental impact assessment); (2) nature conservation; (3) industry and environment; (4) marine environment; (5) environmental education and training; and (6) environmental information. By the inception of ASEP III in 1988, this listing

---

167 ASEP I was endorsed at the First ASEAN Ministerial Meeting on the Environment, Manila, Apr. 1981. Its objective was to "ensure the protection of the ASEAN environment and the sustainability of its natural resources, so that it can sustain continued development with the aim of eradicating poverty and attaining the highest possible quality of life for the people of the ASEAN countries": AEGE, *ASEAN Environment Programme III*, at 2. Among the four policy guidelines adopted was the legal development pledge to "[e]ncourage the enactment and enforcement of environmental protection measures in the ASEAN countries": *ibid.* at 3.

168 ASEP II was adopted at the Second ASEAN Ministerial Meeting on the Environment held in Bangkok, Nov. 1984. Considerable emphasis in this period was placed on air pollution monitoring and control, although this was only one of several designated areas of concern: *ibid.* at 7.

169 ASEP III was considered and endorsed by the Tenth Meeting of the ASEAN Experts Group on the Environment and adopted by the Third Ministerial Meeting on the Environment held in Jakarta, Oct. 1987.

170 The 1994 Strategic Plan of Action contains the explicit statement that it is intended to "promote the principles contained in the Rio Declaration on Environment and Development." For a discussion of these principles, see Foo, *supra* note 29.

of priorities was only slightly altered: the purposes of education, training, and information were combined within one priority program area, and a new area, urban environment, was added to the list.[171]

In the period between Stockholm and Rio, numerous high-level ASEAN policy instruments were negotiated as expressions of environmental commitment on the part of the member states, but actions did not necessarily follow the words. For example, at Manila in 1981, through the interministerial Declaration on the ASEAN Environment, the governments agreed to implement the adopted ASEP program and recommended the establishment of a committee on environment "in the context of the restructuring of ASEAN." In practice, however, environment was given a modest status within the new institutional framework: cooperation was entrusted to the ASEAN Experts Group on the Environment (AEGE) under the purview of the ASEAN Committee on Science and Technology (COST). Along with the other non-economic committees, COST reports to the Triennial ASEAN Ministerial Meeting, whereas the five, more influential, economic committees report to the system's powerhouse, the annual ASEAN Economic Ministers Meeting. In 1984, also at the ministerial level, the Bangkok Declaration on the ASEAN Environment lowered the saliency of environmental concerns by adopting the perspective of economic development, calling in rather weakly worded language for the implementation of the ASEAN Development Strategy through "an integrated approach ... with a view to incorporating [an] environmental dimension in development planning ... in order to achieve sustained development and long-term conservation of environmental assets and at the same time improving the quality of life for all."[172] On the specific topic of legal development, the Bangkok Declaration merely envisaged "appropriate legislation to support the proper management and development of the environment."

Stronger and more explicit language of commitment appeared in a legally binding treaty, the Agreement on the Conservation of Nature and Natural Resources, signed by the ASEAN Foreign Ministers at Kuala Lumpur in 1985. This agreement was drafted with the assistance of the IUCN Commission on Environmental Policy, Law and Administration (now re-named the Environmental Law Commission of the World Conservation Union). At one level, this instrument represents a legal breakthrough, since it included "a

171 See AEGE, *supra* note 167 at 24-25. Remote sensing was added as a new priority area for ASEP II, apparently at the suggestion of Thailand, which has a special competence in this area because of its role as the host of the LANDSAT Satellite Ground Receiving Station for the region. However, not much progress in regional cooperation in this area took place in this period, and thereafter it was subsumed under the general heading of "environmental management": *ibid.* at 12-13.

172 *Ibid.* at 3.

number of concepts which were unfamiliar in international agreements,"[173] but at another level the ambitiousness of the language poses an unprecedented challenge to the countries of the region in implementation, especially since most states have had difficulty in enforcing existing legislation with more modest pretensions. For example, in article 1 the parties pledged themselves, as a "fundamental principle," to adopt "measures necessary to maintain essential ecological processes and life-support systems, to preserve genetic diversity, and to ensure the sustainable utilization of harvested natural resources under their jurisdiction in accordance with scientific principles and with a view to attaining the goal of sustainable development."[174] To this end, the parties accepted the obligation to develop national conservation strategies and to "coordinate such strategies within the framework of a conservation strategy for the Region" (art. 1(2)). The following articles contain more specific, state-of-the-art provisions on a wide range of issues: development planning (art. 2), genetic diversity (art. 3), sustainable use (art. 4), endangered and endemic species (art. 5), vegetation cover and forest resources (art. 6), soil (art. 7), water (art. 8), air (art. 9), environmental degradation (art. 10), pollution (art. 11), land use planning (art. 12), protected areas (art. 13), impact assessment (art. 14), scientific research (art. 15), education, training information, and public participation (art. 16), and other concerns. However, disputes arising out of the interpretation or implementation of the Agreement are to be "settled amicably by consultation or negotiation" (art. 30), not by any process of third party settlement or even assistance such as mediation or conciliation. Despite this tentative approach to dispute management, which is consistent with the policy of most ASEAN countries in most contexts,[175] the 1985 Kuala Lumpur Agreement on the Conservation of Nature and Natural Resources is, by far, the region's boldest commitment to

173 W. E. Burhenne, in Foreword to IUCN, *Legislation, supra* note 48 at vii.

174 ASEAN Agreement on the Conservation of Nature and Natural Resources, art. 1 (1), text reproduced in K. L. Koh, comp., *Selected ASEAN Documents on the Environment* (Singapore: APCEL Document Series, 1996) at 27-47.

175 Since their emergence as independent states, most of the countries of Southeast Asia have consistently avoided resort to third party settlement of disputes arising among themselves. ASEAN was originally set up as a conflict avoidance system. Even in the case of disputes involving a party outside the region, third party adjudication is typically accepted by Southeast Asian countries only as an option of the last resort, and usually only in commercial matters that must be resolved in the manner expected by the commercial community. Curiously the reluctance to litigate at the international level is found also in the common law (but only mildly litigious) cultures of Singapore and Malaysia, although it seems strongest in the civil law countries of Indonesia and Thailand. Many Thais, of course, have bitter memories of the outcome of their government's reluctant decision to let the *Temple* dispute with Cambodia go to the International Court of Justice (ICJ). At the time of writing, however, it seems that Singapore and Malaysia may be willing to refer an island sovereignty dispute to the ICJ: see Hoang, *supra* note 125. A similar lawsuit has been entered by Malaysia and Indonesia.

the environment, and is therefore the most demanding indicator of the progress being achieved by the ASEAN countries toward the ultimate goal of sustainability.

On the other hand, to the extent the 1985 Agreement is visionary, idealistic, or aspirational, rather than operational in significance, a more realistic sense of policy development can be gained by tracking the ASEAN decisions and non-treaty declarations endorsed at the ministerial level. For example, two years after the 1985 Kuala Lumpur agreement, a meeting of ASEAN environment ministers adopted the Jakarta Resolution on Sustainable Development, which accepted the guiding principle of sustainable development "to serve as an integrating factor in their common efforts" (para. I), agreed to focus on issues of common concern, including (but not limited to) "the common seas, land resources and land-based pollution, tropical rainforests, air quality, and urban and rural pollution" (para. II), and suggested the establishment of a regional body on the environment of sufficient stature to recommend policy guidelines on the implementation of the principle of sustainable development and to perform related tasks.

More general environmental language was included later in 1987 in the text of the 1987 Manila Summit Declaration, and also in the Langkawi Declaration of 1989. In 1990 the Fourth ASEAN Meeting of Ministers for the Environment, held at Kuala Lumpur, tried once again to promote environmental action as a regional priority by pointing to the global effort to prepare for the UN Conference and Development (UNCED), which was scheduled to be held in Rio in two years' time. Reference was made to the need for "an ASEAN strategy for sustainable development and a corresponding action programme"[176] and for "a common ASEAN position" to be presented to the Ministerial Level Conference on the Environment for Asia and the Pacific before UNCED.[177]

However, the depth of political reluctance to move swiftly on environmental policy within certain sectors of ASEAN was more truly revealed in north-south contexts such as the Second Ministerial Conference of Developing Countries on Environment and Development, which was held at Kuala Lumpur in April 1992, just weeks before the convening of UNCED at Rio. In his opening speech, Prime Minister Mahathir of Malaysia used the occasion to mount an angry assault on the developed countries for their negotiating positions on various issues in preparation for UNCED, which he denounced as proof of a self-interested, exploitative strategy directed against the developing countries.[178] In the Kuala Lumpur Declaration on Environment and

176 1990 Kuala Lumpur Accord on Environment and Development, para. 1(a), text in Koh, *supra* note 174 at 65-67.

177 *Ibid.*, para. 4.

178 "Freedom is a commodity much touted by the North. Woe betide any country in the developing world which does not grant freedom to its citizens. Yet the North

Development, which was adopted at that meeting, more softly worded language expressed disappointment with the UNCED negotiations. For example, the delegations stressed that "sustainable development makes it incumbent on developed countries to take major steps to transform their production, consumption and distribution patterns towards environmentally sound development," whereas for developing countries "sustainable development implies the right to development with due regard to the ecological processes."[179] The Kuala Lumpur Declaration insisted that Agenda 21 programs should not be used "as a new form of conditionality in access to development support or any attempts to review national policies or strategies";[180] and it took a particularly strong position, in alignment with Malaysia, on forestry issues, emphasizing that "forest ecosystems and resources are part of the national patrimony to be managed, conserved and developed by each country in accordance with its national plans and priorities in the exercise of its sovereign rights."[181]

Certainly Southeast Asian agreement with these reservations was not confined to Malaysia. Yet perhaps a more accurate account of the majority sentiment within ASEAN on environmental policy issues was reflected in the Singapore Resolution on Environment and Development endorsed by the ASEAN Ministers Responsible for the Environment, who had met several months earlier in February 1992. In this document it was agreed to:

- introduce policy measures and promote institutional development that will encourage the integration of factors in all developmental processes
- work closely on the interrelated issues of environment and development
- cooperate in setting basic environmental quality standards and regulations at national level, work towards harmonized environmental quality standards in the region, and adopt long-term quantitative goals relating to ambient air quality and river water quality
- harmonize policy directions and step up operational and technical cooperation on environmental matters such as transboundary air and water pollution, natural disasters, forest fires, oil spills, and the transboundary

considers it right and proper to deprive the people in the developing countries of their freedom to exploit their own natural wealth. In campaigning against tropical timber and in boycotting it, they are denying us our freedom to make a living, to extract what little wealth we have, and to free ourselves from hunger, disease, and poverty": speech by Prime Minister Dr. Mahathir at the Official Opening of the Second Ministerial Conference of Developing Countries on Environment and Development, Kuala Lumpur, 27 Apr. 1992, para. 33. Dr. Mahathir's anger was provoked by foreign criticisms of Malaysia's forest management practices. For a study, see Murteza Mohamed and Chuan Ti-tieow, "Managing ASEAN's Forests: Deforestation in Sabah," in Seda, *supra* note 141.

179 Kuala Lumpur Declaration on Environment and Development, para. 7.

180 *Ibid.*, para. 10.

181 *Ibid.*, para. 15.

movements and disposal of toxic chemicals and hazardous wastes, and undertake joint actions to address the anti-tropical timber campaign.[182]

Special emphasis was given to several issue contexts of concern to ASEAN: for example, protection of the ecosystems of oceans and seas from pollution; protection of freshwater resources; sustainable management of all forests; conservation of biological diversity; and support for the Basel Convention on the Control of Transboundary Movements of Hazardous Wastes and their Disposal.[183]

After UNCED, the potential facilitative role of ASEAN in the environment field expanded under the shared commitment to promote the principles contained in the Rio Declaration on Environment and Development and to implement Agenda 21. To these ends, the ASEAN Ministers of the Environment agreed, in the 1994 Bandar Seri Begawan Resolution on Environment and Development, to (1) adopt and implement ASEP IV, the ASEAN Strategic Plan of Action on the Environment; (2) to broaden general awareness and public participation in the area of the environment; (3) to adopt a set of harmonized environmental quality standards for ambient air and river quality, and implement the needed measures to attain these standards by the year 2010; and (4) to strengthen cooperation among ASEAN countries to ensure "effective implementation of the decision of the Second Conference of the Parties" to the Basel Convention.[184]

The current ASEAN Strategic Plan of Action on the Environment for the 1994-98 period was prepared by the ASEAN Secretariat at the request of the Fourth Meeting of the ASEAN Senior Officials on the Environment (ASOEN) held in Bangkok in 1993. The Plan was designed to take into account the need to harmonize the objectives of ASEAN's various environment-related working groups to strengthen existing institutional arrangements, to identify regional priorities (including the environmental implications of AFTA, the ASEAN Free Trade Agreement), and to "establish ASOEN's position in international fora such as the Commission on Sustainable Development (CSD) and the Inter-Governmental Committee on the Convention on Biological Diversity (ICCBD)."[185] Of the ten strategies incorporated into this Plan, five are of particular relevance to the tasks of legal development and the ideal of convergence of the legal systems of the region in the environmental sector. First, Strategy 1 calls for the development of "a regional

182 Singapore Resolution on Environment and Development, 18 Feb. 1992, text reproduced in Koh, *supra* note 174 at 70-76.

183 *Ibid.* at 73-75.

184 Bandar Seri Begawan Resolution on Environment and Development, paras. 1-4, text reproduced in Koh, *supra* note 174 at 77-79.

185 ASEAN Strategic Plan of Action on the Environment, 1994-98, para. 3, text in *ibid.* at 182-230.

framework that will ensure the integration of environment and development concerns in the respective national decision-making processes," including "appropriate policies and legal frameworks."[186] Second, Strategy 4 emphasizes the objective of strengthening "institutional and legal capacities to implement international agreements on environment," to participate effectively in the review of existing international instruments and in the negotiation of new ones.[187] Third, legal development tasks are implicit, rather than explicit, in Strategy 5 to establish "a regional framework on biological diversity conservation and sustainable utilisation of its components";[188] in Strategy 6 to promote "the protection and management of coastal zones and marine resources";[189] and in Strategy 7 to promote "environmentally sound management of toxic chemicals and hazardous wastes, and control of transboundary movement of hazardous wastes."[190]

It should also be noted that earlier, during the period of ASEP III (1988-92), the first on the list of twelve projects designated as "very high priority" was the "comparative study of environmental law in ASEAN countries."[191] This task was not in fact accomplished at that time, but later, in 1996, an initiative was taken by the new Asia-Pacific Centre on Environmental Law of the National University of Singapore (APCEL), in collaboration with IUCN's Environmental Law Commission in Bonn, to undertake the training of environmental law teachers in the region on the basis of materials from the countries of ASEAN as well as international materials of global origin. The work of APCEL will also emphasize the kind of comparative environmental law research envisaged by ASEAN during ASEP III, albeit within the academic community. This kind of initiative is, of course, consistent with ASEAN's policy of broadening participation in the area of environment, one of the four objectives adopted under the 1994 Bandar Seri Begawan Resolution.

PROSPECTS

The Question of Values and Interests

The projection of environmental law development in Southeast Asia in the next decade must surely begin with the assumption that the region will continue to be driven by the vision of fast economic growth. Imported wisdom on the merit of sustainable development will not be allowed to change this overriding priority, particularly since the 1997 revelation of the region's

186 *Ibid.*, Executive Summary, para. 7, in *ibid.* at 183.
187 *Ibid.*, para. 10, in *ibid.* at 185.
188 *Ibid.*, para. 11, in *ibid.*
189 *Ibid.*, para. 12, in *ibid.* at 186.
190 *Ibid.*, para. 13, in *ibid.* at 187.
191 See Table I referred to in ASEAN Environment Programme III (ASEP), para. 29.

new vulnerability to foreign investor sentiment. Industry will not be easily shackled, and governments of the region may be even more reluctant than before to accept the costs of major environmental programs.

Singapore will be looked to by its ASEAN fellow members chiefly as a model of economic growth, especially since its status as the region's least vulnerable economy was recently reaffirmed. Although it could also serve as a model of environmental foresight, it will probably not. Even if this part of the Singaporean success story were equally admired, the greening of a city-state has only a limited relevance to the other, much larger, more ruralized, and less governable, countries of the region. Even those countries with strong leaders will continue to operate small and relatively inexpensive government systems that are either too small or too weak to maintain effective, top-down, regulatory regimes of the kind needed to implement and enforce stringent pollution control and other environmental policies.

Respect for nature is not deeply embedded in the psyche of the people of Southeast Asia. On the other hand, respect for education is, especially in the case of the Confucian cultures and increasingly elsewhere in the region as the lessons of the Asian economic miracle are absorbed.[192] Environmental values will have to be implanted in the educational systems of Southeast Asia, if enlightened environmental policy is to have room to grow. But the conversion of cultural attitude toward the environment will not be easy, given the financial rewards available for those who perform best at school with numbers.

How, then, if at all, can Southeast Asia be expected to respond to the environmental ethos of Brundtland and UNCED? To what extent can it be expected that the countries of this region will comply, reasonably or substantially, in the coming years with emergent norms and other concepts negotiated and apparently accepted at the global level of environmental diplomacy? These questions are complicated by the diversity of indicators available at four different levels of behaviour: the global level of diplomatic negotiation; the regional level of diplomatic consultation; the national level of environmental policy-making and legislation; and the household, local, industrial, or communal level of environmental practice. Each of these levels reflects a distinct combination of values and interests.

At the level of global diplomacy, there is clearly some evidence of tension between Western and Asian values in the environmental context, even if

---

192 An insightful foreign observer of the "tiger" economies of East Asia has suggested that the emphasis on basic schooling and total literacy has been a major factor in their "miracle." J. Rohwer, *Asia Rising* (New York: Simon and Schuster, 1995) at 56-57. But in most of these East Asian countries it was left primarily to families to finance their children's secondary and post-secondary education. Accordingly, the state in these countries has acquired little influence over the promotion of environmental education at these critically important levels.

one acknowledges the relative vagueness of the concept of "Asian," and perhaps also of "western." Yet there is also abundant evidence of willingness on the part of Southeast Asian (and other non-Western) states to engage in "alignment diplomacy" within the global diplomatic arena, even as they challenge the Western presumption of "leadership." Often, it seems, it is not values but national interests – political, economic, and strategic – that determine whether a state will accept the suggested language in draft treaties and other international instruments. Under the interest pressures generated in the arena, developing non-Western states are usually obliged to accept the fact of at least political commitment to the compromise or consensus language that eventually emerges as the outcome of global negotiations over issues perceived as having a north-south dimension. The actual significance of such commitment remains to be determined in the light of interests and values that may have a greater impact at the other sub-global levels: interests and values that are detached from the culture of professional diplomacy, which tends to reflect the ethic and energy of system convergence. The apparent advantage of non-binding instruments like Agenda 21 is that these other determinative, sub-global, interests and values are ostensibly given less scope to intervene in the absence of a post-arena mechanism such as treaty ratification.[193]

At the level of regional consultation, such as that practised within ASEAN, greater weight is likely to be given to intra-regional sensitivities than is normally possible within the global arena, where the countries of Southeast Asia are often pulled in two or more different directions. At the global level, the question is often whether to be seen to be (at least weakly) committed to a particular course of policy development, and thus to live with rather diffuse international standards of accountability. At the regional level of ASEAN, a closer degree of bonding is usually called for, and a higher degree of care may be taken in crafting the language of collective pledges where national reputation is more regularly on the line. On certain issues, such as deforestation and the role of the lending institutions, ASEAN-style bonding may be made more difficult by the necessity to become engaged in other, more complicated or more polemical, regional fora such as those of the developing countries in general, or of Asia-Pacific or APEC. It may not be easy, in certain contexts, to avoid giving the impression of offering

193 The general view of the role of ratification under the international law of treaties is that it affords to a signatory state the sovereign prerogative of withholding its final formal consent, if it finds in the last analysis that the national interest – or more often a combination of special interests – is not served by granting consent. In the case of a non-binding instrument, the opportunity to avoid commitment does not arise, but an "ethical" non-binding instrument like Agenda 21 may be more popular in civil society than it is in government circles, where the right to grant or withhold consent resides.

different postures in two or more regional fora. The exact commitment one ends up with may owe more to the dynamics of negotiation within the particular arena than to one's actual national policy. Where does policy reside? If policy is inferred chiefly or partly from a combination of negotiated commitments, the coexistence of multiple regional arenas with the global arena adds to the problem of precise policy identification. On environmental issues, the governments of highly developed countries with strong environmental NGOs may find that consistent pressure from the latter may help them to maintain a higher degree of consistency than is easily maintained by the governments of developing countries.

The national level of legislation is usually regarded, at least by lawyers and most government officials, as the crucial level of policy-making. In this orthodox or official view of things, it is assumed that environmental policy should be articulated in statutory, or even constitutional, form, as if legal form were the best or only reflector of environmental practice or reality. In fact, the national level of behaviour almost always presents the most complicated, and often the most sensitive, array of competing interests and even conflicting values. But national political cultures vary enormously in their capacity to accommodate these differences, and different environmental issues have widely varying impacts within each national society. Singapore may be one of the few countries that can usually enact environmental legislation, or at least pollution control legislation, with a high degree of assurance that these laws, especially those that impinge directly on a target industry, will be obeyed. In most other countries of Southeast Asia, national environmental legislation tends to be either weak, when it reflects the difficulty of effecting top-down enforcement or bottom-up compliance, or aspirational, when it reflects an overly bold course of policy that simply cannot be delivered at the operational level of environmental practice. The operational significance of environmental legislation is, to a very large extent, the product of legal culture,[194] and legal cultures vary so widely within the legal mosaic of

194 One experienced consultant, who has been actively involved in the effort to promote environmental law in Thailand, Malaysia, and the Philippines, explains the frustrations by reference to the basic characteristics of these legal cultures. In Thailand, he suggests, text may be of little importance. The 1974 Constitution of that country devoted eight articles to the importance of maintaining environmental integrity, but there was no mention of the environment in the 1976 and 1977 Constitutions. Nevertheless, environmental problems have been taken more seriously since 1976! J. N. Shane, "Environmental Law in the Developing Nations of Southeast Asia," in MacAndrews and Chia, *supra* note 48, 15 at 17. Thailand, he suggests, tends to be "naturally resistant to the imposition of new regulatory controls. As a result, the regulation of environmentally significant activities in Thailand has traditionally relied more heavily on negotiation than on strict, inflexible enforcement": *ibid.* at 21-22. In such a setting the utility of modern legal instruments "may be questionable, at least in the near term": *ibid.* at 22. Malaysians and Filipinos, on the other hand, are "likely to accept rigorous administrative requirement more readily and mandatory penalties might therefore produce results in both countries": *ibid.* Deforestation he cites as "the

Southeast Asia that the evidence of convergence and of non-convergence must be looked for at community, industrial, local, and even household levels of behaviour: at the level of "living laws."[195]

Modern formal environmental laws, both of the weak and aspirational kinds, usually arise in response to bold, culturally blind or economically controversial commitments negotiated and accepted by the state at the global level under the pressures of the diplomatic arena. The prospect of persuading interest holders and value bearers outside government to accept such laws, and to adapt their behaviour accordingly, seems to depend on such factors as public education and participation, local community involvement, capacity-building, governmental sophistication, political courage, a willingness to tolerate a degree of civic dissent, and a bureaucratic capacity to innovate experimentally with programs of decentralization. In some Southeast Asian countries, some progress is in evidence: the media have assumed an increasingly important role in public education;[196] environmental NGOs are becoming more sophisticated in both the internal and external politics of the environment;[197] governments are being forced to acquiesce in certain, reasonable modes of conditionality imposed by lending institutions, if not by trading partners;[198] and courage, sophistication, and ingenuity might seem to be on the increase as a result of constant reinforcement of environmental commitments and ideas through participation on numerous international networks, both formal and informal.[199] On the whole, moderate environmentalists may be justified in placing their faith in the prospect of steady incremental progress toward the goal of sustainability.

Strategies of Commitment and Inducement to Comply

In the light of the above views, it seems that the most realistic strategy for

---

best example of a problem attributable less to the inherent deficiency of legal structure than to the unwillingness or inability of the governments concerned to enforce the existing measures adequately": *ibid.* at 29.

195 Sociologists and anthropologists have not quite abandoned the effort to convince lawyers that unwritten informal laws may come closer to reflecting reality than those of the formal written sort.

196 See e.g. Ubonrat, *supra* note 115.

197 See generally Finger and Princen, *supra* note 35, and Parnwell and Bryant, *supra* note 35.

198 It seems easier to argue convincingly that business (or sport or entertainment) should not be treated as a part of politics than to argue that lenders are not entitled to impose reasonable or principled conditions on their willingness to lend. On the other hand, lending by a world community institution like the World Bank might be distinguished from commercial lending on the ground that the former is constrained as a mode of assistance based on the "right to development."

199 If it is true that professional diplomacy tends to breed like-mindedness, then it may be that "track-two" diplomacy organized under non-governmental auspices serves to bring in new ideas from outside and also encourage new thinking by government officials who are off-the-record.

cultivating sophisticated and effective environmental policy and legislation in Southeast Asia, in accordance with worldwide commitments, is through environmental education coordinated under ASEAN auspices. An educational approach is a slow approach to any difficult problem, but the idea that there may be an environmental "fast track" seems unrealistic. ASEAN is, first and foremost, a system of consultation built around economic priorities. Foreign policy and defence policy issues come second and third. Environment is somewhat lower, perhaps on a par with education. By combining forces, the ASEAN Ministers of Environment and Education may have a better chance of influencing regional economic policy-making than the Ministers of Environment can on their own. Environment tends to generate a huge volume of official documentation, disproportionate to the impact that it is likely to have on environmental practice. The problem is getting from policy on paper to action in practice.

The suggested emphasis on education seems to condemn the region to slow action on the environmental front, but it may not be as slow as it sounds. One of the most striking features of the Asian economic miracle is the speed with which the educational systems of the "tiger" economies of East Asia were adapted to the overriding objective of economic growth. With the sad exception of Thailand, the more affluent countries of Southeast Asia have devoted more money to primary and secondary education than to any other sector of social welfare, and through education have moved with pace toward the formation of a substantial middle class.[200]

Although ASEAN does not seem perfectly equipped to take the lead in environmental affairs in Southeast Asia, it is difficult to identify an alternative forum with better credentials. The APEC forum gives at least as much priority to economic issues as ASEAN and is too heterogeneous to provide an environmental focus. Canada as a member of APEC is trying to foster a sense of environmental priorities within this grouping and hopes that Singapore might be willing to join it in this initiative, but Asian APEC member states have displayed reluctance to blur the focus on economic issues.

As to the problem of inducement to comply with environmental treaty and legislative commitments, the prospects are also bleak. The prevalence of weak and aspirational legislation is a feature of most countries of the region. If the solution to the implementation problem depended entirely on enforcement and other forms of negative sanctioning, then pessimism would be justified. Experience in southern Europe has shown, however, that a judicious combination of positive and negative sanctions – of carrots and sticks – can be very effective in bringing about a high level of nationwide

200 This is one of the themes developed in Rohwer, *supra* note 192.

awareness of environmental concerns, and even reform the traditional set of cultural attitudes.[201]

Despite these discouragements, it must be supposed that the raising of environmental standards in Southeast Asia depends to a large extent on the successful promotion of the idea of convergence of laws and standards at the regional level. If the legal systems of East Asia are looked at as a single phenomenon, it is unlikely that convergence can be predicted simply because of cultural affinity or economic comparability.[202] But in the specific context of environmental law, legal systems that are otherwise resistant to pressures to conform might be expected to be pulled gradually in the direction of compatibility, even if only as a result of environmental conditions imposed externally on development assistance projects and of the trickle-down effects of global diplomacy.

Finally, one returns to the question of "sacred text." In Southeast Asia, perhaps only the Indonesian culture might be receptive to the idea of a revered text that would encapsulate the ethos of sustainability and related constructs of the 1990s.[203] It may simply be beyond the political capacity and imagination of the leaderships represented at ASEAN meetings to rally around such an initiative. "Pragmatism" is still in vogue as the favourite brand of wisdom. Yet the challenge of negotiating an eloquent Declaration of Environmental Responsibility, which could assume an ethical status in all the cultures of the region, would be a bold stroke that could stir the hearts and minds of the peoples of Southeast Asia and give their political leaders a unique sense of collective purpose and commitment.[204]

---

201 In 1982 a few Greek oil tanker owners led by George P. Livanos initiated a nationwide campaign to clean up the seas, or specifically the Mediterranean. After focusing initially on the human factor (mistake and negligence), this organization, the Hellenic Marine Environment Protection Association (HELMEPA) shifted its emphasis to the motivation of individuals, recognizing the limitations of laws, rules, and regulations. The success of HELMEPA has led to the foundation of similar initiatives in Cyprus (CYMEPA) and Turkey (TURMEPA). Not the least of HELMEPA's achievements is its public awareness campaign with its special focus on environmental education for school children, including its project "HELMEPA Junior" aimed at children aged 8-13. Like HELMEPA, CYMEPA has endorsed an Action Plan, which includes research objectives. TURMEPA plans to become involved primarily with efforts to combat the threat of land-based marine pollution. All three contribute to legal development by promoting relevant marine pollution control agreements.

202 A. B. L. Phang, "Convergence and Divergence: A Preliminary Comparative Analysis of the Singapore and Hong Kong Legal Systems" (1993) 23 Hong Kong L.J. 1.

203 See e.g the idealism represented in Danusoputro Sutan Munadjat, *Towards an ASEAN Environmental Law* (Jakarta: Binacipta, 1984). The idea of concerted policy development under some kind of inspirational guidance seems implicit in much of the literature that looks at Southeast Asian environmental problems from a comparative regional perspective. See e.g. L. S. Chia, ed., *Environmental Management in Southeast Asia: Directions and Current Status* (Singapore: Nat. Univ. of Singapore, 1987).

204 Phang, *supra* note 202.

10
Indigenous Peoples and the Law: The Colonial Legacy in Australia, Canada, New Zealand, and the United States

*Hamar Foster**

> The law is a hard, queer thing. I do not understand it.
> – Poundmaker, a Cree chief, addressing the court at his trial for treason, 17 August 1885

INTRODUCTION

Colonial Law

The colonization process in the four countries listed in the title of this essay was an unavoidably painful one. It usually involved repression, it often led to violence, and it occasionally ended in extinction. In the United States, for example, the Indian tribes tenaciously resisted being removed to reservations, and fought wars against the U.S. cavalry throughout much of the nineteenth century.[1] In New Zealand, Maori warriors battled settler and imperial troops on and off from the 1840s through the 1860s, with some pockets of resistance holding out much longer.[2]

Although – with the exception of the Riel Rebellion of 1885 – this sort of large-scale military resistance did not occur in Canada and Australia, there was violent conflict in those countries as well.[3] The effects of such conflict,

---

* The author would like to thank Steve McKeon for his research assistance with respect to New Zealand and Australian case law.

1 See *inter alia* D. Brown, *Bury My Heart at Wounded Knee: An Indian History of the American West* (New York: Henry Holt, 1970) and R. H. Glassley, *Indian Wars of the Pacific Northwest* (Portland: Binfords and Mort, 1972).

2 For details, see K. Sinclair, *The Origins of the Maori Wars* (Auckland: New Zealand Univ. Press, 1957) and J. Belich, *The Victorian Interpretation of Racial Conflict. The Maori, the British, and the New Zealand Wars* (Montreal: McGill-Queen's Univ. Press, 1989).

3 Massacres of Aborigines took place with disturbing regularity in Australia, and in British Columbia gunboats often laid waste to coastal Indian villages in order to enforce compliance with the law, usually to induce the inhabitants to hand over alleged criminals. See e.g. J. Bassett, "The Faithful Massacre at the Broken River, 1838" (1989) 24 J. of Australian Studies, 18-34; S. B. Harring, "The Killing Time: A History of Aboriginal Resistance in Australia" [1994] 26 Ottawa L. Rev. 385; and B. Gough, *Gunboat Frontier:*

and of the disease and social dislocation that inevitably accompanied imperial expansion, were just as devastating. As a consequence, aboriginal populations entered the twentieth century in a stricken state. Some, notably the Beothuks of Newfoundland, the Aborigines of Tasmania and some American tribes, did not enter it at all.[4]

As Chief Poundmaker clearly suspected, law was an important part of these highly successful and costly attempts to displace aboriginal people. It was also deeply implicated in much less successful (but equally costly) attempts to assimilate them. Indeed, some years before and thousands of miles to the southwest of Saskatchewan, a Maori leader made an observation about the colonial process in New Zealand that was not unlike Poundmaker's. Aproro, a Ngati Maniapoto chief, complained that the law of the English was "a bad dog [that] devours many."[5]

Such laments reflect the fact that the law was believed to lay down three important things about colonization: that upon contact aboriginal people had lost their sovereignty;[6] that upon contact aboriginal people had either ceased to have any rights in their lands, or at least could no longer sell their lands to anyone but the new government;[7] and that upon contact traditional means of dispute resolution and resource allocation among Aboriginal people had either been swept away, or soon would be.[8] Because these propositions, if true, rendered legal what would otherwise have been naked usurpation, they conferred a measure of respectability upon the colonization process. Ironically, this was even true in the United States, where by the early 1830s the Supreme Court had significantly modified at least two of them.[9] As Alexis de Toqueville put it, people in the United States

---

British Maritime Authority and Northwest Coast Indians, 1846-1890 (Vancouver: U.B.C. Press, 1984).

4 In his annual message for 1851, California Governor Peter H. Burnett stated "[t]hat a war of extermination will continue to be waged between the two races until the Indian race becomes extinct, must be expected" (quoted in R. F. Heizer and A. F. Almquist, *The Other Californians: Prejudice and Discrimination under Spain, Mexico, and the United States to 1920* (Berkeley: Univ. of California Press, 1971) at 26. On the Beothuks, see L. F. S. Upton, "The Extermination of the Beothuks of Newfoundland," in R. Fisher and K. Coates, eds., *Out of the Background: Readings on Canadian Native History* (Toronto: Copp Clark Pitman, 1988) at 45-65.

5 Quoted in D. V. Williams, "The Subordination of Maori Social Formations, New Zealand 1840-1894" (Ph.D. Dissertation, Law, Univ. of Dar es Salaam, 1983) c. 3.

6 See art. 1 of the English version of the Treaty of Waitangi, 1840 (New Zealand); *Mabo v. Queensland (No. 2)* (1992), 175 C.L.R. 1 (H.C.) (Australia); *R. v. Sparrow* (1990), 56 C.C.C. (3d) 263 at 283 (S.C.C.) (Canada); and contrast the rather different view of the Supreme Court of the United States in *Worcester v. Georgia*, 31 U.S. (6 Pet.) 515 (1832).

7 See art. 2 of the Treaty of Waitangi, as interpreted (New Zealand); *Mabo v. Queensland (No. 2)*, *supra* note 6 (Australia); the Royal Proclamation of 1763 (U.K.), R.S.C. 1985, Appendix II, No. 1 (Canada); and *Johnson v. M'Intosh* 21 U.S. (8 Wheat.) 543 (1823) (United States).

8 This was more of a corollary than an explicit legal proposition.

9 See "Trends in Civic and Economic Law," *infra*.

possessed a peculiar and "chaste affection for legal formalities." Spain, he declared, had tried to exterminate the Indians but had not even succeeded in preventing them from having rights; Americans, on the other hand, had "attained both these results with wonderful ease, quietly, legally, and philanthropically ... It is impossible to destroy men with more respect to the laws of humanity."[10]

Whatever the truth of that observation, it is clear that the law was an important part of the cycle of resistance and response in all four jurisdictions. As a New Zealand bishop concluded in 1845, colonial government for the Maori had become "a thing of soldiers, barracks, constables and gaols," and similar observations may be found in archives in Australia, Canada, and the United States.[11] But, for colonization to have this leaden effect, it was not necessary that it involve such obvious excesses as the bombardment of Indian villages, as in British Columbia, or the periodic massacres that occurred in Australia and the United States.[12] It was enough that, whether aboriginal title was being legally extinguished (as in the United States, New Zealand, and parts of Canada) or simply ignored (as in Australia and other parts of Canada), the law was seen to have put its imprimatur upon the marginalization and assimilation of whole peoples, languages, and cultures.[13]

Yet, most tribes survived, and so did powerful feelings of loss and determination. Just as important, by the third decade or so of the twentieth century the plummeting aboriginal populations of the Pacific Rim had bottomed

---

10 A. de Toqueville, *Democracy in America* (Garden City: Doubleday, 1969) at 324.

11 Bishop G. A. Selwyn to Governor Fitzroy in Nov. 1845, quoted in P. Adams, *Fatal Necessity: British Intervention in New Zealand 1830-1847* (Auckland: Auckland Univ. Press, 1977) at 233. An exception may be the role that the North West Mounted Police played in defeating the whisky trade on the Canadian prairies during the 1870s. The Indians of that region appear to have been genuinely grateful for such protection, although relations deteriorated once non-aboriginal settlement began to increase. See generally P. F. Sharp, *Whoop-Up Country: The Canadian-American West* (Norman: Univ. of Oklahoma Press, 1973).

12 See notes 3 and 4, *supra*. With respect to the situation in British Columbia, Gilbert Malcolm Sproat, who was Indian reserve commissioner from 1876 to 1880, asked: "What would be said if a white Nova Scotian village were bombarded and plundered by one of Her Majesty's ships on the obligation [sic?] of policemen that they had been roughly treated in attempting to arrest an alleged criminal in the village?" (quoted in T. Loo, "Tonto's Due: Law, Culture, and Colonization in British Columbia," in H. Foster and J. McLaren, eds., *Essays in the History of Canadian Law, vol. VI: British Columbia and the Yukon* (Toronto: The Osgoode Society, 1995) 128 at 158 (note).

13 As an old Maori saying has it, "'Let's assimilate' is what the shark said to the *kahawai* [a salmon-like fish] before he ate him for breakfast" (quoted in P. G. McHugh, *Maori Land Laws of New Zealand: Two Essays* (Saskatoon: Univ. of Sask. Native Law Centre, 1983) at 39.

Although the correct phrase in the United States is "Indian title" and "Indian law," and although Australians and New Zealanders speak of "Native title," in most contexts the more generic "aboriginal title" and "aboriginal law" will be used in this essay.

out. By the seventh decade, their leaders were renewing the struggle to redress the past and, ironically, were using the same legal system that had oppressed them to assert both their sovereignty and their title.

The Sectors of Legal Development

This aspect of the colonization process is one reason that legal development for indigenous peoples has been inextricably bound up with addressing historical grievances. As a consequence, important and strategic questions arise about (1) the extent to which rights and remedies laid down a hundred or two hundred years ago should be re-interpreted today and (2) the extent to which reliance should be placed upon the law of the settler state, as opposed to other, less genteel means of changing the status quo.[14] Legal development for indigenous populations is also "cross-sectoral" in a way that distinguishes it from many of the other topics considered in this book. That is to say, the behavioural aspects of law – for example, crime and punishment, custody and adoption, and family law generally – are very closely related not only to questions of sovereignty, self-government and diversity (the civic sector), but also to economic issues such as resource development, trade, and the transfer of property, both *inter vivos* and by testate or intestate succession.[15] Evidence of such interconnectedness is legion, but one recent example must suffice.

In 1992 the British Columbia government appointed the Cariboo-Chilcotin Justice Inquiry to report upon the unhappy relationship between the justice system and the Chilcotin, Shuswap, and Carrier peoples of the central part of the province. The commissioner, Judge Anthony Sarich, soon discovered that aboriginal complaints were not simply about the police and the courts, but "about all non-native authority structures bearing on their lives. These complaints are long-standing and insistent. They are a product of a conflict of cultural values and beliefs and are driven by the past and present conduct of non-native authority figures. And these complaints go back to the first contact with Europeans."[16]

Judge Sarich also found that, notwithstanding the narrow focus of his inquiry,[17] all the people who appeared before him "brought up the issues of land claims, resource management, and control of their own lives," and

---

14 With respect to the first issue see C. F. Wilkinson, *American Indians, Time, and the Law: Native Societies in a Modern Constitutional Democracy* (New Haven: Yale Univ. Press, 1987) and H. Foster, "Canadian Indians, Time, and the Law" (1994) 7 Western Legal History 69.

15 See e.g. the very elaborate provisions of the Canadian *Indian Act* dealing with status and wills, provisions which have been argued to be relevant to land claims cases.

16 *Report on the Cariboo-Chilcotin Justice Inquiry* (Ministry of the Attorney General, B.C., 1993) at 26.

17 *Ibid.* at 48 (terms of reference, item(n)).

expressed a particular bitterness about what they regarded as the theft of their lands. The Chilcotins were also angry and resentful about an event that had taken place in their territories nearly 130 years earlier: the hanging of several of their chiefs for making war against the government.[18]

Such feelings about land and self-determination are not restricted to British Columbia, or to Canada, or to the other three Pacific Rim jurisdictions.[19] They are in fact typical of indigenous people the world over, and they provide a context for the demands for change in the behavioural sector that are increasingly heard today. Indeed, such demands are best seen as a logical outcome of the desire for self-government that is most apparent in Canada and the United States, but that also exists, in a somewhat different context, in both Australia and New Zealand. So before examining some aspects of legal development in the behavioural sector, it is necessary first to look at the civic and economic setting in which aboriginal rights (as these matters now tend to be called) are debated. Accordingly, the next section outlines the history and the constitutional position of indigenous peoples in Canada, the United States, Australia, and New Zealand, and the extent to which their land title and governmental powers have been protected.

TRENDS IN CIVIC AND ECONOMIC LAW

National Experience

With the possible exception of Australia, in all the jurisdictions under consideration the fact that indigenous people inhabited particular territories and were organized into societies was acknowledged.[20] It had to be. Not only did early settlers often depend upon the superior knowledge and survival skills of the aboriginal inhabitants; they also had to live with the possibility of armed attack and even annihilation should they show insufficient respect for their hosts' lands and culture. Moreover, European participants

---

18 *Ibid.* at 8 and 26. At least, to the Chilcotins it was war, because they had not accepted the sovereignty of the Crown. Legally, the colonial government regarded their attacks as murder, purely a criminal matter. For a recent account see T. Loo, "The Road from Bute Inlet: Crime and Colonial Identity in British Columbia," in J. Phillips, T. Loo, and S. Lewthwaite, eds., *Essays in the History of Criminal Law, vol. V: Crime and Criminal Justice* (Toronto: The Osgoode Society, 1994) 112-42.

19 For example, in Australia Commissioner Elliot Johnson, Q.C., concluded that "the desire and capacity of Aboriginal people to put an end to their disadvantaged situation and to take control of their own lives" was the first and foremost prerequisite of aboriginal empowerment: Royal Commission Into Aboriginal Deaths in Custody, *National Report* (Canberra: A.G.P.S., 1991) vol. 1 at 16, quoted in F. Brennan, "Self-Determination: The Limits of Allowing Aboriginal Communities to be a Law unto Themselves" (1993) 16 U.N.S.W. L. J. 245 at 253.

20 See *Calder et al. v. A.G. British Columbia* (1973), 34 D.L.R. (3d) 145 at 156 (S.C.C.), where it stated that "the fact is that when the settlers came, the Indians were there, organized in societies and occupying the land as their forefathers had done for centuries. This is what Indian title means."

in the economic enterprises that preceded settlement, notably the fur trade in North America, needed the aboriginal societies and cultures that made these enterprises possible. For many advocates of emigration to the colonies, this aspect of the fur trade was a sore point. As one English newspaper put it in 1848, the Hudson's Bay Company only wanted "beavers and sables to multiply, hunting grounds to be preserved, and hunters and trappers to thrive. Their function is to perpetuate what it should be the aim of a colony to destroy."[21]

Land and self-governance rights also came to receive varying degrees of recognition and, however reluctantly, legal protection; but the shape this protection took depended upon the relative strength of the aboriginal and settler populations, how these populations perceived each other, and the state of European legal theory (the aboriginal rights component of which dates back to the first Spanish colonies) at the relevant time.[22] It also depended upon how prepared governments were to make the law in the books both clear and well known, and to ensure that it corresponded with what was happening on the ground.

Canada

For the first 150 years or so of its European history, Canada was a French possession. This changed when Britain defeated France in the French and Indian War;[23] as a consequence, Canada and what would soon become the United States shared a short (1763-76) but nonetheless important period of joint subjection to the British Crown and English law. The most significant legal product of this common inheritance for present purposes is the Royal Proclamation of 1763.[24]

A blueprint for the establishment of the new British colonies of Grenada, East and West Florida, and Quebec, the Proclamation laid down two principles respecting aboriginal peoples that proved to be of lasting importance. The first was that lands inhabited by aboriginal peoples are, even after the assertion of British sovereignty, "Indian territory," and that the title of "Nations or Tribes" under that sovereignty should not be "molested or disturbed." The second was that, with the possible exception of seizure

21 *The [London] Times* (21 Aug. 1848).

22 For example, Sir Robert Peel confided in 1848 that if "the obligations of good faith vary with the military skill and prowess of the parties to a Treaty, the [Maori] have put in a claim to be respected which it has become prudent on our part to recognize" (quoted in Adams, *supra* note 11 at 245). On the Spanish pedigree of aboriginal rights law, see F. S. Cohen, "The Spanish Origin of Indian Rights in the Law of the United States" (1941) 31 Georgetown L. J. 1.

23 Known in Europe as the Seven Years War (1756-63).

24 See *supra* note 7 and, most recently, D. Schulze, "The Privy Council Decision Concerning George Allsopp's Petition, 1767: An Imperial Precedent on the Application of the Royal Proclamation to the Old Province of Quebec," [1995] 2 C.N.L.R. 1.

through conquest, aboriginal lands cannot be made available for sale or grant to European settlers until the indigenous occupiers have surrendered their interest in the lands to a lawful representative of the Crown, at a "public Meeting or Assembly" held for that purpose.

As worded, the Proclamation's aboriginal provisions did not apply to all colonies in existence at that time, and some courts have inferred that they also do not apply to colonies established afterwards.[25] Moreover, it was subject to repeal by the Imperial Parliament, and much of it could be repealed even by the Crown acting alone.[26]

Nonetheless, the ideas contained in the Proclamation form the basis of the doctrine of aboriginal title and are responsible for the treaty process in the century or so following the American Revolutionary War. When this phase came to an end in the 1920s, all of Canada except for Quebec, the maritime provinces, the Yukon, most of British Columbia and part of the Northwest Territories was subject to treaties in which First Nations ceded their aboriginal title to vast tracts of land. In return, they received reserves or promises of reserves, annuities, fishing and hunting rights over the ceded territory, and various other benefits. Provincial intransigence, the Great Depression, and the Second World War suspended the treaty process for many years, but resource development pressures (especially in the James Bay area of Quebec) and the Supreme Court of Canada's decision in *Calder v. Attorney-General of British Columbia* re-started it.[27] A number of modern treaties or land claims agreements (as they are now called) have since been made in northern Quebec, Yukon, and the Northwest Territories, and a unique, trilateral process has been put in place in British Columbia.[28]

The Royal Proclamation of 1763 is not the only constitutional provision that is relevant to aboriginal rights issues in Canada. The federation dates from 1867, when, by virtue of the *British North America Act* (*BNA Act*),[29] what became the provinces of Ontario, Quebec, New Brunswick, and Nova Scotia united to form the Dominion of Canada. Section 91(24) of the *BNA Act* provided that the new central government would have exclusive legislative

---

25 Thus in *Delgamuukw v. British Columbia* (1993), 104 D.L.R. (4th) 470, the British Columbia Court of Appeal ruled that the Royal Proclamation did not apply to that province because the Indians there were not "connected" to the Crown in 1763.

26 See *Campbell v. Hall* (1774), 98 E.R. 848 (K.B.), holding that the Crown's undertaking that the colonies created by the Royal Proclamation of 1763 were entitled to representative government could be rescinded only by Parliament.

27 *Supra* note 20.

28 See generally K. Coates, ed., *Aboriginal Land Claims in Canada: A Regional Perspective* (Toronto: Copp Clark Pitman, 1992); on the B.C. process, see the B.C. *Treaty Commission Act*, S.B.C. 1993, c. 4, the Treaty Commission's regular reports, and the recent Report of the Select Standing Committee of the Legislature on Aboriginal Affairs (Victoria: 1997) dealing with the Nisga'a Agreement in Principle and its implications for the treaty process.

29 30-31 Vict. (1867), c. 3 (U.K.) (now the *Constitution Act, 1867*).

jurisdiction over "Indians, and Lands reserved for the Indians," so it was the dominion rather than the provincial governments that made the post-confederation treaties.[30] Two things are worth noting about this. The first is that, instead of viewing s. 91(24) simply as designating the level of government that would enter into relationships with Canada's First Nations, policy makers saw it as subjecting aboriginal people to near-total federal control. Pursuant to this authority, Parliament passed the *Indian Act* of 1876,[31] which formalized a civic and economic framework for almost every aspect of the civil life of those subject to it and initiated a century of regulation and subordination. Needless to say, such an interpretation limits or even prevents Indian bands from claiming "constitutional space" to enact laws other than those authorized by the *Indian Act*.[32] It is therefore increasingly contentious.

The second point worth noting is that s. 91(24) of the *BNA Act* must be read with s. 109, which acknowledges that the provinces control Crown land within their borders. Beginning with the *St. Catherine's* case in 1888,[33] the courts interpreted this to mean that, insofar as land within a province is concerned, although the dominion government has to make the treaties, a surrender of the Indian title conveys nothing to the dominion; it merely removes a burden on the underlying provincial title. Carrying out treaty promises to create Indian reserves within a province therefore became a

30 Pre-confederation land cession treaties were made in Upper Canada (Ontario) and on Vancouver Island; there were also a few treaties in Quebec and the maritime provinces, but these did not involve land cessions. For their legal effect, see *R. v. Simon* (1985), 23 C.C.C. (3d) 238 (S.C.C.) and *R. v. Sioui* (1990), 56 C.C.C. (3d) 225 (S.C.C.).

31 S.C. 1876, c. 18. This Act and its successors apply only to so-called status Indians, i.e. those who fit the statutory definition. It therefore does not apply to Inuit (Eskimos), Métis, and many others who regard themselves as aboriginal. The rather different question of whether Inuit are "Indians" for the purposes of s. 91(24) was answered in the affirmative in *Re Eskimos*, [1939] S.C.R. 104. Had it been enacted, the Charlottetown Accord of 1992 (see following note) would have clarified that Métis, who are aboriginal people for the purposes of s. 35 of the *Constitution Act, 1982* are also "Indians" in this sense.

32 The quoted phrase is from K. McNeil, "Envisaging Constitutional Space for Aboriginal Governments" (1993) 19 Queen's L. J. 95. In *Delgamuukw*, *supra* note 25, the B.C. Court of Appeal ruled that the division of legislative jurisdiction between Ottawa and the provinces that was laid down by the *British North America Act*, 1867, was exhaustive, and left no room for inherent powers of aboriginal self-government. This decision, however, may have been influenced by the fate of the Charlottetown Accord. The Accord, which was the product of the unanimous agreement of the federal government, the ten provinces, the two territories, and four aboriginal organizations, had recommended that the constitution be amended to specifically recognize the inherent right of self government. This was part of an all-or-nothing package of constitutional amendments that was defeated in a nation-wide referendum in 1992. See also *infra* note 41.

33 See *St. Catherine's Milling and Lumber Co. v. The Queen* (1888), 2 C.N.L.C. 541 (J.C.P.C.). See also *Ontario Mining Co. v. Seybold* (1902), 3 C.N.L.C. 203 (J.C.P.C.) and *A.G. Quebec v. A.G. Canada*, [1921] 1 A.C. 401 (J.C.P.C.) (the *Star Chrome Mining* case).

complicated process that was difficult to complete without the cooperation of that province.[34] Such cooperation was not always forthcoming.[35]

Still, by the early 1980s the modern land claims process was well under way, and aboriginal title was conceded to be inherent, in the sense that its legal status did not depend upon state recognition; such title was, however, vulnerable to unilateral extinguishment by the federal Parliament.[36] Aboriginal sovereignty, on the other hand, was not acknowledged; powers of governance enjoyed by Indian bands were seen as contingent – that is, they did not flow from any inherent right of self-government. They were instead the product of federal delegation, notably the bylaw-making authority conferred upon Indian band councils by the *Indian Act*. Moreover, Indians were subject not only to that Act and to federal law generally, but also to provincial law, so long as the provinces did not attempt to legislate specifically in relation to Indians or their lands.[37]

Then, in April of 1982, Canada made some major constitutional changes. One of these was the passage of s. 35(1) of the *Constitution Act, 1982*, which provides that "existing aboriginal and treaty rights of Canada's aboriginal peoples are hereby recognized and confirmed."[38] A year later this was amended to include rights already acknowledged by land claims agreements and rights that "may be so acquired."[39] The legal result is that aboriginal and treaty rights that were not validly extinguished before 1982 are now constitutionalized – that is, they are beyond the reach of the federal as well as the provincial legislatures, although in exceptional circumstances Parliament may regulate the exercise of an aboriginal right.[40] One of the questions this raises is whether s. 35(1) recognizes and affirms an aboriginal right of self-government and, if so, what the content and territorial scope of

34 This was in marked contrast to the federal treaties made on the prairies, where Ottawa retained title to all public lands until 1930, long after the creation of the prairie provinces; and to the land claims agreements made in the 1980s and 1990s north of 60°, in the federal territories.

35 For example, the provincial government did not acknowledge complete federal authority over Indian reserves in British Columbia until 1938: see *B.C. (A.G.) v. Mount Currie Indian Band* (1991), 54 B.C.L.R. (2d) 156 (C.A.), especially the dissenting judgment of Southin J.A. For commentary, see H. Foster, "Road Blocks and Legal History," Parts I and II in (1996) 54 The Advocate 355 and 531.

36 *Calder*, *supra* note 20, established that aboriginal title existed independently of formal state recognition (e.g. by statute, treaty, etc.), and any lingering doubts about this were removed in *Guerin v. R.*, [1984] 6 W.W.R. 481 (S.C.C.).

37 For a succinct discussion of this complex area of Indian law and s. 88 of the *Indian Act*, a key provision, see P. W. Hogg, *Constitutional Law of Canada*, 3rd ed. (Toronto: Carswell, 1992) at 663-78.

38 Schedule B to the *Canada Act* (U.K., 1982, c. 11). "Aboriginal peoples" are defined as including the Inuit, Indian, and Métis peoples.

39 *Constitution Amendment Proclamation, 1983*, s. 2. [now s. 35(3) of the *Constitution Act, 1982*].

40 See *Sparrow*, *supra* note 6 and *R. v. Gladstone*, [1996] 4 C.N.L.R. 65 (S.C.C.).

such a right might be. More particularly, does s. 35 create constitutional space for aboriginal laws governing behaviour, and if it does, how much space? In British Columbia the courts have said that the *Constitution Act, 1867* leaves no such space, at least for an "inherent" right of self-government.[41] Many academics – and some governments[42] – disagree.[43]

The United States

After the American Revolution, the Royal Proclamation faded into the background as the new republic moved to shed itself of the taint of colonial law and jurisprudence. Nonetheless, the Supreme Court of the United States relied on British practice and in fact specifically referred to the Proclamation when it laid the foundations of American Indian law.[44] The result was an emphatic affirmation of an inherent, albeit limited, form of aboriginal sovereignty and title. As Chief Justice John Marshall put it in 1823, the Indian tribes were "admitted to be the rightful occupants of the soil, with a legal as well as a just claim to retain possession of it, and to use it according to their own discretion."[45]

In a series of cases decided between 1810 and 1835, the most important of which was *Worcester v. Georgia*, the chief justice and his court also ruled that the Indian tribes were "domestic dependent nations" whose sovereignty over North America had been restricted by European intrusion in two respects.[46] The tribes could sell their lands only to the European power that other European nations recognized as enjoying sovereignty over such lands, and the tribes could enter into formal relations only with that power – which by then, of course, was the United States. Otherwise they enjoyed a right of

---

41 See *Delgamuukw*, *supra* note 25. Although in its recent ruling in *Delgamuukw* (1997) 153 D.L.R. (4th) 193, the Supreme Court of Canada came out with an emphatic affirmation of aboriginal title as a form of ownership, it left the issue of self-government for a new trial. A year earlier, in *R. v. Pamajewon*, [1996] 4 C.N.L.R. 164 at 171, the Court had stated that "[a]ssuming without deciding that s. 35(1) includes self-government claims," the accused in that case had not shown that such authority extended to regulating casino gambling.

42 Including the federal (Liberal) government of Prime Minister Jean Chrétien, and the provincial (New Democratic) government in British Columbia.

43 See, *inter alia*, K. McNeil, *supra* note 32 and K. McNeil, "The Decolonization of Canada: Moving Toward Recognition of Aboriginal Governments" (1994) 7 Western Legal History 113; B. Slattery, "First Nations and the Constitution: A Question of Trust" (1992) 71 Can. Bar Rev. 279; and, perhaps less forcefully, P. W. Hogg and M. E. Turpel, "Implementing Aboriginal Self-Government: Constitutional and Jurisdictional Issues" (1995) 74 Can. Bar Rev. 187-224. See also Royal Commission on Aboriginal Peoples, *Partners in Confederation: Aboriginal Peoples, Self-Government and the Constitution* (Ottawa: Canada Communication Group, 1993) and the final, multivolume *Report of the Royal Commission on Aboriginal Peoples* (Ottawa: Canada Communication Group, 1996).

44 See e.g., *Mitchel v. United States*, 34 U.S. 711 (9 Pet.) 711 (1835) at 748, *per* Baldwin J.

45 *Johnson v. M'Intosh*, *supra* note 7 at 574.

46 *Supra* note 6. The concept of domestic dependent nations was put forward a year earlier in *Cherokee Nation v. Georgia*, 30 U.S. (5 Pet.) 1 (1831).

occupancy in their traditional territories that amounted to *de facto* ownership, and a right to govern themselves according to their own laws. The United States, on the other hand, had an exclusive right to make treaties with the tribes and to purchase Indian lands within American territory when the aboriginal owners chose to sell.[47] As a result, the individual states had no jurisdiction in what came to be known as "Indian country."[48]

It is true that American courts soon came to articulate a position that was closer to the Canadian view in one respect. They decided that Congress had jurisdiction *over* the tribes as well as simply jurisdiction to treat with them, and that it could unilaterally extinguish aboriginal rights if it so chose.[49] Nonetheless, such rights existed independently. As the leading federal Indian law scholar put it, powers "lawfully vested in an Indian tribe are not, in general, delegated powers granted by express acts of Congress, but rather inherent powers of a limited sovereignty which has never been extinguished."[50] But since there is nothing in American law comparable to Canada's s. 35(1), these rights are not constitutionally protected. Not surprisingly, there have been calls for the United States to move closer to the new Canadian position.[51]

The century between the Marshall decisions and the Roosevelt administration's *Indian Reorganization Act* (1934) saw a serious decline in aboriginal power in both countries.[52] In the United States, Congress made no more treaties with the tribes after 1871, broke up the reservations into individual

---

47 Thus, although the United States paid France $15,000,000 for the Louisiana Territory in 1803, over the succeeding decades the American government spent more than 20 times that much to extinguish the Indian title to those same lands: F. S. Cohen, "Original Indian Title" (1947) 32 Minn. L. Rev. 28 at 34-35.

48 States such as Georgia ceded their western territories to the United States in return for a promise that the latter would extinguish the Indian title to lands within the state. Georgia's intransigence and the litigation in the Cherokee cases was prompted in part by the slowness with which the United States carried out this obligation, and in part by the discovery of gold on Cherokee lands. See H. R. Berman, "The Concept of Aboriginal Rights in the Early Legal History of the United States" (1978) 27 Buffalo L. Rev. 637 at 656.

49 See e.g. *United States v. Kagama*, 118 U.S. 375 (1886), which held that the *Major Crimes Act*, which limited tribal criminal jurisdiction, was validly enacted by Congress. See also *United States v. McBratney*, 104 U.S. 621 (1882), holding that, even in the absence of a Congressional grant of authority, state courts had jurisdiction over the murder of a non-Indian by a non-Indian committed within Indian country, and *Lone Wolf v. Hitchcock*, 187 U.S. 553 (1903), holding that Congress could unilaterally abrogate Indian treaty rights.

50 F. S. Cohen, *Handbook of Federal Indian Law* (Albuquerque: Univ. of New Mexico Press, 1942) at 122. In the original, this passage is in italics.

51 See e.g. M. P. Wells, "*Sparrow* and *Lone Wolf*: Honoring Tribal Rights in Canada and the United States" (1991) 66 Washington L. Rev. 1119, wherein the author proposes that Congress at least enact legislation reflecting the Canadian approach.

52 See Wilkinson, *supra* note 14 and R. W. Johnson, "Fragile Gains: Two Centuries of Canadian and United States Policy Toward Indians" (1991) 66 Washington L. Rev. 643.

allotments, sold "surplus" lands to white settlers, and made serious incursions on tribal sovereignty.[53] After the Second World War there was even an attempt to "terminate" the tribes.[54] But the Marshall decisions were never overruled. Instead, beginning with *Williams v. Lee* in 1959, they were revived and reaffirmed to the extent that today Indian tribal sovereignty "remains a doctrine of considerable vitality."[55] As a result, there are tribal legislatures and tribal courts in the United States that enjoy jurisdiction over various matters in all three legal sectors: civic, economic, and behavioural.[56]

Although over the years both Congress and the courts have imposed significant limits on tribal sovereignty, it remains extensive. One example will suffice. When a female member of the Santa Clara Pueblo brought suit under the *Indian Civil Rights Act* (*ICRA*) in 1978, she alleged that a 40-year-old tribal ordinance withholding membership from children of women who married outside the tribe denied her equal protection under the law.[57] The Supreme Court denied relief, ruling that, except where *habeas corpus* is available, tribal court decisions interpreting the *ICRA* could not be reviewed in federal court. Any other result, the majority held, would be inconsistent with the intent of Congress and would seriously undermine tribal sovereignty – even where, as here, the tribal council that enacted the law was also the tribal court that interpreted it.[58]

Australia

Australia is often portrayed as the odd man out in all this, and not without reason. The principle that European assertions of sovereignty do not extinguish aboriginal title (either because it exists at common law or by tribal law, whether recognized by colonial governments or not) received short shrift in Australia, nor were treaties acknowledging such title made. And although aboriginal title was affirmed by the Supreme Court of New Zealand

53 So did the courts: see note 49, *supra*, and accompanying text.

54 For an explanation of this term see Johnson, *supra* note 52 and Wilkinson, *supra* note 14.

55 See D. H. Getches and C. F. Wilkinson, *Cases and Materials on Federal Indian Law,* 2d ed. (St. Paul: West Publishing, 1986) at 269; *Williams v. Lee*, 358 U.S. 217 (1959).

56 For details see e.g. W. C. Canby, Jr., *American Indian Law in a Nutshell*, 2d ed. (St. Paul: West Publishing, 1988), esp. c. 7.

57 25 U.S.C.A. §1301 *et seq*. The American Bill of Rights applies to Congress and (via the Fourteenth Amendment) the states, but not to the tribes. The *ICRA* was enacted in 1968 in order to apply many of the Bill of Rights' provisions to tribal governments.

58 *Santa Clara Pueblo v. Martinez*, 436 U.S. 49 (1978). Compare *A.G. Canada v. Lavell*, [1974] S.C.R. 1349, in which it was held that a similar provision of the *Indian Act* did not violate the 1960 Bill of Rights. There was no jurisdictional issue because there are no tribal courts in Canada, nor, at the time, did tribes have any say over their membership. See also *Lovelace v. Canada* (1983), 1 *Canadian Human Rights Yearbook* 305, in which the Canadian legal situation was condemned. The *Indian Act* has since been amended.

in 1847 and by the Supreme Court of the United States even earlier,[59] Australian law calmly and deliberately rejected it as recently as 1971, citing pre-*Calder* Canadian law in support and distinguishing the American and New Zealand cases.[60] Because the notion that any indigenous rights survived the planting of the first flag at Botany Bay in 1788 formed no part of Australian law until quite recently, aboriginal sovereignty has also been a non-issue for governments in Australia. The continent was therefore *terra nullius* in every sense.

The High Court of Australia eventually reviewed and departed from the earlier case law on aboriginal title in *Mabo v. Queensland (No.2)*, decided in 1992.[61] This time, precedent from other jurisdictions was cited more favourably, as were emerging international standards of justice. So Australia is no longer quite the exception it once was, especially if one considers that, to varying degrees, other jurisdictions have failed to live up to the law in their books and the words in their treaties. Indeed, in some parts of nineteenth and even twentieth-century North America – the province of British Columbia, for example – governments denied the existence of aboriginal rights every bit as vigorously as Australia did.[62] Moreover, recent research has shown that the imperial government did recognize aboriginal title in Australia, including the right to compensation upon extinguishment of that title.[63] It is simply that Australian colonial governments, not unlike their counterparts in British Columbia, decided to pursue a course of action that was inconsistent with imperial policy and probably with imperial law as well.

Constitutionally, Australia presents another point of contrast with Canada and the United States. As stated above, the two North American federations

59 See *The Queen v. Symonds*, [1847] N.Z.P.C. Cases 387 (New Zealand) and *Johnson v. M'Intosh* (United States), *supra* note 7. The Canadian position is more difficult to state succinctly. The *St. Catherine's* case, *supra* note 33, recognized aboriginal title in territories covered by the Royal Proclamation of 1763, and the governments of Britain, Upper Canada, and the Dominion of Canada adopted a policy of recognizing and extinguishing such title long before that. But it was not until the *Calder* case (*supra* note 20) in 1973 that the courts expressly gave their imprimatur to aboriginal title that exists independently of state recognition.

60 *Milirrpum v. Nabalco and the Commonwealth* (1971), 17 F.L.R. 141 citing, *inter alia*, *Calder* (*supra* note 20) in the B.C. Court of Appeal.

61 *Supra* note 6.

62 See P. Tennant, *Aboriginal People and Politics. The Indian Land Question in British Columbia, 1849-1989* (Vancouver: UBC Press, 1990) and H. Foster, "Letting Go the Bone: The Idea of Indian Title in British Columbia, 1849-1927," in Foster and McLaren, *supra* note 12 at 28-86. Other examples might include Alaska before 1971, Hawaii, and the Republic of Texas. For the latter, see the decision of the U.S. Court of Claims in *Lipan Apache v. The United States* (1967), 180 Ct. Cl. 487.

63 See H. Reynolds, "The *Mabo* Judgment in the Light of Imperial Land Policy" (1993) 16 U.N.S.W. L. J. 27 and J. Cassidy, "A Reappraisal of Aboriginal Policy in Colonial Australia: Imperial and Colonial Instruments and Legislation Recognizing the Special Rights and Status of the Australian Aboriginals" (1989) 10 J. of Legal History 365.

assigned jurisdiction over aboriginal matters to the central government. Part of the rationale for this was that a centre of power far removed from the pressures of the settlement frontier would be better able to do justice to indigenous peoples. Australia, however, did just the reverse: s. 51(xxvi) of the *Commonwealth of Australia Constitution Act* (1900) expressly exempted aboriginal people from the Commonwealth's exclusive authority to make special laws for particular races.[64] As a result, state governments in Australia were accorded an authority over aboriginal people and their lands that American states and Canadian provinces have never enjoyed.[65]

Recently this state of affairs has been significantly modified. Following a national referendum in the 1960s, the restriction in s. 51(xxvi) was removed and in 1975, pursuant to its new authority, the Commonwealth passed a *Racial Discrimination Act* that applied to all persons, including aboriginals.[66] Because federal law is paramount to state law in the event of a conflict, the Commonwealth government now enjoys significant power over aboriginal matters, and the authority of the states has been diminished. This was starkly confirmed in 1988 when the High Court ruled in *Mabo v. Queensland (No.1)* that Queensland's attempt to derail that case before it got to trial ran afoul of the *Racial Discrimination Act*. The state had passed legislation denying that aboriginal title existed, and extinguishing it unilaterally and without compensation if it did. The law was discriminatory because all other titles were unaffected.[67]

Perhaps even more significantly, early in 1995 the High Court ruled that the state of Western Australia's attempt to avoid *Mabo (No. 2)*'s recognition of aboriginal title and of the Commonwealth's statutory scheme for implementing the ruling was unconstitutional. In a decision that was unanimous in the result, the court held that the federal *Native Title Act*, passed in 1993 as a response to *Mabo (No. 2)* was valid legislation under s. 51(xxvi) of the constitution, and that the Western Australian statute purporting to extinguish aboriginal title was inconsistent with both the *Racial Discrimination Act* and the *Native Title Act*.[68] The court's ruling confirms that aboriginal title in Australia is protected from discriminatory action by state

64 See B. Morse, "Aboriginal-Government Relations in Australia and the Implications for Canada," in J. A. Long and M. Boldt, eds., *Governments in Conflict? Provinces and Indian Nations in Canada* (Toronto: Univ. of Toronto Press, 1988) 209 at 212.

65 Except in the Northern Territory, which, like the Yukon and the Northwest Territories in Canada, is under federal jurisdiction.

66 Morse, *supra* note 64 at 213.

67 *Ibid*. See also *Mabo v. Queensland (No. 1)* (1988), 166 C.L.R. 186.

68 See *Western Australia v. Commonwealth* (1995), 128 A.L.R. 1, which holds that aboriginal title in Australia, where it is established, may not be accorded less status than ordinary fee simple title. For commentary see R. H. Bartlett, "The High Court of Australia Upholds the Federal Native Title Act and Rejects Racist State Legislation" [1995] 2 C.N.L.R. 47 and P. Butt, "Native Title Act held valid: the High Court's decision in Western Australia v. Commonwealth" (1995) 69 Australian L. J. 397.

governments, and that the National Native Title Tribunal that was established pursuant to the *Native Title Act* can proceed with its work.[69] As in the United States, however, this protection is not constitutionally entrenched: the federal parliament can amend both the *Native Title Act* and the *Racial Discrimination Act* by ordinary legislation.[70]

Finally, it should be noted that a number of the High Court justices in *Mabo (No. 2)* held that the existence and content of aboriginal title was to be determined according to the laws and customs of the relevant tribal group.[71] It would therefore seem to follow that, if customary land rights can survive the British assertion of sovereignty, other aboriginal laws that meet the *Mabo* criteria can too.[72] Shortly after *Mabo*, however, the High Court held that their decision in that case was inconsistent with even the "limited kind of sovereignty embraced in the notion that [aboriginal people] are a 'domestic dependent nation' entitled to self-government."[73] Aboriginal governance issues in Australia therefore do not appear to have the constitutional cachet that they have in Canada and, to a lesser extent, the United States.[74]

---

69 For a highly critical account of the tribunal's performance to date, see R. H. Bartlett "The National Native Title Tribunal in Australia: Dispossession Not Settlement" [1996] 2 C.N.L.R. 1.

70 The current Commonwealth government appears set to do just that. As a result of the storm of controversy following the High Court's 4:3 decision in *Wik Peoples v. Queensland* (1996), 141 A.L.R. 129, amendments to the *Native Title Act* have been proposed that, if enacted, will seriously affect the rulings in that case. Given that *Wik*, which holds that aboriginal land rights can survive the granting of pastoral leases, does not go as far in protecting aboriginal rights as the B.C. Court of Appeal and the Supreme Court of Canada did in *Delgamuukw* (*supra* notes 25 and 41), this is remarkable. For a comparison of *Wik* and *Delgamuukw* (before the Supreme Court of Canada's decision), see K. McNeil, "Co-existence of Indigenous and Non-Indigenous Land Rights: Australia and Canada Compared in Light of the *Wik* Decision" (1997) 4:5 I.L.B. 4.

71 Other justices based aboriginal title more squarely upon the common law. For discussion, see K. E. Mulqueeny, "Folk-Law or Folklore: When a Law Is Not a Law, Or Is It?" in M. A. Stephenson and S. Ratnapala, eds., *Mabo: A Judicial Revolution: The Aboriginal Land Rights Decision and Its Impact on Australian Law* (St. Lucia: Univ. of Queensland Press, 1993) 165 at 168*ff*.

72 See Mulqueeny, *ibid.*, and F. Brennan, "Mabo and Its Implications for Aborigines and Torres Strait Islanders," in Stephenson and Ratnapala, *ibid.* at 24. See also B. Hocking, "Aboriginal Law Does Now Run in Australia," in *Essays on the Mabo Decision* (Sydney: The Law Book Co. 1993) at 67 and H. A. Amankwah, "Post-*Mabo*: The Prospect of the Recognition of a Regime of Customary (Indigenous) Law in Australia" (1994) 18 Univ. of Queensland L. J. 15.

73 *Coe v. Commonwealth* (1993), 118 A.L.R. 193 at 200.

74 Although the Supreme Court of Canada stated in *Sparrow*, *supra* note 6 at 283, that there has never been any doubt that sovereignty, legislative power, and underlying title vested in the Crown, the justices also affirmed (quoting an essay by Prof. Noel Lyon at 285) that s. 35 of the 1982 Constitution "renounce[d] the old rules of the game under which the Crown established courts of law and denied those courts the authority to question sovereign claims made by the Crown." For a discussion of the Court's belief that there was "never any doubt" about the Crown's authority, see H. Foster,

New Zealand

Aotearoa, or New Zealand, is the only one of the four jurisdictions under consideration that is not a federation. Arguably, it is the most interesting of all.

When the British government reluctantly decided to colonize New Zealand at the close of the 1830s, it had already acknowledged, by statute and otherwise, that the Maori were sovereign and independent.[75] Thus the commission conferred upon Captain William Hobson of the royal navy, who was sent to treat with the "Chiefs of the Confederation of the United Tribes of New Zealand and the ... independent Chiefs," appointed him not only lieutenant-governor of such parts of the country "as may be or hereafter shall be ceded to Her Majesty," but also consul to New Zealand.[76] When the Treaty of Waitangi was executed in 1840, Hobson shook hands with each of the chiefs who signed, and declared that "he iwi tahi tatou" (we are now one people).[77]

The colonial office, however, was somewhat ambivalent about just how sovereign the Maori were, and there is a long-standing debate among legal scholars about whether New Zealand really was a ceded colony – a point of colonial law that determined the legislative powers of the Crown and that, at one time, had important consequences for determining indigenous land rights.[78] That Britain had acknowledged Maori independence and entered into the Treaty of Waitangi would, at first glance, seem conclusive: sovereignty was ceded by treaty.[79] But a closer examination reveals that only some chiefs signed the treaty and that, worried about French designs on New Zealand, Hobson rather suddenly declared the South Island to be Britain's by right of discovery rather than cession. Moreover, when the new colony's Attorney General doubted whether tribes on the North Island that were not parties to the treaty were subject to English law, he was told in no uncertain terms that they were – a pronouncement that hardly seems consistent with Hobson's commission or with the proposition that New Zealand was a ceded,

---

"Forgotten Arguments: Aboriginal Title and Sovereignty in *Canada Jurisdiction Act* Cases" (1992) 21 Manitoba L. J. 343.

75 See 57 Geo. III (1817), c. 53 (U.K.); 4 Geo. IV (1823), c. 96 (U.K.); and 9 Geo. IV (1828), c. 83 (U.K.). As Permanent Undersecretary James Stephen put it, to have annexed New Zealand without negotiating for sovereignty would have been to act "in opposition to our own Statute Book," Stephen to Vernon Smith, 9 July 1840, quoted in Adams, *supra* note 11 at 162.

76 From the Preamble and Article 1 of the Treaty of Waitangi, 1840.

77 Quoted in A. Ward, *A Show of Justice: Racial "Amalgamation" in Nineteenth Century New Zealand* (Auckland: Auckland Univ. Press, 1974) at 42.

78 For a discussion of the significance of the distinction between settled and ceded colonies for aboriginal title, see G. I. Bennett, "Aboriginal Title in the Common Law: A Stony Path Through Feudal Doctrine" (1978) 27 Buffalo L. Rev. 617.

79 See *Hoani Te Heuheu Tukino v. Aotea District Maori Land Board*, [1941] A.C. 308 (J.C.P.C.).

as opposed to a settled, colony.[80] From the outset, therefore, there was confusion about the proper legal interpretation of what had occurred.

The Treaty of Waitangi differs from those made in North America in a number of ways, but the most important is that it acknowledged aboriginal title without extinguishing it. Article 2, in the English version, "confirms and guarantees" to the chiefs and tribes, and to their families and family members, "the full, exclusive and undisturbed possession [in the Maori version, *tino rangatiratanga*] of their lands and estates, forests, fisheries, and other properties," so long as when they wished to sell, they sold to the Crown. Although *rangatiratanga* "implies control of land and resources according to Maori custom,"[81] the settler community sought to have this article interpreted as referring only to village sites and gardens. They even succeeded in persuading a majority of the parliamentary committee formed to examine the question that such an interpretation should be adopted.[82]

But this view did not prevail. In the face of formidable Maori military strength and on the advice of a canny new governor, the Colonial Office decided that Maori law was the law of article 2 of the treaty, and according to Maori law probably "every inch" of land was owned by one *hapu* (subtribe) or another.[83] Soon afterwards, the Supreme Court of New Zealand held in *The Queen v. Symonds* that, quite apart from the Treaty of Waitangi, colonial common law guaranteed that aboriginal title cannot be extinguished "otherwise than by the free consent of the Native occupiers."[84] As a result, land in New Zealand could pass into Pakeha (non-Maori) hands only if it were sold to the Crown (which would then re-sell to settlers) or confiscated in war.[85] Although this meant that there were no unilateral takings such as occurred in Australia and other jurisdictions, such as British Columbia, the Maori eventually lost most of their land. This result was accomplished by the Native Land Court, which began to hear cases after the main hostilities in the war in the Waikato ceased in 1865. According to the leading student

---

80 See D. V. Williams, "The Annexation of New Zealand to New South Wales in 1840: What of the Treaty of Waitangi?" (1985) 2 Australian J. of Law and Society 41 at 49-54.

81 E. Stokes, "The Treaty of Waitangi and the Waitangi Tribunal: Maori Claims in New Zealand," in G. Cant, J. Overton, and Eric Pawson, eds., *Indigenous Land Rights in Commonwealth Countries: Dispossession, Negotiation and Community Action* (Christchurch: Univ. of Canterbury and Ngai Tahu Trust Board, 1993) 66 at 67.

82 See House of Commons, *British Parliamentary Papers: Report of the Select Committee on New Zealand together with the Minutes of the Evidence Appendix and Index, 1844* (Shannon: Irish Univ. Press, 1968).

83 Adams, *supra* note 11 at 178 and 185. The *hapu,* which is larger than the extended family (*whanau*) but smaller than the tribe (*iwi*) is the principle Maori kin group.

84 *Supra* note 59 at 390, Chapman J. To put this case in context, however, see D. V. Williams, "*The Queen v. Symonds* Reconsidered" (1989) 19 Victoria Univ. of Wellington L. Rev. 385.

85 The *raupatu,* or confiscations, took place in 1863-65, as a consequence of the Waikato War.

of this institution, it was a "veritable engine of destruction" for tribal tenure,[86] and the legal regime it developed has made land claims in New Zealand more technically complex than elsewhere.[87]

Self-government issues in New Zealand depend not only upon article 2 of the Treaty but also upon article 1. In the English version of this clause, the chiefs ceded all their sovereignty, "absolutely and without reservation," to the Crown. The Maori version, however, does not refer to *mana* (authority, status, prestige) or *rangatiratanga*, words the chiefs would have understood to mean more or less what "sovereignty" means to English-speakers. Instead the chiefs ceded only their *kawanatanga*, a word coined by the missionaries that translates as "governorship" and which would have connoted something less than sovereignty to Maori ears.[88] There is, therefore, in New Zealand a question of whether and to what extent the sovereignty or *kawanatanga* of the Crown in article 1 is encumbered by confirmation of the *rangatiratanga* of the chiefs in article 2. As many Maori say today, New Zealand may be one nation, but the Treaty – notwithstanding Captain Hobson's pronouncement – recognizes that it is composed of two peoples.[89]

However, the courts and the legislature refused to give the Treaty any teeth, and one nineteenth-century judge even went so far as to call it a "simple nullity."[90] The highest court in what was the British Empire disagreed, ruling some 60 years later in *Hoani Te Heuheu Tukino v. Aotea District Maori Land Board* that it was a valid treaty of cession; but the Judicial Committee of the Privy Council went on to uphold the legal orthodoxy that, because the Treaty had never been incorporated by statute into New Zealand's domestic law, it was not enforceable.[91] As recently as 1992, the majority of the New Zealand Court of Appeal (Cooke P. dissenting) confirmed this doctrine, stating that "[t]reaty rights cannot be enforced in the Courts except in so far as they have been given recognition by statute."[92] This is another point of contrast with North America. Article 6, s. 2 of the Constitution of the United States provides that properly ratified treaties are part of "the supreme law of the land," and s. 35 of Canada's *Constitution Act,*

86 I. H. Kawharu, *Maori Land Tenure: Studies of a Changing Institution* (Oxford: Oxford Univ. Press, 1977) at 15.

87 See e.g. P. G. McHugh, *The Fragmentation of Maori Land* (Auckland: Legal Research Foundation, 1980).

88 *Kawanatanga* would in all likelihood have been associated with the missionaries and with the ineffectual James Busby, the official British Resident in New Zealand in the 1830s, whom the Maori knew had no real authority.

89 Stokes, *supra* note 81 at 66-67.

90 *Wi Parata v. The Bishop of Wellington* (1877), 3 N.Z. Jur. (NS) S.C. 72, Prendergast C.J.

91 *Supra* note 79.

92 *New Zealand Maori Council v. Attorney General*, [1992] 2 N.Z.L.R. 576 at 603. On appeal the appellants relied solely upon statutory arguments, and did not attempt "to challenge or avoid" the principle in *Te Heuheu*: see [1994] 1 N.Z.L.R. 513 at 515 (J.C.P.C.).

1982 goes even further, insulating the treaty rights of aboriginal people from legislative interference.[93]

Even in New Zealand, however, *Te Heuheu* must be put in context. In the first place, there has been significant statutory activity since it was decided. The *Treaty of Waitangi Act, 1975* created a tribunal to inquire into claims based on the principles of the Treaty, and in 1985 the Waitangi Tribunal's jurisdiction was extended to include claims dating from 1840 onwards.[94] Moreover, in the ground-breaking case of *New Zealand Maori Council v. Attorney General*,[95] the High Court ruled that, where the Treaty *is* incorporated by statute, it is a force to be reckoned with. Second, the courts may conceivably be able to do indirectly what the *Te Heuheu* case prevents them from doing directly: they can invoke common law rather than Treaty principles to protect aboriginal rights.[96] Although the nature of customary title and the statutory maze of Maori land law makes this more difficult in New Zealand than elsewhere,[97] such cases as *New Zealand Maori Council v. Attorney General* and *Te Wheehi v. Regional Fisheries Officer*[98] – which held that customary fishing rights that have not been extinguished continue to exist independently of any proprietary right in the foreshore – have revitalized an approach that, since the *Queen v. Symonds*,[99] had been very much in abeyance. Of particular note in this regard is the recent decision of the Court of Appeal in *Te Runanganui o Te Ika Whenua Inc. Society v. Attorney General*.[100]

---

93 The Canadian position goes further because the *Lone Wolf* case, *supra* note 49, established that Congress could unilaterally abrogate Indian treaty rights. Before the enactment of s. 35 in 1982, this was also Canadian law: see *Sikyea v. R.*, [1964] S.C.R. 642 and *R. v. George*, [1966] S.C.R. 267. It must be conceded, however, that in Canada problems with international treaties remain: see e.g. *Francis v. R.*, [1956] S.C.R. 618 and D. Evans, "Superimposed Nations: The Jay Treaty and Aboriginal Rights" (1995) 4 Dalhousie J. of Legal Studies 215.

94 *Treaty of Waitangi Act, 1975* and *Treaty of Waitangi Amendment Act, 1985*, s. 3. For a recent example of the sort of work the Tribunal does, see the *Taranaki Report: Kaupapa Tuatahi* (WAI 143, Waitangi Tribunal Report 1996).

95 [1987] 1 N.Z.L.R. 614. In this case, the Court's ruling resulted in legislation providing that Waitangi Tribunal recommendations that land be resumed by the Crown and restored to the Maori will be binding on the Crown in certain circumstances. However, this law, and the notion of compulsory restoration of land to the Maori, have yet to be put to the test. See generally R. P. Boast, "The Waitangi Tribunal: 'Conscience of the Nation,' or Just Another Court?" (1993) 16 UNSW L. J. 223 at 227-28.

96 Boast may overstate the case a little when he states (*ibid.* at 224) that "after 1986-89 the government could have no confidence that it would succeed in any case that it allowed to go to court." See also 236*ff*.

97 See McHugh, *supra* note 87.

98 *Supra* note 95 and [1986] 1 N.Z.L.R. 680.

99 *Supra* note 59. See also Williams' comment on *Symonds*, *supra* note 84 at 385, and P. G. McHugh, "Case and Comment: Aboriginal Title Returns to the New Zealand Courts" [1987] N.Z.L.J. 39.

100 [1994] 2 N.Z.L.R. 20.

The latter case concerned a proposed transfer of water and hydro-electric rights that was alleged to interfere with Maori interests in the affected rivers. The Court of Appeal dismissed an application to delay the transfer, but in doing so Sir Robin Cooke, speaking for the court, pointed to two possible means of redress. He noted first of all that, because the government had demonstrated a "willingness to remedy past injustices,"[101] the most practical remedy probably lay with a recommendation by the Waitangi Tribunal. Much more interesting, however, is his comment that a remedy might "conceivably" be obtained in a court action based on Maori customary title or fiduciary duty. Referring to Canadian law and to the *Mabo* case in Australia, President Cooke went on to observe that other jurisdictions were increasingly inclined to recognize the justiciability of the claims of indigenous peoples. Moreover, he concluded, not only was the Treaty of Waitangi "acquiring some permeating influence in New Zealand law," but "treaty rights and customary rights tend to be partly the same in content."[102] This suggests that the fact that the Treaty is not directly enforceable may not matter.[103]

But that is to predict the future, a murky business at best.[104] What is somewhat clearer is that in New Zealand the judiciary, the government, and the Waitangi Tribunal have all agreed that the Treaty should be viewed as a partnership that created mutual obligations, and that the task before them is to find the proper balance between the *kawanatanga* of the Crown and the *rangatiratanga* of the chiefs and tribes. Although the latter is conceded to comprise full authority over lands and other property, the Tribunal has stated that it is "satisfied that sovereignty was ceded [under article 1 of the Treaty]" and that *kawanatanga* means the right to govern and to make laws. *Rangatiratanga*, on the other hand, "refers not to a separate sovereignty but to tribal self-management on lines similar to what we understand by local government."[105] So self-governance, although Treaty-based, is limited to the

---

101 *Ibid.* at 27, referring to the controversial Sealord settlement, whereby significant fishing rights were transferred to the Maori. For a brief description of the Sealord deal see Boast, *supra* note 95 at 242-43.

102 *Ibid.*

103 See also A. B. Blades, "Article 27 of the International Covenant on Civil and Political Rights: A Case Study on Implementation in New Zealand" [1994] 1 C.N.L.R. 1 at 31-34. There is a strong Canadian parallel: the Supreme Court of Canada's recent decision in *Delgamuukw*, *supra* note 41, confirms that whether lands are subject to the Royal Proclamation or not will have little or no effect on what Canadian courts say about aboriginal title.

104 Some commentators, it should be noted, take a less sanguine view of the role of New Zealand's judiciary: see J. Kelsey, *infra* note 124, and J. Kelsey, "Globalization and the Demise of the Colonial State: Options for Decolonization in Aotearoa/New Zealand" (Paper presented to the U.S. Law and Society Meeting, Arizona, June 1994) [unpublished].

105 *Orakei Report*, 1987; *Muriwhenua Fishing Report*, 1988.

municipal model, and other rights depend either on the common law or on statute.[106] There is no constitutional protection in the Canadian sense.[107]

Comparative Reflections

In the nineteenth century, the courts played an important part in advancing the legal position of aboriginal people only in the United States, and even in that country their influence was at first more theoretical than real.[108] Elsewhere courts were a relatively minor player, getting involved when aboriginal people accused of crime were brought before them, but not otherwise. Aboriginal individuals and organizations had neither the funds nor the knowledge necessary to gain access to the judicial system until the twentieth century, and even then they faced legal obstacles. In Canada, for example, not only were litigants prevented from suing the Crown unless the Crown consented, but also, in 1927, Parliament made it illegal for anyone to raise money from Indians for the purpose of pursuing their legal claims against government.[109] As a result, aboriginal people brought virtually none of the early actions that dealt, usually obliquely, with aboriginal title: the issue arose only as a necessary stage in resolving issues that concerned the settler community.[110] The only obvious exception is the Cherokee cases heard by the United States Supreme Court in the 1830s.[111]

Governments and legislatures were much more important, but weighed in on the other side. Colonial legislatures were controlled by settlers who by and large believed that they had nothing to gain by advancing or protecting aboriginal interests; and bureaucrats, even if some may have been

106 These findings have been seen as a retreat from the Tribunal's earlier pronouncements on the relationship between *kawanatanga* and *rangatiratanga*: see A. L. Mikaere, "Maori Issues I," [1989] N.Z. L. Rev. 170 at 173.

107 But see P. Havemann, "'What's in the Treaty?': Constitutionalizing Maori Rights in Aotearoa/New Zealand 1975-1993," in K. M. Hazlehurst, ed., *Legal Pluralism and the Colonial Legacy: Indigenous Experiences of Justice in Canada, Australia and New Zealand* (Aldershot, England: Avebury, 1994) at 73-102.

108 Thus, although the Cherokee won a stunning victory in *Worcester*, *supra* note 6, they still lost their traditional lands. They also lost a quarter to a third of their population on the forced trek west to the Indian Territory known as the "Trail of Tears." A sense of what this was like may be found in de Toqueville's moving description of a similar trek made by the Choctaws in 1831: see de Toqueville, *supra* note 10 at 324.

109 The law in question required that the written consent of the general superintendent of Indian affairs had to be obtained before funds could be raised. It was removed from the *Indian Act* in 1951: see Foster, *supra* note 62.

110 The leading cases of *The Queen v. Symonds* (N.Z., *supra* note 59), *Johnson v. M'Intosh* (U.S., *supra* note 7) and *St. Catherine's Milling* (Canada, *supra* note 33) all fit this description.

111 See *supra* note 46 and accompanying text. The Cherokee were one of the so-called "Five Civilized Tribes," which presumably accounts for their ability to initiate and conduct such litigation. On this aspect of the cases, see J. Norgen, "Lawyers and the Legal Business of the Cherokee Republic in the Courts of the United States, 1829-1835" (1992) 10 Law and History Rev. 253-314.

inclined to take a more balanced approach, were usually subject to important institutional constraints. In many colonies, for example, the department in charge of indigenous peoples and their lands was also responsible for opening land for settlement, a hopeless conflict of interest. Even where a degree of institutional separation was achieved – for example, in the Indian Reserve Commission established in British Columbia in 1876 – those who were to represent aboriginal interests invariably found themselves in possession of insufficient authority and influence to counter the powerful forces arrayed against them.[112]

After the Second World War, however, governments came under pressure to establish at home the sorts of rights that their armies had secured abroad, and when this proved to be a slow and difficult process, aboriginal people who were now better educated and organized began to look to the judiciary. Legal development in the latter half of the present century has therefore tended to be court-driven and – with the exception of the United States, where judges rarely refer to case law from other jurisdictions – the courts are self-consciously aware of what is happening elsewhere. Such cases as *Williams v. Lee* in the United States, *Calder* in Canada, *New Zealand Maori Council v. Attorney General* in New Zealand and, most recently and strikingly, *Mabo (No. 2)* in Australia mark turning points in the legal history of its country of origin that also influenced, directly and indirectly, developments beyond its borders. The courts, in turn, have tended to point to governments and to the negotiation process as the real avenue to lasting settlements.[113]

Governments have responded to this call for action, and sometimes even anticipated it. Thus, the Waitangi Tribunal in New Zealand, aboriginal land rights legislation in Australia's Northern Territory, and the process that eventually led to the establishment of the Treaty Commission in British Columbia all *preceded* successful litigation; indeed, in British Columbia and Australia, these initiatives came on the heels of court cases in which the aboriginal plaintiffs *lost*.[114] Public opinion after the Second World War was increasingly, if not always reliably, in favour of redressing aboriginal grievances, although such support tended to increase with geographical distance from

112 See Foster, *supra* note 62 and sources cited therein.

113 See e.g. the remarks of the judges in *Te Runanganui o Te Ika Whenua Inc. Society v. Attorney General, supra* note 100, *Delgamuukw, supra* note 25 and *MacMillan Bloedel Ltd. v. Mullin et al; Martin et al. v. R. in Right of British Columbia et al.* (the "Meares Island" case), [1985] 3 W.W.R. 577 (B.C.C.A.). The Supreme Court of Canada reaffirmed this preference in its reasons in *Delgamuukw, supra* note 41.

114 Although the aboriginal plaintiffs in *Milirrpum, supra* note 60, lost their case, the Commonwealth government enacted legislation providing for aboriginal land rights. In British Columbia the government established the current treaty process a month *before* the Court of Appeal partially overruled the trial judge's decision in *Delgamuukw, supra* note 25. That judge had ruled that there were no aboriginal land rights in British Columbia.

aboriginal communities – a fact that helps to explain why imperial authorities insisted on metropolitan control over aboriginal matters and why both the Canadian and American federations placed such control with the central government. There was also increasing support among the bureaucrats, many of whom had first-hand experience with the failure of the paternalistic and assimilationist policies of the past.

However, because so much is at stake and because opposition to land settlements, compensation, and self-government proposals is usually well-financed and well-organized, most major public initiatives have followed rather than anticipated judicial rulings. Although some legislators may have felt that they should simply do what was right, generally politicians do not choose to act unless they are seen to be reacting: then, if they are called to account, they can argue that they are merely carrying out what the courts have mandated.[115]

Although the pattern of response to this judicial prodding has been similar in each country, there are some notable differences. In Canada there are now constitutional guarantees, a complex land settlements policy, and a gaggle of tribunals and commissions.[116] New Zealand does not have the same sort of land claims to settle, but it too has opted for an administrative approach, relying primarily upon negotiation and the work of the Waitangi Tribunal. In Australia, on the other hand, the *Native Title Act* of 1993 represents a much more ambitious attempt to provide a statutory framework for settlements, and one that is currently seriously threatened by a political backlash.[117] But for aboriginal claimants in all these jurisdictions, the courts remain (apart from direct action such as demonstrations and blockades) the uncertain remedy of last resort.

In the United States, the situation is more difficult to pigeonhole. Much of the work that the other countries are now engaged in was done decades ago, mainly through (1) litigation,[118] (2) the Indian Claims Commission

---

115 Indeed, in British Columbia, whether the government's treaty process goes beyond what has been required by the courts is hotly contested. For a rather one-sided view of this question, see M. H. Smith, *Our Home or Native Land? What Governments' Aboriginal Policy Is Doing to Canada* (Victoria: Crown Western, 1995), cc. 4 and 9. The Supreme Court's decision in *Delgamuukw, supra* note 41, should, but probably will not, mute this debate considerably.

116 In Canada the federal government distinguishes between comprehensive and specific claims, and has established an Indian Claims Commission to make recommendations with respect to the latter. British Columbia has its own tripartite process and Treaty Commission, but the latter – unlike the Indian Claims Commission and the much more influential Waitangi Tribunal in New Zealand – neither investigates claims nor makes recommendations. It is simply the "keeper" (facilitator) of the treaty process.

117 Caused largely by the *Wik* decision: see note 70, *supra*. For a conveyancer's analysis of the Act, see P. Butt, "The Native Title Act: A Property Law Perspective" (1994) 86 Australian L. J. 285-93.

established after the Second World War,[119] and (3) negotiated settlements such as the one billion dollar deal in Alaska in 1971.[120] There is unfinished business, certainly; not only in Hawaii, which is a special case, but also in regions where the treaties are generations old.[121] Indeed, when the Indian Claims Commission shut down in 1978, there were scores of unresolved cases that had to be transferred to the Court of Claims.[122] But the principles of tribal sovereignty and title are much more settled in the United States, and at present one of the more interesting questions appears to be, which institution is most likely to stand by these principles – Congress or the Supreme Court?[123] The answer should be of interest to anyone seeking to understand the delicate institutional balance in Canada, Australia, and New Zealand.

Needless to say, the jurisprudence on aboriginal rights that has jump-started many of these developments is not without its critics. At one end of the spectrum are those who hold that European law has not and cannot do justice to indigenous peoples, arguing that the common law of aboriginal rights is hopelessly compromised by imperialist and even racist premises and assumptions. Or they argue that, even if in theory European law is up to the task, the human beings charged with applying it are not. Such critics allege that the courts have betrayed the promise of the early cases and other sources of law, such as the Royal Proclamation of 1763, that laid the foundations of aboriginal rights law.[124] Often the debate then turns to whether

---

118 For example, the Marshall Court cases (see text with footnotes 44-58, *supra*). See also e.g. *United States v. Creek Nation*, 295 U.S. 103 (1935); *United States v. Shoshone Tribe*, 304 U.S. 111 (1938).

119 Before 1946, the United States' sovereign immunity from suit meant that Congress had to authorize claims litigation on a case by case basis. These suits were heard in the Court of Claims and, by the 1940s, 142 statutes had been passed for this purpose. The *Indian Claims Commission Act* was enacted to avoid this cumbersome procedure: it established a commission that could adjudicate claims permitted by the statute, and its decisions were subject to review by the Court of Claims. The only real remedy, however, was monetary damages. See Getches and Wilkinson, *supra* note 55 at 184-89.

120 *Alaska Native Claims Settlement Act*, 85 Stat. 688. For an early analysis see K. Lysyk, "Approaches to Settlement of Indian Title Claims: The Alaskan Model" (1973) 8 U.B.C. L. Rev. 321-42.

121 See e.g. the *Maine Indian Claims Settlement Act*, 1980; *County of Oneida v. Oneida Indian Nation*, 105 S.Ct. 1245 (1985), and Getches and Wilkinson, *supra* note 55 at 74 and 820-47.

122 See A. Durocher, "Land Claims Reform," [1995] 2 I.C.C.P. 25 at 42-43.

123 In at least one respect in recent years, it has been Congress. In 1990 the Supreme Court ruled that tribal courts not only had no criminal jurisdiction over non-Indians, they also had none over Indians who were not tribal members: see *Duro v. Reina*, 495 U.S. 676 (1990). This decision was quickly reversed by Congress.

124 See e.g. B. Clark, *Native Liberty, Crown Sovereignty: The Existing Aboriginal Right of Self-Government in Canada* (McGill-Queen's Univ. Press, 1990); and J. Kelsey, *A Question of Honour? Labour and the Treaty 1984-1989* (Wellington: Allen and Unwin, 1990) and "Treaty Justice in the 1980s," in P. Spoonley, D. Pearson, and C. MacPherson, eds.,

international law holds out more promise than domestic law, and, here as elsewhere, opinions differ.[125] Certainly organizations such as the Inuit Circumpolar Conference and the United Nations Working Group on Indigenous Populations have been influential, but, at time of writing, the Draft Declaration on the Rights of Indigenous Peoples remains a draft. On the whole, such influences have been indirect rather than direct.[126]

At the other end of the spectrum are those who believe that it is the nation state and liberal concepts of equality that are being betrayed, not aboriginal rights. They see in the jurisprudence of the past few decades a sort of "judicial spree" in which courts have substituted morality for law and preferred their own vision of social justice to precedent and parliamentary democracy. The Hon. P. D. Connolly, Q.C., formerly a justice of the Supreme Court of Queensland, summarized this position somewhat acidly when he described the central holding in *Mabo* as belonging to "the world on the other side of the looking glass." He wondered aloud whether Australian governments would be "so supine as to allow judges to strip from the Crown property rights which the Crown has held and exercised for two hundred years."[127] Other members of this group, who are perhaps reluctant to be quite so outspoken about the judiciary, have targeted instead the governments and bureaucracies whose backbone Connolly so clearly doubts. Like some of the more ardent tracts advocating aboriginal rights, publications in this category seek to inflame as well as to inform, but jeopardize the latter objective by taking similar risks with the facts.[128] They also tend to display an approach to legal philosophy that fails to take into account recent constitutional and jurisprudential developments, and that explicitly rejects the more fluid notions of sovereignty upon which real change in this area depends.

IMPLICATIONS FOR THE BEHAVIOURAL SECTOR

Traditionally, sovereignty in all four countries under consideration has been conceived by the colonizing powers as solely in the Crown, even where this sovereignty is distributed among the Crown in right of the central government and the Crown in right of the governments of the provinces or states making up a federation.[129] Such an approach permits the delegation of powers

Nga Take: Ethnic Relations and Racism in Aotearoa/New Zealand (Palmerston North, N.Z.: Dunmore Press, 1991).

125 See e.g. Brennan, *supra* note 19.

126 For example, in *Mabo (No. 2)*, *supra* note 6.

127 Hon. P. D. Connolly, Q.C., "The Theory of Universal and Absolute Crown Ownership" (1994) 18 Univ. of Queensland L. J. 9 at 11 and 13.

128 See e.g. T. Hewat, *Who Made the Mabo Mess?* (North Brighton: Wrightbooks Pty, 1993) and Smith, *supra* note 115. Since the Supreme Court's decision in *Delgamuukw*, *supra* note 41, Smith has begun criticizing the courts in the Australian fashion.

129 See e.g. *Delgamuukw*, *supra* note 25.

to subordinate levels of administration such as municipalities, but this sort of self-government falls short of what many, perhaps even most, aboriginal people want. Using treaties between the Crown and aboriginal tribes or nations as a model, they seek acknowledgment of their inherent and independent right to govern themselves and to possess powers that, in some areas at least, are equal or even superior to state (provincial) or federal authority.[130] For both historical and constitutional reasons, this position is articulated much more clearly in the United States and Canada, but it also exists to varying degrees in Australia and New Zealand. Not surprisingly, one of the central issues is the extent to which there should be separate aboriginal laws and justice systems.

Put another way, the question is whether the unique situation of aboriginal peoples outlined above means that they have a legal and perhaps even a constitutionally protected right to self-determination, such that they may enact laws and adjudicate disputes without interference – or at least with minimal interference – from the government or governments of the larger states they inhabit.[131] If it does, this has significant implications for the structure of government in all four countries. Below this level of sovereignty, however, there are some more modest, but not insignificant, options. These will be considered first.

At the very least, national legal systems ought to be able to take aboriginal law and custom into account in determining factual issues: for example, justifications and excuses in criminal responsibility, the best interests of the child in custody cases, and the intention of testators in wills cases. Aboriginal law and custom also ought to be relevant to pronouncing sentence in criminal cases, to awarding civil damages, and to decision-making in certain procedural areas.[132] Courts have made these types of concessions to cultural differences, perhaps because they require no acknowledgment of aboriginal sovereignty or that aboriginal law has any binding force.[133] Some

---

130 See e.g. Slattery, *supra* note 43.

131 The issue of whether this might amount to a right of sovereign independence will not be addressed. At the level of international law, which is otherwise noted for its sympathy for aboriginal concerns (see e.g. the *Western Sahara* case (1975) 1 C.J. Reps 6), this sort of sovereignty has been vigorously resisted by governments that are not prepared to see their territorial integrity impaired by aboriginal separatism. Thus, although the International Labour Organization agreed to refer to indigenous "peoples" in redrafting I.L.O. Convention 169, it added that the use of the term should "not be construed as having any implications as regards the rights which may attach to the term under international law." And although the Draft Declaration on the Rights of Indigenous Peoples produced by the United Nations Working Group on Indigenous Populations speaks of indigenous peoples having the "right of self-determination," this right is limited by other provisions: Brennan, *supra* note 19 at 258.

132 See generally Mulqueeny, *supra* note 71.

133 The court records of all four jurisdictions provide evidence of this sort of concession, sometimes because harsh application of European law seemed inappropriate, some-

examples of these concessions follow, although it must be stressed that they do not represent a comprehensive or systematic picture of the situation in all or even one of the four jurisdictions under discussion.

Cases in this category include decisions that (1) elders may be consulted in child custody and criminal cases; (2) a version of the colour of right defence is available to aboriginal defendants charged with offences against property who claim that their belief in their aboriginal rights justified the actions in question;[134] (3) aboriginal custom on the inheritance of real property can be relevant to assessing whether an application to vary a will should succeed;[135] and, (4) in Canada, that "sentencing circles" may be used.[136] Canadian and American judges have also ordered the temporary exile or banishment of aboriginal offenders on a limited number of occasions,[137] and Australian courts have quite regularly taken into account the fact that an aboriginal offender has undergone "payback" (for example, spearing in the thigh) at the hands of the family of the victim, adjusting the sentence accordingly.[138] A Canadian court has awarded civil damages for false arrest in an amount sufficient to enable the plaintiff to hold a feast, in accordance with her tribal law, to expunge the shame of being falsely accused of shoplifting.[139] And an Australian court has ordered a publication ban on the name of the deceased in a manslaughter case because it is contrary to most tribal customs to speak of a dead man by name.[140] Indeed, in Australia there are special rules, the Anunga Rules, for interrogating aboriginal suspects.[141]

---

times, in the early days, because of a fear that it might result in unacceptable retaliation against settlers living in more remote areas. On this latter point see J. Swainger, "A Distant Edge of Authority: Capital Punishment and the Prerogative of Mercy in British Columbia, 1872-1880," in Foster and McLaren, *supra* note 12 at 204.

134 See e.g. *Walden v. Hensler* (1987), 163 C.L.R. 561 (Aust. H.C.), *R. v. Potts*, [1990] O.J. No. 2567 (Ont. Prov. Ct.) and *R. v. Ashini*, [1989] 2 C.N.L.R. 119, rev'd on other grounds (1989), 51 C.C.C. (3d) 329 (Nfld. C.A.).

135 See e.g. *Re Stubbing*, [1990] 1 N.Z.L.R. 428, in which the New Zealand High Court remarked that this appeared to be a case of first impression.

136 See e.g. *R. v. Moses* (1992), 71 C.C.C. (3d) 347 (Yukon T.C.) and, more recently, *R. v. Morin*, [1995] S.J. No. 457 (Sask. C.A.).

137 See *The Economist* (13 Aug. 1994) 29 on a recent American case and *The [Toronto] Globe and Mail* (30 May 1995) A1 to A2 on developments in Canadian law. Banishment is a punishment that some aboriginal councils in Australia wish to impose, as well: see Brennan, *supra* note 19. In all three jurisdictions it remains highly controversial. For example, the Saskatchewan Court of Appeal, e.g., recently reversed – albeit on jurisdictional grounds – what was in effect a sentence of banishment that had been recommended by a sentencing circle: see *R. v. Taylor* (1995), 104 C.C.C. (3d) 346.

138 See e.g. the cases discussed in the text accompanying notes 152-55, *infra* and *R. v. Shannon* (1991), 56 A. Crim. R. 56 (S.A. Ct. Crim. App.), where the accused believed he would be subject to a form of magical revenge.

139 *Forsythe v. Collingwood Sales Ltd.*, [1987] B.C.J. 40 (Co. Ct.).

140 *R. v. Bara Bara* (1992), 87 N.T.R. 1 (S.C.).

141 *R. v. Anunga and others* (1976), 11 A.L.R. 412 (N.T.S.C.). This of course is a practice with long roots; for a Canadian example of a judge in 1916 chastising a B.C. detective for

What these and many other examples that might be cited have in common is that they do not present a direct challenge to the existing legal order. However, as the Australian Law Reform Commission and others have pointed out, such cases can provoke an equal protection or "equality before the law" debate.[142] Thus criminal prosecutions involve the possibility that an aboriginal offender may be treated differently (either more harshly or more leniently) than a non-aboriginal one;[143] and there can be a fine line between taking aboriginal differences into account and creating a defence that is available only to aboriginals.[144] The involvement of the community is also, unless it is very carefully designed and monitored, vulnerable to the criticism that well-meaning but naive non-aboriginal justice officials are being co-opted by regressive and even offending elements of that community;[145] or, less dramatically, that the accused's influence in his community would militate against an appropriate resolution of the issue there.[146] These concerns become especially acute if courts or legislatures go beyond taking facts about aboriginal life into account or asking elders for advice that can be rejected, and recognize, as they have in the United States, that aboriginal or customary law can have a legal status all of its own.

If aboriginal law is to be afforded this degree of recognition in Canada, New Zealand, and Australia, two questions arise: whether an aboriginal law or custom can be shown to exist and, if so, whether it can co-exist with

---

not adapting the standard police warning in a case involving an aboriginal accused, see Loo, *supra* note 12 at 140 and 163-64.

142 J. Blokland, "Commentary on *R. v. Minor*" (1992) 16 Crim. L. J. 362 at 364. Of course, in one form this debate already existed: in both domestic and international legal forums, Canadian and American aboriginal women have invoked bill of rights arguments to challenge federal and tribal laws that discriminate against them: see note 58, *supra*.

143 For an example of a harsher aboriginal penalty see Brennan, *supra* note 19.

144 See e.g. *R. v. Drainville*, [1991] O.J. No. 430 (Prov. Ct.) and *R. v. Ly* (1987), 33 C.C.C. (3d) 31 (B.C.C.A.). In the latter, a murder case involving a Vietnamese accused who claimed that he had been provoked by his wife's infidelity, the court rejected the argument that cultural difference should be relevant to the question whether an ordinary person would have been deprived of his self-control.

145 For a discussion of this aspect of the problem in Canada, see E. La Rocque, "Re-examining Appropriate Models in Criminal Justice Applications," in M. Asch, ed., *Aboriginal and Treaty Rights in Canada: Essays on Law, Equality and Respect for Difference* (Vancouver: UBC Press: 1997) at 75-96. In Australia, see C. Bulbeck, "A Tale of Two Statistics: Evaluating the Findings of the Royal Commission into Aboriginal Deaths in Custody" (Griffith Univ., 1992) [unpublished]. Bulbeck and others argue that aboriginal men who commit serious crimes may receive much less severe penalties than non-aboriginal ones, and notes that even some male elders have remarked upon "the misrepresentation of traditional custom by younger men who assault their wives" (citing a Report of the Aboriginal Coordinating Council, Cairns, *Community Justice in Northern Australia: Problems in Implementation and Development* (1988) at 29.

146 See e.g. *R. v. F.(A.)*, [1995] 2 C.N.L.R. 145, where the Ontario Court of Justice refused to order a sentencing to be held in the accused's home community because of an imbalance of power among the parties that would work to the complainant's disadvantage.

national or state (provincial) law. If the answers to both questions are affirmative, in Canada such a law might also qualify under s. 35(1) of the *Constitution Act, 1982* for protection as an aboriginal right. To varying degrees, academic writers in all three jurisdictions and royal commissions in two of them have recommended the recognition of aboriginal law, but their respective legal systems have been slow to act.[147] Such proposals excite strong feelings about the rule of law and about differential treatment, and raise obvious questions about the necessity for, or at least the desirability of, a uniform system of laws.

There has been some movement, however. In a recent British Columbia case, the Court of Appeal held that a customary adoption according to Gitksan law was sufficient to qualify the elderly plaintiffs as "dependent parents" eligible for death benefits under the province's statutory motor vehicle insurance scheme. The justices overruled the trial judge's decision that customary adoption gives rise only to moral rights, not legal ones.[148] In doing so the court stated that at least some aboriginal rights of "social self-regulation" have survived to the 1990s and that customary adoption rights are recognized and affirmed both by the common law and by s. 35(1) of the *Constitution Act, 1982*.[149]

Australian courts have not gone quite so far, but they have long taken aboriginal law into consideration in sentencing offenders, and in 1986 the Australian Law Reform Commission produced a lengthy report on *The Recognition of Aboriginal Customary Laws*.[150] In it the Commission drew a distinction between treating aboriginal laws as a factor in sentencing and actually incorporating such laws into sentences, recommending against the latter if the aboriginal sanction were contrary to general law. The Commission also was of the view that, in international law, article 7 of the International Covenant on Civil and Political Rights (prohibiting torture and cruel, inhuman, or degrading punishment) would override article 27 (protecting the right of

147 See e.g. the *Report of the Aboriginal Justice Inquiry of Manitoba*, 2 vols. (Winnipeg: Queen's Printer, 1991); the Royal Commission Into Aboriginal Deaths in Custody, *National Report* (Canberra: A.G.P.S., 1991); the *Report of the Royal Commission on Aboriginal Peoples* (*supra* note 43); and M. Jackson "Criminality and the Exclusion of Maori" (1990) 20 V.U.W.L.R. 23. Recognition of aboriginal law in defined circumstances is a *fait accompli* in the United States.

148 *Casimel v. Insurance Corp. of British Columbia*, [1994] 2 C.N.L.R. 22 (B.C.C.A.), discussed in J. Fiske, "The Supreme Law and the Grand Law: Changing Significance of Customary Law for Aboriginal Women of British Columbia" (1995) 105 and 106 B.C. Studies 183 at 184-91. And cf. *Wilson v. Wilson*, discussed at [1991] 4 C.N.L.R. 1.

149 *Casimel*, *ibid.* at 25 and 27. Contrast *Thomas v. Norris*, [1992] 2 C.N.L.R. 139, in which the B.C. Supreme Court rejected an argument that the healing ceremony imposed on the plaintiff was protected by s. 35 and awarded him damages for assault and false imprisonment.

150 Report No. 31 (Canberra: 1986).

minorities to enjoy their own culture, religion, and language).[151] Since then there have been two judicial decisions of particular note. In the first, the Court of Appeal for the Northern Territory appears to have held that courts may take an aboriginal sanction into account, even if it violates the general law, although some members of the court pointed out that payback such as spearing may not be unlawful if the parties consented and if no serious harm was intended.[152] In most jurisdictions this will depend upon how assault is defined by statute;[153] in others it will depend upon the common law.[154] In the second case, the Supreme Court of the Northern Territory made an order that, instead of simply recognizing a past spearing, provided for monitoring a spearing that had yet to take place. This order would seem to amount to incorporating an aboriginal sanction into the sentence of the court.[155]

In New Zealand there seem to have been fewer initiatives in this area, perhaps because there is a higher degree of integration in that country and because the reserve system does not exist there in the way it does in Canada, the United States, and, to a lesser extent, Australia.[156] Nor is the Maori Land Court really an exception: it not only has no jurisdiction apart from its authority over Maori lands, but even its real property jurisprudence is composed not of customary law but of the complex rules that were introduced by the Pakeha to supersede customary forms of tenure.[157] It is true that some New Zealand courts have referred cases to *marae* committees for sentencing and that, by statute, Maori communities may deal with some minor offences.[158] There is also the Te Atatu Maori Committee, which deals with

151 "Article 27 protects the right of a minority to profess or practise religion. It does not in terms protect cruel or inhumane punishments connected with it": see Discussion Paper No. 17 (1980) at 53, cited in S. Bronnit "Recognition of Aboriginal Customary Law – Relevance of 'Payback' in Sentencing in Australia" (School of Law, Australia Nat. Univ., 1995) at 15 [unpublished].

152 See *R. v. Minor* (1992), 79 N.T.R. 1 (Ct. Crim. App.).

153 Bronnit, *supra* note 151 at 11-12 and 17. In Canada the most recent consideration of this question (in a non-aboriginal context) is in *Jobidon v. The Queen* (1991), 66 C.C.C. (3d) 454 (S.C.C.).

154 See e.g. *R. v. Brown* (1993), 97 Cr. App. R. 44 (H.L.) and D. McArdle, "A Few Hard Cases? Sport, Sadomasochism and Public Policy in the English Courts" (1995) 10 Can. J. of Law and Society 109-117.

155 See the case of Wilson Jagamara Walker, discussed in Bronnit, *supra* note 151 at 7-9. It is also reported in *The Independent Monthly* (May 1974) at 37-38 and *The Canberra Times* (27 May 1994) at 3.

156 This state of affairs is in marked contrast to that colony's early history, however. The colonial office contemplated a declaratory law recognizing Maori customs that were not "repugnant" (such as cannibalism). In James Stephens' view, the law was blocked "by the spirit of legal pedantry from which no English society is ever emancipated, and by the contempt and aversion with which the European races everywhere regard the Black races" (quoted in Ward, *supra* note 77 at 62).

157 See Chief Judge E. T. Durie, "Custom Law: Address to the New Zealand Society for Legal and Social Philosophy" (1994) 24 VUWLR 325 at 326. On the Maori (formerly Native) Land Court, see text accompanying notes 86 and 87, *supra*.

young offenders diverted from the regular system in a manner somewhat similar to Canadian sentencing circles.[159] Nonetheless, critics fault the criminal justice system for excluding Maori customs and concerns – a criticism that is, of course, levelled in the other jurisdictions as well.[160]

Notwithstanding such criticism, national governments – except for the United States – remain cautious about according status to aboriginal law and justice systems. Canadian and New Zealand judges and politicians would therefore have no quarrel with the High Court of Australia's pronouncement in *Walker v. State of New South Wales*[161] that aboriginal people in Australia are subject to the general criminal law. But the court's contention that "English criminal law did not, and Australian criminal law does not, accommodate an alternative body of law operating alongside it" is more problematic.[162] This statement does not, of course, apply to the United States, where tribes legislate and adjudicate respecting many civil matters and less serious crimes; but it would also be misleading to try to apply it to Canada, even though, as yet, there are no tribal courts or legislatures. In Canada the issue is still open, not about whether aboriginal people are *presently* subject to criminal or other types of law (they are),[163] but about whether room will be made for some degree of "separateness," either because the constitution requires it or because Parliament so chooses.[164] This question is not being posed in such a stark way in New Zealand, but there are parallels in Australia. Even in Queensland, aboriginal councils are permitted, by statute, to constitute their own courts for dealing with breaches of bylaws, and with disputes that the community regards as governed by their traditional usages and customs.[165]

One focus of the debate about aboriginal justice systems is crime; another

158 *Report of the Aboriginal Justice Inquiry of Manitoba*, vol. I, *supra* note 147 at 301. A *marae* is a traditional meeting place for spiritual and community matters.

159 *Ibid.*

160 See e.g. Jackson, *supra* note 147.

161 (1994), 126 A.L.R. 321 (H.C.) at 323, in which the plaintiff argued, unsuccessfully, that the state parliament could not legislate with respect to aboriginal people without their consent. In Canada, see *R. v. Beboning* (1908), 17 O.L.R. 23 at 25 (C.A.), discussed in Foster, *supra* note 74 at 347, and, more recently, *R. v. Williams*, [1994] B.C.J. No. 2745 (B.C.C.A.).

162 *Walker*, *ibid.* at 323-24.

163 See, however, the unsuccessful arguments made by the accused in *Williams*, *supra* note 161, and by lawyer Bruce Clark (*supra* note 124) in a number of cases in and out of court, including the armed standoff at Gustafsen Lake, B.C., in the summer of 1995.

164 See e.g. the recommendation of the Aboriginal Justice Inquiry of Manitoba (*supra* note 147) in favour of a separate aboriginal justice system in that province, and the adverse and very public reaction to this proposal by a member of the Manitoba Court of Appeal in the Winnipeg *Free Press* (13 Sept. 1992) A7.

165 See Brennan, *supra* note 19 at 246. This is currently more than Canadian band councils may do. The *Indian Act* courts that were first provided for in the 1880s were

is child custody and adoption. In the United States, the *Indian Child Welfare Act* of 1978 provides that, subject to any federal law to the contrary, tribal courts have exclusive jurisdiction over the custody and adoption of children domiciled or residing within the tribal reservation.[166] Even if the child in question resides or is domiciled outside the reservation, tribal courts have a jurisdiction that is concurrent with that of the relevant state; and in cases of foster care placement or termination of parental rights, the state court must transfer the case to the tribal court upon petition, unless there is good cause to retain jurisdiction or either parent objects. Perhaps most important of all, in adoption cases both state and tribal courts must, in the absence of good cause to the contrary, give preference to placing the child with (1) a member of the child's extended family; (2) other members of the child's tribe; or (3) other Indian families.[167]

These issues are also important in the other jurisdictions. Cases in Canada, Australia, and New Zealand reveal a heightened awareness and concern that cultural identity and the rights of the extended family or tribe be considered. In New Zealand, for example, the Maori view that the *whanau* (extended family), *hapu* (sub-tribe) and *iwi* (tribe) have a responsibility for children that may override that of the birth parents is reflected in the policy of the Department of Social Welfare. But it has not been enacted into law.[168] The need to retain cultural ties and tribal identity has also been recognized in Canada[169] and Australia,[170] but when it comes to the forensic crunch the "best interests of the child" are usually interpreted in such a way as to subordinate these factors.[171] Naturally, opinions differ about whether the proper balance has been struck.[172] Only in the United States does the law specifically provide for tribal interests, and only in the United States is it

---

presided over by Indian agents. See generally B. W. Morse, "A Unique Court: S. 107 *Indian Act* Justices of the Peace" (1982) 5: 2 and 3 Canadian Legal Aid Bulletin at 131.

166 25 U.S.C. 1901-68.

167 See Canby, *supra* note 56 at 164 and C. Davies, Q.C., "Native Children and the Child Welfare System in Canada" (1992) 30 Alta. L. Rev. 1200 at 1214-15.

168 See P. F. Tapp, "Family Law" [1990] NZ Recent L. Rev. 102 at 104-108, and cases cited therein, especially the remarks of Borrin J. in *Re Adoption 23/89* (F. C. Porirua, 3 Oct. 1989). For a different perspective, see the critical comments of P. J. Downey, "Race and Adoption" [1993] New Zealand L. J. 425.

169 See e.g. *Racine v. Woods*, [1983] 2 S.C.R. 173 and *Sawan v. Tearoe*, [1994] 1 W.W.R. 419 (B.C.C.A.), leave to appeal dismissed [1994] 2 W.W.R. lxv (S.C.C.).

170 See e.g. *In the Marriage of: McI Husband and McI Wife* (1991), F.L.C. 92-238.

171 As Wilson J. put it in *Racine* (*supra* note 169 at 187): "when the test to be met is the best interests of the child, the significance of cultural background and heritage as opposed to bonding abates over time. The closer the bond that develops with the prospective parents the less important the racial element becomes."

172 Compare e.g. the views of Davies, *supra* note 167, who urges legislators to "think long and hard" before following the U.S. example, and the late Samuel Bull, former chief of the Goodfish Lake Band in Alberta, Canada in "The Special Case of the Native Child" (1989) 47 The Advocate 523.

applied in tribal courts.[173]

The reasons for the growth of tribal law and separate justice systems in the United States are both historical and philosophical. Historically, the tradition of inherent tribal sovereignty took hold in American law in a way that it did not in the other jurisdictions. Not only did it arise as a natural consequence of the military alliances of the late eighteenth and early nineteenth centuries; it also developed as a convenient counter to the states' rights doctrine that federalists, notably the court headed by Chief Justice John Marshall, opposed. Philosophically, it satisfied the need aboriginal and non-aboriginal reformers felt for an alternative to the assimilation and dependency that resulted from the breaking up of the reservations after the 1870s and, much later, of tribal termination in the 1950s.[174] In Canada and New Zealand this process was hindered, almost from the outset, by the view that aboriginal people were British subjects – albeit without many of the rights enjoyed by their fellow subjects; and in Australia, as we have seen, the situation was even worse. In the United States, on the other hand, Indians were legally members of domestic dependent nations, which were regarded as possessing at least a limited sovereignty.[175]

Philosophy is also one of the prime obstacles in the way of New Zealand, Australia, and Canada developing their own versions of the American approach. Tribal sovereignty sits rather uneasily both with liberal individualism and with some versions of rule of law ideology, and is easily portrayed as a demand for special rights or as a denial of equality before the law. In jurisdictions like Canada, where in British Columbia alone there are numerous aboriginal language and ethnic groups, it can even be characterized as a form of balkanization. Nowhere is this controversy more intense than when a dispute pits individual rights against communal or tribal ones; and in both Canada and the United States, the issue of whether tribal governments should be restrained by the same "rights document" that limits the federal and local governments has become a sort of flashpoint.

In the United States, the Bill of Rights binds only Congress and, to a somewhat lesser extent, the states. Accordingly, those who wanted tribal governments to respect individual rights had to secure the passage of the *Indian Civil Rights Act* (*ICRA*) in 1968.[176] This statute, which was enacted in the face of opposition from many Native Americans, imposed most of the restrictions

---

173 A possible exception is the Spallumcheen Indian Band child welfare by-law in British Columbia, which gives the band exclusive jurisdiction over custody of a band child whether on or off reserve: see Davies, *supra* note 167 at 1207-209.

174 The termination process was effectively reversed in subsequent years. See e.g. the case of the Menominee Tribe of Wisconsin, which was terminated in 1961 and "restored" in 1973 (described in Getches and Wilkinson, *supra* note 55 at 148-51).

175 Until well into the twentieth century, many Indians were not U.S. citizens: see Canby, *supra* note 56 at 237-38.

176 See note 57, *supra*.

contained in the Bill of Rights on the tribes, and the federal courts initially viewed it as constituting a congressional waiver of the tribes' sovereign immunity.[177] However, the United States Supreme Court ruling in *Santa Clara* that, in most cases, the tribal court's interpretation of the *ICRA* is final significantly reduced the potential impact of the *ICRA* as a rights document. *Santa Clara* is therefore a controversial decision.[178] In particular, many – although certainly not all – aboriginal women worry that tribal governments dominated by men will not respect their rights unless they are subject to some form of external review and, if necessary, restraint.[179] Similar concerns have been expressed in Australia, although there the emphasis has been upon a renewed customary law.[180]

In Canada this issue gained prominence during the debate over the Charlottetown Accord in 1992, and it is an important aspect of current land claim and self-government talks.[181] Section 32 of the *Constitution Act, 1982* states only that the Canadian Charter of Rights and Freedoms binds the provincial and the federal governments. It would therefore seem that if constitutional space is made for aboriginal governments, the Charter will not apply unless specific provision is made to that effect.[182]

In sum, then, it would seem that the primary obstacle to increased recognition of aboriginal law in the behavioural sector is some form of assurance that an acceptable accommodation between collective and individual rights can be worked out. In the United States and, since 1982, Canada, the debate has been shaped by the existence of entrenched rights documents. The debates in New Zealand and Australia lack this sort of focus, but the issues are much the same, whether it is a question of differential punishment in criminal law or the role of culture in adoption and custody cases. And the context for all this is the contested status of aboriginal sovereignty and aboriginal title: that is, whether and to what extent aboriginal governments will exercise independent, albeit limited, authority over defined territories and/or defined populations within the nation-state.[183] If an aboriginal government

177 But as the Chairman of the Mescalero Apache Tribe is said to have somewhat wryly observed, "Every Indian is opposed to the Indian Civil Rights Act ... until he has been screwed by his tribal council" (quoted in J. De Raismes "The Indian Civil Rights Act of 1968 and the Pursuit of Responsible Tribal Self-Government" (1975) 20 South Dakota L. Rev. 59). For a different perspective see A. J. Ziontz, "In Defense of Tribal Sovereignty: An Analysis of Judicial Error in Construction of the Indian Civil Rights Act" (1975) 20 South Dakota L. Rev. 1. Both articles are pre-*Santa Clara* (*supra* note 58).

178 *Supra* note 58.

179 See e.g. the back-to-back comments, pro and con, by A. Pearldaughter and V. Lindstrom in 6 American Indian L. Rev. 187 and 205 (1978).

180 See Bulbeck, *supra* note 145, and the incident described by Brennan, *supra* note 19 at 250.

181 See note 32, *supra*, and *Native Women's Association of Canada et al. v. Canada et al.* (1995), 173 N.R. 241 (S.C.C.).

182 For a contrary view see Slattery, *supra* note 43; Hogg and Turpel, *supra* note 43.

is perceived as contrived or artificial, its authority to depart from long-established or even relatively recent constitutional protections is seriously compromised. If, on the other hand, it is seen as possessing a sovereignty similar in kind to that of the wider polity, its position on such matters stands a much better chance of being respected, if not entirely accepted.[184]

Related to this is another concern. The demand for recognition of aboriginal law is coming at a time when that same law is in a parlous state.[185] Weakened by decades, even centuries, of social dislocation, its practitioners are trying to re-establish it in an age of change so rapid as to have been unimaginable only a few years ago. If this project is to succeed, it seems likely that the aboriginal peoples of Canada, Australia, and New Zealand will not only have to recover the old law, but re-invent it.[186] Although many doubt whether such regeneration is possible and fear the changes it will involve, many more hope that the result will be legal systems that better meet the needs of everyone, aboriginal and non-aboriginal alike.[187]

---

183 This way of putting it acknowledges that there is also an issue of self-government for urban aboriginal populations: e.g. the Métis in Canada.

184 For a remarkable exploration of the aboriginal perspective on some of the issues raised here, see R. Ross, *Dancing with a Ghost: Exploring Indian Reality* (Markham, Ont.: Octopus Publishing Group, 1992).

185 See e.g. Brennan, *supra* note 19 at 249-53.

186 The only other alternative would appear to be a statute book not unlike those of some of the American tribes, which are modelled very closely on state codes. On these reservations the benefit appears to lie in separate enforcement by Indian – or predominantly Indian – police, judges, and lawyers, rather than in the substantive law. As Ross (*supra* note 184 at 111) puts it, Indian bands in Northern Ontario are "reluctant to see their laws administered by strangers from the outside." One commentator on aboriginal communities in Quebec has made the same observation, noting significant "support for both Canadian and Quebec laws (with the exception of laws related to hunting and fishing). The main problem as perceived was that the system was administered by strangers": *Putting Aboriginal Justice Devolution into Practice: The Canadian and International Experience*, Workshop Report (1995) at 6 [unpublished].

187 See e.g. Ross, *supra* note 184. In Canada, the impact of the Supreme Court's decision in *Delgamuukw, supra* note 41, will be significant because its strong affirmation of aboriginal title as a communal property right suggests governance powers as a corollary. Although the decision was handed down too late to be fully incorporated into the present essay, an assessment of the legal and historical basis for the decision maybe found in Foster, "Aboriginal Title and the Provincial Obligation to Respect It: Is *Delgamuukw* v. *British Columbia* 'Invented Law'?" (1998) 56 *The Advocate* 221-31.

11
Alternative Dispute Resolution in Thailand and Cambodia: Making Common Sense on (Un)Common Ground

Andrew J. Pirie

INTRODUCTION

> The establishment of ADR processes would benefit Nicaragua in both the short and long term. In the short term, ADR would lessen the pressure on administrative and judicial institutions by resolving current post-revolutionary property disputes. In the long-term, ADR would bring more collaborative and problem-solving techniques to Nicaraguan society ... The team believes that a real window of opportunity exists to establish ADR in Nicaragua and make a long-lasting improvement in Nicaraguan society.[1]

> The language was ours, to use as we pleased. The literature that came with it was therefore of peculiar authority; but this literature was like an alien mythology. There was, for instance, Wordsworth's notorious poem about the daffodil. A pretty flower, no doubt; but we had never seen it. Could the poem have any meaning for us.[2]

The expression "alternative dispute resolution" and its acronym ADR grew out of popular dissatisfaction with the administration of justice in the United States in the 1970s. Two decades later, ADR ideas and practices are blossoming not only in the United States but also in Canada, England, and Australia.[3]

However, recently and increasingly, ADR is being promoted in many regions and countries with cultures quite different from the dominant cultures

---

1 Newsletter of the Consortium of Georgia Universities for the Advancement of Conflict Resolution Theory and Education (Atlanta, Georgia: Aug. 1995) at 3.

2 V. S. Naipaul, "Jasmine," in R. Hammer, ed., *Critical Perspectives on V. S. Naipaul* (London: Heinemann, 1977).

3 For a sense of this growth, see *Alternative Dispute Resolution in the United States: A Bibliography* (Washington, D.C.: American Arbitration Association, 1987); "Bibliography Issue" (1994) 9 Ohio State J. on Dispute Resolution 433-619; W. A. McHenry, *We Can Work It Out: A Dispute Resolution Bibliography* (Victoria, B.C.; UVic Inst. for Dispute Resolution, 1989).

of the areas where ADR has flourished.[4] Important questions arise from the increasing incidence of ADR across cultures. For example, what role does culture play in understanding and shaping disputing behaviour, theories and institutions? Are disputing concepts transferable across clear cultural divides? Are there disputing practices that transcend culture, that are just common sense? What is the relationship between alternative dispute resolution and existing legal systems, particularly non-Western legal systems? Are there possibilities of developing global processes of dispute resolution? Should there be concerns about cultural diffusion? Can ADR have any meaning in other countries?

---

4 See e.g. S. T. Wildau, C. Moore, and B. S. Mayer, "Developing Democratic Decision-Making and Dispute Resolution Procedures Abroad" (1992-93) 10 Mediation Quarterly 303; B. E. Barnes, "Conflict Resolution Across Cultures: A Hawaii Perspective and a Pacific Mediation Model" (1994-95) 12 Mediation Quarterly 117; T. Kennedy-Grant, "Dispute Resolution in the Pacific" [1987] New Zealand L. J. 294; "Alternative Dispute Resolution in Papua, New Guinea" (1996) 8 Newsletter of the International Conflict Resolution Centre at 14; J. P. Lederach, "Mediating Conflict in Central America" (1991) 28 J. of Peace Research 85; R. J. Volkerma, "Alternative Dispute Resolution in Brazil" (1989-90) 7 Mediation Quarterly 59; N. Iwai, "Alternative Dispute Resolution in Court: The Japanese Experience" (1990-91) 6 Ohio State Journal on Dispute Resolution 201; "Alternative Forms of Dispute Resolution in Chinese Commercial Transactions" (1994) New Zealand L.J. 187; D. LeResche, "Comparison of The American Mediation Process with a Korean-American Harmony Restoration Process" (1991-92) 9 Mediation Quarterly 323; S. Zaidel, "Challenges Facing the Development of Family Mediation in Israel" (1990-91) 8 Mediation Quarterly 281; L. Diamond and R. L. Fisher, "Integrating Conflict Resolution Training and Consultation: A Cyprus Example" (1995) 11 Negotiation J. 287; T. R. Colosi, "Training East Europeans to Develop ADR and Negotiating Techniques" (1992) 47 Arbitration J. 46; R. Coulson, "Will the Growth of Alternative Dispute Resolution Be Replicated in Europe?" (1992) 9 J. of Int'l Arbitration 39; C. B. Wiggins, "Exporting Process Technology: Transplanting North American Public Interest Mediation to Central Europe" (1992-93), 10 Mediation Quarterly 273; D. Ondrusek, "The Mediator's Role in National Conflicts in Post-Communist Central Europe" (1992-93) 10 Mediation Quarterly 243; J. Olszanska, R. Olszanska, and J. Wozniak, "Do Peaceful Conflict Management Methods Pose Problems in Posttotalitarian Poland" (1992-93) 10 Mediation Quarterly 291; O. A. Tjersland, "Extended Mediation in Norway" (1994-95) 12 Mediation Quarterly 117; R. M. Slim and H. H. Saunders, "Managing Conflict in Divided Societies: Lessons from Tajikistan" (1996) 12 Negotiation J. 31; M. Jackson, "In Search of Pathways to Justice: Alternative Dispute Resolution in Aboriginal Communities" (1992) U.B.C. L. Rev. Special Edition 147; P. Monture-Okanee, "Alternative Dispute Resolution: A Bridge to Aboriginal Experience?" in C. Morris and A. Pirie, eds., *Qualification for Dispute Resolution: Perspectives on the Debate* (Victoria, B.C.: UVic Inst. for Dispute Resolution, 1994) 131; S. Assanand, "Indo-Canadian Diversity Issues in Mediation," *The Mediator*, winter 1993-94, Vancouver, B.C.; J. P. Lederach, *Preparing for Peace: Conflict Transformation Across Cultures* (Syracuse, N.Y.: Syracuse Univ. Press, 1995); K. Avruch, P. Black, and J. Scimeccia, *Conflict Resolution: Cross Cultural Perspectives* (New York: Greenwood Press, 1991); D. W. Augsburger, *Conflict Mediation Across Cultures: Pathways and Patterns* (Louisville, Kentucky: Westminster/John Knox, 1992); M. LeBaron Duryea and J. B. Grundison, *Conflict and Culture: Research in Five Communities in British Columbia* (Victoria, B.C.: UVic Inst. for Dispute Resolution, 1993); K. Cloke, "Conflict Resolution System Design, the United Nations and the New World Order" (1991-92) 9 Mediation Quarterly 343; and, to show you that the sky's the limit, K. H. Brockstiegal, "Settlement of Disputes Regarding Space Activities" (1993) 21 J. of Space Law 1.

This chapter provides an opportunity to consider these and related questions by examining recent ADR initiatives in two Southeast Asian countries, Thailand and Cambodia.[5] The chapter begins by exploring the meaning of alternative dispute resolution, paying special attention to the conflicting motivations behind ADR developments and ADR's ambiguous relationships with existing laws and legal systems. Second, the chapter reviews the notion of culture, and surveys recent work that juxtaposes conflict with culture. Third, with an appreciation of ADR's meaning and in light of these observations on conflict and culture, the chapter examines the details of recent ADR activities in Thailand and Cambodia. It concludes with the suggestion that the real promise of ADR across cultures is not achieved by praising the common sense of ADR but rather by critically examining the complexities and consequences of introducing Western ADR beliefs into diverse cultural settings such as Thailand and Cambodia. Any criticism of works on ADR in other cultures is meant to be constructive and to encourage recognition of the enormous (and still to be identified) challenges to be met in working with dispute resolution practices and principles alongside culture.

THE MEANING OF ALTERNATIVE DISPUTE RESOLUTION

The Modern Emergence of ADR

Before considering ADR experiences in Thailand and Cambodia, it is useful to explore the question – what is ADR? As the name suggests, ADR began as a study of alternatives. Citing a need to avoid the undue cost and delay associated with court adjudication of disputes and to increase access to justice while also drawing attention to the benefits of empowering disputants to resolve their own problems, ADR proponents in the United States looked beyond the adversarial arena of the courtroom and the dominant dispute resolution image of the lawyer as "a knight in shining armour whose courtroom lance strikes down all obstacles."[6] To a substantial degree, informal

5 This chapter does not review the increasing examples of dispute resolution mechanisms and systems being incorporated into trade and other international agreements between and among world countries. There is a growing body of literature that is examining and comparing disputing regimes for resolving inter-nation relations and resulting disputes. For example, see T. L. McDorman, "Using the Dispute Settlement Regime of the Free Trade Agreement: The West Coast Salmon and Herring Problem" (1990) 4 Canada-U.S. Business L. Rev. 177; S. P. Croley and J. H. Jackson, "WTO Dispute Procedures, Standards of Review, and Deference to National Governments" (1996) 90 Amer. J. of Int'l Law 113; R. Knutson, "Dispute Provisions: Recent Developments at FIDIC and the World Bank" (1996) 13 Int'l Construction L. Rev. 174. The relationships between these international disputing arrangements and the more local or internal disputing practices of a country, which are the focus of this chapter, require analysis.

6 Warren Burger, former Chief Justice of the United States Supreme Court, in "Isn't There a Better Way?" (1982) 68 A.B.A.J. 274, from the annual report on the state of the judiciary to the American Bar Association.

methods of dispute resolution became a major focus of ADR, illustrated through, for example, the efforts in the 1970s to establish neighbourhood justice centres as decentralized, deprofessionalized, self-governing community forums.[7]

If informalism or "informal justice" made up the large body of ADR, the heart of the movement clearly was mediation, the antithesis of court adjudication. Folberg and Taylor define mediation "as a voluntary process in which a neutral third party, who lacks authority to impose a solution, helps participants to reach their own agreement for resolving a dispute or planning a transaction."[8] Others simply say mediation is "assisted negotiations." Lon Fuller in an early description of mediation's forms and functions said: "The central quality of mediation is its capacity to reorient the parties toward each other, not by imposing rules on them, but by helping them to achieve a new and shared perception of their relationship, a perception that will redirect their attitudes and disposition toward one another."[9]

Not surprisingly, the perspective that ADR was a necessary response to failings in the existing justice system, more the norm than an alternative,[10] and better to boot, drew initial criticism and hostility. More often than not, these first critics came from a legal profession and judiciary that felt its court-centred procedural and economic structures under attack from ADR and its many non-lawyer supporters. Specific concerns were directed at mediation, a process that was new and unfamiliar to most lawyers.[11]

While the ADR movement was not stopped by these critics, it was changed by them. One important change has been a redefinition of ADR. An example of this new definition is contained in the 1989 Task Force Report on Alternative Dispute Resolution[12] prepared by the Canadian Bar Association (CBA). The Report urges lawyers, and presumably others working with disputes, to see their primary function as problem-solving. Rather than separating ADR procedures from traditional court procedures, this definition urges the problem-solver to evaluate the entire continuum of dispute

7 For example, see R. Danzig, "Toward the Creation of a Complimentary, Decentralized System of Criminal Justice" (1973) 26 Stanford L. Rev. 1.

8 J. Folberg and A. Taylor, *Mediation: A Comprehensive Guide to Resolving Conflict Without Litigation* (San Francisco: Jossey-Bass Inc., 1984).

9 L. L. Fuller, "Mediation – Its Forms and Functions" (1971) 44 Southern California L. Rev. 305 at 325.

10 Professor Carrie Menkel-Meadow makes the obvious point that 90-95% of litigation is settled outside of court and that it is a "misnomer" to label processes such as mediation, negotiation, and arbitration as alternatives. "They are the norm in dispute resolution": C. Menkel-Meadow, "Dispute Resolution: The Periphery Becomes the Core" (1986) 69 Judicature 300.

11 Riskin describes the tension between mediation and the lawyer's "standard philosophical map" in L. L. Riskin, "Mediation and Lawyers" (1982) 43 Ohio State L.J. 29.

12 Canadian Bar Association, *Task Force on Alternative Dispute Resolution, Alternative Dispute Resolution: A Canadian Perspective* (Ottawa: CBA, 1989).

resolution techniques, skills, and resources and then to choose the most appropriate steps to take. In this definition, ADR is an expression of commitment to fair, effective, and accessible dispute resolution, whether that involves using the traditional legal system or not. As the CBA Report states, "alternative dispute resolution will not be viewed as superior or inferior to, or indeed even separate from, court adjudication."[13]

The preferred initials remain ADR, although suggested replacements include better dispute resolution (BDR), enhanced dispute resolution (EDR), innovative dispute resolution (IDR) or, for consistency, appropriate dispute resolution. Whatever the adjective, the emphasis is no longer primarily on alternatives to the court. A 1995 Canadian Forum on Dispute Resolution stated that alternative dispute resolution "should be considered an umbrella term which encompasses litigation, focusing on the appropriate method for resolving any given dispute."[14]

The initiatives and reforms that now qualify as ADR range from mandatory settlement conferences to mini-trials, to private judging, to negotiating, to avoiding disputes. Some writers conceptualize ADR as being made up of "primary" dispute resolution processes, such as adjudication, arbitration, mediation, and negotiation, and "hybrid" processes, such as private judging, neutral expert fact-finding, mini-trial, ombudspersons, and summary jury trial.[15] Riskin and Westbrook categorize the major methods of dispute processing as "adjudicative processes," including court and administrative proceedings, arbitration, and private tribunals; "consensual processes," including ombudspersons, fact finding, negotiation, mediation, and conciliation; and "mixed processes," including med-arb, mini-trial and summary jury trial.[16]

Mediation still remains an integral component of ADR. Although the use of mediation in Canada does not quantitatively rival its applications in the United States, there is no question that mediation is receiving enthusiastic attention in a range of settings, from private disputes involving neighbours and families[17] to enormous experiments in land use and resource

---

13 *Ibid.* at 4.

14 *Charting the Course, Report of the Canadian Forum on Dispute Resolution* (Ottawa: Department of Justice, 1995) at 12.

15 S. B. Goldberg, E. D. Green, and F. E. A. Sander, *Dispute Resolution* (Boston: Little, Brown and Co., 1985) at 7-10.

16 L. L. Riskin and J. E. Westbrook, *Dispute Resolution and Lawyers* (St. Paul, Minnesota: West Publishing Co., 1978) at 2-6.

17 For a review of the literature on neighbourhood justice centres, see C. Morris, ed., *Resolving Community Disputes: An Annotated Bibliography about Community Justice Centres* (Victoria, B.C.: UVic Inst. for Dispute Resolution, 1994). The literature on family mediation is voluminous, but for an overview of family mediation practices, see R. Phegan, "The Family Mediation System: An Art of Distribution" (1995) 40 McGill L.J. 365 and the references therein.

management.[18] This growth and acceptance of mediation is especially evident in the legal profession. The difference a day makes is perhaps best illustrated in the following two quotations, the first from an address by the Chief Justice of the British Columbia Supreme Court in 1989 "putting the boots to ADR," the second from a brochure eagerly promoting a 1994 ADR conference sponsored by the Canadian Bar Association.

> ADR is often supported by well-intentioned people who, for a variety of reasons, are anxious to reorganize society and procedures of courts with naive, theoretical concepts of humanity and efficiency ... society's decent people need the no-nonsense, straightforward procedures of courtroom litigation to fight unreasonable claims and not the "soft" procedures ADR offers.[19]
>
> This symposium is for practitioners, judges, educators, and government officials who have already heard all the arguments and are ready and eager to use these new forms of dispute resolution in appropriate circumstances.[20]

While ADR now covers a lot of ground, one spot on the ADR terrain is much touted and is worth visiting briefly. With ADR's continued emphasis on mediation, attention turned, naturally enough, to the process of negotiation that takes place within a mediation and to what makes an effective negotiator. Although the literature on negotiation is voluminous, one concept has stood out. That concept is interest-based bargaining, which was popularized by Fisher and Ury in *Getting to Yes*.[21] The idea was simply presented by them as follows:

> Consider the story of two men quarreling in a library. One wants the window open and the other wants it closed. They bicker back and forth about how much to leave it open: a crack, halfway, three quarters of the way. No solution satisfies them both. Enter the librarian. She asks one why he wants

---

18 The Commission on Resources and Environment (CORE) in British Columbia is an example of the mega-mediation project. CORE's mandate, set out in the *Commission on Resources and Environment Act,* S.B.C. 1992, c. 34, was to develop a province-wide strategy for land use and related resource and environmental management. To develop plans for Vancouver Island, Chilcotin, East Kootenay, and West Kootenay Boundary, comprising over 10 million hectares of land and home to a long history of land use conflicts, CORE relied heavily on a "shared decision-making" model, meaning that all public interests as well as the provincial government, with the assistance of professional mediators, would work for a limited time in an effort to reach a consensus.

19 Chief Justice Allan McEachern, quoted in "Chief Justice Puts Boots to ADR," *Lawyers Weekly* (26 Oct. 1989) 2.

20 Canadian Bar Association, "Alternative Dispute Resolution in Action in Canada," C.B.A. Conference (11-12 Mar. 1994), Vancouver, B.C.

21 R. Fisher and W. Ury, *Getting to Yes: Negotiating Agreement Without Giving In* (Boston: Houghton Mifflin Co., 1981).

> the window open. "To get fresh air." She asks the other why he wants it closed. "To avoid a draft." After thinking a moment, she opens wide a window in the next room, bringing in fresh air without a draft.[22]

In interest-based bargaining, interests are the needs, desires, concerns, and fears that motivate people. Behind stated positions – what the parties want out of a negotiation – are these underlying interests. By focusing on the interests or needs of the disputants, Fisher and Ury argue that certain benefits follow. First, common ground will be found. While the parties' positions, or what they want, may be in conflict, they may share common interests. For example, a divorcing couple may disagree about who gets custody of the children, but agree that any custody arrangement must, at least, be economically affordable and preserve the children's relationship with both parents. Second, focusing on interests can "create options for mutual gain." In the library example, the solution that satisfied both parties was not immediately apparent until the librarian helped the parties identify their underlying needs – a common interest in a comfortable working environment and individual needs for fresh air and avoiding drafts. Finally, Fisher and Ury argue that agreements that meet underlying interests are more likely to be long-lasting. Interests represent basic human needs including psychological needs. If an agreement satisfies these needs, a change in the agreement will be unnecessary unless needs change. Of course, the achievement of durable agreements means that *all* important interests must be identified and satisfied. While a payment of money to an ex-employee in a wrongful dismissal action may satisfy her or his economic needs, a reasonable monetary settlement offer may be rejected, at least for a time, if psychological concerns around the perceived unfair procedure of dismissal are not addressed. "I'm going to court on principle" may reveal, with careful probing, undisclosed psychological interests that may be just as important, if not more so, to a disputant than substantive monetary concerns.

Interest-based bargaining dominates much popular thinking about negotiation and mediation and, consequently, about ADR. It is common to find this concept to be an integral part of education and training programs in dispute resolution and to underlie public policies for dealing with complex conflicts. Consider the following extract from a report presenting the case for a comprehensive system for resolving land and resource management disputes. "Interest-based negotiation is emerging as an increasingly useful method for resolving disputes that emerge at any stage in land use decision-making and dispute resolution. This technique supports high levels of public participation in the administrative decision-making process, provides a

---

22 *Ibid.* at 41.

means of joint problem-solving within government, and supplements adjudicative processes."[23]

The modern emergence of ADR raises more than the cute distinction between ADR and BDR, the simple conclusion that the new definition of ADR includes courts and other formal justice processes or the growing interest in interests. The history of ADR presents several serious ambiguities that complicate our understanding of what ADR is. These ambiguities need to be explored. They are the accompanying baggage that is often undeclared when ADR travels to other countries.

The Politics and Contradictions of Informal Justice

The ambiguities around ADR are more recognizable when one realizes that the rise of ADR and mediation was not just a fad of the 1970s and early 1980s in the United States and Canada. As a contemporary reaction against formal legal institutions, ADR has both historical and geographical antecedents. For example, Auerbach describes 350 years of alternatives to the courts in the United States,[24] including rich accounts of the Freedman's Bureau, a government agency established to manage the transition from slavery to freedom after the Civil War,[25] industrial arbitration tribunals, which were a part of a search for a peaceful alternative to industrial violence at the end of the nineteenth century,[26] and the Jewish Conciliation Court of America, established to preserve harmony, achieve respectability, and prod immigrants along the road to Americanization.[27] Munger also observes the recurring nature of court reform in the United States. He suggests it is no coincidence "that the major movements for court reform and the most intense debate about the role of adjudication in society have occurred in this century during three periods of political upheaval and realignment."[28] He chronicles court reform initiatives, including the creation of alternative forums to resolve disputes, in response to political crises during the Progressive era (1905-15), the New Deal period (1930s) and the Civil Rights movement (1960s).

In Canada, there are historical accounts of Acadian communities,[29] north western fur traders,[30] and aboriginal peoples[31] resorting to informal justice.

23 Commission on Resources and Environment, *The Provincial Land Use Strategy, vol. 4, Dispute Resolution* (British Columbia: Commission on Resources and Environment, 1995) at 20.

24 J. S. Auerbach, *Justice Without Law? Resolving Disputes Without Lawyers* (New York: Oxford Univ. Press, 1983).

25 *Ibid.* at 58.

26 *Ibid.* at 60.

27 *Ibid.* at 84.

28 F. Munger, "Movements for Court Reform: A Preliminary Interpretation," in P. L. Dubois, ed., *The Politics of Judicial Reform* (Lexington, Mass.: Lexington Books, 1982) 51 at 55.

29 D. G. Bell, "A Perspective on Legal Pluralism in 19th Century New Brunswick" (1988) 37 Univ. of New Brunswick L.J. 84.

Recent research also documents the reliance on traditional methods of conflict resolution by immigrants to Canada from diverse cultural backgrounds.[32] Prior to 1970, Canadian court reform focused almost exclusively on judicial appointment procedures and jurisdictional questions.[33] However, the emergence of administrative agencies in this period to deal with the economic and social problems of a young and developing country clearly represents the delegation of adjudicative authority to non-judicial forums, which often had informal dispute resolution mechanisms.[34] Miller and Baar, in their comprehensive, post-1970 study of judicial administration in Canada,[35] saw court reform, including alternatives such as decriminalization and diversion projects, "largely influenced by its counterparts in the U.S."[36] Informalism also was visible in developing countries as well as in industrialized nations, in the Far East as well as in Europe and North America.[37]

These parallels in reform movements over space and time did not go unnoticed. Observing the cyclical nature of discontent with the courts and the resulting reforms, variously characterized as "informal justice," "community justice," "delegalization," "deinstitutionalization" or now "the programmatic development of alternative dispute resolution,"[38] critics began to look closely at the construction of this newest reform movement. What they saw were politics and contradictions.

The scope of this political critique is very broad. A good starting point is Richard Abel's *The Politics of Informal Justice*.[39] Abel and his co-contributors ask many thorny questions. Why do we find *these* changes? Why are these

30 H. Foster, "Conflict Resolution During the Fur Trade in the Canadian North West, 1803-1859" (1993) 51 The Advocate 871.

31 M. Jackson, "In Search of the Pathways to Justice: Alternative Dispute Resolution in Aboriginal Communities" (1992) Univ. of British Columbia L. Rev., special ed. 147.

32 M. LeBaron Duryea, *Conflict and Culture: A Literature Review and Bibliography* (Victoria, B.C.: UVic Inst. for Dispute Resolution, 1992); M. LeBaron Duryea and J. B. Grundison, *Conflict and Culture: Research in Five Communities in Vancouver, British Columbia* (Victoria, B.C.: UVic Inst. for Dispute Resolution, 1993).

33 P. S. Millar and C. Baar, *Judicial Administration in Canada* (Montreal: McGill-Queen's Univ. Press, 1981).

34 A good example is human rights discrimination. In Canada, early human rights legislation gave federal and provincial commissions the authority to resolve complaints by conciliation or mediation, both during or after initial investigation, in lieu of going to a formal hearing. In addition, labour-management cooperation and the resolution of disputes through conciliation or mediation mechanisms have been obvious features in the workings of labour relations boards.

35 *Supra* note 33.

36 *Ibid.* at 10.

37 M. Cappelletti, ed., *Access to Justice* (Alphen aan den Rijn: Sijthoff and Noordhoff, 1978); D. T. Weckstein, "The Purposes of Dispute Resolution: Comparative Concepts of Justice" (1988) 26 Amer. Business L.J. 605; L. Nader and H. F. Todd, *The Disputing Process: Law in Ten Societies* (New York: Columbia Univ. Press, 1978).

38 C. B. Harrington, *Shadow Justice: The Ideology and Institutionalization of Alternatives to Court* (Westport, Conn.: Greenwood Press, 1985) at 16.

39 R. L. Abel, ed., *The Politics of Informal Justice* (New York: Academic Press, 1982).

changes occurring now? Are they changes at all or have comparable phenomena always existed? If they are changes, are they part of a cycle, or a progression? What do they signify for the central issues of contemporary capitalist society: the problems of democracy, liberty, oppression, and exploitation? Do they equalize the position of disputing parties or do they aggravate existing inequalities? Do they accelerate dispute processes or do they actually delay outcomes? Do they close the gap between the promises of liberalism and the reality, or do they widen it? Do they enhance or undermine the legitimacy of the state?

While the full breadth of this critique is beyond the scope of this chapter, I would like to review one fundamental question posed by the critique. The question is an obvious one, particularly if ADR is not a new phenomenon. What are the reasons for the modern rejection of formal legal institutions, rights, and processes? Or, framed differently, what are modern ADR proponents really trying to achieve?

The question, however stated, focuses our view clearly on the goals and purposes of ADR. The resulting picture, however, is less than clear and strangely uncontroversial, given the powerful legal institutions that are being challenged. The problem with the picture is not caused by the absence or paucity of ADR goals. Expressions of purpose are easy to locate. Goldberg, Green, and Sander discern four separate goals of the alternatives movement: (1) to relieve court congestion as well as undue cost and delay; (2) to enhance community involvement in the dispute resolution process; (3) to facilitate access to justice; and (4) to provide more "effective" dispute resolution.[40]

Other references, more or less ambitious or abstract, see ADR seeking "to reorient the practice of law towards a higher quality, problem-solving approach,"[41] to achieve "extralegal justice, the achievement of goods or rights to which the parties have no legal right,"[42] to promote and maximize "human interactions that are creative, enfranchising, enriching and empowering, rather than alienating and conflict provoking"[43] and to integrate "social justice and peace ... into the fabric of society."[44]

Specific ADR programs identify more specific goals. Court-annexed programs strive, among other things, "to decrease the court's docket, to speed the pace of cases to resolution, to increase litigant satisfaction with the court

40 *Supra* note 15 at 5. Whether these goals were appropriate for ADR in Canada was asked in the Canadian Bar Association Task Force Report on ADR, *supra* note 12 at 6-7.

41 C. A. McEwan, "Pursuing Problem Solving or Predictive Settlement" (1991) 19 Florida State Univ. L. Rev. 77.

42 L. B. Edelman, J. Lande, and H. S. Erlanger, "Internal Dispute Resolution: The Transformation of Civil Rights in the Workplace" (1993) 27 Law and Society Rev. 497 at 503.

43 C. Menkel-Meadow, "Toward Another View of Legal Negotiation: The Structure of Problem Solving" (1984) 31 U.C.L.A. L. Rev. 754 at 763.

44 *Supra* note 12 at 77.

system and to lower recidivism."[45] Neighbourhood justice centres express interest in "improving communication among the parties and clarifying viewpoints, interests and positions."[46] Business people pledge allegiance to ADR because of its cheapness compared with litigation.[47] Governments want to reduce the public costs of dispute processing.

In a very thoughtful piece, Robert Baruch Bush clusters over 50 statements of sub-objectives for ADR into six "quality statement" goals. He suggests ADR programs achieve quality when:

(1) They leave disputing parties feeling that their individual desires, as defined by themselves, have been satisfied, in terms of the experience and the outcome of the process [*individual satisfaction*].

(2) They strengthen the capacity of and increase the opportunity for disputing parties to resolve their own problems without being dependent on external institutions, public or private [*individual autonomy*].

(3) They facilitate or strengthen the control of public and private institutions, and the interests they represent, over exploitable groups and over possible sources of social change or unrest [*social control*].

(4) They ameliorate, neutralize, or at least do not exacerbate existing inequalities in the societal distribution of material wealth and power [*social justice*].

(5) They provide common values, referents, or "texts" for individuals and groups in a pluralistic society, and thereby increase social solidarity among these individuals and groups [*social solidarity*].

(6) They provide opportunities for and encourage individual disputants to experience personal change and growth, particularly in terms of becoming less self-centred and more responsive to others [*personal transformation*].[48]

Several commentators provide greater goal synthesis. Menkel-Meadow distinguishes between quantitative-efficiency claims for ADR – cheaper and faster, versus qualitative-justice claims – better.[49] Galanter reframes Menkel-Meadow's descriptions into production (more with less) goals and quality

45 S. Press, "Building and Maintaining a Statewide Mediation Program: A View from the Field" (1992-93) 81 Kentucky L.J. 1029 at 1035.

46 T. J. Stipanowich, "The Quiet Revolution Comes to Kentucky: A Case Study in Community Mediation" (1992-93) 81 Kentucky L.J. 855 at 917.

47 Through the Center for Public Resources (CPR), founded in 1979, many of the largest U.S. corporations have taken a "pledge" to pursue some form of ADR in disputes with each other but, interestingly, not with non-signatories. The recently formed Canadian Foundation for Dispute Resolution in Calgary, Alberta is pretty much a CPR clone, set up to make the business community and its lawyers more aware of the benefits of ADR.

48 R. A. Baruch Bush, "Defining Quality in Dispute Resolution: Taxonomies and Anti-Taxonomies of Quality Arguments" (1989) 66 Denver Univ. L. Rev. 335 at 347.

49 C. Menkel-Meadow, "Pursuing Settlement in an Adversary Culture: A Tale of Innovation Co-opted or the Law of ADR" (1991) 19 Florida State L. Rev. 1 at 6.

(encompassing valued aspects of a process apart from time, cost, and institutional convenience) goals.[50] Clearly different constituencies have pursued ADR for different purposes and "cheaper and faster is not necessarily the same thing as better."[51]

The problem with this picture is not the array of differing ADR goals. The problem is whether this comfortable collection of ideas provides a full and convincing explanation for a movement to reshape modern justice systems within North America. Two points cast doubt. First, while ADR often is touted as the needed relief for court congestion, there is considerable empirical evidence to suggest that the crisis in the courts is exaggerated. In the United States, Galanter and others question the "hyperlexis" or "too-much-litigation" reading of contemporary American society.[52] While acknowledging "per capita rates of filing civil cases have risen in most localities during recent decades,"[53] Galanter argues that these increases are not proof of runaway litigiousness. Some studies document higher litigation rates during the nineteenth and early twentieth centuries than in the present.[54] Sarat concludes that "viewed over a longer period, the growth in filing rates in state and federal courts has been both gradual and uneven."[55] Others have found "many cases require little court time" and "the average duration of civil cases has sharply declined."[56] When comparing the number of cases to some baseline measure of potential litigation, Galanter finds that "the patterns of use of courts is conservative, departing relatively little from earlier patterns."[57] He criticizes work that focuses almost exclusively on the sheer volume of cases. This "tip of the iceberg" view of the litigation explosion "is the product of a narrow elite of judges (mostly federal), professors, and deans at eminent law schools, and practitioners who practise in large firms and deal with big clients about big cases. Because they are attuned to the 'top' of the

---

50 M. Galanter, "Compared to What? Assessing the Quality of Dispute Processing" (1989) 66:3 Denver Univ. L. Rev. xi at xii.

51 *Supra* note 49 at 10.

52 M. Galanter, "The Day After the Litigation Explosion" (1986) 46 Maryland L. Rev. 3; M. Galanter, "Reading the Landscape of Disputes: What We Know and Don't Know (And Think We Know) About Our Allegedly Contentious and Litigious Society" (1983) 31 U.C.L.A. L. Rev. 4; A. Sarat, "The Litigation Explosion, Access to Justice and Court Reforms: Examining the Critical Assumptions" (1985) 37 Rutgers L. Rev. 319; W. McIntosh, "150 Years of Litigation and Dispute Settlement: A Court Tale" (1980-81) Law and Society Rev. 823; D. S. Clark, "Adjudication to Administration: A Statistical Analysis of Federal District Courts in the Twentieth Century" (1981) 55 Southern California L. Rev. 65; L. M. Friedman and R. V. Percival, "A Tale of Two Courts: Litigation in Alameda and San Benito Counties" (1976) 10 Law and Society Rev. 267.

53 Galanter, "Reading the Landscape," *ibid.* at 40.

54 McIntosh, *supra* note 52 at 823.

55 Sarat, *ibid.* at 330.

56 Clark, *ibid.* at 80-84.

57 Galanter, "Reading the Landscape," *ibid.* at 69-70.

system ... such elites tend to have a limited and spotty grasp of what the bulk of the legal system is really like."[58]

In Canada, there also is little empirical evidence of too much litigation. A 1981 report on judicial administration in Canada[59] referred to a crisis in urban court volumes but conceded "Superior Courts in Canada generally lack both the data base and the capacity to monitor their caseloads."[60] The 1991 report of the Canadian Bar Association on Court Reform in Canada[61] noted survey results that showed "a disturbingly consistent message is that the legal system is perceived to be too slow"[62] but observed "these conclusions, of course, relate not to the reality of what courts do, but to how they are perceived."[63] Given this state of affairs, it is difficult to imagine that "court congestion" and "delay" concerns could realistically account for the rapid and widespread growth of ADR.

Consider a second problem with relying on the full range of stated ADR goals in order to explain ADR developments. If there is inconclusive evidence of court congestion, one would expect that the relief promised by ADR would not be court-related. However, there is increasing evidence to suggest that court efficiency goals are now what really fuel ADR initiatives.

In the United States, Menkel-Meadow concludes that "efficiency has become the more prominent concern ... although the quality of justice proponents actually came first in very recent history."[64] Menkel-Meadow provides strong evidence to illustrate the inattention to, or co-option of, ADR's "quality" goals, including the institutionalization of many ADR devices within the courts to reduce litigation cost and delay, the developing "law of ADR" as courts rule on the legal questions raised by various forms of ADR, and the "colonization" of the alternatives (How to Win at ADR) by traditional adversarial practices. In a recent paper, I echoed Menkel-Meadow's concerns and suggested that the cheaper and faster goals also are beginning to

58 *Ibid.* at 61.

59 *Supra* note 33.

60 *Ibid.* at 210.

61 Canadian Bar Association, *Report of the Canadian Bar Association Task Force on Court Reform in Canada* (Ottawa: C.B.A., 1991). The 1996 Report of the Canadian Bar Association Task Force on Systems of Civil Justice rediscovered these public and litigation counsel concerns with "the speed with which disputes are resolved in the civil courts" and that the speed with which disputes are resolved is "one of the areas most in need of improvement." However, the Report noted that "comparable data about the time required to process civil cases in Canadian courts are not available at present" and "under existing rules of procedure there are no real time standards against which the progress of cases through the civil justice system can be measured." See Canadian Bar Association Task Force, *Systems of Civil Justice Task Force Report* (Ottawa: C.B.A., 1996).

62 *Ibid.* at 36.

63 *Ibid.*

64 *Supra* note 49 at 6.

dominate ADR discourse, particularly in the legal profession, in Canada.[65] Indeed, in a recent response to criticisms of litigation saying "it's too expensive, takes too long, it's too frightening, it's not user-friendly," ADR was boldly labelled "the second coming of litigation."[66]

In light of this confusion about what is actually spurring ADR on, consider whether other, more openly political ideas help explain modern ADR developments. First, Abel provides an overarching explanation for the rise of ADR. From a critical social theory perspective, "the primary business of informal institutions is social control."[67] ADR allows for the expansion of state control but disguises its coercion. Parties are "referred" to mediation. Disputants are made to feel comfortable. Behavioural change, not sanctions, is stressed. Informal justice provides a "haven" from the expense, delay, and humiliation of the formal system. But overall, ADR often permits earlier intervention into disputes, allows scrutiny of disputes not previously subjected to review, and imposes little constraint on the jurisdiction of the informal processes. While ADR or mediation represents an expansion of state power, this form of power differs significantly from traditional mechanisms of state control. The language of the helping professions, the buzz words of inclusiveness and consensus and the symbol of community participation "are not merely masks for state power but are expressions of ... the changing styles of social control."[68]

This new hegemony of social control reflects Foucault's philosophy on power.[69] Power is located in socio-legal concepts and understandings rather than primarily in official punishment or simple brute force. However, the intimate relationship between ADR and social control should not be surprising. The rise of ADR often is equated nostalgically with the demise of

---

65 A. J. Pirie, "Teaching ADR in Canadian Law Schools: The A,B,Cs of ADR" (Paper presented at Canadian Bar Association Conference, Alternative Dispute Resolution in Action in Canada, Vancouver, B.C., 11, 12 Mar. 1994).

66 D. Small, "The Second Coming of Civil Litigation," *The [Ottawa] National*, vol 5 (Jan./Feb., 1996) 20. The 1996 Task Force Report, *supra* note 61, reinforces ADR's ties to the courts when it states that court reforms must "offer a range of procedures, blending the best qualities of traditional and alternative approaches to dispute resolution."

67 *Supra* note 39 at 5.

68 C. B. Harrington and S. E. Merry, "Ideological Production: The Making of Community Mediation" (1988) 22 L. and Society Rev. 709 at 713. L. Nader also sees the "harmony ideology" of ADR as an "insidious exercise of power through indirect controlling processes" and "mind colonization." See L. Nader, "Controlling Processes in the Practice of Law: Hierarchy and Pacification in the Movement to Re-Form Dispute Ideology" (1983) 9 Ohio State J. on Dispute Resolution 1.

69 M. Foucault, *Power/Knowledge: Selected Interviews and Writings, 1972-77*, ed. C. Gordon (New York: Pantheon Books, 1980); H. L. Dreyfus and P. Rabinow, *Michel Foucault: Beyond Structuralism and Hermeneutics,* 2d. ed. (Chicago: Univ. of Chicago Press, 1983).

70 See e.g. the references in Abel, *supra* note 39 at 275. Goldberg, Green, and Sander, *supra* note 15 at 3-4, also acknowledge the "waning role" of the family, the church, and the community as a factor in the current interest in alternatives.

traditional sources of authority and control such as churches, schools, and the family.[70]

If ADR strengthens the state's monopoly on social control, it would not be unusual to find "insiders" or elite professionals in formal legal institutions busy in the movement toward informalism. There are a number of reasons why these professionals would want to send cases elsewhere. Heavy case overloads and unpredictable results rob lawyers and judges of intrinsic rewards. The need to deal with "junk" cases, or those disputes having little economic value, or cases that involve lower class participants and demand few technical skills can reduce professional power. The increasing economic pressures in a global economy demand that legal professionals move cases out of the courts but also maintain control of the "big" cases.[71] While there are examples of grassroots ADR programs,[72] many ADR initiatives are from the top down, and hence lead to the institutionalization of ADR.

The linking of ADR and social control also is consistent with the ideology of informalism. Harrington argues that reform movements ideologically have never sought to replace the legalistic paradigm. Delegalization reforms, on the contrary, have been designed to complement existing adjudication processes. ADR, rather than fundamentally challenging formalism, is really about the nature and scope of judicial power and judicial authority. Harrington calls this "shadow justice"[73]: "the construction of informal ideology is linked to the reconstruction of judicial power and authority"[74] and "the legitimacy of delegalization reforms is still grounded in procedure."[75] Galanter labels ADR "short form formalism."[76]

This ideology should be expected. Modern ADR developments appear to have their genesis in court reform agendas. In the United States, newly-appointed Chief Justice Warren Burger's court reforms in the 1970s had obvious ADR features. Burger proposed eliminating minor and less important disputes from the court system, expanding the use of arbitration, and improving lawyers' negotiating skills. However, these "alternatives" clearly

---

71 "Big" is becoming relative. Aside from the increasing promotion of ADR by lawyers for a wide spectrum of commercial cases, there is interesting evidence that the "junk" cases are shrinking for legal professionals and that lawyers and judges are maintaining hold of such cases, albeit in an ADR setting. Consider recent amendments to the rules governing small claims in British Columbia, which give judges authority to mediate cases in mandatory settlement conferences. See Rule 7 of the Small Claims Rules, made pursuant to the Small Claims Act, S.B.C. 1989, c. 38, as amended.

72 A good example is the Neighbourhood Justice Centre growing out of the work of Danzig, Lowy, Shonholtz, and Wahrhaftig. For a description of early attempts to establish decentralized, deprofessionalized, self-governing community forums, see R. Danzig, *supra* note 7.

73 *Supra* note 38.

74 *Ibid.* at 15.

75 *Ibid.*

76 *Supra* note 50 at xiv.

were part of the rationalization of the court system. Courts would be reserved for only "the truly important conflicts."[77] What was needed were fewer rights being asserted in the courts, not necessarily fewer cases in court.

Viewing ADR as a new form of social control also fits with Max Weber's sociological analysis of the relationship between law and capitalism.[78] Weber saw a direct link between the economic rationality embodied in capitalism – the pursuit of self-interest through the rational calculation of means and ends – and the particular type of legal rationality best able to sustain the capitalist economic order. In an emerging capitalist society, formal legal institutions and guaranteed rights ensured the calculability or predictability necessary for market activity. For Weber, the legitimacy of this formal legal order was based on a belief in the rightness of a "logically formal" or "gapless" system of law in which judges apply abstract rules to individual cases to reach correct decisions. However, increasingly, law as a normative system has come under attack as being too rigid, exploitative, and inequitable. But with the capitalist order firmly entrenched, the legitimacy provided by the ideology of formal justice is no longer required. Weber theorizes that what arises from the anti-formalistic tendencies of modern legal development is not law reform to serve ends such as social justice that underlie the disenchantment with formal law. What arises is the increasing rationalization of law finely tuned to the rationality of advanced capitalism. Accordingly, Weber saw the emergence of particularistic laws and special procedures "to eliminate the formalities of normal legal procedures for the sake of a settlement that would be both expeditious and better adapted to the concrete case" and "the general acceptance of law as an instrumental mechanism that facilitates compromise between conflicting interests."[79] ADR appears to be an obvious component in the rationalization of law. Legitimacy under ADR comes from the instrumental rationality of its individualistic processes, which are promoted to avoid the rigidity and arbitrariness of formal justice and to better support the rational pursuit of self-interest in the marketplace.

A second explanation for the modern emergence of ADR is related to social control. The rise of ADR may be viewed as a reaction to the progressive legal rights victories of the 1960s and 1970s. ADR, and mediation particularly, shift the emphasis from rights to needs.[80] By de-emphasizing

---

77 *Supra* note 28 at 60. Laura Nader's research points to the "harmony ideology" of ADR being strongly influenced by the 1976 Pound Conference: Perspectives on Justice in the Future, a conference essentially about innovations in the administration of justice. See Nader, *supra* note 68.

78 For an overview of Weber's work, see A. Kronman, *Max Weber* (London: Edward Arnold, 1983).

79 S. Ewing, "Formal Justice and the Spirit of Capitalism: Max Weber's Sociology of Law" (1987) 21 Law and Society Rev. 487 at 509.

legal rights and emphasizing party interests and needs, ADR depoliticizes law. Silbey and Sarat describe this shift:

> ADR advances a non-rights based conception of the juridical subject ... Eschewing rights, ADR proponents deploy the discourse of interests and needs. They reconceptualize the person from a carrier of rights to a subject with needs and problems, and in the process hope to move the legal field from a terrain of authoritative decision-making where force is deployed to an arena of distributive bargaining and therapeutic negotiation.[81]

The problem, critics say, is that claims based on rights are generalizable whereas claims based on interests and needs are more often individual in character. Under ADR, "individual demands are satisfied in order to forestall their aggregation."[82] Social reform is thus inhibited. Conflict is individualized because similar experiences by other members of a social group, particularly a group lacking political and social power, become irrelevant. The conflict becomes private, often excluded from public scrutiny, and loses any of its public interest features. ADR, reframing disputes from rights-oriented problems to interpersonal or psychologically based problems,[83] may reproduce societal differences in power and privilege. Customized agreements, unlike court precedents, are not transferable from one context to another. What is transportable is the rationality of the interest-based process.

These political explanations for the modern emergence of ADR raise other critical questions. Who are the people who want better justice through informality rather than the authority of the state to enforce their rights? Does ADR represent "an attempt by the dominant classes to impute wishes to the dominated so that the former can enjoy speedy, inexpensive access to authoritative courts from which the latter has been excluded?"[84] Do informal processes, such as mediation, have highly formalized structures, and follow rigid rules, concealing striking similarities in process and substance to adjudicative processes? Do neutral facilitators hide values and beliefs that

80 For an analysis of this change in emphasis, see S. Silbey and A. Sarat, "Dispute Processing in Law and Legal Scholarship: From Institutional Critique to the Reconstruction of the Juridical Subject" (1989) 66 Denver Univ. L. Rev. 437.

81 *Ibid.* at 479.

82 *Supra* note 39 at 4.

83 Hofrichter and Merry, in studies of neighbourhood and family dispute resolution, found that mediators tend to redefine social problems as interpersonal problems and that the language of therapy and morality is more prevalent than is the language of legal rights. See R. Hofrichter, *Neighbourhood Justice in Capitalist Society: The Expansion of the Informal State* (New York: Greenwood Press, 1987); S. Engle Merry, *Getting Justice and Getting Even: Legal Consciousness among Working Class Americans* (Chicago: Univ. of Chicago Press, 1990).

84 *Supra* note 39 at 8.

commonly are exposed in neutral decision-makers?[85] What community does ADR serve, particularly when it individualizes disputes? Do disputants have more autonomy from professionals or will ADR increase the dependence of lay persons on a new class of professionals?

The political critique of ADR and the questions it raises reveal the contradictions of informal justice. Informal alternatives may possess the potential to be part of a struggle for progressive change or, conversely, may assist in preserving existing social and economic inequalities. Abel summarizes the ambiguity of ADR:

> Yet if the goals of informal justice are contradictory, and if it is incapable of realizing them because of contradictions inherent in advanced capitalism, informalism should not simplistically be repudiated as merely an evil to be resisted, or be dismissed as a marginal phenomenon that can safely be ignored. It is advocated by reformers and embraced by disputants precisely because it expresses values that deservedly elicit broad allegiance: the preference for harmony over conflict, for mechanisms that offer equal access to the many rather than unequal privilege to the few, that operate quickly and cheaply, that permit all citizens to participate in decision-making rather than limiting authority to "professionals," that are familiar rather than esoteric, and that strive for and achieve substantive justice rather than frustrating it in the name of form.[86]

The key to understanding ADR developments surely must rest in appreciating that these contradictions exist and then in evaluating this contemporary reform movement in its social and political context. Does an ADR development embody certain fundamental values: "rapid and thorough airing of controversies, participation by the disputants in resolving their own conflicts, reduction of dependence on professionals, greater involvement of citizens in an essential aspect of democratic governance?"[87] Do social justice, social solidarity, or personal transformation goals really matter? Or

---

85 Evidence of bias in the courts is commonplace. For example, see the selection of essays presented at a symposium at Dalhousie Law School (5 Oct. 1991) to honour the significant contributions of Madame Justice Bertha Wilson of the Supreme Court of Canada in (1992) 15 Dalhousie L.J. 1-260. See also B. Wilson "Will Women Judges Really Make a Difference?" (1990) 28 Osgoode Hall L.J. 507. The decision by Chief Justice MacEachern in *Delgamuukw et al. v. British Columbia et al.* (1991), 79 D.L.R. (4th) 185 (B.C.S.C.), which portrayed aboriginal life as nasty, brutish, and short and suggested that the Gitskan did not exhibit sufficient civilization to exercise dominion over property, inflamed aboriginal people and others across Canada. Reference also can be had to the Royal Commission on the Donald Marshall Jr. Prosecution in *Commissioner's Report: Findings and Recommendations*, vol. 1 (Halifax, Nova Scotia, 1989).

86 *Supra* note 39 at 310.

87 *Ibid.* at 12.

does the ADR initiative attempt to depoliticize the conflict, to disguise the increase in social control, to be mostly cheap and fast, to benefit mostly those with social, economic, and political power?

The politics and contradictions of informal justice provide a more informed view of ADR. They particularly question why changes to the justice system are taking place now, and challenge some conventional and comfortable concepts. The politics and contradictions of ADR bring a critical perspective to the question of whether ADR fits, or doesn't fit, in Thailand and Cambodia.

CULTURE, CONFLICT, AND ADR

Conflict, from the Latin verb, *fligere*, meaning to strike, can conjure up an image of a fight or a struggle. Morton Deutch's definition of conflict evokes this confrontational mind set. Conflict "exists whenever incompatible activities occur ... An action that is incompatible with another action prevents, obstructs, interferes, injures, or in some way makes the latter less likely or less effective."[88] But Deutch's definition is not a universal one. In many countries there is no easy translation for conflict. In some countries conflict is absent from the vocabulary, while in other countries many different words would take its place. At bottom, how conflict is understood and presented can vary considerably.

This fact has obvious consequences for ADR. As a modern response to conflict, ADR surely must be responsive to what conflict is perceived to be. While a face-to-face meeting in mediation to problem solve and share decisions may be ADR for some, others may regard this process as unacceptable if conflict in their culture requires withdrawal, indirectness, submission to or avoidance of authority, respect for elder advice, or, perhaps, more confrontational behaviour. Accordingly, in addition to the politics and contradictions of ADR, another obvious contributor to assessing alternative dispute resolution in Thailand and Cambodia is culture itself. What is culture? Does it play a role in shaping the concept of conflict? And, importantly, what is the relationship between culture and ADR?

The Notion of Culture

Notions of culture open up enormously complex and interdisciplinary lines of inquiry that reveal stark differences in perspective and that, in many respects, have implications for the politics and contradictions of ADR. While the sources of the concept of culture originated in classical antiquity, it was only in the nineteenth century that culture was formulated as an abstract notion. Over a century ago, the anthropologist, E. B. Tylor, provided the

88 M. Deutsch, *The Resolution of Conflict: Constructive and Destructive Processes* (New Haven: Yale Univ. Press, 1973).

classical charter definition. "Culture or civilization ... is that complex whole which includes knowledge, belief, art, law, morals, custom and any other capabilities and habits acquired by man as a member of society."[89] This definition, important in inspiring the study of culture as a separate science, includes non-material products of social life such as folklore, mores, and laws that emerge from social interaction and serve a normative function; material elements in forms ranging from arrowheads to automobiles that represent an obvious product of society; and finally the meaningful relationships between the parts of culture and the symbolic interpretations placed upon them.

But 80 years later, Kroeber and Kluckhohn discovered over 160 different definitions of culture coined before 1950, as well as thousands of statements about culture[90] None of these definitions or statements garnered universal support. Many conflicted with one another. Some of these definitions enumerated the various kind of phenomena that different writers considered as cultural objects, including mental states and processes (knowledge, ideas, beliefs, attitudes, values, morals), patterns of behaviour (habits, customs), part mental, part material acquisitions (language, abilities, art), material and non-material products of human activity (tools, artifacts, songs, stories) and generalized behaviours and attitudes (law, marriage, religion). Other definitions set out the empirical and theoretical criteria necessary to distinguish culture, such as objects or phenomena that are shared, accepted, acquired or handed down – that is, all of the adjustments to life conditions or a collection of traits integrated into a system with varying degrees of correlation between the parts. Still other definitions focused on the creation and survival of culture so that culture became artificial, transmitted independently of genetic inheritance or learned behaviour.[91]

Kroeber and Kluckhohn's synthesis of this definitional morass was as follows:

> [C]ulture consists of patterns explicit and implicit, of and for behaviours acquired and transmitted by symbols, constituting the distinctive achievement of human groups, including their embodiment in artifacts. The essential core of culture consists of traditional (that is, historically derived and selected) ideas and especially their attached values; culture systems may, on the one hand, be considered as products of action, on the other hand as conditioning elements of further action.[92]

---

89 E. B. Tylor, *Primitive Culture* (London: Murray, 1871) at 1.

90 A. L. Kroeber and C. Kluckhohn, *Culture, a Critical Review of Concepts and Definitions* (New York: Vintage Books, 1952).

91 For a fuller analysis of Kroeber and Kluckhohn's collection of definitions, see E. Vermeersch, "An Analysis of the Concept of Culture," in B. Bernardi, ed., *The Concept and Dynamics of Culture* (The Hague: Mouton Publishers, 1977) at 10.

Definitions that reduced culture to mental phenomena or to patterns of behaviour often vied for supremacy. These definitions dichotomized human behaviour into concrete, observable behaviour or into shared values, beliefs, and ideas. The differentiation of non-material products of group life and material elements was critical for still other definitions. Some writers stressed a unique feature of culture such as its symbolic aspects or its learned or intellectual quality. Parsons considered culture as a basic part of a system of action. Culture emerges from social interaction and is a guide to behaviour in subsequent interaction. An individual thus develops a personality that is more or less adjusted to the demands of that society.[93]

While differences in definition existed, classical sociological theory and classical social anthropology generally conceived of culture as being made up of the shared values, norms, beliefs, and attitudes of the entire population or subgroups within the population. Importantly, culture also was coherent and consistent.

New perspectives in the sociology of culture, strongly influenced by other disciplines such as anthropology, political science, literary studies, cultural studies, feminist studies, and ethnic studies, and by perspectives from European sociological theory, such as post-structuralist theories in France, challenge these classical orthodoxies of culture. This powerful body of work[94] rejects culture as a rather narrow ribbon of patterned behaviour that does not extend into social institutions and that is external to a very powerful determining set of material constraints and forces. In fact, these perspectives suggest that theories of culture cannot be separated from cultural critique – that is, from the need to engage with specific cultural problematics in a way that underscores their relevance to the contradictory reproduction of social divisions and hierarchies across the social field.

Accordingly, culture is linked to social constructionism – the theory that much of what we take for granted as objectively real or necessary in social life is actually constructed through social relationships and social behaviour. Hence we see Berger and Luckmann's concern with the social

---

92 *Supra* note 90 at 181.

93 T. Parsons, *The Social System* (Glencoe, Ill.: Free Press, 1951). See F. E. Merrill, *Society and Culture: An Introduction to Sociology* (New Jersey: Prentice-Hall, 1961) for a summary of various representative definitions of culture.

94 For an introduction to this literature, see T. Bennett *et al.*, eds., *Culture, Ideology and Social Process* (London: The Open Univ. Press, 1981); R. Wuthnow *et al.*, *Cultural Analysis: The Work of Peter L. Berger, Mary Douglas, Michel Foucault and Jürgen Habermas* (London: Routledge and Kegan Paul, 1984); M. Ryan, *Politics and Culture: Working Hypotheses for a Post-Revolutionary Society* (London: Macmillan, 1989); J. C. Alexander and S. Seidman, eds., *Culture and Society: Contemporary Debates* (Cambridge: Cambridge Univ. Press, 1990); P. Scannell, P. Schlesinger, and C. Sparks, eds., *Culture and Power* (London: Sage, 1992); D. Crane, ed., *The Sociology of Culture: Emerging Theoretical Perspectives* (Cambridge: Basil Blackwell Ltd., 1994).

construction of implicit culture (social behaviour).[95] European theorists, such as Foucault and Bourdieu,[96] emphasize the social construction of explicit culture such as the media, knowledge, and science, as well as the ways in which these forms of "recorded" culture construct social roles such as those of class, gender, and race. From these perspectives, science, technology, and knowledge generally cease to be viewed unproblematically as truth and become social constructions of particular social groups as well as instruments of power for these groups.

Similarly, culturally oriented historical sociologists focus on cultural change and cultural control – how culture in conjunction with (or independently from) social structures has brought about changes in nation states, in relationships between or within social classes or ethnic groups, or in the conduct of everyday life.[97] A major theme in this work is that of a dominant class imposing a coherent world view on the population, either in the form of an ideology or as hegemony, to such an extent that the world view is accepted unquestioningly as common sense.

For cultural Marxists, like Louis Althusser, culture does not simply express and directly reproduce social power through a distribution of cultural capital. "Culture is the arena in which the contradictions that arise within a capitalist society are resolved in ways that assure the continuation of a ruling group's hegemony."[98] The althusserian theory of culture sees culture more accurately as a function of power and assumes culture is something more than an expressive medium for extracultural social structures.

Swidler rejects the classical view of culture, which sees the individual as a passive recipient of cultural influences that define goals and determine individual behaviour.[99] She argues that culture offers the individual a wide range of choices. Instead of defining goals, culture provides tool kits in the form of "symbols, stories, rituals and worldviews" that people use to solve problems and to organize their activities. While values may be shared, individual behaviour may be very different because the capacity to translate the same values into "strategies of action" varies. Not only do individuals use the same cultural components differently, Swidler also argues that culture is not a unified system that pushes action in a consistent direction. All real cultures contain diverse, often conflicting elements.

---

95 P. L. Berger and T. Luckmann, *The Social Construction of Reality: A Treatise in the Sociology of Knowledge* (New York: Doubleday, 1966).

96 See e.g. P. Rabinow, ed., *The Foucault Reader* (New York: Pantheon, 1984); P. Bourdieu and A. Passeron, *Reproduction* (Los Angeles: Sage, 1977); P. Bourdieu, *Distinction: A Social Critique of the Judgment of Taste* (Cambridge: Harvard Univ. Press, 1984).

97 See E. Morawska and W. Spohn, "Cultural Pluralism in Historical Sociology: Recent Theoretical Directions," in Crane, *supra* note 94.

98 Ryan, *supra* note 94 at 11.

99 A. Swidler, "Culture in Action: Symbols and Strategies" (1986) 51 Amer. Sociological Rev. 273-86.

Other works show culture as determining of materiality, as a force capable of reshaping social life. In Juri Lotman's semiotic theory, culture consists of "a hierarchy of semiotic systems" the purpose of which is "structurally organizing the world around man."[100] The Japanese cultural theorist Tetsuo Kogawa also presents a strong case for cultural determination.[101] Kogawa argues that the "Emperor System" in contemporary Japanese society reshaped social and bodily life along Western capitalist lines in the late nineteenth century and shows how the deliberate use of the Emperor helped establish attitudes of discipline, respect, and obedience that were necessary to the process of modernization and industrialization.

Culture from these critical perspectives becomes inherently contradictory, inconsistent, and complex instead of primarily a global unitary characteristic of the society or group. Abandoning the reduction of culture to mental phenomena and to patterns of behaviour, new perspectives on cultural analysis break down the boundary between the traditional concept of culture and the supposedly extra-cultural realm of materiality, economics, and social reality. These theories present important and stimulating frameworks for defining and conceptualizing culture in all its contemporary ramifications. In turn, these critical frameworks provide obvious vehicles for analyzing the impact of culture on conflict and for understanding the relationship between culture and ADR.

Conflict and Culture

One would expect that the range of perspectives on culture would contribute significantly to a sophisticated understanding of conflict, particularly when studying conflicts in differing countries and most importantly when dealing with conflicts that relate to existing social, economic, and political power structures. However, it appears that much work analyzing conflict across cultures has opted for the classical definition of culture.

For Duryea, in her highly regarded review of work on conflict and culture, culture is matter-of-factly Ralph Linton's 1945 version: "the configuration of learned behaviour and results of behaviour whose components and elements are shared and transmitted by the members of a particular society."[102] This definition is carried forward in a 1994 report on conflict and

---

100 J. Lotman et al., *Theses for the Semiotic Study of Culture* (Lisse: De Ritter, 1975).

101 T. Kogawa, *The Electronic State and the Emperor System* (Tokyo: Kawadeshoboshinsha, 1986).

102 M. LeBaron Duryea, *Conflict and Culture: A Literature Review and Bibliography* (Victoria, B.C.: UVic Inst. for Dispute Resolution, 1992) at 4, referring to R. Linton, *The Cultural Background of Personality* (New York: Appleton-Century, 1945). Some of the literature reviewed by Duryea that also appears to accept the classical view of culture includes: K. Avruch, P. W. Black, and J. A. Scimecca, eds., *Conflict Resolution: Cross Cultural Perspectives* (New York: Greenwood Press, 1991); S. Bochner, ed., *The Mediating Person: Bridges Between Cultures* (Cambidge, Mass.: Schenkman, 1981); P. H. Gulliver, *Disputes*

culture, with the result that culture's fundamental implications are limited to "worldview, language, beliefs, values, concepts of space and time, religion and social and family relationships."[103] Culture becomes, classically, shared behaviour, albeit broadly-based behaviour.

This rather narrow perspective on what culture is means that working with conflict in different cultures requires primarily an inquiry into behaviour. The traditional, shared, or required cultural behaviour in specific conflict settings must be discovered. Once this behaviour is uncovered, dispute resolution methods can be adopted or established so long as they accommodate and respect this behaviour.

As a result of equating culture with behaviour, several classically-inspired models and theories about cultural behaviour have been relied on to explain how different peoples view and respond to conflict. For example, there has been strong reliance on the individualist versus collectivist model. The premise of this model is that differences in cultural behaviour in general can be understood by the degree to which a culture has collectivist or individualist tendencies. Individualism refers to the tendency to be more concerned about one's own needs, interests, and goals, whereas collectivism refers to the tendency to be more concerned about the consequences of one's behaviour for in-group members and to be more willing to sacrifice personal interests for the attainment of collective interests.[104] The common suggestion is that people from Western cultures tend to be more individualistic, and those from Eastern and southern cultures more collectivist.[105]

Duryea sets out some implications of this model for understanding conflict behaviour and for encouraging successful dispute resolution, particularly through the use of mediation:

> [Collectivists] place more importance on resolving disputes amicably than do individualists.[106]
>
> For collectivists ... much more attention is paid to the context of the communication, including verbal associations, gestures, body postures, and the facial muscles of the other person.[107]

---

and Negotiations: A Cross-Cultural Perspective (New York: Academic Press, 1981); J. P. Lederach, "Training on Culture: Four Approaches" (1990) 9 Conciliation Quarterly 6; D. N. LeResche and J. Spruill, "Training on Culture: A Survey of the Field" (1990) 9 Conciliation Quarterly 2. See also M. H. Ross, *The Culture of Conflict* (New Haven: Yale Univ. Press, 1993).

103 B. Lund, C. Morris, and M. LeBaron Duryea, *Conflict and Culture: Report of the Multiculturalism and Dispute Resolution Project* (Victoria, B.C.: UVic Inst. for Dispute Resolution, 1994) at 25.

104 *Ibid.* at 26-27, referring to H. C. Triandis, R. W. Brislin, and C. H. Hui, "Cross Cultural Training Across the Individualism-Collectivist Divide" (1988) 12 Int'l J. of Intercultural Relations 269.

105 Duryea, *supra* note 102 at 39.

106 *Ibid.* at 40.

collectivists are more comfortable than individualists in hierarchical structures. This has implications for the role and acceptance of the third party facilitator.[108]

Collectivists are more likely to agree that it is all right to show respect to people in authority and to direct the actions of those who are junior in age or status. They are also more influenced by familial, tribal or social group connections than individualists. First meetings with collectivists tend to be formal, and payment is frequently in kind rather than in monetary currency.[109]

Collectivists are most comfortable sharing intimacies when the sharing is reciprocal.[110]

Events accompanying marital or familial difficulties in a collective culture may be decided consultatively by relatives and elders in the community, not solely by the immediate parties. The parties, if they are quite traditional, may expect recommendations and decisions from the intervenor, as would occur from elders within their culture.[111]

Once the parties are at the table, the procedural needs of the parties may vary considerably, with the collectivist expecting a broad, leisurely discussion and the individualist a tight, controlled atmosphere.[112]

[Individualists] may be slow to see common ground, while those from collectivist cultures find this natural.[113]

Cultural norms for collectivists emphasize avoidance of confrontation as a means of preserving harmony, while individualists value individualism and directness as signs of strength.[114]

Morris provides a more over-arching view of the conflict perspectives of individualists and collectivists.[115] For the individualist,

Conflict is viewed as an expressed struggle to air out and resolve differences and is seen as both functional and dysfunctional. It is functional when it

107 *Ibid.*
108 *Ibid.* at 41.
109 *Ibid.*
110 *Ibid.*
111 *Ibid.*
112 *Ibid.* at 42.
113 *Ibid.* at 44.
114 *Ibid.* at 45.
115 C. Morris, "Dispute Resolution in the 1990s: An Overview of Principles and Practices in Canada," in Conference Materials, Dispute Resolution in Thailand, 8-9 June 1995, Khon Kaen, Thailand, at 28.

> provides an opportunity to resolve problems. It is dysfunctional when not confronted and allowed to fester.

For the collectivist,

> Conflict is viewed as dysfunctional. Conflict is seen as damaging to social harmony and should be avoided as much as possible. Conflict may be considered to indicate a lack of self-discipline and a sign of emotional immaturity.

A second and similar model is the low context versus high context model.

> Low context cultures generally refer to groups characterized by individualism, overt communication and heterogeneity. The United States, Canada and central and northern Europe are described as areas where low context cultural practices are most in evidence. High context cultures feature collective identity-focus, covert communication and homogeneity. This approach prevails in Asian countries including Japan, China and Korea as well as Latin American countries.[116]

The distinction in cultures tends to suggest that low context cultures perceive conflict in terms of the individual and the striving for individual achievement through self-reliance. Conflict is thus more easily constructed as an "us versus them/me versus you" competitive exchange of adversaries. High context cultures, on the other hand, will perceive of conflict as the disruption of a state of harmony and balance in relationships and, as such, conflict is often seen as requiring the rebuilding and maintaining of relationships.

A third model is the universalist model. Rather than emphasizing differences in cultural behaviour, this model looks for uniformity by positing that there are certain universal behavioural elements that apply to conflict resolution in all cultures. These elements are the universal need for respect, caring, and procedural fairness. While differences may exist in how conflict is understood, behaviour that embodies these three elements is desirable in the resolution of all conflict.[117]

116 Durea, *supra* note 102 at 39.

117 The idea that there are several over-arching universal principles that apply in conflict resolution across cultures appears in Lund, Morris, and Duryea, *supra* note 103 at 26. The source of this thesis that certain behaviours in conflict (i.e. respect, caring, fairness) are acultural and always desirable for good conflict resolution is not disclosed and does not appear supportable based on Duryea's earlier work on conflict and culture. Duryea and Grundison, *supra* note 4 at 202, do raise the notion of pan-cultural values in developing multicultural mediation and refer to the principles of respect and caring called for in the Canadian Code of Ethics for Psychologists.

Ting-Toomey uses the idea of cultural demands and cultural constraints to explain conflict behaviour. Ting-Toomey says that it is these demands and constraints that implicitly dictate what is the appropriate and inappropriate ways of behaving and communicating in a conflict situation. For Ting-Toomey, the application of these cultural demands and cultural constraints depends on "the patterned ways of thinking, acting, feeling and interpreting that constitute the fundamental webs of a culture." Thus, in the classical tradition,

> cultural demands here refer to the set of cultural ideologies or implicit standards that a collective group of individuals more or less ascribe to. They pose as the "oughtness" of how things should be done. The term cultural constraints here can be divided into three types: cultural cognitive constraints, cultural emotional constraints and cultural behaviour constraints. Cultural cognitive constraints refer to belief systems or ideologies that prevent or discourage group members from cognitively thinking in a particular direction. Cultural emotional constraints arise from cultural norms that dictate what sorts of emotional expression (such as anger, frustration or grief) are acceptable or unacceptable to be outwardly displayed in the public cultural context. Finally, cultural behavioural constraints refer to cultural rules and codes that govern the behavioural appropriateness of a given gesture, or words or phrases in a given socio-cultural context.[118]

Culture and the Meaning of ADR

Work that seeks to understand conflict across cultures primarily in behavioural terms – how disputants perceive, approach, process and resolve conflict[119] – has fit nicely with the simple image of ADR as an assortment of different processes that disputants engage in to resolve conflicts. Accordingly, as ADR crosses cultures, the approach essentially has been to adapt or establish ADR processes, particularly the mediation process, in ways that accommodate and respect the behaviour that has been "discovered" to be culturally appropriate in conflict settings.

Lederach's elicitive or "create-a-model" approach is a good example.[120] Rejecting the prescriptive idea of a preconceived, universal model of mediation, Lederach suggests creating a model by eliciting its details from participants in a given cultural setting. The strength of this model would

118 S. Ting-Toomey, "Toward a Theory of Conflict and Culture," in W. B. Gudykunst, L. P. Stewart, and S. Ting-Toomey, eds., *Communication, Culture and Organizational Processes* (Beverly Hills: Sage, 1985) at 73-74.

119 Lund, Morris, and Duryea, *supra* note 103 at 25.

120 J. P. Lederach, "Training on Culture: Four Approaches" (1990) 9 Conciliation Quarterly 6.

be its respect for the cultural knowledge and patterns of behaviour that it manifests.

For Duryea, "the heartbeat of our findings is the importance of a client-centred model for multi-cultural conflict resolution."[121] Agreeing that "effective intervention in any dispute is necessarily elicitive, though the degree of disputant participation in process design will vary,"[122] Duryea proposes treating the dispute resolution process as an "educational experience" because "there is often a great deal of respect accorded to educators in traditional cultures."[123] For Duryea, conflict resolution across cultures appears to resemble the private classroom:

> As the process unfolds, the educator role is experienced by all: the disputants educate the intervenor and each other about their perspectives, and the intervenor educates the disputants about ways they can effectively communicate to address issues of significance to them. The intervenor does this in a way that responds to and respects the needs and values of the disputants.[124]

Whether eliciting the appropriate conflict behaviour or being educated about correct conflict configurations, the image of ADR across cultures ignores contemporary and critical perspectives on what culture is and accordingly omits any analysis that might expose a more profound relationship between culture and conflict. Absent these insights, the interesting connections between culture and conflict, on the one hand, and the politics and contradictions of ADR, on the other hand, remain unexplored. ADR across cultures strives to be just common sense.

ADR IN THAILAND AND CAMBODIA

With these perspectives on culture, conflict, and ADR in mind, I will now examine recent ADR initiatives in Thailand and Cambodia.[125] This analysis should provide a bridge back to the questions raised at the beginning of this chapter as well as an opportunity to consider how the preceding discussion of culture, conflict, and ADR shaped the work in Thailand and Cambodia.

---

121 M. LeBaron Duryea and J. B. Grundison, *Conflict and Culture: Research in Five Communities in Vancouver, British Columbia* (Victoria, B.C.: UVic Inst. for Dispute Resolution, 1993) at xxiv.

122 *Ibid.* at 207.

123 *Ibid.* at 208.

124 *Ibid.*

125 These ADR initiatives in Thailand and Cambodia are not meant to be an exhaustive inventory. These activities are ones that the author was directly involved with and responsible for as Executive Director of the UVic Institute for Dispute Resolution. They provide useful examples to analyze the promise and problems that arise when introducing western disputing beliefs into diverse cultural settings.

ADR in Thailand

Thailand is often referred to as the land of smiles. This inviting image, in part, is a reflection of Thailand's reputation as a country of happy and welcoming people with strong Buddhist traditions and a preference for harmony in human relationships.

Behind the smile[126] is a complex and fiercely independent society of 60 million people that has managed to avoid the colonial invasions experienced by many of its Southeast Asian neighbours. But modern Thailand is rapidly changing under another type of invasion. Once known as an agricultural country, industrialization has accelerated in the past few years bringing Thailand into the ranks of newly industrialized countries such as Hong Kong, Taiwan, Singapore, and South Korea. Bangkok, with its unofficial population unknown but probably well over 10 million, is the centre of Thai commerce and wealth.

Despite modernization, three-quarters of the Thai population still live in the countryside trying to make a living off the land. However, increasing drought, soil erosion, and burgeoning debts have made it more and more difficult to survive off the land alone. Industrialization has added to these woes. Tropical forests, once community resources, have been cleared to grow cash crops such as maize, tobacco, and tapioca. Government reforestation policies cut down natural forests, a vital source of food and firewood, to create eucalyptus tree farms to feed paper pulp markets. Despite a nationwide ban on logging, illegal logging still occurs. Mangrove swamp forests, rich in fish and marine life, have been felled for timber and charcoal production to make way for aquaculture, mainly prawn farms to service the Japanese market. Frozen seafood factories, tobacco-curing plants, pulp and paper mills, and other industries, built near rural communities with promises of increased prosperity, often pollute the air, fish ponds, wells, rice fields, and health of nearby villages. Land speculation, massive hydroelectric dam projects, and dubious designations of national parks displace villagers from their traditional lands.

Although praise is given for Thailand's economic progress, alongside these advances have come stark poverty and an ever-increasing gap between the rich and the poor. Hope for a higher per capita income lures large numbers of people from rural Thailand to Bangkok each year but these migrant workers, including many women and children, often are forced to accept dangerous and oppressive working conditions.

The rapid and often involuntary changes associated with Thailand's commercial development are transforming political, economic, and social systems, many of them rooted in rural life. It is not surprising that protests,

---

126 Sanitsuda Ekachai, *Behind the Smile: Voices of Thailand* (Bangkok: The Post Publishing Co., 1990).

demonstrations, and other examples of open and violent conflict are becoming more evident. While Thailand has well developed political and legal infrastructures, the highly centralized nature of these institutions, along with instances of corruption, make them poorly suited to deal effectively with these conflicts and their rural roots.

In July 1994, the UVic Institute for Dispute Resolution and the Commission on Resources and Environment (CORE) from Canada were invited to visit Thailand by representatives from Khon Kaen University. The purpose of the trip was to discuss dispute resolution. How this visit came about is worth noting. Khon Kaen University is located in Khon Kaen in the northeast of Thailand. The northeast, known in Thai as Isan, is home to approximately 18 million people and accounts for one third or 170,000 square kilometres of Thailand's land area. It is culturally close to its neighbours in Laos and Cambodia with many people speaking Lao, a language similar to Thai.

Most of the people in the northeast are subsistence farmers. Khon Kaen University has a history of working closely with rural communities, largely providing technical assistance from the university's agriculture, engineering, nursing, medical, and other faculties to improve agricultural methods, overcome farming-related problems, and respond to issues around health and welfare. However, Khon Kaen University was finding that technical assistance alone was not resolving the new and complex problems being brought to the university. For example, allegations by villagers of serious pollution and health problems from a recently-built pulp and paper mill were being denied or ignored by the company, despite a university report documenting adverse environmental impacts.[127]

The call for Canadian dispute resolution assistance was not only prompted by the urgency of existing and escalating conflicts in the northeast. Overseas advice on ADR also was sought, in part, as a result of the President of Khon Kaen University reading *Getting to Yes*[128] and concluding that the approach to negotiation lauded in that book might provide a constructive approach to land-use conflicts in the northeast.

Canadian advice was to come from the UVic Institute and the Commission on Resources and Environment (CORE). The UVic Institute is a

---

127 The Khon Kaen University report actually assessed the company's answer to initial complaints that mill wastewater effluent was polluting the Nam Phong River. The company's response, called Project Green, was to use the wastewater effluent for agricultural purposes. Specifically, the effluent was used to irrigate eucalyptus trees being grown for mill raw material. The report found, perhaps not surprisingly, that due to runoff from the cropping area to the streams and the river that water for fishing, irrigation, and domestic drinking did not meet standard values. The report recommended that the project cease until a proper environmental impact assessment could be done.

128 *Supra* note 21.

multidisciplinary research centre based at the University of Victoria in British Columbia. Its mandate is to advance knowledge in the area of dispute resolution through research, education, and community development. The Commission was a statutory body in British Columbia that was created in 1992[129] to "stop the war in the woods" by developing a province-wide strategy for land use and related resource and environmental management. Key to the work of the Commission had been reliance on shared decision-making processes, emphasizing interest-based negotiation and the use of mediators to reach consensus.

Canadian representatives from these organizations visited Thailand and consulted with a number of individuals and organizations in the northeast and in Bangkok, both to share information on ADR and to assess dispute resolution needs in Thailand. Thai interest in supporting some type of further programming in dispute resolution was generally high, although it is probably fair to say, at this point, that there was limited critical analysis of whether Canadian-funded expertise in ADR, particularly around land disputes, could contribute constructively to land use conflicts in Thailand.

The Canadian assessment of dispute resolution needs was

> that there is an acute need, acknowledged by people in a variety of sectors at several levels of society in Thailand, for effective conflict resolution strategies to address conflicts in Thailand. The need is particularly acute in the area of environmental, land-use, and other public policy issues. Also identified is the need for effective dispute resolution methods for smaller scale disputes at the community level, particularly in settings where traditional village dispute resolution mechanisms may not be available or suitable to the scope of particular problems.[130]

Accordingly, general objectives and expected outcomes were set for the project. The general objectives were to

(1) develop knowledge and technique for conflict resolution with reference to conflict contexts to be developed by Khon Kaen University, and including land-use issues
(2) disseminate concept, knowledge, and technique for conflict resolution

---

129 *Supra* note 18. The Commission was disbanded in early 1996, in part due to government funding cutbacks. A full analysis of the demise of this large scale ADR project has yet to be done, but for a preliminary analysis see R.A. Kelly and D. K. Alper, *Transforming British Columbia's War in the Woods: An Assessment of the Vancouver Island Regional Negotiation Process of the Commission on Resources and Environment* (Victoria: UVic Inst. for Dispute Resolution, 1995).

130 UVic Institute for Dispute Resolution, Funding Proposal to the Management for Change Program, Canadian International Development Agency (CIDA) (Ottawa, 31 Oct. 1994) [unpublished].

(3) officially establish a Conflict Resolution Institute at Khon Kaen University
(4) build linkages between UVic, CORE, and Khon Kaen University with respect to conflict resolution, including joint research.

By the end of a three-year project it was expected that there would be a fully operational and independent institute for conflict resolution at Khon Kaen University. At the end of the three-year period, this institute would be engaged in

(1) conflict resolution research, including theoretical, empirical, and action research
(2) conflict resolution education and training
(3) dispute resolution service to the community
(4) continued linkages with the UVic Institute for Dispute Resolution, CORE, and other conflict resolution organizations.

The specific objectives for the first year of the project were to

(1) strengthen personnel and program capacity in the area of conflict resolution
(2) conduct inventory and needs assessment of interested persons and organizations
(3) conduct research on the state of conflict resolution in Thailand including the legal and policy framework for dispute resolution
(4) organize workshops or seminars on conflict resolution with a focus to be developed by issues. Other possible conflict contexts (e.g. rural development or public health) could be selected if considered by KKU to be strategically productive
(5) plan and deliver skills-training workshops in conflict resolution skills.

The following three first-year activities were undertaken to achieve these objectives.

Research and Program Development

In order to avoid an unreflective "give them the goods" approach, the project called for substantial research activities in year one to ensure that future dispute resolution programming would be responsive to the obvious differences between Canadian and Thai societies. Accordingly, representatives from Khon Kaen University visited Canada, where they participated in seminar discussions, received exposure to North American notions of ADR knowledge and skills, and observed mediation processes involving land-use planning. In addition, the project expected that Thai researchers would conduct studies on dispute resolution in Thailand including:

(1) compiling an inventory of persons, organizations, and institutions interested in (or who would be influential in, or affected by) conflict resolution initiatives

(2) conducting a needs assessment about the most important concerns for conflict resolution. This could include surveying the persons and organizations discovered in the above inventory
(3) developing (in consultation with other institutions) an understanding of the legal frameworks needed to support conflict resolution initiatives
(4) reviewing literature on dispute resolution in Thailand, including community participation in public decisions, mandate and exercise of decision-making by public bodies, the legislative framework for dispute resolution, and community dispute resolution.

Unfortunately, there were few concrete results from these research initiatives. Because no coherent review was made of disputing customs, practices, and systems in Thailand, subsequent programming in the project became almost entirely centred on fitting Canadian ADR experiences – particularly experiences with the consensus-building processes – into the Thai context, but without understanding the complexities of that unique cultural context.

Dispute Resolution Conference

A second major programming component was a "buy-in"[131] conference. The project contemplated a two-day symposium that would give an opportunity for an in-depth look at dispute resolution processes in a variety of sectors. The goal of the conference would be "to stimulate and advise broad and high-level support for dispute resolution." The conference, held in June 1995, came to be named Dispute Resolution in Thailand: Working Together for Peace and Prosperity. It attracted academics, government officials, nongovernmental organization leaders, private sector representatives, and people from rural communities throughout Thailand.

The conference program included Thai presenters,[132] who generally acknowledged the increasing level of open and violent conflict in Thailand and the need for political, economic, and social structural changes to respond to these conflicts. The Canadian input, including an environmental mediation role play, primarily provided the conference participants with opportunities to understand and evaluate consensus-based processes for resolving conflicts. For most of the conflicts described at the conference, it

131 This expression was used to describe the conference goal of "stimulating and advising broad and high-level support for dispute resolution" in Thailand. The image of "investing in ADR" or "psychological recruitments" fits with my analysis, *infra*.

132 For the conference proceedings, see S. Laohasiriwong, C. Morris, and W. Kongdee, eds., *Dispute Resolution in Thailand: Working Together for Peace and Prosperity* (Victoria, B.C.: UVic Inst. for Dispute Resolution, 1996). The Thai presenters included Professor Prawet Wasri, Siriraj Hospital Bangkok; Dr. Chaiwat Sata-arnan from Thammasat University; Paiboon Watanasiritham, Chair of the Rural Re-construction and Development Foundation; Bamroong Kayotha, Northeast Small Scale Farmers Assembly; Phra Pisarn Visalo, Buddhist monk.

seemed clear that Thai concerns about centralized government decision-making, corruption, the role of the army, poverty, power imbalances, other systemic inequalities, and Thai traditions of deference to authority made the use of, or even reliance on, Canadian experiences with ADR seriously problematic.

Technical Skills Training

The final first-year activity in Thailand was a five-day in-depth skills training workshop held in November 1995. The goal of the workshop was to "equip future practitioners and educators with specific conflict resolution skills." The first part of the workshop focused on concepts and skills for dispute prevention and resolution. Topics included analyzing the causes of conflict, the continuum of methods for prevention, management and resolution of conflicts, conflict styles, and, not surprisingly, approaches to negotiation including interest-based bargaining. The second part of the workshop described CORE's shared decision-making model for involving interested parties in environmental and public policy decisions and sought to apply this model to Thailand's land use conflicts. A concluding workshop session involved a Buddhist monk who incorporated the language and goals of interest-based negotiation into Buddhist philosophy.

As with the conference, it was made clear in the workshop that there were obvious barriers to the practical adoption or useful adaptation of many ADR concepts in Thailand. Among the chief impediments to working together to resolve public policy disputes were the glaring power imbalances existing between corporate interests and village constituencies concerned with land use and development, gaps in and enforcement problems with public regulatory structures, centrally-appointed local officials who often were unaware of local conditions, corruption, greed, threats of and the use of violence to achieve ends, and, importantly, Thai traditions of deference and consideration or "social place" displayed toward one higher in rank, social status, or age. This latter point, defined in Thai as *krengjai*, seemed particularly incongruent with the Canadian image of a round table at which all interested parties sat equally to share decision-making powers on important public policy issues.

ADR in Cambodia

Cambodia is a country of over 9 million people covering a land mass of 181,000 square kilometres. The country is overshadowed by 60 million Thais to the West and 70 million Vietnamese to the east. During the Angkor Empire from the ninth to the thirteenth centuries, the Khmer kings controlled much of what is now northern Thailand, southern Laos, and southern Vietnam. But since that empire's decline, Cambodia's history has been marked by great conflict with its neighbours and by internal strife among its own people.

Cambodia today is obviously a product of its complex past. The country has been called "still a semi-feudal country, a place of bargaining, survival and lawlessness."[133] "Everywhere, Cambodia is a society of patronage and theft."[134] Whatever the definition of Cambodia's present-day reality, there is no denying the cumulative influence on Cambodian society of factors such as the French-imposed protectorate from 1864 to 1953, the Cambodian monarchy and the fading leadership of King Norodom Sihanouk, the Vietnam war, the Khmer Rouge period from 1975 to 1979, the death of over one million people in the Killing Fields, the Paris Peace Agreement of 1991, the United Nations Transitional Authority in Cambodia (UNTAC), the ongoing conflict with the Khmer Rouge, the 10 million or so land mines that kill or disable 300 people each month, the May 1993 elections, the compromise coalition government in the National Assembly, the absence of developed agriculture, education, health, legal, social, and transportation infrastructures, demographic imbalances, continuing human rights abuses, severe poverty, and over $2 billion in foreign aid. It was into this reality and its many obvious and deadly disputes that ADR was invited.

The invitation to the UVic Institute and CORE to visit Cambodia was carefully arranged. Selected government ministers, senior bureaucrats, and respected non-governmental organization leaders from Cambodia had been invited to attend the dispute resolution conference in Thailand. These representatives obviously saw merit in opening up discussions in Cambodia on how ADR and, particularly, consensus-based processes might contribute to developments in Cambodia.

Again, after a series of meetings with a range of individuals and organizations in Cambodia, it was concluded that "there are significant opportunities for important and practical conflict resolution programming in Cambodia provided that this programming is developed in collaboration with appropriate partners in Cambodia," and that, "while there are enormous complexities, in many ways it is these complexities that stimulate the general expression of acute and pressing needs for effective methods of responding to the serious conflicts that now arise in Cambodia."[135]

It is interesting to note the several barriers to effective conflict resolution that were identified, including an absence of skill in interest-based bargaining:

> Several barriers to more peaceful approaches to conflict resolution identified during the meetings in Phnom Penh that may be addressed by a conflict

---

133 W. Shawcross, *Cambodia's New Deal* (Washington, D.C.: Brookings Institution, 1994) at 2.

134 *Ibid.* at 38.

135 UVic Institute for Dispute Resolution, Funding Proposal to the Management for Change Program, CIDA (Ottawa, 27 July 1995) [unpublished].

resolution project included: structural and systemic issues that discourage or prevent collaborative approaches to conflict; loss or abandonment of traditional Khmer approaches to conflict resolution in some contexts; competitive attitudes developed over the long periods of war in Cambodia; the need for development of the overall level of skills in cooperative problem solving and interest-based negotiation among the relevant interests; the need for development of legal and institutional infrastructures to guide the peaceful resolution of public policy disputes, including the need for monitoring and dispute resolution capacity within and independent of government agencies.[136]

A three-year program was proposed as a joint initiative of the Commission on Resources and Environment, the British Columbia Ministry of the Attorney General, the UVic Institute for Dispute Resolution, the International Ombudsman Institute, and the Cambodia Development Resource Institute.[137] Participation in all Cambodian events by the key coordinators of the dispute resolution project at Khon Kaen University was also proposed "to nurture tripartite linkages among Canada, Cambodia and Thailand."

Major goals by year included:

Year 1: to develop an increased awareness and understanding of conflict resolution principles and practices that could contribute to new and improved approaches for the prevention, management, and resolution of the critical conflicts that presently are arising in Cambodia;

Year 2: to develop training programs in conflict resolution skills and practices and to deliver in-depth skills training workshops for lay government, NGOs, and other key leaders;

Year 3: to develop educational materials and experiences for use in Cambodia at educational levels determined as a result of preceding research and other activities.

The objectives for the first year of the project were to

(1) conduct inventory and needs assessment of persons and organizations working directly with selected conflicts
(2) conduct research for analysis of the nature of conflict resolution in Cambodia, including traditional approaches and existing legal and policy frameworks for conflict resolution
(3) provide five days of training to several selected Cambodians from 6-10 November 1995 in conjunction with activities in Khon Kaen, Thailand, and provide opportunities for assessment of this training for use and adaptation in Cambodia
(4) organize a conference on conflict resolution with focus and content to be developed in collaboration with CDR

136 *Ibid.*

(5) provide advice with respect to specific issues or disputes where appropriate
(6) organize an exchange between Canada and Cambodia of selected personnel to review directly the nature of conflict resolution practices in each country
(7) facilitate the building of dynamic linkages among persons and organizations interested in developing conflict prevention and resolution activities in Cambodia.

The first year of activities in the Cambodia project is summarized in the following sections.

Technical Skills Training

Several selected individuals from Cambodia attended the five-day skills training workshop held at Khon Kaen University. In addition to skill development, it was expected that the Cambodian attendance would provide opportunities for assessment of this training for use and adaptation in Cambodia. Difficulties in providing concurrent translation for the Khmer-speaking attendees reduced considerably the benefits of this particular component.

Dispute Resolution Conference

A two-and-a-half day conference also was proposed for Cambodia as a primary year-one activity. Such a conference would stimulate awareness and discussion of peaceful dispute resolution approaches among the full range of interests within Cambodian society and would "assist in setting the stage for the refinement of the dispute resolution program in subsequent years." Elements proposed for the conference included keynote and panel speeches regarding the need for and barriers to cooperative approaches to the resolution of public policy disputes in Cambodia, an introduction to the theory and techniques of interest-based negotiation, and a workshop on strengths, weaknesses, opportunities, and threats regarding developing cooperative conflict resolution in Cambodia.

The conference called Dispute Resolution in Cambodia: A Road to Peace and Reconciliation was held in Phnom Penh in November 1995.[138] Over 90 representatives from government and non-governmental organizations heard

---

137 The addition of the B.C. Ministry of the Attorney General and the International Ombudsman Institute reflected administrative exigencies only. The Cambodia Development Resource Institute is a well-respected non-governmental organization based in Phnom Penh with a mandate to support and encourage development research and consequential infrastructure building.

138 For the conference proceedings, see E. Mysliwiec and C. Morris, eds., *Dispute Resolution in Cambodia: A Road to Peace and Reconciliation* (Victoria, B.C.: UVic Inst. for Dispute Resolution, 1997).

conference presentations by Khmer speakers on the nature of disputes in the environment, local communities, and urban centres. Interestingly some disputes, such as those around land distribution, were too sensitive to discuss. A senior monk described Buddhist approaches to conflict and conflict resolution, and John McDonnell, author of *Mindful Mediation*,[139] described the Buddha as a mediator while drawing parallels between consensus building and Buddhist philosophy. Khmer actors also presented a dramatization of a "typical" North American mediation of a controversial land use dispute. The Canadian presenters generally described their experiences with shared decision-making processes with an emphasis on resource management disputes. In an effort to demonstrate how shared decision-making might work, the conference participants engaged in and debriefed a multiparty negotiation role play involving conflicts around the siting of a large dam project. The conference concluded with a speech by the Second Prime Minister, who encouraged the study of conflict resolution in Cambodia and the establishment of a centre for this work.

The Cambodian conference on dispute resolution, even more dramatically than in Thailand, raised questions about the relevance of ADR and its interest-based foundation to Cambodia. While connections were made between Buddhism and ADR, the similarities and relationships were, at best, strained. This is not surprising, since Buddhist religion, while containing teachings about approaches to conflict, departs from the ethos of ADR in many respects. One major problem for consensus processes in Cambodia appeared to be the absence of necessary support systems for such an approach to dispute resolution. There is no independent judiciary. Political stability is, at best, still developing. Legislative and regulatory frameworks are non-existent with respect to many areas of public policy conflict. Corruption and violence are quite widespread. The level of trust necessary for many sectors to work together is low or absent. Both human and economic resources are often in short supply. Given the political developments that were taking place in Cambodia at the time of the conference and the violent political coup d'état that was to occur shortly thereafter,[140] the high-level political endorsement of peaceful conflict resolution given at the

139 J. A. McConnell, *Mindful Mediation: A Handbook for Buddhist Peacemakers* (Bangkok: Buddhist Research Inst., 1995).

140 Clearly high level political attention was given to the conference and its content. The Second Prime Minister's support for the study of conflict resolution and the establishment of a conflict resolution centre, at which he said he would teach, came in the midst of rising political conflict involving, *inter alia*, the development of a new political party and an alleged conspiracy to assassinate the Second Prime Minister involving a vocal critic of the Cambodian People's Party. The 1997 coup d'état in which the First Prime Minister was ousted and many leaders and supporters in his political party killed or imprisoned provides further proof that North American notions of ADR's utility in Cambodia for high level disputes are well off track at this time.

conference by the Second Prime Minister was ominously incongruent with many of the democratic notions behind shared decision-making approaches to dispute resolution.

ALTERNATIVE DISPUTE RESOLUTION ACROSS CULTURES: MISSING THE CRITICAL LINKS

At one level, the examples of alternative dispute resolution in Thailand and Cambodia, or for that matter in Nicaragua, South Africa, China, Japan, or Europe are unremarkable. It would be surprising if ADR theories and practices were not shared and compared, given advances in communication technologies. This exchange of information is a common occurrence in law, economics, politics, religion, and other important disciplines. What is remarkable, though, is the way in which ADR mediates this exchange. While conflicting ideas and practices between peoples, geographic regions, and governments are openly acknowledged and accepted in many areas of endeavour, alternative dispute resolution seems to dislike this arrangement. Rather than acknowledging incompatibilities, ADR seeks to reshape itself to accommodate differences and to fit in. The question is not whether ADR is suitable for Thailand, Cambodia, or another country. The question is rather how can ADR contribute to peace, prosperity, reconciliation, or other long lasting improvements in many countries while at the same time maintaining and respecting cultural differences? ADR, it is assumed, can problem-solve its way into diverse communities by promising to achieve desirable goals, by cooperatively negotiating new and improved ADR techniques that accommodate local interests, or by a combination thereof.

This chameleon-like approach is possible for two reasons. First, the uncertainties and contradictions surrounding the meaning of ADR permit varied representations to be made. ADR can occupy the economic efficiency terrain pretty much as easily as the social justice or peace studies fields. While questions are sometimes asked about the empirical evidence demonstrating the achievement of ADR goals,[141] ADR proponents have little difficulty in adjusting their focus depending on the market. ADR can be cheap and fast, it can be socially transformative, or it can ease post-revolutionary pains. Second, ADR also practises what it preaches. While the recognition that ADR cannot ignore cultural differences is a relatively recent development, work on conflict and culture clearly has brought a problem-solving approach to bear on suggestions that ADR's usefulness is limited in cross-cultural settings. Both Lederach's elicitive approach and Duryea's educational approach, previously described, attempt to reshape ADR to

141 For insights into the question of whether ADR is achieving its goals, see J. P. Essex, "Evaluations of Dispute Processing: We Do Not Know What We Think and We Do Not Think What We Know" (1988-89) 66 Denver Univ. L. Rev. 499.

accommodate and respect learned behaviour so that criticisms of cultural insensitivity are met or minimized.

In this light, given ADR's broad scope and apparent willingness to accommodate cultural interests, can there be serious practical or theoretical concern with ADR initiatives in Thailand, Cambodia, or elsewhere? Is it not likely that ADR is transferable, eventually, with necessary cultural modification and that a new disputing world order may emerge from this consensual convergence? I would like to suggest that there are several related problems with fully endorsing exchanges of the type described in Thailand and Cambodia or with assuming that these exchanges can produce uniform dispute resolution, perhaps to be called UDR.

First, there is a problem of transparency. It is possible to allow ADR to remain intellectually amorphous, its status clouded by the many and varied initiatives that claim ADR status. As discussed, these eclectic endeavours and their goals can be narrow or broad. ADR, for example, can be the development of new and cost-effective arbitration procedures for mobile home disputes.[142] ADR also can be legislation that institutionalizes enormous experiments in land use and resource management mediation, not just to save money but to provide more public input into public policy decision-making.[143] As a label for a new, or renewed, examination of systems of justice, ADR may simply resemble a convenient collection of assorted actions from disparate actors, suggesting that countries such as Thailand or Cambodia need only pick and choose from this ADR smorgasbord with its made-in-that-country flavour. ADR makes common sense even on uncommon ground.

But this shapeless nature is not the full picture. It represents an "unreflective" side of ADR. Critical inquiry is dampened because, after all, something is ADR or it isn't. ADR's full image is revealed only if its many and varied initiatives are located within a framework for analysis. One such framework is ideology. There are, of course, many, often contested, understandings of ideology.[144] But if an ideology can be understood as a cluster of beliefs, values, and images through which meanings are attached to people and practices in such a way that power relations in society are established and maintained, then surely ADR is an ideological expression. As an ideological expression, ADR seeks to inform our thought processes about what is natural, normal, and essential about disputing behaviour and disputing institutions, about what is common sense, about how the world is and how the world must be.

As ideology, ADR is more transparent. There is ample room for the politics and contradictions of ADR. There are opportunities to question, in

142 See e.g. *Residential Tenancy Act*, S.B.C. 1984, c. 15, s. 13.
143 *Supra* note 18.
144 See e.g. M. Cormack, *Ideology* (Ann Arbour: Univ. of Michigan Press, 1992).

countries like Thailand and Cambodia, what concepts such as shared decision-making, consensus, and interest-based bargaining actually mean in people's lives when juxtaposed with the reality of severe political, economic, and social inequalities. ADR as ideology, as a matter of course, would inquire whether the fundamental structural changes being sought in these countries is helped or hindered by significant reliance on Western notions of disputing, particularly on ADR's preoccupation with consensus. ADR's impact on existing power structures would be a critical part of any ideological analysis. Contemporary and critical perspectives on culture would make obvious and essential contributions to an analysis of ADR that is grounded in ideology.

Seeing ADR as ideology also provides the opportunity to answer the most interesting question. What is ADR's ideology? What are the beliefs, values, and images that make up ADR? Does the ideal in disputing still mostly involve individuals, with professional representatives, fighting it out to determine who is right or at least who wins? Have economics and economic interests taken over ADR to force inefficient dispute resolution systems, including the courts, to be fiscally responsible or be left behind? Is ADR displacing the state in dispute resolution and substituting a private, market-driven model? Is harmony or preservation of the status quo the ideal, with ADR a coercive mechanism of pacification? Or, is the truth and reality of ADR an alternative image of disputing that more accurately mirrors people's diverse experiences with disputes, that overcomes barriers to appropriately bringing disputes forward, that reduces unnecessary dependence on professional intervenors, that empowers those people who traditionally have been excluded from having their important struggles aired, and that takes a more holistic view of the dispute?

The correct answer is – it depends. What ADR is depends on what is constructed and presented as natural, normal, and essential about disputing and on who does this constructing and presenting. While the answer is not always clear, thinking of ADR as ideology brings a sharper, more critical focus to what is being done or proposed to be done about disputes. ADR as an ideological expression puts the horse before the cart by providing a guiding theoretical framework to better analyze and understand the myriad practical actions that have claimed ADR status.

This type of transparency needs to be present for ADR to move with any degree of legitimacy and effectiveness from one cultural context to another. Seeing ADR as ideology opens up a new approach to the question of whether ADR fits or can be made to fit into Thailand and Cambodia. Rather than simply adopting or modifying ADR techniques, ADR as ideology invites individuals, organizations, and governments to review and compare their own unique, often long-standing disputing theories and practices while having a reflective understanding of ADR's full meaning and makeup in North

America. The outcome may be an acceptance of ADR or some "made in the country" variation. But the more likely result of a careful examination of one's own disputing practices will be the development of a new or renewed understanding of what is and what should be natural, normal, and essential about disputing in the specific country and in the specific context. A fully transparent ADR, abandoning any neo-colonialist attitudes of superiority and acknowledging its own contradictions and ambiguities, could be, but need not be, one of many contributors to a country's own review of its disputing ideas and practices.

There is a second and related problem that further challenges the relevance of exporting ADR to countries such as Thailand and Cambodia. While ADR may offer, with sensitive elicitation, to change shape in order to fit in, a distinguishing and dominant feature usually remains intact. That feature is ADR's emphasis, its insistence, on achieving consensus through interest-based approaches to dispute resolution. This characteristic was a clear and featured component of the ADR activities in Thailand and Cambodia just described and underscored the chapter-opening quotation respecting ADR's promise of long-lasting improvement in Nicaragua. The problem with ADR's consensus and interest-based roots is more than their undisclosed ideology. The problem is practical. Can heavy reliance on achieving consensus through interest-based processes of dispute resolution offer much to countries such as Thailand and Cambodia?

The argument usually made to promote the practical utility of interest-based consensus processes outside North America is simple. These processes work. They can result in the achievement of laudable and diverse goals including economic efficiency and individual transformation. There are numerous and increasing examples of successful programs that use these processes. There is a growing demand for training in "interest-basing" and a corresponding emergence of a new profession.[145] Any lingering concerns about cultural incompatibilities can be met by offering analyses of similarities between interest-based consensus approaches to disputes and the country's own traditional or customary methods of disputing, such as the role of the Thai headman or Buddhism, and also by matter-of-fact observation that the values behind interest-based consensus processes – respect, caring, trust, harmony, relationship and the like – are universal givens in any good and advanced disputing system.

---

145 I chronicle the efforts to create a new profession of "dispute resolutionaries," in A. Pirie, "Manufacturing Mediation: The Professionalization of Informalism," in C. Morris and A. Pirie, eds., *Qualifications for Dispute Resolution: Perspectives on the Debate* (Victoria, B.C.: UVic Inst. for Dispute Resolution, 1994). Transforming what essentially is an adjective describing a theory (interest-based negotiation) into an active verb (interest-basing) seems to fit this move to concretize standards of practice and to legitimize the classical concept of a profession's "special" traits.

This reassuring reasoning misses several important points that cast doubt on the practical transferability of ADR across cultures or, at the very least, that demand more study. Aside from a lack of conclusive evidence proving ADR does achieve its diverse goals,[146] let alone produce peace and prosperity, there is an important, unanswered question about dispute resolution goals. Policy-making and planning in dispute resolution surely depend on clearly-defined goals. The clarification of purposes and objectives will create priorities for addressing certain conflict areas, will influence resource allocation, will shape the measures that are employed and, ultimately, will determine the direction dispute resolution is to take. The process of articulating dispute resolution goals that fit the unique political, economic, and social complexities of Thai and Cambodian conflicts seems an obvious first task that has yet to be completed and articulated.

It may be that a coherent and careful identification of well-defined goals for dispute resolution practices in Thailand and Cambodia would mirror objectives analogous to those that ADR aspires to achieve in North America. But it probably would not. Court congestion is not a pressing problem for many disputants in Thailand and Cambodia. The particular type of personal transformation promised by ADR is probably not a high priority for many disputants in Thailand and Cambodia. It is not clear whether the business communities in either Thailand or Cambodia have urgent needs for less costly dispute resolution procedures. The achievement of harmony through consensus may be an undesirable goal in Thailand and Cambodia if such a result only preserves the status quo. All of this may suggest that ADR's endorsement in North America of interest-based consensus processes loses credibility when taken out of context.[147] At bottom, context-specific dispute resolution goals need to be set in the specific cultural context before the benefits and costs of North American notions of consensus can be properly assessed.

Apart from goals, there are the critics of consensus. Despite the proliferation of mediation and interest-based processes in North America, there have been wide-ranging critiques including concerns about trivializing the public dimensions of lawsuits,[148] about losing formal due process protections,[149]

---

146 *Supra* note 141.

147 I raised the issue of whether obviously American goals behind ADR and its consensus processes are transferable even to the Canadian context in a report for the Law Reform Commission of Canada. See A. Pirie, *Dispute Resolution in Canada: Present State Future Direction* (Ottawa: Law Reform Commission of Canada, 1987) at 14-17.

148 O. Fiss, "Against Settlement" (1984) 93 Yale L.J. 1073.

149 A. W. Alschuler, "Mediation with a Mugger: The Shortage of Adjudicative Services and the Need for a Two-Tier Trial System in Civil Cases" (1986) 99 Harvard L. Rev. 1808; H. T. Edwards, "Alternative Dispute Resolution: Panacea or Anathema" 99 Harvard L. Rev. 668.

about overlooking the pervasiveness of distributive bargaining,[150] about the adverse impact on women,[151] about ethics,[152] fairness,[153] about the effectiveness of mandatory mediation,[154] about professionalization,[155] and about cross-cultural inadequacies.[156]

The relevance of these or other critiques to the use of interest-based consensus processes in Thailand and Cambodia requires further analysis. However, one criticism in particular appears to provide a painfully sharp perspective. Linked to notions of social control, critics have argued that mediation and other consensus processes shunt disputes into private settings where existing power imbalances can be exploited. For women, the poor, indigenous peoples, minorities, or others who generally have been disadvantaged in a society, private consensus processes may offer little assistance to these people and may, in fact, cause great harm. The problem is that inequalities in power, both individually-based and systemic, are often the real cause of the conflict. These conflicts are difficult to resolve by consensus, either because the more powerful party has little incentive to negotiate in good faith because he has a better alternative than voluntarily giving up power in a negotiated agreement, or because the existence of the power imbalance allows the more powerful party to impose an inequitable solution.

This critique may be telling for Thailand and Cambodia. Both countries are experiencing a range of conflicts, increasingly around land use and resource development, in which tremendous economic, political, and social disparities in power are present among the affected parties. A shared decision-making process "in which, on a certain set of issues for a defined period of time, those with authority to make a decision and those affected

150 J. White, "The Pros and Cons of 'Getting to Yes'" (1984) 34 J. of Legal Education 115.

151 See the references in B. Whittington, *Mediation, Power and Gender: A Critical Review of Selected Readings* (Victoria, B.C.: UVic Inst. for Dispute Resolution, 1990); T. Grillo, "The Mediation Alternative: Process Dangers for Women" (1991) 100 Yale L.J. 1545; Phegan, *supra* note 17.

152 See e.g. R. B. McKay, "Ethical Considerations in Alternative Dispute Resolution" (1990) 45 Arbitration J. 15; K. Gibson, "Confidentiality in Mediation: A Moral Reassessment" (1992) J. of Dispute Resolution 25; A. J. Pirie, "The Lawyer as Mediator: Professional Responsibility Problems or Profession Problems?" (1986) 63 Can. Bar Rev. 378.

153 L. L. Riskin, "Towards New Standards for the Neutral Lawyer in Mediation" (1984) 26 Arizona L. Rev. 329; J. L. Maute, "Mediator Accountability: Responding to Fairness Concerns" (1990) 2 J. of Dispute Resolution 347; K. E. Menzel, "Judging the Fairness of Mediation: A Critical Framework" (1991) 9 Mediation Quarterly 3.

154 See e.g. C. Menkel-Meadow, "For and Against Settlement: The Uses and Abuses of the Mandatory Settlement Conference" (1985) 33 U.C.L.A. L. Rev. 485; A. Nelle, "Making Mediation Mandatory: A Proposed Framework" (1992) 7 Ohio State J. of Dispute Resolution 287; L. V. Katz, "Compulsory Alternative Dispute Resolution and Voluntarism: Two-Headed Monster or Two Sides of the Same Coin" (1993) J. of Dispute Resolution 1.

155 For a collection of essays and bibliography on the subject see Morris and Pirie, *supra* note 145.

156 See e.g. P. E. Salem, "A Critique of Western Conflict Resolution from a Non-Western Perspective" (1993) 9 Negotiation J. 361.

by that decision are empowered jointly to seek an outcome that accommodates rather than compromises the *interests of all concerned*"[157] (emphasis added) may be appropriate in some Canadian contexts for land use strategy decisions. However, similar approaches in Thailand and Cambodia for conflicts surrounding the siting of hydro-electric power projects, logging licences, land ownership and distribution, election issues, political structures, or other public policy disputes seem naive or even dangerous unless the power dynamics at play are acknowledged and effectively addressed.

In addition to concerns about mismatched goals and very different power contexts, another doubt can be raised about the practical utility of ADR's interest-based foundation in Thailand and Cambodia. Interest-based approaches to dispute resolution did not magically materialize in *Getting to Yes* with the rise of ADR. The concept has an interesting background.[158] In part, the theoretical framework of interest-based bargaining derives from the work of American legal realists who criticized legal doctrine and rights talk. These theorists tried to build a more realistic jurisprudence through closer attention to behaviour, empirical data, facts, and "the actual doings of judges."[159] Interests or preferences "seemed to more forthrightly demand and empower empirical demonstration and would therefore provide the basis for a more realistic legal science."[160]

Vilhelm Aubert, a Norwegian sociologist, differentiated between conflicts of interest and conflicts of value.[161] Essentially conflicts of interest derived from competition over scarce resources. These conflicts could be resolved through the market or through mechanisms that compromised the demands, gains, and losses to each side and "minimized the likelihood of maximal loss."[162] Solutions to interest conflicts would involve what Aubert called "a natural adjustment of needs."[163] Conflicts of interest "emphasized the similarity of the contestants, their common needs and aspirations."[164] In contrast, conflicts of value arose not from competition but from disagreement "concerning the normative status of a social object."[165] For disagreement and conflicts of value, Aubert suggested that law and courts would provide the most appropriate mode of conflict resolution.

157 This definition was coined by the B.C. Commission on Resources and Environment as the overarching framework for public participation in public policy negotiations.

158 Silbey and Sarat provide insights into what helped shape the concept, *supra* note 80 at 479.

159 *Ibid.* at 480.

160 *Ibid.*

161 V. Aubert, "Competition and Dissensus: Two Types of Conflict and Conflict Resolution" (1963) 7 J. of Conflict Resolution 26.

162 *Ibid.* at 29.

163 *Ibid.* at 34.

164 *Ibid.* at 29.

165 *Ibid.*

Conversely, he hypothesized that law and formal conflict resolution institutions would transform conflicts of interest into conflicts of value, making compromise solutions less possible. Aubert's analysis borrows from standard conceptions of economic markets but adds to the usual variables. At the heart of the dispute decision model is the "conception of the dispute as an arena of competitive decision-making by rationally calculating individuals motivated by utility maximization."[166]

More comprehensive theories of needs have added another layer of complexity to interest-based approaches to dispute resolution. The fundamental premise of these theories is that disputants share essential human requisites and capacities. Based on the work of Ardry and Wilson in sociobiology, Maslow in psychology, as well as stimulus response behaviourism, fundamental human needs are identified that collectively constitute human nature. For example, Burton and Sandole[167] identify several such needs: a need for consistent response, a need for stimulation, a need for security, a need for recognition, a need for distributive justice, a need to appear rational, a need for meaning in response, and a need for role defence.[168] Successful dispute resolution, it is said, must explore these fundamental, deep-seated human needs or "underlying interests." Attention to these needs will reveal grounds of interdependence, reciprocity, and compatibility as well as show that solutions based on needs are not limited and may expand through interaction and exchange. This focus on allegedly universal and core human attributes also raised suggestions that cooperative approaches to dispute resolution meet all people's psychological needs for harmony, peace, autonomy, integrity, dignity, trust, and relationship.[169]

These intellectual underpinnings of interest-based approaches to dispute resolution are not left at home when ADR travels to countries like Thailand and Cambodia. But are their assumptions about disputing behaviour and dispute resolution valid in these new destinations? The core of interest-based approaches to dispute resolution rests on an apparently essentialist view of human needs that transcends cultural differences. Whatever the traditional or dominant cultural mores, there is an assumption behind interest-based dispute resolution of a better, more essential approach to expressing and realizing our needs. Interest-based dispute resolution also assumes the disputants begin at or aspire to a condition of perfect competition for maximizing preferences. There is additionally the inevitable dependency on expert helpers who will specify and service human needs. There is a consequential denying of legitimacy to those who disagree about what

166 Silbey and Sarat, *supra* note 80 at 484.
167 J. W. Burton and D. J. D. Sandole, "Generic Theory: The Basis of Conflict Resolution" (1986) 2 Negotiation J. 333.
168 *Ibid.*
169 Silbey and Sarat, *supra* note 80 at 486-88.

is needed or who is needy. There is the claim that all problems are solvable because a dispute involves the technical and individual problem of matching available means to essential needs. Dispute resolution becomes a technocratic activity[170] that is apolitical and relatively uncontroversial.

These underpinnings of interest-based bargaining need to be tested in the Thai and Khmer context. How do they compare with Thai or Khmer sociological, psychological, anthropological, legal, customary, or other relevant disciplinary notions of disputes and disputing? Do these assumptions reflect what has been, what is or what could be the reality of dispute resolution in Thailand or Cambodia? A closer examination of the premises that have shaped interest-based approaches to dispute resolution may expose ethnocentric biases behind ADR's hype and profound differences in dispute processing theories and practices. The salvation promised by ADR's interest-based disciples may require Thai and Khmer allegiance to foreign and unworkable beliefs.

At bottom, the issues associated with ADR's journeys across cultures seem clearly to cry out for further study. If these issues are overlooked or superficially dealt with, ADR surely cannot contribute constructively to the disputing needs and hopes of complex countries like Thailand and Cambodia. If serious attention is paid to the issues that emerge when diverse disputing worldviews converge, a different role for ADR is likely. Rather than offering a road to peace, prosperity, reconciliation, economic efficiency, or other good and lasting improvements, the real promise of ADR across cultures may be primarily inspirational. Despite its history, politics, contradictions, ambiguities, and critics, alternative dispute resolution has inspired much thinking in many disciplines about the world of disputes, about the many ways in which various disputes are or can be processed and about the application of the practical principles, skills, and hunches that help resolve problems. ADR, at its best, has opened a field of inquiry of such enormous magnitude, fundamental importance, and untapped potential that, at times, it takes your breath away.

The real promise of ADR across cultures should be its encouragement, not its insistence, to share that breathlessness, to consider the reflective, critical, and multidisciplinary work possible on dispute processing, to explore the complex interrelationships between culture and conflict, and not to ignore the long histories and traditions that most peoples and cultures bring to dispute resolution. While globalization is commonplace in many areas of endeavour, the result of ADR's inspiration is likely to be a mosaic of approaches to dispute resolution across cultures. These approaches to dispute resolution, the new ADRs, surely will be as complex, contradictory and inconsistent as the cultures of the disputants themselves.

170 *Ibid.* at 495.

Conclusion: Reflections on the Convergence and Divergence of Legal Systems

Gerry Ferguson and Douglas M. Johnston

INTRODUCTION: THE DIVERSITY OF APPROACH AND FOCUS

The eleven expert studies in this collection have been brought together within the frame of reference described in the Introduction. At first impression they exemplify six of the nine models of comparative law distinguished in that introductory essay. None of the eleven chapters can be characterized as an exercise in purely descriptive scholarship, at one extreme of the formalistic tradition; nor does any one, at the other extreme of empirical field research, attempt to engage in legal ethnology or cross over the line to the sociology of law (as distinct from "law and society" studies). What remains is a mosaic that can be said to reflect a fairly wide approach to contemporary scholarship in comparative law, perhaps not unrepresentative of the intellectual diversity that resides in most North American law schools in the 1990s.

In the order of the nine generations presented in the Introduction, the oldest and most firmly established of the six approaches taken in these studies is the chapter by Robert Howell, who makes a detailed analysis of legal developments, and especially of judicial decisions, in two areas of intellectual property law: that is, parallel importation and reputation spillover. The countries compared – Canada, Malaysia, and Singapore – are all (chiefly) jurisdictions of the common law family and therefore lend themselves to a close textual comparison of this kind. Emphasis is placed on the promotion of doctrinal convergence or non-convergence by common law judges within these specialized areas of the economic sector. This expert appraisal provides the foundation for future comparisons that might be attempted between common law and civil law jurisdictions, and invites speculation on the global prospect of "judicialization" in traditionally non-litigious societies, which would be necessary if micro-convergence at the doctrinal level is to accompany macro-convergence at the statutory level.

No fewer than four of the above chapters represent the sub-field of comparative legislative and constitutional studies. In all four of these studies, however, the language of the formal law is examined with an eye on the milieu that it is intended to serve, and might also be said to reflect the law and society genre of comparative law. In the study of securities law by Mark Gillen and Pitman Potter, the authors are attentive to the range of internal and external influences on the development of this area of the economic law sector in Malaysia, Singapore, Japan, and China. These four countries might be said to represent distinguishable levels of economic development and arguably different degrees of sensitivity to outside pressures for globalization of the marketplace. Each might also be characterized as a legal culture with its own mix of indigenous and imported features. This study raises questions about the role of formal, as distinct from informal, laws and sanctioning techniques in a context crucial to economic development and central to the concerns of the international investment community. To that extent it might also be viewed as representing the "law and development" approach to comparative law. These authors address explicitly a number of legal development hypotheses, and these are discussed later in this concluding chapter.

The chapter by Crane, Gillen, and McDorman focuses on the tradition of parliamentary supremacy in Canada, Malaysia, and Singapore – the same countries chosen for comparison by Howell. For each of these countries, the authors assess attitudes and practices by placing the relevant provisions of written constitutional law and relevant judicial decisions in their historical and cultural perspective. In each case sufficient "law and society" evidence of the distinctiveness of the civic culture is presented to explain divergence between Canada and the two Southeast Asian countries despite their common descent from the same parent of the common law and parliamentary family of formal legal systems. This study can, therefore, be regarded also as a contribution to the genre of Commonwealth legal studies, which specialize in the pattern of diversification emerging in those countries that inherited the Westminster model of government.

The modern political and constitutional history of Thailand provides the background for Ted McDorman's analysis of the 1991 state constitution of that country. Five key elements in the milieu of Thai society are selected to provide a "law and society" perspective on the symbolic as well as operational significance of that recent exercise in law reform. This contextualist approach is designed to save the reader, especially the Western reader, from misjudgments that might arise from a strictly textualist analysis. Arguably, this chapter is above all an explanation of the uniqueness of the Thai political culture, with its proneness to relatively non-violent military intervention in government but also to benevolent intervention by the king in times of political crisis.

Rather similarly, the Harrington-McDorman-Neilson chapter on the 1992 state constitution of Vietnam is as much a study of civic culture as of formal legal text. The same distinction between the symbolic and operational uses of written constitutions is implicit in these authors' cautious treatment of the text. Indeed it is asserted that this revision, like other recent evidences of law reform in Vietnam that are discussed in William Neilson's chapter on the transformation of economic laws in Vietnam, has arisen from the need to provide assurances to the world community, and more particularly to its development assistance and trade-and-investment sectors. Like China, Vietnam is emerging from a period of central government control over a wide range of economic activities, and also from a tragically protracted history of foreign domination and civil war. As in the case of Thailand, the reader is warned against overexpectation. However, the authors seem to conclude with the implied suggestion that, as a new member of ASEAN, Vietnam will be drawn increasingly into a forum where intraregional comparisons will become an important influence on how its state constitution is to be used by the Vietnamese themselves.

None of these chapters belongs to the long-established, but rapidly diminishing field of comparative socialist legal studies, but the above studies on securities law and Vietnamese constitutionalism, along with Neilson's study of Vietnam's recent economic law transformation, concentrate on two countries with a not-yet-repudiated heritage of Marxist-Leninist ideology and a recent history of commitment to a strategy of economic pragmatism. In China and Vietnam, unlike most countries of eastern and central Europe, the political leadership struggles to preserve the legitimacy of the old official ideology, even as it is forced to make major concessions to the demands of the global corporate community. In this sense, these three chapters, taken together, provide a comparative neo-socialist perspective on the role of formal law in effecting transition from socialism to a hybrid form of society that lies outside the parameters of Marx's predictive framework.

The focus on the phenomena of Westernization and modernization, which characterized the law-and-development literature of the 1970s and the early 1980s, is more or less explicit in most of these essays, but perhaps especially in the chapters by Ferguson and Pirie. In providing the foundation for his comparison of different approaches to the legal regulation of mental disorder in seven Asia-Pacific countries, Gerry Ferguson adopts a law-and-society perspective on this intensely ethical and cultural issue, but law-and-development questions about the intrusive nature of external cultural influences arise inevitably. In this context it might be thought that the intrusion takes the form not only of legal models but also of ideas and values inherent in Western psychiatry and cognate disciplines that make up the global "mainstream" literature on mental health. But the reader is reminded that the non-Western countries have an even longer history of social response to mental disorder. An even-handed, cross-cultural observer might conclude that all cultures, East and West, have exhibited their own mix of traditional superstitions and modern myths. The focus on mental health is, to a large extent, a focus on a profession that, like many others, can be regarded as a middle-class urban elite, so that the revisionist law-and-development concern is not so much statist as societal: the intrusion is less centrally that of West on East than that of urban elites on rural and small-town communities, and the intrusion seems on the whole to be benevolent.

Andrew Pirie's study of the spread of alternative dispute resolution (ADR) to non-Western countries such as Thailand and Cambodia brings out even more directly the complexity of the concept of "culture" and the fundamentality of the divide between urban and village societies, especially in non-Western societies. Like modern psychiatry, the field of ADR studies is essentially of Western origin, and law-and-development concerns about the impacts of "cultural imperialism" surface here as well as in the context of mental disorder. But dispute resolution encompasses all three sectors of the formal legal system (economic, civic, and behavioural), and much of its utility lies precisely in its avoidance of undue dependency on state institutions and formal legal procedures. So comparative ADR studies such as this come closest to the literature on informal justice in the sociology of law and legal ethnology, and seem likely to become increasingly empirical in orientation as hypotheses have to be formulated for validation.

As noted earlier, several of the chapters in this work are partly "law and society" in orientation, primarily because of the need to look beyond the written word of formal law. But two in particular, those by John McLaren and Hamar Foster, are fully developed examples of law-and-society scholarship, focusing as they do on current social rather than legal issues, reinforced by insights drawn from social as well as legal history. In the first of these, McLaren compares the social history of the sex trade, West and East, as background for his analysis of how the legal systems of Australia, Canada, and Thailand have responded to the practice of female prostitution. As in other chapters, the reader is shown the extent of Western influences both through direct imitation and intergovernmental promotion, and questions are raised regarding the possibility of a universal, culturally neutral, model around which a campaign for legal convergence could be mounted. But McLaren also notes that solutions to the problems of prostitution in Thailand must be related to cultural realities and political strategies devised in that country, which take into account its own traditions. None of the countries studied is put forward as a possible model for reform, but Thailand in particular is presented as a legitimate target for genuine law reform.

The fate of indigenous peoples as a result of colonialism has become an important theme of comparative legal studies. Nowhere in this book is the adverse impact of formal legal structures more apparent than in Foster's study of the legacies visited upon aboriginal communities in four settler states of the Pacific Rim: Australia, Canada, New Zealand, and the United

States. Here the problem is perceived as the result of the "unavoidably painful" process of colonization. Whereas the treatment of female prostitution under formal law can be criticized for heavy-handed interference with the intimacies of personal behaviour at the urging of middle-class moralists, the treatment of entire indigenous communities can be condemned as an offence with civilizational rather than elitist dimensions. Both are essays in impositionism, but Foster is drawn into the civic and economic, as well as the behavioural, implications of the current legal status of indigenous peoples and of their claims and demands on modern society and the state system that serves to protect it. The law-and-society approach and the use of social and legal history result in an emphasis on the complexity of the problem and the need for accommodation between competing values such as individual versus collective property rights.

Finally, the "harmonization" orientation in contemporary comparative legal studies is evidenced in part by William Neilson's discussion of Vietnam's entry into ASEAN in 1995 and the legal framework that ASEAN has put in place to promote economic cooperation in the region. The harmonization mode of comparative law is more fully represented by Douglas Johnston's overview of current trends in environmental law development in the ASEAN countries of Southeast Asia. Like most such studies, Johnston's study focuses on the evidences of "legal policy" found in national legislation and in treaties and other negotiated instruments, which seem to commit the participating governments to move forward in agreed-upon directions. In the case of Southeast Asia there is little, if any, opportunity to draw upon the judiciary as an engine of legal development in this area of law, and great differences among the bureaucratic systems of these countries make prediction especially hazardous. Moreover, most of these governments are sensitive to the evidences of Western impositionism. Some who are in the law-and-development mode are quick to accuse outsiders, in their attempts to raise environmental law standards, as being motivated by Western interest in putting a brake on rapid development that might reduce the West's currently preponderant share of the marketplace. The approach taken in this study may virtually ensure that it concludes in a mood of guarded pessimism.

THE ECONOMIC SECTOR

Introduction

Some evidence points to a trend, both regionally and globally, towards convergence or similarity in laws and legal structures. In the Introduction, it was suggested that this convergence is most evident in the economic sector and least evident in the behavioural. It is possible to identify a number of influences or factors that may contribute to convergence and a number of others that may impede it, or even foster divergence in laws and legal structures.

The Gillen-Potter comparison of securities law in four Asian countries with its Anglo-American counterpart provides an excellent vehicle for examining the factors that account for convergence and divergence in at least one sphere of economic law. The countries under comparison (Malaysia, Singapore, Japan, China, and the Anglo-American countries) provide significant contrasts in their stages of economic development, their political ideology, their cultures, and their legal systems. In his examination of similarities and differences in the way Singapore, Malaysia, and Anglo-Canadian countries respond to two emerging transnational problem areas in the law of intellectual property, Howell provides evidence of some of the same factors at work through judicial decision-making, albeit of a less dramatic kind. Neilson's chapter on the transformation of Vietnam's economy and economic laws demonstrates the impact that Vietnam's neighbours, and especially the ASEAN community, have had in shaping that country's economic transformation. Taken together, these studies support the thesis that the process of convergence of economic laws is accelerating both regionally and globally. But what factors appear most influential in this trend toward convergence?

Factors Contributing to Convergence

International Competition and Convenience

As the world market expands to encompass virtually all products and services and almost all countries, each country's economy becomes less national and more transnational. This phenomenon appears to make the increased transnationalization or convergence of economic laws almost inevitable.

Transnationalization to promote economic trade is not a new phenomenon. For thousands of years traders have had a common interest in the availability of a common legal language, or official framework of expectations, for the purposes of negotiating transactions and often also for the settlement of disputes. Efforts to respond to this need, both for domestic and external trade purposes, have been made in all legal cultures, although some legal systems have developed the conceptual and institutional responses more formally, more systematically, and more uniformly than others. The feudal components of the law merchant remain as the substratum of modern commercial law in the Western world,[1] and to a large and increasing extent everywhere else by virtue of international codification or

1 See generally L. E. Trakman, *The Law Merchant: The Evolution of Commercial Law* (Littleton, Colo.: F. B. Rothman, 1983).

unification.[2] The trader's interest in uniform or compatible laws is a matter of common sense, rooted in convenience.[3] Legal convergence fosters growth in transnational economic relations, whether in the fields of intellectual property, trading in securities, or other spheres of commercial law. Globalized competition and economic convenience seem to be the most influential factors in the trend towards greater convergence of laws in the economic sector.

In Vietnam, the institutional efforts at economic renovation that began in 1986 were a political response to a command economy that was isolated, stagnating, and collapsing at a time when the economies of Vietnam's ASEAN neighbours were bustling. The imperative to improve its economic condition drove that economic reform, tempered of course by a continuing socialist political regime. As Neilson observes, it is no accident that Vietnam's first major piece of economic legislation in this new era was a foreign investment law designed to create mechanisms and suitable conditions for the attraction of foreign investment.[4] Any significant alteration of domestic legal relationships – land, contract, and local company laws, for example – waited for the second tier of reform, which began after 1990. Indeed, the constitutionality of the 1987 *Foreign Investment Law* was only perfected five years later by the 1992 Constitution.

Predictability, certainty, and stability in securities markets are important in attracting both domestic and foreign capital. The securities laws of Malaysia, Singapore, Japan, China, and Anglo-American countries have striking similarities, even though the countries in question have differing ideologies, cultures, and legal systems and are at different stages of economic development.[5] Could this similarity be explained on the basis that similar securities laws have been selected by diverse countries because those laws embody the optimal solution to creating and regulating securities markets? Gillen and Potter suggest that this would, at best, be only part of the

2 In federal countries such as Canada and the United States, the internal unification of private and commercial law at the national level has often taken precedence over the objective of external unification at the international level. Paradoxically, in the United States, professional interest in international unification has declined in recent years despite the U.S. government's apparently growing interest in fostering the transnationalization of law in various core and peripheral areas of the economic sector: P. Winship, "National Conference of Commissioners on Uniform State Laws and the International Unification of Private Law" (1992) 13 Univ. of Pennsylvania J. of Int'l Business Law 227.

3 From the economist's perspective, the existence of disparate legal systems affecting the international marketing of goods and services creates frictions and inefficiencies, greatly increasing transactional costs, including the costs of negotiation, advertising, and dispute settlement.

4 W. A. W. Neilson, "Vietnam's Economic Law Transformation within the ASEAN Community" (ch. 3 of this book) at 137-38.

5 M. Gillen and P. Potter, "The Convergence of Securities Laws in Asia: Case Studies of Malaysia, Singapore, Japan, and China" (ch. 1 of this book).

explanation, since alternative laws could be used to regulate securities markets and some of these alternatives might be at least as good as existing laws.[6] We are inclined to agree that the "optimal solution" explanation for convergence is of questionable validity, although it provides more explanatory power when viewed as public policy promoted through special interest groups, an issue that we discuss below as the fourth factor contributing to convergence.

Where a country's continued economic development depends upon attracting foreign investment, it will be strongly induced to provide securities laws and structures that are familiar to foreign investors and traders. Uncertainty in the law will impair a country's ability to compete for foreign investment. Gillen and Potter observe that, for this reason, newcomers to the securities field can be expected to avoid most of the problems associated with implementing unique and untested laws by imitating, where possible, the securities laws and structures already in place in the economically powerful countries.[7]

Robert Howell, in his chapter on parallel importation and reputation spillover in trademark law, observes that advances in the technologies of transportation and communications have globalized the marketplace for products and services, thereby forcing nations to consider regulating competitive practices at international or transnational levels.[8] The countries under study, Canada, Malaysia, and Singapore, have similar British common law roots. The transnational accommodation in all three countries has to date come about through traditional common law, judicial decision-making, rather than by specific legislation or treaty-making. Because the decisions of individual judges in individual cases are affected by a multiplicity of visible and invisible influences, there is greater room for different approaches to develop. Notwithstanding this open-ended characteristic of judicial lawmaking, Howell notes a trend in all three countries, albeit in differing degrees, to a considerable uniformity or convergence in the recognition and regulation of the extraterritorial dimensions of parallel importation and reputation spillover.[9]

Legal Traditions and Educational and Commercial Linkages

Although securities laws and intellectual property laws are similar among Western countries, there are also differences of varying degrees of importance. Assuming that competition for foreign capital and marketplace convenience encourage emerging economies to imitate the economic laws of

6 *Ibid.* at 19-22.

7 *Ibid.* at 30.

8 R. G. Howell, "Parallel Importation of Wares and Reputation Spillover: Examples of Transnationalization of Law" (ch. 2 of this book) at 85.

9 *Ibid.* at 127-28.

established economies, what factors influence a country to choose, for example, a British law rather than a U.S. law as its primary model? A number of possible factors are mentioned by Gillen and Potter. We suspect that three of those factors are especially significant[10]: legal tradition, educational linkages, and commercial ties.

In Malaysia and Singapore, the intellectual property laws are modelled after British law, and their securities laws are most closely modelled after the British and Australian laws, with some limited incorporation of certain features of U.S. securities law. The most plausible explanations for this British and Australian modelling are the establishment of a British legal system in Malaysia and Singapore when those countries were colonized by Britain, and the extensive foreign legal (and, to a lesser extent, economic) training, of Malaysians and Singaporeans in England and Australia. The borrowing of parts of U.S. securities law may reflect the educational training of certain Malaysian and Singaporean specialists in the United States as well as the dominance of the United States as an economic world power.

On the other hand, Japanese securities laws are primarily based on U.S., not British, securities laws. This is, almost certainly, attributable to the dominance of the United States as an occupational force in Japan after the Second World War and the extensive Japanese-United States educational links and business contacts that ensued in the years following the War.[11]

In China, securities laws have somewhat diverged from those of the West for a number of reasons. As China shifts in the 1990s from a socialist command economy to a controlled market economy, its previous legal traditions are not the most important factor in shaping securities law. However, many remnants of Soviet-style economic law doggedly remain, as does the modern Chinese tradition of modelling on European civil law codes.[12] Commercial links with Hong Kong provide a British influence, while the commercial and economic importance of the United States and Japan provide U.S. influences on the shape of Chinese law in this area. The Chinese experts most closely associated with the securities regulatory system have received their legal education in the United States and this has surely contributed to the shaping of this area of Chinese legislation.

In the field of its new economic laws, Neilson observes that Vietnam is influenced by the legal experience of its socialist neighbour, China, while at the same time examining and adopting aspects of commercial and economic laws that exist in ASEAN and Western countries. This process of modelling occurs through the short-term importation of foreign legal experts and newfound educational linkages with ASEAN and Western countries.

---

10 Gillen and Potter, *supra* note 5 at 30-34.
11 *Ibid.*
12 *Ibid.* at 77-78.

Ideology

Commercial convenience has served as an explanation for the compatibility of economic laws for thousands of years before the invention of modern ideologies such as capitalism.[13] However, in the modern world the generic concept of capitalist interest has a more exciting, and perhaps more fundamental, connotation, offering livelier explanations, predictions, and prescriptions than could be conjured out of the blandness of commercial convenience. We live in a world, or a period of civilization, committed to one kind of social theory or another. Ideology contributes, often fundamentally, to the shaping of political (and other) attitudes, and to the structuring of the political system. Given the enormous force of economic circumstances in human affairs, it is difficult not to attribute great weight to the influence of capitalism as an ideology on the shaping and re-shaping of the economic sector throughout the world community, especially now that it encounters little in the form of a state-supported counter-ideology.[14]

With the apparent collapse of most socialist economies, one can expect greater convergence in economic laws due to the unipolar pressure and influence of capitalist countries such as the United States. However, as Gillen and Potter note,[15] the development of securities legislation in transitional economies such as China and Vietnam will still be affected by "a continuing controlled-economy mentality" in the minds of some influential bureaucrats. Neilson in his study of Vietnam's economic transformation makes the same point. The new economic laws in Vietnam are still largely administered by Soviet-trained bureaucrats operating under a political system of state management and socialist orientations. For example, the core element of Vietnam's foreign investment strategy is to join foreign capital and investment with state companies. Political pressures in economic affairs are different in these transitional economies than in countries with more traditional market-based economies, and these political influences

13 Concepts of capitalism are, of course, derived from that of capital, conceived as a stock, which is imaginable only in contrast with the flow concepts of income, profit, and interest. Capitalism as a theory of history was impossible before the introduction of capital, income, profit, and interest theories by the classical economists, such as Adam Smith, David Ricardo, Nassau Senior, and John Stuart Mill. Karl Marx developed the hypothesis of "capitalist exploitation" by arguing that capital was merely the embodied labour of the past. Thus profit and interest are characterized by Marx as the result of exploitation by the capitalist (the provider of capital), who skims off the income derived in these forms instead of rewarding the providers of services.

14 It seems premature to announce the end of socialist ideology. The present convergence of governmental (as distinct from political) opinion on the priority of debt reduction in statecraft may not endure, especially if electorates continue to demand a degree of enlightened state benevolence toward the victims of prolonged economic recession. However, communism as a form of authoritarian state control seems to have run its course.

15 Gillen and Potter, *supra* note 5 at 36.

can be expected to result in significant variations in the scope and administration of economic laws.[16]

This phenomenon has been clearly evident in China where current securities legislation is a compromise effort to maintain state control and yet induce investor confidence.[17] For example, although the disclosure requirements under Chinese securities law share some broad similarities to those in Malaysia, Singapore, and Japan, Chinese disclosure laws are unique to the extent that they are designed more with the regulator (i.e., the People's Bank of China) in mind than with the investor. Issuers of securities in China must provide the People's Bank with extensive information during the process of seeking approval.[18] In other jurisdictions it is common to delegate certain aspects of the regulation and enforcement of the securities industry to self-regulatory organizations composed primarily of industry members. What appears unique in China is the extent of government control, particularly through the People's Bank of China, which has ultimate authority to direct financial and monetary policy to achieve state-planned development goals.[19]

Public Policy and Special Interest Groups

One step below official ideology, at a more pragmatic level, sits public policy. Explanations of legal change in the economic sector are usually affected by the way one perceives the political system, the government, the establishment, the ruling elite, the business community, and the market. Idealistically we like to believe, regardless of the nature of the political system, that the outcome of the political process, which may be referred to as public policy, represents a more or less conscientiously contrived balancing of special interests with a view to affirming the common interest. More cynically or more perceptively, we see or sense the existence of elites with preponderant influence on the shaping of what purports to be public policy based on common interest.

The concept of an elite is extremely slippery. On the one hand, the term may be applied to self-serving, acquisitive elites, whose interests are assumed to be competitive with, if not inimical to, the general interest. With equal legitimacy, the term may apply to the best educated or wealthiest class, which may produce most of the social critics, such as the consumerists, environmentalists, and human rights proponents, who keep pressure

16 Neilson, *supra* note 4.

17 Gillen and Potter, *supra* note 5 at 58, n. 144, citing P. Potter, "The Legal Framework for Securities Markets in China: The Challenge of Maintaining State Control, and Inducing Investor Confidence" (1992) 7 China Law Reporter 69.

18 Gillen and Potter, *supra* note 5 at 58.

19 *Ibid.* at 76-77.

on the business establishment and their associates in the bureaucracy on behalf of the general public or particular vulnerable groups.[20]

Western civilization tends to be *confrontational* or adversarial in style and it is a Western notion that formal law is a vehicle for the confrontation of elites. Courts of law, arbitration tribunals, regulatory bodies, and public hearings are familiar Western institutions available in almost every context of economic affairs. In greatly varying degrees, most non-Western cultures have established comparable institutions to curb excessive economic power and influence in economic relationships, but the significance of these institutions in formal law may be much less than appears if the culture is more tolerant of elite dominance.[21] In non-Western cultures, parts of the economic sector of the formal legal system may appear essentially a ground for privileged verbal combat between elites and counter-elites within the central party system, with little relevance to the general public.

Public policy may at one and the same time be promoted out of either national interest or international idealism. Both project a bias, though the former may be more frank in acknowledging the "colour" of the bias. However, the main difference between the two is that the international idealist assumes the *desirability* of a particular kind of outcome, and may be relatively uninterested in the clash of arguments involved in the process, whereas the national interest analyst is bound to be chiefly interested in the process and in the evidence of *leverage* being applied.[22] In the search for explanations, the scholar adopting the teleological approach may unconsciously assign the greatest weight to factors that are conducive to the value goal of legal uniformity, economic integration, or policy harmonization; the alternative kind of explanation pivots on the asymmetry of intergovernmental or intercorporate relations, on sanctions, and the naked development of "leverage diplomacy."[23]

---

20 Among elites, as among traditional monarchs and other manipulators, one may try to distinguish the benevolent from the non-benevolent. It is surely one of the primary purposes of the civic sector of a legal system to provide strong institutional safeguards against manipulation or oppression in any form, however motivated.

21 At the time of writing, the high level of tolerance of traditional, military, party, and commercial elites in Asian countries such as Japan, South Korea, Thailand, Malaysia, Indonesia, the Philippines, Russia, and India seems to be slowly eroding, but there is also evidence that discredited elites are being replaced by new forms of elitism rather than by a new ethos of egalitarianism.

22 Most international lawyers tend to assume that legal uniformity contributes to a better world. By training, political scientists tend to focus on national interest and the deployment of national power or influence at the international level.

23 In the context of driftnet fishing, the emotive nature of the issue persuaded many commentators to insist on the need for prohibition backed up by political force at the global level rather than on the need for regulations through uniform, negotiated principles or guidelines: D. Johnston, "The Driftnetting Problem in the Pacific Ocean: Legal Considerations and Diplomatic Options" (1990) 21 Ocean Development and Int'l Law 5.

As Howell observes, one explanation for transnational convergence or similarity in economic laws is the fact that trade, which is driven by supply, demand, and the potential for profit, establishes its own pattern with minimal regard to political territory.[24] Economic markets in different countries have similar interest groups with similar market objectives. For example, in the securities field, promoters, investors, brokers, dealers, accountants, lawyers, and other special interest groups apply political pressure within their own country to produce a securities market that will have features in common with securities markets and regimes elsewhere.[25] The notion of common goals asserted by similar interest groups seems like a plausible explanation for the convergence of securities laws in Singapore, Malaysia, and Japan, but less plausible in China where interest groups such as these are less well defined and less influential.[26] It is arguable that the absence of these interest groups, connected as that may be to Chinese political ideology, partially explains why Chinese securities laws, though broadly similar to securities laws elsewhere, are less convergent than those of Singapore, Malaysia, Japan, and the Anglo-American countries. The same comments apply equally to explain some of the divergence in Vietnam's economic laws from the economic laws of Western countries.

In the areas of parallel importation and reputation spillover in Canada, Malaysia, and Singapore, a similar range of special interest groups is clearly at work. The fact that trademark law, through either interpretation of legislation or application and refinement of common law, is in effect ultimately developed by one elite group – the judges – puts a premium on country-to-country variations in the degree of judicial independence from government and other special interest groups.

Factors Contributing to Divergence

Several factors may work against convergence and even support divergence in laws and legal structures. Principal among these in the economic sphere are (1) differences in stages of economic development, (2) the acceptance of differential standards in international legal instruments, (3) cultural resistance, and (4) legal system differences.

Differing Stages of Economic Development

It is reasonable to assume that differences in national economic laws may be related to differences in the stage of economic development of each country. Although the black-and-white distinction between developed and developing countries is losing credibility as a description of reality, it is still of

---

24 Howell, *supra* note 8 at 84.

25 Gillen and Potter, *supra* note 5.

26 *Ibid.*

some assistance in stating broad generalities. For example, it is certainly fair to say that the economic needs, priorities, and structures of the least developed countries are far different than they are in the most developed countries. Similarly immense differences may be found between the least and most developed in their reliance upon capital and technology. Under such diverse economic conditions, one might expect to see laws shaped somewhat differently to meet a particular country's economic realities and priorities.

One might expect commercial laws or securities laws, for example, to be less detailed and less complex in countries in the early phases of economic development. Less regulatory detail and less rigorous enforcement may be strategies adopted more or less consciously by developing countries with fledgling securities markets to attract both national and foreign investment. For example, strict monitoring and regulation of insider trading may not take place in a country until the volume of trading is sufficient to justify the administrative costs involved. The securities markets in Malaysia and Singapore developed much later than in the United States. Consequently, insider trading laws also developed much later in Malaysia and Singapore (and in Britain) than in the United States.[27] Some of the differences in Chinese securities laws can be attributed to the fact that China is still in the early stages of developing securities markets. Similarly, some of the differences in Vietnam's economic laws can be attributed to the fact that Vietnam has not yet created the necessary institutional mechanisms to either support or enforce its new laws.[28]

Differing Standards in International Legal Instruments

It is well accepted that flexibility and diversity in negotiating and implementing international legal instruments are essential to accommodate the very real differences in the economic capacities of different countries. In global treaty-making, especially in trade and environment contexts, the trend now is to preserve the commonality of principles and objectives, but to permit differential standards according to the category to which each contracting party has agreed to belong.[29] It is now common for certain global

27 *Ibid.* at 44-45. For a recent practical guide to insider trading legislation in 25 countries, see M. Stamp and C. Welsh, eds., *International Insider Dealing* (London: FT Law and Tax, 1996).

28 Neilson, *supra* note 4.

29 The purpose of the "common but differentiated" approach to global treaty-making is to preserve the parties' shared sense of responsibility, rather than the strict letter of obligation, but at the same time to accept realistically the huge disparity among the parties in their capacity to implement difficult or costly provisions in the short term. Different standards or deadlines are set out for different categories of states in accordance with reasonable and realistic expectations.

treaties to have different Annexes setting out different standards for different countries, based upon economic realities within each country.[30] It appears that the World Trade Organization has no choice but to operate a "common-but-differentiated" regime, and this is likely to postpone, if not prevent, the achievement of convergence in trade-related areas of the economic law sector.[31]

Cultural Resistance

Religious and cultural beliefs are powerful influences on the shape and content of law. Of all the factors tending toward divergence, one might anticipate that cultural differences, or resistance to the imposition of foreign cultural norms, would be a particularly powerful influence. However, this factor seems to have only marginal significance in the economic sector, which in a sense has its own common culture – a culture of growth, development, and profits now fostered almost everywhere under the impact of an increasingly globalized market ideology. Howell observes that parallel importation and reputation spillover are almost exclusively economic or commercial in their impact and influence on society, and any

30 In art. 4 of the 1992 UN Framework Convention on Climate Change, for example, separate commitments are prescribed for "developed country Parties and other Parties included in annex I" (para. 2) and for more affluent (OECD) "developed country Parties and other developed Parties included in annex II" (para. 3). Paragraph 6 provides that in the implementation of their commitments under paragraph 2, "a certain degree of flexibility shall be allowed by the Conference of the Parties to the Parties included in annex I undergoing the process of transition to a market economy." Paragraph 7 notes that the "extent to which developing country Parties will effectively implement their commitments under the Convention will depend on the effective implementation by developed country Parties of their commitments under the Convention related to financial resources and transfer of technology. Parties are agreed to give special attention to the "specific needs and special situations of the least developed countries" (para. 9), and to the "situation of Parties, particularly developing country Parties, with economies that are vulnerable to the adverse effects of climate change," such as those that are "highly dependent on income generated from the production, processing and export, and/or consumption of fossil fuels and associated energy intensive products and/or the use of fossil fuels for which such Parties have serious difficulties in switching to alternatives" (para. 10). Paragraph 8 gives further emphasis to the concept of "specific needs and concerns" by recognizing nine categories of countries: (1) small island countries; (2) countries with low lying coastal area; (3) countries with arid and semi-arid areas, forested areas and areas liable to forest decay; (4) countries with areas prone to natural disasters; (5) countries with areas liable to drought and desertification; (6) countries with areas of high urban atmosphere pollution; (7) countries with areas with fragile ecosystems, including mountainous ecosystems; (8) countries whose economies are highly dependent on income generated from the production, processing and export, and/or consumption of fossil fuels and associated energy-intensive products; and (9) land-locked and transit countries.

31 On the level-playing-field issue in contemporary global trade law and policy, see e.g. R. E. Hudec, "Differences in National Environmental Standards: The Level-Playing-Field Dilemma" (1996) 5 Minn. J. Global Trade 1.

moral or social issues that might be included are essentially peripheral or of marginal significance.[32] Even where religious or cultural beliefs might possibly be expected to impinge on economic laws, they often do not have any observable effect on the formal laws or the way they are interpreted.[33] As Gillen and Potter note, although Islam, which is the dominant religion in Malaysia, has strict concepts concerning matters such as usury, these concepts have not been enacted into Malaysia's legislation on securities or debt instruments.[34]

However, even if the economic sector is treated as a single culture, it can be seen to consist of distinct business sub-cultures. Although Japanese securities law has had the same broadly framed market fraud provision that has been relied upon by U.S. courts in developing a prohibition of insider trading, no similar prohibitory policy emerged in Japan. This contrast has been attributed to different cultural beliefs and values on the part of Japanese and American business communities concerning the appropriateness of insider trading.[35] Legal convergence seems even more unlikely if one takes into account the evidence of divergent corporate micro-cultures.[36]

Legal System Differences

Diversity in law among countries is a phenomenon that one naturally expects. Even within the same country, there may be fundamental differences in law, especially when a country is a federation, like Canada or the United States, with law-making power at both the national and the state or provincial levels. Canada's legal diversity is even more pronounced, accommodating both the civil law system in Quebec and the common law tradition in

---

32 Howell, *supra* note 8 at 128.

33 *Ibid.*

34 Gillen and Potter, *supra* note 5 at 48. Such impingement may occur even in the economic sector in some countries that are more fundamentalist Muslim than Malaysia.

35 *Ibid.* at 51. The failure to apply insider trading laws was apparent in Japan until at least 1988, when, due to external pressure and loss of foreign confidence in the market, Japan tightened up these laws.

36 The literature in the field of business administration suggests that although there may be some universal, cross-cultural truth in the adage that "business is business," management styles and philosophies are often extremely diverse not only between one country (or corporate community) and another, but also between one corporate structure and another within the same country. Accordingly, it seems superficial to compare, say, the "American corporate culture" with the "Japanese corporate culture." This has not prevented writers from stereotyping the Americans as competitive and the Japanese as cooperative in their general social behaviour, and therefore, it is usually agreed, in their management style. On the assumption that each orientation has both strengths and weaknesses, some have argued that American and Japanese corporations can learn from each other. See e.g. J. P. Alston, *The American Samurai: Blending American and Japanese Management Practices* (Berlin and New York: Walter de Grayter, 1986).

the rest of the country. In a situation such as this, system diversity is virtually one of professional mindset or milieu.[37] Legal families or systems are often distinguished one from the other, not so much by substantive content, as by the way in which rules are enunciated and classified, the methods of legal reasoning employed, and the mechanisms and institutions available for the enforcement of laws.[38]

Most comparatists would probably agree that in Western countries there are still three primary legal systems: civil law, common law, and socialist law, although the last of these is eroding. In the Muslim world, Africa, and parts of Asia, indigenous folk law and religious law structures and traditions are also tenacious, and in some countries might be said to constitute a legal system. The very conception of law and its role in society can vary greatly. David and Brierley suggest, perhaps a little too starkly, that in Western, Islamic and Hindu communities,

> law is held to be a necessary part of, indeed a basis for, society. Good social order implies the primacy of law ... Law is therefore venerated, the courts are temples of justice, the judges its oracles. Far Eastern countries reject this view. For the Chinese, law is an instrument of arbitrary action rather than the symbol of justice; it is a factor contributing to social disorder rather than to social order ... Reconciliation is a greater value than justice; mediation must be used to remove conflicts rather than invoking law to resolve them. Laws may exist to serve as a method of intimidation or as a model; but law is not made with a view to being really applied, as in the West."[39]

As relevant as those comments may be to the behavioural and civic sectors of a legal system, they seem to have less relevance to the economic sector, at least at the transnational level. The existence of different legal systems has not prevented a high degree of convergence in economic laws, and the virtual collapse of socialist legal systems seems likely to accelerate this trend. The fact that economic law is predominantly a matter of legislation in common law countries, administered largely by regulatory bodies, tends to blur the significance of the distinction between common law and civil law systems.[40] At least in the area of securities law, legal system differences seem to have had little effect on the design of current economic legislation.

---

37 R. David and J. Brierley, *Major Legal Systems in the World Today*, 3d ed. (London: Stevens and Sons, 1985) use the expression "legal families." See also J. H. Wigmore, *A Panorama of the World's Legal Systems*, library edition (Washington, D.C.: Washington Law Book, 1928 and 1936).

38 David and Brierley, *ibid.* at 20-21.

39 *Ibid.* at 29-30.

40 Gillen and Potter, *supra* note 35-36.

Conclusions

The above analysis seems to support the following conclusions:

(1) Convergence in the economic law sector can be attributed chiefly to conscious imitation by less developed countries of the laws of economically dominant countries in order to facilitate trade and economic growth. This process of imitation is often advocated by like-minded special interest groups acting in the marketplace.

(2) Convergence also results in circumstances where it is economically expedient for developing countries to accept the laws or legal system originally imposed upon them by dominant economic powers, or where the legal and economic elites from developing countries have been educated in these foreign countries.

(3) Convergence is also achieved by direct leverage (often through trade or foreign aid) applied by economically powerful states on less powerful states in order to protect the perceived interests of the former.

(4) Differential economic development is taken into account in the negotiation of global treaties and the setting of standards, postponing hopes for uniformity in related areas of economic law. However, ideology, culture, and legal system differences do not appear to play a significant role in preventing the convergence of economic law. The trend to convergence is all the more evident today with the general demise of socialist economic law and the dominance of market capitalism in the world.

THE CIVIC SECTOR

Introduction

Comparative constitutional studies are of special interest at a time in world history when national governments everywhere are subject to increasing pressures to conform with Western democratic and rule-of-law ideals and practices. The democracy movement is bolstered by the belief that it now has an unprecedented opportunity to take advantage of the demise of repressive Marxist-Leninist regimes and of the added leverage possessed by American diplomacy.

It should not be supposed, of course, that democracy and legalism of the Western sort are necessarily resisted throughout the non-Western world as concepts based on alien sentiments, but, in many non-Western political cultures, democratic demands for a higher standard of *operational* constitutionalism are associated chiefly with identifiable groups. In some countries these demands may be heard only from a small, highly educated elite, which often but not always is Westernized to some degree; in other societies democracy demands may become the most salient feature of student movements, led usually by urban, middle-class sub-elites. In still other political cultures, democracy may become the rallying call in a more generalized popular uprising.

Despite the attractiveness of the concept of universal civic *ideals* and the basic similarities that can be found in the *texts* of most state constitutions, the reality seems to be that national constitutional and other civic *practices* tend to follow their own course, dictated by internal rather than external factors and considerations.[41] Convergence may be apparent, but divergence is real. This seems, at least, to be supported by the three chapters on the civic sector included in this work. The co-authored study of parliamentary supremacy shows recent divergence between Canada, which now favours constitutional supremacy over parliamentary supremacy, despite its direct descent from the mother of all parliamentary systems, and Singapore and even more clearly Malaysia, which favour parliamentary supremacy despite written constitutional provisions that would seem to tilt in the opposite direction.[42] Ted McDorman's chapter on the new state constitution of Thailand offers no hope of sudden conversion to the U.S. "cult" of constitutionalism, and only a modest degree of optimism that we are witnessing a gradual shift away from the "cycle of Thai politics": coups, constitutions, and elections.[43] The co-authored chapter on the new state constitution of Vietnam traces major constitutional changes that, in the Chinese style, reflect changes in public policy from the nationalistic text of 1946, through the ideological but non-directive text of 1960 and the visionary but Party-controlled text of 1980, to the economically motivated but Party-controlled text of 1992.[44]

Factors Contributing to Convergence

The World Community

The combination of democracy and rule-of-law ideals in the Western world has been offered as further evidence of the "ascent of the West," and the defeat of communist authoritarianism has been hailed as the opportunity

41 L. W. Beer, ed., *Constitutional Systems in Late Twentieth Century Asia* (Seattle: Univ. of Washington Press, 1992) shows a high degree of similarity in the texts of state constitutions but a wide discrepancy in their application. Even if one accepts a national constitution as text it projects different images to different observers and to different sets of interests, and indeed changing images over time even from the same perspective. On the multiple images of the Canadian constitution in the present era, see W. E. Conklin, *Images of a Constitution* (Toronto: Univ. of Toronto Press, 1989). The non-textualist approach encourages the view of constitution as practice.

42 C. Crane, M. Gillen, and T. L. McDorman, "Parliamentary Supremacy in Canada, Malaysia, and Singapore" (ch. 4 of this book).

43 T. L. McDorman, "Constitutional Change and Continuity in Thailand in the Aftermath of the 1991 Coup" (ch. 5 of this book).

44 J. Harrington, T. L. McDorman and W. A. W. Neilson, "The 1992 Vietnamese Constitution: Economic Reform, Political Continuity" (ch. 6 of this book). For a similar Chinese pattern see A. H. Chen, *An Introduction to the Legal System of the People's Republic of China* (Hong Kong: Butterworths Asia, 1992) at 39-62.

to promote these civic values aggressively in the arena of global diplomacy. But in the most ambitious versions of these ideals, especially that of the United States, the distinction between human rights and governance issues is easily overlooked, and a written constitution inspired by bold civic aspirations tends to generate overexpectations.

Since the late 1940s the human rights community has been divided between those who assign primacy to the value of individualism and thus to political and civil rights, and those who grant priority to economic and social rights in the name of collective ethic. During the Cold War era it was only too easy to think of this distinction in terms of political ideology, but in the 1990s the gulf remains in so many countries that it seems more accurate to describe it rather in terms of political culture. Many cultures, such as Thailand and Vietnam, may be as far away as ever from accepting a written constitution as "sacred text" and providing effective state machinery to guarantee its operational vitality. Western "world community" pressures on governments such as these have not yet produced any discernible trend to operational convergence within the civic law sector. Symbolic convergence – the appearance of convergence – within this sector may continue for generations to be the only result of external pressures in the name of the world community. The operational significance of constitutional language will continue, it seems, to be culturally contingent.

Western lawyers are, however, professionally trained as well as culturally conditioned to believe in the possibility, if not the inevitability, of civic progress along Western lines. The dominant Western economic powers have acquired enormous leverage over most of the international economic institutions and corporate enterprises that together control the global marketplace – to the extent that control is possible – and recent experience in central and eastern Europe might be interpreted as showing that the "conditionality" strategy in trade and development assistance is beginning to effect a change of civic values in these government systems, if not at the grass roots of their political culture.[45] Thailand and Vietnam may belong to a gradually shrinking category of "symbolically constitutional" states.

Cultural Affinity

In the light of the above argument, the likeliest cause of convergence in the civic law sector may be cultural association. In the co-authored chapter on

---

45 It has been argued that the reconciliation of free trade with environmental responsibility in the new era depends on effective linkages between the WTO and environmental NGOs: W. M. Rachert, "Resolving the Trade and Environment Conflict: The WTO and NGO Consultative Relations" (1996) 5 Minn. J. Global Trade 219. The same argument can be made for the reconciliation of trade and development assistance with human rights through consultation between NGOs and key IGOs such as the WTO, the World Bank, and other institutions.

parliamentary supremacy, it is suggested that Canada's movement away from that ideal to the alternative of constitutional supremacy, since the enactment of its Charter of Rights and Freedoms in 1982, is due to a gradual narrowing of the gap between the Canadian and American political, social, and economic cultures.[46] This trend seems likely to be reinforced by recent economic developments such as NAFTA, as well as by a continual process of the Americanization of popular culture through the mass media.

As implied in the chapter on parliamentary supremacy, gradual civic convergence between Canada and the United States might be predicted on the ground that public respect for the judiciary is deeply rooted in both cultures, as in the British culture, and in all three cultures there is a diminishing trust in the "will of the people" as interpreted manipulatively by the people's elected representatives, who are "merely politicians." For an increasingly large number of those committed to democracy, the people's will is more likely to prevail through participation than through representation. By this reasoning, civic convergence of the operational sort will be the product of cross-cultural affinity, and therefore it will not become a global phenomenon in a world composed of markedly diverse political cultures.

"Judicialization" of Civic Values

It can, however, be argued that over the long run there is likely to be a trend to resort increasingly to international, if not national, courts to secure individual or collective rights set out in a written constitution. Reference can be made to the impact of the European Court of Human Rights, which has granted relief to many complainants who were deprived of a judicial remedy in the courts of their own jurisdiction.[47] As more and more European countries line up to join the Council of Europe, the expansion of that Court might be expected to have an important long-term effect on the convergence of civic law throughout the European continent.[48] Efforts to create

---

46 Crane, Gillen, and McDorman, *supra* note 42.

47 The European Commission of Human Rights hears complaints from individuals but will not forward them to the Court unless the applicant can be shown to have complied strictly with the "local remedies" rule: that is, the rule that a state "should be given the opportunity to redress an alleged wrong within the framework of its own domestic legal system before its international responsibility can be called into question at the international level": A. A. Trindade, *The Application of the Rule of Exhaustion of Local Remedies in International Law* (Cambridge: Cambridge Univ. Press, 1983) at 1.

48 The Council of Europe was established by the Treaty of Westminster in 1949 at the first stage of the "European movement," but fell far short of the European federalists' much bolder plans for regional integration, as later realized in the European Communities and the present European Union. However, membership of the Council of Europe is conditional upon acceptance of the European Convention on Human Rights and creates entitlement to place a judge on the European Court of Human Rights. For a description of the evolution of the Council, see M. J. Dedman, *The Origins and Developments of the European Union, 1945-95: A History of European Integration* (London and New York:

regional courts in Latin America, the Middle East, and other regions are now being made, inspired by the European experience.[49]

However, it is not probable that a trend of this kind elsewhere can become established at the international level in the absence of a corresponding trend to the use of courts for civic purposes at the national level. As the Thai experience demonstrates, even those legal systems that permit a relatively high degree of judicial independence – and from a global perspective this is the exception, not the rule – do not necessarily grant the regular courts of law the power to review the constitutionality of legislation and executive decrees.[50] As in Thailand, a special quasi-judicial body entrusted with this power is less likely to operate with the same degree of detachment from political manipulation.

Factors Contributing to Divergence

Nation-Building Strategy

Crane, Gillen, and McDorman deal with the divergence between Canada, on the one hand, and Malaysia and Singapore, on the other, on the choice between parliamentary and constitutional supremacy. Since all three countries have somewhat comparable textual commitments to the principle of constitutional supremacy, the two Southeast Asian countries can be seen to have diverged also from their own written constitutions, and to that extent from the U.S.-led Western model of constitutionalism. Among the reasons suggested for this phenomenon is the desire of governments, and perhaps also citizens, of countries like Singapore and Malaysia for a strong executive, which can be perceived as a prerequisite to nation-building in general and to rapid economic development in particular. Given the (pre-crisis) economic success of these two countries, it seems entirely plausible that strong leadership, allied with moral authority, has indeed taken precedence in the hearts and minds of the bulk of these electorates.

The need for strong leadership as a national priority may prevail across a wider range of civic issues, including some that involve human welfare

Routledge, 1996) at 27-33. Since the newest members of the Council of Europe are from central Europe, it might be supposed that the civil law tradition on the Court will become increasingly dominant over the common law tradition.

49 The judicialization of civic values might also be reflected in current efforts to bring accused war criminals to justice before *ad hoc* international tribunals, as in the case of former Yugoslavia and Rwanda.

50 McDorman, *supra* note 43.

51 In both Taiwan and South Korea, dissent on the part of students and special interest groups had little effect on the process of democratization until they secured the sympathy and respect of the middle-class, middle-aged mainstream of the electorate, whose civic consciousness seems to have risen along with their level of education and material well-being. There is some evidence to support the view that political motivation is commensurate with widely shared prosperity in its larger sense.

concerns more directly than the struggle for supremacy between the branches of government. Apologists for nation-building strategy as the paramount consideration in public policy for developing countries often wave off protests against the accompanying downgrading of civic values on the ground that the latter will be elevated once a sufficiently comfortable level of affluence has been attained. Recent civic progress in terms of democracy and the rule of law in other tiger economies, such as those of Taiwan and South Korea, might be taken as evidence in support of this proposition.[51] It may be too early to predict when, or if, Singapore and Malaysia will follow in the same direction of civic adjustment.

Civic Apathy

The Crane-Gillen-McDorman study also raises the possibility that divergence on the supremacy issue may be attributable to a lack of political awareness.[52] On this and other issues, the deficiency might be defined more narrowly as a lack of civic or constitutional consciousness. It is conceded by the authors that the electorates of Singapore and Malaysia are well educated and factually well informed on most political developments, but suggested that government control deprives them of access to critical oppositionist opinion.[53] Similar constraints are described in the chapter on Vietnam.[54] On the other hand, nothing could be further from the truth in the case of Thailand, where the media delight in the freedom to report on the often bitter, verbal exchanges across the broad spectrum of the country's many political parties. Yet all four countries diverge conspicuously from the Western models of constitutionalism in many ways. Perhaps what they share is not so much a lack of awareness as a lack of concern. Civic apathy in certain cultures may be the factor that ensures global non-convergence in this sector of formal law, at least as long as the enhancement of material well-being is sustained.[55] It may be worth noting that the recent failures of the Thai, Indonesian, Malaysian, and South Korean governments to sustain material well-being have had different effects on the morale of the citizenry: largely negative in the case of Indonesia but almost positive in the case of Thailand and South Korea.

Respect for Authority

In many non-Western political cultures, civic apathy seems to be concomitant with an inborn respect for authority, which is less frequently found in the more sceptical and disputatious political cultures of the Western world. It might even be suggested that the civic sector of a modern system of

52 Crane, Gillen, and McDorman, *supra* note 42.
53 *Ibid.*
54 Harrington, McDorman, and Neilson, *supra* note 44.
55 Crane, Gillen, and McDorman, *supra* note 42.

formal law is a barometer of the general trust or distrust of those in positions of power and authority. Political or legal history cannot be expected to make full disclosure of the reasons for such trust or distrust, since the writing of any history is itself psycho-culturally conditioned.

Two aspects of respect for authority are commented upon by Crane, Gillen, and McDorman, and also by McDorman in his chapter on the Thai constitution. First, in Malaysia and Singapore the traditionally respectful attitude to authority may have been reinforced by the long period of British residency. By imperial standards, the latter maintained a fairly high degree of moral authority with relatively little resort to military force. Under a strict but relatively fair-minded administration, shared to some extent with the traditional power-holding sultans, the energetic but politically powerless groups on the Malay peninsula were free to concentrate on economic, professional, and other non-civic opportunities. Even today the national bureaucracies of Malaysia and Singapore – and the executive and legislative organs – enjoy a relatively high degree of respect, and there is a fairly widespread acceptance that the running of the country can be left to those in authority. Open public criticism of government is barely tolerated, and for that matter is not widely admired, even among the fully aware members of the academic community. Civic law is generally perceived as an instrument of responsible government rather than as a constraint on civic irresponsibility. In Thailand, it seems, the fully aware have lower expectations of those in authority, both at political and bureaucratic levels, but have not yet found a way within their political culture to use formal civic law as an effective constraint on irresponsibility. This situation may change if the 1997 constitutional amendments acquire the operational significance that is intended.[56]

Second, respect for authority is reflected in attitudes toward the judiciary. Certainly the history of Chinese civilization seems to show a deeply rooted aversion to contact with the heavily penalistic Chinese judicial system.[57]

---

56 The collapse of the ruling coalition under Prime Minister Banharn in 1996 induced the latter to dissolve the Thai Parliament rather than accept a successor to himself as leader of the coalition. The "fully aware" members of the urban middle class, who were mostly hostile to the Banharn government, were seemingly divided on the civic propriety of this course of action. By mid-1997 it appeared that the Bangkok middle class had retained its solidarity in support of the Chuan government, reinforced by approval ratings from the international community.

57 For a detailed and scholarly account of the workings of the traditional Chinese judicial system at the appellate level, see D. Bodde and C. Morris, *Law in Imperial China Exemplified by 190 Ch'ing Dynasty Cases* (Philadelphia: Univ. of Pennsylvania Press, 1973). For a view of how Chinese legal institutions worked on a day-to-day basis, see S. van der Sprenkel, *Legal Institutions in Manchu China: A Sociological Analysis* (London: Athlone Press, 1962). On the role and justification of punishment in traditional Chinese society, see G. MacCormack, *The Spirit of Traditional Chinese Law* (Athens: Univ. of Georgia Press, 1996) at 182-212. On the ethical foundations of the Chinese penal law, see also MacCormack, *ibid.* at 52-68.

Against this ethnic background of avoidance, it should not be surprising that most members of Chinese communities both inside and outside the PRC today seem less than deeply imbued with British-style rule-of-law idealism or with Western-style respect for judicial process within the framework of formal state law. It may not come easily to the Chinese, or for that matter to the Malays, to perceive lawyers in general, or judges in particular, as the natural agents of justice or as the critics and censors of political authority. Operational constitutionalism as a constraint may even be seen as an alien notion that would create an unwanted degree of dissonance in a culture that still puts a premium on the goal of social harmony.[58]

Conclusions

The civic law chapters in this book seem to support the following four conclusions:

(1) All written state constitutions serve symbolic as well as operational purposes, but the ratio between them varies enormously with the values and interests predominant in the political culture.

(2) The vitality of the cognate principles of democracy, constitutionalism, and the rule of law within a "civic culture" must be measured against a wide variety of criteria: for example, universal suffrage; pluralism; rule by consent of the people as a whole and their elected representatives; access to justice through the courts of law; freedom of speech and association; enlightened majoritarianism based on tolerance of ethnic, religious, linguistic, and other minorities; public participation in decision-making; independence of the judiciary; judicial review of the constitutionality of legislation and executive decisions; honesty and efficiency in government; subordination of the military to civilian authority; restriction of police powers; subordination of the majority religion to effective constitutional guarantees of religious freedom; and the non-partisan use of the educational system to promote civic consciousness. Faced with such a variety of value criteria, it is unrealistic to expect anything more than a gradual trend to convergence in the civic law sector.

(3) The build-up of operational, as distinct from symbolic, civic law on the Western (or U.S.) model cannot be expected to happen in the short or medium term in radically different, non-litigious, non-Western legal cultures.

---

58 By the time of Neo-Confucianism in the late Sung dynasty, harmony was seen to depend upon scrupulous respect for the "Three Bonds" between ruler and subject, father and son, and husband and wife. A great deal of codified law from late Sung to late Ch'ing was essentially structured around these three key relationships. Today in all Chinese legal cultures there seems still to be widespread distaste for any form of operational constitutionalism that would encourage or legitimize the undermining of the tradition of respect for authority and for the stability of the family.

(4) Contributions to a gradual development of civic law in these legal cultures depends chiefly on the rise of civic consciousness on the part of urban middle-class elites within these countries.

THE BEHAVIOURAL SECTOR

Introduction

In the behavioural sector, law is generally concerned with more intimately personal and interpersonal aspects of human experience than in either the economic or civic sector. Because of its personal intimacy, behavioural law often touches upon some of the most fundamental beliefs or values within a society. Criminal law, family law, and much of tort law form the core of the behavioural sector, and also of what might be characterized as a *legal culture*.[59] Conduct within the behavioural sphere is often managed from both within and outside the legal system. Extra-legal behavioural norms such as social conventions, religious practices, or cultural taboos operate through institutions such as the family, schools, employers, and social or religious organizations. Prostitution and mental disorder, which are the subjects of separate chapters in this book, are striking examples of behavioural issues that straddle the line between the legal and extra-legal domains. In looking at patterns of convergence and divergence in the behavioural sector, it might be assumed in general that the greater the cultural differences between countries, the greater is the likelihood of divergence in their behavioural laws, but once again it is possible to distinguish specific factors that tend to push or pull in both directions.

Factors Contributing to Convergence

The Global Economy and the Global Village

International trade and the global economy, which are firmly situated in the economic sector, may appear to have little to do with the more intimate

59 "By legal *culture* is meant these historically conditioned, deeply rooted attitudes about the nature of law and about the proper structure and operation of a legal system that are at large in the society. Law is, among other things, an expression of the culture; ideas about law are part of the intellectual history of a people. Such ideas are very powerful; they limit and direct thinking about law, and in this way they profoundly affect the composition and operation of the legal system": J. H. Barton *et al.*, *Law in Radically Different Cultures* (St. Paul, Minn.: West, 1983) at n. 2. On the face of things, a legal culture approach to comparative legal systems can be expected to be of the greatest relevance in the behavioural sector and of least relevance in the economic sector. Yet in many countries around the world, rural transactions especially are still governed by traditional norms, local customs, and informal procedures rather than by formal rules of law, national institutions, and state sanctions. See A. J. Pirie, "Alternative Dispute Resolution in Thailand and Cambodia: Making Common Sense on (Un)Common Ground" (ch. 11 of this book) for a discussion of the role of culture in shaping dispute resolution mechanisms.

and private affairs that fall within the domain of the behavioural sector, but there is in fact a spill-over from the economic to the behavioural. The rapid advance of globalized capitalism and transnational trade, with its associated values of materialism and individualism, poses a threat, or at least a challenge, to the maintenance of other traditional values. The global onslaught of Western culture, propagated through increased international commerce and travel, not to mention the exportation of Western culture through the popular media, has undoubtedly had some influence on creating greater convergence between Eastern and Western cultures. Cultural assimilation throughout the world seems likely, sooner or later, to bring greater convergence in national behavioural laws. On the other hand, it should be noted that the magnitude of the onslaught has had the effect of sharpening the resistance by some fundamentalist leaders to this insidious importation of Western culture.[60] Moreover, it must be remembered that some cultural beliefs and practices are too deeply embedded in Eastern societies to be seriously disturbed by mere surface noises from Western cultures.

Resistance or not, there are definite signs of at least some Western encroachment. In family law, employment law, and human rights law, the Western-promoted principle of equality between the sexes has resulted in changes to behavioural laws in some Eastern countries. Western permissiveness concerning sexual behaviour, communicated world-wide through the popular media, has resulted in changes to substantive laws and enforcement practices in some Eastern countries in such contexts as pornography, abortion, and homosexuality. John McLaren, in his chapter on prostitution, notes that the evolution of sex trade law in Thailand has clearly been influenced by Western concerns and pressures.[61] First, Thai law responded to a Western concern about the spread of venereal diseases through prostitution; later Thai law was changed to respond to the Western concern for the suppression of female sexual slavery (the selling of women and girls across borders for the purpose of prostitution); then there was an expansion of Thai law in an attempt to meet international obligations under the United Nations Convention Ending Discrimination Against Women, and to enhance its image more generally; and finally Thai law changed again to accommodate Western concerns arising from a new source of sexual demand – American servicemen on furlough during the Vietnam War. Currently Thailand grapples with pressure from the international community, especially the West, to give teeth to its laws on child prostitution, a practice that exists in part due to Western demand.

---

60 Resentment of this kind is particularly conspicuous in the popular journals of Southeast Asia.

61 J. McLaren, "Whores, Soiled Doves, or Working Women? Law, Society, and the Sex Trade in Australia, Canada, and Thailand" (ch. 8 of this book) at 387-96.

There is also another, deeply embedded, explanation for convergence: namely, the existence of common patterns of political and social organization through patriarchy. This is clearly evident in the ideology of sexual relationships and gender status in both the East and the West. In the Thai context, McLaren makes the point that traditional elite notions of women being there to satisfy male sexual desires has been transformed into a social ideology of the general availability of women to please and titillate Thai men. Patriarchy is also clearly evident in the socio-legal treatment of prostitution throughout all Western societies.

Other examples of global (usually Western) pressures to adopt common behavioural norms, which may be in conflict with accepted cultural norms in less dominant countries, include international initiatives to promote women's equality, or to curb the use of corporal punishment as a form of discipline or punishment, or to abolish the practice of female genital mutilation as a religious or social custom.

Notwithstanding the evidence of some convergence in a few high-profile behavioural areas, it seems accurate to say that increased globalization of world economies and of modes of telecommunication has not radically ameliorated cultural differences in the behavioural sector of law.

Colonial Legal Tradition

The imposition or adoption of Western laws, as part of the general colonization of Asia that occurred predominantly in the nineteenth and early twentieth centuries, has had a definite impact on the convergence of at least formal laws in all three sectors. As Gerry Ferguson notes in his chapter on mental disorder,[62] there was a clear and fairly systematic adoption or imposition of Western criminal laws in most Asian countries; in particular he describes the process of adoption in India, Malaysia, Singapore, Thailand, Japan, Indonesia, and Taiwan. Criminal law was seen by the Western colonizers as a mechanism to ensure a degree of social control and security that would be familiar and reassuring to foreigners living in and trading with Asian countries. Thus the penal codes and penal laws of the colonizers – Britain, France, Germany, Portugal, and Holland – became for the most part the formal penal laws of the Asian countries in question. These Western penal codes were not generally altered to incorporate much in the way of local, indigenous customs or norms.

In the formal criminal laws of Asian and Western countries a high degree of similarity can be observed. But this formal textual convergence hides the reality of a wide divergence in the actual practice or enforcement of criminal law at the indigenous village level. To a large extent, the imported penal

---

62 G. Ferguson, "Legal Regulation of Mental Disorder: Looking East and West" (ch. 7 of this book) at 298-301.

laws did not actually operate within the local indigenous communities except where there was interaction with the relatively few foreign colonialists; and in other areas of behavioural law, such as family law or the civil regulation of mental disorder, the colonizers felt less of a need to impose Western laws. Consequently, indigenous laws and practices continued in these areas virtually unaffected by Western law.

The Educational Connection

Apart from the direct imposition of foreign laws, juridical convergence between one jurisdiction and another can arise less directly, but very effectively, through educational linkages between these jurisdictions. When many of the academic elite of one country are educated in another country, they tend to promote within their own country many of the ideas and social solutions that they have observed overseas. One can see this process at work in the sphere of economic laws. It also exists but is less pronounced in the behavioural sector. Since behavioural rules are rooted in fundamental values and beliefs, it is extremely uncommon to see a widespread or rapid adoption of a wholly foreign cultural approach to the legal regulation of behavioural activities or problems. It is the experience at least of North American law teachers that foreign students studying law in the West tend to concentrate their studies more on the economic and civic sectors than on the behavioural.

Be that as it may, some areas of human activity within the behavioural sphere have been profoundly affected by foreign knowledge, transmitted largely through foreign educational training. In particular, Western science and technology have had a revolutionary effect on all aspects of life, including the economic, civic, and behavioural. For example, the fairly widespread adoption of Western medicine and psychiatry in Eastern countries over the past 100 years has, as Ferguson discusses in his chapter,[63] altered indigenous beliefs about the nature of the body and the mind and the nature of sickness and health. This alteration, which is more complete in the case of urban elites than among remote village dwellers, has occurred principally through foreign medical training and Western aid in support of Western medical practices and facilities. Similarly, McLaren notes the influence of Western notions of public health in the development of Thai responses to the regulation of prostitution on public health grounds.[64]

Ideology

It seems safe to assert that the greater the concurrence in behavioural or social ideology, the more likely there will be convergence in behavioural

63 *Ibid.* at 290-94.

64 McLaren, *supra* note 61, at 387-90.

laws. Also, the greater the ideological divide, the greater the divergence we should expect to find in behavioural laws. In his study of prostitution and its regulation in Canada, Australia, and Thailand, McLaren, drawing on feminist theory, Foucaultian notions of knowledge as power, and the importance of professional discourse, illustrates how ideology is critical in constructing a society's notions of what constitutes deviant sex.[65]

During the era of Marxist-Leninist ideology, the contrast between the economic laws of socialist and capitalist countries was readily apparent. In the behavioural sector one finds today an equally striking contrast between fundamentalist religious states and purely secular states. Clearly, at that level, state ideologies are reflected in both the content and the enforcement of behavioural laws. At one extreme, in theocratic or quasi-theocratic cultures, such as that of the fundamentalist Islamic states, extensive areas of human experience are deemed to be governed by holy writ and thus subject to regulation and punishment by religious institutions.[66] In these countries the state system is effectively discouraged from intruding in the spiritual domain, especially in the behavioural sector, and sometimes in the economic and civic sectors as well.[67]

In multi-sectarian societies, such as India, where religious conflict always threatens to strip the state of its social cohesion, the secular courts of law often have to walk a narrow line between active neutralization and nonintervention.[68] The need for social cohesion, rationalized in terms of public

---

65 See generally McLaren, *supra* note 61.

66 The Rushdie blasphemy affair has seriously damaged the reputation of Islamic law at the popular level around the world. For a rare sympathetic viewpoint, see A. Bradney, "Taking Sides: Religion, Law and Politics" (1993) 143 New Law J. 434.

67 For example, in all matters relating to the family, including marriage, divorce, maintenance, property, inheritance, and custody and guardianship of children, Muslims in Malaysia are governed by Muslim Law, albeit as modified by Malay custom: M. Siraj, "Marriage and Divorce: The Law Applicable to Muslims," in M. Siraj, ed., *Women and the Law* (University Women's Association, Univ. of Malaya, Kuala Lumpur, Malaysia, 1988). In several Islamic countries, behavioural norms of religious origin impinge upon such transactional areas as real property (detention and perception), personal property (gifts), inheritance, and business transactions (usury): A. A. A. Fryzee, *Outlines of Muhammadan Law*, 4th ed. (Delhi: Oxford Univ. Press, 1974). Through its governance of the criminal justice system in several Islamic countries, religious teaching has a direct influence on the treatment of human rights and related civic issues: M. C. Bassiouni, ed., *The Islamic Criminal Justice System* (London: Oceana Publications, 1982). One should be warned, however, that generalization about "Islamic influences" tends to be misleading: M. Hooker, *Islamic Law in South-East Asia* (Singapore: Oxford Univ. Press, 1984) at 3.

68 Women in particular are often the victims of the clash between Indian secular law and Hindu or Muslim law or custom. See e.g. M. S. Fahn, "Noncompliance with India's Dowry Prohibition Act of 1961: A Society's Reactions to Imposed Law" (1990) 4 Temple Int'l and Comparative L.J. 101, and A. Rahman, "Religious Rights Versus Women's Rights in India: A Test Case for International Human Rights Law" (1990) 28 Columbia J. of Transnational Law 473.

policy or public order, tends to generate impingements by the civic sector upon the behavioural. In theocratic societies, governed by the norms and beliefs of a single, dominant state religion, non-intervention in the behavioural sector may be sacrosanct. In non-sectarian or secular systems, such as those found in most Western countries, there is an established separation of religion and state, although many of the secular state's social values have religious roots. Furthermore, religious groups within the secular state may still constitute a powerful special interest group able to promote its values under the guise of secular laws.[69]

Public Policy and Special Interest Groups

Public policy, and therefore the influence of special interest groups, is no less evident in the behavioural sector than in the civic or economic sectors. In some areas of behavioural law, in particular criminal law, there will be a high degree of concurrence on public policy across cultures. Most societies share a common desire to prohibit and punish conduct such as murder, kidnapping, assault, and robbery. In other areas of conduct, such as alcohol consumption, gambling, and sexual behaviour, or in attitudes to certain sanctions such as maiming, caning, or the death penalty, there is substantial room for divergence in the criminal laws of one country and another. Some countries may use criminal law to promote or maintain a public policy aimed at sexual purity, traditional family values, and unquestioned respect for religious and civil authority. In other, more secular and permissive countries, the dominant public policy may not show the same respect for traditional family values: for example, these countries may permit abortion, ban corporal punishment, and decriminalize homosexual behaviour.[70] Thus, different visions of public policy will normally be reflected in, or result in, differing behavioural laws. But when a behavioural issue is pushed into the international spotlight, there may be global political (or economic) forces at work shaping or demanding a common policy and a common legal approach to behavioural issues that have previously been dealt with in divergent ways. This is currently very evident in the developing international campaign to suppress child prostitution and sex tours.

---

69 For example, the Catholic Church still exerts strong influence on law and public policy in secular countries. Also, much attention has been bestowed recently in U.S. politics on the interests and concerns of what are described as fundamentalist Christians or, more broadly, the "religious right."

70 In the west, some social critics challenge the prohibition of any "consensual crimes" (e.g., gambling, drug use, prostitution, pornography, transvestism, homosexuality, and other unconventional sexual practices) on the ground that the principle of personal freedom should permit any form of intimate behaviour that does not physically harm the person or property of another. See e.g. P. McWilliams, *Ain't Nobody's Business If You Do: The Absurdity of Consensual Crimes in a Free Society* (Los Angeles: Prelude Press, 1993).

Factors Contributing to Divergence

Differing Stages of Economic Development

Although differing stages of economic development may be a significant factor in explaining divergence in economic laws, it is difficult to weigh that factor's influence on the pattern of divergence in behavioural laws. It is sometimes argued that the less economically developed a country is, the less likely Western cultural values will have permeated its indigenous culture and behavioural laws. But this argument is not wholly convincing. Through the popular media, there is still widespread transmission of Western cultural values and modes of expression to even the world's poorest countries.

On the other hand, one of the ideological or public policy hallmarks of economically developed Western countries is the development of the welfare state, with its provision of public welfare benefits.[71] Public welfare benefits in the areas of health, education, and social welfare straddle the civic and behavioural sectors. Divergence will obviously exist in social welfare laws between countries that are economically developed enough to afford such benefits and countries which are not. But social welfare laws are contingent on ideology as well as economics. Many of the economically prospering countries of Asia and South America have been slow to provide public welfare benefits on a scale commensurate with their resources.[72] So economic development does not necessarily explain differences in behavioural laws in the social welfare area.

Differential Standards in International Legal Instruments

Outside the field of human rights, international legal instruments have much less impact on the behavioural area than on either the economic or civic sector. In part, it is the intensely personal, private character of behavioural law, influenced and developed as it is through religious beliefs or other fundamental social norms, that accounts for its relative immunity from the

---

71 Welfare statism had its origins in the mercantilist period of the early seventeenth century, but in its modern systemic form it took root as a virtually unchallenged political philosophy late in the nineteenth century: R. St. J. Macdonald, D. M. Johnston, and G. L. Morris, "The International Law of Human Welfare: Concept, Experience and Priorities," in Macdonald, Johnston, and Morris, eds., *The International Law and Policy of Human Welfare* (Aalphen Aan den Rijn: Sijthoff and Noordhoff, 1978) at 33-45.

72 On the psychic or spiritual side of human welfare, these same, relatively non-philanthropic cultures often display a higher degree of sensitivity to the needs of the individual, not, as in the west, through public policies and state laws, but through informal social networks and support associations at the community, workplace, and interpersonal levels of society. At these levels, the special vulnerabilities of certain individuals may be more easily identified and treated than is likely to be possible at the more impersonal level of state bureaucracy operating within a well-intentioned system of formal laws and public policies. Presumably, too, these social arrangements tend to be more respectful of deeply held beliefs and of the personal value of "intimacy."

interstate system. Thus in many areas of the behavioural sector, it is not a matter of having different standards for different countries under an international legal instrument, but rather it is often a matter of having no international legal instrument at all.

Where international treaties or declarations do exist in fundamental areas of human rights – areas governed by norms widely recognized as basic within a hierarchy of norms – the instruments do not normally recognize different standards for different countries. Fundamental norms such as prohibitions against torture, sanctions against international terrorism, or even guarantees of equality rights, are not contexts in which differential standards are likely to be acceptable at the level of international diplomacy. But the wording of most human rights instruments, even in fundamental areas, is often broad enough to permit divergent interpretations and practices.[73]

Cultural Resistance

We have already emphasized the obvious in asserting that laws within the behavioural sector are often rooted in fundamental religious and cultural beliefs and practices. Because there is significant divergence in world cultures, it only makes sense to expect greater divergence in laws in the behavioural sector than in the somewhat less culturally dependent civic or economic sectors. For explanations of divergence, one need look no further than the current continuation of East-West tension and conflict in contexts touching upon fundamental values. Reacting against the corrupting influences of the West on their youth, some Asians, Arabs, and perhaps other non-Westerners feel that they have already paid too high a price for the

---

73 Whether improvements in state compliance with human rights instruments can be expected may depend on progress in the development of "more flexible and innovative approaches to implementation than has thus far characterized approaches to human rights treaties": P. Alston, "The Legal Framework of the Convention on the Rights of the Child" (1992) 91/2 Bulletin of Human Rights 1. The Convention on the Rights of the Child reflects realistically that implementation might be regarded as a process of genuine effort to move in the direction of strict or substantial compliance rather than as an attainment of such standards. This "progressive" concept of implementation is reflected, for instance, in the parties' recognition not of the child's right to health, but of the child's right to the enjoyment of the highest attainable standard of health. States "do not guarantee the child right of access to medical treatment and rehabilitation services, but undertake to "strive to ensure" that no child is deprived of his or her right of access to health care services": F.-Z. Ksentini, "The Convention on the Rights of the Child: Norms for Protection and an Instrument of Cooperation for the Survival, Development and Well-being of the Child" (1992) 91/2 Bulletin of Human Rights 43 at 49. On the other hand, this kind of flexibility will not prevent cross-cultural differences to arise in the interpretation of the "best interests of the child" if this phrase is considered to undermine parental authority. Some countries will simply not be prepared to incorporate such language into national legislation, and may have to find a substitute such as "welfare of the child": A. Lopatka, "Importance of the Convention on the Rights of the Child" 91/2 Bulletin of Human Rights 56 at 59-60.

"benefits" of Westernization. Some perceive that their own civilization is being undermined by threats in the form of materialistic greed, cynicism, violence, and hedonism. Even as they succumb to the temptations of affluence, they fear the worst. Faced with this Western "virus," one Arab or Islamic reaction has been to insist on the need to elevate the value of *rectitude*.[74] The threat of defilement by the West has served to sharpen their perception of what is, or strives to be, *pure* in their own civilization, at the point of interaction with their God.[75] In Western eyes, severity of punishment, for example in Islamic law, is ascribed to fundamentalism or fanaticism in an intolerant and hence barbaric culture. In Arab or Islamic eyes, Western leniency in criminal law is further evidence of spiritual weakness, a lack of commitment to the God-given concept of purity in human affairs. In Asian eyes, Western permissiveness is self-indulgence. It is a form of self-abasement that reduces the need for others to owe respect, perhaps confirming their belief that the future truly belongs to Asia, in matters spiritual as well as material. In seeming to impose its own cultural values in the name of legal uniformity, the West might be seen to be provoking a "clash of civilizations."[76] The vaunted advantages of "modernization"[77] may, even now, be giving way to a reinforcement of non-Western religious and ethical values, in regions such as the Middle East and Southeast Asia.[78]

The importance of culture in shaping domestic law, whether behavioural or civic, is acknowledged by all but the most naive of law reformers. It is well recognized that normally one cannot successfully transplant laws or legal institutions from one country to another if the social, political, or economic conditions in the two countries are radically different. In his

74 In the Lasswellian sense, one's sense of rectitude results in judgments of responsibility expressed "in terms of right and wrong, good or bad, responsible or irresponsible, ethical or unethical, decent or indecent, depending on the meaning of words in the culture concerned": H. D. Lasswell and M. S. McDougal, *Jurisprudence for a Free Society: Studies in Law, Science and Policy*, vol. 1 (New Haven, Conn.: New Haven Press; and Dordrecht: Martinus Nijhoff, 1992) at 575.

75 Again in Lasswellian terminology, a culture's "strategy of rectitude may be pursued by affirmation or inquiry ... Carried to excess, one strategy can swallow up the other ... The posture of [purity] affirmation can become rigid, dogmatic, negligent of the facts, and contemptuous of what can be gained by observation. The posture of inquiry, on the other hand, can defeat survival by becoming over-detailed, uncorrelated, and deficient in guiding criteria for the solution of the conflicting claims": *ibid.* at 582.

76 S. P. Huntington, "The Clash of Civilizations?" (1993) 72:2 Foreign Affairs at 22-49.

77 On the concept of modernization and related concepts such as secularism and rationalism, see F. R. Von der Mehden, *Religion and Modernization in Southeast Asia* (Syracuse, N.Y.: Syracuse Univ. Press, 1986) at 2-13.

78 The familiar idea that modernization has weakened the force of religion, at least in the short run, has been challenged by recent events, especially in the Islamic world. Yet the phenomenon may be said to have lessened the impact of religion on the "whole life experience" of traditional societies and reduced it to the level of personal significance: *ibid.* at 203.

chapter on alternative dispute resolution mechanisms, Andrew Pirie notes that there are serious barriers and dangers in blindly transferring dispute resolution mechanisms across cultural divides, since such mechanisms are inextricably linked to cultural assumptions and beliefs. For example, dispute resolution mechanisms designed to treat all parties as "equals" may be inappropriate for a culture that values deference to authority or accords respect and power according to age, rank, or social status.[79]

Legal System Differences

The existence of different legal systems in different countries has not been an insurmountable barrier to convergence within the economic law sector. The desire for legal uniformity, as a mechanism to promote transnational trade, has trumped any systemic differences. In the behavioural sector, connected as it is to more indigenous values, legal system differences may be a bit more of a barrier, although not an insuperable one, to convergence of behavioural laws.

Major differences between the common law and civil law systems can contribute to divergence in any sector of the law. Legal system differences may consist of differences in: (1) the conception of legal ideas (for example, the different ways that tort law is conceived in the two systems); (2) the form of law (for example, written versus unwritten law, and comprehensive codification versus *ad hoc*, piecemeal legislation); (3) the style of legislative drafting; or (4) the differences in legal procedures and legal institutions (for example, adversarial versus inquisitorial systems). These differences are often likely to be more operative, and therefore subject to greater resistance to change, in the behavioural sector. For example, it is highly unlikely that common law countries will abandon their adversarial procedures and institutions in criminal law in favour of the inquisitorial procedures and institutions of the civil law system. Nor are civilians likely to abandon many of their fundamental legal conceptions and institutions and adopt those of common law countries. Legal system differences of this type are likely to remain indefinitely.

Differences in civil law and common law systems have also been imported into Asia. To the extent that Western formal laws have been imposed, adopted, or imitated in Asian countries, one sees a replication of these differences. Singapore, Malaysia, and Hong Kong have common law criminal law structures, while Thailand, Indonesia, and Vietnam have civilian criminal law systems.[80] There is very little evidence of a desire for convergence within the region of Southeast Asia: the difference is structural and beyond the reach of harmonization under ASEAN or otherwise.

---

79 Pirie, *supra* note 59.
80 Ferguson, *supra* note 62.

If legal system differences can be seen to contribute to divergence between common law and civil law systems, which share a relatively common Anglo-European history and culture, then they are likely to be of even greater influence when one shifts to legal systems premised on radically different ideology and cultural beliefs, whether they be socialist legal systems, fundamentalist Islamic legal systems, or indigenous customary folk law systems.[81]

Conclusions

The above analysis seems to support the following conclusions:

(1) Convergence or uniformity in the behavioural sector seems much less pronounced than in either the economic or civic sectors, and, as in the civic sector, where there is similarity in the formal laws, that similarity may in fact mask substantial differences in actual practice.

(2) To the extent that convergence does appear in behavioural laws, that convergence appears to be most strongly influenced by the emergence of a global economy, by pressure from the international community, by common technology, and by educational linkages.

(3) Many features of behavioural laws continue to be distinct and nonconvergent. The factors that seem most conducive to divergence in behavioural laws are differences in ideology and culture and differences in legal systems, reinforced by the common desire for political autonomy.

CROSS-SECTORAL OVERLAPS

Introduction

Most of the areas of law – as distinct from issues – covered in this work seem to fall fairly neatly into one of the three sectors distinguished in the Introduction. In each of these areas, issues may arise that involve impingement by one sector on another, but not with such regularity that the area itself cannot be treated as essentially unisectoral. However, a few areas or compartments of law are so clearly characterized by the necessity to respond to cross-sectoral issues that the areas themselves should be regarded as multisectoral. In this book, three chapters, by this test, seem to stand out as cross-sectoral overlaps: those on environmental law, indigenous claims, and alternative dispute resolution (ADR). Of these three, only the first, it might be objected, is a "substantive" area of law that appears to be evolving on the basis of a more or less coherent set of substantive norms; but the area of "native law" is taught, researched, and practised as a distinguishable field of legal specialization that is perceived by specialists to be evolving on the basis of at least an emergent set of substantive norms; and ADR is a recently

81 Bassiouni, *supra* note 67; Fryzee, *supra* note 67; Hooker, *supra* note 67; J. N. Hazard, *Communists and Their Law: A Search for the Common Core of the Legal Systems of the Marxian Socialist States* (Chicago: Univ. of Chicago Press, 1969).

established field derived from a more or less coherent set of institutional and procedural constructs.

Environmental law is presented by Douglas Johnston as a mix, in almost equal parts, of economic, civic, and behavioural elements; and because of the impact upon it of the non-governmental "ethical community" at national, regional, and global levels, it is the focus of highly diverse interests and values. Environmental law is perceived as a conceptual and institutional response to the social need for *accommodation*. In the chapter by Hamar Foster, the field of native law is treated as a mix chiefly of economic (property and commercial) and civic (sovereignty and governance) concepts, but is complicated frequently by the intrusion of behavioural concerns related to crime and punishment, interspousal relations, adoption and custody of children, and spiritual autonomy. Pirie's study envisages ADR as a response to growing dissatisfaction with the existing formal structures for the administration of justice in all areas of human affairs. To the extent that faith in mediation is at the core of the case for informalism, there is no reason to think of ADR as skewed in the direction of any one of the three sectors.

In all three of these areas it might be hypothesized that the behavioural and civic elements will tend to offset, or at least postpone, the trend to convergence that might otherwise prevail by reason of the economic components. It is at least consistent with the general sectoral theory of legal development addressed in the Introduction that a trisectoral area of law will be found to be subject to more internal strain than would be normal in a unisectoral area: namely, the strain created between the push of convergence and the pull of divergence.

Factors Contributing to Convergence

The Transnational Ethical Community

The concept of the transnational ethical community is developed by Johnston in his environmental law chapter to describe the relative cohesiveness of non-governmental "civil society" pressures on virtually all national legal systems: a sustained effort, external as well as internal, to induce change in conformity with what are held out to be ethical demands on formal state laws and structures. If these demands have sufficient mutual consistency and are pressed by enough people with skill and determination, then it might be supposed that they will, sooner or later, serve the purpose of legal convergence.

The reality, however, is likely to be more complicated. First, there are too many kinds of ethical demands – or orders of morality – and too many systems of cultural beliefs and values for a high degree of mutual consistency within the transnational ethical community to be attained over the longer term. Even in the short term, ethical rifts tend to arise, sometimes with opposed factions offering incompatible versions of the morality that should prevail. In whaling and other hunting contexts, for example, the demands of animal rights proponents and other preservationists (as distinct from conservationists) cannot be reconciled with the demands of indigenous people for traditional communal entitlement or even special immunity.[82] The middle ground in that context is as elusive as in that of abortion or euthanasia. In environmental law generally, the case for conservation and regulation is very different indeed from that for preservation and prohibition, and yet there is no axiomatic truth that one is more ethically compelling than the other. Sometimes the competition is rather between reason and sentiment, and morality is generally perceived and felt to be a blend of the two. In native law, civic and economic demands are often, but not always, compatible, but if a traditional lifestyle is seen to be oppressive, these demands may be resisted on behavioural grounds. For native women, a return to the past may not be an improvement on the *status quo* imposed by the structures of the settler state.[83] In ADR situations, notions of informal justice may be as culturally contingent as notions of formal justice, and even the most benevolent ADR interventions into village society may have to accept unwanted comparison with the missionary movement.

Common Legal Principles and Concepts

Of the three cross-sectoral areas dealt with in this book, only environmental law is at present the beneficiary of a systematic legal development effort at the global level. International environmental law is of relatively recent origin, dating essentially from the late 1960s, although of course antecedents can be found much earlier. Normative development, rather than law-making in a strict sense, has been the primary purpose served by the two enormous United Nations environmental mega-conferences of 1972 and 1992.[84] The sophisticated stock of global concepts articulated in Agenda 21 might seem to ensure that the intellectual foundation of national environmental regimes in the coming years will become less and less divergent. The prospect of convergence might seem to be enhanced by the growing number of global treaties and other strenuously negotiated and politically influential

82 It might be said that there are three, not two, orders of morality in collision in the context of whaling, because general conservation or sustainable use is distinguishable both from preservation based on animal rights and from the special interests of highly vulnerable or privileged groups.

83 H. Foster, "Indigenous Peoples and the Law: The Colonial Legacy in Australia, Canada, New Zealand, and the United States" (ch. 10 of this book) at 499.

84 D. M. Johnston, "Environmental Law as 'Sacred Text': Western Values and Southeast Asian Prospects" (ch. 9 of this book).

85 Many of the most ambitious of these treaties, such as the Biodiversity and Climate Change Conventions of 1992, put their faith in the processes of regular global conference diplomacy created for the parties to them, and in the availability of energy, talent, and good will as well as financial resources that would be essential to produce a genuine convergence of national policy and legislation within these frameworks.

instruments coming down from the diplomatic arena.[85] However, an abyss separates the fact of international negotiation from the fact of national implementation, and, as Johnston points out, even the interposition of regional policy instruments, such as those of the ASEAN member states, may not advance the cause of convergence beyond the symbolic or textual level, at least in arenas that have not yet begun to move in the direction of regional economic integration and its corollary of legal harmonization.[86] Some of the potentially uniform norms advanced at the level of global environmental diplomacy, such as the polluter-pays and precautionary principles, are established only at the national level and are the focus of harmonization diplomacy in western Europe, but still contested, ignored, or variously interpreted elsewhere in the world community.[87] It remains to be seen how much cohesive force will be found to inhere in the universally accepted concept of sustainability.[88]

Efforts have also been made to reach out to the global diplomatic arena for assistance in the consolidation of principles and concepts supportive of economic and civic claims by indigenous peoples.[89] It is likely that declaratory instruments of this kind will begin to emerge from the United Nations system in the coming years, creating at least an international climate favourable to future initiatives in convergence diplomacy.

ADR, on the other hand, is concerned with technique rather than legal substance, although it does, of course, rest on the concept of informal justice and seek an affordable alternative to the use of courts of law. Convergence in the use of ADR in radically different legal cultures is unlikely to be facilitated by global treaties, but rather by the international network of NGOs and academic research centres. In the nature of things, it is not to be expected that this kind of conceptual convergence would be clearly reflected in the formal law of non-Western countries.

Factors Contributing to Divergence

Economic Development and Differential Standards

Economic disparity is surely bound to retard the process of convergence

---

86 Johnston, *supra* note 84.

87 International lawyers are divided over the juridical status of these two norms. Some claim that they are "established" in general or customary international law; others maintain that they are "emergent" at the global level; and still others suggest that they are established principles in some countries, emergent norms in others, and merely suggested goals or guidelines in others.

88 Almost all governments seem to have accepted the relevance of the concept of sustainability to economic, industrial, and other development goals. But precision in the use of this term is elusive, and the lack of clear consensus on its operational meaning in certain contexts raises questions about its potential cohesiveness or coherence.

89 For a variety of views on the rights of indigenous peoples, see J. Crawford, ed., *The Rights of Peoples* (Oxford: Clarendon Press, 1988).

within the trisectoral context of environmental law. As Johnston documents, there is considerable political resistance on the part of most developing countries to efforts by Western developed states to impose strict environmental norms and standards in the global arena.[90] As noted earlier, the compromise in recent global environmental instruments is to take a "common but differentiated" approach to the development of environmental regimes, built on the basis of common principles and concepts but also of differentiated standards designed to be equitable and economically realistic in light of the level of economic development attained by the state in question. As a consequence of this compromise, it is politically difficult, and perhaps juridically impossible, to determine precisely the substantive content of a single international standard in the areas of environmental law where this approach has been adopted.[91]

Economic disparity has a less obvious effect on the development of native law. The settler states compared by Foster – Australia, Canada, New Zealand, and the United States – are among the wealthiest countries of the world, and all have shown a willingness to spend large, if insufficient, sums to settle indigenous claims. However, the indigenous grievances that exist in many other countries are mostly ignored or suppressed for a variety of reasons that always emphasize the need for national unity but often include the economic cost of separate or special treatment.

The presence or absence of affluence is also relevant to the prospects of ADR, but it turns not so much on the gross national product of states as on the poverty of subnational rural regions or specific local communities, where recourse to formal (urban) law is unaffordable as well as culturally alien. It may be premature to predict even the short-term outcome of current cross-cultural ADR initiatives, not least because of the interaction between low-income, rural target communities and relatively high-income, urban intervenors, both local and foreign. It might be supposed that the outcome will vary considerably from case to case.

Cultural Resistance

Convergence in all three of these trisectoral areas is likely to be met with cultural resistance, but the concept of culture varies in significance with the context. In the case of ADR, resistance might be encountered as a result of a

---

90 Johnston, *supra* note 84.

91 For example, the concept of "international standards" is frequently invoked in the marine pollution provisions of the 1992 UN Convention on the Law of the Sea, and usually refers to the norm-setting decisions of the International Maritime Organization (IMO). But IMO diplomacy is not sufficiently binding or globalized to guarantee convergence beyond the core of the IMO-observant shipping community. For a knowledgeable but optimistic view of these trends, see B. H. Oxman, "The Duty to Respect Generally Accepted International Standards" (1991) 24 New York Univ. J. of Int'l Law and Policy 109.

variety of tensions, each of which might be characterized in some sense as "cultural": for instance, tensions between foreign and national, between urban and rural, between rich and poor, and between "mainstream" and "peripheral" in the ethnological sense. One must expect a diversity of responses from target communities, creating difficulties in conceptual convergence of the sort that sociologists and anthropologists have had to accept since the beginning of legal ethnology. Admittedly, economic necessity might sound conducive to conformity, and even appear so in certain circumstances, but the behavioural (intimate) and civic (decisional) elements seem more likely to pull in the direction of divergence.

The cultural tension in the field of native rights is, of course, fundamentally perceived as a struggle between dominant and dependent cultures in the civilizational sense of the term. Not all dominant cultures have the same capacity to accept the psychic or economic burden of guilt for their policies of oppression in the distant past, or even for more recent resort to barbarism.[92] Settler and non-settler states are likely to have a different emotional mix but, as Foster shows, even the settler states seem to be following separate courses, while being increasingly aware of the relevance of experiences in other settler states. Countries such as Canada that have accepted the negotiability and separateness of all indigenous land claims seem to have closed the door on the prospect of speedy settlements based on a convergence of legal concepts and principles.[93]

In the field of environmental law, cultural resistance to convergence pressures might be expected to manifest itself in various ways. External pressures to conform to international environmental values might be resisted because of such diverse considerations as general cultural attitudes to state intervention in the economy and to the role of the judiciary, and particular cultural attitudes to animals, wildlife, and wilderness, and the role of human beings as the guardians of nature for the benefit of one's descendants.[94] Except in situations where environmental threats are perceived as hazards, the ethic of environmental responsibility may not be universally

---

92 Some evidence supports the view that sensitivity to aboriginal claims is likely to be most evident in circumstances where the elites share in some degree a sense of collective guilt for historic injustices perpetrated by their predecessors, and where aboriginal claims are seen to enjoy priority in a political culture that caters to special interests.

93 Because there are several hundred bands of aboriginal descent in Canada, most of which are quite tiny by the standards of electoral democracy, the settlement of band claims by separate negotiations will take 40-50 years at the present rate, unless the bands show a willingness to combine forces at the negotiating table.

94 Respect for one's ancestors, which is still a strongly felt obligation in Chinese and many other non-western cultures, sets up a psychocultural block against rapid westernization, especially in rural or semi-rural sectors of society. For instance, the traditionally harsh treatment of animals that was approved and practised by one's immediate ancestors will not be easily altered on the basis of an imported animal welfare ethic.

shareable at the grass roots level, and for that reason may not be enforceable through the use of state mechanisms such as formal law and litigation.

Political Autonomy

Demands for political autonomy, which are themselves a specific manifestation of cultural resistance, may foster divergence in both the civic and behavioural sectors. Claims for political autonomy are often based, at least in part, upon an assertion that "we are different from you, and therefore we want to rule ourselves." The alleged differences will undoubtedly incorporate a number of cultural differences. A further claim will be made that "our cultural survival is dependent upon the right to self-government including the right to enact laws that represent and preserve our culture." Canadians are familiar with such claims in the context of political, legal, and cultural struggles in Quebec.[95]

In Chapter 10 of this book, "Indigenous Peoples and the Law," Foster documents the long-standing demands by aboriginal peoples in Australia, Canada, New Zealand, and the United States for some measure of sovereignty or self-government. In some instances it is a claim for a degree of self-government within the existing nation-state that will permit aboriginal people to enact and enforce laws that are aboriginal rather than colonial in origin. As a strategy to achieve or maintain self-government, it may be necessary to emphasize differences rather than similarities. In the context of those who support aboriginal self-government, there is a renewed interest in articulating differences between colonial and aboriginal conceptions in regard to matters such as property inheritance, adoption and custody within the aboriginal family, concepts of justice related to healing rather than punishment, and different methods of dispute resolution. Thus, claims of political autonomy can result in the creation or maintenance of diversity in laws, especially in the civic and behavioural sectors.

Conclusions

At least two tentative conclusions might be drawn from these observations and from the three cross-sectoral chapters:

(1) The above considerations and counter-considerations make it extraordinarily difficult to predict whether convergence or divergence in these cross-sectoral areas is the more likely trend over the next 20 or 30 years. The long-term view of national interest may ultimately prevail in the environmental field and ensure a gradual convergence of legal systems,

95 Perhaps most commentators outside Canada take the unsympathetic view that the people of Quebec already enjoy the "right of self-determination" within the framework of the Canadian federation, and that cultural survival is unlikely to be secured by the political fact of secession from the rest of Canada.

at least among countries at the upper end of the GNP scale, but a similar prediction is more perilous in the contexts of ADR and native rights.

(2) Because convergence in these complex, cross-sectoral areas is facilitated by NGOs sharing similar ethical views, a convergence trend is more likely to occur in the more open societies that tolerate "civil society" intervention in the decision-making processes controlled by the state.

CONCLUSIONS

New Directions in Comparative Law

Despite the diversity of approach and focus reflected in the studies brought together in this book, the legal development orientation that binds them together has tempted the co-editors to draw tentative conclusions within the trisectoral framework delineated in the Introduction. Even when drawn down from the systemic to the sectoral level, generalizations about trends to convergence or divergence still need to be revised or qualified. Further studies need to be undertaken that would focus on a much wider range of topics and encompass an even greater variety of methodologies and legal systems or cultures. As these gaps are narrowed down and complexities brought into perspective, it will become easier to revise or qualify the generalization.

In the economic law sector, for example, the topics of reputation spillover, parallel importation, and securities regulation may not be "typical." Studies focusing on bills of lading, sale of goods, cargo claims, and other commercial topics that have been the object of unification conventions would undoubtedly provide evidence of a trend toward the global convergence of national economic laws, and European Community studies would exemplify the actual and potential convergence inherent in harmonization diplomacy and legal development at the regional level. Other kinds of studies, focusing more sharply on the gaps between international negotiation, national enactment, and local enforcement, seek to clarify the variance between the law-in-books and the law-in-action, or between law and practice, even in the supposedly convergent context of commercial law. Indeed, even in some areas of economic law, such as banking, investment, and insurance, the idea of global or even regional convergence based on the evidence of formal legal instruments may be a misconception of mythic dimensions.

In the area of civic law, each criterion selected as the most significant indicator of convergence or non-convergence in areas governed by democracy, rule-of-law, or constitutional constructs might produce a rather different picture. For example, most countries practise as well as preach universal adult suffrage, and a growing majority seem now to be committed to political pluralism as a civic principle, but, by most other criteria, "civic progress" is much more uneven, and by a few the rate of convergence may be likened to that of a glacier's descent. A balanced perspective might be sought through comparative civic studies that embrace a dozen or more criteria, but the difficulties in embarking on multifactorial scholarship on this scale may daunt all but the bravest of hearts. It might be more fruitful to limit the testing of the convergence-divergence hypothesis to groupings of relatively like-minded civic cultures that are open to the influences of mutually interactive societies. These might include the EC countries, the Council of Europe countries, the Nordic and Benelux countries, the OECD "club" of wealthy democracies, the Commonwealth, the South Pacific Forum, the Andean Community, and newer groupings such as NAFTA and perhaps even APEC. Such studies would, of course, tend to fortify the case for convergence. To avoid distortion it would be necessary to develop "corrective" studies comparing countries with no obvious cultural affinity or political or economic alignment with one another, so as to permit a return to the global level of trends in legal development.

Behavioural law, on the other hand, seems to require further contextual case studies that would allow the historical and cultural background to be brought into sharper focus. The apparent distinctiveness of this sector of national law seems subject to challenge only in those special circumstances where a group of states, as in western Europe, has formed a political union and to some extent has begun to dissolve the national bonds of their separate social and political histories, even in areas of strong ethical and cultural significance such as capital or corporal punishment, sexual behaviour, welfare entitlement, and the extent of religious freedom.

The Issue of Comparability

Current work in the field of comparative legal studies is increasingly challenged by the issue of comparability: what is worth comparing? Only a certain proportion of legal scholars will be prepared to accept that it is sufficient to compare legislative texts without resorting to supplementary textual (judicial) or contextual (cultural or institutional) studies. As noted above, judicial-doctrinal comparisons at the micro-analytical level tend to be confined to cognate jurisdictions that share descent from the common law or civil law tradition and have case law evolving on the basis of relatively frequent resort to litigation. By and large, therefore, the issue of comparability in comparative law comes down to questions concerning the centrality of contextual differences. If two legal systems or cultures are radically different, the value of comparison may be limited to the benefits that may accrue in the form of jurisprudential insights into the role of law in society.

How comparative lawyers judge what is worth comparing is likely to be affected by at least three considerations. First, the matter may depend essentially on whether the scholar is primarily a specialist in cultural studies or is a subject specialist in a field, discipline, or sub-discipline. In Canada, for example, only a small handful of law teachers – perhaps only two or three – are primarily foreign law specialists with doctoral or equivalent qualifications in the language, history, and culture as well as the law of a foreign country. The ability to carry out effective on-site law-and-society research in the language of a foreign-language country may create not only the opportunity to gain certain insights not available to those untrained in the study of legal cultures, but may also tend to limit comparative inquiry to the scholar's own state of original training and the country or area of specialized training. It is the exception rather than the rule for such a scholar to extend comparison to a third tier of legal systems in which he or she has no particular professional expertise in cultural terms. By far the largest number of legal scholars engaged in transnational studies, including almost all of the contributors to this work, belong to the second category of "subject specialists," who may aspire to cultivating a flair for transnational inquiries through perceptive travel, on-site discussions with colleagues, interactions on the conference or workshop circuit, and project-linked collaborations. Some in this large category may, of course, acquire a fair amount of sophistication after years of exposure to other legal systems, or to certain sectors or subject areas, without the benefit of initial formal academic training. Moreover, extended periods of residence in a foreign-language country normally create a degree of proficiency in that language. In one way or the other, one's degree of cultural sensitivity is likely to affect one's sense of the distinction between real and apparent similarities, and of the potential use of comparison. Other things being equal, those at the "cultural studies" end of the spectrum are inclined to be sceptical of the value of textual comparisons and tend to stress the uniqueness of a legal culture.

Second, the question of comparability may be addressed differently according to the sector of the legal system that is the chief object of one's research. Specialists in areas of economic, or at least commercial, significance may argue that comparative analysis should concentrate mostly on patterns of micro-divergence in areas characterized by macro-convergence. Differences between countries like Malaysia and Singapore in areas such as intellectual property, sale of goods, restraint of trade, regulation of industry, insurance law, and foreign investment might seem to be particularly worthy of close scrutiny. At the other extreme, specialists in topics of behavioural law, such as prostitution or mental disorder, might be likely to regard comparative inquiry as consisting of exercises in comparative legal history that are, almost invariably, bound to result in an emphasis on dissimilarities, if not on separate and unique "narratives." In the civic sector, comparative law might be seen chiefly as an invitation to compare text with context by juxtaposing two or more legal or political cultures that present apparent textual similarities and real contextual dissimilarities. In each sector, a tendency to converge or not to converge might be presumed to be inherent, and the purpose of the comparative research is to validate or invalidate the initial assumption.

Third, the purpose, and therefore the utility, of comparative legal research seems likely to be much influenced, if not determined, by the orientation or mindset of the investigator. The specialist in the textual analysis tradition of comparative law may want to see a basic compatibility in the textual evidences of the formal law of two or more systems or jurisdictions before undertaking the task of close comparison; otherwise the initiative may seem to lack any practical purpose. Closeness of comparison may not appear to be a prerequisite to a contextualist scholar who is chiefly attracted to the contrast between two or more legal cultures or histories. A scholar engaged in theory-based comparative law, on the other hand, may be motivated by the opportunity for conceptual innovation, and the ideology-based jurist by the opportunity to contribute to the ethical challenge of law reform in countries seen to be deficient from the investigator's perspectives.

There is also the factor of the scholar's predisposition. Traditionalists may wish to emphasize the value of dispassionate, detached analysis in comparative law, in the hope of attaining something that approximates objective truth, whereas modernists in the field may claim to bring a more realistic dimension to scholarship by disclosing their own bias, even though the latter may be a good deal more complex than they are able or willing to disclose. The former may tend to underestimate the importance of the comparability issue; the latter may sharpen the dilemma by importing overexpectation out of an exaggerated respect for the governing concepts and values of their own legal culture.

Tensions in Comparative Law

Law is traditionally described as a "normative science," at least in Western societies, and therefore as a blend of concern for values and respect for facts. Today it is more common than in the past to regard comparative law as a vehicle for promoting the values or principles of one's choice. The concept of the "world community" is a useful construct to legitimize one's value preferences, reinforced as they may be by colleagues sharing one's own cultural predispositions. The apparent result is that contemporary comparative law is witness to an exacerbation of the inherent tension between facts and values.

In addition to tensions between facts and values, there may also be fundamental normative tensions between subdisciplines of law. At one time scholars in the field of public international law tended to accept the ideal of uniformity as the paradigm that controlled their sense of progress in the history of legal ideas. Scholars in the fields of legal ethnology and the sociology of law, however, were likely to be compelled by their ideal of autonomy to take pleasure in the discovery of cultural diversity. As shown in the current literature that overlaps these two fields, international lawyers today still tend to argue on the side of absolutism, uniformity, and universality, whereas most comparative lawyers are seen to defend cultural autonomy, even by espousing the philosophically vulnerable concept of cultural, if not moral, relativism.

Some of our final reflections in this chapter may give the impression that we lean toward the ideal of uniformity, rather than that of diversity. But, at least in some contexts, we are content to be cultural relativists, and we sense that our Asianization makes us increasingly sceptical of the overgeneralized argument for the convergence of all law. The truth, we feel, is that the value of comparative law in the late 1990s depends on discovering new modes of transnational and transcommunal scholarship that accommodate the competing demands for better information and value enhancement. Each of the nine models of comparative law has a contribution to make in one direction or the other. The reality of international society is much too heterogeneous to be confused with the ideal of world community, and it seems still to be the duty of comparative lawyers to hold up each order of legitimacy against the others.

Contributors

Molly Cheang is a Professor of Law, Faculty of Law, University of Malaya, Kuala Lumpur, Malaysia.

Cheryl Crane is an Assistant Professor and former Associate Dean at the University of Victoria Faculty of Law. Before joining the faculty in 1990, she practised constitutional law and human rights law with the Saskatchewan Department of the Attorney General and the Canadian Human Rights Commission. She has research interests in administrative law, human rights law, and employment law.

Thamrong Dasananjali is the Deputy Director General of the Department of Medical Services, Ministry of Public Health, Bangkok, Thailand.

Gerry Ferguson is a Professor of Law at the UVic Faculty of Law. He is a specialist in criminal law and mental health law. He has been a visiting professor at a number of law faculties in the Asia-Pacific region, and is a member of the Board of Directors of the International Centre for Criminal Law Reform and Criminal Justice Policy and of the Advisory Council of the Law Commission of Canada.

Hamar Foster is a Professor of Law, and currently the Associate Dean, at the UVic Faculty of Law. Professor Foster is a specialist in the areas of Canadian legal history and Aboriginal law and has written extensively on both topics.

Mark Gillen is an Associate Professor of Law at the UVic Faculty of Law. He is the chair of the Corporate Law Subsection of the Canadian Association of Law Teachers. Professor Gillen is the author of a book entitled *Securities Regulation in Canada*. He is also the author of several articles on Malaysian constitutional law.

Joanna Harrington received her LL.B. degree from the UVic Faculty of Law and is enrolled in the Doctoral program in international and comparative law at Cambridge University. This year she has taken leave from her doctoral studies to work as a legal officer to Lord Lester of Herne Hill, Q.C., focusing on human rights, constitutional reform, and European integration issues.

Dadang Hawari is a Professor in the Department of Psychiatry, Faculty of Medicine, University of Indonesia, in Jakarta.

Robert G. Howell is a Professor of Law at the UVic Faculty of Law. Professor Howell is a specialist in intellectual property and telecommunications law and policy. He is a member of the Advisory Panel of *Tolley's Communications Law* and co-chair of the Intellectual Property Section of the Canadian Association of Law Teachers.

Douglas M. Johnston is the former Chair in Asia-Pacific Legal Relations at the UVic Faculty of Law and the UVic Centre for Asia Pacific Initiatives. At present he is Director of the Policy Research Programme at the National University of Singapore, and Co-Director of the Southeast Asian Programme in Ocean Law, Policy, and Management (SEAPOL), based in Bangkok. Professor Johnston is a specialist in international and comparative law and has published extensively on the law of sea and international environmental law.

Khaw Lake Tee is an Associate Professor, Faculty of Law, University of Malaya, Kuala Lumpur, Malaysia.

Kok Lee Peng is a former Associate Professor in the Department of Psychological Medicine, National University of Singapore, and is currently a partner in a private psychiatric clinic in Singapore.

Ted L. McDorman is an Associate Professor of Law at the UVic Faculty of Law. He has written extensively in the areas of ocean law and policy, trade law, and Asian constitutional law. Professor McDorman is a research associate with the UVic Centre for Asia Pacific Initiatives.

John P. S. McLaren is the Lansdowne Professor of Law at the University of Victoria. His major research passion is legal history. He has specialized in work on the history of vice regulation, the legal history of racial and ethnic discrimination, and the history of environmental regulation.

William A. W. Neilson is a Professor of Law, and former Dean, at the UVic Faculty of Law, and the Director of the UVic Centre for Asia Pacific Initiatives. Professor Neilson has extensive experience directing law reform, legal education, and economic development research and training programs in Southeast Asia. His research interests include international trade and business law, competition law, and Asia-Pacific legal development. He is the co-editor of *Law and Economic Development: Cases and Materials from Southeast Asia* (1992), and author of *The Vietnam Investment Manual* (1995), among other works.

Andrew J. Pirie is an Associate Professor of Law at the UVic Faculty of Law. Professor Pirie was the Executive Director of the UVic Institute for Dispute Resolution from 1989 to 1996. He is a specialist in alternative dispute resolution and is currently completing a book on that topic. He has participated in dispute resolution workshops in Thailand and Cambodia.

Pitman Potter is an Associate Professor at the University of British Columbia and a member of the Bars of Washington and California. He has written extensively on Chinese law, and international and investment law.

Stephan Salzberg is a member of the Faculty of Law and the Centre for Asian Legal Studies at the University of British Columbia in Vancouver.

Index

Note: This index is constructed on a chapter-by-chapter basis.

Chapter 2: Parallel Importation of Wares and Reputation Spillover

Chapter 3: Vietnam's Economic Law Transformation

Chapter 5: Constitutional Change and Continuity in Thailand

Chapter 6: The 1992 Vietnamese Constitution

Chapter 7: Legal Regulation of Mental Disorder

Chapter 8: Whores, Soiled Doves, or Working Women?

Chapter 9: Environmental Law as "Sacred Text"

Chapter 10: Indigenous Peoples and the Law

Set in Stone by Artegraphica Design Co.

Printed and bound in Canada by Friesens

Copy editor: Yvonne Bondarchuk

Proofreader: Edward Wagstaff